Alison

Cheltenham 2000

QOHELET
IN THE CONTEXT OF WISDOM

BIBLIOTHECA EPHEMERIDUM THEOLOGICARUM LOVANIENSIUM

CXXXVI

QOHELET
IN THE CONTEXT OF WISDOM

EDITED BY

A. SCHOORS

LEUVEN
UNIVERSITY PRESS

UITGEVERIJ PEETERS
LEUVEN

1998

ISBN 90 6186 905 6 (Leuven University Press)
D/1998/1869/41
ISBN 90-429-0589-1 (Uitgeverij Peeters)
D/1998/0602/267

Leuven University Press / Presses Universitaires de Louvain
Universitaire Pers Leuven
Blijde Inkomststraat 5, B-3000 Leuven-Louvain (Belgium)

© 1998, Uitgeverij Peeters, Bondgenotenlaan 153, B-3000 Leuven (Belgium)

PREFACE

The book of Qohelet (Ecclesiastes) received a steadily increasing attention during the last two decades. Next to an impressive number of commentaries there is a flood of monographs and articles on the literary structure of the book, on each pericope and every verse, on the central theme or the theological and philosophical teachings of this relatively short and at te same time idiosyncratic work that sometimes has a modern ring to it. It is again becoming to study its connections with Greek philosophy – in whatever sense –, and the investigation of the socio-economical and cultural background in connection with Judaism in the Hellenistic period as well as with the impact of Ptolemaic policy on Judaean society is becoming an important topic in today's research. More recently an analysis of Qohelet in terms of current linguistic and philosophical tendencies, such as deconstruction, is coming to the fore. Hence the decision to devote the 46th session of the *Colloquium Biblicum Lovaniense* to Qohelet was well-advised. The conference took place in Leuven from July 30 to August 1, 1997, and was sponsored by the Katholieke Universiteit Leuven, the Université Catholique de Louvain and the Fonds voor Wetenschappelijk Onderzoek, the Fonds National de la Recherche Scientifique (Brussels). About one hundred participants took part in the colloquium, the programme of which consisted of ten main papers, four seminars, eighteen short papers and a discussion session, the so-called *Carrefour*, which was an animated event. As far as I am aware, most participants agree that we can look back at a successful colloquium.

The present volume contains the text of nine of the main papers, of the seminar papers and of almost all the short papers read at the colloquium, in total 30 contributions written in English (18), German (8) and French (4) by authors from 13 different countries.

I want to express my sincere thanks to all those who contributed to the success of the conference: the readers of the main papers, the directors of the seminars, the readers of short papers. Thanks are also due to those who took care of the technical aspects of this meeting: the secretariate of the Faculty of Theology of the K.U.Leuven, the assistants Bénédicte Lemmelijn, Hans Ausloos and Pierre Van Hecke, who were always there where they were expected to be, and the last mentioned also for his considerable and careful assistance in preparing the volume. Also my wife

Annie Schoors-Broekaert did more than her fair share in the preparation of the volume and in the assemblage of the indexes. The colloquium was held, as usual, in the Paus Adrianus VI-College, where we enjoyed the hospitality and kindness of the President Prof. Lambert Leijssen and his staff. And finally, it is only right to express our appreciation to Professor Emeritus Frans Neirynck, whose part in the organization of the colloquium was invisible for most of the participants, but who for years has been and still is the driving force behind the *Colloquium Biblicum Lovaniense* as well as the BETL-series, and the guardian of the high standards of both these enterprises.

Antoon SCHOORS

CONTENTS

OFFERED PAPERS

INDEXES

INTRODUCTION

The Book of Qohelet (Ecclesiastes) has rarely been the subject of an *ex professo* treatment at earlier sessions of the *Colloquium Biblicum Lovaniense*. Only in the 1978 session, devoted to Wisdom in the Old Testament, did three papers, presented by D. Lys, N. Lohfink and J. Coppens, deal with this intriguing book[1]. But in 1997 the Colloquium was completely devoted to Qohelet, a book that is not the one most frequently read in church, but, although it has never been absent from scientific research, is nowadays the subject of growing attention.

When reviewing the papers published in the present volume, we can say that a rich array of questions typically related to Qohelet have been dealt with.

In his opening address, A. Schoors[2] (Words Typical of Qohelet) discusses the meaning and usage of the four words which score the highest frequency in the book, viz. אדם, "man" (49 occurrences), היה, "to be" (49), ראה, "to see" (47) and טוב(ה), "good" (52). The highly reflective and even philosophical character of the Book of Qohelet finds expression in this typical vocabulary. A semantic study of other words which are typical of Qohelet, such as לב, "heart", עת, "time", הבל, "absurdity", ידע, "to know", etc. will certainly confirm this conclusion. It appears that Qohelet seeks to attain to a critically sound vision (ראה) of everything that happens (היה), but always centered on human existence (אדם), i.e. everything that happens and is done is judged on its value for

---

1. M. Gilbert (ed.), *La Sagesse de l'Ancien Testament* (BETL, 51), Gembloux-Leuven, 1979; Leuven, ²1989: D. Lys, *L'Être et le Temps. Communication de Qohèlèth*, pp. 249-258; N. Lohfink, *War Kohelet ein Frauenfeind? Ein Versuch, die Logik und den Gegenstand von Koh., 7,23-8,1a herauszufinden*, pp. 259-287; J. Coppens, *La structure de l'Ecclésiaste*, pp. 288-292.

2. Of his publications on Qohelet, see *La structure littéraire de Qohéleth*, in *OLP* 13 (1982) 91-116; Kethibh-Qere *in Ecclesiastes*, in J. Quaegebeur (ed.), *Studia Paulo Naster oblata*, II (OLA, 13), Leuven, 1982, pp. 215-222; *The Peshitta of Kohelet and its Relations to the Septuagint*, in C. Laga, J.A. Munitiz & L. Van Rompay (eds.), *After Chalcedon. Studies in Theology and Church History*. FS A. Van Roey (OLA, 18), Leuven, 1985, pp. 347-357; *Koheleth: A Perspective of Life after Death?*, in *ETL* 61 (1985) 295-303; *Emphatic or Asseverative kî in Koheleth*, in H.L.J. Vanstiphout a.o. (eds.), *Scripta signa vocis*. FS J.H. Hospers, Groningen, 1986, pp. 209-216; *The Use of Vowel Letters in Qoheleth*, in *UF* 20 (1988) 277-286; *The Pronouns in Qoheleth*, in *Hebrew Studies* 30 (1989) 71-90; *The Preacher sought to find pleasing words. A Study of the Language of Qoheleth* (OLA, 41), Leuven 1992; *Bitterder dan de dood is de vrouw (Koh 7,26)*, in *Bijdragen* 54 (1993) 121-140; *Qoheleth: A Book in a Changing Society*, in *OTE* 9 (1996) 68-87.

humanity and human beings individually (טוב). The fact that אלהים, "God" is the next most frequent word shows that this philosophical pre-occupation has a strong component of theodicy.

The much debated meaning of Qohelet's הבל-sayings was discussed again by N. LOHFINK[3] (Frankfurt am Main). In discussion with D. Michel he raises the question of the domain of reference of הבל. In Qohelet the word seems not to function in metaphysical or cosmological utterances but only in anthropological ones. But cannot its use be more limited? According to Michel, Qohelet uses the word always when he wants to express an epistemological scepticism. Lohfink agrees with Michel that Qohelet holds such an epistemological scepticism, a pessimism with regard to the possibilities of human knowledge, meaning that human knowledge has its limits. But he contests that this scepticism is expressed in the notion of הבל. This notion is not the expression of epistemological realities. In his opinion, when Qohelet uses this notion he speaks about acts, things, situations, facts, about the objective world and not about the human subject and his epistomological possibilities. This analysis should not be considered as a direct contribution to the elucidation of the real meaning of הבל, but to have determined the domain of application is an indirect contribution anyway.

I.J.J. SPANGENBERG[4] gives a nice review of the paradigm shifts in the study of Qohelet (A Century of Wrestling with Qohelet: The Research

3. See his studies on Qohelet: *War Kohelet ein Frauenfeind? Ein Versuch, die Logik und den Gegenstand von Koh 7,23-8,1a herauszufinden* (n. 1), 1979, pp. 259-287; *Kohelet* (NEB), Würzburg, 1980; *Der Bibel skeptische Hintertür. Versuch, den Ort des Buches Kohelet neu zu bestimmen*, in *Stimmen der Zeit* 198 (1980) 17-31; melek, šallīṭ und môšēl *bei Kohelet und die Abfassungszeit des Buches*, in *Bib* 62 (1981) 535-543; *Warum ist der Tor unfähig, böse zu handeln? (Koh 4,17)*, in *ZDMG.S* 5 (1983) 113-120; *Le temps dans le livre de Qohélet*, in *Christus* 32 (1985) 69-80; *Die Wiederkehr des immer Gleichen. Eine frühe Synthese zwischen griechischem und jüdischem Weltgefühl in Kohelet 1,4-11*, in *Ebraismo, Ellenismo, Cristianesimo*, Padova, 1985, pp. 125-151; *Koh 1,2 "alles ist Windhauch" – universale oder anthropologische Aussage?*, in R. MOSIS & L. RUPPERT (eds.), *Der Weg zum Menschen*. FS A. Deissler, Freiburg, 1989, pp. 201-216; *Kohelet und die Banken: Zur Übersetzung von Kohelet V 12-16*, in *VT* 39 (1989) 488-495; *Qoheleth 5:17-19 – Revelation by Joy*, in *CBQ* 52 (1990) 625-635; *Freu dich, Jüngling – doch nicht, weil du jung bist! Zum Formproblem im Schlußgedicht Kohelets (Koh 11,9-12,8)*, in *Biblical Interpretation* 3 (1995) 158-189; *Grenzen und Einbindung des Kohelet-Schlußgedichtes*, in P. MOMMER & W. THIEL (eds.), *Altes Testament. Forschung und Wirkung*. FS Henning Graf Reventlow, Frankfurt a.M., 1994, pp. 33-46; *Les épilogues du livre de Qohélet et les débuts du Canon*, in P. BOVATI & R. MEYNET (eds.), *"Ouvrir les Écritures". Mélanges offerts à P. Beauchamp* (Lectio Divina), Paris, 1995, pp. 79-96; *Zu einigen Satzeröffnungen im Epilog des Koheletbuches*, in A.A. DIESEL a.o. (eds.), *„Jedes Ding hat seine Zeit…" Studien zur israelitischen und altorientalischen Weisheit*. FS D. Michel (BZAW, 241), Berlin-New York, 1996, pp. 131-147.

4. See his *Die Prediker se uitsprake oor en uitkyk op die dood*, in *Scriptura* 27 (1988) 29-37; *Quotations in Ecclesiastes: an Appraisal*, in *OTE* 4 (1991) 19-35; *Die boek*

History of the Book Illustrated with a Discussion of Qoh 4,17-5,6). He shows that the historical-critical method played a dominant role at the beginning of this century and still does today. He points out the important role of R. Gordis's studies in changing the focus from identifying and eliminating secondary material to reading the book as the work of one author. The shift from the historical-critical paradigm to that of modern literary criticism has had only a limited impact on the exegesis of Qohelet. This is evident when investigating the influences of the paradigm shifts on the exegesis of a passage such as Qoh 4,17-5,6. With his clearly presented rhetorical analysis of this pericope Spangenberg shows that non-historical-critical approaches do hold much promise, but they never replace the former approaches.

Qoh 4,17-5,6 was going to play a central role in the discussions of the Colloquium. Not only is it the topic of a short paper presented by T. Hieke (cf. *infra*), but also D. MICHEL[5] (Mainz) paid special attention to this pericope in his paper *"Unter der Sonne" : Zur Immanenz bei Qohelet*. By means of an analysis of the expression "under the sun" he showed that the object of Qohelet's empirical approach is limited to the immanent world. When in 2,24-26 he no longer acts as an empiricist but reflects (*betrachtet*) on what he sees, Qohelet can speak of God. But Qohelet's experience of absurdity in this world is not resolved by introducing God as the creator. As well as a few other pericopes Michel discusses more thoroughly the central text 4,17-5,6 which ends with the well-known admonition "Fear God". The fear of God is not a reaction to the encounter with God as it is in Psalms, but the result of the realization that one cannot meet the inaccessible God. From 4,17-5,6 we see Qohelet not as a pious, traditionalist Jew, but as a critical sage, who cannot transcend the limits of immanence: "In 4,17-5,6 sehen wir Qohelet nicht als traditionsgebundenen, frommen Juden, sondern als kritischen Weisen. Auch hier bleibt er in den Grenzen der Immanenz." The way he speaks about God shows the limits of theodicy, i.e. of the attempts to build, from his position in this world, statements about God as the cause of that world.

Prediker (Skrifuitleg vir bybelstudent en gemeente), Kaapstad, 1993; *Irony in the Book of Qohelet*, in *JSOT* 72 (1996) 57-69.

5. See especially his *Humanität angesichts des Absurden. Qohelet (Prediger) 1,2-3,15*, in H. FOERSTER (ed.), *Humanität Heute*, Berlin, 1970, pp. 22-36; *Vom Gott, der im Himmel ist (Reden von Gott bei Qohelet)*, in *ThViat* 12 (1973-74) 87-100; *Qohelet-Probleme. Überlegungen zu Qoh 8,2-9 und 7,11-14*, in *ThViat* 15 (1979-80) 81-103; *Qohelet* (Erträge der Forschung, 258), Darmstadt, 1988; *Untersuchungen zur Eigenart des Buches Qohelet* (BZAW, 183), Berlin-New York, 1989.

Also in the German-language seminar on the significance of recently published texts from Qumran for the interpretation of the book of Qohelet, Qoh 4,17-5,6 played a pivotal role. A. LANGE[6] (In Diskussion mit dem Tempel: Zur Auseinandersetzung zwischen Kohelet und weisheitlichen Kreisen am Jerusalemer Tempel), who led the seminar, introduced texts from Qumran which might be of help in interpreting Qohelet, viz. *The Book of Mysteries* (1Q27; 4Q299-301) and the *Sapiential Work A* (4Q416-418) to be dated in the 3rd/2nd centuries B.C. These non-Essene wisdom texts provide new vistas on Jewish wisdom in the 3rd and 2nd centuries B.C. Qoh 6,8 or 6,11 is quoted in 1Q27. The connection between Torah and/as wisdom on the one hand and Eschatology on the other in Qoh 8,5-6; 11,9; 12,12-14 (passages from the second redactor) is also attested in the two Qumranic works under consideration. The latter can be situated in the Temple as well as probably the second redactor of the Book of Qohelet. Qohelet himself takes issue with the *Weisheitsnomismus* in 2,26; 7,26; 4,17-5,6. The background of the last mentioned pericope can be understood in the light of the attention cultic matters receive in Sirach and the Qumran texts under consideration. All these theses were extensively debated but no final agreement could be attained. Everybody agreed that there is some relationship between wisdom and Torah in Qohelet and also in the non-Essene wisdom texts just referred to. The problem, however, remained that it seemed problematic to find a direct relationship between these texts and Qohelet. Yet Lange offers a consistent and well furnished presentation of his approach.

In his paper on "Qohelet et Ben Sira", M. GILBERT[7] discusses two questions. First, can Qoh 12,13bα, "Fear God and keep his command-

---

6. See his *Weisheit und Torheit bei Kohelet und in seiner Umwelt* (Europäische Hochschulschriften, XXIII/ 433), Frankfurt a.M., 1991; and on wisdom literature at Qumran his: *Weisheit und Prädestination. Weisheitliche Urordnung und Prädestination in den Textfunden von Qumran* (Studies on the Texts of the Desert of Judah, 18), Leiden, 1995.

7. With regard to Qohelet and other Wisdom literature, see his *La structure de la prière de Salomon (Sg 9)*, in *Bib* 51 (1970) 301-331; *Volonté de Dieu et don de la sagesse, Sg 9,17s*, in *NRT* 93 (1971) 145-66; *La critique des dieux dans le livre de la Sagesse (Sg 13-15)* (AnBib, 53), Roma, 1973; *L'éloge de la Sagesse (Sir 24)*, in *RTL* 5 (1974) 326-48; *La connaissance de Dieu selon le Livre de la Sagesse*, in J. COPPENS (ed.), *La notion biblique de Dieu. Le Dieu de la Bible et le Dieu des philosophes* (BETL, 41), Leuven, 1976, pp. 191-210; *Comment lire les écrits sapientiaux de l'AT*, in *Morale et Ancien Testament* (Lex Spiritus Vitae, 1), Louvain-la Neuve, 1976, pp. 131-75; *Ben Sira et la femme*, in *RTL* 7 (1976) 426-42; *Le discours de la Sagesse en Prov 8*, in *La Sagesse de l'Ancien Testament* (cf. n. 1), pp. 202-18; *La Sagesse personnifiée dans les textes de l'Ancien Testament*, in *CahEv* 32 (1980) 5-36; *La description de la vieillesse en Qohélet XII 1-7 est-elle allégorique?*, in *SVT* 32 (1981) 96-109; *Les raisons de la modération di-*

ments", allude to Sirach? The answer seems not to be unambiguous: it is possible, but the double precept given by the epilogist is a stereotyped formula, which does not reveal Sirach's rich thinking about the connections between wisdom, fear of God and observation of the Torah. His second point is a comparison between Qohelet's idea of happiness and Sir 14,11-19, the latter to be read together with 13,25-14,10, the portrait of the avaricious pennypincher. When Sirach invites us to enjoy the happines which is our part, it is hard to prove that he depends on Qohelet. His only argument to found his advice is the inescapability of death, whereas Qohelet's invitation to enjoyment originates from his observation of the incongruities of life. When reading Qohelet in connection with possible sources or successors, it appears from such papers as the ones by Gilbert or Michel that an intertextual approach of this book is a tricky business.

The question of Greek influence on Qohelet, which often preoccupied scholars, receives an exemplary treatment on the basis of an exegesis of Qoh 7,15-18 by L. SCHWIENHORST-SCHÖNBERGER[8] (Via media. Koh 7,15-18 und die griechisch-hellenistische Philosophie). He shows with a convincing argumentation that Qoh 7,15-18 recommends some form of via media, a *tertium quid* between righteousness and wickedness, which in the line of Greek philosophy is called "good" (טוב), and in the line of Judaism, "Fear of God" (ירא אלהים). This is a discussion about the va-

vine (Sag 11,21-12,2), in A. CAQUOT & M. DELCOR (eds.), *Mélanges bibliques et orientaux en l'honneur de M. Cazelles* (AOAT, 212), Kevelaer-Neukirchen, 1981, pp. 149-162; *Il cosmo secondo il libro della Sapienza*, in G. DE GENNARO (ed.), *Il cosmo nella Bibbia*, Napoli, 1982, pp. 189-199; *L'adresse à Dieu dans l'anamnèse hymnique de l'Exode*, in V. COLLADO & E. ZURRO, *El misterio de la palabra; homenaje de sus alumnos al professor L. Alonso Schökel*, Madrid, 1983, pp. 207-225; *Wisdom Literature*, in M.E. STONE (ed.), *Jewish Writings of the Second Temple Period* (Compendia Rerum Iudaicarum ad Novum Testamentum, 2,2), Assen, 1984, pp. 283-324; *La figure de Salomon en Sg 7-9*, in R. KUNTZMANN, *Études sur le judaïsme hellénistique* (LD, 119), Paris, 1984, pp. 225-249; *Il giusto sofferente di Sap 2,12-20: figura messianica*, in G. DE GENNARO, *L'Antico Testamento interpretato dal Nuovo: il Messia*, Napoli, 1985, pp. 193-218; *Sagesse de Salomon*, in DBS 11,60 (1986) 58-119; *La relecture de la Genèse 1 à 3 dans le livre de la Sagesse*, in F. BLANQUART, *La création dans l'Orient ancien* (LD, 127), Paris, 1987, pp. 323-344; *L'Ecclésiastique: quel texte? quelle autorité?*, in RB 94 (1987) 233-250; *La procréation; ce qu'en sait le livre de la Sagesse*, in NRT 111 (1989) 824-841; *Le discours menaçant de Sagesse en Proverbes 1,20-33*, in D. GARRONE & F. ISRAEL, *Storia e tradizioni di Israele*, Brescia, 1991, 99-119.
    8. Among his publications on Qohelet, we should mention: *Nicht im Menschen gründet das Glück (Koh 2,24). Kohelet im Spannungsfeld jüdischer Weisheit und hellenistischer Philosophie* (Herders Biblische Studien, 2), Freiburg, 1994, ²1996; *Das Buch Kohelet*, in E. ZENGER u.a., *Einleitung in das Alte Testament*, Stuttgart, 1995, pp. 263-270; *Kohelet: Stand und Perspektiven der Forschung*, in ID. (ed.), *Das Buch Kohelet. Studien zur Struktur, Geschichte, Rezeption und Theologie* (BZAW, 254), Berlin, 1997, pp. 5-31.

lidity claims of traditional ethics or of Torah, probably provoked by a plausibility crisis. It is the expression of reflective ethics, in search of ethical fundaments, even beyond prescriptions or traditions, but in the larger context of the search for happiness. The substance of Judaism is worded in a new paradigm that has been inspired by ancient philosophy: "Der צַדִּיק und der רָשָׁע werden problematisiert, der יְרֵא אֱלֹהִים, der Gottesfürchtige, wird als der jene Alternativen überwindende Dritte etabliert, dessen Verhalten in jedem Fall gut (טוֹב) ist". More than the ideas themselves, the degree of reflectivity we find in Qohelet was provoked by contact with Hellenistic culture and philosophy.

The theme of human knowledge, and particularly the quest for knowledge is the subject of the paper offered by J. CRENSHAW[9] (Qohelet's Understanding of Intellectual Inquiry). His aim was "to tease out some fundamental principles pertinent to a discussion of Qoheleth's epistemology, examine the sapiential language for acquiring wisdom, and explore the sages' acknowledgment of limits imposed on the intellect". In this regard, Qohelet's complex language makes it difficult to ask pertinent questions. The sages had access to a few expressions connoting a teacher, but they compiled an extensive vocabulary for students and their activity. Writing is seldom mentioned, whereas references to observing, listening, reflecting, testing, and drawing conclusions abound. The combination of eye and ear, speech and thought, individual insight and open discussion makes intellectual inquiry a communal effort. Perhaps this acknowledgment that others sharpen one's wits softens the concession that every intellectual endeavour comes up against certain limits, giving rise to the expression that the matter is unfathomable. In his understanding of the intellectual enterprise, Qohelet was quite at home with the sages before or after him, "if his choice of language and recognition of the outer limits of knowledge have any bearing on this issue". With regard to intellectual inquiry, Qohelet may have been less revolutionary than some scholars have thought.

---

9. See his *The Eternal Gospel (Eccl. 3:11)*, in J.L. CRENSHAW & J.T. WILLIS (eds.), *Essays in Old Testament Ethics*, New York, 1974, pp. 23-55; *The Shadow of Death in Qoheleth*, in J.G. GAMMIE (ed.), *Israelite Wisdom: Theological and Literary Essays in Honor of S. Terrien*, Missoula, 1978, pp. 205-216; *Old Testament Wisdom*, Atlanta, 1981; *Qoheleth in Current Research*, in *HAR* 7 (1983) 41-56; *A Whirlpool of Torment*, Philadelphia, 1984; *The Wisdom Literature*, in D.A. KNIGHT & G.M. TUCKER, *The Hebrew Bible and Its Modern Interpreters*, Philadelphia, 1985; *Education in Ancient Israel*, in *JBL* 104 (1985) 601-615; *Ecclesiastes. A Commentary* (OTL), Philadelphia, 1987; *Prohibitions in Proverbs and Qoheleth*, in *Priests, Prophets and Scribes* (JSOT SS, 149), Sheffield, 1992, pp. 115-124. – Professor Crenshaw was not able to attend the Colloquium because of health problems. His paper was read by M.V. Fox.

M.V. Fox[10] (The Inner-Structure of Qohelet's Thought) presented an interesting and provocative paper the thesis of which is that the book of Qohelet is about meaning: he complains about the collapse of meaning and in his counsels and affirmations he attempts to reconstruct and re-cover meanings. In other words: he tears down meaning by uncovering contradictions, but he also seeks ways of reconstructing local meanings within a senseless world. This is illustrated by Qohelet's sayings about עמל and שׂמחה, about wisdom and its advantages and about righteous-ness and its rewards. For Qohelet the anomalies do not undermine the rule but rather the world's rationality. His affirmations are based on a very modest standard: something is good if it is better than its alternative. "Qohelet is not primarily a moralizer, and in this regard he stands far from Proverbs and Ben Sira, who tend to equate wisdom and righteousness". The best he can offer is a temporary, local tactic for coping with the vacuum: When you possess something good, enjoy it immediately.

The subject of the English-language seminar, conducted by R.N. WHYBRAY[11] (Qoheleth as a Theologian), was whether Qohelet should be understood as a Jewish theologian and apologist concerned to present to his readers a version of Judaism that retained the essentials of the Jewish faith while recognizing the necessity to move with the times – that is, as both a conservative and a radical. The discussion ranged widely. Some participants felt that this perception of Qohelet's role went beyond what could be demonstrated from the text. The opinion was also voiced that his radicalism, especially his scepticism about God's concern with the human race, was more subversive of orthodox belief than the author of the introductory paper supposed. The fact of the book's inclusion in the

10. See his *Frame-narrative and Composition in the Book of Qohelet*, in *HUCA* 48 (1977) 83-106; (with B. Porten) *Unsought Discoveries: Qohelet 7:23-8:1a*, in *Hebrew Studies* 19 (1979) 26-38; *The Identification of Quotations in Biblical Literature*, in *ZAW* 92 (1980) 416-31; *The Meaning of* hebel *for Qohelet*, in *JBL* 105 (1986) 409-27; *Aging and Death in Qohelet 12*, in *JSOT* 42 (1988), 55-77; *Qohelet and his Contradictions* (JSOT SS 71), Sheffield, 1989; *Wisdom in Qoheleth*, in *In Search of Wisdom*. Essays in Memory of J.G. Gammie, Louisville, 1993, pp. 115-131.

11. Of his publications on Qohelet mention should be made of the following: *Qoheleth the Immoralist? (Qoh. 7:16-17)*, in J.G. GAMMIE (ed.), *Israelite Wisdom: Theo-logical and Literary Essays in Honor of S. Terrien*, Missoula, 1978, pp. 191-204; *Conservatisme et radicalisme dans Qohelet*, in E. JACOB (ed.), *Sagesse et religion*, Paris, 1979, pp. 65-81; *Two Jewish Theologies: Job and Ecclesiastes*, Hull, 1980; *The Identifi-cation and Use of Quotations in Ecclesiastes*, in *SVT* 32 (1981) 435-451; *Qoheleth, Preacher of Joy*, in *JSOT* 23 (1982) 87-98; *Ecclesiastes 1.5-7 and the Wonders of Nature*, in *JSOT* 41 (1988) 105-112; *Ecclesiastes* (New Century Bible Commentary), London-Grand Rapids, 1989; *"A Time to be Born and a Time to Die". Some Observations on Ecclesiastes 3:2-8*, in *Near Eastern Studies*. FS Prince Takahito Mikasa (Bulletin of the Middle Eastern Culture Center in Japan, 5), Wiesbaden, 1991, pp. 469-483. It is our sad duty to inform our readers that Professor Whybray died suddenly on 15th April 1998.

canon was also thought to be relevant. The view of Qohelet as a theologian in some sense was generally accepted as a valid approach to the book.

A. DE PURY[12] (Genève) dealt with the position of Qohelet within the canon of the *ketubim*: *Qohélet et le canon des* ketubim. He adheres to the paradigm proposed by Leiman and Beckwith, viz. that in a certain Jewish milieu (pharisaic or proto-pharisaic) the present collection of the 12 *Ketubim* was formed about the middle of the 2nd century B.C. But the original collection of the Writings, formed at the end of the 3rd century B.C., probably included only Proverbs, Job, Canticles and Qohelet. In this collection Qohelet seems to be the latest book. According to de Pury the second epilogue (12, 12-14) could go back to the formation of the pharisaic *Ketubim*. But from the first epilogue (12,9-11) one gets the impression that it presents Qohelet-Solomon as the creator of a literary canon, probably not bound up with the Book of Qohelet only. Hence the question: Could Qohelet be the inventor, editor and commentator of the first *Ketubim*? Without Job, Canticles and Qohelet, the Jewish Bible would not have been the literature it is now. The provocative conclusion then is: "Il ne serait donc peut-être pas tout-à-fait absurde de dire que Qohélet est le 'père' de la Bible hébraïque!" Provocative certainly, but also a very speculative supposition, which de Pury himself called "ludique". We regret that we did not receive this paper for publication in the present volume.

Qohelet and the canon was also the topic of the French-language seminar conducted by J.-M. AUWERS[13] (L'épilogue de Qohélet et la réception du livre dans le Canon). In his two introductory lectures, Auwers presented a reading of the two parts of the epilogue (12,9-11 and 12-14). The first question to be discussed was that of the continuity between the book and the epilogue(s). As for 12,9-11, the question may be asked if the "words", mentioned three times, are those of Qohelet or of other sapiential collections. With respect to 12,12-14 we may ask whether it is a conclusion inspired by the book or rather criticizing it. If the epilogist, according to a possible interpretation, is the editor of the book, he may have put on the scene the fictitious character Qohelet and be himself the author of the whole book. Here also the question was raised: Might Qohelet be the editor of the *Ketubim*? Or is he just against Ben Sirach? Although the epilogues tend to contrast with the book in

12. Among his studies on wisdom, see *Sagesse et révélation dans l'Ancien Testament*, in *RTP* 110 (1977) 1-50.
13. See his *La condition humaine entre sens et non-sens. Le bilan de Qohèlèth*, in A. THÉODORIDÈS a.o. (eds.), *Humana condicio. La condition humaine* (Acta Orientalia Belgica, 6), Bruxelles, 1991, pp. 193-211.

form and content, one feels a tendency, in accord with some exegetes, to consider them less alien to the book than it is often suggested.

F. VINEL[14] (Le texte grec de l'Ecclésiaste et ses caractéristiques) offers a lexical study of the Greek text of *Ecclesiastes*, which, in fact is the version of Aquila: Its vocabulary is characterized by its uniformization vis à vis the other biblical books; this uniformization is often obtained by an etymological type of translation, but it does not exclude an occasional translation *ad sensum*. Aquila's vocabulary is also homogeneous with the vocabulary of Greek literature in general. The Greek character of Aquila's vocabulary curiously contrasts with the well-known awkwardness of his syntax. In the second part of her paper Vinel presents the Greek Ecclesiastes as a critical *relecture* of the history of Israelite kingship. The vocabulary shows an evident affinity with several narratives in the books of *Regna*, whereas the sapiential text itself appears as the judgment pronounced on the activity of the kings.

The Dutch-language seminar conducted by P.C. BEENTJES[15] ("Who is like the Wise?" Some Notes on Qohelet 8,1-15) was devoted to a close reading of Qoh 8,1-15. In the first session, Qoh 8,1-9 was discussed.

14. Dr. Françoise Vinel participates in the project "La Bible d'Alexandrie" directed by Marguerite Harl, Gilles Dorival and Olivier Munnich, an abundantly annotated French translation of the Septuagint, for which she prepares the translation of Ecclesiastes.

15. Of his publications on Qohelet and Sirach, see *Sirach 22,27-23,6 in zijn context*, in *Bijdragen* 39 (1978) 144-150; *Recente visies op Qohelet*, in *Bijdragen* 41 (1980) 436-444; *Jesus Sirach 7:1-17: Kanttekeningen bij de structuur en de tekst van een verwaarloosde passage*, in *Bijdragen* 41 (1980) 251-9; *Jesus Sirach 38:1-15: Problemen rondom een symbool*, in *Bijdragen* 41 (1980) 460-5; *Jesus Sirach en Tenach; een onderzoek naar en een classificatie van parallellen, met bijzondere aandacht voor hun functie in Sirach 45:6-26*, Amsterdam, 1981; *Recent Publications on the Wisdom of Jesus Sirach (Ecclesiasticus)*, in *Bijdragen* 43 (1982) 188-198; *De getallenspreuk en zijn reikwijdte; een pleidooi voor de literaire eenheid van Jesus Sirach 26:28-27:10*, in *Bijdragen* 43 (1982) 383-9; *Jesus, de zoon van Sirach*, Averbode, 1982; *The 'Praise of the Famous' and its Prologue; Some Observations on Ben Sira 44:1-15 and the Question on Enoch in 44:16*, in *Bijdragen* 45 (1984) 374-382; *'The Countries Marvelled at You'; King Solomon in Ben Sira 47:12-22*, in *Bijdragen* 45 (1984) 6-13; *De stammen van Israël herstellen; het portret van Elia bij Jesus Sirach*, in *ACEBT* 5 (1984) 147-155; *Some Misplaced Words in the Hebrew Manuscript C of Ben Sira*, in *Bib* 67 (1986) 397-402; *In de marge van manuscript B; kanttekeningen bij de hebreeuwse tekst van Sirach 30:12*, in *Bijdragen* 48 (1987) 132-7; *Hermeneutics in the Book of Ben Sira; Some Observations on the Hebrew Ms. C*, in *EstBib* 46 (1988) 45-59; *The Reliability of Text-Editions in Ben Sira 41,14-16; A Case Study in Repercussions on Structure and Interpretation*, in *Bijdragen* 49 (1988) 188-194; *'Full Wisdom is Fear of the Lord'; Ben Sira 19,20-20,31; Context, Composition and Concept*, in *EstBib* 47 (1989) 27-45; *Hezekiah and Isaiah; A Study on Ben Sira xlviii 15-25*, in A.S. VAN DER WOUDE (ed.), *New Avenues in the Study of the Old Testament* (OTS, 25), Leiden, 1989, pp. 77-88; *'Sweet is his Memory, Like Honey to the Palate'; King Josiah in Ben Sira 49,1-4*, in *BZ* 34 (1990) 262-6; *The Book of Ben Sira in Hebrew; Preliminary Remarks Towards a New Text Edition and Synopsis*, in H. SCHWEIZER a.o. (eds.), *Actes du Troisième Colloque International Bible et Informatique*, Paris, 1992, pp. 471-485; *'How Can a Jug Be Friends with a Kettle?' A Note on the Structure of Ben Sira Chapter 13*, in *BZ* 36 (1992) 87-93; (ed.), *The Book of Ben Sira in Modern Research* (BZAW, 255), Berlin, 1997.

Most attention was paid to אני at the opening of verse 2. The participants
discussed intensively whether this word could be the answer to the twofold question of 8,1: "Who is like the sage? Who knows...?" – "I,
Qohelet". During the second session, some problems of Qoh 8,10-15
were studied, especially verse 10: are there two groups, or only the
רשעים, and what are they doing? There was also a long discussion on the
function and meaning of some אשר-clauses, especially those of vss. 11a
and 12. In this volume Beentjes presents his close reading of this chapter. Of course, one can always ask the question of how this reading fits
in with the rest of the book. However, this type of close reading has a
sobering effect and it is full of detailed remarks which command careful
attention and cannot be passed over in silence.

A variety of short papers were offered by scholars and students representing different approaches to the Book of Qohelet. We can distinguish
between papers devoted to the interpretation of a pericope and other
ones which deal with more general literary, philosophical or theological
themes that concern the whole book.

In the first series, T. HIEKE (Wie hältst du's mit der Religion?
Sprechhandlungen und Wirkintentionen in Kohelet 4,17-5,6) offers an
analysis of the illocutional acts in the pericope under consideration,
which shows that Qohelet opposes his opinion to certain traditions and
religious praxis. In *religiosis* the wise should cultivate the same restraint
and prudence as in daily life: the correct relationship with God consists
in "fear of God", the awareness that he is unattainable and not at one's
disposal. With a careful redaction-critical analysis and a close reading of
Qoh 3,16-21, A.A. FISCHER (Kohelet und die frühe Apokalyptik: Eine
Auslegung von Koh 3,16-21) opposes the thesis that in this pericope
Qohelet polemizes against a certain apocalyptic hope of retribution after
death.

Qoh 1,1-11 has been variously read as a description of the endless repetitiveness of life or, more positively, as a narration of the regular and
dependable cycles of life. L. WILSON (Artful Ambiguity in Ecclesiastes
1,1-11 – A Wisdom Technique?)[16] argues that the positive and negative
readings of this pericope have some foundation in the text, and that the
reader may see both to be true to life. Perhaps the reader should sit with
the enigma of both being right. If life is enigmatic, then הבל might be
rendered as 'enigma' (G. Ogden[17]). R.W. BYARGEON (The Significance

---

16. Dr. Lindsay Wilson was not able to present her paper at the colloquium because of
an illness in her family.

17. G.S. OGDEN, *Qoheleth* (Readings – A New Biblical Commentary), Sheffield,
1987, p. 14.

of Ambiguity in Ecclesiastes 2,24-26) analyzes the lexical and grammatical ambiguities in Qoh 2,24-26. By these ambiguities Qohelet is suggesting that even God's gifts are tinged with ambiguity. The wise man should therefore be driven to a greater awareness of God's sovereignty an a realization "that ultimately pleasure and wisdom are limited by divine will and not capitalized on by humanity's wisdom". J.Y.S. PAHK (The Significance of אשר in Qoh 7,26: "More bitter than death is the woman, *if* she is a snare") defends the thesis that in Qoh 7,26 אשר has conditional force and thus Qohelet appears not to be misogynous. According to K. SMELIK (A Re-Interpretation of Ecclesiastes 2,12b) את אשר functions as a conjunction meaning "if", and the meaning of this verse is that Qohelet's search for wisdom and folly cannot be surpassed and that his conclusions regarding the value of human life are final. A. VONACH (Gottes Souveränität anerkennen: Zum Verständnis der "Kanonformel" in Koh 3,14) considers עולם and "fear of God" as key notions in Qohelet's theology: fear of God is man's faithful response to God, whose work he can recognize but not completely fathom or influence. H.A.J. KRUGER (Old Age Frailty Versus Cosmic Deterioration? A Few Remarks on the Interpretation of Qohelet 11,7-12,8) studies the possibility of a mythological-cosmological approach of this pericope as an alternative to the allegorical approach: It would contain a warning against or speculation on a threatening global natural disaster in the light of wisdom's concern with creation. A.J.O. VAN DER WAL (Qohelet 12,1: A Relatively Unique Statement in Israel's Wisdom Tradition) defends the position that 12,1a is an integral part of Qoh 11,7-12,7 and that in the conclusion of his book, Qohelet calls God "your Creator", thus indicating a personal relation between God and man as a basic security for man.

In the series of papers on general themes, N. KAMANO (Character and Cosmology: Rhetoric of Ecclesiastes 1,3-3,9) first defends the unity of Qoh 1,3-3,9 by identifying certain key rhetorical techniques. Character construction and deconstruction based on cosmology are the chief rhetorical strategies utilized in the book. Qohelet is able to characterize himself as a superior king, to deconstruct this self-characterization in order to re-characterize himself as sage, to correlate human affairs to cosmology, and to prepare his audience for points that he is about to make later.

E. CHRISTIANSON (Qoheleth and the/his Self among the Deconstructed) offers a highly philosophical analysis in which he contends that Qohelet's meta-narrative of the self offers an adequate measure of experience: in his world the causes for the failure of the self are clear; both the world and the way the self relates to it are not as they should be. This places every individual under the vexatious curse of futile toil and circular existence, but the self cannot escape its own very real existence. H.-F. RICHTER (Kohelet – Philosoph und Poet) finds in Qohelet a number of poetical devices, such as onomatopoeia, assonance, rime, chiasmus, which give a certain flavour to his world view. He seems to maintain a cyclical world view. Like Schopenhauer he deems life meaningless and like Epicurus he is favourable to joy, but he has not lost the fear of God. Studying "Qohelet's Minimalist Theology", T.A. PERRY focuses on only one of its aspects, his quietism. From this perspective he examines Qoh 1,3-11 and 8,8. His quietism is of the practical sort: Things must be worked out practically, must be consistent with the quotidian character of our personal existence and reflexion (cf. Qoh 3,1ff: many projects are appropriate in their natural time). V. D'ALARIO (Liberté de Dieu ou destin? Un autre dilemme dans l'interprétation du Qohélet) studies the different perspectives of fate in Qohelet but also its constants. In all its occurrences מקרה refers to death and its levelling effect, and unforseeable chance is characteristic of misfortune and death (9,11-12). On the other hand, Qohelet also accepts the idea of God's mysterious freedom (3,10-15) and his uncomprehensible relation with man (9,1). Chance and God's freedom seem to be the two sides of the same reality. Investigating the relationship between wisdom, sorrow and joy, D. RUDMAN (The Anatomy of the Wise Man: Wisdom, Grief and Joy in the Book of Ecclesiastes) studies Qoh 7,3; 9,3; 11,9-10 in which the terms "good" and "evil" are associated with the mind, and so finds the main thrust of Qohelet's thought on this question. The conclusion is: "While sorrow is experienced in the course of his meditations upon the world, this act leads ultimately to wisdom. This in turn enables the sage to appreciate life's benefits". A. GIANTO (Human Destiny in Emar and Qohelet) attempts to show the bearing of two wisdom texts from Emar (Emar VI.4:767 and VI.4:778) on the interpretation of Qohelet. They appear to share four basic themes with Qohelet: Destinies are fixed by divine force with their own logic; destinies and lots are therefore unalterable; it is a mere illusion to try to change destinies; one thing is worth doing, viz. to try to find meaning in the realities of life.

Finally, J. COOK (Aspects of the Relationship between the Septuagint Versions of Kohelet and Proverbs) compares the two LXX versions on the macro-level (textual issues, order of verses and chapters, syntax), on the micro-level (lexical) and on the "theological/ideological" level. His conclusion is that these translations differ dramatically as far as most facets of their rendering are concerned. Unlike the translator of Proverbs the one of Ecclesiastes stuck to his source text in a litteral manner, but both were intent to render the intention of their source text as clearly as possible.

It is striking that the much debated question of the structure of Qohelet was more or less absent from the programme. It was only obliquely touched upon in the discussion of the exegesis of certain pericopes. There seems to be a certain weariness in examining again and again ingeniously built structures. Perhaps we shall have to content ourselves with agreeing on the function of Qoh 1,3-3,9 as the basic exposition of Qohelet's *Weltanschauung* and be happy to find our way in the logic of its more detailed elaboration in the delineation and the mutual connections of pericopes in the following chapters. Most of us will agree that Qohelet is a highly philosopical book. And, in contrast to many commentaries which deal with the philosophical aspect rather superficially, we heard in the Colloquium quite a number of thorough discussions of Qohelet's philosophical tenets. But at the same time there was a striking interest in the theological significance of Qohelet: "Qohelet as a theologian" was the topic of the English-language seminar and a theological interest came to the fore in a number of (short) papers. Striking also was the significance of Qoh 4,17-5,6 as a central pericope in the book, and we know that it is even the central one in some schemes of the composition of the book, e.g. the one suggested by Lohfink in his commentary, where the pericope receives the title "Religionskritik"[18]. But we should beware of a tendency, which is wrong, in my opinion, to reclaim Qohelet too easily as a proponent of traditional biblical views. This volume contains a rich collection of thorough analyses and different approaches, which will give new incentives to continue exploring this fascinating book of Qohelet.

Dunberg 50   Antoon SCHOORS
B-3210 Lubbeek

---

18. N. LOHFINK, *Kohelet* (Die Neue Echter Bibel), Stuttgart, Echter Verlag, 1980, p. 10.

MAIN PAPERS

WORDS TYPICAL OF QOHELET

As a second part of my work on the language of Qohelet I am preparing a volume on the vocabulary of that book. A number of words occur in Qohelet with such frequency that they can be considered as typical of his vocabulary. I have already dealt with some of them in full detail elsewhere[1], but here I will restrict myself to the philosophical impact of those words.

1. אָדָם

The word אדם is found 49 times in Qohelet[2] whereas, according to M. Dahood, אִישׁ occurs only 7 times. This 7:1 ratio has no match in any other book of the Bible. Dahood is convinced that this points to a Northern provenance of Qohelet, since, as pointed out by Z. Harris, "a lexical specialization peculiar to the Phoenician branch of Northwest Semitic is the preference of אדם over אשׁ, especially in the singular"[3]. This is a rash statement. First of all, Dahood's count is not correct, for אִישׁ is found 10 times in Qohelet (1,8; 4,4; 6,2(bis).3; 7,5; 9,14.15(bis); 12,3). But more importantly, as already objected by R. Gordis, this high frequency needs no linguistic explanation: Qohelet employs אדם, because his main interest is "man" in the generic sense of "mankind", human existence in general[4]. In this book the word has a universalistic meaning, especially when it is used with the article, and this applies to the expression בני האדם too. This is explicitly remarked on by S.H. Auerbach: האדם
"הידוע הוא המין האנושי בכללי" (sic)[5]. This usage is in keeping with the fre-

---

1. Cf. A. SCHOORS, *The Word* אדם *in Qoheleth*, in K. VAN LERBERGHE – A. SCHOORS (eds.), *Immigration and Emigration Within the Ancient Near East*. FS E. Lipinski (OLA, 65), Leuven, 1995, pp. 299-304; ID., *The Verb* ראה *in the Book of Qoheleth*, in A.A. DIESEL et al. (eds.), *"Jedes Ding hat seine Zeit..."* FS D. Michel (BZAW, 241), Berlin-New York, 1996, pp. 227-241.

2. Qoh 1,3.13; 2,3.8.12.18.21(bis).22.24.26; 3,10.11.13.18.19(bis).21.22; 5,18; 6,1. 7.10.11.12(bis); 7,2.14.20.28.29; 8,1.6.8.9(bis).11.15.17(bis); 9,1.3.12(bis).15; 10,14; 11,8; 12,5.13.

3. M. DAHOOD, *Canaanite-Phoenician Influence in Qoheleth*, in *Bib* 33 (1952) 3-52; 191-221, pp. 202-203; cf. Z. HARRIS, *Development of the Canaanite Dialects*, New Haven, 1939, p. 52.

4. R. GORDIS, *Was Kohelet a Phoenician? Some Observations on Methods of Research*, in *JBL* 74 (1955) 103-114, p. 112; cf. F. PIOTTI, *Osservazioni su alcuni usi linguistici dell'Ecclesiaste*, in *BibOr* 19 (1977) 49-56, pp. 49-51.

5. S.H. AUERBACH, *Das Buch Koheleth neu übersetzt mit einem hebräischen Commentar*, Breslau, 1837, p. 37.

quent occurrence of the word with the general meaning of "mankind" in the rest of the Bible, where, for example, his creation by God is emphasized, or where an opposition to other creatures such as animals is suggested, or where in legal texts his duties are fixed. In Psalms the expression בני אדם always has a universalistic meaning. In Job, too, the word is used in connection with man's relation to God and with the general destiny of mankind[6]. The occurrence of the noun without the article is either due to syntax, in particular to the presence of negative particles (7,20; 8,8), or the indefinite word refers to an unnamed individual. There are only a couple of exceptions to this scheme. Here follow a few examples which illustrate this thesis.

The difference between the noun with and without the article can be illustrated by Qoh 2,21-22, where v. 21 provides an example: "Sometimes a man (אדם) who has toiled with wisdom and knowledge and skill must leave all to be enjoyed by a man (אדם) who did not toil for it". Here two individuals are put upon the stage, whereas in v. 22 a general conclusion is drawn: "What has man (לָאָדָם) from all the toil and strain with which he toils beneath the sun". Also in 2,26, the noun without article does not refer to mankind but (an) individual(s), since it is defined by a relative clause: לְאָדָם שֶׁטּוֹב לְפָנָיו.

In 3,13, the universalistic meaning of האדם is strengthened with כל: "every man" (comp. 5,18; 7,2)[7]. A special instance of כל־האדם is found in Qoh 12,13. Although this verse is part of the second addition at the end of the book, it can give us information about the linguistic peculiarities of Qohelet's milieu. The exact meaning of the expression in this context is debatable. The moral exhortation, "Fear God and keep his commandments", concludes with the nominal clause כי־זה כל־האדם. A traditional paraphrase of this enigmatic sentence is: "this is the whole duty of man"[8]. But a great number of scholars rightly defend the thesis that here כל־האדם has the same meaning as elsewhere in the book of

6. Cf. *TWAT* I, 88-89 (Maass).

7. G. WILDEBOER, *Der Prediger*, Tübingen, 1898, p. 134; G.A. BARTON, *Critical and Exegetical Commentary on the Book of Ecclesiastes*, Edinburgh, 1908, p. 138; W.J. FUERST, *The Books of Ruth, Esther, Ecclesiastes*, London, 1975, p. 128. D.A. HUBBARD, *Beyond Futility: Messages of Hope from the Book of Ecclesiastes*, Grand Rapids, 1976, pp. 52 and 85; B. ISAKSSON, *Studies in the Language of Qoheleth. With Special Emphasis on the Verbal System* (Studia Semitica Upsaliensia, 10), Uppsala, 1987, pp. 94 and 96.

8. Cf. AUERBACH, *Koheleth* (n. 5), p. 100: "כי זאת תורת האדם ויותר אין ביכלתו"; C. BRIDGES, *An Exposition of the Book of Ecclesiastes*, London, 1860, p. 309; G. MARGOLIOUTH, *Ecclesiastes XII.8-14*, in *ExpT* 35 (1923-24) 121-124, p. 124; L. GORSSEN, *Breuk tussen God en mens*, Brugge, 1970, p. 91. Cf. LXX: ὅτι τοῦτο πᾶς ὁ ἄνθρωπος; Sym: τοῦτο γὰρ ὅλος ὁ ἄνθρωπος; Vg: hoc est enim omnis homo.

Qohelet and, as a matter of fact, throughout the whole Bible[9]: "all men". And therefore they render the sentence as "this is the duty of all men / every man"[10].

As for the general meaning of האדם, there are exceptions in Qohelet. Thus in Qoh 2,12.18 it appears to refer to an individual, viz. the successor of the king, as suggested by many commentators, the most explicit of whom may well be O.S. Rankin: "The view that the words of vs. 12b refer to the king's successor (see Barton, Hertzberg) can hardly be overcome"[11]. Some critics are of the opinion that in 6,7 האדם does not have a general meaning but refers to the man of whom the preceding verses speak[12]. In that case, the article has an anaphoric force. This exegesis, however, is debatable. The verse sounds very much like a proverb. Some scholars regard it as a later addition. Thus Rankin suggests that "the glossator seeks to counter Qohelet's conclusions on frustrated desire by saying man's longings are the very essence of life"[13]. But others who accept the proverbial character of the sentence, such as V.E. Reichert-A. Cohen and R.F. Johnson give it a function in the context[14]. According to D. Michel, it may express the opinion of Qohelet's interlocutor, who reacts against Qohelet's saying in v. 3 that, if someone's appetite does not get satisfaction from the good things, a still-born child is better off than he. The reaction in v. 7 states that unfulfilled appetite is an essential

9. Cf. Gen 7,21; Ex 9,19; Num 12,3; 16,29.32; Jos 11,14; Jud 16,17; 1 Kgs 5,11; 8,38; Jer 31,30; Ez 38,20; Zech 8,10; Ps 116,11; 2 Chr 6,29.
10. M. LUTHER, *in loc.*; M. GEIER, *In Salomonis Regis Israel Ecclesiasten Commentarius*, Lipsiae, 1668, p. 485; C.D. GINSBURG, *Coheleth Commonly Called the Book of Ecclesiastes*, London, 1861, p. 478; F. DELITZSCH, *Hoheslied und Koheleth*, Leipzig, 1875, p. 422; WILDEBOER, *Prediger* (n. 7), p. 167; A.H. MCNEILE, *Introduction to Ecclesiastes*, Cambridge, 1904, p. 94; BARTON, *Ecclesiastes* (n. 7), p. 201; E. PODE-CHARD, *L'Ecclésiaste*, Paris, 1912, p. 484; R. BRAUN, *Kohelet und die frühhellenistische Popularphilosophie* (BZAW, 130), Berlin, 1973, p. 145; M.V. FOX, *Qohelet and his Contradictions* (JSOT SS, 71), Sheffield, 1989 , p. 329.
11. O.S. RANKIN, *Ecclesiastes*, in *Interpreter's Bible* 5, Nashville, 1956, pp. 37-38. Cf. GINSBURG, *Coheleth* (n. 10), p. 290; P. HAUPT, *Ecclesiastes*, Baltimore, 1905, p. 28; M. THILO, *Der Prediger Salomo*, Bonn, 1923, p. 32; O. LORETZ, *Gotteswort und menschliche Erfahrung*, Freiburg, 1964, p. 134; N. LOHFINK, *Technik und Tod nach Kohelet*, in H. SCHLIER (ed.), *Strukturen christlicher Existenz*, Würzburg, 1968, pp. 27-35, esp. 33; A. BAUM, *Worte der Skepsis*, Stuttgart, 1971, p. 9; FUERST, *Ruth, Esther, Ecclesiastes* (n. 7), p. 110; ISAKSSON, *Language of Qoheleth* (n. 7), p. 77; and many others. For a broader discussion of the reading, cf. A. SCHOORS, *The Preacher Sought to Find Pleasing Words* (OLA, 41), Leuven, 1992, pp. 156-157.
12. GINSBURG, *Coheleth* (n. 10), p. 363; THILO, *Prediger Salomo* (n. 11), p. 36; G.C. AALDERS, *Het boek De Prediker*, Kampen, 1948, p. 131.
13. RANKIN, *Ecclesiastes* (n. 11), p. 62; cf. MCNEILE, *Introduction* (n. 10), pp. 22-24.
14. V.E. REICHERT – A. COHEN, *Ecclesiastes*, in *The Five Megilloth*, London, 1946, p. 147; R.F. JOHNSON, *A Form-Critical Analysis of the Sayings in the Book of Ecclesiastes*, Diss. Emory University, 1973, p. 94.

part of human existence. Qohelet's reply to this is formulated in v. 9: "Better is the sight of the eyes than the wandering of desire" (RSV), i.e. "It is better to be satisfied with what is before your eyes than give rein to desire" (NEB)[15]. But I am not convinced that v. 7, assuming that it has that meaning, could not express Qohelet's own ideas. In any case, there are no serious arguments against a universalistic meaning of האדם in Qoh 6,7[16].

Qoh 6,10 is a difficult verse and the exact meaning of אדם is a moot question. A common translation is "and it is known what man is" (RSV) or "will be"[17]. But this is a somewhat strained interpretation, for אשר is not the normal pronoun introducing an indirect question. B. Isaksson has remarked that it is "surprising that the presence in the same verse of the words נקרא שמו has not directed far more scholars to consider the possibility that אדם in this case is a proper name". And he suggests that Qohelet alludes here to Gen 5,2 ויקרא את שמם אדם[18]. This is in itself a valuable suggestion but, as I have exposed in my grammatical analysis of Qohelet, it does not function very well in the context. I have opted for the solution that the relative pronoun contains its antecedent in itself: "that what man is, is known"[19]. If this is correct, then here indefinite אדם would have the same universalistic meaning as the noun with the article, which is possible in itself and, in view also of Qohelet's erratic use of the article[20], fully acceptable.

In Qoh 8,1 the noun without the article indicates the individual: "the wisdom of a man", for not everybody is wise[21]. Similarly, in 8,9 בָּאדם refers to an individual, viz. the one who is under the power of another one. In 9,15, "no one" is expressed by אדם followed by a negative particle. This is good biblical Hebrew.

15. D. MICHEL, Untersuchungen zur Eigenart des Buches Qohelet (BZAW, 183), Berlin, 1989, p. 150: "Dann wäre 6,7 also nicht die Wiedergabe der Meinung Qohelets, sondern Zitat seiner Gesprächspartner! Zu dieser Annahme paßt nun m.E. ausgezeichnet das weitere Vorkommen von נֶפֶש in v. 9: „Besser das Sehen (= Genießen) der Augen als das Umhergehen (= Umherschweifen) der נֶפֶש (= des Verlangens)!"

16. Cf. also D.C. FREDERICKS, Chiasm and Parallel Structure in Qoheleth 5:9-6:9, in JBL 108 (1989) 17-35, p. 20.

17. Thus H.W. HERTZBERG, Der Prediger (KAT, 17,4), Gütersloh, 1963, p. 135; K. GALLING, Der Prediger (HAT, 1,18), Tübingen, 1969, p.105; A. LAUHA, Kohelet (BKAT, XIX), Neukirchen-Vluyn, 1978, p.118; MICHEL, Untersuchungen (n. 15), pp. 159-161.

18. ISAKSSON, Language of Qoheleth (n. 7), pp. 85-88; also E.H. PLUMPTRE, Ecclesiastes, London, 1890, p. 158; D. LATTES, Il Qohelet o l'Ecclesiaste, Roma, 1964, p. 73; L.G. SARGENT, Ecclesiastes and Other Studies, Birmingham, 1965, p. 53.

19. Cf. SCHOORS, The Preacher Sought (n. 11), pp. 126-127; 140.

20. Ibid., pp. 164-169.

21. Cf. BRAUN, Kohelet (n. 10), p. 131: "eines Menschen".

2. הָיָה

Taking into account Qoh 2,22 הֹוֶה and 11,3 יִהוֹא[22], the verb היה occurs 49 times in Qohelet, which is exactly the same number as for אדם[23]. Again this frequency can be accounted for by the philosophical genre of the book, since philosophy is about "being". However, M.V. Fox has correctly pointed out that "this verb is often best translated 'to happen'. This is a well-established sense of *hayah* (BDB, pp. 224f[24].). The concept of 'being' is not, of course, entirely distinct from 'happening', and often a translation can use either verb."[25] No doubt, the verb can have the meaning "to happen", and it seems to have always meant "to be" in the sense of "to exist" and in the sense of "to come into existence, to happen" at the same time[26]. But in BH the meaning "to happen" is not very often demonstrable[27]. What is typical for Qohelet is the high frequency of the verb היה and the fact that it rather often means "to happen". This illustrates that he is a real philosopher, but more interested in human life than in an ontology of an unalterable metaphysical world. Hence the problem which Qohelet, with all his wisdom, cannot fathom in a satisfactory way, viz. that the God who has preordained human life "under the sun" belongs to the metaphysical world.

Many attestations of the verb היה in Qohelet have a commonplace meaning. Quite often it has the function of a copula[28]. Sometimes היה ל expresses possession or belonging as in 1,11; 2,7; 6,3; 8,12-13. But we are more interested in the occurrences of the verb with an intrinsicly philosophical meaning.

In Qohelet we find several times the phrase מה־שהיה (1,9; 3,15; 6,10; 7,24) and twice its counterpart מה־שיהיה (8,7; 10,14). It seems that the first occurrence in 1,9 sets the lead for understanding the expression:

מה־שהיה הוא שיהיה ומה־שנעשה הוא שיעשה

---

22. Cf. SCHOORS, *The Preacher Sought* (n. 11), pp. 42-43.
23. Qoh 1,9(bis).10(bis).11(ter).12.16; 2,7(ter).9.10.18.19.22; 3,14.15(ter).20.22; 4,3. 16; 5,1; 6,3(bis).10.12; 7,10(bis).14.16.17.19.24; 8,7(bis).12.13; 9,8; 10,14(bis); 11,2. 3.8; 12,7.9.
24. Cf. also *TWAT* II, 393-407, p. 397 (Ringgren).
25. FOX, *Contradictions* (n. 10), pp. 151-152.
26. *TWAT* II, p.397: "Immerhin hat es den Anschein, als habe *hājāh* von vornherein zugleich 'sein' im Sinne von 'existieren, vorhanden sein' (=Gewordenes) und im Sinne von 'entstehen, geschehen' (=Werdendes) bezeichnet".
27. *Ibid.*, p. 398.
28. Qoh 1,10.12.16; 2,7.9.10.18.19; 4,16; 5,1; 6,3; 7,10.14.16.17.19; 9,8; 11,3.8; 12,9.

The verb here clearly has a quite general meaning. It is in this kind of sentence that, according to Fox, the verb specifically means "to happen": Qoh 1,9 "does not mean that a certain entity will once again come into existence, a notion quite foreign to Qohelet. It means that *types of events* recur *ad infinitum*."[29]. In this verse, the parallelism with עשׂה ni. confirms this thesis. N. Lohfink agrees with it, and stresses that the sentence deals with what happens and in the second part with human activity[30]. And both Fox and Lohfink refer to 3,1-8, the "Catalogue of Times" for an illustration of the type of events Qohelet has in mind. The idea of this catalogue is strikingly recapitulated in a sentence that is very close to 1,9, viz. 3,15: "Whatever happens (היה) already has happened, and what is to happen (להיות) already has happened (היה)" (transl. Fox). The question is whether the perfect forms of היה in 1,9 as well as in 3,15 express the present tense. This question is not without importance in a study of the meaning of the verb in Qohelet's language: does he only oppose past to future or does he rather oppose all that is in existence to what is still to come? Isaksson is of the opinion that it is reasonable "to conceive the phrase *maššæhāyā* as having reference to present time, or more properly, to any time (the general present)". This would be confirmed by the general perspective of the text: "The interest is focused on the invariances of life in the midst of things which can be observed"[31]. But if the present is here a general present and if the verb means "to happen", the difference from a past tense is negligible, since the general present would also mean "what has happened up to now", since it is opposed to the future יהיה. On the contrary, in 3,15 the opposition is between the present and the past, expressed by כְּבָר, and then between the future and the past:

מה־שׁהיה כבר הוא ואשׁר להיות כבר היה

This verse has been much debated in scholarly literature particularly because of the somewhat awkward construction with כבר הוא. Isaksson rightly remarks that Qohelet is dealing here with actual life under the sun, and therefore the perfect היה does refer to a gnomic present, as already proposed by a number of critics and as I have also stated in my book on Qohelet's language[32]. This confirms the *RSV* translation: "That

29. Fox, *Contradictions* (n. 10), p. 151.
30. N. Lohfink, *Kohelet* (Die Neue Echter Bibel), Würzburg, 1980, p. 22.
31. Isaksson, *Language of Qoheleth* (n. 7), pp. 75-76. Cf. Podechard, *L'Ecclésiaste* (n. 10), p. 52: "ce qui existe, ce qui arrive".
32. Isaksson, *Language of Qoheleth* (n. 7), p. 82; cf. Schoors, *The Preacher Sought* (n. 11), p. 174; Thilo, *Prediger Salomo* (n. 11), p. 34: "Was ist (היה presentisch), das war längst"; Podechard, *L'Ecclésiaste*(n. 10), p. 300; D. Lys, *L'Ecclésiaste ou que vaut la vie?*, Paris, 1977, p. 366; Lauha, *Kohelet* (n. 17), p. 62.

which is, already has been..." (cf. also the *NEB*). The nominal clause כבר הוא, in which the past meaning is expressed by כבר, is a good Hebrew clause and C.F. Whitley's translation very well renders its meaning: "That which is, is of long ago..."[33]. Probably the second היה in 3,15 has a past meaning because of its adjunct כבר, although a present meaning cannot be excluded. The same applies to 1,10 כבר היה לעולמים, where the verb also means "to happen", since it is a comment on v. 9. In sum, in Qoh 1,9 and 3,15, מה־שהיה refers to the general situation under the sun, in the more dynamic sense of "what happens", rather than in the more static or ontological sense of "what is".

The same analysis applies to the phrase as it occurs in Qoh 6,10. A host of exegetes render it with the verb "to happen"[34]. And again many of them decide in favour of a present tense[35]. The second half of v. 10a makes it clear that the whole verse is about mankind. This has been observed for a long time by several scholars[36] and Isaksson has rightly underlined that "it is evident that the formally impersonal expression *maššæhāyā* in fact refers to mankind and its activities"[37], even if his interpretation of אדם as a proper name is not necessarily correct[38].

The last attestation of מה־שהיה in Qoh 7,24 has been understood in the same line as the previous ones. Again a number of scholars read the verb as meaning "to happen"[39]. But I have the impression that, because of the highly "philosophical" character of the verse, there is a stronger tendency to understand the verb as referring to "existence"[40]. According to G.A. Barton, "'that which exists' seems here to refer to the true in-

---

33. C.F. WHITLEY, *Koheleth. His Language and Thought* (BZAW, 145), Berlin, 1979, p. 34. Cf. E.S. ARTOM, חמש מגילות מפרשות, Tel Aviv, 1967, p. 77, who paraphrases the clause as follows: הוא דבר של כבר,כלומר כבר היה קודם לכן.

34. E.g. GINSBURG, *Coheleth* (n. 10), p. 366; THILO, *Prediger Salomo* (n. 11), p. 37; H.L. GINSBERG, קהלת, Tel Aviv, 1961, p. 94; GALLING, *Prediger* (n. 17), p. 105; BRAUN, *Kohelet* (n. 10), p. 119: "die ewige Gleichförmigkeit des Geschehens"; L. ALONSO SCHÖKEL, *Eclesiastés y Sabiduría*, Madrid, 1974, p. 43; FOX, *Contradictions* (n. 10), p. 224; MICHEL, *Untersuchungen* (n. 15), p. 161.

35. Next to THILO, GINSBERG, GALLING, FOX and MICHEL, also GEIER, *Commentarius* (n. 10), p. 222; PODECHARD, *L'Ecclésiaste* (n. 10), p. 360; WHITLEY, *Koheleth* (n. 33), p. 60; J.L.CRENSHAW, *Ecclesiastes: A Commentary* (OTL), Philadelphia/London, 1987, p. 130; ISAKSSON, *Language of Qoheleth* (n. 7), p. 88.

36. GEIER, *Commentarius* (n. 10), p. 221-2; J. COTTON, *A Brief Exposition ... upon the Whole Book of Ecclesiastes*, London, 1654, p. 112; PLUMPTRE, *Ecclesiastes* (n. 18), p. 158; WILDEBOER, *Prediger* (n. 7), p. 144.

37. ISAKSSON, *Language of Qoheleth* (n. 7), pp. 85-88.

38. Cf. SCHOORS, *The Word* אדם (n. 1), pp. 303-304, and *supra*, p. 20.

39. E.g. *NEB*; ARTOM, חמש מגילות (n. 34), p. 89: "מה שהתרחש בעולם"; GORSSEN, *Breuk* (n. 8), p. 104: "alles wat er gebeurt"; FOX, *Contradictions* (n. 10), p. 240.

40. Cf. DELITZSCH, *Hoheslied und Koheleth* (n. 10), pp. 324-325; REICHERT-COHEN, *Ecclesiastes* (n. 14), p. 157; R. GORDIS, *Koheleth – The Man and His World*, New York, 1955, p. 271: "all that exists".

wardness of things, the reality below all changing phenomena", and further he explains that the expression "usually means events or phenomena which exist (1,9; 3,15; 6,10), but the context makes it necessary to
understand it here as that which underlies phenomena"[41]. This insistence
on "das Wesen der Dinge" (M. Thilo) should not exclude the primarily
dynamic aspect of what is meant here. Thilo himself opens his comment
with the remark "Eigentl. 'was geschieht'"[42]. And Isaksson correctly
renders the bearing of the verse: "True wisdom, which would involve
insight into the real nature of the things *going on* (emphasis mine) under
the sun, is beyond the reach of human intellect, and this is exactly what
is expressed in 7,24"[43]. It is evident then that here again the perfect form
refers to a timeless present[44].

The phrase מה־שיהיה (Qoh 8,7; 10,14) undoubtedly has in view what
will happen in the future[45]. A number of critics render it as "the future"[46]. In 8,7 this applies to the second יהיה as well. As for 10,14, it has
been suggested on the basis of a few manuscripts, LXX, Sym, Syr and
Vg to emend מה־שיהיה to מה־שהיה[47]. But this is based on a wrong understanding of the opposition between the two halves of the sentence:

לא־ידע האדם מה־שיהיה

ואשר יהיה מאחריו מי יגיד לו

There is not necessarily an opposition, for a perfectly synonymous
parallelism is possible. Some commentators see here a distinction between "future in general" in the first member and "what will happen
after his death" in the second[48]. A question quite similar to the one in
10,14bβ is asked in 3,22: מי יביאנו לראות במה שיהיה אחריו, "who can
bring him to enjoy what will be after him?" (RSV)[49], and in 6,12: מי־יגיד
לאדם מה־יהיה אחריו תחת השמש, "who can tell man what will be after

41. BARTON, *Ecclesiastes* (n. 7), pp. 146 and 148.
42. THILO, *Prediger Salomo* (n. 11), p. 38.
43. ISAKSSON, *Language of Qoheleth* (n. 7), pp. 90-91.
44. Cf. GORSSEN, FOX, GORDIS, REICHERT-COHEN, DELITZSCH, BARTON and ISAKSSON
in the preceding notes; also GINSBERG, קהלת(n. 34), p. 102.
45. Cf. PODECHARD, *L'Ecclésiaste* (n. 10), pp. 396-397; GORSSEN, *Breuk* (n. 8),
pp. 106-107; BRAUN, *Kohelet* (n. 10), pp. 84-86.
46. E.g. PLUMPTRE, *Ecclesiastes* (n. 18), p. 177; WILDEBOER, *Prediger* (n. 7), p. 150;
REICHERT-COHEN, *Ecclesiastes* (n. 14), p. 162; H. BRANDENBURG, *Das Buch der Sprüche,
der Prediger und das Hohelied*, Gießen, 1971, p. 168.
47. *BHS*; MCNEILE, *Introduction* (n. 10), p. 155; D. BUZY, *L'Ecclésiaste*, in L. PIROT
& A. CLAMER (eds.), *La Sainte Bible*, VI, Paris, 1941, p. 265. Cf. LXX τὸ γενόμενον;
Syr ܡܐ ܕܗܘܐ; Vg *quid ante se fuerit*.
48. GINSBURG, *Coheleth* (n. 10), p. 438; DELITZSCH, *Hoheslied und Koheleth* (n. 10),
p. 372; cf. PODECHARD, *L'Ecclésiaste* (n. 10), p. 435.
49. Cf. *infra*, p. 26, for ב ראה meaning "to enjoy".

him under the sun?" (*RSV*). J.L. Crenshaw rightly translates מה (שׁי)היה אחריו by "what will *occur* after him/ them" (3,22; 10,14), but "what will occur *afterward*" (6,12) is less felicitous[50]. Another verse that proclaims human ignorance about what will happen in the future is 11,2b: כי לא תדע מה־יהיה רעה על־הארץ, "for you know not what evil will *happen* on earth" (*RSV*)[51].

In Qoh 7,10 מה היה שהימים הראשׁנים היו טובים מאלה, the beginning of the sentence is mostly translated by "How is it that..." or "Why is it that...". I have the impression that – against F. Zimmermann, C.C. Torrey and Isaksson – the verb here again has the meaning "to happen", and I suggest the translation: "Do not say: 'What happened that the former days were better than these?'"[52]. Sometimes the verb expresses more the durable quality of what God does. So in Qoh 3,14 יהיה in combination with עולם.

Qoh 2,22 poses a special problem, for here the participle of the root הוה is used: מה־הֹוֶה לאדם בכל־עמלו, "what has a man for all his toil". According to D. Lys the author has deliberately chosen this root because he wants to express something different from היה, which would mean the banal being, whereas here Qohelet means that toil makes man participate in "l'être". Qohelet would here be posing the problem of ontological being[53]. Lys is right in remarking that this is the only place where Qohelet employs this Aramaic root, but not in looking for an ontological explanation. The reason is rather grammatical: except for Ex 9,3 הֹוָיָה, there is no participle of היה in BH[54]. Michel is closer to the mark, when he compares 2,22 to 1,3:

מה־יתרון לאדם בכל־עמלו שׁיעמל תחת השׁמשׁ 1,3
מה־הוה לאדם בכל־עמלו ובריעיון לבו שׁהוא עמל תחת השׁמשׁ 2,22

This parallelism clearly shows that הֹוֶה replaces יתרון, and that it is used here to stress the enduring character of the gain he is searching for,

50. CRENSHAW, *Ecclesiastes* (n. 35), pp. 101; 130 and 168; cf. AALDERS, *Prediker* (n. 12), p. 135.

51. Cf. BUZY, *L'Ecclésiaste* (n. 47), p. 267; GALLING, *Prediger* (n. 17), p. 118; BRAUN, *Kohelet* (n. 10), p. 136.

52. F. ZIMMERMANN, *The Aramaic Provenance of Qohelet*, in *JQR* 36 (1945-46) 17-45, p. 35; C.C. TORREY, *The Question of the Original Language of Kohelet*, in *JQR* 39 (1948-49) 115-160, p. 159; ISAKSSON, *Language of Qoheleth* (n. 7), pp. 88-89.

53. LYS, *L'Ecclésiaste* (n. 32), pp. 274-275: "Qohèlèth pose le problème que nous appellerions ontologique de l'être, qui se distingue des étants (cf. Heidegger)". Cf. ID., *L'être et le Temps. Communication de Qohèlèth*, in M. GILBERT (ed.), *La Sagesse de l'Ancien Testament* (BETL, 51), Gembloux, 1979, pp. 249-258; A. NÉHER, *Notes sur Qohélet (L'Ecclésiaste)*, Paris, 1951, p. 93. Cf. SCHOORS, *The Preacher Sought* (n. 11), p. 99. There I have also mentioned some attempts to dissociate the root הוה from היה.

54. Cf. SCHOORS, *The Preacher Sought* (n. 11), p.99.

and Michel goes somewhat in Lys's direction, when he suspects the possible influence of Greek philosophical terminology[55]. This connection with יתרון has already been remarked on by C.D. Ginsburg and in a less clear way by F. Delitzsch and, in fact, is reflected in the versions of the Vg and Tg[56].

3. רָאָה

The verb ראה is used 47 times in Qohelet[57]. Therefore it must play an important part in the author's exposé. It is important to look at the forms which the verb takes and the subjects and objects that accompany it.

In Qoh 2,1 occurs the expression ראה בטוב. According to Barton, followed by Gordis, the verb here means "to experience", applied to "the whole gamut of experience from life (9,9) to death (Ps 88,49)". It is frequently followed by the preposition ב (Gen 21,16; 44,34; Jer 29,32; Job 3,9), and Barton explicitly states that "those who hold that ראה ב' denotes enjoyment, are quite mistaken. It is used for any experience, pleasurable or otherwise"[58]. This is correct, but in some instances, the object and the context point to a pleasurable experience, as is the case in 2,1 (cf. Ps 34,13), but Barton is right in pointing out that this enjoyment has an aspect of experience[59]. The same meaning can be given to the verb with טוב(ה) as a direct object. Thus in 2,24, a typical enjoyment conclusion of Qoh, והראה את־נפשו טוב means "and he let his soul enjoy pleasure", i.e. "enjoy himself"[60]. Again 2,24 ראה טוב and 5,17 לראות טובה both mean "to see pleasure, to enjoy"[61]. Finally 6,6 וטובה לא ראה means

55. MICHEL, *Untersuchungen* (n. 15), p. 33: "soll aber doch wohl das Dauernde, Bleibende betonen und damit die Vorstellung eines relativen *jitrôn* abweisen"; n. 85: "Man kann sogar fragen, ob hier nicht Einfluß philosophischer Terminologie des Griechischen anzunehmen ist!"

56. GINSBURG, *Coheleth* (n. 10), p. 298; DELITZSCH, *Hoheslied und Koheleth* (n. 10), p. 254: "Was ist dem Menschen werdend – *resultierend* bei all seiner Arbeit". Cf. Vg: *quid enim proderit homini*; Tg: ארום מא הנאה אית ליה לגבר.

57. Qoh 1,8.10.14.16; 2,1.3.12.13.24(bis); 3,10.13.16.18.22(bis); 4,1.3.4.7.15; 5,7. 12.17(bis); 6,1.5.6; 7,11.13.14.15.27.29; 8,9.10.16(bis).17; 9,9.11.13; 10,5.7; 11,4.7; 12,3.

58. BARTON, *Ecclesiastes* (n. 7), p. 88; GORDIS, *Koheleth* (n. 40), p. 204.

59. Cf. GINSBURG, *Coheleth* (n. 10), p. 276; THILO, *Prediger Salomo* (n. 11), p. 32; R.N. WHYBRAY, *Ecclesiastes* (NCBC), London, 1989, p. 52; WHITLEY, *Koheleth* (n. 33), p. 59; cf. *HAL* III, 1080.

60. Cf. A. STROBEL, *Das Buch Prediger* (Welt Bib, KK, 9), Düsseldorf, 1967, p. 46; BRAUN, *Kohelet* (n. 10), p. 106; GALLING, *Prediger* (n. 17), p. 92; LAUHA, *Kohelet* (n. 17), p. 57; GINSBURG, *Coheleth* (n. 10), p. 300; PODECHARD, *L'Ecclésiaste* (n. 10), p. 280; BARTON, *Ecclesiastes* (n. 7), p. 78; GORSSEN, *Breuk* (n. 8), p. 55; AALDERS, *Prediker* (n. 12), p. 66.

61. GINSBURG, *Coheleth* (n. 10), p. 311; BRAUN, *Kohelet* (n. 10), p. 107; GORSSEN,

"if he finds no joy", as suggested by Gordis, who states that the verb here means "to experience, to taste"[62]. The presence of לֹא־תִשְׂבַּע מִן הַטּוֹבָה in v. 3 in a similar conditional clause enhances this interpretation. Moreover 9,9 רְאֵה חַיִּים עִם־אִשָּׁה is generally understood as "enjoy life with a woman"[63]. The opposite of "see good" is "see evil". We meet this idea in Qoh 4,3, רָאָה אֶת־הַמַּעֲשֶׂה הָרָע, "see the evil work", which means "to experience it, to suffer under it"[64]. In 5,7 "If you see the oppression of the poor and the wresting of justice and right", the meaning is not that of "undergoing, suffering", but only of "perceiving".

Another instance of ראה ב׳ is 3,22 לִרְאוֹת בַּמֶּה שֶׁיִּהְיֶה אַחֲרָיו. The verb can only have a meaning close to יִשְׂמַח in the first part of the verse and the preposition ב confirms this: "There is nothing better than that a man should enjoy (יִשְׂמַח) his work, for that is his lot; who can bring him to *enjoy* (לִרְאוֹת ב) what will be after him?"[65]

Eighteen times the verb occurs in the first person singular of the perfect tense (רָאִיתִי: 1,14; 2,13.24; 3,10.16.22; 4,4.15; 5,12.17; 6,1; 7,15; 8,9.10.17; 9,13; 10,5.7). To this list one can add 1,16 לִבִּי רָאָה, "my heart has seen"; 2,12 פָּנִיתִי אֲנִי לִרְאוֹת, "I turned to see"; 4,1.7 וְשַׁבְתִּי אָנִי וָאֶרְאֶה, "again I saw"; 9,11 שַׁבְתִּי וְרָאֹה "again I saw". The object of these verbs is quite varied.

J.A. Loader has gathered these sentences, together with those introduced by ידע and a few other verbs, into a *Gattung* or basic literary form, called "observation". "The observation is marked by a first person singular style", and it consists in a "report of what has been seen in life"[66]. This supposes that the verb has the same meaning "to see, observe" in all of these contexts. But according to Michel, who has made a somewhat longer analysis of the question,

Breuk (n. 8), p. 128; PODECHARD, *L'Ecclésiaste* (n. 10), p. 298; GALLING, *Prediger* (n. 17), p. 93; AALDERS, *Prediker* (n. 12), pp. 78-79; BUZY, *L'Ecclésiaste* (n. 47), p. 220; LAUHA, *Kohelet* (n. 17), p. 113.

62. GORDIS, *Koheleth* (n. 40), pp. 160 and 249; AALDERS, *Prediker* (n. 12), p. 131; BUZY, *L'Ecclésiaste* (n. 47), p. 239.

63. Cf. *RSV*; *NEB*; GINSBURG, *Coheleth* (n. 10), p. 416; BARTON, *Ecclesiastes* (n. 7), p. 166; GORSSEN, *Breuk* (n. 8), p. 53; PODECHARD, *L'Ecclésiaste* (n. 10), p. 415; GALLING, *Prediger* (n. 17), p. 112; AALDERS, *Prediker* (n. 12), p. 204; BUZY, *L'Ecclésiaste* (n. 47), p. 258; R.B.Y. SCOTT, *Proverbs. Ecclesiastes* (AB, 18), Garden City, 1965, p. 245; GORDIS, *Koheleth* (n. 40), p. 178; J. VAN DER PLOEG, *Prediker* (BOT, VIII,2), Roermond, 1953, p. 58; HERTZBERG, *Prediger* (n. 17), p. 169; J. STEINMANN, *Ainsi parlait Qoheleth*, Paris, 1955, p. 97; MICHEL, *Untersuchungen* (n. 15), p. 125; FOX, *Contradictions* (n. 10), p. 259; LAUHA, *Kohelet* (n. 17), p. 169.

64. GINSBURG, *Coheleth* (n. 10), p. 323; BARTON, *Ecclesiastes* (n. 7), p. 114.

65. Cf. MICHEL, *Untersuchungen* (n. 15), p. 121: "Wer könnte ihn dazu bringen, sich sattzusehen an dem, was nach ihm sein wird?"

66. J. A. LOADER, *Polar Structures in the Book of Qohelet* (BZAW, 152), Berlin, 1979, p. 25.

this is not correct[67]. Already in 1,14, the second half of the verse states the result of the "seeing", which is introduced with הנה. Since this result consists of an appreciation ("All is *hebel* and chasing after wind"), ראה can only mean "(*prüfend*) *betrachten*, look at, examine", an idea which has already been suggested by Delitzsch[68]. The same meaning applies to 2,12, where the expression פניתי לראות implies an active seeing, i.e. examination, and "see by comparing" is also suggested by the juxtaposition of wisdom, madness and folly as objects and by the next verse: "And I saw that wisdom has an advantage over folly" (Barton)[69]. The implication of this would be that in v. 13 the same verb has the meaning "I came to the conclusion". However, v. 14a is a quotation of a traditional proverb, and in v. 13 Qohelet has first given its significance in his own words. It seems that here neither "to examine" nor "to conclude" is the meaning of the verb "to see". The sage has found (he has seen) in traditional wisdom the conviction that wisdom has an advantage over folly, but to this common wisdom he opposes his own opinion in vv. 14b-17.

A similar situation is to be found in Qoh 2,24-25, where again Michel understands ראיתי in the sense of "consider, examine": "Auch das habe ich betrachtet (!), daß dies aus der Hand Gottes kommt"[70]. In his opinion, it is clear that Qohelet does not speak here of an observation and the verb does not refer to the empirical act of "seeing". What, then, is its metaphorical meaning? In v. 24a the sage only repeats the conclusion about the vanity of enjoyment he has reached by his reflections (2,1-11) and in 24b he introduces a new element: he has also examined (ראיתי) the "theological" thesis that enjoyment "is from the hand of God". This thesis is illustrated with the quotation of a proverb in v. 25: "Who can eat or who can have enjoyment/worry apart from him?" Here Michel sees in 24b the reference to some sort of *communis opinio*, which in v. 25 is illustrated with a proverb[71]. But it is hard to prove that v. 25 is a quotation. On the contrary, the idea that either enjoyment or worrying are determined by God, is typical of Qohelet, as appears from 3,13; 5,18. And the inanity or absurdity (v. 26b) consists in the disjunction of

    67. MICHEL, *Untersuchungen* (n. 15), pp. 25-30; 35-7.
    68. MICHEL, *Untersuchungen* (n. 15), p. 21; DELITZSCH, *Hoheslied und Koheleth* (n. 10), p. 235: "ein forschendes Sehen".
    69. Cf. GINSBURG, *Coheleth* (n. 10), p. 288; BARTON, *Ecclesiastes* (n. 7), p. 82; PODECHARD, *L'Ecclésiaste* (n. 10), p. 269; WHITLEY, *Koheleth* (n. 33), p. 59; W. ZIMMERLI, *Prediger* (ATD, 16/1), Göttingen, 1980, p. 155. LXX: Καὶ ἐπέβλεψα ἐγὼ τοῦ ἰδεῖν; Vg: *ad contemplandam*.
    70. MICHEL, *Untersuchungen* (n. 15), p. 35.
    71. MICHEL, *Untersuchungen* (n. 15), pp. 35-40.

effort and result. This exegesis, as proposed by Fox, is more straightforward than the one defended by Michel, and the verb ראיתי here means "to realize"[72], even though Qohelet does not state explicitly how he came to realize it[73]. A comparable use of ראיתי is found in 5,17, where the object is somewhat complicated but has to do with eating, drinking and pleasure. In my monograph on the grammar of Qohelet, I opted for the translation: "Behold, that which I have discovered is good, that it is becoming to eat and drink..."[74] And this implies at the same time that ראה here means "to discover, to realize": it indicates a result of his experience and reflection[75].

In Qoh 3,10 ראיתי את־הענין אשר נתן אלהים לבני האדם, the meaning of the verb can only be "to examine", as suggested e.g. by Ginsburg and Michel[76]. Also for ראיתי in 3,16, Michel defends the meaning "to examine". The verse would again quote a position which is against Qohelet's system: "The place of justice, thither wickedness (must go); the place of righteousness, thither wickedness (must go)". And the sage would open the pericope saying that he has examined this thesis. The verb ראה does not necessarily mean here "to examine, investigate", but "to see, to remark": it refers to Qohelet's experience. In v. 16 he moves the problem of judicial injustice, which he continually sees. In v. 17 he suggests the solution of final judgment, but in 18-21 he points out that this solution does not work. In v. 22 he comes to his practical conclusion that "there is nothing better than that a man should enjoy his work" (*RSV*), again introduced with וראיתי. As it is a conclusion, the verb here can only mean "come to realize" as in 2,24[77].

In Qoh 4,1.7 we find a variant of ראיתי, viz. ושבתי אני ואראה. The verb "to see" refers to Qohelet's experience in the same way as it does in 3,16. In v. 7 the same interpretation applies: "I observed another absurdity under the sun" (Fox)[78]. Of course, in both instances ראה could mean "to

---

72. Cf. also DELITZSCH, *Hoheslied und Koheleth* (n. 10), p. 262: "ein resultatisches".

73. FOX, *Contradictions* (n. 10), pp. 188-90 and 334.

74. SCHOORS, *The Preacher Sought* (n. 11), p. 139; cf. also GINSBURG, *Coheleth* (n. 10), p. 355.

75. Cf. ARTOM, חמש מגילות (n. 34), p. 84: "הרי המסקנה שאליה הגעתי"; GORSSEN, *Breuk* (n. 8), p. 129; WHITLEY, *Koheleth* (n. 33), p. 55; BRAUN, *Kohelet* (n. 10), p. 107; PODECHARD, *L'Ecclésiaste* (n. 10), p. 352; AALDERS, *Prediker* (n. 12), p. 123; BUZY, *L'Ecclésiaste* (n. 47), p. 236.

76. GINSBURG, *Coheleth* (n. 10), p. 307: "a minute inspection of the different employments which God has assigned the children of men"; MICHEL, *Untersuchungen* (n. 15), p. 59: "keine (neue) *Wahrnehmung*, sondern eine (diskursive) *Betrachtung*". Cf. also BRAUN, *Kohelet* (n. 10), p. 107; AALDERS, *Prediker* (n. 12), p. 74.

77. Cf. GINSBURG, *Coheleth* (n. 10), p. 320; REICHERT-COHEN, *Ecclesiastes* (n. 14), p. 130. Cf. Vg: *deprehendi*.

78. GINSBURG, *Coheleth* (n. 10), p. 326: "from jealousy Coheleth proceeds to ava-

examine", as suggested by Michel, but there are no compelling reasons to understand it that way. The situation is the same in 9,11, where the same formula occurs, except for the infinitive absolute וְרָאֹה, which here replaces the imperfect consecutive וָאֶרְאֶה. The object here is expressed by a dependent clause "that under the sun the race is not to the swift, nor the battle to the strong..." (*RSV*). The verse introduces a new experience of Qohelet: he has observed that there is a lot of incongruity in this world.

In Qoh 4,4 again, Michel renders the formula וראיתי אני by "I considered, examined": "Ich betrachtete alles Mühen und den Erfolg alles Tuns: das ist (nur) (Wett)Eifern einer gegen den anderen"[79]. But here also, Qohelet employs his favoured technique of anticipation: אֶת־כָּל עמל ואת כל־כשרון המעשה is the anticipated subject of the following כ-clause[80]. Therefore, the meaning "I have seen, I have experienced" can be retained: "And I saw that all the toil and all skillful activity is one person's jealousy of another" (Crenshaw).

A somewhat peculiar case is Qoh 4,15, where ראיתי does not introduce a new problem but where Qohelet "transports himself into the midst of the scene which he depicts"[81]. From the continuation of the pericope one gathers that "to see" here means "to observe, examine" and that vs. 16 expresses the result of the investigation. The object of the examination is all those who are on the side of the new king and the result is: they are innumerable, but those who come later do not take pleasure in him[82]. Yet, the meaning "to see, experience" cannot be totally excluded, especially when, following Fox and according to the masoretic accents, we understand the structure of the sentence as "I saw all the living (namely, those who go about under the sun) with the next young man..."[83].

---

rice"; BARTON, *Ecclesiastes* (n. 7), p. 115; PODECHARD, *L'Ecclésiaste* (n. 10), p. 325: "la constatation d'une nouvelle anomalie". Vg: *repperi*.

79. MICHEL, *Untersuchungen* (n. 15), p. 46.

80. Cf. SCHOORS, *The Preacher Sought* (n. 11), p. 214; also GINSBURG, *Coheleth* (n. 10), p. 323.

81. GINSBURG, *Coheleth* (n. 10), p. 332; cf. MICHEL, *Untersuchungen* (n. 15), p. 48: "Mit 'ich habe betrachtet' (v. 15) meldet sich Qohelet zu Wort".

82. MICHEL, *Untersuchungen* (n. 15), p. 48; ID., *Qohelet* (Erträge der Forschung, 258), Darmstadt, 1988, p. 141:

> 15 Ich habe mir einmal alle Lebenden angesehen,
> die unter der Sonne geschäftig herumlaufen
> auf der Seite des nachfolgenden Jünglings,
> der an jenes Stelle getreten war:
> 16 Endlos ist die Anhängerschar
> bei jedem, der (gerade) an ihrer Spitze steht —
> (aber est gilt) auch: die Späteren
> sind nicht (mehr) mit ihm zufrieden.

83. FOX, *Contradictions* (n. 10), p. 207.

In Qoh 5,12 the object of ראיתי is a רעה חולה, viz. "wealth is stored up by his owner to his harm" (Fox), a case which is elaborated in the following verses. This elaboration does not necessarily entail the meaning "to examine" of ראה to the exclusion of "to perceive, observe". The same situation is present in 6,1[84]. The object of ראיתי is את־הכל in Qoh 7,15, where it means "both", referring to the two situations that are mentioned in the second half of the verse[85]. Here again the ראה refers to observation and experience as in 3,16; 4,1.7; 5,12; 6,1 etc.[86].

In Qoh 8,9 the meaning of ראה can only be "to examine", since it is explained by the continuation of the verse: ונתון את־לבי לכל־אשר נעשה תחתה שמש, "while applying my mind to all that is done under the sun" (*RSV*). Thus rightly Michel[87]. On the contrary, in the next, quite difficult verse, the verb refers to observation, experience. This means that here, as in 3,16; 4,1.7; 6,1; 7,15, Qohelet opens a section with the description of what he has observed[88].

The syntactical situation of ראיתי in Qoh 8,17 is rather complicated. As I have suggested already, vv. 16-17 consist of one long sentence, in which 16a is the protasis and 17 the apodosis[89]. This is well reflected in Barton's translation: "When I gave my heart to know wisdom and to see the toil that is done upon the earth – for both day and night he sees no sleep with his eyes –, then I saw all the work of God, that man is not able to fathom the work that is done under the sun..." There are also problems with the object of the verb: there seems to be a double object, viz. את־כל־מעשה האלהים and the כי-clause[90]. Some scholars bring the

84. AALDERS, *Prediker* (n. 12), p. 125; R.B.Y. SCOTT, *Proverbs. Ecclesiastes* (n. 63), p. 231.

85. Cf. GINSBURG, *Coheleth* (n. 10), p. 379; BARTON, *Ecclesiastes* (n. 7), p. 145; PODECHARD, *L'Ecclésiaste* (n. 10), p. 374; GALLING, *Prediger* (n. 17), p. 107; AALDERS, *Prediker* (n. 12), p. 153; BUZY, *L'Ecclésiaste* (n. 47), p. 245; WHYBRAY, *Ecclesiastes* (n. 59), pp. 119-120; FOX, *Contradictions* (n. 10), p. 233.

86. HERTZBERG, *Prediger* (n. 17), p. 153; MICHEL, *Untersuchungen* (n. 15), p. 195: "beobachtet".

87. MICHEL, *Untersuchungen* (n. 15), p. 98: "*Rā'îtî* bedeutet hier 'betrachten' und nicht 'sehen'".

88. I.J.J. SPANGENBERG, *Die Boek Prediker*, Kaapstad, 1993, p. 125.

89. SCHOORS, *The Preacher Sought* (n. 11), pp. 135-136; cf. *RSV*; GEIER, *Commentarius* (n. 10), p. 324; GINSBURG, *Coheleth* (n. 10), pp. 407- 408; DELITZSCH, *Hoheslied und Koheleth* (n. 10), p. 344; PLUMPTRE, *Ecclesiastes* (n. 18), pp. 182-183; WILDEBOER, *Prediger* (n. 7), p. 152; MCNEILE, *Introduction* (n. 10), p. 107; BARTON, *Ecclesiastes* (n. 7), p. 157; PODECHARD, *L'Ecclésiaste* (n. 10), pp. 405-406; BUZY, *L'Ecclésiaste* (n. 47), p. 254; AALDERS, *Prediker* (n. 12), p. 194; HERTZBERG, *Prediger* (n. 17), p. 168; SCOTT, *Ecclesiastes* (n. 63), p. 244; GALLING, *Prediger* (n. 17), p. 112; GORSSEN, *Breuk* (n. 8), p. 46; LOADER, *Polar Structures* (n. 66), p. 54; MICHEL, *Untersuchungen* (n. 15), p. 65; SPANGENBERG, *Prediker* (n. 88), p. 132. VAN DER PLOEG, *Prediker* (n. 63), p. 55, is one of the few opponents to this approach.

90. Cf. GK §117h; LAUHA, *Kohelet* (n. 17), p. 161.

two together in one clause, via the figure of prolepsis or anticipation, which is an acceptable parsing[91]. When we keep to our original interpretation of the connection between vv. 16 and 17, whether we accept an anticipation or not, in v. 17 the verb ראה can only express a conclusion: "I realized that...", whereas in vs. 16 לראות refers to Qohelet's observation or examination which led him to that conclusion.

In Qoh 9,13 the object of ראיתי is זה and חכמה. According to Barton, who is followed by many translators and commentators, חכמה here means "a wise act"[92]. As the MT stands, חכמה seems to be a predicative accusative: "This also I saw as an instance of wisdom under the sun" (Gordis)[93]. There can be discussion, whether "an instance of wisdom" announces the little story on the besieged city and the wise man, or the conclusion, which is drawn from it in v. 16. The latter alternative is preferable, because the whole tone of the pericope indicates that what happened in the narrated incident was not wise. But what does the verb "to see" then mean in this position? If "wisdom" announces v. 16, then the verb should mean "I have found" (as a result of my investigation). Finally, in Qoh 10,5.7 ראיתי undoubtedly refers to the sage's observation, as appears from the objects: an evil or error proceeding from the ruler and slaves on horses and princes walking like slaves[94].

In sum, in Qohelet the form ראיתי has not the fixed meaning as suggested by Loader (observation) or Michel (examination), but depending on the object and the context, it can mean either of them and also realization or conclusion.

In Qoh 1,16 the object of the comparable expression לבי ראה is הרבה חכמה ודעת. Here, the subject "my heart" as well as the object seem to exclude the meaning "observe" in the sence of experience[95]. Rather it should refer to some active seeing, such as "examination". Again in 2,3 the clause עד אשר־אראה אי־זה טוב לבני האדם, "till I might see what was

91. Cf. SCHOORS, *The Preacher Sought* (n. 11), p. 215; further GINSBURG, *Coheleth* (n. 10), p. 408: וראיתי כי לא יוכל האדם למצוא את־כל־מעשה האלהים; BRAUN, *Kohelet* (n. 10), p. 68; PODECHARD, *L'Ecclésiaste* (n. 10), p. 406-407; F. ELLERMEIER, *Qohelet, Teil I, Abschnitt 1: Untersuchungen zum Buche Qohelet*, Hertzberg am Harz, 1967, pp. 299-303; BUZY, *L'Ecclésiaste* (n. 47), p. 254; FOX, *Contradictions* (n. 10), p. 255.

92. BARTON, *Ecclesiastes* (n. 7), p. 164; cf. *RSV*; *NEB*; PODECHARD, *L'Ecclésiaste* (n. 10), p. 419; BUZY, *L'Ecclésiaste* (n. 47), p. 260; SCOTT, *Ecclesiastes* (n. 63), p. 247; GORDIS, *Koheleth* (n. 40), p. 180; VAN DER PLOEG, *Prediker* (n. 63), p. 59; STEINMANN *Ainsi parlait Qoheleth* (n. 63), p. 100.

93. AALDERS, *Prediker* (n. 12), p. 209; GORDIS, *Koheleth* (n. 40), pp. 180 and 300; FOX, *Contradictions* (n. 10), p. 262.

94. AALDERS, *Prediker* (n. 12), p. 218: "ראה tekent het euvel als voorwerp van eigen waarneming".

95. *Pace* THILO, *Prediger Salomo* (n. 11), p. 31; F. ZIMMERMANN, *The Inner World of Qohelet*, New York, 1973, p. 139; FOX, *Contradictions* (n. 10), p. 176.

good for the sons of men" (RSV), refers to a conclusion reached by examination and experience. I have already dealt with the problem of the original reading of 3,18 וְלִרְאוֹת, viz. whether it is hif. or qal[96]. For the meaning of the verb this discussion is irrelevant. Whether we read: "God has tested them and shown that they are beasts", or "God has tested them and they see that they are beasts"[97], the verb refers to a conclusion as the result of God's testing. In Qoh 7,13-14 we find twice an imperative רְאֵה followed by the object "the work of God" and by the closely related clause "God has made the one as well as the other" (RSV). Here the meaning undoubtedly is "consider thoughtfully, pay attention to, bear in mind" (cf. Isa 5,12; 22,11; 26,10)[98].

4. טוֹבָה/טוֹב

In the book of Qohelet the word (ה)טוב is used 52 times[99], which is the highest score in the vocabulary of this book. In the Old Testament the most frequent meaning of the adjective טוב is that of suitability or usefulness of a thing or person: the emphasis here is on the functional aspect, i.e. the fact that something is as it should be, that it answers its essence or task[100]. This rather common meaning is very rare in Qohelet. On the contrary, in Qohelet טוב has some specific meanings, which also occur elsewhere in the Bible but have a key function in this book. In connection with Qohelet's quest for abiding profit, the word has the connotation of "beneficial, efficacious, of lasting value", e.g. when it refers to wisdom. It often has an evaluative meaning, especially when used in "better than" proverbs. In 6,12 but more clearly in 7,18.20; 9,2 the word

96. Cf. SCHOORS, The Preacher Sought (n. 11), p. 44.
97. On the parsing of the infinitives לברם and לראות, see SCHOORS, The Preacher Sought (n. 11), pp. 180-1.
98. Cf. GINSBURG, Coheleth (n. 10), p. 377; DELITZSCH, Hoheslied und Koheleth (n. 10), pp. 317-318; PODECHARD, L'Ecclésiaste (n. 10), p. 373; BRAUN, Kohelet (n. 10), p. 108; SCOTT, Ecclesiastes (n. 63), p. 235; BARTON, Ecclesiastes (n. 7), p. 143; GINSBERG, קהלת (n. 34), p. 99; C. LEPRE, Qoheleth, traduzione ritmica dall' originale ebraico e note, Bologna, 1975, p. 96, THILO, Prediger Salomo (n. 11), p. 37; ISAKSSON, Language of Qoheleth (n. 7), p. 89; GORSSEN, Breuk (n. 8), p. 54; GALLING, Prediger (n. 17), p. 106; AALDERS, Prediker (n. 12), p. 150; GORDIS, Koheleth (n. 40), p. 265; VAN DER PLOEG, Prediker (n. 63), p. 46.
99. Qoh 2,1.3.24(bis).26(bis); 3,12(bis).13.22; 4,3.6.8.9(bis).13; 5,4.10.17(bis); 6,3(bis). 6.9.12; 7,1(bis).2.3.5.8(bis).10.11.14(bis).18.20.26; 8,12.13.15; 9,2(bis).4.7.16.18(bis); 11,6.7; 12,14.
100. Cf. TWAT III 315-339 (Höver-Johag), p. 324: "Unter dem Aspekt der Eignung oder des Nutzens einer Sache oder Person liegt der Schwerpunkt dabei auf dem funktionalen Aspekt als etwas, das in der rechten Ordnung steht, seinem Wesen, d.h. seiner Aufgabe, entspricht."

is used with a more "ethical" meaning, referring e.g. to a virtuous person (9,2). Its most striking connotation is that of "enjoyable" in connection with Qohelet's frequent advice to enjoy the good things of life. The substantive (טוב(ה then means "the good things of life" or "prosperity, pleasure".

In Qoh 11,7 וטוב לעינים is the predicate of a clause in which the subject is the infinitival phrase לראות את־השמש: "And it is pleasant for the eyes to behold the sun" (RSV). Here the adjective is parallel with מתוק, "sweet", it expresses a positive evaluation: "pleasing, enjoyable"[101]. Elsewhere we have shown that "to see the sun" means "to live"[102]. Therefore in 11,7 "good" not only refers to what is adapted to the sense of sight, but it qualifies life as "good, pleasing"[103].

In Qoh 7,11 it is said that טובה חכמה עם־נחלה, "Wisdom is good with an inheritance" (RSV), and comparable sentences are found in 9,16.18. The adjective, used as the predicate of a clause with "wisdom" as its subject, is the expression of a value judgment and means "beneficial, efficacious". In 9,16.18 the syntactical position of the adjective is the same but here the nominal clauses are supplemented with the prepositional phrases מגבורה (v. 16) and מכלי קרב (v. 18), in which the preposition מן has a comparative value ("better than"), thus enhancing the evaluative meaning of the predicate: Wisdom is better than might and better than weapons. These sentences belong to the class of the "better than" proverbs[104].

In this literary form antithetic word pairs are put in opposition in a proverbial sentence which has a typical structure: טוב + subject + מן + second term of the comparison. In the "better than" proverbs טוב is again an adjective that functions as the predicate in a nominal clause. Beside 9,16.18 this literary form is found in Qoh 4,3.6.9.13; 5,4; 6,9; 7,1.2.3.5.8. In all of them a certain life situation is said to be of a higher quality (טוב מן) than another related or opposite one. Even if the gram-

---

101. Cf. H.Witzenrath, *Süß ist das Licht... Eine literaturwissenschaftliche Untersuchung zu Koh 11,7-12,7* (ATSAT, 11), St.Ottilien, 1979, pp. 9-10: "Das unspezifisch positiv wertende Adj nimmt zunächst die spezielle Wertqualität des Adj 11,7a auf"; cf. also p. 37; Fox, *Contradictions* (n. 10), p. 65.

102. Schoors, *The Verb* ראה (n. 1), pp. 227-228.

103. G.S. Ogden, *Qoheleth XI 7-XII 8: Qoheleth's Summons to Enjoyment and Reflection*, in *VT* 34 (1984) 27-38, p. 30: "The adjectives *mātôq* and *ṭôb* in parallel, together wit *hā'ôr* and its complement *lir'ôt 'et-haššemeš*, provide the opening forceful statement about the pleasure of life".Cf. M.J.H. van Niekerk, *Qohelet's Advice to the Young of his Time – and to ours Today? Chapter 11:7-12:8 as a Text of the Pre-Christian Era*, in *OTE* 7 (1994) 370-380, p. 372.

104. Cf. G.E. Bryce, *"Better"-Proverbs: An Historical and Structural Study*, in *SBL Seminar Papers* 108,2 (1972) 343-354; G.S. Ogden, *The "Better"-Proverb (Tôb-Spruch), Rhetorical Criticism, and Qoheleth*, in *JBL* 96 (1977) 489-505.

matical subjects are concrete, such as a youngster, a king, a dog and a lion, or oil, they always represent a certain type of life, behaviour or destiny, which are philosopically evaluated. With V. D'Alario we can conclude that in Qohelet the "better than" proverbs "express the system of values which the author invokes when formulating his judgments; the traditional values are contested and we assist at a real reversal of the criteria of valuation"[105].

In Qohelet טוב is used often as a substantive, as happens already at its first occurrence in 2,1 ראה בטוב. A related phrase is found in 2,24; 3,13; 5,17; 6,6. As we have seen, the verb ראה, followed by an object with ב and sometimes also without the preposition, means "to experience" but in these instances it is always an enjoyable experience[106]. In 2,1 this is confirmed by the fact that the word parallel to טוב is שמחה, "pleasure". In 2,24 it appears that this "good" which is to be enjoyed is a gift of God. In 5,17 we find the feminine form טובה, which we shall also meet in other contexts, but in view of the complete equality of the context, there can be no difference in meaning from the masculine forms in 2,24 and 3,13. Qoh 3,13 is the continuation of v. 12 in which we find the phrase לעשות טוב, "to do good". Some commentators understand this in an ethical sense, because of the ethical character of the joy which is recommended in the context[107]. But the close association with לשמוח and the general affinity with the texts we are discussing in this paragraph, make it clear that the meaning is "to enjoy the good things"[108]. The context of 6,6 is different, but the meaning of the phrase ראה טובה is the same. It makes an *inclusio* with v. 3, where we read ונפשו לא־תשבע מן־ הטובה, "if he does not get satisfaction from the good things of life" (*NEB*)[109]. In sum, טוב(ה) operating substantivally means several times the good or pleasurable things of life, which a person should enjoy, should his or her life not be totally worthless. The feminine form טובה used as a substantive also occurs in Qoh 9,18b: "one sinner destroys much good". It is not clear whether the author here means al kinds of

105. V. D'ALARIO, *Il libro del Qohelet. Struttura letteraria e retorica*, Bologna, 1993, p. 196: "si può senz' altro affermare che i detti *ṭôb* esprimono il sistema di valori, ai quali l'autore fa appello nel formulare i suoi giudizi; in essi i valori tradizionali sono contestati e si assiste a un vero e proprio ribaltamento dei criteri di valutazione".

106. Cf. pp. 26-27.

107. E. ELSTER, *Commentar über den Prediger Salomo*, Göttingen, 1855, p. 72; PLUMPTRE, *Ecclesiastes* (n. 18), p. 133.

108. Cf. O. EISSFELDT, *Einleitung in das Alte Testament*, Tübingen, 1964, p. 675; THILO, *Prediger Salomo* (n. 11), p. 34; HAUPT, *Ecclesiastes* (n. 11), p. 29; GORDIS, *Koheleth* (n. 40), p. 222; LOADER, *Polar Structures* (n. 66), p. 105; T.A. PERRY, *Dialogues with Kohelet*, University Park, PA, 1993, p. 91

109. Cf. J.-J. LAVOIE, *La pensée du Qohélet*, Québec, 1992, p. 113.

good or valuable things and situations without further specification. Although there is no enjoyment-formula in the immediate context, there is some reason to suppose that Qohelet here has in mind "happiness, enjoyment", since that is the only practical "good" that is mankind's part in this world and since טובה often has that meaning in Qohelet[110].

Ogden has dedicated an article to the אין טוב form, which occurs on four occasions in Qohelet: 2,24; 3,12.22; 8,15[111]. The common concern of these texts is the enjoyment of life. In each of them טוב functions substantivally rather than adjectivally. The word could be translated as "pleasure, happiness"[112]. Although these sentences show differences in expression, a degree of formal correlation exists between them. The subject matter of these sentences is focussed on the theme of enjoyment, so that we are in the same theme as the clauses about ראה (ב)טוב(ה), which we have just analyzed. The formula itself means "There is no good except", and because of the presence of comparative מן or כי אם, M. Zer-Kabod has interpreted it in the sense of a superlative: "there is no greater good than", but this is common knowledge in most of the translations and commentaries[113].

A verse which, on form-critical grounds cannot be classified as an אין טוב form but shares with it a number of central elements is 5,17[114]:

הנה אשר ראיתי אני טוב אשר יפה לאכול ולשתות ולראות טובה בכל עמלו

In my study on the language of Qohelet I have already discussed the possibility that טוב אשר יפה reflects the Greek phrase καλὸν κἀγαθόν. I have formulated serious doubts about this identification of the two phrases, not because I reject the possibility of Greek influence but because the two formulas are different[115]. In fact, in spite of the Masoretic accentuation, the Hebrew expression does not constitute a phrase but ²אשר nominalizes the following clause setting it in apposition to טוב[116].

110. Cf. *Pléiade*: "un seul pécheur perd beaucoup de bonheur"

111. G.S. OGDEN, *Qoheleth's Use of the "Nothing is Better"-Form*, in *JBL* 98 (1979) 339-350.

112. E.g. LOHFINK, *Kohelet* (n. 30), p. 63: "Es gibt kein Glück für den Menschen unter der Sonne, es sei denn, er ißt und er trinkt und er freut sich..."(8,15; cf. 2,24; 3,12.22).

113. M. ZER-KABOD, קהלת, Jerusalem 1973, p. 55; cf. *RSV*; *NEB*; *Pléiade*; PERRY, *Dialogues,* (n. 108), p. 83; SPANGENBERG, *Prediker* (n. 88), p. 53; O. LORETZ, *Altorientalische und kanaanäische Topoi im Buche Kohelet*, in *UF* 12 (1980) 267-278, pp. 271-274; LOADER, *Polar Structures* (n. 66), p. 106.

114. OGDEN, *"Nothing is Better"* (n. 111), p. 341.

115. Cf. SCHOORS, *The Preacher Sought* (n. 11), p. 139.

116. Cf. FOX, *Contradictions* (n. 10), p. 217-8: "Here is what I have seen to be good: it is appropriate to eat..."

Therefore I preferred and still prefer a translation in the footsteps of Whitley: "Behold that which I have discovered is good, that it is becoming to eat and drink..."[117] In that case טוב no longer operates substantivally, but the translation "Behold what I have seen as/to be a good thing" remains possible and, in fact, it amounts to the same with respect to meaning.

Also outside the אין טוב form we find the same meaning of טוב used substantivally in sentences that deal with the enjoyment which Qohelet recommends time and again. I wonder whether in Qoh 2,3 טוב, which is the object of יעשו in the relative clause, could not indicate the good or valuable things which man can enjoy (עשה) in his life on earth: "till I might see what is the 'good' for the sons of men, which they may enjoy under the sky the numbered days of their life"[118]. In 4,8 טובה undoubtedly has the meaning of the good things of life, pleasurable things, pleasure"[119]. The fact that we have here the feminine form in contrast with 2,3, where the masculine form occurs, does not demand a different meaning in the two verses.

The meaning of טובה in Qoh 7,14 comes close to the one in 4,8: "In the day of prosperity be joyful" (RSV). This interpretation is generally accepted. The feminine substantive means "well-being, prosperity", and the masculine substantive (בטוב) suggests something like "good mood". In 5,10 הטובה means prosperity in its more material form of riches: "When riches multiply, so do those who live off them" (NEB)[120].

Sometimes טוב acquires a deeper or broader meaning than "enjoyable (things), prosperity", when it is used in sceptical questions like Qoh 6,12: מי־יודע מה־טוב לאדם בחיים , "Who knows what is good for man while he lives" (RSV). It is not the question about what is good for mankind always and everywhere, but what is good for the individual in his life[121]. This is the fundamental concern of Israelite wisdom: what in life, what events, actions, attitudes, will eventually proof to be good. Partly the idea comes close to the moral notion of good versus evil but with Qohelet it cannot be dissociated from his question about lasting profit (יתרון) in human life and therefore it must mean "fruitful, efficacious, of lasting value". In 8,12b-13 we find טוב twice in a similar clause: יהיה־

---

117. WHITLEY, Koheleth (n. 33), p. 55; cf. supra, p. 29.

118. Cf. HAUPT, Ecclesiastes (n. 11), p. 27; BJ: "le bonheur des hommes".

119. RSV and FOX, Contradictions (n. 10), p. 204: "pleasure"; NEB: "the good things of life"; BJ: "bonheur"; SPANGENBERG, Prediker (n. 88), p. 73: "aangename dinge".

120. Cf. SPANGENBERG, Prediker (n. 88), p. 90.

121. LOHFINK, Kohelet (n. 30), p. 50; G. BRIN, The Significance of the Form mah-ttôb, in VT 38 (1988) 463.

טוב ליראי האלהים...וטוב לא־יהיה לרשע. These verses with their traditional *Tun-Ergehen-Zusammenhang* seem to clash with the general
mood of the book of Qohelet. Qohelet quotes traditional wisdom, according to which it will be well with the righteous and not with the
wicked. In this context טוב denotes "well-being, happiness"[122].

The meaning of טוב in 7,18 comes close to that in 6,12: "It is good to
hold on to the one thing and not lose hold of the other" (*NEB*). In the
context the verse expresses the idea that it is the right middle way not to
pretend to be perfectly righteous nor to reject moral earnestness[123]. Also
in 7,20 טוב has a moral connotation, since it is connected with righteousness (צדיק) and the opposite of "doing good" (יעשׂה־טוב) is "sin"
(יחטא). The final sentence of the epilogist (12,14) ends with the pair
"good and evil": "For God brings everything we do to judgement, and
every secret, whether good or bad" (*NEB*). In such a saying טוב can only
have a moral meaning.

In a few verses טוב with a moral connotation is applied to human beings. In 9,2 Qohelet affirms that the same fate awaits the righteous and
the wicked, viz. death. He underlines this thesis by listing a number of
opposed moral or cultic attitudes, which lose their importance in death.
Among them we find כטוב כחֹטֶא, "as is the good man, so is the sinner"[124]. In 2,26 and 7,26 we find the phrase טוב לפניו/לפני האלהים. The
moral connotation of this expression is not undisputed. A number of
commentators understand it in a strictly moral sense, and they can invoke the contrasting term חוטא, which in their opinion must be understood as "sinner"[125]. But there is a strong exegetical trend to interpret
חוטא as the one who has missed the mark, the unfortunate, and טוב לפני
האלהים then is the lucky one, whom God likes[126]. In view of Qohelet's

122. Cf. *BJ, Pléiade*.
123. Cf. ELSTER, *Commentar* (n. 107), p. 99: "es ist der richtige Mittelweg, daß du
weder in heuchlerischer Weise eine vollkommene Gerechtigkeit prätendirst, noch aber
auch den sittlichen Ernst, die Strenge der sittlichen Zucht verläugnest"; I. IBN LATIF,
פירוש מגלת קהלת, Jerusalem, 1970, p. 38; LAUHA, *Kohelet* (n. 17), p. 134.
124. לטוב is a later addition: cf. *BHS*; GINSBERG, קהלת (n. 34), p. 113; LORETZ,
Gotteswort und menschliche Erfahrung (n. 11), p. 169; STROBEL, *Prediger* (n. 60), p.
134; LAUHA, *Kohelet* (n. 17), p. 164; MICHEL, *Untersuchungen* (n. 15), p. 174. The ancient versions read "to the good and the evil" (LXX: καὶ τῷ κακῷ; Vg: et malo; Pesh:
ܠܒܝܫܐ), but this is a later adaptation. It is hard to accept that טוב would occur twice in
these antitheses.
125. Cf. ARTOM, חמש מגילות (n. 34), p. 75; DELITZSCH, *Hoheslied und Koheleth*
(n. 10), p. 258; WHYBRAY, *Ecclesiastes* (n. 59), p. 64-65.
126. J. CARLEBACH, *Das Buch Koheleth*, Frankfurt 1936, p. 34: "Pechvogel"; THILO,
Prediger Salomo (n. 11), p. 33 and 38; HERTZBERG, *Prediger* (n. 17), p. 94; GALLING,
Prediger (n. 17), p. 92-93; BRAUN, *Kohelet* (n. 10), p. 51-53; A. BONORA, *Il libro di
Qoèlet*, Roma, 1992, p. 124: "chi ha la fortuna di essere gradito a Dio e di ottenere la sua
protezione...chi invece è sfortunato, fallito".

criticism of the traditional connection between a moral attitude and good fortune (*Tun-Ergehen-Zusammenhang*), we may conclude that in 2,26; 7,26 טוב לפני אלהים (and its opposite חוטא) does not have the traditional moral meaning but denotes an element of divine favour without an ethical connotation.

5. CONCLUSION

The highly reflective and even philosophical character of the Book of Qohelet finds expression in its typical vocabulary. In this paper the four words which occur with the highest frequency have been studied. A semantic study of other words which are typical of Qohelet, such as לב, "heart", עת, "time", הבל, "absurdity", ידע, "know", חכמה/חכם, "wise/wisdom", מעשׂה/עשׂה, "make/happen (ni.)/what happens", עמל, "toil", אמר, "say", כסיל, "fool", מצא, "find (out)", etc. will certainly enhance this conclusion. It appears that Qohelet seeks to attain to a critically sound vision (ראה) on everything that happens (היה), but always centered on human existence (אדם), i.e. everything that happens and is done is judged on its value for humanity and human beings individually (טוב). The fact that אלהים, "God", is the next most frequent word shows that this philosophical preoccupation has a strong component of theodicy.

Faculteit Letteren   Antoon SCHOORS
Blijde-Inkomststraat 21
B-3000 Leuven

IST KOHELETS הבל-AUSSAGE
ERKENNTNISTHEORETISCH GEMEINT?

Das Wort הבל ist nicht gleichunmittelbar zu allen Themen des Buches Kohelet. Es fehlt sofort im großen Einleitungsgedicht 1,4-11, nachdem es das Buch in 1,2 mit einem mächtigen Paukenschlag eröffnet hat. Dann fehlt es bei der Beschreibung von Salomos Weltgestaltung und Glückssuche in 2,3-10. Schließlich zieht es sich im 3. Kapitel von neuem zurück, sobald sich am Ende des 2. Kapitels die Aufmerksamkeit auf Gott und sein Handeln in der Welt konzentriert hat. Soweit im ersten Buchteil[1]. Vom restlichen Buch gilt Ähnliches. Das Wort kehrt zwar immer wieder, da es offenbar symmetrisch über das Buch verteilt sein soll[2], aber es hat seine eingrenzbaren Gebrauchsbereiche. Es hängt an bestimmten Themen. Zu anderen hat es offenbar keine Affinität.

Das war auch früher schon bekannt[3]. Aber meist ist doch der Satz aus Koh 1,2 »alles ist הבל« in der Koheletliteratur die *These,* die das Buch als ganzes beweisen solle, das *Thema,* das überall abgehandelt werde, oder das *gemeinsame Motiv,* das allein die im Buch locker vereinten »Sentenzen« oder »Topoi« miteinander verbinde.

In den letzten Jahren kommt es demgegenüber wieder häufiger zur Frage nach dem Bereich, über den überhaupt הבל-Aussagen gemacht werden. Trotz kleiner Randunschärfen ist man sich, hat man die Frage erst einmal aufgeworfen, weithin auch einig[4]. Vor allem wird die הבל-Aussage nicht über Gott oder die Totenwelt gemacht[5]. Die הבל-Aussage

---

1. Zur Struktur des Buches vgl. N. LOHFINK, *Das Koheletbuch: Strukturen und Struktur,* in L. SCHWIENHORST-SCHÖNBERGER (Hrsg.), *Das Buch Kohelet. Studien zur Struktur, Geschichte, Rezeption und Theologie* (BZAW, 254), Berlin, pp. 39-121, bes. 108-113.

2. Näheres bei *ibid.,* p. 114.

3. Vgl. etwa die Analyse bei E. PODECHARD, *L'Ecclésiaste* (EB), Paris, 1912, p. 233.

4. Vgl., ohne Anspruch auf Vollständigkeit: E.M. GOOD, *Irony in the Old Testament,* Sheffield, [2]1981, pp. 177-182; M.V. FOX, *The Meaning of hebel for Qohelet,* in *JBL* 105 (1986) 409-426, p. 415; ID., *Qohelet and his Contradictions* (JSOT SS, 71), Sheffield, 1989, p. 38; N. LOHFINK, *Koh 1,2 »alles ist Windhauch« — universale oder anthropologische Aussage?,* in R. MOSIS – L. RUPPERT (Hrsg.), *Der Weg zum Menschen. Zur philosophischen und theologischen Anthropologie.* FS A. Deissler, Freiburg, 1989, pp. 201-216, bes. 212-214; T. KRÜGER, *Theologische Gegenwartsdeutung im Kohelet-Buch,* Habilitationsschrift, München, 1990, pp. 18f (mit kritischer Stellungnahme zu Fox und Lohfink).

5. *Ibid.,* p. 19, problematisiert mit Recht die Deutung von 11,8 durch Fox auf den Tod. 2,26 bezieht er gegen Fox (der schwankt) und Lohfink auf Gott. Es dürfte aber in 2,26 doch um den von 2,18 an analysierten innerweltlichen Sachverhalt gehen, vgl. FOX, *Contradictions* (Anm. 4), p. 39: »2:18-26 describes a single situation.« Zu Krüger sei

gehört allein zum Bereich »unter der Sonne»[6]. Doch auch da betrifft sie nicht alle Seienden und alle Ereignisse, sondern nur den Bereich der Menschen (und – in 3,19 – Menschen und Tiere zusammen). Man kann ohne weiteres eingrenzen: הבל dient anthropologischen Aussagen.

Eine noch weitergehende Eingrenzung schlägt Diethelm Michel in seinem Exkurs »Zur Bedeutung von הבל bei Qohelet« vor[7]. Das Wort הבל gehöre innerhalb des menschlichen Bereichs spezifisch zur menschlichen Erkenntnis[8]. Er führt für seine These den philosophischen Fachterminus »erkenntnistheoretisch« ein und spricht von »erkenntnistheoretischem Skeptizismus«[9]. Der Gegenbegriff wäre im Blick auf das Wort »Skeptizismus« dann »erkenntnistheoretischer Optimismus»[10], im Blick auf das Wort »erkenntnistheoretisch« die Verwendung von הבל bezüglich von Handlungen, Ereignissen und Situationen, also bei Aussagen über die objektive Welt[11].

noch angemerkt, daß 2,1 nicht über »Freude und Genuß« geht, sondern über das Bemühen darum. Bringt man diese Korrekturen an, dann bleibt es nach der kritischen Diskussion von Krüger am Ende doch bei den von mir gegebenen Referenzen.

6. Die insgeheim leitende räumliche Welt-Metapher Kohelets scheint neben der שאול eher nur den Bereich unter der Sonne (oder: unter dem Himmel) zu kennen, keinen »räumlichen« Himmel. Wenn Gott בשמים ist (5,1), dann heißt das vielleicht gar nicht »im Himmel«, sondern (was der häufigsten Bedeutung von בשמים in der hebräischen Bibel entspräche) »am Himmel«, da also, wo die Sonne ihren Lauf vollzieht. Zwar wird Gott niemals mit der Sonne identifiziert und erst recht nicht als »Gott Sonne« gekennzeichnet. Aber der Leser wird in der alles tragenden Buchmetaphorik deutlich bis in die Nähe dieser Bildvorstellung geführt (vgl. den gleichen Prozeß in Ps 36,6-10). Das Wort »Sonne« konnotiert unmittelbar »Licht«, und dieses ist, wie am Ende des Buches ausdrücklich gesagt wird, für den Menschen טוב (11,7). »Unter der Sonne« hat also durchaus positive Beiklänge. Das kosmische Geschehen unter der Sonne ist auch so gewaltig, daß die Augen und Ohren des Menschen ihm gar nicht gewachsen sind (1,8). Doch fügt sich an das Wort »Sonne« sofort auch die Gegensatz-Konnotation »Finsternis«. Die Finsternis gehört zur שאול, dringt aber in den Raum unter der Sonne ein durch die Torheit (2,13f), durch böses Geschick (5,16) und vor allem definitiv durch den Tod (11,8 und das ganze Schlußgedicht). Innerhalb dieses komplexen Welt-Raums, des einzigen Ortes, der dem Menschen gegeben ist, ist auch dem Wort הבל gemachte Aussage unterzubringen. Nicht umsonst steht im Parallelismus zu הבל häufig die Wendung רעות רוח, deren Element רוח zumindest assoziativ auf den Wind weist, der unter der Sonne bläst (vgl. 1,6 mit 1,9). – Zu einer anderen, bewußt stärker aufs Negative ausgerichteten Sicht der mit »unter der Sonne« verbundenen Assoziationen vgl. den Beitrag von Diethelm Michel in diesem Band.

7. D. MICHEL, *Untersuchungen zur Eigenart des Buches Qohelet* (BZAW, 183), Berlin, 1989, pp. 40-51.

8. Daß bei Kohelet auch die menschliche Erkenntnis wegen ihrer Grenzen die Qualifikation הבל erhalte, ist auch früher schon gelegentlich vertreten worden. Vgl. z.B. B. PENNACCHINI, *Qohelet ovvero il libro degli assurdi*, in *Euntes docete* 30 (1977) 491-501, pp. 500f. Doch spitzt Michel die Dinge zu, indem er hier den eigentlichen Ort der הבל-Aussage sieht.

9. MICHEL, *Untersuchungen* (Anm. 7), pp. 45, 46, 51; für den Ausdruck ohne direkte Zuordnung zum Wort הבל vgl. *ibid.* pp. 65 und 117.

10. So Michels eigene Formulierung (*ibid.*, p. 45).

11. Zu den Begriffen vgl. A. DIEMER – C.F. GETHMANN *Erkenntnistheorie, Er-*

Sein interpretatorischer Zusammenhang ist der: Michel sieht im Koheletbuch das Zeugnis eines Umbruchs. Hier zeige sich eine Krise des menschlichen »Versuches, mit *Weisheit* alles, was unter dem Himmel geschieht, herauszufinden«[12]. Die Weltsicht der »Weisheit« Israels zerbreche. Kohelet verneine mithilfe des Wortes הבל »die weisheitliche Grundthese, der Mensch könne die von Gott in die Welt hineinverborgenen Gesetzmäßigkeiten *erkennen* und dadurch einen *jitrôn* erlangen«[13].

Nicht alle Kenner der altorientalischen und altisraelitischen »Weisheit« werden sie so radikal auf eine optimistische Weltsicht festlegen[14]. Dennoch wird schon lange und vielfach angenommen, ja es gibt fast einen Konsens darüber, daß im Koheletbuch eine Krise der herkömmlichen »Weisheit« zutage tritt. Das ist also nicht das Neue. Neu ist bei Michel nur eines: Die spezielle Zuordnung des Gebrauchs von הבל zu den Ausführungen des Buches über die Grenzen der menschlichen Erkenntnis. Am deutlichsten ist es in folgendem Satz formuliert:

> Gegenüber diesem Anspruch der Weisheit bezieht Qohelet die Position eines *erkenntnistheoretischen Skeptizismus;* er verwendet das Wort הבל *immer* da, wo er diesen Anspruch der Weisheit als nicht erkennbar nachweist[15].

Der Satz schließt sich an den soeben zitierten Satz an, der die »weisheitliche Grundthese« vor allem als einen Erkenntnisanspruch verstand. Das ganze steht in prominenter Position, nämlich am Ende des Exkurses über die »Bedeutung von הבל bei Qohelet«.

Die Formulierungen von Michel schließen nicht aus, daß es vielleicht auch noch einen Gebrauch von הבל in anderen Aussagezusammenhängen geben könne – obwohl das dann eher ein marginales Phänomen wäre. Herausgestellt wird auf jeden Fall die eigentliche Zuordnung des Wortes הבל zur erkenntnistheoretischen Thematik (»immer«).

Das liefe für das Koheletbuch auf eine weitere Eingrenzung des Bereichs hinaus, von dem הבל ausgesagt wird. Das Wort wäre nicht nur auf anthropologische Aussagen begrenzt, sondern gehörte innerhalb der An-

---

kenntnislehre, Erkenntniskritik, in *Historisches Wörterbuch der Philosophie* 2 (1972) 683-690 und A.A. LONG – M. ALBRECHT, *Skepsis, Skeptizismus,* in *Historisches Wörterbuch der Philosophie* 9 (1995) 938-974.

12. MICHEL, *Untersuchungen* (Anm. 4), p. 43 (Hervorhebung von mir).

13. *Ibid.*, p. 51 (Hervorhebung von mir). Es geht also nicht ums Erkennen allein, doch ist dieses als der entscheidende Punkt im weisheitlichen Anspruch verstanden («und dadurch»).

14. Vgl. in diesem Band etwa die differenzierendere Sicht von Schwienhorst-Schönberger.

15. MICHEL, *Untersuchungen* (Anm. 4), p. 51 (Hervorhebung von mir).

thropologie zumindest ureigenst noch genauer in den Bereich erkenntnistheoretischer Aussagen. Sollte mein Verständnis der Sicht von Michel ein Mißverständnis sein, dann bleibt das aufgeworfene und offenbar
bei Michel zumindest herauslesbare Sachproblem. Die nun folgende
Diskussion dieses Problems wird am Ende tatsächlich zu einer weiteren
Restriktion des Bereiches führen, auf den sich הבל bezieht, wenn auch
nicht auf die, die Michel anzunehmen scheint.

Ich möchte der These, Kohelet drücke seinen »erkenntnistheoreti-
schen Skeptizismus« da, wo er ihn äußert, *immer* unter Benutzung des
Wortes הבל aus, zwei andersartige Thesen entgegenstellen, die Michels
Sicht teilweise zustimmen, ihr teilweise aber auch widersprechen:

1. Kohelet vertritt wirklich Grenzen der menschlichen Erkenntnis.
2. Er gebraucht jedoch, um diese zu bewerten, nicht das Wort הבל.

Die Thesen implizieren nun natürlich umgekehrt, daß das Wort הבל stets
Aussagen über die objektive Welt dienstbar ist. Sie führen also ebenfalls
zu einer weiteren Eingrenzung des Bereichs der Gegenstände, von denen
הבל im Koheletbuch ausgesagt wird, aber zur entgegengesetzten. Das
Wort dient zwar anthropologischen Aussagen, doch in diesem Bereich
keinen erkenntnistheoretischen.

Ich versuche, die beiden Thesen am Text zu begründen. Zu diskutieren sind 14 Stellen, in denen spezifisch und zugleich mit negativem
Urteil von den Möglichkeiten menschlicher Erkenntnis gesprochen
wird[16]. Hinzu kommt eine weitere Stelle, die ich selbst nicht für relevant halte, die aber in dem Zusammenhang gern herangezogen wird[17].
Von der Diskussion auszuschließen sind negative Aussagen mit der
Wurzel חכם allein, ohne daß speziell das Moment der Erkenntnis betont wäre. Da חכם semantisch umfassender ist und außer dem Erkenntnis-
moment auch stets das Moment des praktischen Handelns und Sich-in-
der-Welt-Verhaltens mitumschließt, zumindest das der praktischen
Handlungsanweisung, kann, wo der Kontext nicht selbst die Dinge genauer spezifiziert, nicht geklärt werden, ob in solchen Belegen die negative
Aussage aus dem Erkennen oder aus anderen Momenten resultiert[18]. Es

16. Koh 1,8.9-11 (ראה, שמע, 2 x זכרון); 3,11 (מצא); 3,21f (ראה, ידע); 6,11f (נגד, ידע);
7,14 (מצא); 7,23f (מצא, עמק, רחוק); 7,25a.26-29 (6 x מצא); 8,7 (נגד, ידע); 8,16f (... מצא,
מצא, [ידע]); 9,1 (ידע); 9,12 (ידע); 10,14 (נגד, ידע); 11,2 (ידע); 11,5f (3 x ידע).
17. Koh 1,13.
18. Die gründlichsten und differenziertesten Ausführungen zum Thema habe ich bei
Fox, *Contradictions* (Anm. 4), pp. 79-120, gefunden (»Chapter 3: The Way to Wisdom:
Qohelet's Epistemology«). Vgl. seine ältere Arbeit: ID., *Qohelet's Epistemology*, in
HUCA 58 (1987) 137-155. Meine folgenden Ausführungen gehen jedoch nicht, wie er,
von der Annahme aus, daß חכמה einfach mit »Erkennen« und »Erkenntnis« gleichzusetzen sei. Ferner beschränke ich mich auf das, was Kohelet über die Erkenntnis sagt, ja so-

gibt sogar Belege, wo im Zusammenhang das Wissenselement eher positiv auftritt[19].

THESE 1:
KOHELETS »ERKENNTNISTHEORETISCHER SKEPTIZISMUS«

Michel hat völlig recht, wenn er betont, daß die menschliche Erkenntnis, und zwar speziell deren Grenze, bei Kohelet ein prominentes Thema sei. Leicht lassen sich vom Beginn des Buches bis zu dessen Ende die Belege dafür aufreihen. Sie zeigen sogar einen gewissen systematischen Zusammmenhang. Ich will versuchen, ihn unterwegs mitzuvermitteln.

1. Sofort im Eröffnungsgedicht 1,4-11 steht dem ewig kreisenden herrlichen Kosmos[20] der Mensch gegenüber, der diesen zwar durch Sinne und Wort bewältigen sollte, seiner Aufgabe aber nicht gewachsen ist (1,8), ja sich über die ewige Wiederkehr auch alles Menschlichen täuscht, da die einander ablösenden Generationen mit ihrem Erkenntnisbemühen stets wieder bei Null anfangen müssen (1,9-11). Der Text relativiert zumindest die Möglichkeiten menschlicher Erkenntnis erheblich.

2. Liest man 1,13b in Abhebung von 1,13a als neuen Satz – was ich allerdings für falsch halte –, so lautet er nach Michel:

> Das ist eine böse Mühe, die Gott den Menschen gegeben hat, sie damit zu plagen[21].

Der Satz ist dann eine Art Stoßseufzer oder Nebenbemerkung. Worüber seufzt Kohelet-Salomo? Bezieht man den Satz – was ich wiederum für

gar noch genauer, was er über deren Grenzen sagt. Die Frage, auf welche Weise Kohelet selbst Erkenntnis vollzieht, berühre ich nur ganz am Rande. Als Stellungnahme zu den Ausführungen von Fox vgl. den Beitrag von Crenshaw in diesem Band. Nicht mehr berücksichtigen konnte ich M.P. SCIUMBATA, *Peculiarità e motivazioni della struttura lessicale dei verbi della 'conoscenza' in Qohelet. Abbozzo di una storia dell'epistemologia ebraico-biblica*, in *Henoch* 18 (1996) 236-249.

19. Vgl. unten zu 2,3.9. Ferner vgl. 9,13-18. Zuspitzung auf Erkenntnis findet sich bei חכם in 7,11f; 7,23; 7,25; 8,16f; 9,1; 9,11; 10,12. Die Aussagen über Erkenntnis finden sich für diese Stellen alle auf meiner Liste.

20. Zu diesem nach meiner Meinung einzig richtigen Verständnis vgl. C.D. GINSBURG, *Coheleth, Commonly Called the Book of Ecclesiastes*, London, 1861; Reprint: New York, 1970, pp. 260-267; N. LOHFINK, *Die Wiederkehr des immer Gleichen. Eine frühe jüdische Synthese zwischen griechischem und jüdischem Weltgefühl in Kohelet 1,4-11*, in *AF* 53 (1985) 125-149; R. MICHAUD, *Qohélet et l'hellénisme* (Lire la Bible, 77), Paris, 1987, p. 135; R.N. WHYBRAY, *Ecclesiastes* (NCBC), London, 1989, pp. 39f; L. SCHWIENHORST-SCHÖNBERGER, *»Nicht im Menschen gründet das Glück« (Koh 2,24). Kohelet im Spannungsfeld jüdischer Weisheit und hellenistischer Philosophie« (HBS, 2), Freiburg, 1994, pp. 25-40; F.-L. HOSSFELD, *Die theologische Relevanz des Buches Kohelet*, in L. SCHWIENHORST-SCHÖNBERGER (Hrsg.), *Das Buch Kohelet. Studien zur Struktur, Geschichte, Rezeption und Theologie* (BZAW, 254), Berlin, pp. 377-389, bes. 383.

21. MICHEL, *Untersuchungen* (Anm. 4), p. 9.

falsch halte – nicht auf die direkt davor genannte Größe (also auf »alles, was unter dem Himmel geschieht«), sondern auf die Forschertätigkeit Salomos בחכמה, von der ganz am Anfang des Verses die Rede war, dann wird in der Tat über das Erkenntnisstreben geseufzt. Dieses wird als ענין רע klassifiziert. Selbst dann bleibt noch offen, ob man das als erkenntnistheoretische Aussage verstehen muß. Das menschliche Erkenntnisstreben könnte ja nicht wegen Erfolglosigkeit, sondern wegen der mit ihm verbundenen Anstrengung als ענין רע qualifiziert sein. Doch ich möchte die Stelle in unserem Zusammenhang zusätzlich mitbehandeln, da sie für Michel ein Schlüsseltext ist[22].

3. Wissen und weisheitliches Handeln werden dann bald deutlicher zum Thema: ankündigend in 1,16-18, voll ausgeführt in 2,12a.13-17. Doch die Fragestellung ist in diesen Texten nicht erkenntnistheoretisch. Gebildeter und Ungebildeter werden verglichen, und es zeigt sich, daß sie angesichts des Todes alle gleich sind. Bei der Darstellung der Weltgestaltung Salomos fallen in 2,3 und 9 sogar sehr positive Urteile über die Hilfe, die ihm seine חכמה gewährt hat. Sie ist in diesem Fall ja sicher vor allem technisches Wissen. Auch später wird es durchaus Passagen geben, die in konkreten Zusammenhängen positiv vom menschlichen Erkennen sprechen – man denke etwa an die Gegenüberstellung des Wissens der Lebenden und des Wissens der Toten in 9,5, oder an den Weisen, der arm war und eine belagerte Stadt hätte retten können, wenn man auf ihn gehört hätte, in 9,13-15[23]. Die Problematisierung, die sich hier anschließt (9,16-18), bezieht sich nicht auf Grenzen seiner Erkenntnis, sondern auf die Grenzen seiner gesellschaftlichen Akzeptanz. Doch zurück zum ersten Buchteil! Die menschliche Erkenntnis in ihrer Begrenztheit kommt erst wieder im theologischen Abschnitt 3,1-15 zur Sprache.

4. Und zwar in 3,11, das Michel so übersetzt:

> Alles hat er [= Gott] schön (angemessen?) gemacht zu seiner Stunde – aber auch die Ewigkeit hat er in ihren [= der Menschen] Verstand gesetzt, ohne

---

22. Vgl. *ibid.*, pp. 43f. Von dieser Stelle aus entwickelt er, genau besehen, seine Theorie vom »erkenntnistheoretischen Skeptizismus« Kohelets. Er springt von 1,13 unmittelbar zu 8,14, das er von 8,17 her deutet (einer Stelle, wo הבל nicht vorkommt). Die gründlichste und treffendste Analyse von 1,13 finde ich bei SCHWIENHORST-SCHÖNBERGER, *Glück* (Anm. 20), pp. 45-51. Dort auch die Positionen der älteren Literatur. Für meine Sicht vgl. LOHFINK, *Qoheleth 5:17-19 – Revelation by Joy*, in *CBQ* 52 (1990) 625-635, p. 628, und demnächst ausführlicher ID., *Kohelet übersetzen. Berichte aus einer Übersetzerwerkstatt* (im Druck), 7. Abschnitt.

23. Diese Charakterisierung entspricht der Alternativübersetzung, die die *Einheitsübersetzung* angibt. Die im Haupttext gegebene Übersetzung führt aber in unserem Fall zu den gleichen Folgerungen.

daß der Mensch das Werk, das Gott tut, von Anfang bis Ende herausfinden kann[24].

Die Aussage schließt sich, wie auch einiges in den folgenden Versen, deutlich an das Eröffnungsgedicht an und führt dessen Aussagen über die Erkenntnisgrenzen des Menschen weiter[25], nun unter Einführung der Größe »Gott«. Da das Schlüsselwort des Verses עולם »endlose Zeiterstreckung« zu sein scheint[26], geht es wohl vor allem darum, daß sich das Erkennen des Menschen nicht sehr weit in Vergangenheit und Zukunft erstreckt. Auf jeden Fall kommt er nie an den zeitlichen Anfang und das zeitliche Ende. Hier erscheint auch zum erstenmal das negierte Verb מצא »finden«, das später in erkenntnistheoretischen Aussagen eine führende Rolle spielen wird[27].

5. Doch diese Aussagen lassen erst einmal auf sich warten. Nach Abschluß des ersten Buchteils in 3,15 werden zunächst andere Themen behandelt, vor allem gesellschaftlicher Art. Höchstens in 3,21

> Wer weiß, ob die רוח der einzelnen Menschen wirklich nach oben steigt, während die רוח der Tiere ins Erdreich hinabsinkt?

könnte das Thema für einen Augenblick anklingen, vielleicht sogar bis zum Ende von 3,22[28]. Doch dann führt erst der dritte Buchteil, der sich

---

24. D. MICHEL, *Qohelet* (EdF, 258), Darmstadt, 1988, p. 137. Als Analyse unter erkenntnistheoretischem Gesichtspunkt vgl. ID., *Untersuchungen* (Anm. 7), pp. 64f. Auch hier wird sofort wieder 8,16f herangezogen, und zwar im Zusammenhang des Themas יתרון, obwohl auch dieses Wort dort nicht vorkommt. 3,10 wird übrigens in der Parallelfassung von 1,13 zitiert, also *mit* dem Wort רע, das in 3,10 signifikant *nicht* steht. Zu meiner eigenen Übersetzung und Auslegung von 3,10f vgl. N. LOHFINK, *Kohelet* (NEB, 1), Würzburg, 1980; [4]1993, pp. 32f; ID., *Joy* (Anm. 22), pp. 628-630.

25. Hierzu vgl. vor allem A.A. FISCHER, *Beobachtungen zur Komposition von Kohelet 1,3-3,15*, in *ZAW* 103 (1991) 71-86.

26. עלם zu emendieren scheint mir nach den Regeln der Textkritik nicht erlaubt zu sein. Auch die neuerdings bei ID., *Skepsis oder Furcht Gottes? Studien zur Komposition und Theologie des Buches Kohelet* (BZAW, 247), Berlin, 1997, pp. 233-237, noch einmal zusammengestellten Gründe für die Metathese zu העמל kommen gegen die eindeutige Bezeugung nicht auf, falls der Text nicht absolut unsinnig ist. Das ist er aber nicht. Zu den Autorenmeinungen vgl. ebd., p. 226, n. 5. Ich selbst folge F. ELLERMEIER, *Qohelet. Teil 1, Abschnitt 1. Untersuchungen zum Buch Qohelet*, Herzberg, 1967, pp. 309-322. Doch für die jetzige Diskussion ist das keine notwendige Voraussetzung. Auch ein ins Bewußtsein der einzelnen Menschen eingesenktes Wissen um die unendlich ausgedehnte Zeit erlaubt meine hier gemachte Analyse.

27. Vgl. einerseits die Schlüsselstellen 7,14, 7,24 und 8,17 (dort 3 mal), andererseits die חשבן-Passage 7,26-29, wo das Wort Leitmotiv ist (6 mal, mit 7,24 sieben mal).

28. Es handelt sich aber eher um die Frage, ob eine bestimmte Ansicht über das, was nach dem Tod geschieht, richtig oder falsch sei, nicht um die grundsätzliche Frage nach den Grenzen menschlicher Erkenntnis. Das würde erst anders, wenn man streng beim masoretischen Text bliebe, also nicht mit zwei Pendenskonstruktionen und nicht bei העלה und הירדת jeweils mit einem ה-*interrogativum* rechnete (zur Möglichkeit eines solchen ohne Emendation vgl. Lev 10,19; Jes 27,7; Hiob 23,6). Dann wäre zu übersetzen: »Wer

von 6,10 bis – je nach Theorie – 8,15, 8,17 oder 9,10 erstreckt[29], das Thema »Erkenntnis« wieder herauf.

6. Dieser Teil ist im Sinne der klassischen Rhetorik die *refutatio*[30]. Er setzt sich mit der weisheitlichen Tradition auseinander, und zu ihr gehörte zweifellos auch ein gewisser erkenntnistheoretischer Optimismus. Zwar geht es zunächst um anders orientierte Spruchweisheiten und Prinzipien dieser Tradition, doch die einleitende oder besser überleitende[31] Passage 6,11-12 bereitet durch locker hingeworfene Voraus-Anspielungen auch schon auf die in 7,14 dann erstmals wiederkehrende Problematisierung der menschlichen Erkenntnis vor[32]:

kennt denn die Menschenseele, die (bekanntlich) nach oben steigt, und die Tierseele, die (bekanntlich) ins Erdreich hinabsinkt?« Vermutlich haben die Masoreten den Text so verstanden, um die Unsterblichkeit der Seele zu retten. Dann würde behauptet, die menschliche Erkenntnis könne die Menschen- und Tierseele innerlich nicht wirklich ergründen. Aber darauf will Michel mit Sicherheit nicht hinaus, er emendiert sogar: vgl. *Untersuchungen* (Anm. 7), p. 116, Anm. 4. Soweit zum Philologischen. Michel sieht im gesamten Abschnitt 3,16-22 die Ablehnung der Vorstellung von einer *Vergeltung* im Jenseits, vgl. *Ibid.*, pp. 116-118 und 248-251. In 3,21 würde also bezweifelt, ob wir wissen könnten, daß den Menschen im Gegensatz zum Tier ein Jenseitsgericht erwarte. Hätte das nicht deutlicher gesagt werden können? Im ganzen scheint mir diese Deutung auch nur möglich zu sein, wenn man mit Michel mehrere Textkorruptionen und spätere Zusätze annimmt. Dann ist man natürlich nicht mehr beim Endtext, den wir in Händen haben. Dieser bleibt allerdings schwierig. Vgl. zur Passage jetzt Alexander A. Fischer in diesem Band. Wichtig für spätere Überlegungen dieses Referats scheint mir zu sein, daß den Abschnitt – sei es in streng logischem Zusammenhang, sei es eher assoziativ – in 3,22b eine wie 3,21 מי anlautende Frage abschließt: »Wer könnte es ihm ermöglichen, zu sehen, was nach ihm sein wird?« oder, wohl besser, »Wer könnte es ihm ermöglichen, etwas zu genießen, was erst nach ihm da sein wird?« Diese ebenfalls schwer zu entziffernde Aussage weist, wenn auch weniger wahrscheinlich im Zusammenhang mit menschlichem Erkenntnisvermögen, auf jeden Fall eines auf: Es geht um Zukunft. Das Thema »Zukunft« wird in der Frage nach der Erkenntnis mehrfach wiederkehren. Vgl. 6,12; 7,14; 8,7; 9,12; 10,14; 11,2.6. Im nächsten für die Erkenntnistheorie relevanten Text (6,12) werden aus 3,21f folgende Stichworte aufgegriffen: היה אחריו – אדם – טוב – מי יודע. Das ist zuviel, um Zufall zu sein. Der Leser soll die Verbindung zweifellos sehen. Doch wird man mit inhaltlichen Folgerungen vorsichtig sein. Vielleicht soll der Leser am Anfang des dritten Buchteils auch nur anaphorisch an den Anfang des zweiten Buchteils erinnert werden. Dann wüßte er: Jetzt wird ein Faden aufgenommen, der dort liegengeblieben war.

29. Zur Frage der strukturellen Grenze zwischen 3. und 4. Buchteil vgl. zuletzt LOHFINK, *Struktur* (Anm. 1), pp. 106-108.

30. Vgl. L. SCHWIENHORST-SCHÖNBERGER, *Kohelet: Stand und Perspektiven der Forschung*, in ID. (Hrsg.), *Das Buch Kohelet. Studien zur Struktur, Geschichte, Rezeption und Theologie* (BZAW, 254), Berlin, pp. 5-38, bes. 11f.

31. Vgl. FISCHER, *Skepsis* (Anm. 26), pp. 7-9 (»Brückentext«). Zu den Rückgriffen in diesem Text vgl. LOHFINK, *Struktur* (Anm. 1), p. 67 (dort wäre zu 6,11 noch zu ergänzen: מי יודע vgl. 2,19; 3,21).

32. Vgl. 7,14 מי יגיד לו, מה־שהיה, ; מי יודע ,יודע, מה־שהיה;8,7; ומי יודע 8,1; מי, מה־שהיה;7,24 אחריו, אדם, טוב; אין יודע האדם 9,1; לדעת 8,16f. In dieser Liste sind praktisch alle eigentlich erkenntnistheoretischen Aussagen des dritten Buchteils vertreten. Sie sind dann durch andere Lexeme, die sich in 6,11-12 nicht finden, noch enger miteinander verknüpft, etwa מצא.

Denn es gibt viele Worte, die nur den הבל vermehren. Was nützt das dem Menschen? Denn wer kann erkennen, was für den Menschen besser ist im Leben?
Die wenigen Tagen seines Lebens voll הבל – er verbringt sie wie ein Schatten. Denn wer kann dem Menschen verkünden, was nach ihm geschehen wird unter der Sonne?[33]

Auf der Aussagenebene wird Erkenntnis hier zunächst nur problematisiert, indem die Zuverlässigkeit der bald folgenden traditionellen טוב-Sprüche angezweifelt wird[34], und dann noch durch den lockeren Hinweis darauf, daß doch wohl keiner da ist, der mitteilen könnte (מי־יגיד), was die Zukunft bringt[35].

7. Wir springen sofort zu 7,14:

> Am Glückstag erfreue dich deines Glücks, und am Unglückstag sieh ein: Auch diesen hat Gott geschaffen, genau wie jenen. (Zu beidem muß man auffordern,)[36] darum weil der Mensch von dem, was nach ihm kommt, gar nichts herausfinden kann.

---

33. Zur Pendenskonstruktion vgl. F.J. BACKHAUS, »*Denn Zeit und Zufall trifft sie alle*«. *Studien zur Komposition und zum Gottesbild im Buch Qohelet* (BBB, 83), Frankfurt, 1993, p. 11.

34. Das Wort טוב findet sich in 7,1-18 zwölf mal, davon mehrfach in Zitaten traditioneller Sprüche. So dürfte 6,12 die Sicherheit, mit der solche Sprüche weitergegeben werden, schon im voraus anzweifeln. Der unmittelbare Kontext macht es weniger wahrscheinlich, daß 6,12a in Form einer rhetorischen Frage eine Grundsatzaussage machen wolle, etwa des Inhalts, was für den Menschen gut sei, könne nicht erkannt werden. Das wäre im Koheletbuch auch einmalig. Ja, es stünde im Gegensatz zum sonstigen Buch: Kohelet selbst macht in seinen שׂמחה-Passagen klare Aussagen darüber, was für den Menschen in diesem Leben gut sei. Zu Michels Annahme, 6,12a sei ein Gegnerzitat, vgl. BACKHAUS, *Zeit* (Anm. 33), p. 217, Anm. 10.

35. נגד Hifil kommt hier erstmals vor. Ähnliche Begründungen von negativen Aussagen über die menschliche Erkenntnisfähigkeit unter Verwendung des gleichen Verbs finden sich noch in 8,7 und 10,14. Denkt Kohelet an das weisheitliche Traditionswesen, wo die »Wahrheit« dem Schüler einfach zum Auswendiglernen mitgeteilt wurde? Oder ist noch eine zweite Front vorhanden, nämlich gegen Prophetie und Apokalyptik? Das Verb spielt bei Deuterojesaja im Zusammenhang mit der prophetischen Ankündigung der Zukunft eine Rolle. Zur möglichen Bezugnahme Kohelets auf Deuterojesaja vgl. T. KRÜGER, *Dekonstruktion und Rekonstruktion prophetischer Eschatologie im Qohelet-Buch*, in A.A. Diesel u.a. (Hrsg.), *»Jedes Ding hat seine Zeit...« Studien zur israelitischen und altorientalischen Weisheit*. FS. Diethelm Michel (BZAW, 241), Berlin, 1996, pp. 107-129. Existiert diese weitere Frontstellung, dann wäre der vierte Beleg des Verbs in 10,20, der ziemlich bald auf 10,14 folgt, vielleicht recht sarkastisch: Der einzige Bereich, in dem Verborgenes unter der Sonne mit Erfolg weitergegeben und mitgeteilt wird, sind die Geheimdienste der politischen Machthaber.

36. Es geht um beide Ratschläge, nicht nur um den Schlußgedanken des zweiten. על־דברת ש ist »darum weil« zu übersetzen: vgl. FISCHER, *Skepsis* (Anm. 26), pp. 113f. Die Begründung von Ratschlägen durch Hinweis auf die Grenzen menschlicher Erkenntnis ist sonst typisch für den vierten Buchteil; vgl. unten. Vorher scheint der Fall nur vielleicht in 3,22 und dann hier in 7,14 vorzukommen.

Auch in 7,14b handelt es sich eher um eine – im Zusammenhang natürlich durchaus wichtige – Randaussage, welche die in 7,14a gegebenen Ratschläge begründet. Vielleicht wird sie auch deshalb gemacht, damit das Thema »Grenzen der Erkenntnis« nicht in Vergessenheit gerät. Sowohl in 6,12 als auch in 7,14 geht es darum, daß der Mensch die Zukunft nicht erkennen kann[37].

8. Das ist anders in 7,23f, wo die Erkenntnisthematik voll einsetzt:

> All das habe ich mit der חכמה versucht. Ich habe gesagt: Ich will ein חכם werden. Aber sie (= die חכמה) blieb fern von mir. Fern ist (alles), was geschehen ist, und tief, tief versunken – wer könnte es finden?

Hier geht es zunächst um die Weisheit im ganzen. Doch konzentriert sich der Text schnell auf eine ihrer Komponenten, das Erkennen. Und zwar auf das Erkennen alles Vergangenen. Aus 1,9 wird die Formulierung מה־שהיה »was immer geschehen ist«[38] aufgenommen, und aus 3,11 מצא »finden«,[39] das Stichwort des Satzes, daß dem Menschen Anfang und Ende des göttlichen Tuns in der Welt unerkennbar bleiben. 7,24 schließt sich also an die erkenntnistheoretischen Ausführungen an, die den ersten Buchteil rahmten.

9. Doch die Aussage über die nicht gelingende Erkenntnis des Vergangenen dient Kohelet nur als Ausgangspunkt, um sich zwei anderen Untersuchungen zuzuwenden, die er in 7,25 in einer Art Dispositionsangabe andeutet (... ולדעת ... סבותי אני ולבי לדעת)[40]. Die zweite – um das zunächst hinter uns zu bringen – lautet:

> zu erkennen, ob רשע mit mangelnder Bildung und Unwissen mit Verblendung zusammenhängt[41].

Hier steht die Wurzel רשע, die dann in 8,8-14 gehäuft vorkommen wird[42]. Es geht daher wohl um 8,1-15, wo – nach einem Anlauf über die

---

37. Gemeinsames Stichwort: אחריו »nach ihm« oder »später«. In 7,14 unterscheidet allein dieses Wort den Satz von dem, was in 9,5 über die Toten gesagt wird: Diese erkennen überhaupt nichts mehr, und zwar unter jeder Rücksicht.

38. Daß es sich um vergangenes Geschehen handelt, ist hier und in 3,15 durch Oppositionen gesichert. Das nachfolgende כבר in 6,10 schließt es nicht aus. Weitere Belege gibt es nicht. So ist die Wendung zweifellos auch in 7,24 vergangenheitlich gemeint.

39. Inzwischen in 7,14 schon vorweisend neu eingeführt.

40. Hierzu N. LOHFINK, *War Kohelet ein Frauenfeind? Ein Versuch, die Logik und den Gegenstand von Koh., 7,23-8,1a herauszufinden*, in M. GILBERT (Hrsg.), *La Sagesse de l'Ancien Testament* (BETL, 51), Gembloux – Leuven, 1979, pp. 259-287, bes. 274f; ID., *Struktur* (Anm. 1), pp. 76f.

41. Es kann hier offenbleiben, ob vielleicht nur Objekte aufgereiht werden: »zu erkennen רשע und mangelnde Bildung, Unwissen und Verblendung.«

42. Koh 8,8.10.13.14.14. Nimmt man 7,25 selbst und das nachklingende 9,2 hinzu, so hat man im Kontext 7 Belege.

Probleme von Beratern bei Hof – die Lehre vom Tun-Ergehen-Zusammenhang kritisiert wird. Dabei tritt die Erkenntnisproblematik nur kurz in 8,5 in einem Gegnerzitat auf, das aber schnell unter Anspielung auf früher Gesagtes zurückgewiesen wird[43].

Unter erkenntnistheoretischer Rücksicht wichtig ist dagegen der erste in 7,25 angekündigte Teil. In ihm geht es nach der Ankündigung um die Beurteilung von חכמה וחשבון (7,25a), was ich als Hendiadyoin betrachte und etwas neuzeitlich klingend mit »berechnend-summierende Wissenschaft« übersetzen würde:

> forschend und suchend zu erkennen, was חכמה, insofern sie als חשבון auftritt, (wert) ist[44].

Es muß wohl so etwas wie induktive Wissenschaft und aus ihr erwachsende menschliche Technik gemeint sein, denn nachher ist offenbar von Belagerungsmaschinen die Rede[45]. חשבון kehrt in 7,27 und, abgewandelt, in 7,29 wieder. Der angekündigte Text über diesen Typ von Erkenntnis ist daher 7,26-29[46].

Dieser Text ist nach üblicher Auffassung eine reichlich misogyne Darlegung über das weibliche Geschlecht. Er spricht in der Tat von »der Frau«. Aber die Frau scheint nur der Beispielfall zu sein, an dem ein Problem der menschlichen Erkenntnis abgehandelt wird. Auch wird die Frau nur dann geschmäht, wenn man die Zitations-Theorie ablehnt. Und auf jeden Fall sind מצא und חשבון die eigentlichen Leitworte. Die »Frau« würde vielleicht am besten in das Bild passen, wenn sie insgeheim die »Frau Weisheit« wäre. Thomas Krüger hat das vertreten[47]. Ich kann hier zu diesem vielverhandelten Text keine neue Theorie entwikkeln[48]. Das ist auch nicht nötig. Es genügt die Feststellung, daß der mit dem Wort חשבון signalisierte spezielle Typ menschlicher Erkenntnis, der wahrscheinlich zu den Errungenschaften der neuen hellenistischen Kultur gehörte, nicht besonders positiv abzuschneiden scheint. Später kommt Kohelet nie mehr darauf zurück, außer daß nach 9,10 auch in der Unterwelt nicht nur Tun, Wissen und Bildung, sondern auch חשבון nicht mehr da sein werden. Es handelt sich auf jeden Fall nicht um die menschliche Erkenntnisfähigkeit als solche, sondern um eine spezielle

---

43. Für die Erkenntnisaussage wird in 8,7 auf 6,12 angespielt. Näheres bei LOHFINK, *ibid.*, pp. 71f.

44. Auch hier kann offen bleiben, ob vielleicht nur gesagt ist: »zu erkennen חכמה, insofern sie als חשבון auftritt.«

45. Koh 7,29. Vgl. ID., *Frauenfeind* (Anm. 40), pp. 284-286.

46. Man kann diskutieren, ob 8,1a noch dazugehört. Vgl. *ibid.*, pp. 260f.

47. KRÜGER, »*Frau Weisheit*« in Koh 7,26?, in Bib 79 (1992) 394-403.

48. Vgl. in diesem Band den Beitrag von Johan Y.S. Pahk.

Ausformung derselben. Kohelet scheint diesem Phänomen gegenüber eine gewisse Skepsis zu haben, doch ist es, wie gesagt, ein Teilphänomen.

10. Damit sind wir schon bei 8,16-17, dem nächsten großen Brückentext, der wohl zugleich zum dritten Buchteil als Schluß und zum vierten und letzten als Anfang gehört. Die Verse zeigen das Ende des dritten, polemischen Buchteils an, indem sie das Ergebnis des ersten Buchteils hinsichtlich der menschlichen Erkenntnis wiederholen und dabei noch vertiefen[49]. Das Verb ידע »erkennen« rahmt sie ein. Formal sind sie eine narrative Rückblende: Was vorn im ersten Teil erzählt worden war, wird, durch neue Elemente bereichert, noch einmal aufgegriffen[50].

Anknüpfungspunkte sind in 8,16 vor allem die identischen Teile der Verse 1,13 und 3,10, die die ganze Salomotravestie[51] umklammern:

> Als ich mir vorgenommen hatte,... zu beobachten, welches Geschäft eigentlich auf der Erde[52] getätigt wird...

Wie 3,10 sofort in 3,11 die Aussage von der Begrenztheit der menschlichen Erkenntnis provoziert, so folgt diese Aussage auch hier sofort in 8,17 als Nachsatz:

> Was das Ganze des Tuns Gottes angeht, so kann der Mensch das Tun, das unter der Sonne getan wird, nicht finden; deshalb strengt der Mensch beim Suchen sich an und findet doch nicht; selbst wenn der Weise behauptet, er erkenne – er kann nicht finden.

Das eine לא ימצא האדם von 3,10 erscheint hier in höchster Emphase als dreifaches

לא יוכל האדם למצוא
ולא ימצא
לא יוכל למצוא

Stärker läßt sich das Nein zur Möglichkeit des Erkennens kaum ausdrücken.

---

49. Die neueste, ausführlichste und gründlichste Untersuchung von 8,16f findet sich bei J.Y.-S. PAHK, *Il canto della gioia in Dio. L'itinerario sapienziale espresso dall'unità letteraria in Qohelet 8,16-9,10 e il parallelo di Gilgameš Me. iii* (Istituto Universitario Orientale, Dipartimento di Studi Asiatici, Series Minor, 52), Neapel, 1996, pp. 15-21 und 75-128. Dort Literaturangaben. Zur Frage der Erkenntnis speziell pp. 108-117.

50. Vgl. LOHFINK, *Struktur* (Anm. 1), pp. 72f.

51. Zu deren Umfang vgl. *ibid.*, pp. 91-95. Gesamtliste der lexematischen Rückbezüge in 8,16f: *ibid.*, p. 67.

52. Die Rede von etwas, was »auf der Erde getan wird«, findet sich im Koheletbuch nur in 8,14 und 8,16. Wegen der Nähe der beiden Stellen zueinander ist anzunehmen, daß 8,16 sich hier – nun natürlich verallgemeinernd und früher im Buch Gesagtes einbringend – auch an die direkt vorausgehenden Überlegungen anschließt, also an Gedanken über Schicksalsabläufe, die der Überzeugung vom Tun-Ergehen-Zusammenhang in keiner Weise entsprechen und deshalb הבל sind.

Doch was ist es, das der Mensch, der Tag und Nacht aus Drang nach Erkenntnis auf den Schlaf verzichtet (8,16b), dennoch nicht finden kann?[53]

Die erste Aussage von 8,17 ist sehr sperrig formuliert. Das Objekt des Nichtfindenkönnens ist zunächst in einer Pendenskonstruktion vorangestellt. Es ist כל־מעשה האלהים. Doch im nachfolgenden Satz wird es nicht, wie in solchen Fällen möglich, durch ein Pronomen aufgenommen, sondern wird noch einmal voll genannt, und zwar jetzt in der Form: המעשה אשר נעשה תחת־השמש. Diese Wendung bezieht sich im Koheletbuch auf die innerweltlichen Geschehnisse, ihre Träger sind Menschen. Hier werden also die gleichen Handlungen sowohl als Tun Gottes als auch als Tun von Menschen bezeichnet[54].

Diese Identität war auch schon im ersten Buchteil angedeutet, wenn auch verhaltener. In 1,13 war Salomos Ausgangspunkt eine zu überprüfende fremde Meinung, nach welcher ein Gott den Menschen ein übles Geschäft zugeteilt habe (נתן), und davor und danach nannte er die gleiche Sache המעשה אשר נעשה תחת־השמים (1,13a, ähnlich 1,14). Doch als er das Thema in 3,10 abermals aufgriff, knüpfte er zwar an die Formulierung von dem Geschäft, das ein Gott den Menschen zugeteilt haben solle, an, aber dann redete er ohne Übergang vom Tun Gottes weiter: המעשה אשר־עשה האלהים und את־הכל עשה יפה בעתו (3,11). Eigentlich konnte man hier schon entnehmen, daß ein und dasselbe Geschehen für Kohelet sowohl menschliches Tun als auch göttliches Tun ist.

Doch jetzt in 8,16 wird das durch die doppelte Objektformulierung für das Nicht-erkennen-Können – einmal von Gott her und einmal von den Menschen her – noch klarer. Falls Johan Yeong-Sik Pahk mit seiner Auslegung von 9,1 im Recht ist[55], wird der Gedanke dort mit der Bildaussage weitergeführt, daß die »Gerechten und die Weisen und ihre Werke, sei es Liebe, sei es Haß« sich »in der Hand Gottes« befinden. Später wird Kohelet sich dieser Metaphysik nur in 11,5 noch einmal nähern:

---

53. Fox, *Contradictions* (Anm. 4), pp. 106-112, will vor allem aus 8,17 herausarbeiten, daß Kohelet nicht nur die Erkenntnis der Zukunft für unmöglich hält, sondern darüber hinaus vertritt, daß der Sinn des Lebens dem Menschen unbegreiflich bleibt. Ich sehe nicht, daß Kohelet das hier oder an anderer Stelle direkt sagt. Vielleicht kann man es aus seinen Aussagen folgernd heraushören, doch mehr kaum. Und selbst wenn der Mensch den letzten Sinn nicht ergründen kann, er weiß, daß dieser von Gott her da ist: vgl. 3,11.

54. Vgl. *ibid.*, p. 107.

55. PAHK, *Canto* (Anm. 49), pp. 22-26 und 129-153. Dort weitere Literatur. Pahk, dem ich hier folge, macht auch aus »Liebe wie Haß« noch ein nachgeholtes Stück des Subjekts des Nominalsatzes von 9,1aβ. Für die hier verhandelte Frage ist es jedoch nicht entscheidend, ob man auch in diesem Punkt mit ihm geht oder nicht.

Wie du den Weg des Windes ebensowenig wie das Werden des Kindes im Leib der Schwangeren erkennen kannst, so kannst du auch das Tun Gottes nicht erkennen, der alles tut[56].

Der Ton liegt auf «alles».

Ist also dieses Mysterium der doppelten Trägerschaft aller Ereignisse – in der Sprache der scholastischen Philosophie das Problem des *concursus Divinus* – das, was der Weise nie »finden« kann, da es undurchschaubar ist? Ich glaube nicht. Dieses Mysterium ist für Kohelet selbstverständliche Voraussetzung seines Denkens. Er bringt es mit großer Scheu und eher indirekt zur Sprache, wenn die Rede darauf kommen muß. Er spürt kein Bedürfnis, es reflex zu erörtern.

Worauf es in 8,16-17 ankommen dürfte, ist das kleine Wort כל, das ja auch in 3,11 stand und sich dort wohl auf die Vielfalt der menschlichen Handlungsfiguren bezog, die das Gedicht in 3,2-8 aufgezählt hatte[57]. In 11,5 wird כל bei der gleichen Sache wiederkehren. An allen diesen Stellen will Kohelet auf eines hinaus: Der Mensch kann zwar einzelnes erkennen, aber nicht die Gesamtheit dessen, was in der Wirklichkeit vor sich geht. Nach 3,11 entgehen ihm gerade der »Anfang« und das »Ende« des göttlichen Tuns, also die zeitlich entfernteren Vorgänge und Wirklichkeiten, sowohl in der Vergangenheit als auch in der Zukunft. Durch diese Grenze seiner Erkenntnis ist aber seine Möglichkeit zur Zukunftsplanung durchkreuzt.

Am schwersten wiegt das Dunkel der Zukunft. Das hat sich schon in 3,21f, 6,11f und 7,14 gezeigt. In 7,24 ging es dann um versunkene Vergangenheit. In 8,7 war es schon wieder die Zukunft. Auch in allen jetzt im Buch noch folgenden Aussagen über die Grenzen der menschlichen Erkenntnis geht es stets um die Dunkelheit der Zukunft – ausgenommen vielleicht im direkt folgenden Vers 9,1.

11. Der Text von 9,1 ist sehr schwierig. Ich möchte deshalb nur gerade festhalten, daß es gegen Ende heißt:

אין יודע האדם
der Mensch erkennt nicht

Wieder sind also die Grenzen der Erkenntnis das Thema. Die Wörter הכל לפניהם, wenn sie das Objekt des negierten Erkennens bezeichnen sollten und zeitlich aufzufassen wären, müßten nach dem durchgehen-

---

56. Man könnte fragen, ob hier את־הכל nicht »beides« meint und sich nur auf den Weg des Windes und das Werden des Kindes bezieht. Aber dann verlöre der Satz völlig seine Beziehung zum Kontext, in dem sein יודע אינך eine argumentative Funktion für das יודע אינך von 11,6 haben muß.

57. Das heißt: את־הכל in 3,11 nimmt das לכל von 3,1 auf.

den temporalen Gebrauch von לפני in die Vergangenheit (die »Vor-Zeit«) weisen[58].

12. Die weiteren Aussagen über die Begrenztheit der menschlichen Erkenntnis, die im vierten und letzten Teil des Buches nun noch folgen[59], sprechen alle von der undurchschaubaren Zukunft. Es sind 9,12; 10,14; 11,2 und 11,5f[60]. Dabei geht es zum Teil um Dinge wie den Todestag, zum Teil aber auch um sehr konkrete und gar nicht ferne Dinge wie die Ernte aus der Saat, die man gerade aussät. Die Begrenztheit der menschlichen Erkenntnis wird als bekannt vorausgesetzt und nach Bedarf eingeführt. In 9,12, 11,2 und 11,5f leitet begründendes כי die Aussage ein[61], und 10,14 ist gar nur ein Rückverweis auf die Aussagen von 6,11f und 8,7[62].

13. So läßt sich jetzt die Summe ziehen. Das Koheletbuch handelt an insgesamt 14 oder 15 Passagen von den Grenzen des menschlichen Erkennens. Das Thema ist also sicher nicht unwichtig. Es wird auch mit einer gewissen Systematik behandelt. Es steht am Anfang und am Ende des grundsätzlichen ersten Teils des Buches, kehrt dann im dritten, eher polemischen Teil wieder, wobei es bei dessen Schlußtext seinen Höhepunkt erreicht, und im vierten Teil klingt es immer wieder neu nach, meist um Ratschläge, die Kohelet gibt, zu begründen[63].

58. Hier kann ich Pahk nicht folgen, der לפניהם in Analogie zu 8,17 תחת־השמש räumlich verstehen will. Vgl. *ibid.*, p. 151f. Aus der Parallelität der beiden Konstruktionen folgt nicht notwendig auch eine Parallelität im Aspekt »Raumvorstellung«. Ich folge Pahk auch nicht ganz in der syntaktischen Großkonstruktion. Die beiden oder die drei Nominalsätze in 9,1aβ.b haben (nach den Theorien von D. Michel) von der Stellung von Subjekt und Prädikat her folgende Qualitäten: Nebensatz – Hauptsatz (- Nebensatz), wobei man von der Zuordnung von גם־שנאה גם־אהבה abstrahieren kann. Eine Übersetzungsmöglichkeit wäre also zum Beispiel: »da (auch) die Gerechten und die Weisen und ihre Werke in der Hand Gottes sind, […], erkennt der Mensch überhaupt nichts aus früherer Zeit.« Eine andere: »auch wenn die Gerechten und die Weisen und ihre Werke in der Hand Gottes sind, […], bleibt dem Menschen Erkenntnis verschlossen, weil alles vergangen ist.« Es gibt noch weitere Möglichkeiten.

59. FISCHER, *Skepsis* (Anm. 26), p. 20, Anm. 75, nennt noch mehr Stellen. Doch kann ich nicht entdecken, wieso in ihnen die Aussage »Der Mensch weiß es nicht« vorkommt.

60. In 11,5 wird die zunächst generell klingende Aussage sowohl durch den Kontext als auch speziell durch 11,6 auf die Zukunft zugespitzt.

61. Zu 9,12 כי גם vgl. WHYBRAY, *Ecclesiastes* (Anm. 20), p. 146. In 11,5f ist 11,5 vorangestellt; den logischen Anschluß an das Hauptthema liefert das כי am Anfang von 11,6b. In 11,2 und 11,5f werden Ermahnungen begründet.

62. Vgl. LOHFINK, *Kohelet* (Anm. 24), p. 77; MICHEL, *Untersuchungen* (Anm. 7), p. 266.

63. Zum begründenden Charakter der Aussage vgl. schon 3,22 und 7,14. 3,22a ist zwar kein Rat, sondern eine Feststellung. Doch auf Sprechaktebene hat diese Feststellung durchaus den Charakter eines Rats. Die dann folgende rhetorische Frage (3,22b), die die Erkennbarkeit der Zukunft leugnet, wird mit כי eingeführt. So wird man auch hier schon einmal von einer verdeckten Funktion der Aussage über Erkenntnisgrenzen als Begründung eines Ratschlags sprechen können. Zu 7,14 vgl. oben.

Die negativen Aussagen sind oft hart. Sie klingen sehr grundsätzlich. Dennoch sind es – im Gegensatz zur Aussage über die völlig fehlenden Erkenntnismöglichkeiten der Toten in 9,5 – niemals Aussagen über eine absolute Erkenntnisunfähigkeit des Menschen. Es geht nur um die Grenzen der menschlichen Erkenntnisfähigkeit, und zwar speziell bezüglich von Ereignissen der Vergangenheit und der Zukunft. Am bedrückendsten scheint nach Kohelet das Dunkel der Zukunft zu sein. Daneben stehen durchaus auch Aussagen über gelingende Erkenntnis und vorhandenes Wissen.

14. Es kommt hinzu, daß das Buch im Vollzug seiner Aussage niemals daran zweifelt, daß es selbst mit seinen Thesen die Wirklichkeit trifft. Und diese Thesen bestreichen nicht nur den Raum der Empirie, sondern reichen tief in die Unterwelt hinein. Vor allem sparen sie auch Gott nicht aus[64]. Die Sicherheit, mit der sie vorgetragen werden, erlaubt es noch nicht einmal, Kohelet als einen »Empiriker« zu bezeichnen, wenigstens wenn man den Sinn des Wortes wahren will, den es in Handbüchern der Philosophiegeschichte hat[65].

Im Blick auf den in der Philosophiegeschichte üblichen Sprachgebrauch wäre ich auch mit dem Etikett »erkenntnistheoretischer Skeptizismus« vorsichtig. Es klingt nach Grundsätzlicherem, als das ist, was wir bei Kohelet vorfinden. Wenn ich die Wendung dennoch weiter benutze, dann nur mit all den Einschränkungen, die ich jetzt gemacht habe.

Nachdem sie gemacht sind, läßt sich jedoch klar mit Michel sagen, daß der Kohelet des Koheletbuchs seine in Erkenntnisfragen vielleicht viel optimistischeren Zeitgenossen mit deutlicher Stimme auf die Basis eines erkenntnistheoretischen Skeptizismus zurückpostiert. Damit steht die zweite Frage an, die sich nicht auf die Sache, sondern auf ein Wort bezieht, das allerdings ein Schlüsselwort ist: Verwendet Kohelet *immer und gerade dann,* wenn er den weisheitlichen Erkenntnisoptimismus bezüglich des Weltenlaufs in Frage stellt, das Wort הבל?[66] Die Antwort ist, soweit ich sehen kann, eindeutig: Nein.

THESE 2:
DAS FEHLEN VON הבל BEI ERKENNTNISTHEORETISCHEN AUSSAGEN

Selbstverständlich: Wenn man schon vor jeder Einzelprüfung der Meinung ist, im ganzen Koheletbuch werde von überhaupt nichts anderem

---

64. Zu den theologischen Dimensionen des koheletschen Erkenntnisanspruchs vgl. den Beitrag von Crenshaw in diesem Band.

65. Dies ist ein weiterer Terminus, den Michel benutzt. MICHEL, *Untersuchungen* (Anm. 7), p. 273 beschließt den eigentlichen Text seines Buches mit dem Satz: »Er ist ein konsequent im Bereich des Empirischen bleibender Philosoph«.

66. Ich lehne mich bei dieser Formulierung an die schon eingangs zitierten Aussagen aus MICHEL, *ibid.,* p. 51, an.

geredet als von הבל, dann ist die Frage geklärt. Wer hierauf festgelegt ist, dem haben alle bisherigen Analysen und das, was noch folgt, nichts mehr zu sagen. Wer nicht so denkt, müßte bereit sein, die Texte zu überprüfen. Es handelt sich natürlich wieder um die selben Texte, jene, die von den Grenzen der Erkenntnis sprechen. Wird die Begrenztheit der menschlichen Erkenntnis in diesen Texten als הבל bezeichnet oder nicht?

1. Zunächst sei die Frage in der ihr angemessenen Form gestellt: Gibt es Aussagen über die Begrenztheit der menschlichen Erkenntnis, die als Basis für ein הבל-Urteil dienen? Wird die Begrenztheit der Erkenntnis vielleicht wenigstens auf die Weise, die in späteren Teilen des Buches möglich ist, einfach schon mit dem Terminus הבל eingeführt? Die Antwort ist negativ. Es gibt diesen Fall nicht.

2. Er liegt *auch* nicht in 1,13b vor, dem Text, den ich deshalb zusätzlich erwähnt habe, weil er nach Michel ebenfalls von den Grenzen der Erkenntnis handelt. Hier folgt bekanntlich schon im nächsten Vers, 1,14, die erste הבל-Aussage des Buches, wenn man vom »Rahmenvers« 1,2 absieht. Sie steht allerdings in 1,14b und folgt als Schlußfolgerung auf eine Kurznotiz in 1,14a. Diese sagt, daß Salomo Beobachtungen angestellt hat. Das Objekt seiner Beobachtungen ist jedoch nicht die menschliche Erkenntnis, sondern die Gesamtheit des Handelns unter der Sonne. Der Text als ganzer lautet in der Übersetzung von Michel:

> Ich sah an (betrachtete) alle Werke, die unter der Sonne geschehen: Siehe, alles ist *hæbæl* und Haschen nach Wind[67].

«Alles« in der הבל-Aussage bezieht sich notwendig auf »alle Werke, die unter der Sonne geschehen,« zurück, dazu noch auf »alles, was unter dem Himmel geschieht« von 1,13, nie jedoch auf die Erkenntnisbemühung, von der 1,13 am Anfang spricht und wo das Wort »alles« nicht vorkommt[68]. Selbst wenn man also mit Michel 1,13b als Aussage über die menschliche Erkenntnis liest, gilt das nicht von dem הבל-Urteil

---

67. So *ibid.*, p. 9. Michel legt in seiner Monographie hohen Wert darauf, daß ראה bei Kohelet in vielen Fällen »betrachten« im Sinne von »untersuchen, überprüfen« bedeutet. Das trifft hier sicher auch zu. Für die Gesamtheit der Stellen vgl. A. SCHOORS, *The Verb* ראה *in the Book of Qoheleth,* in A.A. DIESEL *Studien* (Anm. 35), pp. 227-241.

68. Die Kommentierung bei MICHEL, *Untersuchungen* (Anm. 7), p. 10, lautet, bei dem von ihm als selbständiger Satz aufgefaßten 1,13b ansetzend: »Der um Verstehen bemühte Leser steht etwas ratlos vor dieser Feststellung – warum um alles in der Welt soll solches Bemühen um Erkenntnis eine böse Mühe sein, obendrein noch eine solche, die Gott den Menschen gegeben hat, sie damit zu plagen? Er muß diese Ratlosigkeit, dieses Fragen nach einer Begründung aushalten bis 3,10-15; dort erst wird dieses Urteil einsichtig begründet. Jetzt erhält er auf sein Fragen im folgenden Vers nur eine *sachliche Wiederholung* und also Bekräftigung.« Es folgt ein Zitat von 1,14, dann Bemerkungen zum Sinn des Wortes הבל. Unterstreichung von mir.

in 1,14, so nah die Dinge beieinander stehen. Inzwischen hat das Thema gewechselt.

3. Damit könnte unsere Frage als beantwortet gelten. Doch sei zur Absicherung noch ein zweites Mal gefragt, etwas lockerer. Wird in den 14 Stellen, die von der Begrenztheit der menschlichen Erkenntnis handeln, zwar nicht eine formelle הבל-Aussage gemacht, aber die Sache vielleicht doch in den Umkreis oder den Dunstkreis der ganzen הבל-Thematik gebracht?

Fragt man so, dann verstärkt sich eher der bisherige Eindruck. Die ersten beiden Belege auf unserer Liste finden sich genau in jenen Bereichen des ersten Buchteils, für die ich anfangs das Fehlen der הבל-Thematik feststellen mußte: im Anfangsgedicht 1,4-11 (nämlich 1,8.9-11) und im theologischen Teil 3,1-15 (nämlich 3,11). Da alle späteren Stellen an diesen beiden Stellen hängen, sollte auch für sie alles klar sein. In der Tat findet sich auch später nirgends in den Texten oder in unmittelbarer Nachbarschaft das Wort הבל – mit einer einzigen Ausnahme, die ich deshalb jetzt genauer besprechen muß.

4. Es handelt sich um den Brückentext 6,11-12, der, möglichst viele Stichworte ineinander verwebend, zugleich an Früheres anknüpft und zum dritten, andere Meinungen diskutierenden Teil des Buches hinüberführt. Daß bei dieser Stichwortverknotung auch הבל vorkommen muß, ist fast zu erwarten. Denn das Wort הבל spielt nicht nur vorher, sondern auch im nun beginnenden dritten Teil bei den Urteilen über die traditionelle Spruchweisheit eine wichtige Rolle. Einerseits dient es dort zur Beurteilung der Tradition. Es qualifiziert ein zitiertes Sprichwort negativ (7,6), und es charakterisiert Gegenbeobachtungen (8,10.14.14). Andererseits charakterisiert es den Erfahrungsraum, in dem die Gegenbeobachtungen Kohelets sich zeigen, durch den Ausdruck ימי הבלי »meine הבל-Tage«. Auf den ersten Gebrauch von הבל spielt im Ankündigungstext wohl 6,11 an, wenn es dort heißt: »Es gibt viele (Sprich-)Wörter, die den הבל vervielfachen«[69], den zweiten nimmt 6,12a vorweg, wenn es von den »wenigen Tagen des הבל-Lebens« eines Menschen spricht. Doch zur formalen Konstitution der Aussage über die Grenzen der menschlichen Erkenntnis in 6,12b tragen alle diese Aussagen nichts bei. Es handelt sich um zwecks möglichst intensiver Voraus-

---

69. Die דברים dürften, wie sich dem Leser zumindest bald zeigen wird, die Sprichwörter sein, die jetzt kommentiert werden. Wichtig ist, daß nicht gesagt wird, diese Sprichwörter *seien* הבל, sondern sie *vermehrten* הבל. Man könnte sie ja zumindest als Objektivationen des Erkennens betrachten. Würde also gesagt, sie *seien* הבל, dann wäre das eine Aussage über das Erkennen. Doch sie *vermehren* הבל. Vermutlich ist der Gedanke der, daß diese Spruchweisheit in ihrem Optimismus die Menschen immer wieder zu falschem und dann enttäuschtem Handeln bringt. Nichtentsprechung von rationaler Erwartung und Effekt ist aber Absurdität, הבל.

Verknüpfung Miterwähntes, um mehr nicht. So ist es verständlich, daß in diesem einen Fall von 6,11-12 zweimal das Wort הבל vorkommt. Doch auch hier soll nicht angedeutet werden, die Begrenztheit der menschlichen Erkenntnis selbst sei הבל.

Auch unter der sehr lockeren Fragestellung nach dem einfachen Vorkommen des Wortes הבל an den einschlägigen Stellen läßt sich also nicht sagen, Kohelet verwende das Wort הבל *immer da, wo* er den Erkenntnisanspruch der Weisheit ablehne.

Schluss

Es ging um das Wort הבל bei Kohelet. Wofür wird es verwendet, für welchen Bereich von Aussagen? Als einigermaßen sicher kann gelten, daß הבל weder metaphysischen noch kosmologischen Aussagen dient, sondern nur anthropologischen. Doch stellt sich die Frage, ob der Gebrauch von הבל nicht noch stärker eingeschränkt sei. Nach Michel benutzt Kohelet das Wort הבל immer da, wo er im Gegenzug zur traditionellen Weisheit seinen erkenntnistheoretischen Skeptizismus zum Ausdruck bringen will. Diese Annahme sollte überprüft werden.

In der Tat lehrt Kohelet einen erkenntnistheoretischen Skeptizismus, wenn man dieses Wort in diesem Zusammenhang vielleicht auch etwas abgeschwächt gebrauchen muß. Doch das Interessante ist: In den 14 Aussagen, die er zu diesem Thema macht, spielt das Wort הבל keine Rolle. Es dient im Koheletbuch also nicht der Qualifizierung der Grenzen der menschlichen Erkenntnis.

Diese negative Formulierung läßt sich ins Positive wenden: Wenn Kohelet von הבל spricht, dann spricht er über Handlungen, Dinge, Situationen, Ereignisse. Er spricht von objektiver Welt, nicht vom Subjekt und seinen Erkenntnismöglichkeiten.

Mit diesem Ergebnis ist zwar kein direkter Beitrag zur Frage geliefert, was הבל im Koheletbuch nun wirklich bedeute. Aber für eine Klärung dieser Frage könnte es schon wichtig sein, wenn der Bereich, auf den sich das Wort bezieht, genauer umschrieben ist. Eine Hoffnung, in der Deutung dieses schwierigen und doch so faszinierenden Buches weiterzukommen, haben wir wohl nur, wenn wir uns zu solchen kleinen Schritten der Analyse entschließen. Auch eine provozierende These, die sich nicht bewährt, kann dann sehr hilfreich sein.

Phil.-Theol. Hochschule Sankt Georgen   Norbert LOHFINK SJ
Offenbacher Landstraße 224
D-60599 Frankfurt am Main

A CENTURY OF WRESTLING WITH QOHELET

The Research History of the Book
Illustrated with a Discussion of Qoh 4,17-5,6[1]

I. INTRODUCTION

Although a number of research histories on Qohelet[2] have been written this century, none of the researchers employed paradigms and paradigm shifts as a guiding principle in their investigations. Most scholars only investigated short periods of research and mainly identified the dominant themes and trends in the respective periods[3]. This endeavour gives a brief presentation of a century's research on Qohelet structuring it on the basis of paradigms and paradigm shifts. In order to accomplish this, a brief presentation of the paradigm shifts which have occurred in the field of Biblical Studies since the Reformation is offered. This is followed by a reflection on how the paradigms and paradigm shifts influenced the research on the book. The last section of the article illustrates the previous sections by looking at interpretations of Qoh 4,17-5,6.

II. CURSORY SURVEY OF THE PARADIGM SHIFTS IN BIBLICAL STUDIES

The notion of Thomas Kuhn[4] that growth in scientific knowledge does not take place through *accumulation,* but by means of *revolutions,* exerted a stimulating influence on various disciplines. Theology is one

1. The author hereby acknowledges grants received from the Centre for Science Development of the Human Sciences Research Council and the University of South Africa which enabled him to attend the *Colloquium Biblicum Lovaniense.*

2. K. GALLING, *Stand und Aufgabe der Kohelet-Forschung*, in *TR* 6 (1934) 355-373; S. BRETÓN, *Qoheleth Studies*, in *BTB* 3 (1973) 22-50; P.C. BEENTJES, *Recente visies op Qohelet*, in *Bijdragen* 41 (1980) 436-444; O. KAISER, *Judentum und Hellenismus*, in *VuF* 27 (1982) 68-88; J.L. CRENSHAW, *Qoheleth in current research*, in *HAR* 7 (1983) 41-56; D. MICHEL, *Qohelet* (EdF, 258), Darmstadt, WBG, 1988; N. WHYBRAY, *Ecclesiastes* (Old Testament Guides), Sheffield, JSOT Press, 1989; R.E. MURPHY, *Recent Research on Proverbs and Qoheleth*, in *Currents in Research, Biblical Studies* 1 (1993) 119-140.

3. Diethelm Michel's research history (*Qohelet* [EdF, 258]) is an exception. He, however, mainly gives an overview of the historical-critical research done until 1987.

4. T.S. KUHN, *The Structure of Scientific Revolutions* (International Encyclopedia of Unified Science, Vol. 2, No. 2), Chicago, University of Chicago Press, ²1970.

such area. Küng[5] indicated convincingly that systematic theology reflects such revolutions. Paradigms and paradigm shifts have indeed influenced this discipline.

A number of scholars have endeavoured to indicate paradigms and
paradigm shifts in the fields of Old and New Testament research.
Robertson[6] distinguished *four paradigm shifts* in the reading of the
Tanakh/Old Testament, observing that[7]:

> The first [paradigm shift] occurred when the Jewish people began to read it
> [the Tanakh] not simply as diverse writings in Hebrew but as scripture, as
> writings which, when taken as a whole, represent a canon of religious doc-
> trine and practice. The second happened when Christians read it not as
> Jewish but as Christian scripture. The third, the shift brought about by
> modern critical investigation of the Bible, represented in one way a return
> to the first point of view, the Old Testament as applied writings in Hebrew;
> the new element was the study of it according to the criteria of critical
> historiography. Reading it as literature is now another and fourth major
> paradigm shift.

According to Vorster[8], a New Testament scholar, it is possible to distinguish a pre-critical, a critical and a post-critical paradigm in the field of
Biblical Studies. Lategan[9] also identifies three paradigms, linking these
to the model of communication designed by Jakobson: *sender — message — receiver*, or in the case of literature: *author — text — reader*.
According to Lategan, historical-critical studies represent the first phase
in the history of biblical research. During the heyday of the historical-
critical paradigm, scholars focussed on questions about origins: sources,
authorship, *autographa* and the reconstruction of texts. The first paradigm shift occurred with the advent of structuralism and scholars' focus
now shifted to the text. A second paradigm shift occurred when scholars
realised that readers of texts play an important role in constituting meaning. Reader-response criticism was born, representing the third paradigm
in interpretation.

5. H. Küng, *Was meint Paradigmenwechsel?* in H. Küng & D. Tracy (Hrsg.),
Theologie – Wohin? Auf dem Weg zu einem neuen Paradigma (Ökumenische Theologie,
2), Zürich, Benziger, 1984, pp. 19-25; Id., *Paradigmenwechsel in der Theologie:
Versuch einer Grundlagenerklärung*, in *op. cit.*, pp. 37-75.
    6. D. Robertson, *The Old Testament and the Literary Critic* (Guides to Biblical
Scholarship), Philadelphia, Fortress, 1977.
    7. *Ibid.*, p. 4.
    8. W.S. Vorster, *Towards a post-critical paradigm: Progress in New Testament
scholarship?* in J. Mouton, A.G. Van Aarde & W.S. Vorster (eds.), *Paradigms and
Progress in Theology* (HSRC Studies in Research Methodology, 5), Pretoria, Human Sciences Research Council, 1988, pp. 31-48.
    9. B.C. Lategan, *Current issues in the hermeneutical debate*, in *Neotestamentica* 18
(1984) 1-17.

This notion of a shift in the various foci as points of departure, indicated by Lategan, has now almost become axiomatic. Scholars employing reader-response criticism often use the communication model to explain the shifts[10]. However, in my opinion, these divisions misrepresent the paradigm shifts that occurred in Biblical Studies during this century. This century reflects only two paradigm shifts in Biblical Studies – the historical-critical and modern literary criticism. However, scholars working in the field of modern literary criticism (*Literaturwissenschaft*) have witnessed a shift in their discipline which can be described as a shift in focus from *author* to *text* to *reader*.

Although there have been these *two paradigm shifts* during the twentieth century, scholars have worked within *three paradigms*. These three paradigms are: the pre-critical paradigm (or what I would like to call the *Word-of-God paradigm*), the historical-critical paradigm, and the new literary criticism paradigm. The three paradigms should not be confused with the shifts in focus that occurred in modern literary criticism (*Literaturwissenschaft*).

The paradigm shift that led to the historical-critical paradigm had a long prehistory. To obtain a clear picture of this shift and the resultant paradigm, it is necessary to go as far back as the Reformation. I therefore provide a brief historical survey of the paradigm shifts which have occurred in the field of Biblical Studies from the Reformation onwards.

1. *The paradigm shift of the Reformation*

The paradigm shift which took place during the Reformation is sometimes described by the statement: "The Reformers dethroned the Pope and enthroned the Bible"[11]. However, this is a misleading characterisation of the revolution, since the Catholic Church *also emphasised the authority* of Scripture. The Reformers merely accepted that the *individual believer* could also be *a legitimate interpreter* of the Bible. The Reformers were convinced that it was not only popes and councils that could claim the guidance of the Spirit for the correct interpretation of the Bible[12]. An individual believer could also claim the guidance of the Spirit. As support for their viewpoint the Reformers emphasised the

10. Cf. D.J.A. CLINES, *What Does Eve Do to Help? and Other Readerly Questions to the Old Testament* (JSOT SS, 94), Sheffield, JSOT Press, 1990, pp. 9-10; M.G. BRETT, *The Future of Reader Criticisms?* in F. WATSON (ed.), *The Open Text: New Directions for Biblical Studies?*, London, SCM, 1993, pp. 13-31, esp. 14.

11. R.H. BAINTON, *The Bible in the Reformation*, in S.L. GREENSLADE (ed.), *The Cambridge History of the Bible, Volume 3: The West from the Reformation to the Present Day*, Cambridge, Cambridge University Press, 1963, pp. 1-37, esp. 1.

12. *Ibid.*, p. 4.

clarity of Scripture (*"perspicuitas"*) and furthermore asserted that be-
lievers need not turn to all kinds of interpretation (e.g. the fourfold
meaning of Scripture) in order to understand the Bible and apply it to
their daily living. The *historico-literal interpretation* and the *guidance of
the Holy Spirit* were sufficient for a correct understanding and application of Scripture.

2. The historical-critical paradigm

The paradigm shift brought about by the Reformation had hardly
taken place, when a number of crises[13] arose which seriously threatened
the paradigm.

The first crisis occurred on account of the Copernican revolution. The
Reformers (like their contemporary Catholic theologians) believed in a
geocentric universe: the earth stood still while the sun revolved around
it. This presupposition was challenged when Galileo Galilei (1564-1642)
claimed that the heliocentric viewpoint was no longer merely an hypothesis, but a fact. Those who espoused these novel ideas were condemned
because they (according to the prevailing interpretation) relegated the
Holy Spirit to a liar and undermined the authority of Scripture[14]. After
all, it was the Holy Spirit who inspired the Bible authors to write that the
earth stood still, while the sun revolved around it (Josh 10,12-13; Qoh
1,4-5). The new cosmology did not only affect the Protestant view of
Scripture, but also the Catholic view. Scripture was also authoritative for
the Catholic Church and for this reason they condemned Galileo
Galilei[15].

A second crisis was brought about by the philosophy of René Descartes
(1596-1650), when he propounded that man could doubt everything except the fact *that it is he who doubts*. Underlying his famous dictum,
"cogito ergo sum", was the conviction that people could only obtain
certainty about a matter by means of their mental ability. This brought
about a new concept of truth. Truth was no longer that which was guaranteed by one or other institution of authority, but that which is clear to
human reason[16]. Church traditions and viewpoints were challenged since
reason could doubt everything – even the truths that were formulated on
the basis of the Bible. Church authorities reacted fiercely against this

---

13. KUHN, *op. cit.*, pp. 66-91.
14. K. SCHOLDER, *The Birth of Modern Critical Theology: Origins and Problems of
Biblical Criticism in the Seventeenth Century*, London, SCM, 1990, p. 55.
15. I.J.J. SPANGENBERG, *Galileo Galilei en die boek Prediker: 'n Les uit die kerkge-
skiedenis*, in *ThEv (SA)* 26 (1993) 121-131.
16. SCHOLDER, *op. cit.*, pp. 111-113.

new philosophy. Some theologians asserted emphatically that they would rather err along with Scripture than adhere to these new ideas[17]. Protestant Orthodoxy is an example of this counter reaction and in "Kuhnian" terms, one may say that Protestant Orthodoxy endeavoured to formulate rules to protect the biblical paradigm of the Reformation[18].

The third crisis came about during the eighteenth and nineteenth centuries when scholars developed a stronger historical consciousness. They began to ask all kinds of questions about history and historiography with the result that within a few decades a revolution took place in the field of historiography[19]. Soon it was clear that the chronology inferred from biblical data (viz. Adam was the first person and the creation took place 4 004 years BCE) just did not concur with new discoveries and theories. Furthermore, the principles according to which historical documents were evaluated, were now also applied to the Bible and this had serious implications for theology. Krentz summarised the crisis as follows: "The Bible was no longer the criterion for the writing of history; rather history became the criterion for understanding the Bible"[20]. The realisation that the biblical books were written by people who had a different culture and maintained other religious convictions, gradually increased.

On account of these three crises a new paradigm emerged, namely the historical-critical paradigm[21]. During the last decades of the nineteenth century several biblical scholars started working in the new paradigm. However, those who paved the way were often accused of heresy and were condemned. Some of these were: Samuel Davidson (1856-57), John William Colenso (1863), William Robertson Smith (1881), Crawford Howell Toy

---

17. *Ibid.*, p. 120.

18. KUHN, *op. cit.*, p. 47.

19. A. RICHARDSON, *The Bible in the Age of Science*, London, SCM, 1964, pp. 47-49; E. KRENTZ, *The Historical-Critical Method* (Guides to Biblical Scholarship), Philadelphia, Fortress, 1975, pp. 22-30.

20. KRENTZ, *op. cit.*, p. 30.

21. Mark Noll summarises this shift excellently: "Kuhn's discussion of 'normal science,' 'paradigm shift,' and 'revolutionary' situations has been applied promiscuously to far too many historical developments. But here at least it seems to fit. A period in which normal science proceeded under a secure paradigm (the Bible is the Word of God to be interpreted by the conventions of common sense) gave way to a period when anomalies in the old theories seemed to proliferate (new knowledge about world religions, new conceptions of historical development, new advances in research, new standards of professional study – and all exacerbated by social and enonomic changes in the community experiencing the anomalies). After a brief period of dialogue between those working in the old paradigm and those struggling toward something different (roughly 1880 to 1900), a new paradigm emerges for the practice of normal science (the Bible, however sublime, is a human book to be investigated with the standard assumptions that one brings to the discussion of all products of human culture)." Cf. M.A. NOLL, *Between Faith and Criticism: Evangelicals, Scholarship, and the Bible*, Leicester, Apollos, 1991, p. 45.

(1879), Charles Augustus Briggs (1890), Johannes Geelkerken (1926) and Johannes du Plessis (1930).

3. *The paradigm of modern literary criticism*

Since the late sixties[22] and the beginning of the seventies of this century[23] a new paradigm in the field of Biblical Studies announced itself. This paradigm is linked to modern literary criticism and the shift in focus which took place in that field of study[24]. In modern literary criticism the focus moved from the *author* to the *text*, and eventually to the *reader*[25]. Old and New Testament scholars found these shifts sufficiently valid to apply them to biblical texts. Literary critics themselves produced publications in which they applied the new ways of reading and studying texts, to biblical material[26]. It was, therefore, not on account of a failure on the part of the historical-critical method that scholars redirected their focus, but because some scholars realised that the historical approach is not the only possible approach to biblical literature. Presently, scholarly journals literally teem with articles in which the newer methods and insights are applied to the literature of the Bible. Articles with headings in which the following descriptors appear: "narratological analysis", "rhetorical analysis", "deconstruction", "intertextuality", "reception-critical approach", are no longer strange[27]. Even a new journal[28] has been launched to cater for those scholars who work in the new paradigm and scholars are already reflecting on the relationship between the two paradigms, and the respective methods of interpretation[29].

22. Cf. A. van der Kooij, The "critical method" of Abraham Kuenen and the methods of Old Testament research since 1891 up to 1991 (Some considerations), in P.B. Dirksen & A. van der Kooij (ed.), Abraham Kuenen (1828-1891). His major Contributions to the Study of the Old Testament, Leiden, Brill, 1993, pp. 49-64, esp. 58-61.

23. David Clines describes this period as follows: "[A] wave of uncertainty, from the late 1960s onward, was sweeping the scholarly world about all sorts of historical-critical conclusions (the sources of the Pentateuch, the Israelite amphictyony, the Solomonic Enlightenment, and so on), and one needed strong nerves to go on insisting there was no problem." Cf. Clines, op. cit., pp. 10-11.

24. Cf. Brett, op. cit., pp. 20-21; M.A. Powell, The Bible and Modern Literary Criticism: A Critical Assessment and Annotated Bibliography, London, Greenwood, 1992, p. 14.

25. Cf. Powell, op. cit., p. 6; Clines, op. cit., pp. 9-10.

26. H.R. Jauss, The Book Jonah – a paradigm of the "hermeneutics of strangeness", in JLS 1/4 (1985) 1-19; I. Gräbe, Theory of literature and Old Testament studies – narrative conventions as exegetic reading strategies, in OTE 3 (1990) 43-59.

27. Cf. the annotated bibliography in Powell, op. cit., pp. 41-363.

28. I'm referring to the journal, Biblical Interpretation published by E.J. Brill in Leiden. To some extent the journal Semeia falls within the same category.

29. J. Barton, Historical Criticism and Literary Interpretation: Is there any common ground? in S.E. Porter, P. Joyce & D.E. Orton (eds.), Crossing the Boundaries: Essays in Biblical Interpretation in honour of Michael D. Goulder, Leiden, 1994, pp. 3-15; P. Joyce, First Among equals? The Historical-critical Approach in the Marketplace of Methods, ibid., pp. 17-27.

In summary, the following diagram portrays these developments.

Diagrammatic overview of paradigm shifts in Biblical Studies

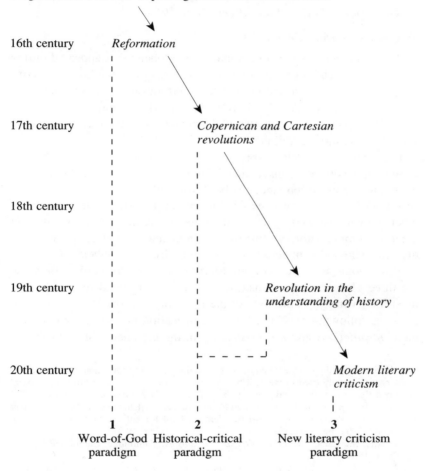

III. PARADIGM SHIFTS AND THE HISTORY OF RESEARCH
ON THE BOOK OF QOHELET

As the above presentation indicates, we can identify two paradigm shifts in Biblical Studies this century. The one occurred at the turn of the century, and the other almost three quarters of a century later[30]. I would

30. In a recent article, Brevard Childs argued that between 1920 and 1940 Old Testament scholars in Germany were searching for a new paradigm. In my opinion this was not a search for a new paradigm, but rather a struggle of German Old Testament scholars working in the tradition of the Reformation to come to grips (theologically) with the his-

now like to focus on how these paradigm shifts influenced the research
that has been done on the Book of Qohelet.

1. *The historical-critical paradigm: 1901-1960*

a) Research during 1901-1920

When one peruses the commentaries on Qohelet that appeared during
the first two decades of this century, it is evident that the historical-critical paradigm played a dominant role during those years. Scholars such
as McNeile in England[31], Barton in America[32] and Podechard in
France[33], espoused the view that Qohelet was a sceptical work with considerable glossarial additions[34].

These views were also expressed in a monograph written by Jastrow
of the University of Pennsylvania[35]. He is representative of the research
done during this period since his book was published at the close of the
second decade. Moreover, he tried to popularise the research results of
other scholars. According to him there were a number of commentators:
a pious commentator, a "maxim" commentator, and a conventional
moralist who added material to the original Book of Qohelet. These additions amount to more than one-fourth of the present book[36]. Between
the three glossators, the "maxim" commentator added the most – almost forty verses "in the style of the Book of Proverbs"[37]. Jastrow supplies the following reasons for the identification of these additions: (1)
the *contradictions* and *inconsistencies* in the arguments of Qohelet, (2)

torical-critical paradigm. One could also say that during those years some Old Testament
scholars in Germany tried to create a hybrid between the traditional Word-of-God paradigm and the historical-critical one. Cf. B.S. CHILDS, *Old Testament in Germany 1920-
1940: The search for a new paradigm*, in P. MOMMER & W. THIEL (eds.), *Altes Testament
Forschung und Wirkung:* Festschrift für Henning Graf Reventlow, Frankfurt am Main,
Peter Lang, 1994, pp. 233-246.
   31. A.H. McNEILE, *An introduction to Ecclesiastes.* Cambridge, Cambridge University Press, 1904.
   32. G.A. BARTON, *A Critical and Exegetical Commentary on the Book of Ecclesiastes*,
Edinburgh, T & T Clark, 1912.
   33. E. PODECHARD, *L'Ecclésiaste* (EB), Paris, Victor Lecoffre, 1912.
   34. These scholars differ on how many editors and glossators tampered with the original book. A.H. McNEILE (*op. cit.*, pp. 21-27) believed that three persons added material to
the original work: an editor, a wisdom teacher and a pious Jew. G.A. BARTON (*op. cit.*, p.
46) opines that only two hands have made additions to the book – an editor "deeply imbued in the wisdom literature", and one "deeply imbued with the spirit of the Phari-
sees".
   35. M. JASTROW, *A Gentle Cynic: Being a Translation of the Book of Koheleth commonly known as Ecclesiastes stripped of later Additions, also its Origin, Growth and Interpretation*, Philadelphia, J.B. Lippincott, 1919.
   36. *Ibid.*, p. 12.
   37. *Ibid.*, p. 76.

the *interruptions* of some of the arguments, and (3) the *form* of the maxims and sayings[38]. Moreover, he dismisses the idea that the maxims and sayings could be quotations on account of their large number[39]. In answer to the question "What was the intent of these additions?", Jastrow replies: "[T]o make the figure of Solomon as the reputed author of the book conform to the Solomon of orthodox tradition, and to give to the book the character of being a collection of sayings, edifying and suitable for general reading like the Book of Proverbs"[40].

The following issues were also debated during the first two decades of this century: (1) the date of origin; (2) the notion that the original author was influenced by Greek philosophical thought; (3) the question whether the book was written in prose or poetry[41]; (4) the nature of the Hebrew in which the book was written. These issues eventually became part and parcel of the historical-critical research of the book.

b) Research during 1921-1940

No major changes in the historical-critical research on Qohelet are reflected in the publications of the twenties and thirties[42]. Scholars did their research along the same lines as their predecessors. Some paid attention to the additions[43], whilst others discussed the alleged Greek philosophical influences[44]. However, these years witnessed a growing interest in the Israelite wisdom literature as a literary corpus, which was possibly influenced by Egyptian wisdom. The interest was sparked off by the 1923 publication of facsimiles of Egyptian hieratic papyri in the

---

38. *Ibid.*, pp. 79-80.

39. *Ibid.*, p. 108: "If we had only a few of such sayings, we *might* assume that Koheleth is introducing them as apt quotations, but their large number precludes the reasonableness of such an inartistic procedure on the part of a skillful writer."

40. *Ibid.*, p. 118.

41. V. ZAPLETAL, *Das Buch Kohelet: Kritisch und metrisch untersucht, übersetzt and erklärt*, Freiburg, Universitäts-Buchhandlung, 1905; P. HAUPT, *Koheleth oder Weltschmerz in der Bibel. Ein Lieblingsbuch Friedrich des Grossen. Verdeutscht und erklärt*, Leipzig, 1905.

42. Kurt Galling gave a thorough overview of the research done up to the early thirties. Cf. GALLING, *Stand und Aufgabe der Kohelet-Forschung*, in *TR* 6 (1934) 355-373.

43. Although the tendency to identify additions and interpolations still existed, the number that scholars pinpointed, declined. Volz identified more or less fifteen additions and thirty interpolations. Cf. P. VOLZ, *Hiob und Weisheit (Das Buch Hiob, Sprüche und Jesus Sirach, Prediger) übersetz, erklärt und mit Einleitungen versehen*, (Die Schriften des AT, 3.2), Göttingen, 1921. Odeberg on the other hand, identified only two additions (11,7-12,7; 12,9-14) and three interpolations (7,19; 9,17-10,4; 10,8-13). Cf. H. ODEBERG, *Qohaelaet: A commentary on the Book of Ecclesiastes*, Uppsala, Almqvist & Wiksells, 1929, pp. 83-85. Galling attributed the interpolations to the second epilogist or redactor (QR²). These were 3,17a; 8,5.12b; 11,9b-12,1a. Cf. K. GALLING, *Der Prediger* (HAT, 18), Tübingen, 1940.

44. H. RANSTON, *Ecclesiastes and the early Greek wisdom literature*, London, 1925.

British Museum containing "The Teaching of Amen-em-ope", and its discussion by Erman at a session of the Prussian Academy in 1924[45]. A number of prominent Old Testament scholars[46] then took part in the research on, and discussion of, the Israelite wisdom literature. Although these studies did not have an immediate effect on the research on the Book of Qohelet it eventually influenced scholars' opinion about Qohelet being a wisdom book and its relation to other wisdom literature. Gemser's commentary published in the early thirties[47], gives evidence to this effect, as well as the commentary by Galling published in 1940[48].

During these decades two monographs were published which reflect a somewhat different slant than those previously mentioned. One was written by Vischer[49] and the other one by Gottfried Kuhn[50]. Both of these scholars took cognisance of the results of historical-critical studies, but tried to incorporate these results in the old *Word-of-God paradigm*[51].

c) Research during 1941-1960

Not many historical-critical commentaries appeared during the fourties and fifties[52]. Most scholars discussed the issues which the historical-critical studies had tabled previously, but they did not work ex-

---

45. Cf. R.B.Y. Scott, *The study of wisdom literature*, in *Interpr* 24 (1970), p. 23; R.N. Whybray, *The social world of wisdom writers*, in R.E. Clements (ed.), *The World of Ancient Israel: Sociological, Anthropological and Political Perspectives*, Cambridge, Cambridge University Press, 1989, pp. 227-250, esp. 230; C. Westermann, *Forschungsgeschichte zur Weisheitsliteratur 1950-1990*, (Arbeiten zur Theologie, 71), Stuttgart, Calwer, 1991, p. 10.

46. A. Erman, *Das Weisheitsbuch des Amen-em-ope*, in *OLZ* 27 (1924) 241-252; H. Gressmann, *Israels Spruchweisheit im Zusammenhang der Weltliteratur*, Berlin, Karl Curtis, 1925; W.O.E. Oesterley, *The Wisdom of Egypt and the Old Testament in the light of the newly discovered "Teaching of Amenemope"*, London, McMillan, 1927; J. Fichtner, *Die altorientalische Weisheit in ihrer Israelitisch-jüdischen Ausprägung*, Gießen, Töpelmann, 1933; W. Baumgartner, *Die israelitische Weisheitsliteratur*, in *TR* 5 (1933) 259-288; W. Zimmerli, *Zur Struktur der alttestamentlichen Weisheit*, in *ZAW* 51 (1933) 177-204.

47. B. Gemser, *Spreuken II: Prediker en Hooglied van Salomo* (Tekst en Uitleg), Groningen, Wolters, 1931.

48. K. Galling, *Der Prediger* (HAT, 18), Tübingen, Mohr, 1940.

49. W. Vischer, *Der Prediger Salomo übersetzt mit einem Nachwort und Anmerkungen*, München, 1926.

50. G. Kuhn, *Erklärung des Buches Koheleth* (BZAW, 43), Gießen, 1926.

51. Barr characterises Vischer's way of reading the Old Testament as follows: "The logic was: if you want a Reformational exposition written by a modern scholar, this is what you get. If you do not like it, then you stand outside the circle of the Reformation." Cf. J. Barr, *Wilhelm Vischer and Allegory*, in A.G. Auld (ed.), *Understanding Poets and Prophets: Essays in honour of George Wishart Anderson* (JSOT SS, 152), Sheffield, Sheffield Academic Press, 1993, pp. 38-60, esp. 47.

52. The commentaries of D. Buzy (*L'Ecclésiaste*, in *La Sainte Bible VI*, Paris, 1946) and F. Nötscher (*Ekklesiastes oder Prediger*, Würzburg, 1948) are the only commentaries that I am aware of.

clusively within that paradigm. Aalders, for example, does not hesitate to mention that he is writing as a Reformed theologian and is thus working in the traditional *Word-of-God paradigm*[53]:

> De schrijver van dezen commentaar is als Gereformeerd theoloog niet alleen van de eenheid van compositie in het boek De Prediker, maar eveneens van de eenheid der gansche H. Schrift overtuigd; en daarom heeft hij hier niet bloot het woord van den anonymen volksleeraar die zichzelf alleen maar Qohelet noemt, maar allereerst en allermeest het woord van den levenden God zelf trachten te beluisteren.

The commentary by van der Ploeg can be characterised as a hybrid approach[54]. He wrote as a Catholic scholar, and his commentary clearly reflects the traditional *Word-of-God paradigm*, but he discussed issues prevalent in historical-critical commentaries.

During these years Gordis' commentary[55] gave new life to an old viewpoint: the book contains a number of wisdom sayings quoted by the author. What some scholars previously demarcated as *additions* he identified as *quotations*[56]. This hypothesis did not meet with much enthusiasm, and for a number of years scholars still followed the old trend and argued a case for *additions*. One might even go so far as to say that Gordis' arguments were ignored during those years[57], but they eventually contributed towards reading the book as a unity written by someone who stood in the wisdom tradition[58]. This was already reflected in the inaugural lecture of Wilhelm Rudolph on November 12, 1958 at the University of Münster when he maintained[59]:

> Einer dieser Weisen ist auch Kohelet, und tatsächlich finden sich bei ihm Klugheitsworte der Spruchweisheit für alle möglichen Fälle im Leben, die geradeso im Proverbienbuch oder im Sirach stehen könnten. Damit tut sich kund, dass er im Strom der Tradition steht. Aber nicht selten zitiert er sie nur, um sie zu ironisieren oder gegen sie zu polemisieren.

---

53. Cf. G.Ch. AALDERS, *Het boek De Prediker*, Kampen, Kok, 1948, p. 19.

54. J. VAN DER PLOEG, *Prediker* (BOT, 8/2), Roermond, Romen & Zonen, 1953.

55. Although Robert Gordis already expressed this view in 1940 (cf. R. GORDIS, *Quotations in wisdom literature*, in *JQR* 30 [1939/40] 123-147), his commentary was published in the fifties (cf. R. GORDIS, *Koheleth – the Man and his World: A Study of Ecclesiastes*, New York, 1955.)

56. This was not a totally new hypothesis since Levy and Gemser also held this viewpoint; cf. L. LEVY, *Das Buch Qoheleth: Ein Beitrag zur Geschichte des Sadduzäismus*, Leipzig, 1912; GEMSER, *op. cit.*, pp. 67-68.

57. As will be indicated later on, Gordis' ideas were only taken seriously during the seventies and eighties.

58. James Crenshaw regards this hypothesis as "a decisive step forward" in the research of the book; cf. J.L. CRENSHAW, *Qoheleth in current research*, in *HAR* 7 (1983) 41-56, esp. p. 46.

59. W. RUDOLPH, *Vom Buch Kohelet: Vortrag, gehalten anlässlich des Rektoratsantritts am 12. November 1958*, Münster, Verlag Aschendorff, 1959, esp. p. 11.

However, Gordis not only convincingly argued the case for quotations, in another work he also gave a thorough analysis of the social world of wisdom literature. According to him wisdom literature reflects an indisputable upper-class orientation[60]. Nevertheless, this study also did not have an immediate effect on research on Qohelet. It appears as though Gordis was ahead of his time. The historical-critical, and the traditional *Word-of-God paradigm*, had so many scholars in their sway, that only a small number took cognisance of the research done by this Jewish scholar[61].

2. Winds of change: 1961-1980

The sixties and seventies can be classified as a period of transition in the history of Qohelet research. As has already been pointed out, these two decades witnessed a paradigm shift in Old Testament studies and this shift had an effect on Qohelet studies as well.

The first Old Testament scholar who tried his hand at making a literary critical study of Qohelet was Good. In the preface to his book *Irony in the Old Testament* (1965), he draws a clear distinction between literary criticism as practised by biblical scholars and literary criticism as defined and practised by modern literary critics[62]. In the essay on Qohelet he dismisses the practice of solving the contradictions in the book by postulating an original author, one or more glossators and an editor or two. According to him[63] there is a basic unity of thought in the book and the incongruities are a mere reflection of irony. The author used irony to lay bare the limitations of wisdom and to criticise an acquisitive society "that sees the meaning of man's life in his assertive achievement"[64]. A decade later he illustrated how meaning is discovered during the act of reading, and used the opening poem of Qohelet for this purpose[65]. Good, however, was not the only scholar whose work dif-

---

60. R. GORDIS, *The social background of wisdom literature*, in *HUCA* 18 (1944) 77-118.

61. No scholar who contributed to *Wisdom in Israel and in the Ancient Near East: Festschrift for H.H. Rowley*, Leiden, Brill, 1955 – except W.F. Albright – referred to Gordis' article: *The social background of wisdom literature*.

62. "We have taken literary criticism to mean the distinction of sources, the analysis of forms, the separation of secondary from primary materials, and theological exegesis. These are all worthwhile and necessary tasks, but they do not comprise literary criticism." Cf. E.M. GOOD, *Irony in the Old Testament*, London, SPCK, 1965, p. 9.

63. *Ibid.*, p. 172.

64. *Ibid.*, p. 183.

65. E.M. GOOD, *The unfilled sea: Style and meaning in Ecclesiastes 1,2-11*, in J.G. GAMMIE, W.A. BRUEGGEMANN, W.L. HUMPHREYS, & J.M. WARD, (eds.), *Israelite Wisdom: Theological and Literary Essays in honor of Samuel Terrien*, New York, Scholars Press, 1978, pp. 59-73.

fered from those of his predecessors. Witzenrath pertinently calls her study of the closing poem of the book (11,7-12,7): *Eine literaturwissenschaftliche Untersuchung*[66]. She makes a thorough literary analysis of the poem, and gives attention to the repetition of words and phrases indicating that there are two themes: (1) "to rejoice" and (2) "to remember". The study by Loader (*Polar Structures in the Book of Qohelet*) which has been hailed as "an original and fascinating contribution to the study of Ecclesiastes"[67], may also be characterised as a literary study[68]. According to Loader "[f]orm and contents should first be analyzed... and only then historical perspectives... [should] be brought to bear on the problems that present themselves"[69]. The contradictions which some scholars identify are merely contrasting viewpoints used by the author to contend against a simplistic view of life. When Loader explains the occurrence of polar structures in the book, he uses Schmid's[70] idea of development in the wisdom tradition. In the early phase of the wisdom tradition *relativity* plays an important role. Then follows the *dogmatic phase*, during which relativity is abandoned and hard and fast rules become the norm. During the *crisis phase*, wisdom teachers protest vehemently against the idea of hard and fast rules. Qohelet evidently belongs to the *crisis phase* in the development of the wisdom tradition[71].

The best example which reflects the paradigm of the modern literary criticism is the one by Fox: *Frame-narrative and composition in the Book of Qohelet*[72]. He acknowledges that Qohelet is wisdom literature, but emphasizes that it is also narration. When reading a narrative one

66. H. WITZENRATH, *Süss ist das Licht...Eine literaturwissenschaftliche Untersuchung zu Kohelet 11:7-12:7*, (ATSAT, 11), St. Ottilien, EOS, 1979.

67. The description of R.N. Whybray in his review of Loader's study on Qohelet in *The Society for Old Testament Study, Booklist 1980*, p. 71; Kaiser says the following in his review: "Die Untersuchung von *James A. Loader* stellt den wesentlichsten Beitrag zur Kohelet-Forschung seit der Monographie von Ellermeier aus dem Jahre 1967 dar." Cf. O. KAISER, *Judentum und Hellenismus*, in *VuF* 27 (1982) 68-88, esp. p. 78.

68. One may even say that Loader is at home in the literary and the historical-critical paradigm. His monograph clearly reflects aspects of both of these paradigms. J. Barton thus misses the mark somewhat with his conclusion that the work "merely adds structuralist ideas to the historical-critical tool-box." Cf. J. BARTON, *Reading the Old Testament: Method in Biblical Study*, London, Darton, Longman & Todd, 1984, p. 131.

69. J.A. LOADER, *Polar Structures in the Book of Qohelet* (BZAW, 152), Berlin, De Gruyter, 1979, pp. 1-2.

70. H.H. SCHMID, *Wesen und Geschichte der Weisheit: Eine Untersuchung zur altorientalischen und israelitischen Weisheitsliteratur* (BZAW, 101), Berlin, Töpelmann, 1966.

71. Cf. LOADER, *op. cit.*, pp. 117-123.

72. M.V. FOX, *Frame-narrative and composition in the Book of Qohelet*, in *HUCA* 48 (1977) 83-106.

should be able to distinguish between the different speakers (or voices) in the work. Different voices do not necessarily come from different hands. A speaker may tell a story about someone else and use this character's voice in the narrative. Applying this to the Book of Qohelet, Fox argues as follows[73]:

> I suggest that all of 1,2-12,14 is by the same hand – not that the epilogue is by Qohelet, but that *Qohelet* is "by" the epilogist. In other words, the speaker we hear from time to time in the background saying "Qohelet said"... is the teller of the tale, the external narrator of the "story" of Qohelet.

The different voices that we hear in the book are thus the voice of the frame-narrator who tells us about Qohelet, and the wisdom teacher (Qohelet) who tells about his life experiences. Fox supplies a number of parallels in ancient literature where "an anonymous third-person retrospective frame-narrative [encompasses] a first-person narrative or monologue"[74].

There are, however, not only two voices in the book, but three. When reading a narrative one should also take cognisance of the implied author. The implied author "is the voice behind the voices that speak in a work of literature, the person whose feelings, ideas and values are ultimately to be conveyed"[75]. When reading the Book of Qohelet, we cannot simply identify the author with Qohelet. Qohelet is a character in the work and we learn more about this character through the eyes of the frame-narrator. However, the opinion of the frame-narrator does not cancel Qohelet's scepticism and the implied author leaves the reader the choice to identify either with the voice of the frame-narrator or with the voice of Qohelet.

The sixties and seventies also witnessed other trends in the research. Crüsemann criticises German scholars for not reflecting on the social background of Old Testament literature[76]. He then takes this task on himself and comes to the conclusion that the book addresses affluent readers/hearers[77]. Stockhammer, Bickerman and Lang, independent of

73. Fox, *op. cit.*, p. 91.
74. *Ibid.*, pp. 92-93.
75. *Ibid.*, p. 104.
76. F. Crüsemann, *Die unveränderbare Welt: Überlegungen zur "Krisis der Weisheit" beim Prediger (Kohelet)*, in W. Schottroff & W. Stegemann (eds.), *Der Gott der kleinen Leute: sozialgeschichtliche Auslegungen*, München, Kaiser, 1979, pp. 80-104.
77. Crüsemann relies on the studies of Robert Gordis (*The social background of wisdom literature*, in HUCA 18 [1943/44] 77-118), Martin Hengel (*Judentum und Hellenismus*, Tübingen, 1969) and Elias Bickerman (*Kohelet [Ecclesiastes] or the philosophy of an acquisitive society*, in Id., *Four Strange Books of the Bible*, New York, 1967).

each other, read the book as a philosophical text[78] while the maverick Qohelet scholar, Zimmermann, made a psychological analysis of the character and personality of Qohelet and came to the conclusion that he was haunted by a number of neuroses[79].

3. *The paradigm of modern literary criticism: 1981-1996*

Although the studies of Gordis, Good, Loader, Fox and Witzenrath had an impact on the study of Qohelet and most scholars nowadays agree that the book is essentially the work of one author[80], only a few scholars really work within the new paradigm. Newsom is correct in her assessment "that scholarly work on Ecclesiastes has remained, with very few exceptions, the province of traditional historical criticism"[81].

When one peruses the publications of the last two decades of this century, less than ten scholars have written studies which reflect some influence of the new paradigm. Williams linked up with the view of Gordis (quotations) and combined this with Fox's idea of three voices and wrote about Qohelet in *The Literary Guide to the Bible*[82]. Fisch and Spangenberg paid attention to *irony* in the book, and thus followed the trend set by Good[83]. Gottcent reflected on the philosophical personality of the narrator in Qohelet[84]. Perry took his cue from Fox, as well as from other earlier scholars and wrote about the voices in the book[85]. However, it was Ogden, Fox and Fredericks who were the

---

78. M. STOCKHAMMER, *Koheleths Pessimismus*, in *Schopenhauer Jahrbuch* 41 (1960) 52-81; E. BICKERMAN, *op. cit.*, 1967; B. LANG, *Ist der Mensch hilflos? Zum Buch Kohelet* (Theologische Meditationen, 53), Zürich, Benziger Verlag, 1979.

79. F. ZIMMERMANN, *The Inner World of Qohelet (with Translation and Commentary)*, New York, Ktav, 1973.

80. Cf. R.N. WHYBRAY, *The social world of the wisdom writers*, in R.E. CLEMENTS (ed.) *The World of Ancient Israel: Sociological, Anthropological and Political Perspectives*, Cambridge, Cambridge University Press, 1989, pp. 227-250, esp. p. 242.

81. C.A. NEWSOM, *Job and Ecclesiastes*, in J.L. MAYS, D.L. PETERSEN & K.H. RICHARDS (eds.), *Old Testament Interpretation – Past, Present, and Future: Essays in honor of Gene M. Tucker*, Nashville, Abingdon, 1995, pp. 177-193, esp. p. 184.

82. J.G. WILLIAMS, *Proverbs and Ecclesiastes*, in R. ALTER & F. KERMODE (eds.), *The Literary Guide to the Bible*, London, Fontana Press, 1989, pp. 263-282.

83. H. FISCH, *Qohelet: A Hebrew ironist*, in ID., *Poetry with a Purpose: Biblical Poetics and Interpretation*, Indianapolis, Indiana University Press, 1988, pp. 158-178; I.J.J. SPANGENBERG, *Irony in the Book of Qohelet*, in *JSOT* 72 (1996) 57-69.

84. J.H. GOTTCENT, *Ecclesiastes: Disillusionment and our philosophical personality*, in ID., *The Bible: A Literary Guide*, Boston, Twayne, 1986, pp. 82-88.

85. T.A. PERRY, *Dialogues with Kohelet: The book of Ecclesiastes. Translation and commentary*, Pennsylvania, Pennsylvania State University Press, 1993.

most adventurous by publishing monographs which reflect aspects of the new paradigm[86].

4. *The historical critical-paradigm: 1961-1996*

Concurrently with the previous periods in which winds of change were blowing (1961-1980) and modern literary criticism was applied to Qohelet (1981-1996), the historical-critical approach still dominated the research. The final overview of the historical-critical research will thus be divided into these two periods as well.

a) Research during 1961-1980

Some of the best historical-critical commentaries and monographs were published during the sixties and seventies. However, scholars became more and more reluctant to identify secondary material. Almost every scholar regarded Qoh 1,1; 7,27 and 12,9-14 as later additions, but they differ on the verses which were previously regarded as secondary. Zimmerli for example held the view that 3,17 and 11,9 might have been added at a later stage[87], whilst Scott regarded 8,12-13 and 11,9 as possible additions[88]. Lohfink doubted whether 11,9 forms part of the original book[89]. Hertzberg argued cogently that Qoh 1,2-12,8 was written by only one author[90].

The thesis of Gordis, that the author quoted traditional proverbs or sayings with a wisdom perspective, was slowly gaining ground. Kroeber, Zimmerli, Scott, Hertzberg, Lauha and Lohfink took notice of this and endorsed it in certain sections of their commentaries. Towards the end of the seventies Beentjes observed as follows concerning the question of wisdom sayings in the Book of Qohelet[91]:

> Dat Qohelet in discussie treedt met *topoi*, wijsheidsspreuken die in zijn tijd de ronde doen, staat vast. Vaak (o.a. in 1,23; 4,6.12) gebruikt hij ze als conclusie om een bepaalde gedachte af te ronden, soms (bijv. 7,1;

---

86. G. OGDEN, *Qoheleth* (Readings – A New Biblical Commentary), Sheffield, JSOT Press, 1987; M.V. FOX, *Qohelet and his Contradictions* (JSOT SS, 71), Sheffield, Almond, 1989; D.C. FREDERICKS, *Coping with Transience: Ecclesiastes on Brevity in Life* (The Biblical Seminar, 18), Sheffield, JSOT Press, 1993.

87. W. ZIMMERLI, *Prediger* (ATD, 16/1), Göttingen, Vandenhoeck & Ruprecht, 1962, pp. 171, 238.

88. R.B.Y. SCOTT, *Proverbs. Ecclesiastes* (AB, 18), New York, Doubleday, 1965, pp. 243, 254.

89. N. LOHFINK, *Kohelet* (NEB), Stuttgart, Echter Verlag, 1980, p. 81.

90. H.W. HERTZBERG, *Der Prediger* (KAT, 17/4-5), Gütersloh, Gütersloher Verlagshaus, 1963, p. 41.

91. P. BEENTJES, *Recente visies op Qohelet*, in *Bijdragen* 41 (1980) 436-444, esp. p. 444.

10,12.18) opent hij een perikope met zo'n citaat uit de traditie. Tegenstrijdigheden in Qohelets denken blijken vaak *citaten van anderen* te zijn, die hij aanvalt, verwerpt, bijschaaft of verder nuanceert.

Most commentaries and monographs published during these years contained a section on the wisdom movement and literature. It appeared that scholars realised that a study of wisdom was essential for understanding the Book of Qohelet[92]. A number of important monographs on Israelite and Ancient Near Eastern wisdom were also published, and reflect the growing interest in a field that was once the "stepchild" of Old Testament research[93]. Contrary to this trend in Qohelet research, Braun set out to prove the notion that Qohelet can best be understood when read in conjunction with popular Hellenistic philosophies[94]. In his study of the language of the book Whitley endorsed the view that the author was influenced by Greek authors from the Homeric era onwards[95].

During this period a small number of scholars remained loyal to the traditional *Word-of-God paradigm*. Kroeber calls the introduction to his commentary (*Eine*) *historisch-literarische Einleitung* and agrees with Delitzsch that the book should be regarded as *das Hohelied der Gottesfurcht*[96]. The critical outlook which is so evident in the Book of Qohelet is almost ignored. This clearly reflects that Kroeber was inclined towards the traditional *Word-of-God paradigm*. The same may be said of Kidner[97].

b) Research during 1981-1996

The last two decades of this century have witnessed a proliferation of publications dealing with the Book of Qohelet. Typical historical-critical issues were once again researched. Two studies on the wisdom forms in the

---

92. The monograph of Oswald Loretz revealed more than any other study that the book of Qohelet should be read and studied in conjunction with the Israelite wisdom literature, as well as the wisdom literature of the Ancient Near East. Cf. O. LORETZ, *Qohelet und der Alte Orient: Untersuchungen zu Stil und theologischer Thematik des Buches Qohelet*, Freiburg, Herder, 1964.

93. The following monographs could be mentioned: H.H. SCHMID, *Wesen und Geschichte der Weisheit* (BZAW, 101), Berlin, Töpelmann, 1966; G. VON RAD, *Weisheit in Israel*, Neukirchen-Vluyn, Neukirchener Verlag, 1970; R.N. WHYBRAY, *The Intellectual Tradition of the Old Testament* (BZAW, 135), Berlin, De Gruyter, 1974.

94. R. BRAUN, *Kohelet und die frühhellenistische Popularphilosophie* (BZAW, 130), Berlin, De Gruyter, 1973.

95. C.F. WHITLEY, *Koheleth: His Language and Thought* (BZAW, 148), Berlin, De Gruyter, 1979, esp. pp. 165-175.

96. R. KROEBER, *Der Prediger* (Schriften und Quellen der alten Welt, 13), Berlin, Akademie Verlag, 1963, pp. 1, 141.

97. D. KIDNER, *A time to mourn, and a time to dance: Ecclesiastes and the way of the world* (The Bible speaks today), Leicester, Inter-Varsity Press, 1976.

book were published, one by Murphy and a second by Klein[98]. Qohelet's language also came under scrutiny in the studies of Isaksson, Fredericks and Schoors[99]. Possible Hellenistic influences were researched by Michaud and Schwienhorst-Schönberger[100]. Three studies focussed on important themes in the book. Schubert wrote about creation theology[101], Lange on wisdom and folly[102], and Backhaus on the structure and Qohelet's idea of God[103]. Michel gave us an overview of the historical-critical research[104], whilst Whybray guided us through the most important historical-critical issues[105].

In this period sixteen commentaries were published[106]. Those who were written for the scholarly guild followed (with the exception of two

98. R.E. MURPHY, *Wisdom literature: Job, Proverbs, Ruth, Canticles, Ecclesiastes, and Esther* (FOTL, 13), Grand Rapids, Eerdmans, 1981; C. KLEIN, *Kohelet und die Weisheit Israels: Eine formgeschichtliche Studie* (BWANT, 132), Stuttgart, Kohlhammer, 1994.

99. B. ISAKSSON, *Studies in the language of Qoheleth, with special emphasis on the verbal system* (Acta Universitatis Upsaliensis. Studia Semitica Upsaliensia, 10), Stockholm, Almqvist & Wiksell, 1987; D.C. FREDERICKS, *Qohelet's language: Re-evaluating its nature and date* (Ancient Near Eastern Texts and Studies, 3), New York, Edwin Mellen, 1988; A. SCHOORS, *The Preacher Sought to Find Pleasing Words: A Study of the Language of Qoheleth* (Orientalia Lovaniensia Analecta, 41), Leuven, Peeters, 1992.

100. R. MICHAUD, *Qohélet et l'hellénisme. La littérature de Sagesse. Histoire et théologie, II* (Lire la Bible, 77), Paris, Cerf, 1987; L. SCHWIENHORST-SCHÖNBERGER, *"Nicht im Menschen gründet das Glück (Koh 2:24)." Kohelet im Spannungsfeld jüdischer Weisheit und hellenistischer Philosophie* (HBS, 2), Freiburg, Herder, 1994.

101. M. SCHUBERT, *Schöpfungstheologie bei Kohelet* (Beiträge zur Erforschung des Alten Testaments und des antiken Judentums, 15), Frankfurt am Main, Peter Lang, 1989.

102. A. LANGE, *Weisheit und Torheit bei Kohelet und in seiner Umwelt: Eine Untersuchung ihrer theologischen Implikationen* (Europäische Hochschulschriften Reihe 23, Theologie, 433), Frankfurt am Main, Peter Lang, 1991.

103. F.J. BACKHAUS, *"Denn Zeit und Zufall trifft sie alle" – Studien zur Komposition und zum Gottesbild im Buch Qohelet* (BBB, 83), Frankfurt, Anton Hain, 1993.

104. D. MICHEL, *Qohelet* (EdF, 258), Darmstadt, WBG, 1988.

105. R.N. WHYBRAY, *Ecclesiastes* (Old Testament Guides), Sheffield, JSOT Press, 1989.

106. The following can be mentioned (in chronological order): D. BERGANT, *Job, Ecclesiastes* (Old Testament Message, 18), Willmington, 1982; M.A. EATON, *Ecclesiastes* (TOTC), Leicester, Inter-Varsity Press, 1983; M.A. BEEK, *Prediker, Hooglied* (POT), Nijkerk, Callenbach, 1984; J.A. LOADER, *Prediker* (Tekst en Toelichting), Kampen, Kok, 1984; R. DAVIDSON, *Ecclesiastes and the Song of Solomon* (The Daily Study Bible), Philadelphia, 1986; G. OGDEN, *Qoheleth* (Readings – A new Biblical Commentary), Sheffield, JSOT Press, 1987; J. NEGENMAN, *Prediker* (Belichting van het bijbelboek), Boxtel, Katholieke Bijbelstichting, 1988; J.L. CRENSHAW, *Ecclesiastes* (OTL), London, SCM, 1988; M.V. FOX, *Qoheleth and his Contradictions* (JSOT SS, 71, Bible and Literature Series 18); Sheffield, Almond, 1989; F. VAN DEURSEN, *Prediker: Leven met vergankelijkheid* (Telos, 234), Amsterdam, Buijten & Schipperheijn, 1989; R.N. WHYBRAY, *Ecclesiastes* (New Century Bible Commentary), London, Marshall, Morgan & Scott, 1989; K.A. FARMER, *Who knows what is good? A Commentary on the Books of Proverbs and Ecclesiastes* (ITC), Grand Rapids, Eerdmans, 1991; J.-J. LAVOIE, *La pensée du Qohélet. Etude exégétique et intertextuelle* (Héritage et projet, 49), Montréal, Fides, 1992; R.E. MURPHY, *Ecclesiastes* (WBC, 23a), Dallas, Word Book, 1992; T.A. PERRY, *Dialogues with Kohelet: The Book of Ecclesiastes. Translation and Commentary*, Pennsylvania, Pennsylvania State University Press, 1993; I.J.J. SPANGENBERG, *Die boek Prediker* (SBG), Kaapstad, NG Kerk-Uitgewers, 1993.

or three), the historical-critical approach. Certain commentaries written for the lay person, evidence knowledge of historical-critical issues. Others, however, betray the traditional *Word-of-God paradigm*[107] or an attempt to keep as close as possible to that paradigm[108].

IV. QOHELET 4,17-5,6

In this last section of the article I would like to focus on a specific section of Qohelet and indicate how the paradigm shifts influenced scholars' interpretation. I also want to offer a rhetorical analysis. The text which I chose for this endeavour is Qoh 4,17-5,6 – a section which was once regarded as an addition to the original book but is now believed to be the pivotal section.

17 שְׁמֹר רַגְלֶיךָ כַּאֲשֶׁר תֵּלֵךְ אֶל־בֵּית הָאֱלֹהִים
וְקָרוֹב לִשְׁמֹעַ מִתֵּת הַכְּסִילִים זָבַח
כִּי־אֵינָם יוֹדְעִים לַעֲשׂוֹת רָע:

1 אַל־תְּבַהֵל עַל־פִּיךָ וְלִבְּךָ אַל־יְמַהֵר
לְהוֹצִיא דָבָר לִפְנֵי הָאֱלֹהִים
כִּי הָאֱלֹהִים בַּשָּׁמַיִם וְאַתָּה עַל־הָאָרֶץ
עַל־כֵּן יִהְיוּ דְבָרֶיךָ מְעַטִּים:

2 כִּי בָּא הַחֲלוֹם בְּרֹב עִנְיָן וְקוֹל כְּסִיל בְּרֹב דְּבָרִים:

3 כַּאֲשֶׁר תִּדֹּר נֶדֶר לֵאלֹהִים אַל־תְּאַחֵר לְשַׁלְּמוֹ
כִּי אֵין חֵפֶץ בַּכְּסִילִים אֵת אֲשֶׁר־תִּדֹּר שַׁלֵּם:

4 טוֹב אֲשֶׁר לֹא־תִדֹּר מִשֶּׁתִּדּוֹר וְלֹא תְשַׁלֵּם:

5 אַל־תִּתֵּן אֶת־פִּיךָ לַחֲטִיא אֶת־בְּשָׂרֶךָ
וְאַל־תֹּאמַר לִפְנֵי הַמַּלְאָךְ כִּי שְׁגָגָה הִיא
לָמָּה יִקְצֹף הָאֱלֹהִים עַל־קוֹלֶךָ וְחִבֵּל אֶת־מַעֲשֵׂה יָדֶיךָ:

6 כִּי בְרֹב חֲלֹמוֹת וַהֲבָלִים וּדְבָרִים הַרְבֵּה
כִּי אֶת־הָאֱלֹהִים יְרָא:

1. *Interpretation during 1901-1960*

It is possible to identify three main trends in commentaries on Qohelet written during the first five decades of this century. Most Old Testament scholars worked in the *historical-critical paradigm* and their commentaries reflect a trend to identify secondary material. Some scholars, however, did their research in the traditional *Word-of-God paradigm*. They

---

107. Cf. van Deursen, *op. cit.*
108. Cf. Eaton, *op. cit.*; Davidson, *op. cit.*; Negenman, *op. cit.*

held the conviction that nobody tampered with the original work. A third group tried to establish a middle way between the two paradigms. Their commentaries bore a striking resemblance to the commentary of Gordis, the Jewish scholar. They all took cognisance of the research done by historical-critical scholars but *formulated other solutions* to the issues of contradictions, wisdom sayings and statements about God's retribution.

Historical-critical scholars were convinced that glossators and redactors *added* material to the original work, and thus it is not strange to hear about interpolations, additions and redactions. McNeile was convinced that a pious Jew (one of the *Ḥasidim*) added this entire section to the book[109]. Barton differed from him and maintained that the section came from the hand of the original author – except the proverbs in 5,2 and 5,6a which were added by the *Ḥokma* glossator[110]. Podechard and Buzy supported this view[111]. Jastrow, on the other hand, believed that the entire section was written by the original author – except the last four Hebrew words (כִּי אֶת־הָאֱלֹהִים יְרָא) which were added by the pious commentator[112].

A number of scholars held different viewpoints. Zapletal was convinced that the book is the product of one author[113]. Contrary to the previous commentators he believed that the book was not written in prose but in poetry[114]. On account of a verse analysis he discovered a few glosses and 5,6a was one of them[115]. Gemser and van der Ploeg also held the viewpoint that the book is the product of one author, but they were convinced that he wrote in prose. The book, however, had a few quotations in verse form – *inter alia* 5,2 and 5,6a[116]. Van der Ploeg differed in one respect from Gemser. He held the opinion that 2,26; 3,17; 8,12b-13 and 11,9b were interpolations[117]. Galling was also convinced that the book contained interpolations. However, he attributed these to the second epilogist or redactor (QR^2) of the book. These interpolations expressed the traditional view of retribution. The first epilogist or redactor

109. McNeile, *op. cit.*, p. 25.
110. Barton, *op. cit.*, pp. 123-125.
111. Podechard, *op. cit.*, p. 338; Buzy, *op. cit.*, p. 169.
112. Jastrow, *op. cit.*, p. 217.
113. Zapletal, *op. cit.*, pp. 14-35.
114. According to him Qoh 4,17-5,6 consists of bicola with a 2+2 stress pattern; cf. Zapletal, *op. cit.*, p. 151.
115. *Ibid.*, p. 155.
116. Gemser, *op. cit.*, pp. 67-68, 112; van der Ploeg, *op. cit.*, p. 11.
117. Cf. van der Ploeg, *op cit.*, p. 13: "Het is alleen maar nodig het bestaan van een epilogist aan te nemen terwijl met de mogelijkheid van enkele kleine toevoegingen aan Qohelets tekst rekening moet of kan worden gehouden... die storend Qohelets gedachtengang onderbreken."

(QR[1]) was a pupil of the author and he was responsible for the "publication" of the book, as well as for the sequence of the different sections[118]. According to Galling, Qoh 5,6a might be the only gloss which the first redactor (QR[1]) added to the book[119].

As a Jewish scholar, Gordis had the advantage of a thorough knowledge of rabbinical literature, and this influenced him to conclude that the book of Qohelet consists of quotations. He was trained in a tradition which was not dominated by historical-critical research. Although he took cognisance of the studies of historical-critical scholars, he was able to distance himself from their conclusions. In my opinion, he may be called a herald of the new literary criticism. According to him Qoh 5,2 is a proverb which is quoted from traditional wisdom material[120].

The commentaries of Vischer, Kuhn, Aalders and Lamparter, all from the traditional *Word-of-God paradigm*, added nothing new to the interpretation of this section[121]. According to them Qoh 4,17-5,6 advises readers to think twice, when taking part in cultic activities. These scholars regarded this entire section as the work of the original author.

2. *Interpretation during 1961-1980*

Although winds of change were blowing through Old Testament studies during the sixties and seventies, they did not radically influence the interpretation of Qoh 4,17-5,6. Most Qohelet scholars worked within the historical-critical paradigm and supported the view that 4,17-5,6 is an integral section with no interpolations or additions. Others endorsed the view of Gordis: *Qohelet often quotes wisdom sayings.*

Zimmerli argued that Qoh 4,17-5,6 consists of four motivated admonitions (*begründete Mahnsprüche*)[122], while Scott supported the view of Gordis and argued that the writer quoted a popular proverb in 5,2 (and probably in 5,6b as well)[123]. Lauha agreed with Zimmerli and Scott's delimitation, but identified only three aphorisms (*drei Aphorismen*): 4,17; 5,1-2; 5,3-6. He was, however, convinced that Qohelet quoted existing proverbs in 5,2 and 5,6a[124].

---

118. GALLING, *op. cit.*, p. 76.
119. *Ibid.*, p. 101.
120. GORDIS, *op. cit.*, pp. 101, 248.
121. VISCHER, *op. cit.*; KUHN, *op. cit.*; AALDERS, *op. cit.*; H. LAMPARTER, *Das Buch der Weisheit, Prediger und Sprüche* (BAT, 16), Stuttgart, Calwer Verlag, 1955.
122. ZIMMERLI, *op. cit.*, p. 182.
123. SCOTT, *op. cit.*, p. 227.
124. A. LAUHA, *Kohelet* (BK, 19), Neukirchen-Vluyn, Neukirchener Verlag, 1978, p. 97.

Hertzberg who read the book as poetry, considered Qoh 4,17-5,8 as an integral unit, consisting of two subsections: 4,17-5,6 and 5,7-8. His view of the structure of the first subsection, corresponds to that of Zimmerli: Qoh 4,17-5,6 contains four warnings (*Warnungen*) and two proverbs[125]. Loader's structural analysis brought him to the same conclusions as that of Hertzberg: 4,17-5,6 is a subsection of 4,17-5,8[126]. The first subsection has four warnings and two sayings "in typical chokmatic fashion"[127]. However, the theme (or "polar structure" as he prefers to call it) is "talk and silence" and not "*höre und schweige*" as Hertzberg maintained[128]. But Loader's thesis of "polar structures", is not merely a variation of the quotation theory as Crenshaw would have us believe[129]. Loader is adamant that the author formulated the sayings himself.

Although Rofé acknowledges that Qoh 4,17-5,6 is a unit, he has a completely different understanding of its content. According to him, Qoh 5,5 is a "Do not say" admonition. In such an admonition a sage usually quotes his pupil's erratic opinion in order to refute it. He translates 5,5: "... And do not say: 'The angel (goes) before me' – because this is a blunder; why should God be angered by your talk and destroy your possessions?" Thus this unit consists of a deprecation of three acts of worship of fools (sacrifice, prayer, and vows) and a condemnation of two superstitions (dreams and angels)[130].

At the end of the seventies, when Lohfink's commentary was published, the viewpoint that Qoh 4,17-5,6 was a unit without any additions was well established. Whitley was the only scholar who held the view that 5,6b (כִּי אֶת־הָאֱלֹהִים יְרָא) was probably a later addition[131]. Then Lohfink came with an innovative idea. According to his analysis the book has a chiastic structure, and Qoh 4,17-5,6 is the pivotal section[132]. Things have changed dramatically in eighty years. It amounts to nothing less than a complete reversal of opinion. At the turn of the previous century a number of scholars regarded the entire section as secondary, whilst others believed that only one or two verses were secondary. These

125. HERTZBERG, *op. cit.*, pp. 118-124.
126. LOADER, *op. cit.*, pp. 73-76.
127. *Ibid.* p. 75.
128. HERTZBERG, *op. cit.*, p. 118.
129. J.L. CRENSHAW, *Qohelet in current research*, in *HAR* 7 (1983) 41-56, esp. 48.
130. A. ROFÉ, *'The angel' in Qohelet 5,5 in the light of a wisdom dialogue formula*, in *Eretz-Israel: Archaeological, Historical and Geographical Studies*. H.L. Ginsberg Volume, Jerusalem, Israel Exploration Society, 1978, pp. 105-109.
131. C.F. WHITLEY, *Kohelet: His Language and Thought* (BZAW, 148), Berlin, De Gruyter, 1979, p. 50.
132. N. LOHFINK, *Der Bibel skeptische Hintertur. Versuch, den Ort des Buchs Kohelet neu zu bestimmen*, in *Stimmen der Zeit* 198 (1980) 17-31; cf. also his commentary p. 10.

ideas faded as the years went by, and more and more scholars became convinced that 4,17-5,6 is an integral unit. Lohfink will be remembered as the Qohelet scholar whose analysis indicated that the section should be regarded as a poem, standing at the centre of the book[133].

3. Interpretation during 1981-1996

Commentaries and monographs of the last sixteen years, reflect no major changes from how scholars interpreted the section in the two previous decades. An overview of a number of important commentaries will suffice to support this conclusion. Michel who is an exponent of the quotation hypothesis, considers 4,17-5,6 to be a unit, consisting of three subsections. Although he supports the view that 5,2 is a quotation (*ein verfremdetes Zitat*[134]), he nevertheless believes that 5,6b has been added by the second epilogist[135]. Fox who firmly rejects the quotation hypothesis and worked within the new literary criticism paradigm, also considers 4,17-5,6 to be a unit. This unit (according to him) consists of four elements: two admonitions (4,17; 5,6a) and two warnings (5,1-2; 5,3-5). Both warnings contain "vows" as their theme, and 5,2 is "a parenthetical remark of proverbial character"[136]. Ogden (also an exponent of the new literary criticism) distinguishes four admonitions, each supported by a motive clause. The four admonitions are: 4,17; 5,1-2, 5,3-4, and 5,5-6. There are quotations or comments in some of the admonitions "which add force to the appeal"[137]. Whybray's analysis to a large extent concurs with this analysis[138].

In spite of the criticism which was levelled at Loader's delimitation and interpretation of Qoh 4,17-5,8[139], he stayed with his argument in his commentary[140], based on his monograph[141]. According to him, Qoh

133. According to his analysis the poem consists of four subsections. The contents of the four admonitions reflect a chiasm: 4,17 can be linked with 5,5, and 5,1 with 5,3-4. However, the admonitions also reflect a parallel structure when the repetition of similar words is taken into account. Cf. N. LOHFINK, *Kohelet* (NEB), Stuttgart, Echter Verlag, 1980, p. 40; ID., *Warum is der Tor unfähig, böse zu handeln? (Koh 4:17)*, in *ZDMG.S* 5 (1983) 113-120.
134. MICHEL, *op. cit.*, p. 142.
135. *Ibid.*, p. 143.
136. FOX, *op. cit.*, p. 221.
137. OGDEN, *op. cit.*, pp. 75.
138. WHYBRAY, *op. cit.*, pp. 91-97.
139. Cf. N. LOHFINK, *Umschau und Kritik: Alttestamentliche Rezensionen*, in *BZ* 8 (1981) 112-113.
140. J.A. LOADER, *Prediker* (Tekst en toelichting), Kampen, Kok, 1984 (E.T. *Ecclesiastes*, Grand Rapids, Eerdmans, 1986).
141. J.A. LOADER, *Polar Structures in the Book of Qohelet* (BZAW, 152), Berlin, De Gruyter, 1979.

4,17-5,6 is a subsection consisting of four admonitions and Qoh 5,2 is a proverb – *not a quotation*. Qohelet formulated the proverb to support his argument[142]. Crenshaw also regards Qoh 4,17-5,8 as an integral unit, but he does not refer to any subsections. He identifies Qoh 5,2 to be "an aphorism" which reflects the viewpoint of traditional wisdom teachers[143].

Murphy's commentary should be read in conjunction with his monograph[144], in order to appreciate his viewpoint fully. He regards Qoh 4,17-5,6 as a subsection of a larger unit and considers the larger unit to be Qoh 4,17-6,9. The other subsections are 5,7-8 and 5,9-6,9[145]. In the monograph he identifies the genre of the first subsection to be "an instruction". The instruction consists of a command (4,17a); a comparative saying (4,17b); a prohibition (5,1); a quoted proverb (5,2); a prohibition (5,3); a "better" saying (5,4); two prohibitions (5,5a); a reason in the form of a rhetorical question (5,5b); a quoted proverb (5,6a); and a command (5,6b)[146].

One may conclude that three viewpoints still dominate the interpretation of this section: (1) Qoh 4,17-5,6 is a unit with three or four subsections; (2) Qoh 4,17-5,6 consists of subsections, but a verse or a section of a verse has been added; (3) Qohelet 4,17-5,6 is a subsection of a larger unit.

4. *A different approach to Qohelet 4,17-5,6*

The question that now arises is whether one can still make any new contribution to the interpretation of Qoh 4,17-5,6? Is there a road less travelled? The foregoing research history clearly indicates that the historical-critical paradigm still dominates the research and interpretation of Qohelet. Thus further research calls for a literary and rhetorical analysis. This analysis will endeavour to indicate how the implied author influences the implied reader's outlook on religion and religious activities.

a) Qoh 4,17-5,6 – an integral unit

This section is an integral unit, since it contains a number of admonitions and has a definite conclusion. A few commentators would, however, include 5,7-8 since it contains the same structure and theme, and thus forms part and parcel of the previous admonitions. At least two ob-

---

142. LOADER, *Prediker*, p. 70.
143. CRENSHAW, *op. cit.*, pp. 114-119.
144. R.E. MURPHY, *Wisdom Literature: Job, Proverbs, Ruth, Canticles, Ecclesiastes, and Esther* (FOTL, 13), Grand Rapids, Eerdmans, 1981.
145. MURPHY, *Wisdom Literature*, p. 138; ID., *Ecclesiastes*, pp. 44-56.
146. MURPHY, *Wisdom Literature*, p. 138.

jections negate this demarcation: (1) 5,7-8 deals with political and not with religious matters; (2) 4,17-5,6 does not focus on the plight of the oppressed.

b) Qoh 4,17-5,6 – prose rather than poetry

Although some scholars maintain that this section should be read as poetry, they differ on the length of the cola and the metre or stress patterns. Based on Watson's criteria to distinguish between prose and poetry, I consider this section (with the exception of 5,2 and 5,6a) as prose[147]. There are, however, a few verses which can perhaps be classified as "rhythmic prose"[148].

c) Analysis of the components

The entire section is an instruction, and consists of four distinct admonitions (4,17; 5,1; 5,3-4; 5,5.6b) and two proverbs (5,2.6a). Each of the admonitions has three elements: (1) a prohibition, (2) a motivation, and (3) a conclusion/reason/advice. The components can be arranged as follows:

Admonition 1: Concerning sacrifices (4,17)

Prohibition: שְׁמֹר רַגְלֶיךָ כַּאֲשֶׁר תֵּלֵךְ אֶל־בֵּית הָאֱלֹהִים
                 Guard your steps when you go to the house of God.

Motivation: וְקָרוֹב לִשְׁמֹעַ מִתֵּת הַכְּסִילִים זָבַח
                 Drawing near to listen is better than when fools offer sacrifice,

Reason: כִּי־אֵינָם יוֹדְעִים לַעֲשׂוֹת רָע
                 for they do not know how to do evil[149].

Admonition 2: Concerning hasty speech to God (5,1)

Prohibition: אַל־תְּבַהֵל עַל־פִּיךָ וְלִבְּךָ אַל־יְמַהֵר
                 לְהוֹצִיא דָבָר לִפְנֵי הָאֱלֹהִים
                 Do not be hasty with your mouth,
                 and let not your heart rush to utter a word in the presence of God,

---

147. W.G.E. WATSON, *Classical Hebrew Poetry: A Guide to its Techniques* (JSOT SS, 26), Sheffield, JSOT Press, 1986, pp. 44-55.

148. Cf. B. GEMSER, *Spreuken II, Prediker en Hooglied van Salomo*, Groningen, Wolters, 1931, p. 68; A. LAUHA, *Kohelet* (BK 19), Neukirchen-Vluyn, Neukirchener Verlag, 1978, p. 97.

149. This clause is a *crux interpretum*. I consider it to be an ironical comment about fools.

Motivation: כִּי הָאֱלֹהִים בַּשָּׁמַיִם וְאַתָּה עַל־הָאָרֶץ
                 for God is in heaven and you are on earth.

Conclusion: עַל־כֵּן יִהְיוּ דְבָרֶיךָ מְעַטִּים
                 Therefore let your words be few.

Proverb 1: 5,2   כִּי בָּא הַחֲלוֹם בְּרֹב עִנְיָן וְקוֹל כְּסִיל בְּרֹב דְּבָרִים:
                 For a dream comes with much business
                 and foolish talk with many words.

Admonition 3: Concerning hasty vows (5,3-4)

Prohibition: כַּאֲשֶׁר תִּדֹּר נֶדֶר לֵאלֹהִים אַל־תְּאַחֵר לְשַׁלְּמוֹ
                 When you make a vow to God, do not delay to pay it,

Motivation: כִּי אֵין חֵפֶץ בַּכְּסִילִים אֵת אֲשֶׁר־תִּדֹּר שַׁלֵּם
                 for there is no pleasure in fools. What you have vowed –
                 pay!

Advice: טוֹב אֲשֶׁר לֹא־תִדֹּר מִשֶּׁתִּדּוֹר וְלֹא תְשַׁלֵּם
                 It is better that you should not make a vow than that you
                 make a vow and do not pay.

Admonition 4: Concerning sincere speech (5,5.6b)

Prohibition: אַל־תִּתֵּן אֶת־פִּיךָ לַחֲטִיא אֶת־בְּשָׂרֶךָ
                 וְאַל־תֹּאמַר לִפְנֵי הַמַּלְאָךְ כִּי שְׁגָגָה הִיא
                 Do not let your mouth cause you to sin,
                 and don't admit in the presence of the messenger: ''It was a
                 mistake.''

Motivation: לָמָּה יִקְצֹף הָאֱלֹהִים עַל־קוֹלֶךָ וְחִבֵּל אֶת־מַעֲשֵׂה יָדֶיךָ
                 Why should God [have to] be angry at your words and de-
                 stroy the work of your hands?

Advice: כִּי אֶת־הָאֱלֹהִים יְרָא
                 Rather, fear God!

Proverb 2: 5,6a   כִּי בְרֹב חֲלֹמוֹת וַהֲבָלִים וּדְבָרִים הַרְבֵּה
                 For as many dreams are senseless
                 so much talking as well.

d) Close reading

In the Masoretic Text the second proverb (5,6a) does not conclude the
section, but stands between the motivation (5,5c) and the advice (5,6b)
of the fourth admonition. There is no need to alter the text and move the

second proverb to the end of the section. In the above analysis, the proverb was merely moved out of its context to indicate that the fourth admonition also consists of three elements. The כִּי at the beginning of 5,6b should be read as an adversative to the negative imperatives in 5,5a[150]. However, the position of the second proverb in the Masoretic Text has an important rhetorical function. (This will be discussed in more detail when a rhetorical analysis is given below.)

The second proverb is extremely terse and scholars differ on how it should be translated. Most scholars agree that there is a link between the two proverbs as both are about "words" (דְּבָרִים) and "dreams" (חֲלֹמוֹת). Although the possibility of an ellipsis has been dismissed, it still seems a viable option[151]. Thus הֲבָלִים should be read twice. Therefore one may translate: "For as many dreams are senseless, so much talking is senseless too." The emphasis actually falls on דְּבָרִים "many words". One should, however, make two small emendations to the Hebrew text: (1) change the בְ of the word בְרֹב into a כְ so that it could read כְּרֹב[152]; (2) delete the ו in front of the word הֲבָלִים[153]. The gist of the proverb is: "Much talking is just as nonsensical as much dreaming"[154]. The suggestion by Galling to add the noun הֶבֶל to the first half of the proverb, amounts to the same as my suggestion of הֲבָלִים being elliptical[155].

A close reading of the section reveals that not only do the proverbs share the same words, but the admonitions as well. The first and the third admonitions have the following in common: the words אֱלֹהִים and כְּסִילִים (4,17ab and 5,3ab); a comparative sentence or saying (4,17b and 5,4); a clause which is introduced by כַּאֲשֶׁר (4,17a and 5,3a); a negative statement which is introduced by כִּי אֵין (4,17c and 5,3b). The second and the fourth admonitions have the following in common: the nouns פִּיךָ and הָאֱלֹהִים (5,1b and 5,5c); the phrase לִפְנֵי הַמַּלְאָךְ / לִפְנֵי הָאֱלֹהִים (5,1b and 5,5b); both admonitions have two negative commands each (5,1a and 5,5ab). These repetitions discovered by the close reading, may be

150. Cf. Fox, *Qohelet and his Contradictions*, p. 212.
151. Watson defines ellipsis as follows: "Ellipsis is the omission of a particle, word or group of words within a poetic or grammatical unit, where its presence is expected." Cf. Watson, *op. cit.*, pp. 303-304.
152. Fox, *op. cit.*, p. 209
153. Hertzberg, *op. cit.*, p. 120.
154. I endorse the recommendation that the rendering of *hebel* should be varied "to bring out the particular shades of meaning in different contexts." Cf. Scott, *op. cit.*, p. 202.
155. He translated the proverb as follows: "Nichtigkeit ist bei vielen Träumen und völlige Nichtigkeit bei vielen Worten!" Cf. Galling, *op. cit.*, p. 100.

summarised as follows (note the possible intended parallellism between admonitions one and three, two and four, and the two proverbs, respectively):

Admonition 1 (4,17)   ◄ - - - ►   Admonition 3 (5,3-4)

אֱלֹהִים
כְּסִילִים
כַּאֲשֶׁר
כִּי אֵין / כִּי־אֵינָם
"Better"-saying

Admonition 2 (5,1)   ◄ - - - ►   Admonition 4 (5,5.6b)

פִּיךָ
הָאֱלֹהִים
לִפְנֵי הַמַּלְאָךְ / לִפְנֵי הָאֱלֹהִים
Two negative commands

Proverb 1 (5,2)   ◄ - - - ►   Proverb 2 (5,6a)

חֲלֹמוֹת / הַחֲלוֹם
דְּבָרִים

e) Rhetorical analysis

On account of the components analysis and the close reading, one may conclude that the section reflects an intended parallel structure. The second part (5,3-6) of the section has the same components as the first part (4,17-5,2): two admonitions (each with three elements) and a proverb.

The first admonition (4,17) is about the bringing of sacrifices to the Temple reminiscent of 1 Sam 15,22 and Hos 6,6. This admonition also corresponds to that of other wisdom teachers (cf. Prov 15,8; 21,3.27) except that the emphasis in this case falls on "*to listen*". To listen to what? Different answers are given to this question, but "*to listen*" is probably only a typical wisdom topos.

The second admonition (5,1) is about religious speech and this can take the form of either "intercession, lament, or praise"[156]. Qohelet warns against the use of too many and unnecessary words when conversing with God.

---

156. OGDEN, *op. cit.*, p. 77.

The first proverb (5,2) may be a traditional saying since it is pithy, terse, telling, and complete in itself and corresponds to Prov 10,19. It fulfills the following rhetorical and structural functions: it divides the entire section into two parts, and substantiates the contents of the first two admonitions. The distinctive characteristic of a fool is his unmeditated verbosity. Even when taking part in religious activities one could act like a fool.

The third admonition (5,3-4) is about vows. The prohibition (5,3a) agrees almost verbally with Deut 23,22.

כַּאֲשֶׁר תִּדֹּר נֶדֶר לֵאלֹהִים אַל־תְּאַחֵר לְשַׁלְּמוֹ   Qoh 5,3

כִּי־תִדֹּר נֶדֶר לַיהוָה אֱלֹהֶיךָ לֹא תְאַחֵר לְשַׁלְּמוֹ   Deut 23,22

The only disagreements between the two texts are the fact that Qohelet does not use the proper name of God (יהוה) and he does not refer to ''your God'' (אֱלֹהֶיךָ), but only to ''God'' (אֱלֹהִים). However, this is in line with Qohelet's reference to God throughout his book. When reading the motivation (which refers to fools, 5,3b) and the advice (which is in the form of a ''better''-proverb, 5,4) one is immediately reminded of the first admonition, of which the motivation (4,17b) also refers to fools and is cast in the form of a ''better''-saying.

The fourth admonition (5,5.6b) is about sincere speech or promises made to a representative of God (maybe a priest?). This admonition reminds one of the second one: it also has two prohibitions (5,1). The motivation of the fourth admonition, however, reflects an urgency which is not present in the second admonition. The motivation within the second admonition only states that God is in heaven and humans are upon the earth. The motivation within the fourth admonition, emphasises that one should still be aware of God's retribution. Although God is in heaven He is still able to inflict his wrath – therefore one should fear him. This advice is not immediately given, but is kept almost as a surprise.

The second proverb (5,6a) – cast in the mould of the quoted proverb (5,2) – reminds one of the typical הֶבֶל-conclusions which end a section. However, it stands between the motivation and the advice of the fourth admonition (5,5.6b) and fulfills an important rhetorical function – it creates tension and expectation. The reader may wonder: Is this the conclusion, or should I expect another? Where is the third element of the admonition? When the final conclusion or advice follows, the reader is caught unawares.

Portrayal of the flow of the instruction:

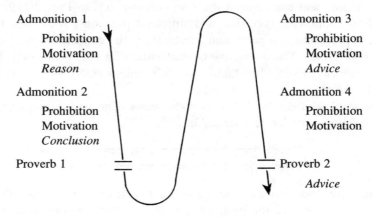

Admonition 1
    Prohibition
    Motivation
    Reason

Admonition 2
    Prohibition
    Motivation
    Conclusion

Proverb 1

Admonition 3
    Prohibition
    Motivation
    Advice

Admonition 4
    Prohibition
    Motivation

Proverb 2
    Advice

When reading Qohelet's admonitions, the implied author engenders assent to his viewpoint of religion and religious activities. The proverbs play an important role in cementing this viewpoint. The first one, is not a mere summary of the content of the first two admonitions – it reflects the tone of the entire section: to be loquacious is a sign of a fool. When taking part in religious activities one should act wisely: "Be silent!" The first proverb functions as a short break in the instruction. The second one (which may seem superfluous since it recaps the thought of the first proverb) creates tension. Then the final injunction comes unexpectedly: "Fear God!" Looking back at the other admonitions one may say that Qohelet was preparing for this injunction all along, but it still comes as a surprise to the implied reader and this reader cannot but endorse Qohelet's view and advice.

CONCLUSION

This survey of the history of research in the field of Old Testament studies found that the various paradigm shifts did impact on the research of the Book of Qohelet. It is also noticeable that the historical-critical approach, to a large extent still dominates. This is especially evident when investigating the influences of the various paradigms on the interpretation of a passage such as Qoh 4,17-5,6.

Although influence of the latest paradigm within which literary approaches are meant to hold sway can hardly be detected, there are some promising signs of change which indicate the employment of not only the literary, but even of other approaches of the new paradigm[157]. That non-historical-critical approaches do hold much promise is undeniable, as could be clearly illustrated when, for instance, employing a rhetorical analysis to Qoh 4,17-5,6.

Department of Old Testament   I.J.J. SPANGENBERG
UNISA
P.O. Box 392
0003 Pretoria
South Africa

---

157. Cf. the intertextual study of Hubert Tita and the article of Robert Harrison concerning the contribution of sociological studies. H. TITA, *Ist die thematische Einheit Koh 4,17-5,6 eine Anspielung auf die Salomoerzählung? Aporien der religionskritischen Interpretation*, in *BN* 84 (1996) 87-102; C.R. HARRISON, *Qoheleth among the sociologists*, in *Biblical Interpretation* 5 (1997) 160-180.

»UNTER DER SONNE«

ZUR IMMANENZ BEI QOHELET

Zum Wesen der menschlichen Sprache gehört es, daß es eine Differenz zwischen dem *Gemeinten* und dem *Ausgedrückten* gibt: Der Mensch kann immer mehr meinen, als er mit den ihm überlieferten sprachlichen Mitteln explizit ausdrücken kann. Durch dieses über die vorhandenen sprachlichen Möglichkeiten hinausgehende Gemeinte ist Fortschritt im menschlichen Denken überhaupt erst möglich – sonst müßten wir ja immer nur das denken und wiederholen, was andere vor uns gedacht und gesagt haben.

Dieses allgemein geltende sprachliche Phänomen wird natürlich dann besonders wichtig und folgenreich, wenn jemand etwas denkt, was die vorgegebenen Bahnen sprengt, wenn er etwas sagen will, für das es in seiner Umgebung und unter seinen »Vordenkern« (das Wort hier einmal in seinem ursprünglichen Sinn genommen!) keine Beispiele gibt und also keine sprachlichen Aussagemuster.

Notwendigerweise muß er dann Sprachschwierigkeiten bekommen, muß versuchen, mit den überlieferten Sprachmitteln anderes zu sagen, als bisher mit ihnen gesagt worden ist. Er kann dann nur darauf hoffen, daß der Kontext einzelner Aussagen und Wortverwendungsweisen den neuen, von ihm gemeinten Sinn klarmacht. Und wenn das nicht klappt, muß er eben damit leben, mißverstanden zu werden.

Und damit haben wir nach meiner Überzeugung grob die Problematik von Qohelet skizziert. Er steht ja in einer bestimmten geistigen Tradition: er denkt in einer Spätphase der sog. »Weisheit«. In ihr haben wir den Niederschlag menschlicher Urbemühungen, gemachte Erfahrungen auszuwerten und in der Fülle der Erscheinungen Regeln zu finden. Sie sollen dann dem Menschen hilfreich sein, wenn sich analoge Situationen wiederholen. Aber während sonst die Weisheitsschriften im Allgemeinen von einem Optimismus getragen werden, der – etwas abgekürzt gesprochen – sich darin äußert, daß man glaubt, es gebe einen Zusammenhang zwischen dem Tun eines Menschen und seinem Ergehen (einen »Tun-Ergehen-Zusammenhang«), ist diese optimistische Annahme bei Qohelet ins Wanken geraten. Er gehört in die Spätzeit der Weisheit, in der man eine Enttäuschung darüber verarbeiten muß, daß die mittels unseres Verstandes gewonnenen Erkenntnisse doch nicht in dem Maße ein glückliches Leben garantieren können, wie man früher glaubte. So wid-

met er denn einen ganzen Traktat der Frage »Was für einen Gewinn hat
der Mensch bei all seinen Mühen, mit denen er sich unter der Sonne abmüht?« (1,3-3,15). Um diese Frage nach dem Sinn weisheitlichen Mühens zu beantworten, *betrachtet* er prüfend, was es an weisheitlichen Ergebnissen bereits gibt. Und hier kommen wir zu einer Besonderheit
Qohelets, die man vielleicht *die* Besonderheit Qohelets nennen kann: er
ist von einem *Weisen*, der die Welt ansieht und beobachtet, um daraus
hilfreiche Regeln zu gewinnen, zu einem *Philosophen* geworden, der die
Beobachtungsergebnisse anderer betrachtet und wertet. Das ist vielleicht
etwas zugespitzt formuliert, dürfte aber nach meiner Überzeugung den
Kern des Problems treffen.

Daß Qohelet mit einem über das bisher übliche Denken hinausgehen-
den Denken neue Gedanken sagen will, kann man schon daran sehen,
daß er einen Sprachgebrauch hat, der für ihn charakteristisch ist. Nur
zwei Beispiele: Er verwendet das Wort הֶבֶל, das im üblichen Sprachgebrauch »Windhauch« und übertragen wohl auch »Vergänglichkeit« be-
deutete, in einem neuen Sinn, über den ich mich hier nicht im einzelnen
auslassen will, der aber jedenfalls für ihn und sein Denken typisch ist.
Ein anderes Beispiel: Das Verb ראה[1], das sonst im Hebräischen »sehen« in der Bedeutung der sinnlichen Wahrnehmung meint, kann bei
ihm natürlich auch diese Bedeutung haben, es kann aber auch bedeuten
»ansehen«, »betrachten«, »prüfend ansehen oder betrachten«, »realize«
(Fox). Daß diese andere Bedeutung vorliegt, wird durch kein sprachliches Mittel angezeigt – es ist von dem verständigen und verstehens-
willigen Hörer oder Leser aus dem Kontext zu erkennen.

Nach diesen kurzen Bemerkungen nun zum Thema.

Eigenartigerweise ist bisher eine Besonderheit der Sprache des Buches Qohelet noch nie zum Gegenstand einer besonderen Untersuchung
geworden, und gerade sie scheint mir für sein Denken typisch und auf-
schlußreich zu sein: Nur im Buche Qohelet findet sich im AT die Wendung »unter der Sonne«, und zwar gleich 29 mal! Den 29 Belegen bei
Qohelet stehen also 0 (!!) Vorkommen im gesamten sonstigen Alten
Testament gegenüber – und das schreit doch nach einer Erklärung!
Denn sonst läßt sich ja zeigen, daß Qohelet seine Wörter sehr bewußt
wählt und verwendet. Weshalb also verwendet er und er allein im ganzen Alten Testament diese Wendung?

---

1. Hierzu vgl. Antoon SCHOORS, *The Verb* ראה *in the Book of Qoheleth*, in Anja A.
DIESEL u.a. (Hgg.), »*Jedes Ding hat seine Zeit...*« FS Diethelm Michel (BZAW, 241),
Berlin, 1996, S. 227-241.

Keine Antwort auf diese Frage ist mit einer Klärung des mehrfach diskutierten Problems gelungen, ob hier griechischer Spracheinfluß vorliege oder nicht. Während man dies früher häufig unter Hinweis auf das im zeitgenössischen Griechisch häufige ὑφ' ἡλίου positiv beantworten zu müssen meinte, hat dem Loretz unter Hinweis auf einige altorientalische Texte widersprochen: »Als beendet ist auch der Streit um das vieldiskutierte *tḥt hšmš* – «unter der Sonne», dieser Lieblingswendung Qohelets, zu betrachten. Eine Ableitung vom gleichbedeutenden griechischen Ausdruck ὑφ' ἡλίου oder gar von einer ägyptischen Formulierung ist durch den Nachweis dieser Formulierung im semitischen Bereich als nicht mehr aufrechtzuerhalten bewiesen worden«[2]. Braun[3] hat dem widersprochen; nach seiner Meinung »wird man das Urteil von Loretz als etwas zu voreilig bezeichnen müssen, wenn man weiß, wie es um die Datierung und geistesgeschichtliche Lokalisierung der von ihm herangezogenen Inschriften bestellt ist, welche zeigen, daß auch hier griechischer Einfluß nicht auszuschließen ist«[4]: die Eschmunazarinschrift und die Tabnitinschrift gehören beide nach ihm ins 3. Jh. v. Chr. und somit dem phönizischen Kulturbereich an[5]. Loretz hat denn auch keineswegs allgemein überzeugen können; Lohfink z.B. sieht in der Wendung תַּחַת הַשֶּׁמֶשׁ weiterhin einen Gräzismus: »...bei »unter der Sonne« hört man das ὑφ' ἡλίου der Schulschriftsteller (in normalem Hebräisch hieße es »unter dem Himmel«) – es ist, wie wenn heute bei Journalisten und Intellektuellen englische Wortmünzen durchschimmern«[6].

Hier liegt offenkundig eine petitio principii vor: Wer meint, wenn semitische Belege der Formel vorlägen, seien sie grundsätzlich als Quelle allen anderen vorzuziehen, kann sich kaum mit jemandem einigen, der meint, wenn zeitgenössische Belege aus der griechischsprechenden Umwelt vorlägen, seien sie grundsätzlich als Quelle anzusehen, da Qohelet als ein gebildeter Mensch ja sicherlich Griechisch beherrscht oder mindestens gekannt habe und dort der Wendung begegnet sei.

Lassen wir also dahingestellt, ob sich in Qohelets Lieblingswendung »unter der Sonne« altes semitisches Erbe zu Worte meldet oder ob hier

---

2. Oswald LORETZ, *Qohelet und der Alte Orient. Untersuchungen zu Stil und theologischer Thematik des Buches Qohelet*, Freiburg, 1964, S. 46.

3. Rainer BRAUN, *Kohelet und die frühhellenistische Popularphilosophie* (BZAW, 130), Berlin, 1973.

4. A.a.O. S. 49f.

5. Diese Datierung ist allerdings wahrscheinlich falsch; die Inschriften dürften ins 5. Jhdt v.Chr. gehören; vgl. z.B. O. KAISER, *Judentum und Hellenismus*, in *VuF* 21 (1982) 68-88; S. 71 unter Hinweis auf B. PECKHAM, *The Development of the Late Phoenician Scripts* (HSS, 20), Cambridge/Mass., 1968.

6. Norbert LOHFINK, *Kohelet* (NEB), Würzburg, 1980, S. 20.

eine zeitgenössische Modewendung vorliegt – vielleicht kann man sich
am einfachsten vorstellen, daß eine durch semitische Sprachtradition be-
reitgestellte Wendung unter Einfluß des Griechischen (re)aktiviert und
vielleicht sogar modisch geworden ist. Wichtiger scheint mir die Beantwortung der Frage zu sein, was denn Qohelet, der ja sonst seine Worte
sehr überlegt wählt, mit dem häufigen Gebrauch dieser Wendung ausdrücken wollte.

Zuvor der Vollständigkeit halber eine weitere Feststellung: Neben der
nur bei Qohelet im AT vorkommenden Wendung »unter der Sonne«
findet sich noch dreimal die Wendung »unter dem Himmel« (1,13; 2,3;
3,1); diese Wendung findet sich im sonstigen AT noch neunmal: Gen
6,17; 7,19; Ex 17,14; Dtn 2,25; 4,19; 9,14; 25,19; 29,19; 2 Kön 14,27.
In 3,1 bringt Qohelet diese Wendung innnerhalb des Zitates eines
Weisheitstextes, wie Whybray[7] gezeigt hat. Die beiden Vorkommen in
1,13 und 2,3 sind textlich unsicher, vgl. den Apparat. Ein Bedeutungs-
unterschied zu »unter der Sonne« ist nicht erkennbar.

Im folgenden gebe ich einen Überblick über die Stellen, an denen »unter
der Sonne« vorkommt:

Die Wendung ist an folgenden Stellen belegt: 1,3.9.14; 2,11.17.18.20.22;
3,16; 4,1.3.7; 5,12.17; 6,12; 8,9.15(2x).17; 9,3.6.9(2x)11.13; 10,5. Die
Verteilung ist nicht gleichmäßig; in Kap. 7 und ab 10,6 fehlt die Wendung; in den übrigen Kapiteln lassen sich Häufungen feststellen, besonders in 2,11-22 (5 Belege in 11 Versen), 8,9-17 (4 Belege in 8 Versen)
und 9,3-13 (6 Belege in 10 Versen).

Die Wendung findet sich vor allem in Texten, in denen Qohelet nicht
zitiert, sondern selber argumentiert; sie muß deshalb als für den Autor
und Denker Qohelet typische und aufschlußreiche Wendung angesehen
werden, selbst wenn sie durch den Sprachgebrauch seiner Zeit (hellenistischer Einfluß!) beeinflußt sein sollte. Wenn man sich dieses verge-
genwärtigt, kann man nur sagen, daß in den bisherigen Untersuchungen
über Qohelet diese Wendung nicht gebührend gewürdigt worden ist.

Da ich eben einleitend zum grundsätzlichen Verstehensproblem von
neuen Wendungen gesagt habe, der verständige und verstehenswillige
Hörer oder Leser müsse versuchen, ihren Sinn aus dem Kontext zu erkennen, will ich im folgenden einmal den Versuch einer Aufgliederung
der Belege unter inhaltlichen Gesichtspunkten vorführen – in der Hoff-

---

7. Roger N. WHYBRAY, *'A time to be born and a time to die'. Some Observations on
Ecclesiastes 3:2-8*, in *Near Eastern Studies. Dedicated to H.I.H. Prince Takahito Mikasa*
(Bulletin of the Middle Eastern Culture Center in Japan, Vol. V), Wiesbaden, 1991, S.
469-483.

nung, daß man schon aus den jeweiligen Kontexten etwas vom Sinn er-
ahnen kann. Ich teile dabei die Belege in vier Gruppen ein:

1. »Unter der Sonne« steht zusammen mit מעשׂה »Werk, Tun« oder
מעשׂים »Werke« als generalisierende Beschreibung der Gesamtheit dessen, was geschieht; 9,3 und 9,6 wird das Generalisierende durch »alles,
was unter der Sonne geschieht« ausgedrückt; 1,9 und 2,11 liegt dieser
Sinn auch ohne מעשׂה oder »alles« vor:

> 1,9 Was gewesen ist, wird wieder sein,
> und was getan worden ist, wird wieder getan werden.
> Es gibt nichts Neues unter der Sonne.
>
> 1,14 Ich betrachtete alle Werke, die unter der Sonne getan werden.
> Ergebnis: alles ist absurd und Haschen nach Wind.
>
> 2,11 Doch dann dachte ich nach über all meine Werke,
> die meine Hände geschaffen hatten,
> und über die Mühe, die ich aufgewendet hatte, etwas zu schaffen.
> Ergebnis: Alles ist absurd und Haschen nach Wind.
> Es gibt keinen Gewinn unter der Sonne.
>
> 2,17 Da empfand ich Verdruß über das Leben,
> denn übel lag auf mir das Geschehen, das unter der Sonne geschieht.
> Ja, alles ist absurd und Haschen nach Wind.
>
> 4,3 Und für noch glücklicher als die beiden halte ich den,
> der noch gar nicht ins Dasein getreten ist –
> er sieht nämlich das schlimme Tun nicht,
> das unter der Sonne geschieht.
>
> 8,9 All dies betrachtete ich, indem ich meinen Verstand befaßte
> mit allem Tun, das unter der Sonne geschieht:
> (es gibt) eine Zeit, in der der Mensch Macht hat über den Menschen
> ihm zum Bösen.
>
> 8,17 Da betrachtete ich also das Tun Gottes in seiner Ganzheit:
> fürwahr, nicht kann der Mensch herausfinden
> das Werk/Tun, das unter der Sonne geschieht...
>
> 9,3 Das ist etwas Schlimmes bei alledem, was unter der Sonne geschieht,
> daß einerlei Geschick alle trifft...
>
> 9,6 Auch ihr Lieben, ihr Hassen und Eifern ist schon längst vergangen,
> und einen Anteil auf ewig gibt es für sie nicht mehr
> an allem, was unter der Sonne geschieht.

2. zusammen mit der Wurzel עמל »sich abmühen« bzw. »Mühe, Ertrag
der Mühe«:

> 1,3 Was für einen Gewinn hat der Mensch bei all seinem Mühen,
> mit dem er sich unter der Sonne abmüht?
>
> 2,18 Da empfand ich Verdruß über (die Frucht) meine(r) Mühe,
> für die ich mich abgemüht habe unter der Sonne
> und die ich einem Menschen hinterlassen muß, der nach mir kommt.
>
> 2,20 Da ging ich dazu über, meinen Verstand der Verzweiflung zu überlassen
> hinsichtlich all der Mühe, mit der ich mich unter der Sonne abgemüht habe.

2,22 Nun: Was bleibt dem Menschen von all seiner Mühe
und dem Plagen seines Verstandes, mit dem er sich unter der Sonne
abmüht?

5,17 Hier ist, was ich als gut (im Sinne von) angemessen betrachtet habe:
zu essen und zu trinken und es sich gut sein zu lassen
bei aller Mühsal, mit der man sich unter der Sonne abmüht
in der begrenzten Frist seines Lebens, die einem Gott gegeben hat:
Fürwahr, das ist sein Teil.

9,9 ... Ja, eben dies ist dein Teil im Leben
und (zwar?) bei deiner Mühe, mit der du dich unter der Sonne abmühst.

3. zusammen mit ראה »betrachten«:

1,14 Ich betrachtete alle Werke, die unter der Sonne getan werden.
Ergebnis: Alles ist absurd und Haschen nach Wind.

3,16 Und weiterhin betrachtete ich unter der Sonne:
(An den) Ort des Gerichts – dort(hin) (muß) das Unrecht,
(an den) Ort des Rechts – dort(hin) muß das Unrecht.

4,1 Und ich wandte mich und betrachtete alle Bedrückungen,
die unter der Sonne geschehen:
Es gibt Tränen von Bedrückten, ohne daß einer sie tröstet,
und von ihren Bedrückern erfahren sie Gewalt, ohne daß einer sie tröstet.

4,7 Und ich wandte mich und betrachtete eine Absurdität unter der Sonne...

5,12 Es gibt ein schlimmes Übel, das ich unter der Sonne betrachtet habe:
Reichtum, der von seinem/für seinen Besitzer gehütet wurde
mit einem schlimmen Ende für ihn.

5,17 Hier ist das, was ich jedenfalls
als gut (im Sinne von) angemessen betrachtet habe:
zu essen und zu trinken und es sich gut sein zu lassen
bei all seiner Mühsal, mit der man sich unter der Sonne abmüht
in der begrenzten Frist seines Lebens,
die einem Gott gegeben hat: Fürwahr, das ist sein Teil.

9,11 Und erneut betrachtete ich unter der Sonne:
Nicht die Schnellen machen das Rennen...

9,13 Auch dies betrachtete ich als (ein Beispiel von) Weisheit unter der Sonne...

10,5 Es gibt auch ein Übel, das ich unter der Sonne betrachtet habe. ...

4. restliche Stellen

6,12 Wer weiß denn, was für den Menschen gut ist
während der begrenzten Frist seiner sinnlosen Tage,
die er wie einen Schatten verbringt?
Wer kann nämlich dem Menschen kundtun,
was nach ihm sein wird unter der Sonne?

8,15 So preise ich denn die Freude, die darauf beruht,
daß es für den Menschen unter der Sonne nichts Gutes gibt
außer zu essen und zu trinken und sich zu freuen.

8,15 ... Das kann ihm bleiben bei seiner Mühe
in den Tagen seines Lebens, die Gott ihm unter der Sonne gegeben hat.

9,9 Genieße das Leben mit einer Frau, die du liebst,
alle Tage deines sinnlosen Lebens,
die er dir gibt unter der Sonne. ...

Zur Deutung:

Wenn man wiederholt und damit betont von einem Bereich »unter der
Sonne« spricht, dann wird damit ein bestimmter Bereich ausgegrenzt
und von einem oder mehreren anderen abgegrenzt. Dieser Sprachgebrauch ist deutlich in den phönizischen Inschriften belegt: In einer
Fluchandrohung heißt es in der Tabnitinschrift[8]:

> »... und wenn du doch über mir (d.h. meinen Sarg) öffnest und mich doch
> störst, so soll dir nicht Nachkommenschaft (Same) im Leben unter der Son-
> ne sein und (auch nicht) eine Ruhestätte bei den Totengeistern«[9].

Hier wird deutlich das »Leben unter der Sonne« abgegrenzt gegenüber der Unterwelt, der Sche'ol. Die Eschmunazarinschrift[10] bringt folgende Fluchandrohung:

> »... nicht sei ihnen eine Wurzel unten noch eine Frucht oben noch Anse-
> hen im Leben unter der Sonne«[11].

Was mit »Wurzel unten« gemeint ist, weiß ich nicht, aber »eine
Frucht oben« bezieht sich sicherlich auf den Bereich der Götter, während »Leben unter der Sonne« demgegenüber die »normale, diesseitige« Existenz des Menschen bezeichnet. Eben diese Bedeutung hat die
Wendung auch in der Fluchformel aus Elam, die in das 13. Jhdt. v.Chr.
gehören soll:

> »Seine Nachkommenschaft möge unter der Sonne nicht gedeihen«[12].

Daß תחת השמש bei Qohelet diese nächstliegende Bedeutung habe,
findet sich denn auch häufig als Feststellung in den Kommentaren; als
Beispiele seien Delitzsch und Lauha zitiert: »'Unter der Sonne' ist die
diesem Buche eigene Bezeichnung der irdischen Welt, der Welt des
Menschen, welche wir die untermondliche (sublunarische) zu nennen
gewohnt sind«[13]. »Dem alten Weltbild gemäß bedeutet der Ausdruck
'auf der Erde' und bezeichnet den Bereich, in dem sich das menschliche Leben abspielt«[14]. Von moderneren Kommentatoren sei stellvertretend Schwienhorst-Schönberger genannt. Er schreibt zu 1,3: »Der
universale anthropologische Fragehorizont wird unterstrichen durch
die Umstandsangabe תַּחַת הַשֶּׁמֶשׁ 'unter der Sonne'.... 'Unter der Sonne'
meint das diesseitige Leben des Menschen im Unterschied zum Ort der

---

8. *KAI* 13.
9. Übersetzung nach LORETZ, *Qohelet und der Alte Orient* (vgl. Anm. 2), S. 46.
10. *KAI* 14.
11. Nach LORETZ, a.a.O. S.46.
12. Nach LORETZ, a.a.O. S.47.
13. Franz DELITZSCH, *Hoheslied und Koheleth* (BC, 4,4), Leipzig, 1875, S. 228.
14. Aarre LAUHA, *Kohelet* (BK, 19), Neukirchen, 1978, S. 33.

Finsternis, aus der er kommt und in die er geht (vgl. 6,4; 9,10; 11,7f; 12,2)«[15].

Daß Qohelet mit »unter der Sonne« eine Bezeichnung dieser unserer Welt im Gegensatz zur »Unterwelt« und zu einer »höheren Welt im Himmel« bietet, kann und soll nicht bestritten werden. Aber diese Erklärung kann noch nicht die Häufigkeit dieser Wendung verständlich machen. Die Frage bleibt: Weshalb verwendet Qohelet, der sonst seine Wörter sehr bewußt wählt, als einziger Schriftsteller des AT diese Wendung, und zwar so überaus häufig?

Es muß dafür einen sachlichen Grund geben, und der läßt sich nach meiner Überzeugung vor allem in den unter Nr. 3 angeführten Stellen finden, wo Qohelet sein Lieblingswort »betrachten« in Verbindung mit seiner Lieblingswendung »unter der Sonne« verwendet. Im folgenden will ich mein Verständnis der Wendung und der sich daraus ergebenden Probleme kurz an einigen Texten vorführen:

1,3

3   מַה־יִּתְרוֹן לָאָדָם בְּכָל־עֲמָלוֹ שֶׁיַּעֲמֹל תַּחַת הַשָּׁמֶשׁ׃

Was für einen Gewinn hat der Mensch bei all seinem Mühen,
mit dem er sich unter der Sonne abmüht?

Qohelet bemüht sich bis 2,23, eine Anwort auf diese Frage zu finden, ohne daß »Gott« dabei eine Funktion hätte. Wie Hans-Peter Müller gezeigt hat[16], redet Qohelet so von Gott, daß er ganz bestimmte Verben verwendet, vor allem: Gott »gibt« oder Gott »macht«. Und wenn man diese Stellen genau ansieht, dann wird Gott als Verursacher von dem eingeführt, was Qohelet mit seinem Verstand bereits erkannt hat. Ein Beispiel: Wenn er der Überzeugung ist, menschliches Nachdenken über den Sinn menschlichen Tuns sei eine »böse Mühe und die Menschen müßten sich damit abplagen«, kann er reden von der »bösen Mühe, die Gott den Menschen gegeben hat, sie damit zu plagen« (1,13). Wenn er findet, daß zu seiner Zeit das dem Menschen Widerfahrende »angemessen« (schön) ist, kann er sagen: »Gott hat alles angemessen gemacht zu seiner Zeit« (3,11). Gott wird also als »Urheber« dessen eingeführt, was der Denker mit seinem Verstand bereits erkannt hat, und natürlich als eine innerweltliche, als eine immanente Gegebenheit erkannt hat. Was sonst sollte ein empirischer Philosoph zum Gegenstand seines Nachdenkens machen. Er beschäftigt sich mit dem, was wir »immanent« nennen. Und wenn er konsequent bei solchen immanenten Tatbeständen

---

15. Ludger SCHWIENHORST-SCHÖNBERGER, *Nicht im Menschen gründet das Glück (Koh 2,24). Kohelet im Spannungsfeld jüdischer Weisheit und hellenistischer Philosophie* (HBS, 2), Freiburg, 1994, S. 20f.

16. Hans-Peter MÜLLER, *Wie sprach Qohälät von Gott?*, in *VT* 18 (1968) 507-521.

ansetzt, kann er von Gott nur als von dem Urheber des von ihm Erkann-
ten reden.

Diese Beschränkung (!) des Bereiches, mit dem er sich denkend beschäftigt, meint Qohelet, wenn er von »Betrachten unter der Sonne« redet. Welche Konsequenzen das für die Auslegung haben muß, will ich
an dem Text 2,24-26 kurz demonstrieren.

2,24-26

אֵין־טוֹב בָּאָדָם שֶׁיֹּאכַל וְשָׁתָה וְהֶרְאָה אֶת־נַפְשׁוֹ טוֹב בַּעֲמָלוֹ   24
גַּם־זֹה רָאִיתִי אָנִי כִּי מִיַּד הָאֱלֹהִים הִיא:

כִּי מִי יֹאכַל וּמִי יָחוּשׁ חוּץ מִמֶּנִּי: 25

כִּי לְאָדָם שֶׁטּוֹב לְפָנָיו נָתַן חָכְמָה וְדַעַת וְשִׂמְחָה וְלַחוֹטֶא   26
נָתַן עִנְיָן לֶאֱסוֹף וְלִכְנוֹס לָתֵת לְטוֹב לִפְנֵי הָאֱלֹהִים גַּם־זֶה
הֶבֶל וּרְעוּת רוּחַ:

24   Es liegt nicht als ein Gutes in der Verfügungsgewalt des Menschen,
     daß er ißt und trinkt und sein Verlangen Gutes sehen läßt bei seiner
     Mühsal.
     Auch das habe ich betrachtet (!), daß dies aus der Hand Gottes
     kommt.
25   Denn: »Wer kann essen und wer sich sorgen ohne mich?«
26   Fürwahr: einem Menschen, der ihm gefällt,
     gibt er Weisheit und Erkenntnis und Freude -
     und dem Sich-Verfehlenden gibt er die Mühe, zu sammeln und anzu-
     häufen –
     und das dann dem zu geben, der Gott gefällt.
     Auch das ist absurd (*häbäl*) und Haschen nach Wind.

Bis 2,23 hatte Qohelet die Frage von 1,3 zu klären versucht: »Was für
einen Gewinn hat der Mensch bei all seinem Mühen, mit dem er sich
unter der Sonne abmüht«. In 2,24a faßt er dieses Ergebnis noch einmal
zusammen. Bis jetzt hat er in 1,9.14; 2,11.17.18.20.22 wohl von »unter
der Sonne« geredet, von »Gott« aber nur in dem einleitenden Vers 1,13,
sonst nicht mehr. Aber jetzt geht er einen Schritt weiter: »Auch das
habe ich gesehen/betrachtet, daß es aus der *Hand Gottes* kommt«. Es ist
nach meiner Überzeugung nicht zufällig, daß Qohelet hier seine
Lieblingswendung »unter der Sonne« nicht verwendet! Denn er argumentiert jetzt nicht mehr als Empiriker. Es liegt alles an der Einsicht,
daß Qohelet hier nicht berichtet, was er gesehen hat (wie sollte er das
»sehen«?), sondern eine »Betrachtung«[17] vorführt, und er begründet
dieses Vorgehen mit einem Satz, der wohl ein Zitat sein muß: »Wer
kann essen und sich sorgen ohne mich?« (Vgl. z. B. das deutsche Kir-

17. A. Schoors will zwar hier im Anschluß an M. Fox, *Qohelet and his Contradictions*, Sheffield, 1989, S. 188ff., eher die Bedeutung »I realized« finden, aber mir
scheint dennoch immer noch »betrachten« textgemäßer.

chenlied: Oh Gott, du frommer Gott, du Geber aller Gaben, ohn' den nichts ist, was ist, von dem wir alles haben!)

Und wenn man in eine Sinnlosigkeit, die man durch eine immanente Analyse erkannt hat, Gott als Urheber (ohn' den nichts ist, was ist) einführt, wird diese Sinnlosigkeit dadurch nicht sinnvoller. Das zeigt Qohelet in v.26. Es ändert sich nur die Terminologie: aus einem Toren wird ein Sich-Verfehlender, aus einem Klugen/Weisen wird einer, der gut vor ihm ist = der Gott gefällt.

Ein Gegenargument gäbe es freilich noch. Diese von dem Urhebergott verursachte Sinnlosigkeit könnte sinnvoll sein, wenn es mehr gäbe als die unserem Verstand zugängliche Welt, wenn z.B. nach dem Tode, der von Qohelet als entscheidendes Argument für die letzte Sinnlosigkeit menschlichen Mühens angeführt wird, ein Teil des Menschen zu Gott kommen könnte, wenn es also so etwas wie eine Auferstehung gäbe. Das wäre freilich das große Fragezeichen an die Grundhaltung, den Sinn des menschlichen Lebens lediglich durch Fragen und Betrachten »unter der Sonne« zu bestimmen. Und genau dieses Gegenargument betrachtet Qohelet in 3,16-4,3. Aus Zeit- und Raumgründen muß ich auf die schwierigen Verse 3,17-19[18] verzichten – das ist m.E. hier vertretbar, weil der Sinn auf jeden Fall aus vv.20-22 deutlich wird, die zu der Einheit gehören:

3,16.19-22; 4,1-3

וְעוֹד רָאִיתִי תַּחַת הַשָּׁמֶשׁ	16
מְקוֹם הַמִּשְׁפָּט שָׁמָּה הָרֶשַׁע	
וּמְקוֹם הַצֶּדֶק שָׁמָּה הָרָשַׁע:	
כִּי מִקְרֶה בְנֵי־הָאָדָם וּמִקְרֶה הַבְּהֵמָה וּמִקְרֶה אֶחָד לָהֶם	19
כְּמוֹת זֶה כֵּן מוֹת זֶה וְרוּחַ אֶחָד לַכֹּל	
וּמוֹתַר הָאָדָם מִן־הַבְּהֵמָה אָיִן כִּי הַכֹּל הָבֶל:	
הַכֹּל הוֹלֵךְ אֶל־מָקוֹם אֶחָד	20
הַכֹּל הָיָה מִן־הֶעָפָר וְהַכֹּל שָׁב אֶל־הֶעָפָר:	
מִי יוֹדֵעַ רוּחַ בְּנֵי הָאָדָם הָעֹלָה הִיא לְמַעְלָה וְרוּחַ הַבְּהֵמָה	21
הַיֹּרֶדֶת הִיא לְמַטָּה לָאָרֶץ:	
וְרָאִיתִי כִּי אֵין טוֹב מֵאֲשֶׁר יִשְׂמַח	22
הָאָדָם בְּמַעֲשָׂיו כִּי־הוּא חֶלְקוֹ כִּי	
מִי יְבִיאֶנּוּ לִרְאוֹת בְּמֶה שֶׁיִּהְיֶה אַחֲרָיו:	
וְשַׁבְתִּי אֲנִי וָאֶרְאֶה אֶת־כָּל־הָעֲשֻׁקִים אֲשֶׁר נַעֲשִׂים תַּחַת הַשָּׁמֶשׁ	4:1
וְהִנֵּה דִּמְעַת הָעֲשֻׁקִים וְאֵין לָהֶם מְנַחֵם	
וּמִיַּד עֹשְׁקֵיהֶם כֹּחַ וְאֵין לָהֶם מְנַחֵם:	

18. Die schwierigen Probleme dieses Textes können hier nicht erörtert werden; vgl. vorläufig Diethelm MICHEL, *Untersuchungen zur Eigenart des Buches Qohelet* (BZAW, 183), Berlin, 1989, S. 248-252.

2 וְשַׁבֵּחַ אֲנִי אֶת־הַמֵּתִים שֶׁכְּבָר מֵתוּ מִן־הַחַיִּים אֲשֶׁר הֵמָּה חַיִּים עֲדֶנָה:

3 וְטוֹב מִשְּׁנֵיהֶם אֵת אֲשֶׁר־עֲדֶן לֹא הָיָה אֲשֶׁר לֹא־רָאָה
אֶת־הַמַּעֲשֶׂה הָרָע אֲשֶׁר נַעֲשָׂה תַּחַת הַשָּׁמֶשׁ:

16 Und weiterhin *betrachtete(!) ich unter der Sonne:*
An den Ort des Gerichts – dorthin (muß) das Unrecht,
an den Ort der Gerechtigkeit – dorthin (muß) das Unrecht.

(...)

19 Denn was das Geschick der Menschen und das Geschick des Viehs angeht:
einerlei Geschick haben sie.
Wie der eine stirbt, so stirbt auch der andere;
einerlei »Geist« haben sie beide,
und einen Vorzug des Menschen vor dem Vieh gibt es nicht.
Denn alles ist *häbäl* (vergänglich/absurd).

20 Alle gehen zu demselben Ort.
Alles ist aus Staub entstanden und alles kehrt wieder zu Staub zurück.

21 Wer weiß denn, ob der Geist des Menschen nach oben steigt
und ob der Geist des Viehs nach unten zur Erde hinabsteigt.

22 Und ich sah/betrachtete, daß es nichts Besseres gibt,
als daß der Mensch sich an seinen Werken (seinem Erworbenen) freue:
Fürwahr, das ist sein Teil.
Denn wer kann ihn dahin bringen, daß er (mit Freude) sähe, was nach
ihm kommt?

4,1 Und ich wendete mich und betrachtete alle Bedrückungen,
die unter der Sonne geschehen:
Es gibt Tränen der Bedrückten, ohne daß sie einer tröstet,
und von ihren Bedrückern erfahren sie Gewalt, ohne daß sie jemand
tröstet.

2 (In diesem Fall) halte ich die Toten, die längst gestorben sind,
für glücklicher als die Lebenden, die noch am Leben sind.

3 Und für noch glücklicher als die beiden halte ich den,
der noch gar nicht ins Dasein getreten ist -
er sieht nämlich das schlimme Tun nicht,
das unter der Sonne geschieht.

Festzuhalten ist, daß Qohelet als *unter der Sonne* denkender Empiriker keineswegs sagt, es gebe keine Auferstehung. Er beschränkt sich auf
die skeptische Frage: »Wer weiß denn, ob der Geist des Menschen nach
oben steigt und der Geist des Viehs nach unten zur Erde hinabsteigt?«
Ja, wer weiß das denn aus eigener Anschauung? Wer kann darüber etwas aus seiner Erkenntnis »unter der Sonne« sagen?

Und konsequent wendet sich Qohelet dann in 4,1-3 wieder[19] dem Geschehen »unter der Sonne« zu und betrachtet einen Grenzfall menschlichen Leides. Er ist, wie man an etlichen Wendungen zeigen kann, ein

---

19. Das hebr. וְשַׁבְתִּי ist nach meiner Überzeugung hier verwendet, um eine Änderung
in der Betrachtungsrichtung anzuzeigen, ähnlich 4,7. Dazu vgl. demnächst meinen Kommentar in ATD.

»Denker von den Grenzfällen her«[20]. Ohne die Einführung des Gedankens der Totenauferstehung kann man »unter der Sonne« das Problem unstillbaren Leidens nicht lösen. Im folgenden deutet er an, daß menschliches Miteinander eine Hilfe sein kann – »zwei sind besser als einer...« (4,9) – aber das ist hier nicht unser Thema. Ich will und kann hier lediglich andeuten, daß Qohelet konsequent mit seinem Denken und Argumentieren »unter der Sonne« bleiben will, daß er also die Immanenz nicht verlassen kann und will. Wenn er unter dieser Voraussetzung das Problem unstillbaren Leidens betrachtet, muß es unlösbar sein – dann ist es besser, nicht geboren zu sein. Und es dürfte kaum zufällig sein, daß er bei diesem »Betrachten unter der Sonne« nichts von Gott sagt. Er bleibt in der Immanenz.

Aber nun gibt es ja einen Abschnitt im Buche Qohelet, in dem es nach Meinung der meisten Ausleger »um das religiöse Verhalten«[21] geht: 4,17-5,6. Man sieht in diesem Abschnitt häufig einen deutlichen Hinweis auf ein Bleiben Qohelets in der Tradition seiner Väter. Nach Lohfink ist dieser Abschnitt, den er »Religionskritik« nennt, gar kompositorisch und inhaltlich das Zentrum des Buches Qohelet, wobei er freilich in dem Text im wesentlichen Kritik an »religiös Emsigen« findet. Das einzig wirklich Positive ist bei ihm in 5,6 die Aufforderung »Du fürchte Gott!«. Die Gottesfurcht ist »die geheime Essenz jedes Augenblicks des normalen Lebens«[22]. Viel mehr noch will Otto Kaiser aus dem Abschnitt 4,17-5,6 heraushören: »Dabei ist die Bedeutung der Reflexion 4,17-5,6 für das Gesamtverständnis des Predigers nicht zu unterschätzen: Der Lehrer, der das aufmerksame Hören im Tempel den Opfern verordnet [sic! lege »vorordnet« Mi] (vgl. 1 Sam 15,22; Prov 31,8; 15,8; Sir 34,21-23; ferner Merikare 305ff.; Pl.Leg.St. 716d-717a) und in v.3 das Gelübdegebot der Tora Dtn 23,22 zitiert, kann schwerlich mit dem Schriftglauben und der Gesetzesfrömmigkeit seines Volkes gebrochen haben«[23]. Und jüngstens hat der Kaiser-Schüler Alexander A. Fischer in seiner Dissertation folgendes zu dem Abschnitt geschrieben: (es ist) »offensichtlich, daß Kohelet hier kaum die Grenzen der herkömmlichen Weisheit und selbst deuteronomistischer Theologie überschreitet. Ein Weiser, der zustimmend die Tora zitiert, kann ihr wohl nicht allzu fern gestanden haben.«[24]

---

20. Dazu vgl. MICHEL, *Untersuchungen* (vgl. Anm. 18), S.184ff.
21. So z.B. SCHWIENHORST-SCHÖNBERGER, a.a.O. S. 136.
22. LOHFINK, *Kohelet* (vgl. Anm. 6), S. 10 und S. 40.
23. Otto KAISER, *Die Botschaft des Buches Kohelet* in ETL 71 (1995) 48-70, S. 64.
24. Alexander A. FISCHER, *Skepsis oder Furcht Gottes?* (BZAW, 247), Berlin, 1996, S. 48.

Ob Qohelet wirklich »zustimmend die Tora zitiert«, werden wir gleich sehen. Jetzt will ich nur einleitend sagen, daß die ersten drei Einheiten durch das Stichwort כְּסִיל »Tor, Einfältiger« zusammengehalten werden; hier haben wir anscheinend das geheime und gemeinsame Thema dieser Abschnitte.

4,17

17 שְׁמֹר רַגְלֶיךָ [רַגְלְךָ] כַּאֲשֶׁר תֵּלֵךְ אֶל־בֵּית הָאֱלֹהִים
וְקָרוֹב לִשְׁמֹעַ מִתֵּת הַכְּסִילִים זָבַח
כִּי־אֵינָם יוֹדְעִים לַעֲשׂוֹת רָע:

Bewahre deinen Fuß, wenn du ins Gotteshaus gehst,
(und) Nahen, um zu hören, (ist besser), als *wenn Toren Opfer geben*:
[und näher ist man beim Hören, als *wenn Toren Opfer geben*]
denn sie sind unverständig, so daß sie Schlechtes tun.

Der Text bietet schwierige exegetische Probleme, die ich hier nur andeuten kann. Erfreulicherweise kann man sich jetzt über die verschiedenen Verstehensmöglichkeiten der schwierigen Wendungen gut bei Antoon Schoors informieren[25]; ich kann mich deshalb hier relativ kurz fassen. וְקָרוֹב ist entweder ein Infinitiv (dann wäre טוֹב zu ergänzen) oder Adjektiv (dann wäre ein Subjekt »man« o.ä. zu ergänzen)[26]. Inhaltlich folge ich Michael Fox: »*Qarob* apparently means 'near to God's favor', i.e. 'acceptable'«[27]. Leider nennt Qohelet nicht das Objekt des Hörens. Meistens nimmt man an, es sei die Thora gemeint – was sonst soll man im Tempel hören? Aber weshalb sagt Qohelet das nicht? Oder sollte er mit שְׁמֹעַ auf 1 Sam 15,22 hinweisen wollen? Es ist doch gut vorstellbar, daß »Hören« gerade in weisheitlicher Sprache noch etwas anderes meint als auf die Thora hören. Hier verdient der Hinweis von Gordis[28] weitere Überprüfung: »More probably it has the meaning here 'to understand'. Koheleth is not interested in preaching religious obedience, but in contrasting the need of understandig with the conforming, empty piety of those he regards as fools.«
Und nun zu dem Schlußsatz כִּי־אֵינָם יוֹדְעִים לַעֲשׂוֹת רָע. Er ist sprachlich mehrdeutig[29] und sachlich so schwierig, daß kein Geringerer als Norbert Lohfink ihm einen ganzen Aufsatz gewidmet hat[30]. Sprachlich scheint

25. Vgl. Antoon SCHOORS, *The Preacher Sought to Find Pleasing Words* (OLA, 41) Leuven, 1992.
26. Vgl. weiter SCHOORS, a.a.O. S. 171; 179; 208.
27. Michael V. FOX, *Qohelet and his Contradictions* (JSOT SS, 71), Sheffield, 1989. S. 210.
28. Robert GORDIS, *Koheleth – the Man and his World* (TSJTSA, Vol. XIX) New York, ³1962, S. 237.
29. Vgl. die Möglichkeiten bei SCHOORS, a.a.O. S. 182f.
30. Norbert LOHFINK, *Warum ist der Tor unfähig, böse zu handeln?*, in *ZDMG.S* 5 (XXI. Deutscher Orientalistentag), 1983, S. 113-120.

die auf Delitzsch zurückgehende Auffassung »sie sind unwissend/unver-
ständig, so daß sie Böses/Schlechtes tun« die nächstliegende zu sein.
Die sprachlich auch mögliche Auffassung »Sie wissen/verstehen nicht,
Böses zu tun« scheint mir trotz Lohfinks Aufsatz eher unwahrscheinlich, auch mit dem von Gordis angenommenen ironischen Beiklang:
»'who do not know how to do evil.' They are good – because they lack
the brains to do evil!«[31]

Man weist in der Auslegung zu לִשְׁמֹעַ häufig auf 1 Sam 15,22 hin
(vgl. z.B. oben das Zitat von Otto Kaiser!): »Gehorsam ist besser als
Opfer und Aufmerken besser als das Fett von Widdern« (הִנֵּה שְׁמֹעַ מִזֶּבַח
טוֹב לְהַקְשִׁיב מֵחֵלֶב אֵילִים). Aber dann entsteht ein Problem, das, wenn ich
nichts übersehen habe, nur Michael Fox in seinem Kommentar zu »besser als wenn Toren Opfer geben« nennt: »To be sure, obedience is
better than *anyone's* sacrifice«, von daher hält er הַכְּסִילִים für eine
»superfluous addition of >fools<«[32]. Was aber, wenn dieses Wort keineswegs eine «superfluous addition« ist, sondern hier gerade der
Skopus von Qohelet läge!? Dann würde er generell Opfer als Werk von
Unwissenden ansehen – und genau das ist der Sinn des Schlußsatzes כִּי־
אֵינָם יוֹדְעִים לַעֲשׂוֹת רָע in dem von Delitzsch u.a. angenommenen Sinn:
Die Toren, die ein Opfer bringen statt zu »hören«, sind unverständig,
so daß sie Schlechtes (nicht: Böses!) tun. Und »den Fuß bewahren
(hüten), wenn man zum Gottesdienst geht« dürfte dann kaum meinen,
man solle sich vorsehen nicht zu stolpern. Und שְׁמֹר heißt nicht »zu-
rückhalten«!

5,1-2

5:1 אַל־תְּבַהֵל עַל־פִּיךָ וְלִבְּךָ אַל־יְמַהֵר
לְהוֹצִיא דָבָר לִפְנֵי הָאֱלֹהִים
כִּי הָאֱלֹהִים בַּשָּׁמַיִם וְאַתָּה עַל־הָאָרֶץ
עַל־כֵּן יִהְיוּ דְבָרֶיךָ מְעַטִּים:

2 כִּי בָּא הַחֲלוֹם בְּרֹב עִנְיָן וְקוֹל כְּסִיל בְּרֹב דְּבָרִים:

1 Überstürze dich nicht mit deinem Munde
und dein Herz beeile sich nicht, eine Sache vor Gott zu bringen.

2 Denn Gott ist im Himmel und du bist auf der Erde,
darum seien deiner Worte wenig!
Denn: *Ein Traum kommt bei (zu) viel Mühe*
und die Stimme eines Toren (wird erkennbar) bei zu vielen Worten.

Beginnen wir mit dem begründenden *ki*-Satz in v.2: »Ein Traum
(kommt) bei (zu) viel Mühe und die Stimme eines Toren (wird erkennbar) bei zu vielen Worten«! Qohelet wendet hier ein Verfahren an, das

31. GORDIS, a.a.O. S. 238.
32. FOX, a.a.O.

er auch sonst benutzt: er verwendet Sprichwörter (aus der Weisheitstradition!?) als Beweise. »Ein Traum kommt bei zu vielen Mühen«
dürfte dann etwa meinen, daß man sich bei zu großen Anstrengungen
leicht Illusionen macht, sich Luftschlösser vorgaukelt. – Und »die Stimme eines Toren bei zu vielen Worten« dürfte die allgemein weisheitliche
Erfahrung wiedergeben, daß es oft besser ist, zu schweigen als zu reden:
»Reden ist Silber, Schweigen ist Gold« – hier aber viel härter formuliert: »bei vielen Wörtern (hört man) die Stimme eines Toren«: o si
tacuisses philosophus mansisses. Das ist eine allgemein weisheitliche
Erfahrung, sicherlich. Aber brisant wird sie, wenn man sie mit dem Beten zusammenbringt! Was wir hier nicht behandeln konnten, will ich
kurz nachholen: in 3,14 sagt Qohelet, man könne dem Handeln Gottes
nichts hinzufügen und von ihm nichts wegnehmen – Gott aber handle so,
daß man sich vor ihm fürchte! Wenn man diese Wörter ernst nimmt,
kann man auch durch Beten oder Gelübde nichts an Gottes Handeln än-
dern – was denn sollte er sonst in diesem Zusammenhang meinen! Die
Aufforderung in v.2 »Gott ist im Himmel und du bist auf der Erde, darum (!!) seien deiner Worte wenig« ist sehr grundsätzlich und umfassend
– es ist also die Frage, ob Qohelet an unserer Stelle wirklich nur vor dem
Geplapper beim Beten warnen will, wie das Jesus ja später getan hat.
Auch beim Beten kann die Stimme eines Toren erkennbar werden!

　　Und nun zu der Stelle, wo Qohelet als frommer Jude die Thora zitieren soll (vgl. die Zitate von Kaiser und Fischer!)

　　5,3-4

3　כַּאֲשֶׁר תִּדֹּר נֶדֶר לֵאלֹהִים אַל־תְּאַחֵר לְשַׁלְּמוֹ
　כִּי אֵין חֵפֶץ בַּכְּסִילִים אֵת אֲשֶׁר־תִּדֹּר שַׁלֵּם׃

4　טוֹב אֲשֶׁר לֹא־תִדֹּר מִשֶּׁתִּדּוֹר וְלֹא תְשַׁלֵּם׃

3　Wenn du ein Gelübde darbringst, dann zögere nicht, es zu erfüllen,
　　denn man hat keinen Gefallen an Toren!
　　Was du gelobst, das erfülle!
4　Besser, du gelobst nicht,
　　als daß du gelobst und nicht erfüllst.

Wir vergleichen den Qohelettext mit dem Text aus Dtn 23,22, den er
»zitieren« soll:

Dtn 23,22	לֹא תְאַחֵר לְשַׁלְּמוֹ	כִּי־ תִדֹּר נֶדֶר לַיהוָה אֱלֹהֶיךָ	
Qoh 5,3	כַּאֲשֶׁר תִּדֹּר נֶדֶר לֵאלֹהִים אַל־תְּאַחֵר לְשַׁלְּמוֹ		

Dtn 23,22	כִּי־דָרֹשׁ יִדְרְשֶׁנּוּ יְהוָה אֱלֹהֶיךָ מֵעִמָּךְ וְהָיָה בְךָ חֵטְא	
Qoh 5,3	כִּי אֵין חֵפֶץ בַּכְּסִילִים אֵת אֲשֶׁר־תִּדֹּר שַׁלֵּם	

Dtn: *Wenn* du ein Gelübde gelobst für *Jahwe, deinen Gott,*
Qoh: *Falls* du ein Gelübde gelobst für *Gott,*

Dtn: *darfst* du nicht zögern, es zu erfüllen.
Qoh: *sollst* du nicht zögern, es zu erfüllen.
Dtn: Denn *gewiß wird es Jahwe, dein Gott, von dir einfordern, und es wird dir eine Verfehlung sein.*
Qoh: Denn *man hat kein Gefallen an Toren – was du gelobst, das erfülle!*

Wenn man die Unterschiede zwischen beiden Texten vergleicht, so wird klar: die Abweichungen sind deutlich zahlreicher als die Übereinstimmungen. Wenn Qohelet hier wirklich »zitieren« wollte, würde das seinem Gedächtnis kein gutes Zeugnis ausstellen. Was aber, wenn er gar nicht zitieren wollte, sondern durch einen bewußten Eingriff in den (ihm und seinen Lesern bekannten!) Text neue Akzente setzen wollte? Dann wiegt es schwer, daß die beiden Vorkommen des Namens »Jahwe« verschwunden sind – und noch schwerer wiegt es, daß die religiöse Begründung durch eine anthropologische ersetzt worden ist: wenn man Gott ein Gelübde ablegt, soll man es halten, weil es keinen Gefallen an Toren gibt! Ein Gelübde abzulegen und dann nicht zu erfüllen wird also aus dem religiösen und kultischen Bereich in den Bereich der Anthropologie transferiert! Unzuverlässige Menschen, Toren machen so etwas, und an denen hat man kein Gefallen. Ob man wirklich hier mit der Einheitsübersetzung und Lohfink »übersetzen« soll: »Die Ungebildeten gefallen Gott nicht«?

Ist das wirklich das Thorazitat eines gesetzestreuen Juden? Oder ist nicht wahrscheinlicher, daß Qohelet hier in den Text eingegriffen und aus einer religiösen Anweisung einen anthropologischen Ratschlag gemacht hat!?

5,5-6

אַל־תִּתֵּן אֶת־פִּיךָ לַחֲטִיא אֶת־בְּשָׂרֶךָ 5
וְאַל־תֹּאמַר לִפְנֵי הַמַּלְאָךְ כִּי שְׁגָגָה הִיא
לָמָּה יִקְצֹף הָאֱלֹהִים עַל־קוֹלֶךָ וְחִבֵּל אֶת־מַעֲשֵׂה יָדֶיךָ:
כִּי בְרֹב חֲלֹמוֹת וַהֲבָלִים וּדְבָרִים הַרְבֵּה 6
כִּי אֶת־הָאֱלֹהִים יְרָא:

5 Laß deinen Mund dich nicht in Verfehlung bringen
und sage nicht vor dem Boten: Es war (nur) ein Versehen!
Wozu sollte Gott über deine Stimme zürnen
und das Werk deiner Hände verderben?
6 [Denn] *Ja, bei vielen Träumen gibt es*
sowohl Sinnlosigkeiten als auch viele Worte.
[denn] *Ja, fürchte Gott!*

Zu v.6 schreibt Schoors: »This verse is very difficult and also the ancient versions were desperate when they had to translate it«[33]. Wir

---

33. SCHOORS, a.a.O. S.103.

brauchen die Probleme hier nicht näher zu diskutieren, denn eines scheint mir auf jeden Fall klar zu sein: V.6 bezieht sich auf v.2 zurück. Dort wurde gesagt: »Ein Traum kommt bei (zu) viel Mühe und die Stimme eines Toren (wird erkennbar) bei (zu) vielen Worten« – hier wird eingesetzt bei »(zu) vielen Träumen«, vermutlich sind die folgenden Wörter der Nachsatz: »(gibt es) sowohl Sinnlosigkeiten als auch viele Worte«. Das schwierige Problem des Verses ist die Frage, wie sich der folgende durch כִּי eingeleitete Satz zu dem vorhergehenden verhält. Ist dieses כִּי parallel zu dem כִּי aus v.6a? Oder soll man v.6a insgesamt als Vordersatz zu v.6b ansehen? So z.B. Gordis: »With all the dreams, follies and idle chatter, this remains – fear God!«[34]

Wie immer man auch das Verhältnis von v.6a zu v.6b bestimmen mag – auf jeden Fall kommt hier im Kontext die Aufforderung zur Gottesfurcht überraschend. Wenn man keine spätere Glosse annehmen will, sollte man erwarten, daß sie im bisherigen Text von Qohelet vorbereitet worden ist. Wir wollen also versuchen, festzustellen, was Qohelet bisher über Gott und Furcht Gottes gesagt hat. Mit welchen Informationen und Erwartungen kommt ein verständiger Leser zu diesem Vers?

Sicherlich hat er noch im Ohr aus demselben Vers:

> »Wozu sollte der Gott über deine Stimme zürnen und das Werk deiner Hände vernichten?!«

Und ebenfalls aus demselben Abschnitt 5,1f und 4,17:

> »Überstürze dich nicht mit deinem Munde
> und dein Herz beeile sich nicht, eine Sache vor Gott zu bringen.
> Denn Gott ist im Himmel und du bist auf der Erde – darum seien deiner Worte wenig!
> Bewahre deinen Fuß, wenn du in das Haus Gottes gehst...

Was ein Leser bei den nächstvorigen Erwähnungen Gottes gedacht hat (3,17 und 3,18), vermag ich nicht zu sagen:

> Ich selber (?!) sprach in meinem Herzen:
> Den Gerechten und den Schuldigen richtet Gott,
> denn es gibt eine Zeit für jedes Geschäft
> und für jedes Tun (gibt es?) ein Dort.
> 18 Ich sprach in meinem Herzen:
> Um der Menschen willen???[35] der Gott,
> um zu sehen, daß sie Vieh sind, sie selbst (?)

---

34. A.a.O. S. 154, vgl. S. 239f.
35. Zu den Problemen vgl. SCHOORS, a.a.O. S. 112-114.

Nach diesen schwierigen Stellen führt der Rückweg zu 3,14:

14   יָדַעְתִּי כִּי כָּל־אֲשֶׁר יַעֲשֶׂה הָאֱלֹהִים הוּא יִהְיֶה לְעוֹלָם
עָלָיו אֵין לְהוֹסִיף וּמִמֶּנּוּ אֵין לִגְרֹעַ
וְהָאֱלֹהִים עָשָׂה שֶׁיִּרְאוּ מִלְּפָנָיו:

Ich erkannte, daß alles, was Gott tut, für den ᶜolam ist.
Dem kann man nichts hinzufügen und von dem kann man nichts weg-
nehmen.
Die Gottheit aber handelt so, daß man sich vor ihr fürchte.

Über die Gottesfurcht bei Qohelet sind etliche Aufsätze geschrieben
worden. Mir scheint jedenfalls deutlich zu sein: Anders als etwa in den
Psalmen, wo Gottesfurcht die Reaktion auf die Begegnung mit Gott ist,
ist bei Qohelet Gottesfurcht das Ergebnis der Einsicht, daß man dem un-
zugänglichen und unbeeinflußbaren Gott nicht begegnen kann. Das geht
aus diesem Vers hervor.

Entscheidend ist, daß v.14 die Aussage aus 3,11 voraussetzt:

11   אֶת־הַכֹּל עָשָׂה יָפֶה בְעִתּוֹ גַּם אֶת־הָעֹלָם נָתַן בְּלִבָּם
מִבְּלִי אֲשֶׁר לֹא־יִמְצָא הָאָדָם אֶת־הַמַּעֲשֶׂה אֲשֶׁר־עָשָׂה הָאֱלֹהִים
מֵרֹאשׁ וְעַד־סוֹף:

Alles hat er schön gemacht zu seiner Zeit – aber (!) auch den עֹלָם hat
er in ihr Herz (= ihren Verstand) gegeben, ohne daß der Mensch das
Werk, das Gott tut, von Anfang bis Ende herausfinden kann.

Was dort dem Menschen unzugänglich ist, ist hier das Wesen des
Handelns Gottes – wegen dieser Unzugänglichkeit kann der Mensch
Gott nur fürchten!

Und wie v.11 zu verstehen ist, geht aus der Einleitung (!) v.10 hervor:

Ich sah/betrachtete die Mühe, die Gott dem Menschen gegeben hat, daß er
sich (damit) abplage!

Dieses Fazit aus 3,1-10 greift 1,13 wieder auf:

Ich setzte meinen Verstand daran, mit Weisheit zu erforschen und zu er-
kunden, was unter dem Himmel geschieht: das ist eine böse Mühe, die
Gott den Menschen gegeben hat, sie damit zu plagen.

Ich kann und will in diesem Zusammenhang all die erwähnten Texte
nicht gründlich auslegen – aber schon ein erstes Hinhören auf sie macht
m.E. klar, daß der so vorbereitete Leser den Schlußsatz aus 5,6 kaum als
Aufforderung zu einer Frömmigkeit, wie man sie in traditionsgebundenen Kreisen pflegte, verstehen konnte.

Auch hier haben wir also keine Übernahme von traditioneller Frömmigkeit.

Fazit:

1. In 4,17-5,6 sehen wir Qohelet nicht als traditionsgebundenen, frommen Juden, sondern als kritischen Weisen. Leitwort in diesem Abschnitt ist כְּסִיל »Tor«: mit diesem Wort werden diejenigen charakterisiert, die bestimmte religiöse Handlungen ausüben. Hier findet sich
   vermutlich eine Anthropologisierung frommer Vorstellungen. Damit
   bleibt er also auch hier in den Grenzen der Immanenz.
2. In seinem gesamten Werk will Qohelet die Welt unter den Gesetzmäßigkeiten erforschen, »die unter der Sonne« = in der Immanenz gelten. Das will er durch den häufigen Gebrauch der Wendung »unter
   der Sonne« betonen. Er will mit dieser Wendung mehr sagen, als sie
   in ihrem reinen Wortlaut hergibt. Er betont das durch ihre ständige
   Wiederholung.
3. In diesem Sinne ist er ein empirischer Philosoph.

Fischtorplatz 20   Diethelm MICHEL
D-55116 Mainz

IN DISKUSSION MIT DEM TEMPEL

ZUR AUSEINANDERSETZUNG ZWISCHEN KOHELET UND WEISHEITLICHEN KREISEN AM JERUSALEMER TEMPEL[1]

Im folgenden soll untersucht werden, inwieweit das Buch Kohelet als ein »unheimlicher Gast«[2] im atl. Kanon mit der Weisheit seiner Zeit im Gespräch stand. Für diesen Zweck lassen die vor kurzem veröffentlichten Weisheitstexte aus Qumran[3] neue Einblicke in die jüdische Weisheit des 3. und 2. Jh. v.Chr. erhoffen. Es soll gezeigt werden, daß Kohelet[4] sich nicht nur mit Gedanken aus dem hinter diesen Texten stehenden Tradentenkreis auseinandersetzt, sondern auch umgekehrt von ihm rezipiert und kritisiert worden ist. Hierzu wird im folgenden zuerst nach der Kohelet-Rezeption gefragt:

1. Der vorliegende Aufsatz basiert auf einem im deutschsprachigen Seminar des Colloquium Biblicum Lovaniense gehaltenen Vortrag. Den Teilnehmern des Seminars möchte ich für die lebhafte und anregende Diskussion sowie für viele konstruktive Anregungen ausdrücklich danken. Eine gekürzte Fassung des ersten Teils erscheint in englischer Sprache unter dem Titel *Eschatological Wisdom in the Book of Qohelet and the Dead Sea Scrolls* in dem von L.H. SCHIFFMAN, E. TOV und J.C. VANDERKAM herausgegebenen Sammelband des Jerusalemer Kongresses anläßlich des fünfzigjährigen Fundjubiläums der Texte vom Toten Meer (»The Dead Sea Scrolls – Fifty Years After Their Discovery. Major Issues and New Approaches, The Israel Museum, Jerusalem, July 20–25, 1997).

2. H.-P. MÜLLER, *Der unheimliche Gast*, in ZTK 84 (1987) 440–464; = ID., *Mensch – Umwelt – Eigenwelt. Gesammelte Aufsätze zur Weisheit Israels*, Stuttgart et al., W. Kohlhammer, 1992, pp. 169–193; cf. O. KAISER, *Die Botschaft des Buches Kohelet*, in ETL 71 (1995) 48–70, p. 48.

3. B.Z. WACHOLDER/M.G. ABEGG, *A Preliminary Edition of the Unpublished Dead Sea Scrolls. The Hebrew and Aramaic Texts from Cave Four*, Fasz. 2, Washington, Biblical Archaeology Society, 1992, pp. 1–203; Übersetzungen finden sich bei J. MAIER, *Die Qumran-Essener. Die Texte vom Toten Meer*, Bd. 1–3 (Uni-Taschenbücher, 1862–1863.1916), München/Basel, Ernst Reinhardt Verlag, 1995–1996 und F. GARCÍA MARTÍNEZ, *The Dead Sea Scrolls Translated. The Qumran Texts in English*, Leiden et al., E.J. Brill, 1994. Eine erste Einleitung in das Material bietet D.J. HARRINGTON, *Wisdom Texts from Qumran* (The Literature of the Dead Sea Scrolls), London/New York, Routledge, 1996. Die 4QMyst-Handschriften werden im folgenden nach der allen bislang veröffentlichen Übersetzungen zugrundeliegenden Edition von B.Z. WACHOLDER/M.G. ABEGG gezählt. Die jüngst erschienene Edition von L.H. SCHIFFMAN weist eine leicht abweichende Zählung der Fragmente auf (*Mysteries*, in T. ELGVIN ET AL., *Qumran Cave 4 XV. Sapiential Texts, Part 1* [DJD, 20], Oxford, Clarendon Press,1997, pp. 31–123).

4. Dem allgemeinen Konsens folgend wird das Buch Kohelet im folgenden in die Mitte des 3. Jh. v.Chr. datiert.

KOHELET-REZEPTION UND DIE WEISHEITSTEXTE AUS QUMRAN

»Und des vielen Bücherschreibens ist kein Ende« – der allseits zitierte und bekannte Satz ist Teil des Schlußkommentars der zweiten Redaktion des Buches Kohelet (Koh 12,12–14)[5]. Wer war dieser scharfe Kriti-

5. Daß es sich bei Koh 12,12–14 um eine redaktionelle Schlußbemerkung orthodoxen
Charakters handelt, ist, von wenigen Ausnahmen abgesehen, eine *opinio communis* der
Kohelet-Forschung und bedarf daher hier keiner ausführlichen Begründung. Zur Sache
s. u.a. E. PODECHARD, *L'Ecclésiaste*, Paris, Librairie Victor Lecoffre, 1912, pp. 150–
170.472; R. KROEBER, *Der Prediger. Hebräisch und Deutsch* (Schriften und Quellen der
Alten Welt, 13), Berlin, Akademie Verlag, 1963, pp. 38.157f.; M. HENGEL, *Judentum und
Hellenismus. Studien zu ihrer Begegnung unter besonderer Berücksichtigung Palästinas bis
zur Mitte des 2.Jh.s v.Chr.* (Wissenschaftliche Untersuchungen zum Neuen Testament, 10),
2. Aufl., Tübingen, J.C.B. Mohr (Paul Siebeck), 1973, pp. 235f.; R. BRAUN, *Kohelet und
die frühhellenistische Popularphilosophie* (BZAW, 130), Berlin/New York, Walter de
Gruyter, 1973, p. 145; A. LAUHA, *Kohelet* (BKAT, 19), Neukirchen-Vluyn, Neukirchner
Verlag, 1978, pp. 222f.; W. ZIMMERLI, *Das Buch des Predigers Salomo. Übersetzt und er-
klärt*, in H. RINGGREN & W. ZIMMERLI, *Sprüche/Prediger. Übersetzt und erklärt* (ATD,
16.1), 3. Aufl., Göttingen, Vandenhoek & Ruprecht, 1980, pp. 121–249, pp. 123.135.246f.;
G.T. SHEPPARD, *Wisdom as a Hermeneutical Construct. A Study in the Sapientializing of the
Old Testament* (BZAW, 151), Berlin/New York, Walter de Gruyter, 1980, pp. 121f.; N.
LOHFINK, *Kohelet* (NEB), Würzburg, Echter Verlag, 1980, pp. 13f.86; J.L. CRENSHAW,
Ecclesiastes. A Commentary (OTL), London, SCM Press, 1988, pp. 24.48.189–191; D. MI-
CHEL, *Qohelet* (EdF, 258), Darmstadt, Wissenschaftliche Buchgesellschaft, 1988, pp. 117f.;
ID., *Untersuchungen zur Eigenart des Buches Qohelet* (BZAW, 183), Berlin/New York,
Walter de Gruyter, 1989, pp. 268f.275; L. SCHWIENHORST-SCHÖNBERGER, *Nicht im Men-
schen gründet das Glück (Koh 2,24). Kohelet im Spannungsfeld jüdischer Weisheit und hel-
lenistischer Philosophie* (HBS, 2), 2. Aufl., Freiburg et al., Herder, 1996, p. 10; F.J.
BACKHAUS, *»Denn Zeit und Zufall trifft sie alle«. Zu Komposition und Gottesbild im Buch
Qohelet* (BBB, 83), Frankfurt a.M., Anton Hain, 1993, pp. 344–351; ID., *Der Weisheit letz-
ter Schluß! Qoh 12,9–14 im Kontext von Traditionsgeschichte und beginnender
Kanonisierung*, in *Biblische Notizen* 72 (1994) pp. 28–59; O. KAISER, *Botschaft*, pp. 62–66.
H.W. HERTZBERG (*Der Prediger* [KAT, 17.4], Gütersloh, Gütersloher Verlagshaus
Gerd Mohn, 1963, pp. 41f.) möchte in Koh 12,9–14 drei Redaktoren am Werk sehen (cf.
O. EISSFELDT, *Einleitung in das Alte Testament unter Einschluß der Apokryphen und
Pseudepigraphen sowie der apokryphen- und pseudepigraphenartigen Qumrān-Schriften*,
3. Aufl., Tübingen, J.C.B. Mohr [Paul Siebeck], 1964, p. 677), und M. JASTROW spricht
von nicht weniger als acht Redaktoren (*A Gentle Cynic. Being a Translation of the Book
of Kohelet Commonly Known as Ecclesiastes Stripped of Later Additions Also its
Growths and Interpretation*, Philadelphia, J.B. Lippencott Co., 1919, pp. 71ff.). Was die
redaktionelle Überarbeitung des Buches Kohelet angeht, ist C.L. SEOW am zurück-
haltendsten (*Ecclesiastes. A New Translation with Introduction and Commentary* [AB,
18C], New York et al., Doubleday, 1997): Für ihn sind die Worte סוֹף דָּבָר הַכֹּל נִשְׁמָע ein
»closing formula« (p. 390). »... we have a call to obey God's commandments and an
allusion to eschatological judgment – both new elements in the book. Indeed, 12:13a
sounds decisively final: «end of matter; everything has been heard.» This may have been
the original ending of the book to which an additional text (12:13b–14) was tacked on«
(p. 38; cf. pp. 390.394–396). Laut A.A. FISCHER (*Skepsis oder Furcht Gottes? Studien
zur Komposition und Theologie des Buches Kohelet* [BZAW, 247], Berlin/New York,
Walter de Gruyter, 1997, p. 21 Anm. 78) hat den sekundären Charakter von Koh 12,9–14
als erster J.C. DÖDERLEIN erkannt (*Salomons Prediger und Hoheslied neu übersetzt mit
kurzen erläuternden Anmerkungen*, Jena 1784, p. 161).

ker? Wie lautete seine Alternative zum Denken Kohelets? Kann man über die wenigen Zeilen der zweiten Redaktion hinaus mehr von ihm wissen? Ausgangspunkt zur Beantwortung dieser Fragen muß sicherlich die zweite Redaktion selbst sein:

Neben polemischen Sätzen gibt sie auch darüber Auskunft, was ihr theologisch wesentlich ist:

סוֹף דָּבָר הַכֹּל נִשְׁמָע אֶת הָאֱלֹהִים יְרָא וְאֶת מִצְוֹתָיו שְׁמוֹר כִּי זֶה כָּל הָאָדָם כִּי
אֵת כָּל מַעֲשֶׂה הָאֱלֹהִים יָבֹא בְמִשְׁפָּט עַל כָּל נֶעְלָם אִם טוֹב וְאִם רָע

»Am Ende des Wortes wird das Wesentliche vernommen:
Gott fürchte und seine Gebote beachte.
Wahrlich, dies gilt jedem Menschen,
daß Gott jedes Werk ins Gericht bringt.
Über alles Verborgene ergeht es, sei es gut oder böse.

Zweierlei ist demnach für den zweiten Redaktor zentral: die sich in Gebotsobservanz realisierende Gottesfurcht und die Gewißheit eines allumfassenden göttlichen Gerichts.

Die Wendung שמר מצוה fordert in Spr 4,4; 7,1f.; 19,16 zur Beachtung des Gebots des Weisheitslehrers auf[6] und kann sich in 1 Kön 2,43 auf

---

Für jene Exegeten, die Koh 12,9–14 heute noch als eine einheitliche Redaktion betrachten, sei stellvertretend G. OGDEN genannt (*Qoheleth* [Readings–A New Biblical Commentary], Sheffield, JSOT Press, 1987, p. 16f.; cf. R.E. MURPHY, *Ecclesiastes* [WBC, 23A], Dallas, Word Books, 1992, pp. XXXIII.126–130): »The purpose of the Epilogue then is clear. It is not an orthodox «corrective» to Qohelet's work to bring it into line with acceptable theology. Qoheleth, according to the commendation of the Editor, already stands within the broad theological parameters of the pluriform Judaism of the post-Exilic period. The Editor has recognized that, and his purpose in adding these two notes is none other than to commend it to others, perhaps in particular to his own students« (OGDEN, p. 213). Für ursprünglich werden die Verse Koh 12,9-14 dagegen von M.V. FOX gehalten (*Frame-Narrative and Composition in the Book of Qohelet*, in HUCA 48 [1977] pp. 83–106; *Qohelet and his Contradictions* [JSOT SS, 71], Sheffield, Sheffield Academic Press, 1989, pp. 311–329; cf. C.L. SEOW, pp. 38ff.391–394 [unter Ausschluß von Koh 12,13b–14]): »I suggest that all of 1:2–12:14 is by the same hand – not that the epilogue is by Qohelet, but that *Qohelet* is «by» the epilogist. In other words, the speaker we hear from time to time in the background saying «Qohelet said» ... is the teller of the tale, the external narrator of the «story» of Qohelet« (*Frame-Narrative*, p. 91).

Auf eine semantische Besonderheit, die den eigenständigen Charakter von Koh 12,12–14 noch unterstreicht und in der Diskussion bislang unberücksichtigt geblieben ist, hat A. SCHOORS aufmerksam gemacht (*The Preacher Sought to Find Pleasing Words. A Study of the Language of Qoheleth*, Teil 1: *Grammar* [OLA, 41], Leuven, Peeters Press/Department of Orientalistiek, 1992, p. 62): »The feminine form *qᵉtīlā* is very common in MH as a *nomen actionis* for the qal, but in BH it is very rare as a verbal substantive, both in early and in late texts. The only attestation of it in Qoh is יְגִעָה, «weariness» [12,12].«

6. Zu מצוה in Spr 19,16 als Bezeichnung für »das Wort des Weisheitslehrers« s. u.a. H. RINGGREN, *Sprüche. Übersetzt und erklärt*, in H. RINGGREN & W. ZIMMERLI, *Sprüche/Prediger. Übersetzt und erklärt* (ATD, 16.1), 3. Aufl., Göttingen, Vandenhoek & Ruprecht, 1980, pp. 1–120, p. 79; O. PLÖGER *Sprüche Salomos (Proverbia)* (BKAT, 17), Neukirchen-Vluyn, Neukirchner Verlag, 1984, p. 224 und A. MEINHOLD, *Die Sprüche*, Teil 1–2 (Züricher Bibelkommentare, AT 16.1–2), Zürich, Theologischer Verlag Zürich, 1991, p. 319.

einen Befehl Salomos beziehen. In hellenistischer Zeit meint sie jedoch ausschließlich die Observanz gegenüber dem am Sinai gegebenen Gebot Gottes (cf. u.a. Sir 15,15; 32,22 [35,27]; 37,12; 44,20a; 1QH^a XVI$_{13.17}$; 1QSb I$_1$; CD II$_{18}$; III$_2$; XIX$_2$; 1QpHab V$_5$)[7]. Das sich auf das vorhergehende האלהים beziehende Suffix der 3. Pers. sing. (»seine [= Gottes] Gebote«) zeigt, daß die Wendung שמר מצוה auch in Koh 12,13 entsprechend gebraucht wird[8].

Mit dem Stichwort Gottesfurcht nimmt der zweite Redaktor ein im Buch Kohelet mehrfach belegtes Thema auf. In Koh 3,14 ist die Aufforderung zur Gottesfurcht Konsequenz der im vorhergehenden dargelegten Erkenntnisunfähigkeit des Menschen und der daraus resultierenden Unberechenbarkeit Gottes. Gerade weil es einen Gott gibt, sein Handeln aber dem Menschen intransparent bleibt, gilt es ihn zu fürchten. Dem entspricht Koh 5,6: Wenn man zum Hause Gottes geht, gilt es, Vorsicht zu wahren (4,17)[9]. Besser als das Opfer der Toren ist nicht das Opfer des Gerechten, sondern nahe zu treten und zu hören (4,17). Beim Gebet soll man sich nicht übereilen, »etwas vor Gott zu reden«, denn dieser ist im Himmel, der Beter aber auf der Erde (5,1–2). Gelübde sind ohne Verzug zu erfüllen, doch besser ist es, Gott nichts zu geloben, denn ob es als שְׁגָגָה (unwissentlich begangene Sünde) anerkannt wird, muß fraglich bleiben (5,3–6). Da Gott auf diese Weise als ferne, unberechenbare und dem Menschen entrückte Macht dargestellt wird, kann das zusammenfassende »wahrlich Gott sollst du fürchten« (5,6) nicht als ein aus der Gottesbeziehung resultierendes ethisches Handeln verstanden werden, sondern nur als Gottesangst, die dazu auffordert, im Angesicht Gottes möglichst unauffällig zu bleiben[10]. Diese Einstellung spricht auch aus 7,16–18:

> »Sei nicht sehr gerecht und werde nicht sehr weise, warum willst du dich zugrunde richten. Frevele nicht viel und sei kein Tor. Warum willst du vor deiner Zeit sterben? Es ist gut, an dem einen festzuhalten, und auch von dem anderen deine Hand nicht zu lassen, denn wer Gott fürchtet, entgeht allen beiden.«

Wiederum realisiert sich Gottesfurcht nicht in weisem und gerechtem Handeln. Vor Gott gilt es, das eine zu tun und das andere nicht zu lassen. Weil Kohelets ferner Gott undurchschaubar ist, empfiehlt es sich,

---

7. Zu Koh 8,5 s.u., p. 118.
8. Zu Koh 12,13 als Aufforderung zur Observanz gegenüber dem Sinaigesetz s. schon J. FICHTNER, *Die altorientalische Weisheit in ihrer israelitisch-jüdischen Ausprägung. Eine Studie zur Nationalisierung der Weisheit in Israel* (BZAW, 62), Gießen, Alfred Töpelmann, 1933, pp. 89f.; cf. u.a. A. LAUHA, p. 223.
9. Zu שְׁמֹר רַגְלֶיךָ als Mahnung zur Vorsicht s.u., p. 151 Anm. 129.
10. Zu Koh 4,17–5,6 s.u., pp. 150ff.

ein bißchen zu sündigen und ein bißchen gerecht zu sein. Auch der Beleg Koh 8,12 widerspricht diesem Verständnis der Gottesfurcht bei Koh nur scheinbar. Koh zitiert hier die weisheitliche Lehrmeinung[11]: »obwohl auch ich weiß, daß den Gottesfürchtigen Gutes entsteht, weil sie sich vor ihm fürchten, aber dem Frevler nichts Gutes und ihm die Tage nicht lang werden wie der Schatten, weil er keine Furcht vor Gott hat« (8,12f.). Im Kontext stellt Koh dem seine eigene Sicht der Dinge gegenüber: Den Frevlern geht es gut und sie leben lange (8,9–11). Absurderweise (הבל)[12] ergeht es den Gerechten nach den Werken der Frevler und den Frevlern nach den Werken der Gerechten (8,14). Das Fazit ist wohl bekannt: »Und ich sprach: Auch dies ist absurd«[13].

Der zweite Redaktor will dieses Verständnis von Gottesfurcht offensichtlich revidieren. Gottesfurcht realisiert sich für ihn in der Erfüllung der am Sinai gegebenen Gebote. Sie ist nicht das-Gute-Tun-und-das-Böse-nicht-Lassen, sondern ist ausschließlich auf die Erfüllung des in der Tora formulierten Willen Gottes ausgerichtet[14]. Diese Position artikuliert der zweite Redaktor nicht nur am Schluß des Buches, sondern trägt sie auch in den Text selbst ein.

11. K. GALLING (*Der Prediger*, in E. WÜRTHWEIN ET AL., *Die fünf Megilloth* [HAT, 18], 2. Aufl., Tübingen, J.C.B. Mohr [Paul Siebeck], 1969, pp. 111f.), A. LAUHA (p. 157) und C. KLEIN (*Kohelet und die Weisheit Israels. Eine formgeschichtliche Studie* [BWANT, 132], Stuttgart et al., W. Kohlhammer, 1994, p. 115 Anm. 10) möchten in Koh 8,12b–13 einen dem zweiten Redaktor zuzuweisenden »orthodoxen Protest« (A. LAUHA, p. 157) gegen die Ausführungen Kohelets sehen. Demgegenüber ist darauf hinzuweisen, daß Kohelet ידע an dieser Stelle – anders als sonst, wenn er eigene Erkenntnisse referiert – nicht als Perfekt sondern als Partizip bildet. Es geht nicht um das Ergebnis eines eigenen Erkenntnisprozesses, sondern um das Wissen einer landläufigen Meinung. Die Wendung כִּי גַּם־יוֹדֵעַ אָנִי weist Koh 8,12b–13 somit als Referat einer weisheitlichen Lehrmeinung aus (cf. u.a. H.W. HERTZBERG, p. 174; ZIMMERLI, p. 216; N. LOHFINK, p. 62; D. MICHEL, *Untersuchungen*, p. 196; R.E. MURPHY, p. 85; L. SCHWIENHORST-SCHÖNBERGER, p. 189; C.L. SEOW, pp. 288.294f.).

12. Zur Übersetzung von הבל mit »absurd« im Sinne des Camus'schen Absurditätsbegriffs s. D. MICHEL, *Humanität angesichts des Absurden. Qohelet (Prediger) 1,2–3,15*, in H. FÖRSTER (ed.), *Humanität heute*, Berlin, 1970, pp. 22–36; ID., *Qohelet*, p. 86; ID., *Untersuchungen*, pp. 40–51.280 und M.V. FOX, *The Meaning of HEBEL for Qohelet*, in *JBL* 105 (1986) 409–427; ID., *Contradictions*, pp. 29–48.

13. Zur Gottesfurcht bei Koh s. H.-J. BLIEFFERT, *Weltanschauung und Gottesglaube im Buche Kohelet*. Darstellung und Kritik, Diss., Rostock, 1938; E. PFEIFFER, *Die Gottesfurcht im Buche Kohelet*, in H. GRAF REVENTLOW (ed.), *Gottes Wort und Gottes Land*. FS H.W. Hertzberg, Göttingen, Vandenhoeck & Ruprecht, 1965, pp. 133–158; H.-P. MÜLLER, *Wie sprach Qohälät von Gott?*, in *VT* 18 (1968) 507–521, pp. 515f.; D. MICHEL, *Vom Gott, der im Himmel ist (Reden von Gott bei Qohelet) (1)*, in *Theologia Viatorum. Jahrbuch der Kirchlichen Hochschule Berlin* 12 (1973/1974) 87–101, p. 97; ID., »*Unter der Sonne*«. Zur Immanenz bei Qohelet, im vorliegenden Band, pp. 93–111; L.G. PERDUE, *Wisdom and Cult. A Critical Analysis of the Views of Cult in the Wisdom Literatures of Israel and the Ancient Near East* (SBLDS, 30), Missoula, Scholars Press, 1977, p. 180; C. KLEIN, p. 201.

14. Cf. F.J. BACKHAUS, *Zeit und Zufall*, p. 349; ID., *Weisheit*, p. 37f.

Nachdem in Koh 8,2–4 ganz im Sinne von Koh 5,3–6 ausgeführt wurde, man solle sich beim Gotteseid verhalten wie beim Wort eines mächtigen unberechenbaren Königs, thematisiert Koh 8,5 das Halten des Gebots. Die Wendung מצוה שמר kann sich nicht auf den im vorhergehenden genannten Befehl des Königs beziehen[15], da sie – wie oben gezeigt (s.o., pp. 115f.) – in hellenistischer Zeit nur bezüglich des sich im Sinaigesetz artikulierenden Gebots belegt ist. Es kommt zu einem inhaltlichen Bruch: Während die vorhergehende Verse Gott, bei dem ein Eid geschworen wird, mit einem unberechenbaren König vergleichen, hat Koh 8,5f. die unbedingte Gebotsobservanz zum Gegenstand. Erst in Koh 8,7f. wird die Argumentation aus 8,2–4 fortgeführt. Dabei knüpft die Feststellung, daß kein Mensch über den Wind oder über den Tag seines Todes Macht hat (שליט und שלטון), an das Motiv von der Macht des Königs (שלטון) in Koh 8,4 an. Koh 8,7 ist durch Form (אין-Spruch) und Inhalt (niemand kennt seine Zukunft) untrennbar mit 8,8 verknüpft.

W. ZIMMERLI möchte in Koh 8,5 eine von Koh aufgenommene und Spr 19,16 entsprechende weisheitliche Tradition finden[16]. Demgegenüber fällt die sorgfältige sprachliche Verknüpfung von Koh 8,5f. mit dem unmittelbaren Kontext auf: שׁוֹמֵר (Koh 8,5) hat sein sprachliches Pendant in שְׁמוֹר (Koh 8,2), während sich דְּבַר רָע (Koh 8,5) wörtlich in Koh 8,3 findet und חֵפֶץ (Koh 8,6) das יַחְפֹּץ aus Koh 8,3 aufnimmt. Eine sprachliche Verknüpfung zum folgenden Kontext leistet das doppelte יָדַע in Koh 8,5 (cf. יֹדֵעַ; Koh 8,7). Diese sorgfältige Verknüpfung mit dem Kontext entspricht in keiner Weise der Art, wie Koh weisheitliche Tradition zitiert. Er achtet im Gegenteil darauf, daß ein Zitat sich sprachlich und formal deutlich von seinem Kontext unterscheidet und leitet es gegebenenfalls mit einer Zitationsformel ein.

Bei den Versen Koh 8,5f. handelt es sich somit um das Ergebnis einer sprachlich kunstvollen und auf hohem Niveau durchgeführten Redaktion[17]. Ausweislich der auch in Koh 12,13 belegten Wendung מצוה שמר dürfte sie dem zweiten Redaktor zuzuschreiben sein. Gott wird im vorhergehenden Kontext (Koh 8,2–4) mit einem machtvollen und willkürli-

---

15. Gegen L. LEVY, *Das Buch Qoheleth. Ein Beitrag zur Geschichte des Sadduzäismus*, Leipzig, J.C. Hinrichs'sche Buchhandlung, 1912, p. 113; W. IRWIN, *Ecclesiastes 8:2–9*, in *Journal of Near Eastern Studies* 4 (1945) 130–131, p. 130; H.W. HERTZBERG, p. 165; J.L. CRENSHAW, p. 151; G. OGDEN, p. 130; M.V. FOX, *Contradictions*, p. 247; A. LANGE, *Weisheit und Torheit bei Kohelet und in seiner Umwelt. Eine Untersuchung ihrer theologischen Implikationen* (EurHS. 23: Theologie, 433), Frankfurt a.M. et al., Peter Lang, 1991, p. 162; C.L. SEOW, pp. 281.292.

16. P. 213; cf. J.L. CRENSHAW, p. 151; D. MICHEL, *Untersuchungen*, pp. 96–99 und A. FISCHER, p. 222.

17. Koh 8,5 wird auch von K. GALLING (p. 110) für eine Glosse des zweiten Redaktors gehalten (cf. A. LAUHA, p. 149).

chen König verglichen. Die Ausführungen über das menschliche Unwissen und das Ergehen von Frevler und Gerechtem gipfeln im folgenden Kontext in einem verhaltenen Votum für die törichte Lebensfreude
(Koh 8,15) und der resignierten Feststellung menschlicher Erkenntnisunfähigkeit (Koh 8,16f.). Demgegenüber will der zweite Redaktor zeigen, daß es eine klare Richtschnur für das menschliche Handeln gibt,
nämlich das am Sinai offenbarte Gebot Gottes: »Wer das Gebot Gottes
beachtet, erfährt nichts Böses, aber ein weises Herz erkennt Zeitpunkt
und *mišpāt*, denn für jedes Ding gibt es Zeit und *mišpāt*. Wahrlich das
Böse des Menschen lastet schwer auf ihm.« מִשְׁפָּט ist wegen seiner hier
bewußt eingesetzten Vieldeutigkeit nicht übersetzbar: Das vorhergehende עֵת einerseits nimmt das Gedicht über die Zeiten aus Koh 3,1–8 auf
und verbindet מִשְׁפָּט so mit dem Gedanken einer weisheitlichen Urordnung. – Die Zusammenstellung von עֵת und מִשְׁפָּט erinnert an Jer 8,7, wo
das Heimkehren der Zugvögel zum ihnen bestimmten Zeitpunkt (עֵת) der
Unkenntnis des Volkes Israel von Jahwes Ordnung (מִשְׁפָּט) gegenübergestellt wird. – Das einleitende שׁוֹמֵר מִצְוָה andererseits stellt מִשְׁפָּט in den
Schatten des Sinaigesetzes. Auf diese Weise wird gesagt, es gibt eine
von Gott festgesetzte Ordnung der Welt. Sie ist dem Weisen in Form des
Sinaigebotes zugänglich. Daher kann erkannt werden: Das Böse lastet
schwer auf ihm und wird bestraft.

Dementsprechend ist das Ergehen des Frevlers das zweite Anliegen
des Schlußredaktors:

כִּי זֶה כָּל הָאָדָם כִּי אֶת כָּל מַעֲשֶׂה הָאֱלֹהִים יָבָא בְמִשְׁפָּט עַל כָּל נֶעְלָם אִם טוֹב
וְאִם רָע

»Wahrlich, dies gilt jedem Menschen,
daß Gott jedes Werk ins Gericht bringt.
Über alles Verborgene ergeht es, sei es gut oder böse.« (Koh 12,13b–14)

Die Wendung הביא משפט (Hiob 14,3) bzw. בוא משפט (Jes 3,14; Ps
143,2; Hiob 9,32; 22,4) trägt juridische Konnotationen und beschreibt
einen Gang Gottes mit den Ältesten seines Volkes, mit David oder
Hiob ins Gericht. Hiob 9,32 spricht andererseits von der Unfähigkeit
Hiobs, mit Gott ins Gericht zu ziehen. Mit diesen Belegen verglichen
ist Koh 12,14 wesentlich allgemeiner formuliert. Hier gilt das Gericht
nicht einer einzelnen Person oder Gruppe sondern allem Verborgenen.
Während die biblischen Belege sämtlich mit soziativen Präpositionen
konstruiert werden (אֶת [Ps 143,2], יַחְדָּו [Hiob 9,32], עִם [Jes 3,14; Hiob
14,3; 22,4]), findet sich in Koh 12,14 die *nota accusativi* (cf. das
Objektsuffix in Koh 11,9c). Der allgemeinere Charakter des Gerichts,
die veränderte Semantik der Wendung הביא משפט und das futurisch zu

interpretierende Imperfekt יָבֹא machen es wahrscheinlich, daß מִשְׁפָּט »hier schon in der Weise eines Endgerichtes« über das ganze Leben gemeint ist[18].

Auf welche Taten diese Gerichtsandrohung besonders bezogen ist, wird in Koh 11,9c deutlich:

וְדָע כִּי עַל־כָּל־אֵלֶּה יְבִיאֲךָ הָאֱלֹהִים בַּמִּשְׁפָּט

»und erkenne, daß Gott dich wegen all diesem ins Gericht bringen wird«

Auch dieser Vers ist nach der *opinio communis* sekundär und dem zweiten Redaktor zuzuschreiben[19]. Im seinem unmittelbaren Kontext fordert Koh zu ungebremstem Lebensgenuß in der Jugend auf (Koh 11,9f.). Was danach kommt, stehe unter dem Schatten von Alter und Tod (Koh 12,1–7). Dem setzt der zweite Redaktor die im Kontext von Koh 12,14 wohl eschatologisch zu verstehende Warnung entgegen, Gott werde den Jugendlichen »um all dieser Dinge willen ins Gericht bringen.« Daß der zweite Redaktor die Glosse im Zentrum der letzten Aufforderung Kohelets zur Lebensfreude plaziert, gibt ihr über den konkreten Kontext hinaus Geltung. Nicht nur die Spitzenaussagen von Koh 11,9f. werden unter den Schatten des eschatologischen Gerichts gestellt, das Verdikt gilt der ganzen von Koh mühsam erkämpften, aber immer noch verhaltenen und gebrochenen Option für die Lebensfreude.

In der Forschungsgeschichte wurden dem zweiten Redaktor häufig weit mehr Verse zugeordnet: Als Beispiele aus der neueren Literatur seien hier K. GALLING (zusätzlich zu Koh 11,9c; 12,12–14 noch 1,1b; 3,17aβ; 8,5.12bf.; 9,3b; 11,10b–12,1a; p. 76.84.113); A. LAUHA (zusätzlich zu Koh 11,9c; 12,12–14 noch Koh 2,26a.bα; 3,17; 5,18; 7,26b; 8,12b.13; p. 7), O. KAISER (zusätzlich zu Koh 11,9c; 12,12–14 noch

---

18. W. ZIMMERLI, p. 240. Zur eschatologischen Interpretation von Koh 12,14 cf. u.a., *op. cit.*, p. 246f.; A. LAUHA, p. 223; O. KAISER, *Botschaft*, p. 66; C.L. SEOW, pp. 38.395.

19. Zur Sache s. u.a. K. GALLING, p. 121; R. KROEBER, pp. 38.158; M. HENGEL, p. 235; W. ZIMMERLI, pp. 238.240; A. LAUHA, pp. 205.209; J.L. CRENSHAW, p. 184; D. MICHEL, *Qohelet*, pp. 166f.; C. KLEIN, p. 151; L. SCHWIENHORST-SCHÖNBERGER, p. 226; A.A. FISCHER, pp. 20.35. Anders H.W. HERTZBERG, pp. 208f.; R.E. MURPHY, p. 117; T. KRÜGER, *Dekonstruktion und Rekonstruktion prophetischer Eschatologie im Qohelet-Buch*, in A.A. DIESEL ET AL., *»Jedes Ding hat seine Zeit ...«. Studien zur israelitischen und altorientalischen Weisheit*. FS D. Michel (BZAW, 241), Berlin/New York, Walter de Gruyter, 1996, pp. 107–129, p. 116; ID., *Die Rezeption der Tora im Buch Kohelet*, in L. SCHWIENHORST-SCHÖNBERGER (ed.), *Das Buch Kohelet. Studien zur Struktur, Geschichte, Rezeption und Theologie* (BZAW, 254), Berlin/New York, Walter de Gruyter, 1997, pp. 303–325, p. 309; C.L. SEOW, pp. 40.350.371, die 11,9c u.a. unter Hinweis auf Koh 3,17; 8,5f. mit dem Rest des Buches für vereinbar halten. Zu Koh 8,5f. als Einfügung des zweiten Redaktors s.o., pp. 118f. Zu Koh 3,17 als zitierter Lehrmeinung s.u., p. 122.

Koh 3,17; 7,27aα; 11,9b.10b und 12,1)[20] und A. FISCHER (zusätzlich zu Koh 11,9c; 12,12–14 noch Koh 3,17; 6,10; 8,8b; 9,3b; pp. 20[Anm. 76].35.160[Anm. 558]) genannt[21]. Solche Versuche, einzelne Verse des Buches Kohelet, teilweise nur aus inhaltlichen Gründen, dem zweiten Redaktor als einem orthodoxen Überarbeiter zuzuweisen, begegnen zwei Schwierigkeiten: Zum einen rühren, wie M.V. FOX gezeigt hat, die inneren Widersprüche des Buches Kohelet aus der Wirklichkeitswahrnehmung seines Verfassers her.

> »As I see it, Qohelet's contradictions state the problems rather than resolving them, and the interpreter likewise must leave many of the observations in tension. Qohelet does not, however, embrace the contradictions as paradoxes that, like Zen koans, can give enlightenment in the inexpressible. He sees paradoxes in the truths he discovers, but they are a dead-end road. He observes them, insists on them, then moves on. Never does he suggest that meditation on them gives new types of insight into God's nature«[22].

Zum anderen versteht es der zweite Redaktor, wie die Analyse von Koh 8,5f. gezeigt hat, sich sprachlich gut an das Buch Kohelet anzupassen[23].

---

20. *Grundriß der Einleitung in die kanonischen und deuterokanonischen Schriften des Alten Testaments*, Bd. 3: *Die poetischen und weisheitlichen Werke*, Gütersloh, Gütersloher Verlagshaus, 1994, p. 86.

21. Auf die ältere literarkritische Diskussion (zur Sache s. die Referate bei D. MICHEL, *Qohelet*, pp. 17–21 und H.W. HERTZBERG, pp. 39–42) braucht hier nicht eingegangen zu werden. Ihre Bemühungen, die inneren Widersprüche des Buches Kohelet auf eine unterschiedliche Anzahl von Redaktionen zurückzuführen, verkennen seinen Charakter. D. MICHEL stellt zu Recht fest: »Der Versuch, mit Hilfe der Literarkritik die Schwierigkeiten des Buches Qohelet zu lösen, hat sich totgelaufen – er wird heute von keinem der maßgeblichen Exegeten mehr vertreten« (*Qohelet*, pp. 20f.; zur Sache cf. z.B. auch O. KAISER, *Einleitung in das Alte Testament. Eine Einführung in ihre Ergebnisse und Probleme*, 5. Aufl., Gütersloh, Gütersloher Verlagshaus, 1984, p. 397). Hinzuweisen ist noch auf neuere Versuche, Koh als das Ergebnis einer sekundären Zusammenstellung ursprünglich genuiner Kohelet-Texte zu verstehen (R.N. WHYBRAY, *Ecclesiastes* [Old Testament Guides], Sheffield, Sheffield Academic Press, 1989, p. 40; A.A. FISCHER, pp. 5–55). M.V. FOX (*Frame-Narrative*, passim und *Contradictions*, pp. 311–321) geht noch einen Schritt weiter und sieht das gesamte Buch Kohelet als Wiedergabe der Lehren Kohelets durch den Epilogisten an seine Schüler: »This narrator looks back and, using the common stance of wisdom teacher, tells his son about the sage Qohelet, transmitting to him Qohelet's teachings, then appreciatively but cautiously evaluating the work of Qohelet and other sages. The body of the book is formally a long quotation of Qohelet' words« (*Contradictions*, p. 311). Zur Diskussion neuerer literarkritischer Ansätze zum Buch Kohelet s. F.J. BACKHAUS, *Widersprüche und Spannungen im Buch Qohelet. Zu einem neueren Versuch, Spannungen und Widersprüche literarkritisch zu lösen*, in L. SCHWIENHORST-SCHÖNBERGER (ed.), *Das Buch Kohelet. Studien zur Struktur, Geschichte, Rezeption und Theologie* (BZAW, 254), Berlin/New York, Walter de Gruyter, 1997, pp. 123–154.

22. *Contradictions*, p. 11; cf. J.A. LOADER, *Polar Structures in the Book of Qohelet* (BZAW, 152), Berlin/New York, Walter de Gruyter, 1979, pp. 29ff. und R.N. WHYBRAY, p. 26.

23. Zur Sache cf. G.T. SHEPPARD, pp. 124f.; L. SCHWIENHORST-SCHÖNBERGER, p. 10.

Daher erscheint es mir nur dann gerechtfertigt, Texte für die Interpretation der zweiten Redaktion heranzuziehen, wenn sie sich aus sprachlichen und formalen Gründen als sekundär ausweisen und sie in Vokabular und Motivik direkte Bezüge zu Koh 12,12–14 besitzen (z.B. die Wendungen שמר מצוה und יביא במשפט in Koh 8,5; 11,9c).

Von den oben genannten Stellen weisen lediglich Koh 3,17 und 8,12b.13 solche Bezüge auf[24]. Wie schon gezeigt wurde (s.o., p. 117), handelt es sich bei Koh 8,12b.13 um das Referat einer weisheitlichen Lehrmeinung. Zur Bewertung von Koh 3,17[25] kann auf L. SCHWIENHORST-SCHÖNBERGER verwiesen werden. Er sieht in dem vorhergehenden Vers 16b »eine von Kohelet zitierte Meinung« (p. 116), die betont, daß Gottes Gericht dem Frevel gilt: »an den Ort des Gerichts – dorthin muß der Frevel, und an den Ort der Gerechtigkeit – dorthin muß der Frevel«[26]. Koh 3,17 betont demgegenüber »daß sich das göttliche Endgericht nicht nur auf die Frevler, sondern auch auf die Gerechten erstreckt und sich damit der im Zitat 3,16b implizit unterstellte Unterschied von Frevlern und Gerechten aufhebt.«[27] Schwierig scheint mir lediglich L. SCHWIEN-HORST-SCHÖNBERGERS Interpretation auf das eschatologische Gericht. Der Vers Koh 3,17 dürfte eher – ähnlich Sir 16,12 und Ps 1,5 – das gegenwärtig ergehende Gericht meinen[28].

Der zweite Redaktor widerspricht somit zwei wesentlichen Themen des Buches Kohelet. Die von Koh angesichts eines fernen und willkürlichen Gottes angenommene Intransparenz des Seins gegenüber der ihm zugrundeliegenden sinnstiftenden Ordnung gibt es nicht. Die von Gott gestiftete weisheitliche Ordnung der Welt ist für den Weisen in der Tora erkennbar[29]. Ihrem Gebot gilt es gottesfürchtig zu folgen. Während Koh angesichts eines unberechenbaren Gottes dazu auffordert, die Lebens-

---

24. Zu den von D. MICHEL (*Qohelet*, p. 143; *Untersuchungen*, p. 257; cf. M. JASTROW, p. 217 und C.F. WHITLEY, *Kohelet. His Language and Thought* [BZAW, 148], Berlin/New York, Walter de Gruyter, 1978, pp. 49f.) dem zweiten Redaktor zugewiesenen Versen Koh 5,5.6b s.u., pp. 155 Anm. 148. 157 Anm. 152.

25. Zu Koh 3,17 als orthodoxer Glosse des zweiten Redaktors cf. auch W. ZIMMERLI, p. 171; D. MICHEL, *Qohelet*, p. 138; J.L. CRENSHAW, p. 102 (ohne den Vers dem zweiten Redaktor zuzuweisen).

26. Zur Übersetzung cf. D. MICHEL, *Qohelet*, p. 138

27. L. SCHWIENHORST-SCHÖNBERGER, p. 117; zur Sache s. *op. cit.*, pp. 115–118.

28. Zur nichteschatologischen Interpretation von Koh 3,17 cf. u.a. H.W. HERTZBERG, p. 110; R.E. MURPHY, p. 36 und C.L. SEOW, pp. 166.175.

29. T. KRÜGERS (*Rezeption der Tora*, pp. 303–306) Vorschlag, »die Mahnung Gott zu fürchten und seine Gebote zu halten, [nicht] als Fazit ... des Koheletbuches, sondern der ebenso zahlreichen wie (nach V. 12) ermüdenden religiösen Literatur seiner Zeit« zu verstehen, und nicht das Buch Kohelet, sondern eben diese Literatur angegriffen zu sehen, darf angesichts der bewußt gesetzten Bezüge der zweiten Redaktion zum Buch Kohelet als widerlegt gelten.

freude immer dann zu ergreifen, wenn sie sich dem Menschen ergibt, unterliegt für den zweiten Redaktor alles Tun des Menschen und damit auch die Lebensfreude dem eschatologischen Gericht. Den Kern weisheitlichen Gedankenguts bilden für ihn somit die Tora und das eschatologische Gericht.

Erste Hinweise, wo dieser durch Eschatologie und eine Verbindung von Weisheit und Tora charakterisierte zweite Redaktor möglicherweise zu lokalisieren ist, können aus der frühen Kohelet-Rezeption gewonnen werden. Paulus ist hierbei nicht nur deshalb von Bedeutung, weil er Verse aus dem von Koh selbst verfaßten Text aufnimmt (Koh 7,20 in Röm 3,10 und die *hæbæl*-Aussage aus Koh 1,2 u.ö. in Röm 8,20), sondern auch, weil 2 Kor 5,10 der älteste erhaltene Beleg für eine Verarbeitung der zweite Redaktion des Koheletbuches ist (Koh 12,14)[30]. Diese muß somit vor dem Wirken des Paulus erfolgt sein. Spätere Texte bleiben daher im folgenden unberücksichtigt[31].

Vorpaulinische Rezeptionen des Koheletbuches sind denkbar selten. H.C. KEE verweist in seiner Übersetzung der TestXII bei TestNaph 8,8 auf Koh 3,5[32]:

עֵת לַחֲבוֹק וְעֵת לִרְחֹק מֵחַבֵּק

»Es gibt eine Zeit für das Umarmen und eine Zeit sich fernzuhalten vom Umarmen« (Koh 3,5).

---

30. Zur Sache s. E. NESTLE/K. ALAND, *Novum Testamentum Graece*, 26. Aufl., Stuttgart, Deutsche Bibelgesellschaft, 1979, p. 479; H. HÜBNER, *Vetus Testamentum in Novo*, Bd. 2: *Corpus Paulinum*, Göttingen, Vandenhoek & Ruprecht, 1997, p. 353.

31. Der sogenannte Weisheitstext aus der Kairoer Genizah nimmt zwar immer wieder Gedanken des Buches Koh auf und zitiert das Werk, ist aber gegen K. BERGER (*Die Weisheitsschrift aus der Kairoer Geniza. Erstedition, Kommentar und Übersetzung* [Texte und Arbeiten zum neutestamentlichen Zeitalter, 1], Tübingen, Franke Verlag, 1989, pp. 51–79; ID., *Die Bedeutung der wiederentdeckten Weisheitsschrift aus der Kairoer Geniza für das Neue Testament*, in New Testament Studies 36 [1990] 415–430, pp. 419–430; ID., *Die Bedeutung der wiederentdeckten Weisheitsschrift aus der Kairoer Geniza für das Alte Testament*, in ZAW 103 [1991] 113–121, p. 113) nicht um 100 n.Chr. in Ägypten verfaßt worden, sondern als »ein Produkt des mittelalterlichen jüdischen Neuplatonismus« zu verstehen (H.P. RÜGER, *Die Weisheitsschrift aus der Kairoer Geniza. Text, Übersetzung und philologischer Kommentar* [Wissenschaftliche Untersuchungen zum Neuen Testament, 53], Tübingen, J.C.B. Mohr [Paul Siebeck], 1991, p. 17; zur Sache s. op. cit., pp. 1–19) und der Piyyutliteratur zuzurechnen (s. G.W. NEBE, *Text und Sprache der hebräischen Weisheitsschrift aus der Kairoer Geniza* [Heidelberger Orientalistische Studien, 25], Frankfurt a.M. et al., Peter Lang, 1993, pp. 287–406; ID., *Die wiederentdeckte Weisheitsschrift aus der Kairoer Geniza und ihre »Nähe« zum Schrifttum von Qumran und zu den Essenern*, in G.J. BROOKE [ed.], *New Qumran Texts and Studies. Proceedings of the First Meeting of the International Organization for Qumran Studies, Paris 1992* [STDJ, 15], Leiden et al., E.J. Brill, 1994, pp. 241–254, pp. 243–249).

32. *Testaments of the Twelve Patriarchs (Second Century B.C.). A New Translation and Introduction*, in J.H. CHARLESWORTH (ed.), *The Old Testament Pseudepigrapha*, Bd. 1: *Apocalyptic Literature and Testaments*, New York et al., Doubleday, 1983, pp. 775–828, p. 814.

Καιρὸς γὰρ συνουσίας γυναικός καὶ καιρὸς ἐγκρατείας εἰς
προσευχὴν αὐτοῦ
»Denn es gibt eine Zeit für das Zusammenkommen mit der Frau und
eine Zeit der Enthaltsamkeit für sein Gebet« (TestNaph 8,8).

Wie der Vergleich beider Verse unschwer erkennen läßt, gehen ihre Gemeinsamkeiten nicht über das Thema körperlicher Nähe und die Vorstellung, daß jede Handlung ihre Zeit habe, hinaus. Da diese Vorstellung jedoch nicht auf Koh 3,1–8 beschränkt ist[33] und es sich bei Koh 3,1–8 mit
hoher Wahrscheinlichkeit um eine von Koh aufgenommene Tradition
handelt[34], scheint ein Zitat von Koh 3,5 in TestNaph 8,8 unwahrscheinlich.

Auf gemeinsame Tradition und nicht literarische Abhängigkeit dürften auch die u.a. von R. KROEBER (pp. 64–66), H.W. HERTZBERG (46–
49)[35] und jüngst J. MARBÖCK[36] angenommen Koheletzitate bei Ben Sira
zurückzuführen sein. An dieser Stelle kann auf die Arbeiten von T.
MIDDENDORP[37] und F.J. BACKHAUS[38] verwiesen werden. Beide fassen
ihre Ergebnisse wie folgt zusammen:

> »Ben Sira und Qo haben manche Themen gemeinsam. Beide lassen auf
> den Einfluss griechischer Literatur (Theognis im besonderen) schliessen.
> Dass Ben Sira den Prediger verwendet hat, liess sich nicht nachweisen;
> dass Qohelet das Büchlein Ben Sira kannte, ebensowenig« (T. MIDDEN-
> DORP, 89).

33. Zum *theologumenon* s. G. VON RAD, *Weisheit in Israel*, 3. Aufl., Neukirchen-
Vluyn, Neukirchner Verlag, 1985, pp. 182–188.337–363.
34. Zur Sache s. G. VON RAD, p. 338; A.G. WRIGHT, *The Riddle of the Sphinx. The
Structure of the Book of Qohelet*, in *CBQ* 30 (1968) 313–334, p. 327; G. OGDEN, p. 52;
R.N. WHYBRAY, *»A Time to be Born and a Time to Die«. Some Observations on
Ecclesiastes 3:2–8*, in *Bulletin of the Middle Eastern Culture Centre in Japan* 5 (1991)
469–483, pp. 473–477; A. LANGE, *Weisheit und Torheit*, p. 99; J. BLENKINSOPP,
Ecclesiastes 3.1–15. Another Interpretation, in *JSOT* 66 (1995) 55–64, pp. 57–60; A.A.
FISCHER, p. 221.
35. Zustimmung fand H.W. HERTZBERG bezüglich Sir 40,11 jüngst noch bei H.-P.
MÜLLER: »H. W. Hertzberg fand in Sir 40,11 wohl mit Recht eine wörtliche Übereinstimmung mit 3,20f und 12,7 (scil. Koh), die danach zumindest im ersteren Falle auf literarischer Abhängigkeit beruht« (*Weisheitliche Deutungen der Sterblichkeit. Gen 3,19 und
Pred 3,21;12,7 im Licht antiker Parallelen*, in ID., *Mensch – Umwelt – Eigenwelt. Gesammelte Aufsätze zur Weisheit Israels*, Stuttgart et al., W. Kohlhammer, 1992, pp. 69–
100, p. 82). H.-P. MÜLLER selbst zitiert jedoch pp. 90–96 eine Vielzahl von Parallelen aus
der griechischen und lateinischen Literatur (die älteste ist eine athenische Inschrift aus
dem Jahr 432 v.Chr.), die zu Teilen verblüffende Ähnlichkeiten in Wortlaut, Motivik und
Inhalt mit Koh 3,20f. und Sir 40,11 aufweisen.
36. *Kohelet und Sirach*, in L. SCHWIENHORST-SCHÖNBERGER (ed.), *Das Buch Kohelet.
Studien zur Struktur, Geschichte, Rezeption und Theologie* (BZAW, 254), Berlin/New
York, Walter de Gruyter, 1997, pp. 275–301.
37. *Die Stellung Jesu ben Siras zwischen Judentum und Hellenismus*, Leiden, E.J.
Brill, 1973, pp. 85–91.
38. *Qohelet und Sirach*, in *Biblische Notizen* 69 (1993) 32–55.

»*Wie die Kurzanalysen gezeigt haben, beweisen die aufgeführten Textstellen nicht mit Sicherheit, daß es zwischen Qohelet und Sirach direkte literarische Bezüge gibt. Insofern sind auch keine einseitigen noch gegenseitigen literarische Entlehnungen festzustellen*« (F.J. BACKHAUS, *op. cit.*, p. 45).

»Finden sich in beiden Werken gleiche Aussagen, dann zeigt dies einerseits, daß Qohelet und Sirach in derselben Weisheitstradition stehen und Einzelthemen daraus für ihr Anliegen verwenden, andererseits, daß z.Zt. der Abfassung der beiden Weisheitswerke gleiche oder ähnliche Zustände in der Gesellschaft bzw. im Wirtschaftsleben herrschten« (*op. cit.*, pp. 50f.)[39].

Ein echtes Koheletzitat findet sich dagegen in einem der nichtessenischen Weisheitstexte aus Qumran, dem *Book of Mysteries* (*Myst*)[40].

מה הוא היותר לֹֹ[...]

»Was ist es, das bleibt dem [...]« (1Q27 1 II₃).

Obwohl die Handschrift an der zitierten Stelle starke Beschädigungen erlitten hat, weist die Konstruktion יותר ל den Beleg als Koh-Zitat aus. Sie findet sich im antiken *corpus hebraicum* lediglich in Koh 6,8.11; 7,11[41]. Davon ist nur in Koh 6,8.11 ein vorgehendes מָה belegt:

כִּי־מַה־יוֹתֵר לֶחָכָם מִן הַכְּסִיל מַה לֶּעָנִי יוֹדֵעַ לַהֲלֹךְ נֶגֶד הַחַיִּים

»Denn was bleibt dem Weisen vor dem Toren, was dem Elenden[42] vor dem, der versteht vor dem Leben zu wandeln?« (Koh 6,8)

כִּי יֵשׁ דְּבָרִים הַרְבֵּה מַרְבִּים הָבֶל מַה־יֹּתֵר לָאָדָם

»Denn je mehr Worte, je mehr Absurdes! Was bleibt dem Menschen?« (Koh 6,11)

Welcher der beiden Verse in *Myst* zitiert wird, kann wegen der Textbeschädigungen nicht mehr gesagt werden.

Ein weiterer Hinweis auf eine Koh-Rezeption im *Book of Mysteries* könnte in 1Q27 6₂f. zu finden sein:

[...]שׁיהמֹה [י]כפר על שגגoooooל[...]   2

[...]עֹד עולם לפניו לכפר ה[...]   3

»[...]*šyhmh* [er] wird sühnen eine unwissentlich begangene Sünde°°°°*l*[...]

[...]bis in Ewigkeit vor ihm, um zu sühnen[...]«

---

39. Zur Sache cf. auch M. GILBERT, *Qohélet et Ben Sira*, im vorliegenden Band, pp. 161–179.

40. Eine literarische Abhänigkeit des Buches Kohelet von *Myst* kann wegen des jüngeren Abfassungsdatums von *Myst* ausgeschlossen werden (s.u., pp. 131f.).

41. Cf. Koh 7,16: וְאַל תִּתְחַכַּם יוֹתֵר לָמָּה תִּשּׁוֹמֵם (»Und sei nicht übermäßig weise – warum willst du dich zugrunde richten?«

42. 𝕲, α, β (cf. 𝕾) lesen διότι ὁ πένης οἶδεν πορευθῆναι κατέναντι τῆς ζωῆς (»weil der Arme weiß, vor dem Leben zu wandeln«). Die Lesart erklärt sich aus einer nachträglichen Verbesserung der schwer verständlichen elliptischen Konstruktion von 𝔐.

Die im Text thematisierte Sühne für unwissentlich begangene Sünde
(s. Lev 4–5; Num 15,22–31)[43] wird auch in Koh 5,5 diskutiert:

אַל־תִּתֵּן אֶת־פִּיךָ לַחֲטִיא אֶת־בְּשָׂרֶךָ וְאַל־תֹּאמַר לִפְנֵי הַמַּלְאָךְ כִּי שְׁגָגָה הִיא

»Gib deinen Mund nicht dazu, dein Fleisch zu versündigen und sage
nicht vor dem Boten[44], daß es eine unwissentlich begangene Sünde
war.«

Neben diesen beiden Belegen könnte lediglich noch ein weiterer, aus
dem in Frage kommenden Zeitraum bekannter Weisheitstext die *šᵉgāgâ*
thematisiert haben[45], der *mûsar lammēbîn*[46]. In 4Q417 2 II$_{14}$ findet sich
die Wendung בלוא צוה נבונות אל תשגכה. Bei תשגכה handelt es sich entweder um einen Jussiv Pi. oder Hi. (2. Pers. sing. mask.) der Wurzel שגה
mit Objektsuffix der 2. Pers. sing. (»du sollst dich nicht groß machen« =
»du sollst nicht hochmütig sein«)[47] oder um einen Jussiv Qal (2. Pers.
sing. mask.) der Wurzel שגה mit Objektsuffix der 2. Pers. sing. mask.
(»du sollst nicht irrtümlich handeln«)[48]. Wegen des zerstörten Kontextes
ist eine sichere Interpretation nicht mehr möglich. Das durch das *kāph*
notwendige Objektsuffix scheint jedoch eher für die Wurzel שגה zu sprechen.

Da das *Book of Mysteries* und der *mûsār lammēbîn* sowohl für die
Frage nach der Identität des zweiten Redaktors des Buches Kohelet als
auch für die Frage nach Kohelets Gesprächspartnern von großer Bedeutung sind, erscheint es sinnvoll, an dieser Stelle in einem Exkurs die Ein-
leitungsfragen zu den noch relativ unbekannten Werken zu diskutieren:

43. Das so nur in Lev 5,18 belegte כפר על שגגה legt nahe, daß in 1Q27 6$_2$ auf Lev 5,18
angespielt wird.
44. Gemeint ist ein Priester oder Tempelbote; so u.a. H.W. HERTZBERG, p. 123; R.
KROEBER, p. 117; A. LAUHA, p. 100; W. ZIMMERLI, p. 185; R.B. SALTERS, *Notes on the
History of the Interpretation of Koh 5,5*, in *ZAW* 90 (1978) 95–101, p. 100; J.L.
CRENSHAW, *Ecclesiastes*, p. 117; G. OGDEN, p. 79; D. MICHEL, *Qohelet*, p. 142; R.E.
MURPHY, pp. 50f. und C.L. SEOW, p. 196.
45. Da der Kontext von Hiob 12,16 nicht kultisch orientiert ist und die Wurzeln שגה
und שגה und ihre Derivate auch ohne kultische Konnotationen belegt sind, dürfte Hiob
12,16 nicht auf die *šᵉgāgâ* hin zu interpretieren sein.
46. Zur Benennung des Werkes s.u., p. 127 Anm. 49.
47. So A. LANGE, *Weisheit und Prädestination. Weisheitliche Urordnung und Prädestination in den Textfunden von Qumran* (STDJ, 18), Leiden et al., E.J. Brill, 1995,
p. 54.
48. So F. GARCÍA MARTÍNEZ, p. 387; J. MAIER, Bd. 2, p. 441 und B.Z. WACHOLDER/
M.G. ABEGG/J. BOWLEY, *A Preliminary Edition of the Unpublished Dead Sea Scrolls. The
Hebrew and Aramaic Texts from Cave Four*, Fasz. 4: *Concordance of Fascicles 1–3*,
Washington D.C., Biblical Archaeology Society, 1996, p. 346.

EXKURS I

Der mûsār lammēbîn[49] *und das* Book of Mysteries

Von dem *mûsār lammēbîn* wurden in Qumran mindestens 6 Handschriften gefunden: 1Q26; 4Q415–418; 423[50]. Abgesehen von einigen größeren Fragmenten in 4Q416; 4Q417 und 4Q418 sind alle Handschriften stark beschädigt. »All the manuscripts are written in the Herodian formal hand of the late first century BCE or early first century CE.«[51] Nach mündlicher Auskunft von A. STEUDEL bewahren nach einer von ihr gemeinsam mit B. LUCASSEN erstellten materialen Rekonstruktion die Fragmente 4Q416 1 und 4Q417 2 den Beginn ihrer jeweiligen Handschriften. Da 4Q416 1 ein eschatologisches Geschehen schildert (s.u., p. 141), während 4Q417 2 I eine weisheitliche Lehrrede über die Erkenntnisfähigkeit des מבין bietet (s.u., pp. 137f.), ist davon auszugehen, daß der *MLM* eine Redaktion erfahren hat. Welchen Umfang diese Redaktion hatte, kann erst nach der Veröffentlichung der *editio princeps* von D.J. HARRINGTON/J. STRUGNELL und der materialen Rekonstruktion

49. Bis vor kurzem trug der Text den vorläufigen Namen *Sapiential Work* A (cf. E. TOV/S.J. PFANN, *Companion Volume to the Dead Sea Scrolls Microfiche Edition*, 2. Aufl., Leiden et al., E.J. Brill/IDC, 1995, p. 43 und S.A. REED/M.J. LUNDBERG, *The Dead Sea Scrolls Catalogue. Documents, Photographs and Museum Inventory Numbers* [SBL RBS, 32], Atlanta, Scholars Press, 1994, pp. 110–112). Die Herausgeber, D.J. HARRINGTON und J. STRUGNELL schlagen in ihrer noch in Vorbereitung befindlichen Edition den Namen *mûsār lammēbîn* vor (*Qumran Cave 4 XXIV. Sapiential Texts Part 2* [DJD 34], Oxford, Clarendon Press). T. ELGVIN nennt das Werk dagegen in seinem Vortrag auf dem Jerusalemer Kongress anläßlich des fünfzigjährigen Fundjubiläums der Texte vom Toten Meer *4QInstruction* (*Wisdom and Apocalypticism in the Early Second Century BCE. The Evidence of 4QInstruction*, in *Abstracts. The Dead Sea Scrolls – Fifty Years After Their Discovery. Major Issues and New Approaches*, The Israel Museum, Jerusalem, July 20–25, 1997, Jerusalem, The Israel Museum/Israel Antiquities Authority/The Hebrew University of Jerusalem/Israel Exploration Society, 1997, p. 27).

50. S. u.a. D.J. HARRINGTON, *Wisdom Texts from Qumran*, p. 40. D.J. HARRINGTON beschreibt in einer früheren Publikation auch 4Q419 als *MLM*-Handschrift (*Wisdom at Qumran*, in E. ULRICH/J. VANDERKAM [eds.], *The Community of the Renewed Covenant. The Notre Dame Symposium on the Dead Sea Scrolls* [Christianity and Judaism in Antiquity Series, 10], Notre Dame, University of Notre Dame Press, 1994, pp. 137–152, pp. 139f.). T. ELGVIN (*Admonition Texts from Qumran Cave 4*, in M.O. WISE ET AL. [eds.], *Methods of Investigation of the Dead Sea Scrolls and the Khirbet Qumran Site. Present Realities and Future Prospects* [Annals of the New York Academy of Sciences, 722], New York, Academy of Sciences, 1994, pp. 179–196, p. 180; *The Reconstruction of Sapiential Work A*, in *RQ* 16 [1993–1995] 559–580, pp. 570–572) will auf Grund kleinerer Wortidentitäten zwischen 4Q418 2 und 213, sowie zwischen 4Q418, 167 und einem bislang unveröffentlichten Fragment, und zwischen 4Q418, 33 und 167 in 4Q418 Reste von zwei Handschriften sehen.

51. D.J. HARRINGTON, *Wisdom Texts from Qumran*, p. 40.

von B. LUCASSEN/A. STEUDEL beantwortet werden[52]. Inhaltliche Ähnlichkeiten zwischen 4Q416 1 und 4Q418 69 II auf der einen und 1Q27 1 I auf der anderen Seite erlauben jedoch Spekulationen, ob die in 4Q416 bezeugte Version des *MLM* etwa zur Abfassungszeit des Mitte des 2. Jh.v.Chr. verfaßten und aus dem gleichen Tradentenkreis wie der *MLM* stammenden (zur Sache s.u., p. 134) *Books of Mysteries* erfolgt sein könnte. Bei der von 4Q416 bezeugten Version des *MLM* würde es sich dann um die jüngere Fassung handeln.

In beiden Versionen des *MLM* sind sowohl weisheitliche Formen als auch weisheitliches Vokabular bezeugt: So finden sich in 4Q417 2 I$_{1\text{-}18}$ par 4Q418 43; 4Q417 2 I$_{18}$–II$_5$; 4Q418 69 II par 4Q417 18; 4Q418 81; 4Q418 103 II und 4Q418 126 II weisheitliche Lehrreden verschiedenen Inhalts mit teils stark ausgeprägtem paränetischen Charakter. Lange Paränesen, die größere zusammenhängende Passagen mit Einzelsprüchen kombinieren und bisweilen traktatartige Züge annehmen können, sind in 4Q416 I–IV par 4Q417 1 I–II par 4Q418 7–10 und 4Q418 88 erhalten. Traktate selbst könnten in 4Q418 55 und 4Q418 77 bezeugt sein. Ein großer Teil des *MLM* kann wegen starker Textzerstörungen keiner Gattung mehr zugeordnet werden.

Das gehäufte Vorkommen weisheitlichen Vokabulars in beiden Versionen des *MLM* mag die folgende Liste illustrieren:

:אויל	4Q417 18$_{1.5}$; 4Q418 58$_1$; 69 II$_{4.8}$; 4Q418 205$_2$
:אולת	4Q415 9$_6$; 4Q416 2 II$_3$; 4Q418 220$_3$; 278$_2$; 4Q423 5$_8$
:בין	4Q415 11$_{4f.11}$; 4Q416 1$_{16}$; 2 III$_{14}$; 4$_3$; 4Q417 2 I$_{1.12.18.25}$; 2 II$_{10.14}$; 3$_3$; 4Q418 2$_{7f.}$; 68$_5$; 69 II$_{15}$; 77$_3$; 81$_{15.17}$; 102$_3$; 123 II$_{4f.}$; 126 II$_{12}$; 147$_{5f.}$; 158$_4$; 164$_3$; 168$_4$; 176$_3$; 189$_2$; 221$_{2f.5}$; 227$_1$; 238$_3$; 4Q423 5$_7$; 7$_7$
:בינה	4Q416 2 III$_{13}$; 4Q417 27$_2$; 4Q418 9$_{14}$; 55$_{6.9}$; 58$_2$; 69 II$_{11}$; 88$_6$; 148 II$_6$; 162$_2$; 165$_2$; 177$_4$; 193$_1$
:דעה	4Q418 43$_6$; 55$_5$; 69 II$_{4.11f.}$
:דעת	4Q416 2 III$_{13}$; 4Q417 2 I$_{22}$; 4Q418 9$_{13}$; 55$_{10}$; 69 II$_{11}$; 95$_3$; 117$_1$; 148 II$_{5.7}$; 221$_5$
חכם (adj.):	4Q418 81$_{20}$
:חכמה	4Q416 2 II$_{12}$; 4Q417 2 I$_6$; 4Q418 8$_{13}$; 81$_{15.19}$; 102$_3$; 115$_3$; 137$_2$; 139$_2$
:מוסר	4Q416 2 III$_{13}$; 4Q418 9$_{13}$; 169$_3$; 257$_1$
:משכיל	4Q417 2 I$_{25}$; 4Q418 21$_2$; 81$_{17}$; 238$_1$

---

52. Ob sie, wie T. ELGVIN annimmt (*Wisdom and Apocalypticism*), alle eschatologischen und revelatorischen Passagen des Werkes umfaßte, scheint mir jedoch fraglich.

סכל: 4Q417 20$_2$

שׂכל (Verb): 4Q418 43$_1$; 69 II$_2$; 81$_{20}$; 161$_7$; 165$_2$; 174$_3$; 184$_3$; 197$_1$; 4Q423 2$_{1f.}$; 5$_8$

שׂכל (Nomen): 4Q416 19$_2$; 4Q417 20$_6$; 4Q418 55$_{10}$; 81$_9$; 149$_6$; 158$_6$; 4Q423 5$_{7.9}$

Neben der Vorstellung von einer als רז נהיה bezeichneten weisheitlichen Urordnung dualen Charakters, die sich im Sinaigesetz und in einer Enosch gegebenen Vision offenbart (zur Identifikation von Weisheit und Tora s.u., pp. 137ff.), und die zumindest in der redaktionellen Version des *MLM* auch kosmologische und eschatologische Züge trägt, ist insbesondere der angemessene Lebenswandel ein zentrales Anliegen des *MLM* (s. z.B. 4Q416 I–IV par 4Q417 1 I–II par 4Q418 7–10; 4Q418 126 II und 127). In die Ermahnungen zu einem solchen Lebenswandel werden mehrfach, und für die ältere Weisheit völlig untypisch, Zitate aus und Anspielung auf den Pentateuch eingeflochten (s.u., pp. 139f.). An Prov 3,19 und Ps 104,24 erinnert der Satz ...וגם לוא נהיו בלוא רצונו ומחו]ל[מתו («und sie sind auch nicht entstanden ohne seinen Willen und aus [seiner] Weish[eit...«; 4Q418 126 II$_5$)[53]. Der schon aus der älteren Weisheit vertraute ethische Dualismus wird zumindest in der jüngeren Version des *MLM* dualistisch und eschatologisch weiterentwickelt[54]. D.J. HARRINGTON skizziert den *MLM* daher wie folgt:

> This Qumran sapiential work is a wisdom instruction expressed in small units and put together without much apparent concern for logical or thematic progression. In some places the sage's appeal is to pragmatism or to reward and punishment at judgment, while in other places there are deductions from Scripture and symbolic uses of Scripture. In form and content it is similar to Sirach, parts of Proverbs (especially chaps. 22–23), late Egyptian wisdom writings, Jesus' instructions in the Synoptic Gospels, and the letter of James[55].
>
> One of the most striking features of the document is its extensive vocabulary with regard to poverty: the nouns *maḥsor* and *rîš / rê(')š*, and the adjectives *rîš* and *'ebyôn*. Yet poverty is presented not so much as an ideal or a more perfect state as it is a symbol of human limitation and mortality. Though this vocabulary appears in other wisdom texts, it is particularly prominent in this work. Another prominent term is *raz nihyāh* (or *nihyeh*). We have been translating it as »the mysteries of what is to be (or, come)« since in some contexts it appears to refer to the eschatological plan of God[56].

53. Rekonstruktion nach J. MAIER, Bd. 2, p. 467.

54. Zum Dualismus im *MLM* s. J. FREY, *Different Patterns of Dualistic Thought in the Qumran Library. Reflections on their Background and History*, in M. BERNSTEIN et al. (eds.), *Legal Text and Legal Issues. Proceedings of the Second Meeting of the International Organization for Qumran Studies Cambridge 1995*. FS J.M. Baumgarten (STDJ, 23), Leiden et al., E.J. Brill, 1997, pp. 275–335, pp. 299f.

55. *Wisdom at Qumran*, p. 144.

56. *Op. cit.*, p. 145.

Daß 1QH^a X$_{27f.}$ den in 4Q418 55$_{10}$ erhaltenen Text zitiert[57], und daß 1QH^a I$_{26f.}$ auf den in 4Q417 2 I$_8$ bezeugten Text anspielt, schließt eine Datierung des *MLM* wesentlich nach der Mitte des 2. Jh. v.Chr. aus. Späte Vokabeln und Konstruktionen wie das persische Lehnwort רז (älteste Belege im Hebräischen sind Sir 8,18; 12,11), das aramäische Lehnwort כשר (die ältesten Belege der Wurzel im Hebräischen sind Est 8,5; Koh 2,21; 5,10; 11,6; Sir 13,4), das Part. Hi. der Wurzel בין (die ältesten Belege im Hebräischen sind 1 Chr 15,22; 2 Chr 34,12; Dan 8,23; Sir 10,1; 38,4; 42,21; 4Q381 45$_1$) und im temporalen Sinn gebrauchtes עם mit Infinitiv (עם התהלכו 4Q417 2 I$_{12}$; die ältesten Belege im Hebräischen sind Esr 1,11; Sir 38,23; 40,14) zeigen, daß der *MLM* nicht viel früher als vor dem Ende des 3. Jh. v.Chr. verfaßt worden sein kann. Wird in Rechnung gestellt, daß eine gewisse Zeit vergeht, bevor ein Text zitiert und redaktionell überarbeitet wird, so dürfte der *MLM* gegen Ende des 3. oder zu Beginn des 2. Jh. v.Chr. entstanden sein.

Gegen eine mehrfach von T. ELGVIN angenommene[58] und zeitweise auch von D.J. HARRINGTON vertretene[59] essenische oder protoessenische Herkunft des *MLM* spricht, daß sich im Text weder für essenische Texte typisches Vokabular[60] noch essenische *theologumena* finden. Mit D.J. HARRINGTON sind dagegen die Ausführungen zu den Eltern und zum Umgang mit der Ehefrau in 4Q416 2 III–IV in essenischen Texten kaum denkbar[61]. Gegen einen essenischen Ursprung des *MLM* spricht auch die Beobachtung T. ELGVINs: »The work does not reflect a hierarchically

---

57. So zuerst *op. cit.*, pp. 142f.

58. *Admonition Texts*, pp. 185f.191f.; *Wisdom, Revelation, and Eschatology in an Early Essene Writing*, in *SBL SP* 34 (1995) 440–463, pp. 443ff.; *Early Essene Eschatology. Judgment and Salvation according to Sapiential Work A*, in D.W. PARRY/S.D. RICKS [eds.], *Current Research and Technological Developments on the Dead Sea Scrolls. Conference on the Texts from the Judean Desert, Jerusalem, 30 April 1995* [STDJ, 20], Leiden et al., E.J. Brill, 1996, pp. 126–165, pp. 128–134). Cf. auch D. DIMANT, *The Qumran Manuscripts. Contents and Significance*, in ID./ L.H. SCHIFFMAN (eds.), *Time to Prepare the Way in the Wilderness. Papers on the Qumran Scrolls by Fellows of the Institute for Advanced Studies of the Hebrew University, Jerusalem, 1989–1990* (STDJ, 16), Leiden et al., E.J. Brill, 1995, pp. 23–58, p. 43.

59. *Wisdom Texts from Qumran*, pp. 41f.

60. Einzige mögliche Ausnahme ist das 4Q415 11$_3$; 4Q416 2 IV$_5$; 4Q418 167$_{5f.}$; 172$_3$; 199$_1$ belegte Nomen יחד. Leider sind davon die Belege 4Q415 11$_3$; 4Q418 167$_{5f.}$; 172$_3$; 199$_1$ wegen Textzerstörungen nicht mehr sicher zu interpretieren und 4Q416 2 IV$_5$ beschreibt es – für den essenischen Sprachgebrauch sehr ungewöhnlich – die Vereinigung mit einer Frau. Der in 4Q408 bezeugte und mit einer gewissen Wahrscheinlichkeit nichtessenische Text zeigt ferner, daß die Vokabel zumindest vor der Gründung der essenischen Bewegung auch in nichtessenischen Texten benutzt wird (zu 4Q408 s.u., p. 152 Anm. 132).

61. *Wisdom at Qumran*, p. 144.

structured community, as the *yaḥad* does. Only two small passages deal with purity matters or priestly traditions.«[62]

Aufschluß über die Herkunft des *MLM* geben demgegenüber die Hinweise auf ein für weisheitliche Texte ungewöhnlich starkes kultisches Interesse:

- die Bemerkungen zum Erstlingsopfer (4Q423 3_4 par 1Q26 2_4)
- die Ausführungen zum Auflösen des Gelübdes einer Ehefrau durch ihren Mann (4Q416 2 IV$_{8f.}$ par 4Q418 $10_{8f.}$)
- die Erörterung zur Vermischung unter Aufnahme von Lev 19,19; Dtn 22,9-11 (4Q418 103)
- die Belege zu Festen und Kalenderfragen in 4Q416 1_3; 4Q418 118_3; 4Q418 211_3; 4Q423 5_6
- die Belege von נדה in 4Q417 4 II$_2$; 4Q418 20_2
- die Beschreibung der Erwählung eines/der Gerechten als von Gott mit Hilfe des Losorakels vorherbestimmt (הפיל גורלכה; 4Q418 81_5).

Der gegen Ende des 3. oder zu Beginn des 2. Jh. v.Chr. verfaßte *MLM* dürfte somit am Jerusalemer Tempel zu verorten sein.

Vom *Book of Mysteries* wurden in Qumran vier Handschriften gefunden (1Q27; 4Q299–4Q301), wovon 1Q27 und 4Q299–4Q300 überlappen[63]. Paläographisch können alle Handschriften herodianischen Schriftformen zugeordnet werden[64]. Das im Text verwandte Vokabular legt eine späte Datierung nahe: Die ältesten Belege des persischen Lehnwortes רז im Hebräischen sind Sir 8,18; 12,1, während das Nomen מוֹלָד sogar erst in der Mischna belegt ist[65]. Für die Datierung des Werkes ist fer-

62. *Early Essene Eschatology*, p. 128.

63. 4Q301 wird von L.H. SCHIFFMAN für die Handschrift eines anderen, der Hechalotliteratur zuzurechnenden Werkes gehalten (*Reclaiming the Dead Sea Scrolls. The History of Judaism, the Background of Christianity, the Lost Library of Qumran*, Philadelphia/Jerusalem, Jewish Publication Society, 1994, p. 206; ID., *4QMysteries^a. A Preliminary Edition and Translation*, in Z. ZEVIT et al. [eds.], *Solving Riddles and Untying Knots. Biblical, Epigraphic, and Semitic Studies in Honor of Jonas C. Greenfield*, Winona Lake, Eisenbrauns, 1995, pp. 207–260, p. 207; ID., *4QMysteries^b. A Preliminary Edition*, in *RQ* 16 [1993–1994] 203–223, p. 205; ID., *Mysteries*, pp. 31.113f). Jedoch fällt auf, daß 4Q301 mit den anderen *Myst*-Handschriften seltene Redewendungen und Lexeme, wie שורשי בינה (4Q301 1_2; 2_1) und שורש חוכמה (4Q300 1 II$_3$) oder תומכי... (4Q301 1_2) und תומכי רזין... (4Q299 2 II$_9$; 6 II$_4$; 40$_2$; 4Q300 8_5) gemeinsam hat, und ihnen stilistisch in der Aneinanderreihung rhetorischer Fragen ähnelt (letzteres beobachtet auch L.H. SCHIFFMAN [*Mysteries*, p. 42]). Sogar die Vorstellung von der verborgenen Weisheit ist – gegen L.H. SCHIFFMAN, *Mysteries*, p. 114 – kein Proprium der Handschrift 4Q301, sondern findet sich u.a auch in 4Q300 1 II$_{2-5}$ und 4Q300 5_5. Mit dem ersten Herausgeber der 4QMyst-Handschriften, J.T. MILIK, ist 4Q301 daher als eine weitere Handschrift des *Book of Mysteries* anzusehen (zur Sache s. B.Z. WACHOLDER/M.G. ABEGG, pp. 35ff.).

64. Zur Sache s. L.H. SCHIFFMAN, *4QMysteries^a*, p. 209; ID., *4QMysteries^b*, p. 205; ID., *Mysteries*, pp. 33.99.114.

65. Cf. D. BARTHÉLEMY/J.T. MILIK, *Qumran Cave I* (DJD, 1), Oxford, Clarendon Press, 1955, p. 104; L.H. SCHIFFMAN, *4QMysteries^b*, p. 214 und M. JASTROW, A

ner die Anspielung auf Nebukadnezzars Traum (Dan 2) in 4Q300 1 II$_1$ von Bedeutung. Das *Book of Mysteries* wäre somit in das 2. oder 1. Jh. v.Chr. zu datieren. Dieser Zeitraum kann durch inhaltliche Bezüge des Werkes zur Zwei-Geister-Lehre (1QS III$_{13}$–IV$_{26}$) weiter eingeengt werden[66]. Da sowohl Dualismus als auch Eschatologie der Zwei-Geister-Lehre als eine Weiterentwicklung des in *Myst* geäußerten Gedankengutes[67] verstanden werden können, dürfte das *Book of Mysteries* vor der Zwei-Geister-Lehre entstanden sein, die gegen Mitte des 2. Jh. v.Chr. oder etwas später zu datieren ist[68].

Eine essenische Herkunft wurde für *Myst* von I. RABINOWITZ[69], O. BETZ[70], J. BECKER[71] und E. TOV[72] vorgeschlagen. Dagegen spricht a), daß sich in *Myst* weder zentrale Themen des *yaḥad*, noch *yaḥad*-typische Sprache, noch zentrale Figuren aus der Geschichte des *yaḥad* finden, b) das häufige Vorkommen der in essenischen Texten vermiedenen Wurzel חכם, und c) die in dem Satz ‏וני[כבד אל בעם קודשו‏] (»[und] Gott [wird] sich durch sein heiliges Volk ehren« 4Q301 3$_6$) belegte und für essenische Texte untypische gesamtisraelitische Perspektive.

Das in *Myst* häufig anzutreffende weisheitliche Vokabular (‏ודעה תמלא‏ ‏תבל ואין שם לע[ו̊]ד] אולת‏ [»und Erkenntnis wird die Welt erfüllen, und Torheit wird es dort nimmermehr geben«; 1Q27 1 I$_7$]; ‏חכם וצדיק‏ [»weise und gerecht«; 4Q299 2 II$_4$]; ‏חכמת ערמת רוע‏ [»Weisheit der frevelhaften Klugheit«; 4Q299 2 II$_5$]; ‏החכמה‏ [»die Weisheit«; 4Q299 39$_4$]; ‏ב[כסלכמה‏ [»in ihrer Torheit«; 4Q300 1 II$_2$]; ‏בבינה‏ [»in ihrer Einsicht«;

Dictionary of the Targumim, the Talmud Babli and Yerushalmi, and the Midrashic Literature, Nachdruck, Brooklyn, P. Shalom, 1967, 742.

66. Zur Verwandtschaft der Zwei-Geister-Lehre mit *Myst* s. J. BECKER, *Das Heil Gottes. Heils- und Sündenbegriffe in den Qumrantexten und im Neuen Testament* (Studien zur Umwelt des Neuen Testaments, 3), Göttingen, Vandenhoek & Ruprecht, 1964, p. 94 und A. LANGE, *Weisheit und Prädestination*, pp. 128–130.

67. Zum Dualismus in *Myst* s. J. FREY, p. 299.

68. Zur Datierung der Zwei-Geister-Lehre s. A. LANGE, *Weisheit und Prädestination*, p. 130.

69. *The Authorship, Audience, and Date of the de Vaux Fragment of an Unknown Work*, in *JBL* 71 (1952) 19–32, p. 32; *Sequence and Dates of the Extra-Biblical Dead Sea Scroll Texts and »Damascus« Fragments*, in *VT* 3 (1953) 175–185, p. 185.

70. *Offenbarung und Schriftforschung in der Qumransekte* (Wissenschaftliche Untersuchungen zum Neuen Testament, 6), Tübingen, J.C.B. Mohr (Paul Siebeck), 1960, p. 57.

71. P. 94.

72. *Letters of the Cryptic A Script and Paleo-Hebrew Letters Used as Scribal Marks in Some Qumran Scrolls*, in *DSD* 2 (1995) 330–339, p. 331; *Scribal Markings in the Texts from the Judean Desert*, in D.W. PARRY/S.D. RICKS (eds.), *Current Research and Technological Developments on the Dead Sea Scrolls. Conference on the Texts from the Judean Desert, Jerusalem, 30 April 1995* (STDJ, 20), Leiden et al., E.J. Brill, 1996, pp. 41–77, pp. 57f.

ibid.); בשורש חוכמה [»in die Wurzel der Weisheit«; 4Q300 1 II$_3$]; חכמה
נכחדת [»verborgene Weisheit«; 4Q300 1 II$_{4f.}$]; כול חוכמתם [»all ihre
Weisheit«; 4Q300 3$_3$]; מחשבת בי[נה] [»Gedanke der Ein(sicht)«; 4Q300
5$_1$]; חכמה נכחדת [»verborgene Weisheit«; 4Q300 5$_5$]; שׁוֹרשי בינה
[»Wurzeln der Einsicht«; 4Q301 1$_2$]; משפטי כסיל ונחלת חכמ]ים [»Ge-
richte eines Toren und Erbteil der Weisen«; 4Q301 2$_1$]; בׁשׁוׁשׁי בינה
[»in Wurzeln der Einsicht«; *ibid.*]) und die trotz des schlechten Erhal-
tungszustands der Handschriften noch vorhandenen Hinweise auf weisheitliche Lehrreden (1Q27 1 I; 4Q299 2 II$_{9ff.}$; 4Q299 6 II; 4Q300 1 II;
4Q301 1 und 4Q301 2)[73] sowie das hymnische Lehrgedicht auf Gott als
den Schöpfer des geordneten Kosmos in 4Q299 6 I weisen *Myst* als einen weisheitlichen Text aus. Weisheitliche Themen dürften von *Myst*
u.a. in 1Q27 1 II$_{3ff.}$ (Tun-Ergehen-Zusammenhang), 4Q299 8 (epistemologische Erörterung), 4Q299 2 II$_{10f.}$; 6 I und 4Q300 1 II$_2$ (weisheitliche Urordnung) behandelt werden.

Neben weisheitlichen Lexemen, Gattungen und Inhalten sind in *Myst*
auch priesterliche Sprache, Motivik und Themen belegt: 1Q27 3$_2$ erwähnt Priester (לו לכוהֹנֹיֹם; »für ihn, für Priester«). In 1Q27 6$_{2f.}$ findet
sich zweimal die Wurzel כפר. 1Q27 6$_2$ thematisiert in Anspielung auf
Lev 5,18 das Ritual zur Sühne versehentlich begangener Sünden (s.o.,
p. 125). 4Q299 52$_5$ spricht im Zusammenhang mit dem Dienst im Tempel von der Sühne (עבו]דֹת קודשו ולכפר עׁל ∞[; »Dien]st seines Heilig-
tums und um zu entsühnen ∞[...«). Priesterliches findet sich ferner in
4Q299 2 II$_3$ par 4Q300 5$_4$ (וכול מעשה צדׁיׁק הטמ]אה; »alles Tun eines
Gerechten wird verunrei[nigt ...«) und in 4Q299 66$_3$ (לחול; »für Unhei-
liges«)[74]. Desweiteren dürften die in 4Q299 65$_2$ erwähnten Urim und
Thummim im Zusammenspiel mit dem א]חת בשנה (»ei]nmal im Jahr«;
4Q299 65$_1$) auf den Rest einer Schilderung der Yom Kippur-Feier oder
eines vergleichbaren Ritus hinweisen[75]. 4Q299 75$_{6f.}$ erwähnt schließlich
»Aaron and the offering of sacrifices«[76]. *Myst* dürfte somit in

---

73. Die für weisheitliche Lehrreden typischen Einleitungsformeln könnten in folgenden Textresten bezeugt sein: שמעו תומכי רׁוׁזׁי (»hört, die ihr ergreift die Ge[heimnisse
der«; 4Q299 2 II$_9$);]ועתה[(»und nun«; 4Q299 41$_3$);]...[אׁיׁכם אשמיע (»...]eure, ich will hören lassen«; 4Q299 50$_{11}$); פ[ועתה] (»und nun«; 4Q299 76$_2$); ...א]בׁיׁעה רוחי ולמיניכם
אׁחלקה דברי אליכם[... (»Ich will sprudeln lassen meinen Geist, und nach euren Arten
meine Worte euch zuteilen[...«; 4Q301 1$_1$).
74. Zu חל im Gegensatz zu קֹדֶשׁ cf. auch Lev 10,10; 1 Sam 21,5.6; Ez 22,26; 42,20;
44,23; CD VI$_{17f.}$; XII$_{20}$.
75. So L.H. SCHIFFMAN, *Mysteries^a*, p. 251; ID., *Mysteries*, p. 82.
76. ID., *Mysteries^a*, p. 255. L.H. SCHIFFMAN (*op. cit.*, pp. 251.255; ID., *Mysteries*,
pp. 82.88) bestreitet auf Grund der priesterlichen Thematik von 4Q299 65; 75 die Zugehörigkeit dieser Frg. zu 4Q299. Da priesterliches Gedankengut und Vokabular aber auch
an anderen Stellen des Werkes belegt ist, überzeugt das Argument nicht.

weisheitlichen Kreisen verfaßt worden sein, deren kultisches Interesse auf eine Nähe zum Tempel deutet[77].

Sowohl das *Book of Mysteries* als auch der *mûsār lammēbîn* teilen viele Besonderheiten. Hier ist nicht nur das für weisheitliche Texte außergewöhnlich starke kultische Interesse der beiden Werke zu nennen, sondern auch die Tatsache, daß sie anders als die meisten Weisheitstexte Vorschriften aus dem Pentateuch zitieren. Ferner sind Parallelen in der Eschatologie beider Werke auffällig, wie die endzeitliche Offenbarung und Realisierung der weisheitlichen Urordnung (s.u., pp. 135ff.141ff.). Neben inhaltlichen Parallelen fallen aber auch Gemeinsamkeiten im Vokabular auf; als Beispiele seien hier die sonst kaum jemals belegten Wendungen רז נהיה (1Q27 1 I$_4$ par 4Q299 3$_4$)[78] und שורשי בינה (»Wurzeln der Einsicht«; 4Q418 55$_9$; 4Q301 1$_2$; 2$_1$; cf. שורש חוכמה 4Q300 1 II$_3$) genannt. Beide Werke dürften daher aus dem gleichen am Tempel zu lokalisierenden weisheitlichen Tradentenkreis stammen[79]. Ein weiterer diesem Tradentenkreis zuzurechnender Text ist wegen Ähnlichkeiten in Vokabular und Inhalt die etwas später als *Myst* zu datierende Zwei-Geister-Lehre (1QS III$_{13}$–IV$_{26}$)[80].

❊ ❊ ❊

Das Koh zitierende *Myst* bezeugt ein starkes Interesse an Tora und Eschatologie: Zwar findet sich in den erhaltenen Resten des Werkes keine ausgeführte Identifikation von Weisheit und Tora, jedoch nimmt *Myst* Toravorschriften auf. So ist das *š^{e}gāgâ*-Opfer (Lev 4–5; Num 15,22–31;

---

77. Die ohne nähere Begründung von D. BARTHÉLEMY/J.T. MILIK (p. 103), A. DUPONT-SOMMER (*Die essenischen Schriften vom Toten Meer*, Tübingen, J.C.B. Mohr [Paul Siebeck], 1960, pp. 353.355), J. BECKER (p. 94), D.S. RUSSEL (*The Method and Message of Jewish Apocalyptic: 200 BC – AD 100* [OTL], London, SCM Press, 1964, p. 47) und M. HENGEL (p. 400) vorgenommene Zuordnung von *Myst* zur Apokalyptik darf nach Bekanntwerden aller Handschriften aus den oben genannten Gründen als gescheitert gelten (zur Sache cf. J. CARMIGNAC, *Qu'est-ce que l'Apocalyptique? Son emploi à Qumran*, in *RQ* 10 [1979–1981] 3–33, pp. 26f. und H. STEGEMANN, *Die Bedeutung der Qumranfunde für die Erforschung der Apokalyptik*, in D. HELLHOLM [ed.], *Apocalypticism in the Mediterranean World and the Near East. Proceedings of the International Colloquium on Apocalypticism Uppsala, August 12–17, 1979*, 2. Aufl., Tübingen, J.C.B. Mohr [Paul Siebeck], 1989, pp. 495–530, p. 513).

78. Zu den Belegen der Wendung im *MLM* s. B.Z. WACHOLDER / M.G. ABEGG / J. BOWLEY, p. 331.

79. Zur Verwandtschaft von *Myst* mit dem *mûsār lamēbîn* cf. L.H. SCHIFFMAN, *4QMysteries^b*, p. 203; ID., *4QMysteries^a*, 207f.; ID., *Reclaiming the Dead Sea Scrolls*, 206; ID., *Mysteries*, p. 31; T. ELGVIN, *Admonition Texts*, p. 179; ID., *Wisdom, Revelation, and Eschatology*, pp. 447f.; ID., *Early Essene Eschatology*, pp. 132.153–157.

80. Zur Sache und zur Datierung der Zwei-Geister-Lehre s. A. LANGE, *Weisheit und Prädestination*, pp. 126–130.

Koh 5,5) in 1Q27 6₂ Gegenstand der weisheitlichen Reflexion – wobei der erhaltene Textbestand eine Anspielung auf Lev 5,18 wahrscheinlich macht (s.o., p. 126 Anm. 43). Daß in 4Q299 65 die Urim und Thummim im Zusammenhang mit der Wendung בשנה אַחת[א (»einmal im Jahr«) belegt sind, läßt möglicherweise darauf schließen, daß *Myst* sich hier dem in Lev 16 beschriebenen Yom Kippur-Ritus widmet[81]. Auf einen halachischen Zusammenhang dürfte schließlich auch die Tatsache hinweisen, daß in 4Q299 66 חוק und חול kurz aufeinander folgen[82]:

$$
\begin{array}{rc}
1 & [\ldots]\text{ם} \mathring{ק}\text{וּם} \mathring{ת}\text{ם}\circ[\ldots] \\
2 & [\ldots]\circ\text{ולֹא ידעתם}[\ldots] \\
3 & [\ldots \text{ולֹחול ואת}\text{ם}[\ldots] \\
4 & [\ldots]\text{ל עם אשמ}\mathring{ה}[\ldots] \\
\end{array}
$$

(1) »[…]∘*tm* Gebot[…]
(2) […]ihr habt nicht erkannt ∘[…]
(3) […]für profanes und ih[r …]
(4) […]*l* mit Schuld[…]

Die Eschatologie ist in *Myst* zumindest an einer Stelle von zentraler Bedeutung, 1Q27 1 I₅₋₇ par 4Q300 3₄₋₆ schildert die eschatologische Offenbarung der Weisheit und die eschatologische Vernichtung des Frevels:

כי יהיה

5 וֹזֹה לכם האות בהסגר מולדי עולה וגלה הרֹשע מפני הצדק כגלות
[חושׁ]ך מפני

6 אור וכתום עשן וא[י]ננו עוד כן יתם הרשע לעֹד והצדק יגלה כשמׁשׁ תכון

7 תבֹל וכול תומכי רזי פלא אינמה עוד ודעה תמלא תבל ואין שם לעֹ[נ]ד
אולת

»(5) Und dies soll ihnen das Zeichen sein, daß es so sein wird: Wenn die Kinder des Frevels ausgeliefert werden werden, dann wird der Frevel entschwinden vor der Gerechtigkeit, wie die Finsternis entschwindet vor (6) dem Licht. Und wie Rauch verfliegt[83] und n[icht] mehr ist, so wird der Frevler für immer vergehen[84]. Und die Gerechtigkeit wird offenbart werden, wie die Sonne aufgeht[85] über (7) der

---

81. Zur Sache s. L.H. SCHIFFMAN, *4QMysteries^a*, pp. 251f.; ID., *Mysteries*, p. 82.

82. Ob die weiteren Belege von חוק im *Book of Mysteries* (4Q299 18₁; 58₂) auf die Gebote des Sinaigesetzes bezogen werden können, kann wegen starker Textbeschädigungen nicht mehr sicher gesagt werden.

83. Wörtlich »aufhört«.

84. Wörtlich »aufhören«.

85. תכון ist Impf. fem. Ni. (3. Person) von כון (cf. G. VERMES, *The Dead Sea Scrolls in English*, 3. Aufl., Sheffield, Sheffield Academic Press, 1987, p. 239). Wörtlich wäre zu übersetzen »wie die Sonne sich hinstellt in Bezug auf die Erde.« A. DUPONT–SOMMER (p. 354) nimmt wohl das Nomen תכון an und übersetzt mit »Norm«. L.H. SCHIFFMAN möchte תכון als »measure« verstanden wissen und übersetzt »(throughout) the full measure of the world« (*4QMysteries^b*, p. 214; cf. ID., *Mysteries*, p. 105). F. GARCÍA

Erde. Und alle, die die wunderbaren Geheimnisse festhalten[86], werden nicht mehr sein. Und Erkenntnis wird die Welt erfüllen, und Torheit wird es dort nimmermehr geben.

Nach einer eschatologischen Prophezeiung über die Vernichtung der Frevler beschreiben die Zeilen, woran das Eintreffen dieser Prophezeiung zu erkennen ist: »Wenn die Kinder des Frevels ausgeliefert werden werden, dann wird der Frevel entschwinden vor der Gerechtigkeit, wie die Finsternis entschwindet vor dem Licht« (Zeile 5f.). Erst nach dem eschatologischen Untergang des Frevels wird dann die präexistente weisheitliche Ordnung des Seins verwirklicht werden: »Und wie Rauch verfliegt und n[icht] mehr ist, so wird der Frevler für immer vergehen. Und die Gerechtigkeit wird offenbart werden, wie die Sonne aufgeht über der Erde. Und alle, die die wunderbaren Geheimnisse festhalten, werden nicht mehr sein. Und Erkenntnis wird die Welt erfüllen, und Torheit wird es dort nimmermehr geben« (Zeile 6f.).

Eschatologisch könnten auch die Zeilen 4Q299 56$_{1-5}$ zu interpretieren sein: Dort werden im Kontext der Wendung במשפט יריב א[ות (»im Gericht wird er streiten m[it«; Zeile 2) Personen erwähnt, die »se[in] Gebot übertreten (בכול עוברי גי[ה]ו; Zeile 3) und dem Frevel beistehen« (עוזרי רשעה; Zeile 4)[87].

Die eschatologische Zerstörung des Frevels und Inthronisierung Israels wird auch in 4Q301 3$_{6ff.}$ thematisiert[88]:

[... הדר]וֹנ[ו וחמתֹו ברוב] הוא[ן וגדו]ל אפי[ון ב]א[ן הוֹא וֹנ[כֹב]ֹה[...]	6
[...]ה[וֹא]ה בהמון רחמיו ונורא הואה במֹזמת אפו נכבֹד הוא[ה...]	7
[... הֹואה ונֹהֹדר ובֹעֹם אל בֹעֹם וֹנֹ[כֹבֹד אֹל בֹעֹם קֹודשו ונֹהֹדר הֹ[ואה ...]	8
[...יֹו]בברכות הואה גֹדול קֹ[ן]דֹש ... הואה ונֹהֹדֹרֹ[ן בֹחֹירֹין...]	9
[...ועשות] רשעה קֹ[ץ ו]בֹכלוֹ[ת...]וֹתֹן ה[ֹדרם ו...]	10

6   […]h und er wird geehrt um seiner Langmut willen, [und] er ist [groß] in der Fülle [seines] Zorns, [und] er [wird verherrlicht …]

7   […]ist er wegen des Reichtums[89] seines Erbarmens, aber er wird gefürchtet wegen des Plans seines Zorns. Er wird geehrt […]

MARTÍNEZ dagegen interpretiert תכון verbal und übersetzt »like a sun which regulates the world« (p. 399).
    86. Zur Übersetzung cf. A. DUPONT–SOMMER, p. 354. G. VERMES (p. 239) nimmt einen Euphemismus an und übersetzt statt »wunderbare Geheimnisse« »mysteries of sin«. Dies erscheint mir jedoch unwahrscheinlich, da kurz vorher (Zeile 2) die רזי פשע genannt werden.
    87. Gegen L.H. SCHIFFMAN, *4QMysteries*^{a}, p. 247: »Again we encounter the motif of God's doing justice against those who violate his commandments.«
    88. Zur Transkription s. A. LANGE, *Physiognomie oder Gotteslob? 4Q301 3*, in DSD 4 (1997), 282-294, pp. 287ff.
    89. Zur Übersetzung cf. D.J.A. CLINES, *The Dictionary of Classical Hebrew*, Bd. 2: ו–ב, Sheffield, Sheffield Academic Press, 1995, p. 569.

8 [...]*bw* und weil er es am Ende zur Herrschaft einsetzen wird, [und] Gott wird sich durch sein heiliges Volk ehren, und er wird verherrlicht [...]

9 [...]Erwählte und [er] wird verherrlicht[...] sein [hei]liges. Er ist groß wegen [seiner] Segnungen[...]

10 [...]ihre [Pr]acht *wt*[...]wenn er beendet die Zeit des Frevels und macht[...]

Noch deutlicher als in *Myst* ist die Kombination von Eschatologie und einer Identifikation von Weisheit und Tora in dem besser erhaltenen und aus dem gleichen Tradentenkreis stammenden *mûsar lammēbîn* bezeugt. Das Werk bindet Toravorschriften mehrmals in Paränesen und weisheitliche Reflexionen ein und identifiziert die weisheitliche Urordnung mit der Tora. Zumindest zu Beginn der wohl älteren Version des Werkes (4Q417 2 par 4Q418 43)[90] spielt das Sinaigesetz und ein als »Vision der Erklärung« (חזון ההגוֹּה 4Q417 2 I$_{16}$) bezeichnetes halachisches Werk eine bedeutende Rolle. In dem dieser Version des *MLM* als epistemologische Einleitung vorangestellten Abschnitt wird begründet, warum ein als מבין bezeichneter weisheitlicher Lehrer[91] Gottes Herrlichkeit, seine machtvollen Taten, seine wunderbaren Geheimnisse und die eigene Bedeutungslosigkeit erkennen kann: Es wird ausgeführt, daß Gott die Welt mit Hilfe dualer Unterscheidungen geordnet und geschaffen habe. Dies wird am Beispiel von Mann und Frau verdeutlicht. Für den Weisen ist Erkenntnis anhand dieser, hier als רז נהיה oder מחשבה bezeichneten dualen Ordnung möglich (4Q417 2 I$_{8-12}$). In einer zweiten Begründung für die Erkenntnisfähigkeit des מבין legt der *MLM* dar, daß dem Weisen diese Ordnung aufgrund von zwei Offenbarungen zugänglich ist. Die erste Offenbarung wird in Anspielung auf Ex 32,16 geschildert: »[denn] eingehauen hat er das Ge[b]ot [geb]racht und einschlagen lassen hat er alle Heimsuchung (כי ה[בא ח]ר[וֹ]ת החוקִֹ֫ים הֿחקיק כול הפקודֿה; 2 I$_{14}$)[92]. Die dem Sein zugrundeliegende duale weisheitliche Ordnung der Welt wurde somit Mose in Form der Tora offenbart.

Auch die zweite Begründung verweist mit der »Vision der Erinnerung« auf ein schriftlich fixiertes Werk:

15 כי חרות מחוקק לאל עֿל כול עֿ[וֹלוֹת] בני שית וספר זכרון כתוב לפניו

---

90. Zu 4Q417 2 als Anfang der Handschrift 4Q417 und den verschiedenen Versionen des *MLM* s.o., p. 127.

91. Zu מבין als Bezeichnung eines Weisheitslehrers s. A. LANGE, *Weisheit und Prädestination*, pp. 55–57.

92. Daß hier auf Ex 32,16 und keinen anderen Vers der Sinaiperikope angespielt wird, ist durch das im AT nur dort bezeugte חרות belegt.

עם

16 לשמרי דברו והוֹאה חזון ההגֹה ס֠פר זכרון וינחילה לאנש עם רוח [כי]א

17 כתבנית קדושים יצרו ועוד לוֹא נֹתֹן הגֹה לרוח בֹשׂר כי לא ידע בין

18 טֹוֹב לרֹע כמשפט [ר]וחו *vacat* ואתה בן מב[ין] הֹבֹט *vacat* ברז נהיה ודע

»(15) denn Eingemeißeltes wurde eingehauen von[93] Gott um all der
F[revel] der Söhne Seths willen, und das Buch der Erinnerung wurde
vor ihm geschrieben (16) für die, die auf sein Wort achten, und die
Vision der Erklärung ist das Buch der Erinnerung. Und er hat es
Enosch[94] gemeinsam mit dem Volk des Geistes zum Erbteil gegeben,
[den]n (17) gemäß der Gestalt der Heiligen ist seine [Ge]sinnung.
Doch die Erklärung wurde nicht dem Geist des Fleisches gegeben,
denn er vermag nicht, zwischen (18) Gut und Böse zu unterscheiden
gemäß dem Gesetz seines Geistes.

Bei der zweiten Offenbarungsform der dualen weisheitlichen Urordnung
handelt es sich also um eine Enosch gegebene Offenbarung. Diese wird
als חזון ההגה (»Vision der Erklärung«) bezeichnet und mit dem ספר זכרון
(»Buch der Erinnerung«) aus Mal 3,15f. identifiziert (4Q417 2 I$_{15f.}$). In
den essenischen Texten von Qumran wird dieser חזון ההגה als ספר ההגו
(»Buch der Erklärung«; 1QSa I$_{6f.}$; CD X$_6$; XIII$_{2f.}$; XIV$_{6-8}$) bezeichnet.
Daß CD XIV$_8$ das »Buch der Erklärung« mit der Tora parallelisiert, belegt seinen halachischen Charakter und seine autoritative Geltung. Die
halachische Natur der »Vision der Erklärung« wird für den *MLM* durch
die Wendung לשמרי דברו (»für jene, die auf sein Wort achten«) bestätigt. Eine Stichwortverknüpfung mit dem kurz vorher erwähnten Sinaigesetz wird durch das חרות in Zeile 15 hergestellt. Da es nach Darstellung des *MLM* Enosch, dem Sohn Seths (Gen 4,26), offenbart wird,
handelt es sich um eine ältere Form des Gesetzes als die Sinaitora. Laut
dem *MLM* wurde es von Gott eingemeißelt (מחוקק לאל; Zeile 15) bzw.
vor ihm geschrieben (כתוב לפניו; ibid.) und erscheint daher als ein
himmlisches Buch. חרות und מחוקק zeigen, daß es sich um die himmlischen Tafeln handelt. Das Sinaigesetz und die »Vision der Erklärung«,
bzw. das »Buch der Erinnerung«, stellen also zumindest stückhafte Ko-
pien der auf den himmlischen Tafeln festgelegten dualen weisheitlichen
Ordnung des Seins dar. Diese Identifikation der weisheitlichen
Urordnung mit der auf den himmlischen Tafeln festgehaltenen Tora erinnert an Jub 1, wo die Entstehung des Jubiläenbuchs und der Tora der-

93. »Bei Vben (sic) im Pass. nennt לְ den Urheber ...« (L. KOEHLER/W. BAUM-
GARTNER/J.J. STAMM/B. HARTMANN, *Hebräisches und Aramäisches Lexikon zum Alten
Testament*, 3. Aufl., Leiden et al., E.J. Brill, 1967–1996, p. 485). Zu אל als logischem
Subjekt von מחוקק cf. auch die Übersetzung von D.J. HARRINGTON, *Wisdom at Qumran*,
p. 144; cf. ID., *Wisdom Texts from Qumran*, p. 53.
94. Zur Übersetzung von אנוש als Eigennamen, s. A. LANGE, *Weisheit und Prädestination*, pp. 86f.

gestalt beschrieben sind, daß sie Mose am Sinai von einem Engel von den himmlischen Tafeln diktiert worden sind[95]. Neben Jub 1 sind besonders enge Berührungen mit Sir 24 und Bar 3,9–4,4 vorhanden.

Anders als das Buch Ben Sira und Bar 3,9–4,4 orientiert sich der *MLM* jedoch im Hauptteil des Werkes an konkreten Geboten der Tora: So werden in dem stark beschädigten Fragment 4Q415 2 die Gebote des Bundes (ובחוקי ברית; II₃) thematisiert, dazu gemahnt, den heiligen Bund nicht unbeachtet zu lassen (פן תפרעו ברית קד[ש »damit ihr nicht unbeachtet laßt den heiligen Bund«; II₄), und Bund und Tempel parallelisiert (בבית מכו[ני]כה]ובבריתך ת[»im Haus [deiner] Stä[tte]und in deinem Bund t[«; II₇). Auf Gebotsobservanz könnten auch die Mahnungen in 4Q416 2 II₈.₉f. par 4Q417 1 II₁₁.₁₂f.; 4Q418 8₈.₉f. hinweisen: וחוקיכה אל תרף וברזיכה השמר (»deine Gebote verlasse nicht und deine Geheimnisse beachte«)[96]; תנומה לעיניכה עד עשותכה [מצו...] (»Schlummer für deine Augen, bis du [das/ein Gebot] getan hast[...]«). Vor dem Hintergrund des Sinaigesetzes (Ex 20,12; Dtn 5,16) dürfte auch die Ermahnung, Vater und Mutter zu ehren (כבוד אביכה ברישכה ואמכה במצעדיכה »ehre deinen Vater in deiner Armut und deine Mutter bei deinen Schritten«; 4Q416 2 III₁₅f. par 4Q418 9₁₇), zu verstehen sein. 4Q417 6₂ belegt die Wendung]ל[חוקי אול (»]für Gebote Got[tes«). 4Q417 19₃ spricht im Zusammenhang mit dem Begriff מצוה (»Gebot«) vom Wandeln in Gerechtigkeit mit dem Freund (יתהל[ך בצדק את רע[הו)[97]. In 4Q418 81₇ mahnt der *MLM* im Kontext von Erwählungsaussagen und Aufforderungen zur Heiligung dazu, von jedem Gottes Gesetze zu erfragen (ואתה דרוש משפטיו מיד כול), dabei mag durch den Gebrauch von דרש bewußt ein exegetischer Ton in die Paränese eingetragen worden sein. Wenn in der folgenden Zeile von Gottes Liebe, ewiger Gnade und Erbarmen »wegen aller, die sein Wort beachten« (על כול שומרי דברו), gesprochen wird, dürfte ein weisheitlich-nomistischer Tun-Ergehen-Zusammenhang thematisiert sein, der sich an der Erfüllung des Gebots orientiert. Ohne daß der Kontext eine Interpretation erlauben würde, sind ברית und חוק in 4Q418

---

95. Zu den himmlischen Tafeln im Jubiläenbuch cf. F. GARCÍA MARTÍNEZ, *The Heavenly Tablets in the Book of Jubilees*, in M. ALBANI/J. FREY/A. LANGE (eds.), *Studies in the Book of Jubilees* (TSAJ, 65), Tübingen, Mohr Siebeck, 1997, 243–260; zu den himmlischen Tafeln im antiken Judentum cf. A. LANGE, *Weisheit und Prädestination*, 69–79.

96. השמר ist wegen des parallel gebrauchten תרף als Imperativ Hif'il und nicht als Imperativ Nif'al zu verstehen (gegen J. MAIER, Bd. 2, p. 432).

97. Ob in Zeile 2 des Fragments vom Allerheiligsten (דבירה »in ihrem Allerheiligsten«; so B.Z. WACHOLDER/M.G. ABEGG, p. 72 und J. MAIER, Bd. 2, p. 444) oder von einer Biene gesprochen wird (דבורה »mit ihrer Biene«; so D.J. HARRINGTON/J. STRUGNELL in ihrer in Vorbereitung befindlichen Edition der Handschrift), kann wegen starker Textbeschädigungen nicht mehr geklärt werden.

120₂ und 4Q418 123 I₃ belegt. Das עֹ[ם ראשית פרי בטנכה ובכור כל
בהמתכה] (»mi]t dem Ersten der Frucht deines Leibes und dem Erstgebo-
renen von all deinem Vieh«; 4Q423 3₄ par 1Q26 2₄) bezieht sich wohl
auf eine der Bestimmungen des Pentateuchs zum Erstlingsopfer (Ex
13,15; 22,28f.; 34,19f.; Lev 3,13; Num 18,15; 28,26ff.; Dtn 18,4;
26,1ff.; cf. Neh 10,37). Da die Wendung רֵאשִׁית פְּרִי sonst nur in Dtn
26,2.10[98] belegt ist, handelt es sich wahrscheinlich um Dtn 26,1ff. Eine
landwirtschaftliche Vorschrift aus dem Sinaigesetz wird in einem anderen Fragment des *MLM* aufgenommen: »So also in one of the agricul-
tural texts (4Q418 103) the best preserved part invokes the biblical law
of «mixed things» from Leviticus 19:19 and Deuteronomy 22:9–11 ...
The biblical ruling is adapted to the format of the wisdom instruction
and used as a consideration ... in sapiential advice.«[99] Und schließlich
sind noch die Ausführungen zum Gelübde in 4Q416 2 IV₈f. (par 4Q418
10₈f.) zu erwähnen:

וכל שבועת אסרה לנֹֹ[ו]דֹרֹ נֹֹדֹ[ר ...] הפר על מוצא פיכה וברצונכה הניא[ן...]

»und jedes ihrer Enthaltungsgelübde für den, [der] ein Gelübde
gelo[bt ... er hat aufgehoben die Äußerungen deines Mundes und
durch deinen Willen hat er gewehrt ...«

Das Vokabular (נדר, אסר, נוא Hi., פרר Hi.) findet sich in dieser Zusammenstellung in den Bestimmungen zu Gelübden und Schwü-
ren Num 30,2–17[100]. Die Wendung שְׁבֻעַת אִסָּר findet sich im Alten Testament nur in Num 30,14. מוצא פיכה (Zeile 9) kann mit כָּל־מוֹצָא שְׂפָתֶיהָ
(Num 30,13) verglichen werden. Da im Kontext das Verhältnis von
Mann und Frau thematisiert ist, dürfte der *MLM* an dieser Stelle die Bestimmungen zum Eid einer verheirateten Frau von Num 30,11–16 in seine Erörterung eingebunden haben (cf. 11QTᵃ LIII₇–LIV₃)[101].

Der *MLM* zeigt somit deutlich, daß im Tradentenkreis von *MLM* und
Myst Weisheit und Tora nicht nur miteinander identifiziert wurden, sondern – für die weisheitliche Literatur außergewöhnlich – die einzelnen
Gebote der Tora auch Gegenstand weisheitlicher Reflexion und Paränese
waren. Dies entspricht dem oben geschilderten Befund der zweiten Redaktion des Buches Koh.

98. In Dtn 26,2 wird die Lesart מֵרֵאשִׁית פְּרִי nur von einem Teil der masoretischen
Texttradition, 𝔐 und 𝔊 bezeugt, die anderen Textzeugen lesen מֵרֵאשִׁית כָּל־פְּרִי.
99. D.J. HARRINGTON, *Wisdom Texts from Qumran*, p. 59; zur Sache cf. J. MAIER, Bd.
2, pp. 463f.
100. Zum Gelübde im *MLM* cf. auch 4Q417 1₁.
101. Beim momentanen Editionsstand des *MLM* muß unklar bleiben, ob das Werk
sich an dieser Stelle auf die m.E. im 3. Jh. v.Chr. verfaßte Tempelrolle oder, wohl wahrscheinlicher, Num 30 bezieht.

Eschatologisches ist im *MLM* in 4Q416 1 und 4Q418 69 II themati-
sisiert[102]: Die Zeilen 4Q416 1$_{1-9}$ sind zwar stark beschädigt, die erhaltenen Textreste lassen aber noch Vermutungen über ihren Inhalt zu: Die
Wendung מועד במועד (»Festzeit um Festzeit«; Zeile 3) könnte auf einen
kultischen Hintergrund hinweisen, während das וצבא השמים הכין (»und
das Heer des Himmels hat er aufgestellt«; Zeile 7) auf ein himmlisches
Geschehen deutet. וכל פקודתהמה (Zeile 9) könnte eschatologisch zu verstehen sein und dann mit »ihre ganze Heimsuchung« zu übersetzen sein,
jedoch sind auch die Übersetzungen von J. MAIER (»all ihr Auftrag«,
Bd. 2, p. 430) und F. GARCÍA MARTÍNEZ (»all his commands«, *Dead Sea
Scrolls*, p. 383) keinesfalls auszuschließen. Eindeutig eschatologischen
Charakter haben erst die Zeilen 10–14. Sie schildern ein endzeitliches
Gericht mit kosmologischen Dimensionen:

בשׁמים ישפוט על עבודת רשעה וכל בני אמת ירצו עֹ[...   10

קצה ויפחדו ויריעו כל אשר התגללו בה כי שמים יראֹה[...   11

מים ותהמות פחדו ויתערערו כל רוח בשר ובני השמי[ם...   12

[מש]פטה וכל עולה תתם עוד ושלם קץ האמֹ[ת...   13

בכל קצי עד כי אל אמת הוא ומקדם שנֹ[...   14

»(10) Im Himmel wird er über den Freveldienst richten, aber alle
Söhne der Wahrheit werden wohlgefällig angenommen werden ʹ[...]
(11) sein (scil. des Frevels?) Ende. Und es werden sich fürchten und
schreien alle, die sich in ihm (scil. dem Frevel?) wälzen, denn sie sind
solche die Furcht setzen[...(12) Wasser und Fluten beben, und aller
Geist des Fleisches wird geschleift werden[103], und die Söhne des
Himme[ls ...] (13) sein (scil. des Frevels?) [Ur]teil/[Ger]icht. Und aller Frevel wird dauerhaft enden, und die Epoche der Wahrh[eit] wird
er vollständig machen[...] (14) in allen Epochen der Ewigkeit. Denn
er ist ein Gott der Wahrheit und von Urzeit her *šny*[...]

Die Ausführungen von Zeile 10, daß Gott im Himmel über den Freveldienst richten werde, während er alle Söhne der Wahrheit wohlgefällig

---

102. T. ELGVINs Auslegungen von 4Q416 1 und 4Q418 69 II im Kontext des
essenischen Dualismus (*Wisdom, Revelation, and Eschatology,* pp. 456–459; *Early
Essene Eschatology,* pp. 146–164) basieren im wesentlichen auf seiner materialen Rekonstruktion der Handschriften 4Q416 und 4Q418 (*The Reconstruction of Sapiential Work A,*
pp. 563–568.570–574). Diese erscheint jedoch nach den Ergebnissen der materialen Rekonstruktion der MLM-Handschriften von A. STEUDEL und B. LUCASSEN problematisch.
Bis zur Veröffentlichung ihrer Arbeit gilt es daher, sich bei der Interpretation der Fragmente 4Q416 1 und 4Q418 69 ausschließlich auf den Text dieser Fragmente selbst zu beschränken. Zum Dualismus im *MLM* cf. J. FREY, pp. 298f.

103. ויתערערו ist als Hitpalpel von ערר zu verstehen (cf. Jer 51,58). Alternativ könnte
es ein Nitpalpel von ערר II sein (»entblößt werden«; so F. GARCÍA MARTÍNEZ, *Dead Sea
Scrolls,* p. 383 [zum Bedeutungsspektrum von ערר II im Nitpalpel s. M. JASTROW,
Dictionary, pp. 1121f.]).

aufnehme (וכל בני אמת ירצו), zeigen, daß die Eschatologie des *MLM* zumindest in der in 4Q416 bezeugten Version von einem ethischen Dualismus geprägt ist. Dies wird durch die Hoffnung, aller Frevel werde dauerhaft enden und Gott werde die Epoche der Wahrheit vollständig machen (Zeile 13), erhärtet. Eine kosmische Dimension erhält diese an einem ethischen Dualismus orientierte Eschatologie durch das Motiv vom Beben der Wasser und Fluten (Zeile 12). Mit dem *kî*-Satz in Zeile 14 beginnt eine hymnische Begründung dieses eschatologischen Gerichts, deren Ende nicht mehr erhalten ist. Die Wendung להכין צדק בין טוב לר[ע] (»um Gerechtigkeit festzusetzen zwischen Gut und Böse«; Zeile 15) könnte im Zusammenspiel mit dem מקדם (»von Urzeiten her«) aus Zeile 14 auf Gottes Festsetzen der Ordnung der Welt vor und während der Schöpfung deuten. י]צר בשר הואה (»ein [Ge]bilde von Fleisch ist er«; Zeile 16) erinnert an die Niedrigkeitsdoxologien der Hodayot. Die Begründung für das eschatologische Gericht könnte also auf die Gerechtigkeit und Wahrhaftigkeit Gottes, sein Festsetzen einer gerechten Seinsordnung und die menschliche Niedrigkeit und Nichtigkeit abheben. Falls im vorhergehenden Kontext himmlische Ordnung und Kult thematisiert sein sollten, erscheint es möglich, daß der begründende Hymnus hierauf zurückgreift und das Gerichtsszenario inkludiert. Auf diese Weise würde dann die Vollkommenheit und Gerechtigkeit der himmlischen Ordnung mit der menschlichen Nichtigkeit kontrastiert.

In 418 69 II finden sich, jeweils auf ein *vacat* folgend, drei Anreden: ואתם אוילי לב (»und nun, ihr Toren des Herzens«; Zeile 4), ואתם בחירי אמת ורודפי] (»und ihr Erwählten der Wahrheit und Verfolger von [«; Zeile 10), ואתה בן [מבין] (»und du Sohn des [Lehrers«; Zeile 15). Sowohl *vacat* als auch Anrede machen deutlich, daß es sich bei 4Q418 69 II$_{4-9.10-15.15ff.}$ um eigenständige Abschnitte handelt. Da jede Anrede mit ו eingeleitet wird, dürfte im nicht mehr erhaltenen Text zumindest noch eine weitere Gruppe angesprochen worden sein. Das verknüpfende ו weist die Zeilen 4Q418 69 II$_{?-4}$; 4Q418 69 II$_{4-9}$; 4Q418 69 II$_{10-15}$ und 4Q418 69 II$_{15ff.}$ ferner als Unterabschnitte einer längeren Paränese aus, die verschiedene Adressaten anspricht. Für die Frage nach der Bedeutung der Eschatologie im *MLM* ist die Ermahnung jener, die törichten Herzens sind, von Interesse (4Q418 69 II$_{4-9}$):

4	...]הֹם ובדעה כול גליהם *vacat* ועתה אוילי לב מה טוב ללוא
5	[מה] השקט ללוא היה ומה משפט ללוא נוסד ומה יאנחו מתים על מ[...]ם
6	וֹתֹמֹ[...]ל נוצרתם ולשחת עולם תשובתם כי תקˢˢ[...] וֹאֹכֹם[...]
7	מחשכיֹםֹ יצרחו על רובכם וכול נהיה עולם דורשי אמת יעורו למשפט]ˢ[...]

8 ישמדו כול אוילי לב ובני עולה לוא ימצאו עו̇ד[וכ]ול מחזיקי רשעה י̇בש[ו ...]

9 במ̇שפטכם ירו̇עו מוסדי הרקיע וירעמו כול צנ[...]ל[...].[...]ל̇ אהב̇י̇[...]

»(4) [...]*hm* und mit Erkenntnis all ihre Wogen. *vacat* Und nun, ihr
Toren des Herzens, was ist gut ohne (5) [... was] ist Ruhe ohne Werden und was Recht, ohne daß es gegründet wird, und was stöhnen
Tote über *m*[...]*m* (6) und vollendet[...]*l* ihr wurdet geformt und zu
ewigem Verderben ist eure Rückkehr, denn *tq∞*[...]*w'km*[...] (7)
dunkle Plätze schreien über eurer Menge und alles wird in Ewigkeit
sein. Die nach Wahrheit suchen werden erwachen zum Gericht°[...]
(8) und sie werden alle Toren des Herzens ausrotten, und Söhne des
Frevels wird man nicht mehr finden, [und al]le die Frevel ergriffen
haben werden zuschand[en ...]. (9) Während eures Gerichts werden
die Fundamente des Firmaments aufschreien und donnern alle
z[...]*l*[...]*l* die lieben[...]«

Das eschatologische Gericht dient in diesem Abschnitt als Begründung
der Ermahnung jener, die törichten Herzens sind. Die Eschatologie des
MLM ist hier von einem ethisch-kosmologischen Dualismus geprägt. Die
ethische Komponente tritt in den Ermahnungen an die Toren des Herzens
zutage, daß ihre Rückkehr zu ewigem Verderben sein wird (Zeile 6), daß
jene, die nach Wahrheit suchen, zu ihrem Gericht erwachen werden (Zeile
7), daß alle Toren des Herzens ausgerottet werden, daß man alle Söhne
des Frevels nicht mehr finden werde und daß alle, die Frevel ergriffen haben, zu Schande werden (Zeile 8). Die kosmologische Komponente wird
in den Vorhersagen, dunkle Plätze würden über ihrer Menge schreien
(Zeile 7) und während ihres Gerichts würden die Fundamente des Firmaments aufschreien (Zeile 9), deutlich. Für die Frage nach der Identität des
zweiten Redaktors von Koh ist es von Interesse, daß das eschatologische
Gericht über die Toren wie in Koh 11,9c; 12,14 als משפט bezeichnet wird
(Zeile 7 und 9). Daß Gott im erhaltenen Text keine aktive Rolle in diesem
Gericht übernimmt, mag an seinem Erhaltungszustand liegen, denn in
4Q416 1 ist Gott unzweifelhaft selbst der eschatologische Richter.

Zwei weitere Weisheitstexte bezeugen eine ähnliche Kombination
von Eschatologie und einer Verschmelzung von Weisheit und Tora[104]:
In 4Q525 3(E. PUECH 2)[105] II findet sich eine an Ps 1 angelehnte Identifi-

104. Zwar finden sich auch bei Ben Sira neben seiner u.a. in Sir 24 belegten Identifi-
kation von Weisheit und Tora eschatologische Aussagen (Sir 48,22–25). Sie sind jedoch
Teil des von ihm aus der Tradition übernommenen und um Sir 49,14–50,26 erweiterten
Lobpreises der Väter und sind auch dort nur im Zusammenhang mit dem Propheten Jesaja
belegt. Henoch wird dagegen in Sir 44,16 auffälligerweise ohne einen Hinweis auf
Eschatologisches gerühmt. Zu den inhaltlichen Parallelen zwischen Koh 12,13 und Ben
Sira cf. M. GILBERT, im vorliegenden Band, pp. 161–179.

105. Zur alternativen Fragmentenzählung von E. PUECH s. *4Q525 et les péricopes des
béatitudes en Ben Sira et Matthieu*, in *RB* 98 (1991) 80–106, p. 83.

kation von Weisheit und Tora, während in 4Q525 5$_{5ff.}$ der rechte Lebenswandel von Weisen (חכמׂים; Zeile 7), Gottesfürchtigen (י[ראי
אלוהים; Zeile 8) und Einsichtigen (נבונים; Zeile 9) als an ihren (scil. der
Tora) Geboten und Zurechtweisungen (חוקיה ובתוכחותיה; Zeile 9) orientiert geschildert wird. 4Q525 15 und 4Q525 22$_{1-3}$ können in ihrer
Motivik durchaus im Sinne eines eschatologischen Strafgerichts verstanden werden. Signifikant ist auch die wohl ins 1. Jh. v.Chr. oder ins 1. Jh.
n.Chr. zu datierende und evtl. in Ägypten entstandene *Sapientia
Salomonis*[106]: Auf eine Schilderung des Schicksals von Guten und Bösen im Endgericht (Weish 4,16–5,23) folgt eine Ermahnung der Herrschenden, nach Weisheit zu suchen (Weish 6,1–23). Diese wird in
Weish 6,17f. (cf. 6,4) mit der Tora identifiziert. Eine, in welcher Form
auch immer vermittelte Beeinflussung der *Sapientia Salomonis* durch
den hinter *MLM* und *Myst* stehenden Tradentenkreis oder die Werke
selbst erscheint mir nicht ausgeschlossen[107]. Anders als in dem *Book of
Mysteries* findet sich in beiden Werken jedoch kein Koh-Zitat. Es erscheint mir daher wahrscheinlicher, den zweiten Redaktor des
Koheletbuches im Tradentenkreis von *MLM* und *Myst* zu lokalisieren.

Der einzige signifikante Unterschied zwischen dem zweiten Redaktor
des Koheletbuches und den beiden letztgenannten Texten ist eschatolo-
gischer Natur. Auffälligerweise fehlt der besonders im *MLM* belegte
ethisch-kosmische Dualismus in der zweiten Redaktion des Koheletbuches. Der Grund hierfür scheint mir in ihrem Charakter zu liegen. Wie
insbesondere Koh 8,5f. und 12,12f. zeigen, bemüht sie sich in Sprache
und Motitivik dem Buch Kohelet selbst zu entsprechen[108]. Daher dürfte
sie auch auf den Gebrauch dualistischer Motivik oder ausgeführte
Gerichtsszenarien verzichten[109].

106. Zu Datierung und Abfassungsort s. O. EISSFELDT, p. 815; L. ROST, *Einleitung in
die alttestamentlichen Apokryphen und Pseudepigraphen einschließlich der großen
Qumran-Handschriften*, Heidelberg, Quelle & Meyer, 1971, p. 43; D. WINSTON, *The
Wisdom of Solomon. A New Translation with Introduction and Commentary* (AB, 43),
New York, Doubleday, 1979, pp. 20–25; C. LARCHER, *Le Livre de la Sagesse ou la Sagesse de Salomon*, Bd. 1–3 (EB, nouvelle série, 1), Paris, Gabalda, 1983-1985, Bd. 1,
pp. 148–161; O. KAISER, *Grundriß*, Bd. 3, pp. 114–116; S. CHEON, *The Exodus Story in
the Wisdom of Solomon. A Study in Biblical Interpretation* (Journal for the Study of the
Pseudepigrapha Supplement Series, 23), Sheffield, Sheffield Academic Press, 1997,
pp. 125–149; L.L. GRABBE, *Wisdom of Solomon* (Guides to Apocrypha and
Pseudepigrapha), Sheffield, Sheffield Academic Press, 1997, pp. 87–91.

107. Um das Verhältnis der *Sapientia Salomonis* zum *mûsar lammēbîn*, dem *Book of
Mysteries* und dem hinter diesen Texten vermuteten Tradentenkreis zu klären, bedürfte es
einer eigenen Untersuchung, die an dieser Stelle nicht geleistet werden kann, jedoch mehr
als wünschenswert wäre.

108. S.o., p. 118; cf. auch G.T. SHEPPARD, pp. 124f. und L. SCHWIENHORST-SCHÖNBERG-
ER, p. 10.

109. G.T. SHEPPARD vergleicht Koh 12,12–14 mit Sir und kommt zu dem Schluß:

Zusammenfassend kann man sagen, daß im *Book of Mysteries* eine in hellenistischer Zeit äußerst seltene Koh-Rezeption belegt (1Q27 1 II₃) ist. Sowohl *Myst* selbst, wie auch der aus dem gleichen Tradentenkreis stammende *MLM* verschmelzen Weisheit und Tora miteinander und machen einzelne Gebote der Tora zum Gegenstand weisheitlicher Reflexion. In beiden Werken ist die Eschatologie von einiger Bedeutung. Wie der zweite Redaktor des Koh sind beide Werke weisheitlicher Natur. Der zweite Redaktor von Koh dürfte daher mit einiger Wahrscheinlichkeit in jener weisheitlichen Gruppe zu verorten sein, aus der auch *Myst* und *MLM* stammen. Da sowohl der *MLM* als auch *Myst* wegen des in ihnen für weisheitliche Texte ungewöhnlich stark dokumentierten kultischen Interesses am Tempel lokalisiert werden können, ist wohl auch der zweite Redaktor des Buches Kohelet hier zu verorten.

KOHELETS KRITIK AN DER TEMPELWEISHEIT

Die Bedeutung des in *Myst* und *MLM* greifbaren, am Jerusalemer Tempel beheimateten weisheitlichen Tradentenkreises für die Exegese des Buches Koh beschränkt sich m.E. nicht auf die Identifikation seines zweiten Redaktors. In den nichtessenischen Weisheitstexten aus Qumran dokumentiert sich vielmehr auch eine von Koh kritisierte weisheitliche Schule, die ich im folgenden als Tempelweisheit bezeichnen möchte:

Wie ich schon an anderer Stelle zu zeigen versuchte[110], setzt sich Kohelet neben der traditionellen Weisheit auch mit der Verschmelzung von Weisheit und Tora auseinander. Neben der noch zu besprechenden Aufnahme der Bestimmungen zum Gelübde (Dtn 23,22–24; s.u., pp. 154f.) und zum *šᵉgāgâ*-Opfer (s. Lev 4–5; Num 15,22–31; s., pp. 125.155f.) aus dem Pentateuch sprechen hierfür vor allem Koh 2,26; 7,26. An beiden Stellen nimmt Koh eine im Zusammenhang mit der Toraerfüllung belegte Formel auf und wandelt sie signifikant ab: Sie ist im Dtn und im dtr Geschichtswerk in der Form עָשָׂה טוֹב וְיָשָׁר בְּעֵינֵי יהוה belegt (z.B. Dtn 6,18; 12,28; 1Kön 15,11; 2 Kön 20,3; MMT C 31f.) und wird in den Chronikbüchern, sofern ihnen nicht das DtrG zugrundeliegt, zu וַיַּעַשׂ הַטּוֹב וְהַיָּשָׁר וְהָאֱמֶת לִפְנֵי יהוה אֱלֹהָיו (2Chr 31,20) abgewandelt. Das Buch Kohelet nimmt diese ihm etwa gleichzeitig belegte Vari-

---

»only Sirach has exactly the same ideology as Qoh. 12:13–14« (p. 127). Seiner Meinung nach hat der zweite Redaktor daher entweder Sir gekannt oder unabhängig von ihm seine Überzeugungen geteilt. Gegen diese Auffassung muß jedoch betont werden, daß Sir die in Koh 12,12–14 bezeugten eschatologischen Gerichtsvorstellungen nicht kennt, daß sich die Theologie Ben Siras also in einem wichtigen Punkt von derjenigen des zweiten Redaktors unterscheidet.

110. Cf. *Weisheit und Torheit*, pp. 95ff.

ante auf und kürzt sie um die Elemente עָשָׂה und וְהַיָּשֶׁר וְהָאֱמֶת (Koh 2,26; 7,16: טוֹב לִפְנֵי הָאֱלֹהִים bzw. Koh 2,26 טוֹב לְפָנָיו) (2,26). Mit der Streichung von עָשָׂה will er zum Ausdruck bringen, daß das in Koh 2,26; 7,26 thematisierte gute bzw. schlechte Ergehen eines Menschen – in Koh 7,26 als Entrinnen bzw. Gefangen-Genommen-Werden von der Frau beschrieben – nicht von seinem Handen abhängt. Unabhängig davon ist allein entscheidend, ob Gott jemanden als gut betrachtet. Vor diesem Hintergrund dürfte auch die Kürzung des וְהַיָּשֶׁר וְהָאֱמֶת zu verstehen sein. Anders als das theologisch wertneutralere טוֹב dürfte die Wendung für Kohelet eine Orientierung an der Tora impliziert haben[111].

Die auf diese Weise von Koh angesprochene Identifikation von Weisheit und Tora ist schon vor dem 3. Jh. v.Chr. belegt und war zu seiner Zeit weitverbreitet. Es kann an wohlbekannte Belege wie Dtn 4,6; Ps 1; 19B; 119; Sir 24 und Bar 3,9–4,4 so wie an die oben erörterten Texte in *MLM*; *Myst*; und 4Q525 erinnert werden. Darüberhinaus sind das *Aramaic Levi Document* und das henochitische *Buch der Wächter* von Interesse: Das aus priesterlich-levitischen Kreisen stammende *Aramaic Levi Document* endet nach der Rekonstruktion von R.A. KUGLER[112] nach einem Bericht über die Einsetzung Levis zum (Hohen)priester, der ihm von Isaak vermittelten Kulthalacha und einer kurzen Familiengeschichte mit einem Preis der Weisheit und einer Paränese an Levis Nachkommen. Die Einleitung zum *Buch der Wächter* (1Hen 1–36) schildert in 1Hen 2,1–5,3, wie die Natur sich nach einer ihr vorgegebenen Ordnung verhält. Anschließend wird den Frevlern vorgeworfen: »Aber ihr habt nicht durchgehalten und das Gesetz des Herrn nicht erfüllt, sondern übertreten und habt mit großen (= hochmütigen) und harten (= trotzigen) Worten aus eurem unreinen Mund gegen seine Majestät geschmäht« (1Hen 5,4)[113]. Daher droht den Frevlern eschatologische Vernichtung, während den Auserwählten das eschatologische Heil gilt. Die Weisheit gilt dem Buch der Wächter dabei als ein eschatologisches Gut: »Und dann wird den Auserwählten Weisheit verliehen werden, und sie alle werden leben und nicht mehr sündigen, weder aus Pflichtvergessenheit noch aus Überheblichkeit, sondern die weise sind, werden demütig sein« (1Hen 5,8)[114].

111. Zur Sache s. A. LANGE, *Weisheit und Torheit*, pp. 109–111.155; gegen R. BRAUN, pp. 51–53.

112. Zur Textfolge cf. R.A. KUGLER, *From Patriarch to Priest. The Levi-Priestly Tradition from Aramaic Levi to Testament of Levi* (Society of Biblical Literature Early Judaism and Its Literature, 9), Atlanta, Scholars Press, 1996, pp. 23–59.

113. Übersetzung nach S. UHLIG, *Das Äthiopische Henochbuch* (JSHRZ, 5.6), Gütersloh, Gütersloher Verlagshaus Gerd Mohn, pp. 513f.

114. Übersetzung nach *op. cit.*, p. 515.

Bei den sich im 3. und frühen 2. Jh. v.Chr. häufenden Belegen für eine Identifikation von Weisheit und Tora und der schon oben beobachteten Auseinandersetzung Kohelets mit dieser Position erscheint es wahrscheinlich, daß sie auch im Hintergrund steht, wenn er sich in Koh 4,17–5,6 mit kultischen Riten beschäftigt und dabei sogar eine Vorschrift aus dem Deuteronomium zitiert, Dtn 23,22 (Koh 5,3). Im folgenden soll daher in einem Exkurs gefragt werden, ob das Kultische in der Weisheit im Zusammenhang mit der sich ab 3. Jh. v.Chr. immer stärker verbreiteten Verschmelzung von Weisheit und Tora an Gewicht gewinnt.

EXKURS II

Weisheit, Tora und Kult

Schon vorexilische Weisheitstexte widmen sich kultischen Themen[115]. Spr 15,8; 21,3.27 haben die Vorzüge gerechten Handelns gegenüber dem Opfer des Toren zum Gegenstand (cf. Spr 17,1), während Spr 15,29; 28,9 über das Gebet des Frommen und des Toren sprechen. Spr 20,25 warnt vor einem unbedachten Gelübde (נֶדֶר; zum Gelübde cf. auch Spr 31,2). Spr 16,33 betont, daß ein durch das Losorakel vermitteltes Gebot von JHWH selbst kommt, und nach Spr 16,6 geschieht Sühne durch חֶסֶד und אֱמֶת.

Nachexilisch kann auf die im Hiobrahmen erwähnten Opferungen (Hiob 1,5; 42,8) verwiesen werden, die aber keiner Opferbestimmung des Pentateuch entsprechen. Erste Anklänge an Kultvorschriften der Tora könnten sich dagegen in der Aufforderung finden, JHWH von seinem Besitz zu ehren und ihm das Erstlingsopfer zu bringen (כַּבֵּד אֶת יְהוָה מֵהוֹנֶךָ וּמֵרֵאשִׁית כָּל־תְּבוּאָתֶךָ; Spr 3,9)[116].

Für das 3. Jh. v.Chr. belegt die von Ben Sira in Sir 24 aus der Tradition übernommene Aretalogie der Weisheit ihre Integration in den Kult: ἐν σκηνῇ ἁγίᾳ ἐνώπιον αὐτοῦ ἐλειτούργησα καὶ οὕτως ἐν Σιων ἐστηρίχθην (»im heiligen Zelt diente ich vor ihm und so wurde ich auf dem Zion eingesetzt«; Sir 24,10)[117]. So verwundert es nicht, wenn Ben

---

115. Zum Kult in ägyptischen und akkadischen Weisheitstexten s. L.G. PERDUE, pp. 19–133.

116. Zur Sache s. H. RINGGREN, p. 21; G. BAUMANN denkt an einen Bezug zu Dtn 28,8 (*Die Weisheitsgestalt in Proverbien 1–9. Traditionsgeschichtliche und theologische Studien* [FAT, 16], Tübingen, J.C.B. Mohr [Paul Siebeck], 1996, pp. 106f.); anders O. PLÖGER, p. 34; zu Spr 3,9f. cf. auch A. MEINHOLD, pp. 76f.

117. Zum traditionellen Charakter des Selbstpreises der Weisheit s. W. BAUM-

Sira in seinem Hymnus auf Simon II berichtet, wie dieser bei einer Yom Kippur Feier aus dem Allerheiligsten tritt (Sir 50,5ff.)[118]. Die Schilderung erweckt den Eindruck, daß Ben Sira im innersten, nur den Priestern vorbehaltenen Vorhof[119] zugegen war. Ben Sira wäre damit selbst Priester gewesen[120]. Dieser priesterliche Hintergrund Ben Siras wird auch in Sir 34,21–35,12 (31,21–32,15) deutlich, wo er – Spr 15,8; 21,3.27 aufnehmend – die Opfer von Frevlern und Gerechten miteinander vergleicht[121].

Die nichtessenischen Weisheitstexte aus Qumran zeigen, daß Sir 24,10 und das Buch Sir keine Einzelfälle darstellen. Trotz der teils schlecht erhaltenen Handschriften wird ein kultischer Einfluß deutlich. Für den *MLM* wurde schon oben auf den parallelen Gebrauch von Bund und Tempel in 4Q415 2 II$_7$, die Ausführungen zum Erstgeburtsopfer in 4Q423 3$_4$ par 1Q26 2$_4$ und zu dem Gelübde einer verheirateten Frau in 4Q416 2 IV$_{8f.}$ par 4Q418 10$_{8f.}$ sowie die Aufnahme der Vermischungsverbote aus Lev 19,19 und Dtn 22,9–11 in 4Q418 103 hingewiesen (pp. 131.139f.). Auf ein kultisches Interesse deuten ferner – wie in der Einleitung in den Text ausgeführt (s. p. 131) – die Wendungen מועד במועד (»Festtermin um Festtermin«; 4Q416 1$_3$) und לכול מעדיה (»für alle Festzeiten«; 4Q418 118$_3$). Daß in 4Q423 5$_6$ zur Einhaltung der Sommerfestzeiten gemahnt wird (פקוד מועדי הקיץ »beachte die Sommerfesttermine«), dürfte auf eine Beschäftigung des *MLM* mit jahreszeitlich orientierten Festen deuten. In diesem Zusammenhang könnte auch die Erwähnung von Interkalationen in 4Q418 211$_3$ (בכול עיבור̊תהמה »in all ihren Interkalationen«)[122] vor

GARTNER, *Die literarischen Gattungen in der Weisheit des Jesus Sirach*, in ZAW 34 (1914) 161–198, p. 173; J. MARBÖCK, *Weisheit im Wandel. Untersuchungen zur Weisheitstheologie bei Ben Sira* (BBB, 37), Bonn, Peter Hanstein Verlag, 1971, pp. 45–47.77; G. VON RAD, p. 316 Anm. 14.

118. Zur Identität des Hohenpriesters Simon in Sir 50 s. u.a. T. MIDDENDORP, p. 168; P.W. SKEHAN/A.A. DI LELLA, *The Wisdom of Ben Sira. A New Translation with Notes, Introduction, and Commentary* (AB, 39), New York, Doubleday, 1987, p. 550.

119. Zum innersten, nur den Priestern vorbehaltenen Vorhof cf. die utopischen Entwürfe bei Ezechiel (46,1f.) und in der Tempelrolle (11QT^a XXXV$_?$–XXXVIII$_{11}$), aber auch mMid 5,1f.; mKel 1,9; bZev 55b–56a.

120. Zum Tempel als dem Ort des Buches Sir cf. H. STADELMANN, *Ben Sira als Schriftgelehrter. Eine Untersuchung zum Berufsbild des vor-makkabäischen Söfer unter Berücksichtigung seines Verhältnisses zu Priester-, Propheten- und Weisheitslehrertum* (Wissenschaftliche Untersuchungen zum Neuen Testament 2. Reihe, 6), Tübingen, J.C.B. Mohr (Paul Siebeck), 1980, pp. 4–26; cf. auch B.G. WRIGHT III, *»Fear the Lord and Honor the Priest«. Ben Sira as Defender of the Jerusalem Priesthood*, in P.C. BEENTJES (ed.), *The Book of Ben Sira in Modern Research. Proceedings of the First International Ben Sira Conference 28–31 July 1996 Soesterberg, Netherlands* (BZAW, 255), Berlin/ New York, Walter de Gruyter, 1997, pp. 189–222.

121. Zum Kult bei Ben Sira cf. J.G. SNAITH, *Ben Sira's Supposed Love of Liturgy*, in VT 25 (1975) 167–174; H. STADELMANN, pp. 40–176 und B.G. WRIGHT III, pp. 192–196.

122. Zur Interpretation von 4Q418 211$_3$ cf. J. MAIER, Bd. 2, p. 478. Zur Sache cf.

einem kultischen Hintergrund zu verstehen sein. Ferner ist auf die Belege von נדה in 4Q417 4 II$_2$; 4Q418 20$_2$ und den kultischen Mythos, daß
Gott den/die Gerechten mit Hilfe des Losorakels erwählt hat (הפיל
גורלכה »er hat dein Los gefällt«; 4Q418 81$_5$) hinzuweisen[123].

Auf kultische Interessen des *Myst* weisen – wie oben dargelegt (pp.
133.135f.) – die Erläuterungen zum *šᵉgāgâ*-Opfer (1Q27 6$_{2f.}$), die Nen-
nung eines Priesters (1Q27 3$_2$), die Erwähnung von Sühne im Zusammenhang mit dem Tempeldienst (4Q299 52$_5$), die Yom-Kippur-Thema-
tik (4Q299 65) ebenso hin, wie die Tatsache daß in 4Q299 75$_6$ von
Aaron die Rede ist.

Unreinheit könnte genauso in dem *Ways of Righteousness* genannten
Weisheitstext Gegenstand weisheitlicher Reflexion (נדׄותיו »seine Un-
reinheiten«; 4Q420 1 II$_7$) sein[124] wie das Losorakel (יצׄא הגוׄרׄל הרישׄון
»herausgekom]en ist das erste Los«, 4Q421 1 I$_4$). Besonders auffällig ist
die Erwähnung von Brand– und Schlachtopfer (]אׄ העולות והזבחים [כׄל
»alle Brand- und Schlachtopfer«) in 4Q421 13$_2$[125]. T. ELGVIN beschreibt
das Fragment 4Q421 13 daher sogar als »priestly halakha on the Temple
service.«[126]

Priester sind schließlich auch in 4Q525 belegt (]ובׄכוהניׄ; 4Q525 6$_3$),
jedoch erlauben die Textbeschädigungen keine weiteren Aussagen zum
Text.

Neben dieser Integration des Kultischen in die Weisheit kann auch
umgekehrt die Aufnahme weisheitlichen Gedankenguts in einem eher
priesterlich-levitischen Text festgestellt werden: Wie schon oben erwähnt, endet das zum Großteil mit der Einsetzung Levis zum Hohenpriester und der ihm von Isaak vermittelten Kulthalacha beschäftigte
Aramaic Levi Document mit einem Preis der Weisheit und einer
Paränese an Levis Nachkommen (s.o., p. 146).

Zumindest drei der genannten Textzeugen stammen mit einiger Wahrscheinlichkeit aus dem 3. Jh. v.Chr., das *Aramaic Levi Document*[127], Sir

---

auch M. ALBANI, *Zur Rekonstruktion eines verdrängten Konzepts. Der 364-Tage-Kalen-
der in der gegenwärtigen Forschung*, in M. ALBANI ET AL. (eds.), *Studies in the Book of
Jubilees* (TSAJ, 65), Tübingen, Mohr Siebeck, 1997, pp. 79–125, pp. 109f. Anm. 105.

123. Zur Interpretation cf. D.J. HARRINGTON, *Wisdom Texts from Qumran*, p. 57.

124. Zur Transkription cf. B.Z. WACHOLDER/M.G. ABEGG, p. 159 und die Übersetzung von J. MAIER, Bd. 2, p. 488. T. ELGVIN (*Ways of Righteousness*, in ID. ET AL.,
Qumran Cave 4 XV. Sapiential Texts, Part 1 [DJD, 20], Oxford, Clarendon Press, 1997,
pp. 173–202, p. 175) liest – wohl wegen des folgenden גבול – שׄדותיו (»seine Felder«).
Eine sichere Transkription ist bei den erhaltenen Textresten nicht möglich.

125. Cf. 4Q421 13$_6$ [... בנים]הׄקׄ לׄ בלׄ[ו]ל שׄ[...] (»[...]mit all[e]n Op[fern ...]«).

126. *Ways of Righteousness*, p. 201.

127. Zur Datierung des *Aramaic Levi Document* s. M. STONE, *Scriptures, Sects and
Visions. A Profile of Judaism from Ezra to the Jewish Revolts*, Philadelphia, Fortress
Press, 1980, pp. 37f.75; ID., *Enoch, Aramaic Levi and Sectarian Origins*, in ID., *Selected*

24,19 und der *MLM*, und sind somit fast zeitgleich mit Kohelet anzusetzen.

Anders als sonst in weisheitlichen Texten werden dabei zumindest in
zwei der genannten Weisheitstexte, dem *mûsar lammēbîn* und dem *Book
of Mysteries*, Toravorschriften aufgenommen: 1Q27 6_2 bezieht sich auf
Lev 5,18, und in 4Q299 65 steht Lev 16 im Hintergrund. Die Argumentation in 4Q416 2 $IV_{8f.}$ par 4Q418 $10_{8f.}$ nimmt Num 30,11–16 auf, während 4Q418 103 im Kontext der Verbote von Lev 19,19 bzw. Dtn 22,9–
11 zu verstehen ist, und 4Q423 3_4 par 1Q26 2_4 wohl auf Dtn 26,1ff.
Bezug nimmt.

Der festgestellte Befund macht es möglich, die oben gestellte Frage
nach einem Zusammenhang zwischen der ab dem 3. Jh. vermehrt auftre-
tenden Verschmelzung von Weisheit und Tora und dem regeren Interesse der Weisheit am Kultischen positiv zu beantworten. Die Identifikation
von Weisheit und Tora dürfte zumindest die theologischen Grundlagen
für das steigende Interesse der Weisheit am Kultischen gelegt haben.
Ferner läßt sich beobachten, daß – soweit der erhaltene Textbestand
Überlegungen zum Abfassungsort eines Textes zulassen – alle oben un-
tersuchten weisheitlichen Texte mit kultischem Interesse wahrscheinlich
am Tempel beheimatet sind. Hierin dürfte eine weitere Ursache für das
steigende Interesse der Weisheit am Kult liegen.

✻ ✻ ✻

Das erreichte Ergebnis erhärtet den Verdacht, daß Kohelets Auseinan-
dersetzung mit kultischen Vorgängen in Koh 4,17–5,6 vor dem Hinter-
grund der Verschmelzung von Weisheit und Tora zu sehen ist. Diese
These gilt es nun, an Koh 4,17–5,6 selbst zu überprüfen und zu präzisie-
ren[128]. Hierbei fällt auf, daß alle dort genannten kultischen Handlungen
(Opfer, Gebet, Gelübde und *šᵉgāgâ*-Opfer) auch in den oben referierten
Weisheitstexten thematisiert werden. Dabei fallen jedoch signifikante
Unterschiede zu Koh ins Auge.

Wie schon festgestellt, wird über das in Koh 4,17 genannte Opfer der
Toren sowohl in der traditionellen Weisheit als auch bei Ben Sira nach-

---

*Studies in Pseudepigrapha and Apocrypha. With Special Reference to the Armenian Tra-
dition* (Studia in Veteris Testamenti Pseudepigrapha, 9), Leiden et al., E.J. Brill, 1991,
pp. 247–258, pp. 247f. Anm. 2, und R.A. KUGLER, p. 134.
    128. Zur Forschungsgeschichte zu Koh 4,17–5,6 cf. I.J.J. SPANGENBERG im vorliegen-
den Band (*A Century of Wrestling with Qohelet. The Research History of the Book
Illustrated with a Discussion of Qoh 4,17–5,6*). Zu Koh 4,17–5,6 cf. im vorliegenden
Band ferner D. MICHEL, *»Unter der Sonne«*, und T. HIEKE, *Wie hältst du's mit der Religion? Sprechhandlungen und Wirkintentionen in Kohelet 4,17–5,6.*

gedacht (s.o., pp. 147f.). Während Ben Sira und Spr 15,8; 21,3.27 die ethische Disposition des Opfernden als entscheidend ansehen, bzw. sogar gute Taten dem Opfer vorziehen, fehlen solche Alternativen bei Koh. Er stellt dem Opfer des Toren weder das Opfer bzw. Gebet des Gerechten noch gerechtes Handeln gegenüber. Stattdessen rät er zu einer von Vorsicht geprägten[129] rein passiven Teilnahme am Opferkult[130]: »Nahetreten, um zu hören, ist besser als das Opfer der Toren.«[131] Vergleicht man dies gar mit der positiven Einstellung zum Opferkult, wie sie sich z.B. in der Kulthalacha des *Aramaic Levi Document*; 4Q299 65 oder 4Q421 13$_{2.6}$ dokumentiert, wird der Unterschied noch deutlicher. Weder findet sich bei Koh die in Spr und Sir belegte Priorität des Ethischen vor dem Opfer, noch vermag er zu einem aktiven Opferkult aufzufordern. Er kommt über die Empfehlung eines passiven Hörens nicht hinaus.

Daß Koh nach dem Opfer des Toren in Koh 5,1f. das Gebet thematisiert, erinnert an Spr 15,8:

זֶבַח רְשָׁעִים תּוֹעֲבַת יְהוָה וּתְפִלַּת יְשָׁרִים רְצוֹנוֹ

»Das Opfer von Toren ist dem Herrn ein Greuel, aber das Gebet von Gerechten ist nach seinem Willen.«

Koh orientiert sich in der Abfolge von 4,17–5,2 an Spr 15,8. Der Grund hierfür, wird deutlich, wenn nach der Bedeutung des Gebets in den Weisheitstexten aus seiner Zeit gefragt wird. Während sich in Spr noch keine ausgeführten Gebete finden und das Thema nur selten behandelt wird, ist dies in den nichtessenischen Weisheitstexten aus Qumran, bei Ben Sira und in den Weisheitspsalmen völlig anders. Allein schon die Tatsache, daß Weisheitstexte in den Psalter aufgenommen worden sind, weist auf einen aktiven Beitrag der Weisheit zum Gebetsleben hin. Die

129. שְׁמֹר רַגְלֶיךָ (Punktation mit Ketib) ist mit H.W. HERTZBERG, p. 121; G. OGDEN, p. 76; M.V. FOX, *Contradictions*, p. 210 und C.L. SEOW, pp. 197f., als Aufforderung zur Vorsicht zu verstehen.

130. שמע kann wegen seiner Parallelen Stellung zu שְׁמֹר רַגְלֶיךָ (das *wāw* zu Beginn von 4,17b ist beiordnend) nicht »gehorchen« meinen (so u.a. K. GALLING, p. 101; R. KROEBER, p. 139; M.V. FOX, *Contradictions*, pp. 209.211; R.E. MURPHY, p. 50), sondern ist die »Empfehlung einer nur passiven Teilnahme am Kult« (A. LAUHA, p. 98; cf. W. HERTZBERG, p. 121). W. ZIMMERLIS vom Rechtfertigungsgedanken geprägte Auslegung, Koh 4,17 warne davor, »im Tempel einen eigenen frommen Weg der Ermöglichung einer menschlichen Leistung« zu suchen und gestehe demgegenüber »im schweigenden Hören die Unmöglichkeit eines eigenen Werkes« zu, geht an der Problemstellung des Textes vorbei und ist als protestantische Eisegese abzulehnen.

131. Koh bleibt an dieser Stelle also gerade nicht im Rahmen der traditionellen Weisheit (so z.B. W. ZIMMERLI, pp. 182f.; R.E. MURPHY, p. 50; C. KLEIN, p. 98; A. FISCHER, p. 48 und C.L. SEOW, p. 198), der genaue Vergleich zeigt, daß ihm die sowohl in den Weisheitstexten seiner Zeit als auch der älteren Weisheit gebotene Alternative zum Opfer des Toren fehlt.

Weisheitstexte des 3. und frühen 2. Jh. v.Chr. verstärken diesen Eindruck[132]:

–   Bei Ben Sira ist das Gebet Gegenstand von Lehrreden und Paränesen: So
    kann er Sir 7,10 formulieren: »Fasse dich nicht kurz beim Gebet (בתפלה),
    noch zögere bei Rechtschaffenheit«. Nach Sir 17,8–10 hat Gott den Men-
    schen Furcht vor ihm ins Herzen gegeben, damit sie die Größe seiner Wer-
    ke erkennen und ihn wegen seiner Wunder rühmen, damit sie Großtaten
    seiner Werke erforschen und seinen Namen preisen. Nach Sir 34,31 (31,31)
    wird das Gebet dessen, der wegen seiner Sünden fastet und wieder sündigt,
    nicht erhört. Und Sir 34,29 (31,29) stellt das Gebet in rhetorischer Frage
    über den Fluch: »Einer betet und einer flucht, wessen Stimme wird der
    Herrscher erhören?« Neben der Paränese zum und der Reflexion über das
    Gebet finden sich ferner meist hymnische Gebetstexte. Hier sind besonders
    Sir 18,1–14; 24,1–22; 36,1–17 (33,1–13; 36,17–22); 39,13–25.35; 42,15–
    43,33; 50,22–24 und Sir 51,1–12 zu nennen[133].
–   Für die erste Hälfte des 2. Jh. v.Chr. ist eine hymnische Praxis weisheit-
    licher Texte auch im *Book of Mysteries* belegt[134]. In 4Q299 6 finden
    sich Reste eines Schöpfungshymnus[135], und der in 4Q299 8 belegte
    Hymnus »emphasizes the notion that all knowledge and discernment
    comes from God. All is at the same time predestined. At the end the
    fragment appears to turn to the wonders of creation.«[136] In 4Q301 3$_{4ff}$.
    findet sich dagegen ein Hymnus auf Gottes Gnade und Zorn sowie sein
    eschatologisches Heilshandeln an seinem heiligen Volk.
–   Um einen wegen seines freien Gebrauchs des Tetragramms nichtesseni-
    schen Weisheitshymnus dürfte es sich auch bei dem einzigen Fragment

132. Die einen Hymnus bezeugende Handschrift 4Q408 wird in den Handschriften-
katalogen von E. Tov/S.J. Pfann (p. 43) und S.A. Reed/M.J. Lundberg (p. 110) als
»sapiential work« beschrieben, jedoch findet sich kein weisheitliches Vokabular, daß
diese Bezeichnung rechtfertigen könnte. Daß in 4Q408 1$_{8ff}$. Gott als Schöpfer von Tag
und Nacht gepriesen wird, ist andererseits auch außerhalb weisheitlicher Literatur denkbar. Die Beschreibung »liturgisch« würde eher zum erhaltenen Textbestand von 4Q408
passen (s. A. Steudel, *4Q408: A Liturgy on Morning and Evening Prayer. Preliminary
Edition*, in *RQ* 16 [1994] 313–334, pp. 331f.). In Frgm. 1$_3$ wird davon gesprochen, daß
Gott ganz Israel als einen *yaḥad* geschaffen habe (כ]ל ישראל [וה?]בֿרֿא הוא לֿיֿחֿדֿ[ו]). Zwar
könnte dies, wegen des nominalen Gebrauchs von יחד, auf einen essenischen Ursprung
des Werkes hindeuten – insbesondere, wenn der in den Zeilen 7ff. belegte Licht-Finster-
nis-Dualismus bedacht wird – jedoch wäre dann die gesamtisraelitische Perspektive ungewöhnlich. Mir erscheint daher eine nichtessenische Herkunft wahrscheinlicher. Hierfür
könnte auch der für essenische Texte ungewöhnliche freie Gebrauch des Tetragramms
sprechen: »The Tetragrammaton is corrected in frg.1,6 with dots around it. Six dots are
still visible, but the others have disappeared with the damaged leather. Above the line 'TH
'DNY is written (1.6a)« (*op. cit.*, p. 316). Falls יהוה א[תֿ in 4Q408 6$_1$ mit J. Maier (Bd. 2, p.
419) ebenfalls als ein Beleg des Tetragramms gedeutet werden kann, darf trotz der korri-
gierenden Punkte in 1$_6$ angenommen werden, daß das Werk das Tetragramm frei gebraucht (zur Sache cf. A. Steudel, pp. 333f.).
133. Hymnisch dürften wohl auch die nur in der Handschrift B bezeugten und in ihrer
Authentizität umstrittenen Verse Sir 51,12a–o zu verstehen sein.
134. Zur Datierung und Verfassern von *Myst* s.o., pp. 131-134.
135. Cf. L.H. Schiffman, *4QMysteries^a*, p. 226; Id., *Mysteries*, p. 48.
136. L.H. Schiffman, *4QMysteries^a*, p. 228; cf. Id., *Mysteries*, p. 50.

der Handschrift 4Q411 handeln. Weitergehende Angaben zum Text sind nicht möglich, da von den 16 Zeilen des Fragments nur jeweils ein bis drei Worte Text erhalten sind[137].

– Auch der erhaltene Text von 4Q413 ist zu stark beschädigt, als daß er sicher zugeordnet werden könnte. Er bezeugt einen hymnischen Einfluß auf die weisheitliche Lehre: »The first word or two («a psalm, a song,»' see Psalms 66, 67) may designate it as a hymn, though in form what survives has more in common with the wisdom instructions or admonitions we have already seen. The instructor speaking in the first person singular addresses listeners in the second person plural. The instructor promises knowledge about God's plans for humankind, God's will regarding their actions, and the rewards and punishments that God will mete out.«[138]

– Zeitlich näher an Koh ist der *mûsar lammēbîn* anzusiedeln[139]. Das Werk bezeugt nicht nur mehrere Hymnen, sondern thematisiert auch anderweitig Gebete und fordert zum Gotteslob auf: In 4Q415 2 II_8 ist das Nomen תהלה (»Lobgesang«) belegt. In 4Q416 2 $III_{10f.}$ par 4Q418 9_{11} mahnt der *MLM* dazu, Gott Ehre zu geben und seinen Namen immerfort zu preisen (למכבדיכה תן הדר ושמו הלל תמיד »dem der dich ehrt, gib Ehre, seinen Namen preise immerdar«). Als eine solche Mahnung zum hymnischen Gotteslob dürfte auch den Textrest 4Q416 3_5 zu interpretieren sein: [...מאד[...] ש]מכה הלל מאד[...] (»[...]deinen [N]amen. Lobpreise sehr[...]«). 4Q418 81 1 ermahnt zum Gotteslob an ewiger Quelle: שפתיכה פתח מקור לברך קודשים ואתה במקור עולם הלל (»deine Lippen hat er geöffnet als Quelle, Heilige zu preisen, daher lobsinge an ewiger Quelle«). 4Q418 126 II_{10} schließlich sagt von den Söhnen des Lebens (בני חיה Zeile 9): ובאמונתו ישיהו כול היום תמיד יהללו שמו (»und seine Treue loben sie den ganzen Tag, immerdar preisen sie seinen Namen«). Daneben fügt *MLM* in seine Paränesen und Lehrreden auch Teile von Hymnen oder ganze Hymnen ein: »In 4Q417 1 i 14–17 is found a *Niedrichkeitsdoxologie* (sic) ...: "For before His wrath nobody can stand, and who can be deemed righteous in His judgement? And how can the poor one [stand] without forgiveness?"«[140] In 4Q417 2 II_{6-11} folgt auf die einleitenden Lehrreden des *MLM* an den *mēbîn* (4Q417 2 I_{1-18}) und seinen Schüler (בן מבין]; 4Q417 2 I_{18}; 4Q417 2 I_{18}–II_5) ein mit ברך שמו (»preise seinen Namen«) eingeleiteter Hymnus, der Gottes Barmherzigkeit, Richten, Schöpfungshandeln und Fürsorge thematisiert.

– Der אשרי-Spruch אולת בדרכי יביעו ולוא בה הגלים אש]רין[(»Glücklich, die über sie jauchzen und nicht hervorsprudeln die Wege der Torheit«; 4Q525 3 II_2) empfiehlt in 4Q525 einen hymnischen Preis der mit der Weisheit identifizierten Tora. Wobei die auf diese Empfehlung folgen-

---

137. Zur Handschrift s. A. STEUDEL, *411. 4QSapiential Hymn*, in T. ELGVIN ET AL., *Qumran Cave 4 XV. Sapiential Texts, Part 1* (DJD, 20), Oxford, Clarendon Press, 1997, pp. 159–162.

138. D.J. HARRINGTON, *Wisdom Texts from Qumran*, p. 64; zu einer anderen Auslegung des Textes s. E. QIMRON, *A Work concerning Divine Providence: 4Q413*, in Z. ZEVIT ET AL. (eds.), *Solving Riddles and Untying Knots. Biblical, Epigraphic, and Semitic Studies in Honor of Jonas C. Greenfield*, Winona Lake, Eisenbrauns, 1995, pp. 191–202.

139. Zur Datierung des *MLM* s.o., p. 130.

140. T. ELGVIN, *Wisdom, Revelation, and Eschatology*, p. 442.

de Seligpreisung der Tora und des Menschen, der sich mit ihr beschäftigt (4Q525 3 II), eben dieses empfohlene Lob darstellen könnte.

Vor dem Hintergrund dieser Texte ist Koh 5,1f. zu interpretieren: Nachdem Koh sich schon in Koh 4,17 deutlich von weisheitlichen Opfervorstellungen seiner Zeit distanziert hatte, negiert er auch die in Spr 15,8 dem Opfer des Toren gegenübergestellte Alternative. Während sich für die Weisheit zur Zeit Kohelets ein gewisser Gebetsenthusiasmus, insbesondere für das hymnische Gotteslob, feststellen läßt, steht das Gebet für Koh unter dem Schatten des fernen Gottes. Dem Beter wird geraten, sich beim Gebet nicht zu eilen. Dies erfährt eine doppelte Begründung: a) Durch die Ferne Gottes ist das Gebet in Frage gestellt, »denn Gott ist im Himmel und du auf der Erde, daher seien deine Worte wenige« (Koh 5,1b)[141], b) In Koh 5,2 fährt Koh mit einem Sprichwortzitat fort[142], das durch die Traummetapher die Flüchtigkeit und Sinnlosigkeit des Gebets betont[143]. Ein deutlicherer Hiatus zu den jüdischen Weisheitstexten aus der Zeit Kohelets läßt sich kaum noch denken.

Besonders deutlich unterscheiden sich die Einstellungen Kohelets und des *MLM* zum Gelübde. Während letzterer unter Aufnahme von Num 30,11–16 das Auflösen eines Gelübdes für möglich hält (4Q416 2 IV$_{8f.}$ par 4Q418 10$_{8f.}$; s.o., p. 140), mahnt Koh zur unbedingten Einhaltung[144]. Dabei ist es signifikant, daß er, wie alle Kommentatoren bemerken, in Koh 5,3 Dtn 23,22 zitiert[145]. Dtn 23,22 empfiehlt jedoch lediglich, Gott

141. Zu dieser Interpretation von Koh 5,1b cf. u.a. W. ZIMMERLI, p. 184; L.G. PERDUE, pp. 183f.; A. LAUHA, pp. 98f.; D. MICHEL, *Untersuchungen*, p. 255. Andere Ausleger wollen in Koh 5,1b nicht Gottes Ferne gegenüber dem Menschen, sondern unter Hinweis auf Ps 115,3 seine Transzendenz betont sehen (so z.B. G. OGDEN, p. 77; R.E. MURPHY, p. 50 und C.L. SEOW, pp. 198f.).

142. Zu Koh 5,2 als Zitat s. u.a. W. ZIMMERLI, p. 184; A. LAUHA, p. 99; D. MICHEL, *Qohelet*, p. 142; R.E. MURPHY, p. 50; C. KLEIN. pp. 70f.

143. Zum Traum als Metapher für Flüchtigkeit in Koh 5,2 cf. die auf altorientalische Parallelen gestützte Auslegung bei C.L. SEOW, pp. 199f.: »So this is how one ought to take the mention of dream in our verse: it is that which is unreal and ephemeral. The significance of «dream» here approximates *hebel* – it is something ephemeral and unreliable ... The point of the aphorism, then, is that much preoccupation amounts to nothing more than a dream, and many words produce nothing more than the hollow sound of the loquacious fool« (*op. cit.*, p. 200). Zusätzlich zu den von C.L. SEOW genannten Belegen kann noch auf Sir 42,22 hingewiesen werden, wo eine (Nacht)vision mit einem Funken verglichen wird.

144. T. KRÜGER (*Rezeption der Tora*, p. 307) hält es sogar für möglich, daß Koh hier »auf der Grundlage von Dtn 23,22ff an anderen Bestimmungen der Tora Kritik übt. Die Forderung, seine Gelübde unverzüglich zu erfüllen, läßt nämlich die in Num 30 eingeräumte Möglichkeit der Aufhebung von Gelübden ... ebenso problematisch erscheinen wie die Bestimmungen zur Erleichterung der Erfüllung von Gelübden in Lev 27.«

145. Die einzige mir bekannte Ausnahme ist M. WEINFELD, der Koh 5,3f. von einer auch in Spr 20,25 und Sir 18,22 belegten weisheitlichen Tradition abhängen läßt, die wiederum auf Dtn 23,22–24 eingewirkt haben soll (*Deuteronomy and the Deuteronomic*

Gelobtes einzuhalten, wobei das Gelübde als solches nicht hinterfragt wird. Koh hingegen geht einen Schritt weiter: Besser ist es nicht zu geloben, als zu geloben und nicht zu erfüllen[146]. »Während der genannte Gesetzestext das Gelübde für etwas Empfehlenswertes und den Verzicht darauf für die Ausnahme hält, setzt Kohelet demgegenüber die Akzente umgekehrt: der Verzicht auf Gelübde überhaupt ist diejenige Alternative, die der Weise bevorzugt.«[147] Hierfür eignete sich, anders als der im *MLM* aufgenommene Beleg Num 30,11–16, das Zitat aus Dtn 23,22 besonders gut, weil es mit seiner Mahnung, einmal Gelobtes auch zu erfüllen, die Frage nahelegt, was passiert, wenn dies nicht geschieht.

Dies beantwortet Koh in Vers 5 durch eine Anspielung auf das *š^egāgâ*-Opfer (cf. Lev 4–5; Num 15,22–31)[148]: Bei einem versehentlich nicht eingehaltenen Gelübde bleibt dem Menschen keine Möglichkeit, sich mit Hilfe des Opfers für unbewußt begangene Verfehlungen zu entsühnen. In Form einer rhetorischen Frage macht Koh vielmehr deutlich, daß jemand, der selbst unwissentlich ein Gelübde bricht, den Zorn Gottes zu fürchten hat. Dieser Wirkungslosigkeit der *š^egāgâ* bei Koh[149] steht

School, Nachdruck der Aufl. Oxford, Oxford University Press, 1972, Winona Lake, Eisenbrauns, 1992, pp. 270–272). Bei der von M. WEINFELD angenommenen traditionsgeschichtlichen Abhängigkeit können die wörtlichen Übereinstimmungen zwischen Koh 5,3 und Dtn 23,22 nicht erklärt werden. Den ganzen Abschnitt Koh 4,17–5,6 hingegen unter deuteronomistischem Einfluß zu sehen, wie R. KROEBER dies vorschlägt (pp. 138–141), scheint mir eine Überinterpretation des Befundes zu sein. Geringe Ähnlichkeiten in der Motivik – beispielsweise zwischen Koh 5,1 und Dtn 4,39 – reichen hierzu keinesfalls aus. Der oben herausgearbeitete Bezug von Koh 4,17–5,2 auf Spr 15,8 unterstreicht dies.

146. Der von C. UEHLINGER (*Qohelet im Horizont mesopotamischer, levantinischer und ägyptischer Weisheitsliteratur der persischen und hellenistischen Zeit*, in L. SCHWIEN-HORST-SCHÖNBERGER [ed.], *Das Buch Kohelet. Studien zur Struktur, Geschichte, Rezeption und Theologie* [BZAW, 254], Berlin/New York, Walter de Gruyter, 1997, pp. 155–247, pp. 225f.) als Parallele zu Koh 5,3f. angeführte Beleg aus dem Papyrus Louvre 2414 (»Wer im Angesicht Gottes eine Sache verspricht, sie ihm aber nicht gibt, wird sie ihm [dennoch] geben [müssen], und zwar zur eigenen Schande«) entspricht eher der Mahnung zur Einhaltung eines abgelegten Gelübdes in Dtn 23,22–24 als der grundsätzlicheren Haltung Kohelets.

147. A. LAUHA, pp. 99f.; cf. J.L. CRENSHAW, p. 117 und L. SCHWIENHORST-SCHÖNBERGER, p. 137.

148. Zum Zusammenhang von Koh 5,4 und 5,5f. cf. u.a. A. LAUHA, p. 100; J.L. CRENSHAW, p. 117; M.V. FOX, *Contradictions*, p. 212; C.L. SEOW, p. 201. D. MICHELS Erwägungen (*Qohelet*, p. 143; *Untersuchungen*, p. 257), Koh 5,5 als orthodoxe Glosse des zweiten Redaktors zu nehmen, basieren ausschließlich auf einem von ihm angenommenen inhaltlichen Widerspruch. Sprachliche Argumente kann er nicht vorbringen. Ferner dürfte es kaum als orthodox bezeichnet werden können, wenn in Koh 5,5 die Wirksamkeit des immerhin im Sinaigesetz festgelegten *š^egāgâ*-Ritus bezweifelt wird.

149. Die bei Koh prinzipiell gemeinte Aussage schließt N. LOHFINKS Interpretation des Verses auf einen Mißbrauch des *š^egāgâ*-Ritus aus: »Es dürfte die bei den religiös Emsigen offenbar sehr häufige Szene ins Auge gefaßt sein, wo jemand wieder einmal durch Ablieferung eines *š^egāgāh*-Opfers bei dem zuständigen Kultbeamten, dem «Boten», sein schwer unsoziales Verhalten verharmlost« (*Warum ist der Tor unfähig, Böse*

die Anspielung auf Lev 5,18 im *Book of Mysteries* gegenüber (1Q27 6$_2$; s.o., p. 125). Zwar ist der Beleg stark zerstört, doch läßt das ‏על כפר‏[‏ו‏] [...]‏שגג‏ (»er [wird] entsühnen eine unwissentlich begangene Sün[de«) auf eine positive Einstellung zum *s̆e͑gāgâ*-Opfer schließen[150].

Es kann festgehalten werden, daß alle vier in Koh 4,17–5,6 diskutierten kultischen Praktiken auch im *mûsar lammēbîn* und dem *Book of Mysteries* reflektiert werden. Dieser Befund ist um so auffälliger, da die beiden letztgenannten Werke nur in zu Teilen stark beschädigten Handschriften erhalten sind. Bei der weitreichenden Überschneidung kann es sich kaum um einen Zufall handeln. Kohelet rät grundsätzlich zur Vorsicht im Umgang mit allen vier Kultpraktiken und bezweifelt sogar ihre Wirksamkeit, während der *mûsar lammēbîn* und das *Book of Mysteries* allen Praktiken grundsätzlich positiv gegenüberstehen. Literarische Abhängigkeiten von Kohelet zu dem nah bei Koh zu datierenden *MLM* konnten jedoch nicht festgestellt werden. Einzelne Kultpraktiken aus Koh 4,17–5,6 werden auch in anderen Weisheitstexten aus hellenistischer Zeit positiv reflektiert (Sir; 4Q420–4Q421). Der Gesamtbefund deutet darauf, daß Koh sich u.a. in Koh 4,17–5,6 mit einem am Tempel zu lokalisierenden weisheitlichen Tradentenkreis auseinandersetzt. Seine positive Haltung zum Kult vermag er nicht zu teilen[151]. Worin Kohelets ängstlich-vorsichtiger Umgang mit dem Kultischen begründet liegt, wird wohl am deutlichsten in Koh 5,1b: »denn Gott ist im Himmel und du auf der Erde«. Die Partizipation am Kult verbindet den Menschen nicht mit seinem Gott, sondern wird gerade durch dessen Ferne hinterfragt. Nicht Heil erlebt der Mensch im Kult, sondern gerade seine Abwesenheit, ja er muß sogar mit der Möglichkeit des Zorns der fernen Gottheit rechnen. Das von Koh angeratene Verhalten des Menschen im Kult ist von dieser Sicht der Dinge ge-

---

zu handeln? [Koh 4,17], in F. STEPPAT (ed.), *XXI. Deutscher Orientalistentag vom 24. bis 29. März 1980 in Berlin. Vorträge* (ZDMG.S, 5), Wiesbaden, Franz Steiner Verlag, 1983, pp. 113–120, p. 119).

150. Weitere Hinweise auf eine Auseinandersetzung Kohelets mit dem Kult finden sich in Koh 8,10 und 9,2. Jedoch lassen sich von den beiden Versen keine Brücken zum erhaltenen Textbestand des *MLM* oder *Myst* schlagen, so daß nicht sicher ist, ob Kohelet hier mit dem weisheitlichen Tradentenkreis, dem diese beiden Texte zugehören, diskutiert oder nicht.

151. Der Vergleich zwischen der Rolle des Kultischen in den nichtessenischen Weisheitstexten aus Qumran, bei Ben Sira und im Buch Kohelet widerlegt auch die Einschätzung A. LAUHAS: »Im Verhältnis zum Kult liegt er (scil. Koh) auf der gleichen Linie wie die Weisheitsliteratur überhaupt: formell wird das traditionelle Brauchtum respektiert, aber das ganze Kultwesen ist nur von beiläufigem Interesse. Bei Kohelet ist der Ton noch zurückhaltender« (p. 101; cf. O. KAISER, *Botschaft*, p. 64; A.A. FISCHER, p. 48); zur Kritik an dieser Position cf. D. MICHEL im vorliegenden Band (*»Unter der Sonne«*, pp. 104ff.).

prägt. Es gilt Vorsicht walten zu lassen und sich vor Gott zu fürchten[152] (Koh 5,6c)[153].

AUSBLICK

Im Kontext des oben Erörterten, erscheinen kanongeschichtliche Zugänge zu Koh 12,12–14, wie sie von G.H. WILSON[154] und F.J. BACKHAUS[155] vorgeschlagen wurden, problematisch. Wenn die zweite Redaktion des Koheletbuches ein Produkt des hinter dem *mûsār lammēbîn* und dem *Book of Mysteries* stehenden Tradentenkreises ist, sollte sie nicht wesentlich später als in der Mitte des 2. Jh. v.Chr. datiert werden[156]. Hierfür spricht u.a., daß es nach und während der sogenannten hellenistischen Religionsreformen unter den Hohenpriestern Jason und Menelaos 175–163 v.Chr. zu großen Umgruppierungen am Jerusalemer Tempel kam, wie u.a. das Entstehen der drei großen »Religionsparteien« Sadduzäer, Pharisäer und Essener belegt. Ferner sind alle dem angesprochenen Tradentenkreis sicher zuzuordnenden Texte, der *mûsār lammēbîn*, das *Book of Mysteries* und die Zwei-Geister-Lehre (1QS

---

152. Zu dieser Interpretation von Koh 5,6 cf. jüngst F.J. BACKHAUS, *Zeit und Zufall*, pp. 183f. und C. KLEIN, p. 112. Den כי-Satz in Koh 5,6 aus inhaltlichen Gründen als Glosse des zweiten Redaktors zu betrachten (so M. JASTROW, *Gentle Cynic*, p. 217; C.F. WHITLEY, p. 50 und D. MICHEL, *Qohelet*, p. 143; cf. ID., *Untersuchungen*, p. 257), erscheint bei diesem Verständnis von Koh 5,6c unnötig. Der Vers fügt sich den anderen Gottesfurchtbelegen im Buch gut ein (zur Gottesfurcht im Buch Koh s.o., pp. 116f.).. D. MICHEL scheint seine literarkritische Hypothese daher im vorliegenden Band zurückzunehmen; cf. »*Unter der Sonne*«, p. 108.

153. Gerade der Abschnitt Koh 4,17–5,6 stellt die These T. KRÜGERs in Frage, daß im Buch Kohelet »einzelne Bestimmungen der Tora aufgenommen werden, weil und insofern sie vernünftig erscheinen. Das Konzept der Tora als einer letztinstanzlich-normativen, «kanonischen» Weisung Gottes für die menschliche Lebensführung wird jedoch theologisch kritisiert und relativiert ... Anders (und kürzer) gesagt: Das Koheletbuch rezipiert die Tora nicht als kanonischen, sondern als klassischen Text« (*Rezeption der Tora*, p. 321). Daß einzige wirkliche Torazitat im Buch Kohelet, wird von Koh gerade nicht angeführt, weil er es für vernünftig und daher befolgenswert hält. Gerade weil die Tora vorschreibt, ein einmal gegebenes Gelübde unbedingt zu halten, gilt es, sich angesichts eines bedrohlichen und undurchschaubaren Gottes so zu verhalten.

154. »*The Words of the Wise*«. *The Intent and Significance of Qohelet 12:9–14*, in *JBL* 103 (1984) 175–192.

155. *Der Weisheit letzter Schluß*, passim.

156. M. HENGEL will die zweite Redaktion schon vor der Mitte des 2. Jh. v.Chr. abgeschlossen sehen, weil das Koheletbuch sonst für die Gemeinschaft Qumran, die eine Abschrift aus der Mitte des 2. Jh. v.Chr. besaß, nicht akzeptabel gewesen wäre (p. 213). Jedoch zeigen die seit M. HENGELs Publikation bekannt gewordenen Handschriften aus Qumran, daß in der dortigen Bibliothek auch den Essenern sicherlich zuwiderlaufende Texte aufbewahrt wurden, etwa ein sogenanntes Brontologion – ein astrologischer Text, der mit Hilfe des Donners die Zukunft vorhersagt.

III$_{13}$–IV$_{26}$)[157] vor oder etwa in die Mitte des 2. Jh. v.Chr. zu datieren[158].
Wenn F.J. BACKHAUS ausführt: »Qoh. 12,12-14 gehört nicht mehr in die
vorkanonisch anzusiedelnde Traditionsgeschichte der Schrift Qohelet,
sondern in Qoh. 12,12-14 spiegelt sich schon ein Kanonbewußtsein wider«[159], widerspricht dies auch dem Befund von *MMT*. In dem ebenfalls
aus der Mitte des 2. Jh. v.Chr. stammenden Brief der essenischen Gemeinschaft von Qumran an den Jerusalemer Hohenpriester ist eine
»Kanonformel« belegt, die als dritten Kanonteil nur den (davidischen)
Psalter kennt: בספר מוש֯ה [ו]בסספר]י הנ]ביאים ובדו֯ד (»im Buch Mose
[und] in den Bücher[n der P]ropheten und in Davi[d«; MMT C 10)[160].

Vor dem Hintergrund der Kanonformel aus MMT C 10 scheint mir
auch G.H. WILSONs These, daß Koh 12,9-14 das Buch Kohelet und das
Buch Proverbien zu einer kanonischen Einheit zusammenbinden will,
um weitere Salomonische Schriften aus dem Kanon auszuschließen, problematisch. Wie MMT C 10 zeigt, gab es in der Mitte des 2. Jh. v.Chr.
noch keine Sammlung der Ketubim, lediglich der (davidische?) Psalter
wurde als eine eigene kanonische Einheit verstanden. Erst das Vorwort
der griechischen Übersetzung zu Ben Sira (Ende 2. Jh. v.Chr.) erwähnt
für den dritten Kanonteil eine Schriftengruppe: διὰ τοῦ νόμου καὶ τῶν
προφητῶν καὶ τῶν ἄλλων τῶν κατ᾽ αὐτοὺς ἠκολουθηκότων (»durch
das Gesetz und durch die Propheten und durch die anderen [Schriften],
die auf sie folgten«); εἴς τε τὴν τοῦ νόμου καὶ τῶν προφητῶν καὶ
τῶν ἄλλων πατρίων βιβλίων ἀνάγνωσιν (»auf das Lesen des Gesetzes und der Propheten und der anderen Bücher der Väter«). Die Erweiterung des dritten Kanonteils um weitere Schriften neben dem
(davidischen) Psalter begann also erst nach Abschluß der zweiten Redaktion des Koheletbuches[161].

N. LOHFINKS Hypothese, daß der erste Epilog (Koh 12,9–11) der Niederschlag einer Diskussion um das Buch Kohelet als Textbuch für die
Tempelschule in Fragen des Hellenismus sei[162], und daß der zweite Epi-

---

157. Zur Zugehörigkeit der Zwei-Geister-Lehre zum Tradentenkreis vom *MLM* und
Myst s.o., p. 134.

158. Zur Datierung der genannten Texte s.o. den Exkurs zum *MLM* und *Myst*.

159. *Der Weisheit letzter Schluß*, p. 50.

160. Zu Transkription und Rekonstruktion s. E. QIMRON/J. STRUGNELL, *Qumran Cave
4 V. Miqṣat Maʿaśe ha-Torah* (DJD, 10), Oxford, Clarendon Press, 1994, p. 58. Zur Datierung von *MMT* s. *op. cit.*, pp. 109–121.

161. Dieser Befund verbietet es auch, Koh als Erschaffer einer im 3. Jh. v.Chr. datier-
ten kanonischen Grundsammlung der Ketubim (Spr, Hiob, Hld, Koh) zu verstehen und
den zweiten Epilog auf die Zusammenstellung des pharisäischen Kanons zurückzuführen
(so A. DE PURY *Qohélet et le canon des Ketubim*, in seinem Vortrag auf diesem
Colloquium).

162. *Kohelet*, p. 12–14; ID., *Les épilogues du livre de Qohélet et les debuts du canon*,
in P. BOVATI (ed.), *Ouvrir les Écritures. Mélanges offerts à Paul Beauchamp*, Paris,

log sich dementsprechend nicht gegen das Buch Kohelet sondern gegen die Ideen des Buches Ben Sira richte[163], wird durch das oben Diskutierte ebenfalls in Frage gestellt. Kohelet selbst kritisiert, wie durch Koh 4,17–5,6 und Koh 2,26; 7,26 belegt, die Ideen einer am Tempel beheimateten weisheitlichen Gruppe. Umgekehrt fügt dieser Tradentenkreis in Koh 8,5f.; 11,9c; 12,12–14 ein kritisches Korrektiv in das Koheletbuch ein. Daß Kohelet unter diesen Umständen in der von N. LOHFINK angenommenen und doch wohl weisheitlichen Tempelschule als Textbuch diente, erscheint mir unwahrscheinlich. Da Ben Sira ferner selbst am Tempel zu verorten ist[164] und in einigen Punkten der Theologie von *MLM*, *Myst* und dem zweiten Redaktor ähnelt, dürfte er im gleichen Tradentenkreis wie *MLM* und *Myst* beheimatet sein, wenn auch eher an seinem Rand. Daß sich unter diesen Umständen die zweite Redaktion des Koheletbuches gegen Ben Sira und nicht gegen Kohelet richtet, kann ausgeschlossen werden.

Institut für antikes Judentum   Armin LANGE
    und hellenistische Religionsgeschichte
Liebermeisterstraße 12
D-72076 Tübingen

Editions du Cerf, 1995, pp. 77–96. Cf. D. MICHEL, *Qohelet*, pp. 117f.; J. MARBÖCK, *Kohelet und Sirach*, p. 282.
    163. *Les épilogues*, pp. 94f.
    164. Dazu s. H. STADELMANN, pp. 4–26.

QOHELET ET BEN SIRA

I. Introduction

Voilà plus d'un siècle que les exégètes se demandent quels rapports il faut voir entre Qohelet et Ben Sira. La question a regagné de l'intérêt depuis qu'en 1896 les premiers textes hébreux de Ben Sira ont été retrouvés[1].

On ne peut envisager ici de rouvrir tout ce dossier. Laissant donc de côté la thèse de Charles F. Whitley, qui, en 1979, tentait de montrer l'antériorité de Ben Sira par rapport au Qohelet[2], thèse que Antoon Schoors ne suivra pas[3], je ne reviendrai pas davantage sur le problème de savoir si Ben Sira a cité l'œuvre de Qohelet. Sur ce point, Franz Joseph Backhaus a donné, en 1993, une réponse négative fondée sur de bons arguments[4].

Mon propos est plus simple, moins ambitieux. Je ne retiens que deux problèmes. Le premier concerne l'épilogue du livre de Qohelet: fait-il allusion à Ben Sira? Autrement dit, et un peu brutalement, y a-t-il du Ben Sira dans Qohelet? Je m'attacherai à la fameuse phrase: «Crains Dieu et observe ses commandements» (Qo 12,13bα).

L'autre problème, déjà traité par Emmanuel Podechard en 1912[5], alors que la majorité des textes hébreux de Ben Sira avaient été publiés, puis, récemment, par F. J. Backhaus, en 1993[6], l'autre problème, dis-je, concerne le thème de la joie et du plaisir. Si 14,11-19 sont-ils un écho de Qohelet? Cette question me permettra de faire le point des études récentes consacrées à ce thème chez Qohelet.

---

1. Pour la bibliographie ancienne, cf. E. PODECHARD, *L'Ecclésiaste* (EB), Paris, 1912, pp. 55-56.

2. C.F. WHITLEY, *Koheleth. His Language and Thought* (BZAW, 148), Berlin, 1979, pp. 122-131 et 163-164.

3. Cf. A. SCHOORS, *The Preacher Sought to Find Pleasing Words. A Study of the Language of Qoheleth*. Part I. *Grammar* (OLA, 41), Leuven, 1992, pp. 12-13 et 121-122; ID., *Qohelet. A book in a Changing Society*, in *Old Testament Essays* 9/1 (1996) spéc. pp. 68-72. Pour rappel, les fragments qumrâniens de Qo datent du milieu du IIe s. avant notre ère.

4. F. J. BACKHAUS, *Qohelet und Sirach*, in *BN* 69 (1993) spéc. pp. 32-45. Cf. aussi J. MARBÖCK, *Kohelet und Sirach. Eine vielschichtige Beziehung*, in L. SCHWIENHORST-SCHÖNBERGER (ed.), *Das Buch Kohelet. Studien zur Struktur, Geschichte, Rezeption und Theologie* (BZAW, 254), Berlin, 1997, spéc. pp. 275-281.

5. PODECHARD, *L'Ecclésiaste* (n. 1), pp. 62-64.

6. BACKHAUS, *Qohelet und Sirach* (n. 4), pp. 45-47.

II. Qo 12,13 ET BEN SIRA

1. Les deux derniers versets du livre de Qohelet font-ils allusion au livre de Ben Sira? Gerald T. Sheppard[7] et Norbert Lohfink[8] le pensent. Par contre, F.J. Backhaus considère que Ben Sira a pu faire partie du cercle de ceux qui ont rédigé Qo 12,13ba et, tout récemment, Johannes Marböck reconnaît que l'hypothèse de N. Lohfink est «plausible»[9].

Sans entrer dans la discussion complète de l'hypothèse que N. Lohfink propose pour l'interprétation de tout l'épilogue du livre de Qohelet, je me demanderai seulement s'il est pensable que Qo 12,13ba fasse allusion au livre de Ben Sira: «Crains Dieu et observe ses commandements» peut-il renvoyer à l'œuvre de Ben Sira?

Ce qui m'étonne surtout, c'est que cette phrase de Qo 12,13ba n'est pas analysée pour elle-même par les commentateurs récents que j'ai pu consulter[10], en tout cas par ceux qui y voient quelque lien avec la sagesse de Ben Sira.

Il est clair qu'avec ses deux éléments – «crains Dieu et observe ses commandements» – cette phrase ne se retrouve pas ailleurs dans le livre de Qohelet. Pris séparément, chacun des deux éléments, par contre, se lit sous la plume de Qohelet. «Crains Dieu» se trouve à la fin de Qo 5,6, en conclusion d'une péricope, 4.17–5,6, consacrée au comportement en matière religieuse. Si, comme le pense N. Lohfink[11], cette péricope est au centre du livre, la centralité du thème de la crainte de Dieu dans l'œuvre de Qohelet en est plus évidente. Il n'empêche que la syntaxe de Qo 5,6 n'est pas limpide[12], ce qui donne place à plusieurs interprétations, et dès lors la portée exacte de «Crains Dieu» ne peut être déterminée à coup sûr. Quant à la deuxième partie de Qo 12,13ba, «Observe les comman-

---

7. G. T. SHEPPARD, *Wisdom as a Hermeneutical Construct. A Study in the Sapientializing of the Old Testament* (BZAW, 151), Berlin, 1980, spéc. pp. 126-128.

8. N. LOHFINK, *Les épilogues du livre de Qohélet et les débuts du canon*, in P. BOVATI – R. MEYNET (éd.), *Ouvrir les Écritures. Mélanges offerts à Paul Beauchamp* (LD, 162), Paris, 1995, spéc. pp. 93-95.

9. BACKHAUS, *Qohelet und Sirach* (n. 4), p. 45; MARBÖCK, *Kohelet und Sirach* (n. 4), pp. 282 et 296.

10. Pas même par E. PFEIFFER, *Die Gottesfurcht im Buche Kohelet*, in H.G. REVENTLOW (ed.), *Gottes Wort und Gottes Land*. FS H.-W. Hertzberg, Göttingen, 1965, pp. 135-158; il renvoie (p. 153) à Dt 13,3; 17,9; 28,58; 31,12-13; Lv 19,14.32; 25,17.36.43, et signale (n. 155) que J. HÄNEL, *Die Religion der Heiligkeit*, Gütersloh, 1931, p. 128, renvoie à Ps 112,1; 119,63.79.161; Pr 13,13; Esd 10,3. A.A. FISCHER, *Skepsis oder Furcht Gottes. Studien zur Komposition und Theologie des Buches Kohelet* (BZAW, 247), Berlin, 1997, p. 243, n. 83, ne fait qu'un renvoi à quelques Pss, dont Ps 103,17-18; 128,1, et à Ben Sira.

11. N. LOHFINK, *Kohelet* (Die Neue Echter Bibel, 1), Würzburg, 1980, p. 10.

12. Cf. J.L. CRENSHAW, *Ecclesiastes. A Commentary* (OTL), Philadelphia, Westminster —London, 1987, p. 118.

dements», on ne la trouve pas ailleurs telle quelle dans le livre. Le seul texte qui s'en rapproche met le singulier: «Qui observe le commandement...» en 8,5, mais, comme le relèvent N. Lohfink et James L. Crenshaw[13], on ne peut savoir si le commandement est celui du roi (8,2) ou celui de Dieu. En outre, Qohelet cite-t-il la sagesse traditionnelle ou exprime-t-il sa propre opinion? Bref, le livre de Qohelet n'aide guère à interpréter la phrase en question de l'épilogue.

Le rapprochement de la crainte de Dieu et de l'observance des préceptes n'est pas davantage le fait du livre des Proverbes et je ne crois pas que Gerald H. Wilson ait raison de voir dans les préceptes paternels, souvent mentionnés en Pr 1–9, les préceptes de la torâ[14]. Il y a, certes, l'un ou l'autre passage de Pr 1–9 qui rappelle tel ou tel texte du Deutéronome, mais, pour l'auteur ou les auteurs de Pr 1–9, ce qui fonde l'autorité des préceptes paternels est bien plus, à mon sens, la Sagesse elle-même, telle qu'elle est mise en scène en Pr 1; 8; 9.

2. Pour trouver l'origine de la formule de Qo 12,13bα, on peut s'appuyer sur une des plus anciennes interprétations de ce stique. Dans le talmud Babli, au traité sur le Shabbath, 30b, on nous apprend que Rabbi Judah répondait aux objections sur la canonicité de Qohelet par le fait, entre autres, que Qo 12,13 reprenait l'enseignement de la torâ[15]. Cette piste, qu'à ma connaissance, nul n'a encore suivie, nous réservera quelque surprise. De fait, plusieurs renvoient à quelques phrases du Deutéronome[16]. Je rappelle ici ces textes:

> *Ah! si leur cœur pouvait toujours être ainsi, pour* me craindre et garder mes commandements *en sorte qu'ils soient heureux à jamais, eux et leurs fils* (Dt 5,29).
> *C'est Yahvé votre Dieu que vous suivrez et* c'est lui que vous craindrez, ce sont ses commandements que vous garderez, *c'est à sa voix que vous obéirez, c'est lui que vous servirez, c'est à lui que vous vous attacherez* (Dt 13,5).

Nous avons ici la théologie de l'alliance, avec sa stipulation fondamentale. Cette parénèse se retrouve encore dans d'autres passages du Deutéronome, où le rapprochement de la crainte du Seigneur et de l'observance de ses commandements est moins strict:

---

13. LOHFINK, *Les épilogues* (n. 8), p. 94, et CRENSHAW, *Ecclesiastes* (n. 12), p. 151.

14. G. H. WILSON, *«The Words of the Wise»: The Intent and Significance of Qohelet 12:9-14*, in *JBL* 103 (1984) 175-192, spéc. p. 183.

15. Cf. K. J. DELL, *Ecclesiastes as Wisdom: Consulting Early Interpreters*, in *VT* 44 (1994), pp. 314-315.

16. Par exemple, PFEIFFER, *Die Gottesfurcht* (n. 10), p. 153, et L. DEROUSSEAUX, *La crainte de Dieu dans l'Ancien Testament* (LD, 63), Paris, 1970, p. 343, n. 138.

Ainsi, si tu crains Yahvé ton Dieu *tous les jours de ta vie*, si tu observes toutes *ses lois et* ses commandements *que je t'ordonne aujourd'hui, tu auras longue vie, toi, ton fils et le fils de ton fils* (Dt 6,2).

Garde les commandements de Yahvé ton Dieu *pour marcher dans ses voies et* pour le craindre (Dt 8,6).

Et maintenant, Israël, que te demande Yahvé ton Dieu, sinon de craindre Yahvé ton Dieu, *de suivre toutes ses voies, de l'aimer, de servir Yahvé ton Dieu de tout ton cœur et de toute ton âme*, de garder les commandements de Yahvé *et ses lois que je te prescris aujourd'hui pour ton bonheur?* (Dt 10,12-13)

(A propos du roi:) *(Cette loi) ne le quittera pas; il la lira tous les jours de sa vie pour apprendre* à craindre Yahvé son Dieu en gardant toutes *les paroles de cette loi, ainsi que ces règles pour les mettre en pratique. Il évitera ainsi de s'enorgueillir au-dessus de ses frères, et il ne s'écartera pas de ces commandements ni à gauche ni à droite. A cette condition, il aura, lui et ses fils, de longs jours sur le trône en Israël* (Dt 17,19-20).

Dans aucun de ces textes on ne retrouve, à strictement parler, le double impératif de Qo 12,13bα. Seul, Dt 8,6 donne un impératif, mais, comme Dt 17,19, ce texte établit une relation entre la crainte de Dieu et l'observance de ses commandements: l'observance est la façon concrète de prouver que l'on craint le Seigneur. Par ailleurs et à l'inverse de Qo 12,13bα, la plupart de ces textes du Deutéronome font de la crainte et de l'observance la condition de la bénédiction ou, plus exactement, du bonheur futur. Font exception Dt 8,6, qui évoquait l'épreuve subie au désert, et Dt 13,5, qui met en garde contre le polythéisme.

Dans l'histoire deutéronomiste, un texte s'inspire de ces passages du Deutéronome. Il s'agit d'une addition ancienne qui achève le jugement porté sur le royaume du Nord déchu. Dans ce texte, il est question des Israélites infidèles:

Ils ne craignaient pas Yahvé *et ils n'agissaient pas selon ses règles et ses rites, selon la loi et selon* les commandements que Yahvé avait ordonnées *aux fils de Jacob... Yahvé avait conclu avec eux une alliance et il leur avait fait cette prescription: Vous ne craindrez pas les dieux étrangers... C'est seulement* Yahvé, *qui vous a fait monter du pays d'Égypte..., que vous craindrez, que vous vénérerez et auquel vous sacrifierez.* Vous observerez *les règles et les rites, la loi et* les commandements qu'il vous a donnés... (2 R 17,34-37).

Il faut attendre l'époque tardive pour retrouver un nouvel écho des textes du Deutéronome, si l'on met à part le début du Ps 112, qui semble postexilique: «*Heureux* l'homme qui craint Yahvé et *se plaît grandement* à ses préceptes» (v. 1)[17]. Cinq textes tardifs peuvent être avancés.

---

17. Egalement Ps 119,63. Les autres renvois fournis par PFEIFFER, HÄNEL et FISCHER (cf. *supra*, n. 10) me paraissent peu probants: leurs formulations sont soit incomplètes soit trop différentes.

Le plus ancien ouvre le livret des Bénédictions qui termine la Règle de la Communauté de Qumrân:

> *Parole de bénédicti[on] pour l'homme intelligent, pour bénir* ceux qui craign[ent Dieu *et qui font] Sa volonté*, qui observent Ses commandements *et sont fermement attachés à son Alliance sainte…* (1 Q 28b, I 1-2).

Les quatre suivants sont difficiles à dater. On lit dans la recension longue de la version grecque d'Esther:

> *Mardochée lui (= à Esther) avait recommandé* de craindre Dieu et d'observer ses commandements *comme au temps où elle était avec lui* (2,20).

La version latine, Vieille latine, de l'Ecclésiastique ajoute en 2,21 (Gr 17) le verset suivant:

> Qui timent Dominum custodiunt mandata illius
> *et patientiam habebunt usque ad inspectionem illius*[18].

Ce texte doit faire partie de l'édition revisée et complétée du livre, édition qui a pu se réaliser déjà au 1er siècle avant notre ère en hébreu et en Judée.

Dans sa traduction latine, la Vulgate, du livre de Tobie, Jérôme aurait suivi un texte araméen[19]. On trouve ainsi en 2,13 le texte suivant, inconnu des autres formes du livre, à propos de l'aveugle:

> *Nam cum ab infantia sua semper* Deum timuerit, et mandata eius custodierit, *non est contristatus contra Deum quod plaga caecitatis evenerit ei.*

Enfin, le dernier texte de cette série se trouve dans le Pasteur d'Hermas, écrit chrétien du IIème siècle. Parmi les préceptes transmis par l'Ange de la pénitence, on lit celui-ci:

> Crains, *dit-il*, le Seigneur et garde ses commandements (37,1).

Le texte grec n'est pas celui de Qo 12,13bα dans la version tardive, on le sait, qui se trouve dans la Septante[20]. Hermas met le verbe en tête de chaque proposition et le premier est à l'aoriste, tandis que la version de la Septante le met au présent. L'Ange de la pénitence développe, un peu plus avant, le même précepte:

---

18. Le second stique est connu en grec: cf. O. WAHL, *Der Sirach-Text der Sacra Parallela* (FzB, 16), Würzburg, 1974, p. 48. Sur sa portée eschatologique (comparez avec Qo 12,14), cf. Núria CALDUCH BENAGES, *En el crisol de la prueba. Estudio exegético de Sir 2,1-18* (Associación Bíblica Española, 32), Estella (Navarra), 1997, p. 265.

19. J.-P. MIGNE (ed.), *Hieronymi Opera Omnia*, vol. 3 (Patrologia Latina, 29), Paris, 1846, c. 25A-26A.

20. Il n'est donc pas évident que Hermas cite Qo 12,13bα, comme le laisse penser R. JOLY, l'éditeur de HERMAS, *Le Pasteur* (SC, 53bis), Paris, ²1968, p. 175.

> *Tous* ceux qui le craindront et observeront ses commandements *vivront pour Dieu....* Ce sont donc ceux qui le craignent et qui observent ses commandements *qui vivent auprès de Dieu* (37,4-5).
> *Ecoutez-moi donc et* craignez celui *qui peut tout sauver et perdre*, et observez ses commandements *et vous vivrez pour Dieu* (49,3).

On aura observé que la majorité des textes de cette série d'époque tardive utilise le terme Dieu, comme Qo 12,13bα, plutôt que Seigneur, et que le rapprochement de crainte de Dieu et d'observance est le plus souvent beaucoup plus étroit que dans les textes deutéronomistes, hormis Dt 5,29 et 13,5. Enfin à Qumrân comme chez Hermas la bénédiction est présente comme dans la plupart des textes cités du Deutéronome. Mais ce qui frappe le plus, c'est que les textes de cette seconde série ont presque une formule stéréotypée et que celle-ci n'apparaît qu'après la rédaction de Qohelet. Dès lors, l'épilogue avec Qo 12,13bα n'appartient-il pas à cette même seconde série? Quelle date faut-il assigner à l'épilogue en question?[21]

3. Jusqu'à présent, je n'ai cité aucun texte propre à Ben Sira, alors que c'est à lui que G.T. Sheppard et N. Lohfink pensent en lisant Qo 12,13bα[22]. Voyons tout d'abord quels sont les textes de Ben Sira qui méritent la comparaison avec ce verset de l'épilogue.

Nos deux interprètes renvoient à Si 1 et particulièrement, si l'on ajoute le thème du jugement de Qo 12,14, en Si 1,26-30. L'analyse critique permet de reconstituer le texte hébreu manquant et de le traduire de la façon suivante:

> *Dans les trésors de la sagesse sont des proverbes de prudence,*
> *mais elle est une abomination pour le méchant*, la crainte du Seigneur.
> *Tu désires la sagesse?* Garde le commandement
> *et le Seigneur te la prodiguera.*
> *Car elle est sagesse et éducation*, la crainte du Seigneur
> *et sa faveur va à la fidélité et à la douceur.*
>
> *Ne sois pas rebelle à la crainte du Seigneur*
> *et ne t'approche pas d'elle avec un cœur double.*
> *Ne sois pas hypocrite devant les gens*
> *et veille sur tes lèvres.*
> *Ne t'élève pas, de peur que tu ne chutes*
> *et n'amènes le deshonneur sur toi-même:*

21. La datation de l'épilogue ne peut être précisée actuellement. BACKHAUS, *Qohelet und Sirach* (n.4), p. 45, considère que Qo 12,13bα pourrait provenir du cercle des théologiens auquel Ben Sira pouvait appartenir. Mais si l'on suit LOHFINK, *Les épilogues* (n. 8), Qo 12,13bα est postérieur à l'édition du livre de Ben Sira (après 175 av. J.-C.?).

22. Cf. *supra*, n. 7 et 8.

> *le Seigneur révélerait tes secrets*[23]
> *et en pleine assemblée te ferait tomber,*
> *car tu ne te serais pas approché de la crainte de Dieu*
> *et ton cœur serait plein de fraude.*

Pour notre propos d'éclairer Qo 12,13bα, les trois premiers vers suffisent. On observera tout d'abord le singulier du mot «commandement». En effet, on est en droit de penser que Ben Sira utilise normalement le singulier (cf. 6,37; 10,19; 32(35),23b.24a; 37,12; 45,5. Le pluriel de 45,17 s'explique aisément par son objet, la torâ)[24]. Deuxièmement, il n'est pas explicitement question, dans ces versets, de la torâ: le précepte (1,26) est un de ces proverbes de prudence (1,25) qui, s'il est fidèlement gardé, assure la bonne éducation (1,27). La crainte du Seigneur porte à garder le précepte et ce comportement conduit à la sagesse. Pour Ben Sira, l'essentiel est la sagesse, sur laquelle il ouvre son livre, et, quoi qu'en ait dit Josef Haspecker[25], le sujet principal de son œuvre, c'est bien la sagesse. Mais pour l'acquérir, il faut l'ouverture, la disponibilité, l'accueil de l'action de Dieu, qui est précisément la crainte du Seigneur, que J. Haspecker a bien mise en lumière. Celle-ci pousse à la mise en pratique du précepte divin.

Autre texte, mais où l'observance est présentée négativement (10,19):

> *La race digne d'honneur, quelle race d'hommes est-ce?*
> *La race digne d'honneur, ce sont ceux qui craignent le Seigneur.*
> *La race digne de mépris, quelle race d'hommes est-ce?*
> *La race digne de mépris, ce sont ceux qui transgressent le précepte.*

Ce qui revient à dire que seuls sont dignes d'honneur ceux qui observent le précepte.

Pancratius C. Beentjes[26] a montré, à propos de Si 18,15–23,27, l'importance de la conjonction des trois thèmes: sagesse, crainte du Seigneur et torâ. On la trouve dans trois textes-clés. Le premier (19,20) introduit la péricope sur la vraie sagesse comparée à la fausse:

---

23. LOHFINK, *Les épilogues* (n. 8), p. 95, n. 36, restitue ici נעלם, comme en Si 11,4 mss A et B. Mais la version syriaque de Si 1,30c oriente plutôt vers le mot hébreu מסתריך, comme en Si 3,22 et 4,18: cf. R. SMEND, *Die Weisheit des Jesus Sirach erklärt*, Berlin, 1906, p. 17; M.S. SEGAL, *Sefer Ben Sira hashshalem*, Jerusalem, ²1958, *ad loc.*, et A.S. HARTOM, *Ben Sira*, Tel Aviv, 1969, p. 17.

24. Cf. G.L. PRATO, *Il problema della teodicea in Ben Sira* (AnBib, 65), Roma, 1975, pp. 243-244.

25. J. HASPECKER, *Gottesfurcht bei Jesus Sirach. Ihre religiöse Struktur und ihre literarische und doktrinäre Bedeutung* (AnBib, 30), Rom, 1967, contre qui G. VON RAD, *Israël et la Sagesse*, Genève, 1970, p. 282, s'était élevé.

26. P. C. BEENTJES «*Full Wisdom is Fear of the Lord*». *Ben Sira 19,20–20,31: Context, Composition and Concept*, in *Estudios Bíblicos*, 47 (1989) 27-45, spéc. 30-34.

Toute sagesse est crainte du Seigneur
et toute sagesse est accomplissement de la torâ.

Puis en introduisant la comparaison du sage et de l'insensé, Ben Sira écrit (21,11):

Celui qui garde *la torâ contrôle ses instincts;*
la perfection de la crainte du Seigneur, *c'est la sagesse.*

Enfin, après avoir montré la culpabilité de la femme adultère, Ben Sira conclut (23,27):

Rien ne vaut la crainte du Seigneur,
rien n'est plus doux que de s'attacher à son commandement.

Ce dernier est certainement celui de la torâ (23,23).

Ces trois textes ont cette caractéristique de se référer à la torâ elle-même. Encore un dernier texte tiré d'une péricope sur la crainte du Seigneur:

En toutes tes actions veille sur toi-même,
car celui qui agit ainsi garde le précepte (cf. Pr 19,16a).
Celui qui tient la torâ veille sur lui-même
et qui fait confiance au Seigneur ne rougira pas.
Celui qui craint le Seigneur, *le mal ne le frappe pas,*
car même dans ses épreuves il sera délivré.
Il n'est pas sage celui qui hait la torâ... (32,23–33,2).

L'enseignement que Ben Sira formulait en 1,25-27 se répète donc à travers toute son œuvre, même s'il précise à un certain moment que le précepte est celui de la torâ. Pourtant, dès 2,15-17, il ajoute une dimension que seul G.T. Sheppard[27] a relevé comme en passant, celle de l'amour:

Ceux qui craignent le Seigneur *ne désobéissent pas à ses paroles,*
ceux qui l'aiment observent *ses voies.*
Ceux qui craignent le Seigneur cherchent à lui plaire,
ceux qui l'aiment se rassasient de sa torâ.
Ceux qui craignent le Seigneur ont le cœur prêt
et devant lui s'humilient.

J. Haspecker[28] a montré que, loin de s'opposer, craindre le Seigneur et l'aimer sont une seule attitude aux facettes complémentaires. Mais il n'a pas montré l'enracinement dans la tradition biblique de la séquence amour-observance.

---

27. SHEPPARD, *Wisdom as Hermeneutical Construct* (n. 7), p. 127.
28. HASPECKER, *Gottesfurcht bei Jesus Sirach* (n. 25), pp. 282-290. Cf. aussi CALDUCH BENAGES, *En el crisol de la prueba* (n. 18), pp. 192-208.

4. En effet, à côté de la séquence crainte-observance, les textes bibliques et la littérature intertestamentaire en connaissent une autre: amour-observance.

Le texte de base semble être celui qui, dans le décalogue, termine le précepte sur le service exclusif de Yahvé. Celui-ci se déclare miséricordieux jusqu'à mille générations envers «*ceux qui m'aiment et gardent mes commandements* » (Ex 20,6 = Dt 5,10). Ce texte est cité par le Livre des Antiquités Bibliques en 11,6. Mais Dt 7,9 y revient déjà en utilisant la 3ème personne du singulier: «*ceux qui l'aiment et gardent ses commandements*»; cette forme est citée en Néhémie 1,5 et dans l'Ecrit de Damas, B, I, 1-2, tandis que Daniel 9,4 met la 2ème personne du singulier: «*ceux qui t'aiment et gardent tes commandements*». C'est sous cette forme qu'on la trouve à Qumrân, dans l'Hymne A', XVI, 13 et 17.

Par contre, Dt 11,1 donne la forme au futur:

> Tu aimeras Yahvé ton Dieu et tu observeras *ses préceptes, ses lois, ses ordonnances et* ses commandements *tous les jours*.

La forme impérative se lit dans le livre des Jubilés, 20,7, cité ici selon la version latine:

> Diligite Deum et *adherete omnibus* mandatis eius.

Le second verbe a été modifié. Par contre, il est resté dans le Testament de Benjamin, 3,1:

> *Maintenant donc, mes enfants, vous aussi*, aimez le Seigneur, *le Dieu du ciel et de la terre*, et gardez ses commandements, *imitant Joseph, cet homme bon et saint*.

Citons encore trois textes où la formule s'exprime un peu différemment. Le premier est une addition latine à l'Ecclésiastique (3,1 Vg):

> *Les fils de la sagesse, c'est l'assemblée des justes;*
> *leur race est obéissance et amour.*

De nouveau, ce texte doit avoir une origine hébraïque et l'on pourrait le dater du Ier siècle avant notre ère. Notez le cadre explicitement sapientiel.

Le Psaume de Salomon XIV,12, à dater des dernières décennies avant notre ère, donne:

> Le *Seigneur est fidèle envers* ceux qui l'aiment *dans la vérité,*
> *qui se soumettent à son châtiment,*
> *qui marchent dans la justice de* ses commandements,
> *dans la loi qu'il nous a imposée pour que nous en vivions.*

A la même époque, la Sagesse de Salomon, dans le célèbre sorite, écrit:

> *L'amour (de la Sagesse), c'est l'observance de ses lois* (6,18).

Nous en aurons fini avec cette série quand nous aurons cité deux textes johanniques. On lit dans le discours après la Cène:

> Si vous m'aimez, vous garderez mes commandements.... Celui *qui a mes commandements* et qui les garde, c'est celui-là qui m'aime (Jn 14,15.21).

Et Jean écrit dans sa première épître:

> *Nous reconnaissons que nous aimons les enfants de Dieu à ce que* nous aimons Dieu et que nous *pratiquons* ses commandements. Car l'amour de Dieu consiste à garder ses commandements (5,2-3).

5. On le voit, la séquence aimer-observer, en matière religieuse, est assez analogue à la première craindre-observer. Toutes deux apparaissent dans la torâ, principalement dans le Deutéronome (Dt 10,12 rapproche même les deux verbes craindre et aimer). Elles ne reviennent qu'après l'exil et le plus souvent entre la crise maccabéenne et le second siècle de notre ère. Mais Qohelet ne se sert jamais des mots aimer et amour en matière religieuse (cf. Qo 3,8; 5,9; 9,1.6.9). C'est ce qui le distingue de Ben Sira. En écrivant: «Crains Dieu et garde ses commandements» (Qo 12,13bα), l'épiloguiste utilise bien la langue de Qohelet: l'accusatif avec את, précédant le verbe[29]. Il met l'article au mot Dieu (cf. formules semblables en Gn 42,18; Ex 1,17-21; 1 Ch 13,12; Ne 7,2). Cependant, Qohelet aurait-il pu écrire ce double précepte? Outre qu'il n'est pas sûr qu'il ait jamais invité à observer les préceptes divins (8,5 n'est pas évident à ce propos), il n'a probablement pas la même perception de la crainte de Dieu. Pour la tradition, deutéronomiste ou récente, il n'y a de crainte de Dieu réelle que dans la relation d'alliance, qui est elle-même amour, et c'est par là que se fonde l'observance des préceptes de l'alliance. Pour Qohelet, confronté aux mystères de l'existence qu'il perçoit plus que d'autres, et sans hargne, il ne reste qu'à révérer ce Dieu dont il a perdu la trace parce que trop haut pour lui, homme d'ici-bas. Cela, encore une fois, le distingue de Ben Sira. Mais puisque Qo 12,13bα n'est pas de Qohelet, l'épiloguiste a-t-il pu viser Ben Sira?

Il est exact que Ben Sira a tenté d'articuler entre elles crainte du Seigneur, observance des préceptes et sagesse. A ce sujet, il me semble toujours qu'il faut éviter d'attribuer à Ben Sira une identification entre sa-

---

29. Cf. SCHOORS, *The Preacher Sought* (n. 3), p. 160.

gesse et torâ[30]. En citant Dt 33,4 Lxx, Si 24,23bc ne fait que reconnaître, à mon sens, que la révélation biblique est l'expression de la Sagesse divine dans son projet.

Je vois pourtant quelques difficultés:

a. Certes, pour Ben Sira, la crainte du Seigneur ne va pas sans l'observance du précepte. Mais réduire l'originalité du sage de Jérusalem à son enseignement sur la crainte de Dieu et l'observance de ses préceptes, cela me paraît un peu court. La thèse de J. Haspecker a eu le mérite de montrer l'importance et les harmoniques de la crainte de Dieu dans l'œuvre de Ben Sira, mais on ne le suit pas quand il entend que la crainte de Dieu en est le thème principal. Lire en Qo 12,13bα une allusion à Ben Sira, c'est suivre trop J. Haspecker.

b. La séquence crainte-observance, telle qu'elle est formulée en Qo 12,13bα, n'apparaît pas dans l'œuvre de Ben Sira, alors qu'elle est connue ailleurs.

c. Enfin, Ben Sira connaît aussi la séquence amour-observance, jumelée à l'autre, crainte-obervance. De cela, Qo 12,13bα ne laisse rien entrevoir. Dès lors, s'il fallait voir en Qo 12,13bα une allusion à Ben Sira, j'y reconnaîtrais une allusion réductrice à l'excès.

III. LA PART DE BONHEUR SELON QOHELET ET SI 14,11-19

Les sept textes de Qohelet ont été analysés en 1982 par R.N. Whybray[31] et plus récemment par Johan Y. Pahk[32]. Le rapprochement avec Si 14 a été suggéré par E. Podechard en 1912[33] et analysé par F.J. Backhaus en 1993[34]. Ce dernier propose également une structure littéraire de Si 14,5-19, sur laquelle je crois devoir revenir.

Commençons donc par le texte de Ben Sira. Ce texte nous est connu par le manuscrit A en hébreu[35], mais celui-ci présente des difficultés

30. Ce que plusieurs répètent; ainsi F.J. BACKHAUS, *Der Weisheit letzter Schluss. Qoh. 12,9-14 im Kontext von Traditionsgeschichte und beginnender Kanonisierung*, in *BN* 72 (1994) 38, n. 30 et LOHFINK, *Les épilogues* (n. 8), p. 94 et n. 35.

31. R.N. WHYBRAY, *Qoheleth, Preacher of Joy*, in *JSOT* 23 (1982) 87-98.

32. J. Y. PAHK, *Il canto della gioia in Dio. L'itinerario sapienziale espresso dall'unità letteraria in Qohelet 8,16–9,10 e il parallelo di Gilgameš Me. III* (Istituto Universitario Orientale. Dipartimento di Studi Asiatici, Series Minor, LII), Napoli, 1996, pp. 197-271.

33. PODECHARD, *L'Ecclésiaste* (n. 1), pp. 63-64. De même, par O. LORETZ, *Qohelet und der Alte Orient*, Freiburg, 1964, p. 119.

34. BACKHAUS, *Qohelet und Sirach* (n. 4), pp. 45-47.

35. Cf. P.C. BEENTJES, *The Book of Ben Sira in Hebrew. A Text Edition of all Extant Hebrew Manuscripts and A Synopsis of all Parallel Hebrew Ben Sira Texts* (SVT, 68), Leiden, 1997, pp. 42-43.

que seul le recours aux versions grecque et syriaque permet de résoudre.

Avec Moshé S. Segal[36], je crois que la péricope débute en fait en Si 13,25. Quatre versets servent d'introduction:

> 25   *C'est le cœur de l'homme qui change son visage*
> *soit en bien soit en mal[37].*
> 26   *Signe d'un cœur joyeux, une mine radieuse;*
> *soucis et préoccupations[38]: pensées de peine.*
> 1   *Heureux l'homme que n'afflige pas sa propre bouche*
> *et ne veut pas que la tristesse[39] atteigne son cœur.*
> 2   *Heureux l'homme qui ne se prive pas lui-même*
> *et dont l'espoir ne s'évanouit pas.*

Il y a donc deux catégories de personnes, les unes bien dans leur peau, les autres à la mine affligée. Tout vient du cœur, où se prennent les options de vie. La suite du texte décrira chacun des deux groupes. Tout d'abord, le groupe au choix négatif:

> 3   *Au cœur chiche la richesse ne convient pas*
> *ni à l'homme au regard cupide ne convient l'or.*
> 4   *Qui se prive soi-même amasse pour un autre*
> *et de ses biens exultera un étranger.*
> 5   *Qui est mauvais pour soi, à qui fera-t-il du bien?*
> *Il ne jouit même pas de ses propres biens.*
> 6   *Qui est mauvais pour soi, il n'y a pas pire que lui.*
> *Aussi l'accompagne la rançon de sa méchanceté.*
> 7   *Même s'il fait le bien, il le fait par mégarde*
> *et au terme ressort sa méchanceté.*
> 8   *Il est mauvais, celui qui a le regard envieux,*
> *qui détourne le visage et méprise les gens[40].*
> 9   *Au regard du cupide[41], elle est trop petite, sa part.*
> *La cupidité dessèche l'âme[42].*
> 10   *L'œil de l'envieux[43] louche sur le pain*
> *et la famine est sur sa table![44]*

Il ne s'agit plus du pauvre que des péricopes précédentes (10,19–11,6; 13,1-24) opposaient au riche. Ici c'est l'avare qui est mis en scène. Sim-

---

36. Segal, *Sefer Ben Sira* (n. 23), p. 87.

37. Ce stique ne dépend pas de Qo 12,14: cf. Backhaus, *Qohelet und Sirach* (n. 4), p. 36.

38. Dans le ms. A, le deuxième mot de ce stique débute par un *waw*, au lieu d'un *yod*.

39. La deuxième lettre doit être un *waw*, au lieu du *yod*.

40. Les versets 7-8 manquent dans le ms. A. On les restitue d'après le grec.

41. Le deuxième mot de ce stique, dans le ms. A, ne semble pas original.

42. Pour ce stique, le texte du ms. A ne semble pas authentique. On suit ici le grec, mais en lisant עין, au lieu de עון.

43. Omettre le second עין.

44. Les stiques c-d du ms. A ne sont pas authentiques: cf. le syriaque.

ple portrait. Aucun précepte formel. L'avare a l'œil mauvais. S'il est riche, il se prive. Mauvais pour soi, il l'est aussi pour autrui. Il est avide de fortune ou d'un simple bien, comme le pain, mais il est incapable d'en jouir: il amasse, mais s'astreint à la misère!

En contraste, Ben Sira formule son enseignement:

> [11] *Mon fils[45], si tu en as les moyens, fais-toi du bien*
> *et, selon ton pouvoir, rassasie-toi.*
> [12] *Souviens-toi que[46] la mort ne tardera pas*
> *et que le temps fixé pour aller au shéol ne t'a pas été révélé.*
> [13] *Avant de mourir, fais du bien à ton ami*
> *et, autant que tu le peux, donne-lui.*
> [14] *Ne te refuse pas le bonheur présent*
> *et à une part désirable[47] ne te dérobe pas.*
> [15] *Ne laisseras-tu pas ta fortune à un autre*
> *et le fruit de ton labeur à ceux qui tireront au sort?*
> [16] *Donne, prends[48] et régale-toi,*
> *car ce n'est pas au shéol qu'on cherche du plaisir[49].*

Le contraste de cet enseignement est flagrant. Pour Ben Sira, au lieu d'épargner à l'excès, jusqu'à vivre misérablement et n'avoir sur autrui qu'un regard envieux, le disciple, qu'il interpelle directement, cette fois, est invité à user des biens dont il dispose pour lui-même et pour autrui, à ne pas refuser non plus le bien qu'on lui offre (le stique 14b, selon l'hébreu, est conjectural). La raison est celle qui valait pour l'avare (v. 4), à savoir qu'à la mort, tous les biens du défunt passent en d'autres mains. A quoi, Ben Sira ajoute ici que nul ne sait la date de sa mort et que le shéol n'est pas un lieu de jouissance.

La conclusion revient sur le thème de la mort, en soulignant qu'elle attend tous les humains, l'avare comme celui qui jouit de ses biens:

> [17] *Toute chair s'use comme un vêtement*
> *et la loi perpétuelle, c'est: ils mourront!*
> [18] *Comme les feuilles poussent sur un arbre verdoyant,*
> *tantôt se flétrissent, tantôt croissent,*
> *ainsi les générations de chair et de sang:*
> *l'une expire et l'autre prend vigueur.*
> [19] *Toutes ses œuvres pourriront*
> *et l'ouvrage de ses mains s'en ira à sa suite.*

---

45. Omettre le reste de ce stique du ms. A, ainsi que le *waw* qui ouvre le deuxième stique.

46. Omettre le reste de ce stique du ms. A: dittographie de 14,16b.

47. Cf. *infra*.

48. Au lieu de לאה, lire וקח ou לקח וקח. Omettre וְתֵן: dittographie.

49. La suite du texte du ms. A est une addition provenant du syriaque.

La perspective de la mort inéluctable pour tous justifie, tant qu'il est encore l'heure, l'invitation à fuir l'avarice et à lui préférer l'usage des biens dont on dispose.

Cette lecture de la péricope s'éloigne de celle qu'a proposée F.J. Backhaus, lequel a tort, à mon sens, de s'appuyer sur l'interprétation de Sir 14,14 proposée en 1975 par Tadeusz Penar[50]. En ne cherchant à structurer que les versets 5-10.11-12 et 13-15.16-19, F.J. Backhaus n'a pas vu ce que J. Haspecker[51] avait déjà relevé en 1967, à savoir que Ben Sira reprend ici sa façon caractéristique d'opposer du négatif et du positif. Les versets introductifs sont déjà clairs à cet égard, tandis que les versets conclusifs reprennent l'argument fondamental, déjà brièvement suggéré à propos de l'avare (v. 4) et explicité dans le message adressé au disciple (v. 12-13.15-16): cet argument vaut pour tous et ne donne à l'avare aucune justification de son comportement.

E. Podechard[52] met Si 14,1-19 et surtout 14,11-17, qu'il traduit d'après l'hébreu, en rapport avec les textes où Qohelet invite à la jouissance. Le thème est identique de part et d'autre, écrit-il, et n'a pas de parallèles ailleurs dans l'Ancien Testament, si ce n'est pour le blâme (Is 22,13); quelques expressions sont en outre analogues chez les deux auteurs: se faire du bien (Si 14,11 et Qo 3,12;11,9), le bonheur présent (Si 14,14 et Qo 7,14) et la référence au shéol (Si 14,12.16 et Qo 9,6.10). Podechard s'oriente donc vers une dépendance, Qohelet, pour qui le thème «sort [...] des entrailles mêmes du sujet»[53], devant être la source.

Par contre, F.J. Backhaus[54] exclut toute influence de Qohelet sur Ben Sira pour quatre motifs, à son avis: sont absents, chez Ben Sira, la formule אין טוב, la triade manger-boire-voir ce qui est bon, la question: quel avantage y a-t-il?, et, enfin, le lexème חלק.

Ce dernier motif, absence du mot «part, portion», me paraît sujet à caution. En effet, pour ne pas avoir vu que les conseils de Si 14,11-16 faisaient pendants avec la description de l'avare en 14,3-10, Backhaus ne prend pas en considération la présence de ce lexème en Si 14,9a, le second stique y insistant d'ailleurs lourdement et, semble-t-il, erronément dans Ms A. A cette observation s'ajoute que Backhaus s'attarde à montrer que Si 14,14b, selon le même Ms A, qui ne donne pas le mot חלק, à l'inverse de la version grecque, peut parfaitement être compris

50. BACKHAUS, *Qohelet und Sirach* (n.4), pp. 46-47; T. PENAR, *Northwest Semitic Philology and the Hebrew Fragments of Ben Sira* (Biblica et Orientalia, 28), Rome, 1975, p. 44.

51. HASPECKER, *Gottesfurcht bei Jesus Sirach* (n. 25), pp. 55 et 129.

52. PODECHARD, *L'Ecclésiaste* (n. 1), pp. 63-64.

53. *Op. cit.*, p. 64.

54. BACKHAUS, *Qohelet und Sirach* (n. 4), pp. 46-47.

comme le proposait T. Penar, à savoir: «*Aber vom Verdienst eines Nächsten ziehe nichts ab*», ce que Penar traduisait: «*and from brother's fixed earnings do not substract*». A mon sens, cette interprétation, que nul autre jusqu'à présent n'a retenue, est un effort désespéré pour sauver deux mots du Ms A que tous les commentateurs ont tenté de comprendre depuis le début du siècle. En effet, si, d'une part, faire de לקח un substantif au sens de gain, profit, avoir, est une hypothèse que Si 42,7 Ms B justifie peut-être, bien qu'une note en marge du manuscrit apporte une correction, d'autre part, garder le mot אח au sens de frère, c'est ne pas observer ce qu'avait noté Israël Lévi[55] en 1901, à savoir que le copiste du Ms A commet le même type d'erreur en 14,16a, où il écrit לאח «au frère», à la place de וקח, «et prends», qu'ont lu les versions grecque et syriaque. Tous les autres interprètes ont vu dans le premier mot du Ms A (ובהלקח) une erreur du copiste qui devait avoir devant lui un mot comportant le lexème חלק[56]. Quelques-uns[57] y voient un complément d'objet direct, sans la préposition ב, tandis que d'autres[58] gardent la préposition, avec raison, me semble-t-il. Quant au second mot de Si 14,14b selon le Ms A, אח, je laisse de côté le recours au mot אָח que la TOB et Antonino Minissale[59] traduisent par «marmite»: le mot n'apparaît qu'en Jr 36,22-23 TM, mais au sens de «brasero»[60]. Par contre, Norbert Peters[61] avait déjà pensé en 1902 qu'il fallait lire, non pas אח, mais אוה, à savoir אַוָּה, désir, ainsi que le proposait la version grecque. Moshé S. Segal et Hans-Peter Rüger[62] proposent, quant à eux, de lire le mot plus courant תַּאֲוָה, au même sens de désir, objet de désir. Pour l'expression comprenant les

55. I. LÉVI, *L'Ecclésiastique ou la Sagesse de Jésus, fils de Sira. Texte original hébreu édité, traduit et commenté* (Bibliothèque de l'École des Hautes Études, Sciences religieuses, 10,2). Paris, 1901, p. 104.

56. Le passage tiré du texte médiéval de l'*Alphabet de Ben Sira*, cité par SMEND, *Die Weisheit des Jesus Sirach erklärt* (n. 23), p. 134, porte bien la racine חלק.

57. LÉVI, *L'Ecclésiastique* (n. 55), p. 104. En suivant le grec: N. PETERS, *Das Buch Jesus Sirach oder Ecclesiasticus* (Exegetisches Handbuch zum Alten Testament, 25), Münster, 1913, pp. 119 et 123-124.

58. R. SMEND, *Die Weisheit des Jesus Sirach hebräisch und deutsch*, Berlin, 1906, p. 17 de la partie hébraïque; H.-P. RÜGER, *Text und Textform im hebräischen Sirach* (BZAW, 112), Berlin, 1970, p. 19; G.L. PRATO, *Il problema della teodicea in Ben Sira* (n. 24), p. 390 («forse»).

59. *Traduction œcuménique de la Bible. Ancien Testament*, Paris, 1975, p. 2135, n. *u*; A. MINISSALE, *La versione greca del Siracide* (AnBib, 133), Roma, 1995, p. 196.

60. Sur les difficultés du passage, cf. D. BARTHÉLEMY, *Critique textuelle de l'Ancien Testament. 2. Isaïe, Jérémie, Lamentations* (OBO, 50/2), Fribourg – Göttingen, 1986, pp. 715-716.

61. N. PETERS, *Der jüngst wiederaufgefundene hebräische Text des Buches Ecclesiasticus*, Freiburg im Breisgau, 1902, p. 82.

62. SEGAL, *Sefer Ben Sira* (n. 23), p. 91; RÜGER, *Text und Textform* (n. 58), p. 19, suivi par G. SAUER, *Jesus Sirach (Ben Sira)* (Jüdische Schriften aus Hellenistisch-römischer Zeit, 3), Gütersloh, 1981, p. 541.

deux mots, il me semble que la proposition de Rüger est la plus acceptable: ובחלק תאוה, c'est-à-dire: «à une part désirable», ce qui rejoint le
grec et ne suppose que la confusion entre ח et ה, de même qu'entre ח et
ת, supposition très acceptable quand on se rappelle l'état du Ms A de
Ben Sira en hébreu.

En acceptant la lecture de Rüger, j'exclus l'hypothèse de Backhaus et
considère donc que le lexème «part, portion» n'est pas absent du texte
de Ben Sira lorsqu'il traite de carpe diem. En cela, il ne se distingue
donc pas de Qohelet, bien qu'en un tel contexte le mot «part» soit classique (Gn 14,24; Dt 18,8; Jb 17,5).

Et pourtant il y a entre Qohelet et Ben Sira de sérieuses différences
qui n'ont pas toutes été notées par Backhaus.

L'invitation à profiter du bonheur qui nous est offert en ce monde
jaillit, chez Qohelet, de l'observation des absurdités de l'existence et de
la société, observation qui le conduit à comprendre que seules quelques
parcelles de bonheur nous restent accessibles. Ben Sira ignore cette pro-
cédure. Il ne porte pas sur le monde et l'existence humaine un regard critique et désabusé. Son message positif en tout cas n'en est pas la consé-
quence comme chez Qohelet. Chez Ben Sira, l'opposition entre la description de l'avare et l'appel à profiter du bien présent est davantage de
l'ordre moral que de la réflexion existentielle. Il ne dira donc pas qu'il
n'y a de bien que dans la jouissance accessible.

Les raisons qui conduisent concrètement Qohelet au *carpe diem* ont
été résumées par R.N. Whybray[63] de la façon suivante:

1. vanité du labeur et de l'effort humain (1,12–2,26),
2. vanité de l'ignorance humaine sur le futur (3,1-15),
3. vanité de la présence d'injustices dans le monde (3,16-22),
4. vanité de la poursuite des richesses (5,9-19),
5. vanité de la méchanceté impunie (8,10-15),
6. vanité du fait que tous les humains partagent un même destin (9,1-10),
7. vanité de la brièveté de la vie humaine (11,7–12,7).

Pour sa part, J. Pahk[64] les synthétise comme suit:

1. la fatigue ou mieux son résultat qui ne peut être maintenu
   comme possession exclusive de qui la supporte (2,12-23; 5,12-
   16),

---

63. WHYBRAY, *Qoheleth, Preacher of Joy* (n. 31), pp. 91-92.
64. PAHK, *Il canto della gioia in Dio* (n. 32), p. 242.

2. l'injustice existentielle, pour laquelle il n'y a pas de jugement adéquat sur terre (3,16-21; 8,9-14),
3. l'agir de Dieu sur le monde et l'intention humaine de connaître cet agir. A cet égard, l'homme demeure ignorant (3,9-11; 8,16–9,6),
4. la brièveté de la vie ou la mort (11,7 ss).

Le seul argument que Ben Sira avance est celui de la mort inéluctable. Il en souligne trois aspects:

1. tu ignores le jour de ton décès (14,12),
2. à ta mort, tes biens reviennent à d'autres (14,15 et déjà 14,2),
3. au shéol, pas de plaisir (14,16).

Le premier aspect se trouve en Qo 8,8 et 9,12. Je note que Qo 8,8 est introduit par 8,7 où l'on trouve le verbe נגד au hifil qui en Si 14,12b se trouve au hofal. En Qo 9,12, le mot «son temps» se réfère au jour de la mort, mais Ben Sira parle de «décret» fixant cette date, terme que Qohelet n'utilise pas.

Le deuxième thème se trouve aussi chez Qohelet, mais avec d'autres nuances. Pour Ben Sira, cela n'a pas de sens de se priver des biens qu'on possède; autant en profiter de son vivant avant qu'ils passent à d'autres. Pour Qohelet, le problème, c'est qu'on ignore la qualité de l'héritier (2,18-19), ou que le temps de jouir de sa fortune n'est pas accordé (6,1-2), ou encore qu'il n'y a pas d'héritier direct (4,8). Dans ce dernier texte, Qo 4,8, on trouve l'expression «se priver» qui paraît en Si 14,2a, mais dans un contexte qui n'exclut pas des héritiers.

Le troisième thème ne se lit pas comme tel chez Qohelet, pour qui il n'y a au shéol ni activité, ni connaissance, ni science, ni sagesse (9,10), pas plus que de récompense (9,5).

Quant à la conclusion de Si 14,17-19, elle ne s'inspire pas de Qohelet. La comparaison avec le vêtement qui s'use vient du Ps 102,27. Si 14,18 semble bien s'inspirer d'Homère, *Iliade*, 6,146-149, ainsi que le proposent Jack T. Sanders, à la suite de Theophil Middendorp[65]:

Comme naissent les feuilles, ainsi font les hommes. Les feuilles, tour à tour, c'est le vent qui les épand sur le sol, et la forêt verdoyante qui les fait naître, quand se lèvent les jours de printemps. Ainsi des hommes: une génération naît à l'instant même où une autre s'efface[66].

65. J.T. SANDERS, *Ben Sira and Demotic Wisdom* (SBL MS, 28), Chico (CA), 1983, p. 39; Th. MIDDENDORP, *Die Stellung Jesu Ben Siras zwischen Judentum und Hellenismus*, Leiden, 1973, p. 19.
66. HOMÈRE, *Iliade*, t. I (Chants I-VI), texte établi et traduit par Paul MAZON e.a. (Collection des Universités de France), Paris, 1937, pp. 158-159.

Enfin, le dernier verset, Si 14,19, va plus loin que Qohelet en déclarant vouées à la pourriture toutes les œuvres humaines.

Face à la mort inéluctable, Ben Sira invite le disciple à se faire du bien, mais aussi à en faire à son ami (14,11.13). Qohelet ne pensait pas à celui-ci. Ben Sira se montre plus altruiste, l'attitude qu'il conseille étant aux antipodes de celle de l'avare qui ne fait du bien à autrui que par inadvertance (14,7). Certes, Qohelet incite le jeune homme à se donner du bonheur (11,9), et l'expression désigne ailleurs (Jg 19,6.9; Rt 3,7; 1 R 21,7) le bon temps qu'on se donne après avoir pris un bon repas. Il en est probablement de même chez Ben Sira. En effet, Si 14,10 parle de nourriture et de table. Pour Qohelet le seul bonheur accessible dans le présent est celui de boire et de manger. Par contre, alors que Qohelet utilise fréquemment le mot שמחה, joie, comme voie de solution aux difficultés de l'existence, Ben Sira ne l'utilise pas dans ce chapitre; le mot, chez lui, n'a pas une portée précise, bien qu'il apparaisse en contexte analogue (Si 30,22).

Mais surtout Qohelet voit dans cette part de bonheur un don de Dieu. Cela, Ben Sira ne le dit pas et c'est, à mon sens, ce qui le distingue le plus de son prédécesseur.

Ben Sira se serait-il donc inspiré de Qohelet? Il est exact que ces deux maîtres de sagesse ont appelé leurs disciples à profiter des plaisirs simples qu'offre l'existence, ce que nul autre sage en Israël n'avait fait avant eux. Mais les différences entre Qohelet et Ben Sira sont telles qu'on peut hésiter à parler d'une influence du premier sur le second. Au reste, l'air du temps, l'impact de la pensée hellénistique[67], peut expliquer les quelques analogies, sans qu'il faille rechercher les sources de Ben Sira. Il a assez de génie, lui aussi, pour s'exprimer en son propre nom. Si quelques-unes de ses tournures en rappellent telle ou telle de Qohelet, les démarches intellectuelles des deux sages sont profondément différentes. On peut, je crois, en rester là.

IV. Conclusion

Les deux enquêtes menées dans ces pages conduisent à des résultats assez négatifs. S'il fallait, pour d'autres motifs qu'on n'a pas discutés ici, reconnaître en Qo 12,13bα une allusion à Ben Sira, ce ne pourrait être vrai que jusqu'à un certain point, car le double précepte de

---

67. Cf. O. KAISER, *Der Mensch unter dem Schicksal* (BZAW, 161), Berlin, 1985, pp. 138-139, sans oublier *Gilgamesh Me. III*, étudié par PAHK, *Il canto della gioia in Dio* (n. 32).

l'épiloguiste est loin de donner, par sa formule stéréotypée, toute la richesse de la pensée de Ben Sira sur les rapports qu'il a mis entre sagesse, crainte de Dieu et observance de la torâ. Et quand Ben Sira invite à profiter du bonheur qui s'offre, on ne parviendra peut-être pas à exclure toute influence de Qohelet, mais prouver cette influence rencontre de telles objections qu'on se prend à douter.

Rue J. Grafé, 4/1   Maurice GILBERT, S.J.
B-5000 Namur

VIA MEDIA
KOH 7,15-18 UND DIE
GRIECHISCH-HELLENISTISCHE PHILOSOPHIE

I. TUGENDETHIK

Der Titel meines Vortrages verbindet zwei Größen miteinander: Kohelet und die hellenistische Philosophie. Die Verbindung kann historisch-genetisch verstanden werden: Wir können nach Bezugnahmen, Beeinflussungen oder inhaltlichen Abhängigkeiten fragen. Der Titel meines Vortrages kann aber auch rein komparatistisch verstanden werden: Zwei Größen werden miteinander verglichen mit dem Ziel, die Eigenart einer jeden der beiden klarer zu erkennen und schärfer zu fassen. Es gibt noch eine dritte Möglichkeit. Sie soll im Rahmen dieses Vortrages entwickelt werden.

Dabei möchte ich nicht das ganze Buch Kohelet ins Auge fassen, wie ich es an anderer Stelle getan habe[1], sondern mich auf *einen* Text beschränken: Koh 7,15-18. Hier – so sagen viele Exegeten – ruft Kohelet auf, zwischen den Extremen übermäßiger Gerechtigkeit und übermäßiger Ungerechtigkeit den goldenen Mittelweg zu gehen. Damit stoßen wir unwillkürlich auf das formale Prinzip dessen, was die abendländische Tradition als Tugend bezeichnet[2].

Die Tugendlehre erlebt gegenwärtig ein Comeback. Soziologen, Psychologen, Ethiker greifen im Rahmen ethischer Grundlagenreflexion direkt oder indirekt auf die klassische abendländische Tugendlehre zurück. Ich denke an den Theoretiker der reflexiven Moderne, den britischen Soziologen und Direktor der London School of Economics and Political Science Anthony Giddens[3], an die Psychoanalytiker Josef Rattner[4] und

---

1. L. SCHWIENHORST-SCHÖNBERGER, *»Nicht im Menschen gründet das Glück« (Koh 2,24). Kohelet im Spannungsfeld jüdischer Weisheit und hellenistischer Philosophie* (HBS, 2), Freiburg, Herder, 1994, ²1996.

2. Cf. ARISTOTELES, *Eth. Nic.* 1106a-1107a.

3. A. GIDDENS, *Jenseits von Links und Rechts. Die Zukunft radikaler Demokratie*, Frankfurt a.M., Suhrkamp, 1997. Cf. ID. in einem Interview, in *Die Zeit* 17, 18.04.1997, pp. 49-50. Er sagt von sich, daß er die »Idee einer »radikalen Mitte« propagiere.« »Das ist nur dann ein Widerspruch, wenn man als Mitte irgendeinen Kompromiß zwischen den politischen Polen Links und Rechts versteht.« Man vergleiche ARISTOTELES, *Eth. Nic.* 1106a-1107a. Zu den Begriffen »radikales Denken« und »mittlerer Weg« vergleiche man die zwanzig Jahre ältere Äußerung von F. CRÜSEMANN im Zusammenhang mit Koh 7,15-18 weiter unten Anm. 23.

4. J. RATTNER, *Was ist Tugend, was ist Laster? Tiefenpsychologie und angewandte Ethik*, München, Knesebeck & Schuler, 1988.

Theodor Seifert, an den amerikanischen Philosophen Alasdair MacIntyre, der die Rückkehr zur aristotelischen Tugendlehre propagiert[5], an den Moraltheologen Dietmar Mieth[6] und nicht zuletzt auch an Hans Küng[7]. Theodor Seifert zitiert in einem Aufsatz in einer psychologischen Fachzeitschrift das Buch des katholischen Philosophen Josef Pieper »Das Viergespann. Klugheit, Gerechtigkeit, Tapferkeit, Maß« aus dem Jahre 1964[8]. Josef Pieper hat in diesem Buch vor allem im Rückgriff auf seinen »Meister« Thomas von Aquin die klassische Lehre von den vier Kardinaltugenden in ihrer Aktualität erschlossen. Allerdings bringt der Münsteraner Philosoph in der Vorbemerkung seines Buches einen Einwand gegen dieses Unternehmen zur Sprache. Er weist zunächst darauf hin, daß die Tugendlehre in den elementaren Bestand des europäischen Bewußtseins eingegangen sei, »und dies auf Grund einer jahrhundertelang durchgehaltenen Denkbemühung, an welcher sämtliche Ursprungskräfte des sich gründenden Abendlandes teilhaben, sowohl die Griechen [Platon, Aristoteles] wie die Römer [Cicero, Seneca] und das Judentum [Philon] nicht anders als das Christentum [Clemens von Alexandrien, Augustin]. Gerade diese Herkunft freilich hat die Tugendlehre später einer christlichen Kritik als etwas allzu sehr »Philosophisches« verdächtig gemacht, vor allem als etwas zu wenig »Biblisches«. Und man hat darauf bestanden, statt von den menschlichen Tugenden von »Geboten« und »Pflichten« zu reden.«[9]

In der Tat findet sich im Alten Testament keine reflektierte Tugendlehre[10]. Allerdings scheint es einen Reflexionsansatz zu geben, der in

5. A. MacIntyre, *After Virtue. A Study in Moral Theory*, Notre Dame, University of Notre Dame Press, 1981, ²1984; dt. Üb. *Der Verlust der Tugend. Zur moralischen Krise der Gegenwart*, Frankfurt a. M., Suhrkamp, 1995. Cf. auch W.C. Spohn, *Current Theology – Notes on Moral Theology*, 1991 – *The Return of Virtue Ethics*, in *Theological Studies* 53 (1992) 60-75.

6. D. Mieth, *Die neuen Tugenden. Ein ethischer Entwurf*, Düsseldorf, Patmos, 1984. Cf. auch E. Schockenhoff, *Bonum hominis. Die anthropologischen und theologischen Grundlagen der Tugendethik des Thomas von Aquin* (Tübinger Theologische Studien, 28), Mainz, Grünewald, 1987.

7. H. Küng, *Projekt Weltethos*, München, Piper, ³1996. Seine ethischen Argumentationen kreisen im Grunde um einen »vernünftigen Weg der Mitte« (cf. *ibid.*, p. 83). Wichtig war der Aufsatz von Max Scheler, *Zur Rehabilitierung der Tugend*, in Id., *Abhandlungen und Aufsätze*, Leipzig, Verlag der weisen Bücher, 1915, pp. 3-38. Ferner sei verwiesen auf K. Rahner / B. Welte (eds.), *Mut zur Tugend. Über die Fähigkeit, menschlicher zu leben*, Freiburg, Herder, 1979.

8. Th. Seifert, *Verwirrt von 10 000 Dingen. Ethisches Handeln, on-line mit dem Selbst*, in *Transpersonale Psychologie und Psychotherapie* 3 (1997) 19-31, p. 27.

9. J. Pieper, *Das Viergespann*, München, Kösel, 1964, p. 9. B. Schüller, *Die Begründung sittlicher Urteile. Typen ethischer Argumentation in der Moraltheologie*, Düsseldorf, Patmos, 1973, ²1980, pp. 299-305, geht auf den Vorwurf ein, in seiner »Ethik des Handelns« die Tugenden als eine »Ethik der Grundhaltungen« nicht berücksichtigt zu haben. Kritisch dazu D. Mieth, *Neue Tugenden* (Anm. 6), pp. 52-55.

10. Die vier Kardinaltugenden werden einmal in der Bibel (LXX) genannt: Weish 8,7.

diese Richtung geht: Koh 7,15-18. Besteht die Grundeinsicht der Tugendlehre darin, daß die Sittlichkeit menschlichen Handelns im rechten Maß, in der rechten Mitte zwischen zwei zu verwerfenden Extremen liegt, so scheint gerade dies in Koh 7,15-18 ausgesprochen zu sein. Und nicht wenige Exegeten sehen gerade in diesem Text den Entwurf einer Ethik des goldenen Mittelweges, so z.B. F. Delitzsch, K. Galling, R. Gordis, H.W. Hertzberg, A. Lauha, J. Vilchez[11]. Andere wie z.B. N. Lohfink, M. Fox, R. Lux lehnen gerade diese Interpretation ab[12].

Viele Exegeten, vor allem diejenigen, die Koh 7,15-18 als eine Empfehlung des goldenen Mittelweges verstehen, vertreten die Ansicht, daß die hier entworfene Ethik in eklatantem Widerspruch zum übrigen Alten Testament stehe[13]. E. Wölfel spricht in diesem Zusammenhang von einem skrupellosen Immoralismus, ja vom »Bankrott der Ethik«[14], A. Lauha von einer Kapitulation vor den Forderungen Gottes[15].

Einen eigenen Interpretationsansatz hat R.N. Whybray vorgelegt. Kohelet – so R.N. Whybray – warne nicht vor Gerechtigkeit, sondern vor *Selbst*gerechtigkeit (self-righteousness) und nicht vor Weisheit, sondern vor *angemaßter* Weisheit (pretensions to wisdom)[16]. Dem haben

---

11. F. DELITZSCH, *Hoheslied und Koheleth,* mit Excursen von Consul D. Wetzstein (BC IV, 4), Leipzig, 1875, pp. 318-321. K. GALLING, *Kohelet-Studien,* in ZAW 50 (1932), p. 277. R. GORDIS, *Koheleth – The Man and his World* (TSJTSA, 19), New York, 1968, pp. 178. 275-278. A. LAUHA, *Kohelet* (BK, 19), Neukirchen-Vluyn, 1978, pp. 131-136. J. VILCHEZ, *Ecclesiastes o Qohelet* (Nueva Biblia Española, Sapienciales, 3), Estella, Editorial Verbo Divino, 1994, pp. 315-318.

12. N. LOHFINK, *Kohelet* (NEB), Würzburg, 1980, [4]1993, p. 55: »... das meint weder paradoxes Handeln noch einen hier oft zitierten »goldenen Mittelweg«, sondern so etwas wie gesellschaftlichen Ekklektizismus, der der Situation der Gleichzeitigkeit und des Ineinander verschiedener gesellschaftlicher Systeme und Weltdeutungen einzig entspricht«. Etwas weiter spricht N. LOHFINK im Zusammenhang mit dem Begriff der Gottesfurcht von »Situationsethik«. M. FOX, *Qohelet and his Contradictions* (JSOT SS, 71), Sheffield, Sheffield Academic Press, 1989, p. 233. R. LUX, *Der »Lebenskompromiß« – ein Wesenszug im Denken Kohelets? Zur Auslegung von Koh 7,15-18,* in JUTTA HAUSMANN & HANS-JÜRGEN ZOBEL (eds.), *Alttestamentlicher Glaube und Biblische Theologie.* FS Horst Dietrich Preuß zum 65. Geburtstag, Stuttgart, Kohlhammer, 1992, pp. 267-278, spec. 275f, kommt in der Sache meiner Interpretation nahe, formuliert allerdings *ibid.,* p. 275 den Satz: »Hier wird gerade nicht der »goldene Mittelweg« gesucht, ein ethisch indifferentes Verhalten nahegelegt. Vielmehr wird der Leser... zu äußerster ethischer Verantwortlichkeit herausgefordert«. Das Problem solcher und ähnlicher Sätze besteht in der dem Ausdruck »goldener Mittelweg« unterstellten Bedeutung. Cf. dazu meine Ausführungen in Kapitel »III. Aristoteles: Nikomachische Ethik«.

13. A. LAUHA, *Kohelet* (Anm. 11), p. 135: »An Stelle der für das Alte Testament charakteristischen Unbedingtheit wertet er alle Dinge relativ«.

14. E. WÖLFEL, *Luther und die Skepsis,* München, Chr. Kaiser, 1958, pp. 70-74. »... zeigt sich Kohelet als jenseits von Gut und Böse«, *ibid.,* p. 73. V. 18b (»Gott fürchten«) ist für E. WÖLFEL sekundär (*ibid.,* p. 71, n. 1).

15. A. LAUHA, *Kohelet* (Anm. 11), p. 136.

16. R.N. WHYBRAY, *Qoheleth the Immoralist? (Qoh 7: 16-17),* in J.G. GAMMIE &

allerdings W.A. Brindle, M. Fox, Th. Krüger und R.E. Murphy widersprochen[17].

Vor dem Hintergrund der hier in aller Kürze skizzierten Forschungssituation[18] lohnt es sich, den Text erneut zu analysieren. Dabei möchte ich vor allem auf die Form der ethischen Argumentation achten. Sie gibt uns – so scheint mir – einen Hinweis auf die Stellung des Buches Kohelet innerhalb der jüdischen Tradition und in bezug auf die griechisch-hellenistische Philosophie.

II. KOH 7,15-18: GANG DER ARGUMENTATION

V.15a leitet eine Beobachtung ein. Die Determination der generischen Partikel כֹּל hat kataphorische Funktion: »*das* alles...«. Aus den in V.15b mitgeteilten *zwei* Beobachtungen ergibt sich für כֹּל im Nachhinein dualische Bedeutung[19]. Auch im vorangehenden V.14 werden zwei Dinge besprochen: der gute und der böse Tag. Auf beide wird in V.14b mit זֶה ... זֶה Bezug genommen. So ist der Leser also schon von V.14 her auf dualische Bedeutung eingestellt. Diese Beobachtung ist wichtig, weil das Wort כֹּל am Ende der Texteinheit, und zwar als letztes Wort von V.18, wieder auftaucht. Hier ist es mit dem Suffix der 3. Ps. M. Pl. versehen. Die suffigierte generische Partikel כֹּל trägt hier ebenfalls – durch die vorangehende Erörterung meines Erachtens eindeutig angezeigt – dualische Bedeutung[20]. Der Text diskutiert somit eine Alternative im strengen Sinne des Wortes (alter...alter); seine Pointe besteht allerdings darin, daß er ein Drittes konstituiert. Dabei arbeitet der Text auf subtile Weise mit dem Auf- und Abbau von Erwartungshorizonten. Doch damit

W.A. BRUEGGEMANN & W.L. HUMPHREYS & J.M. WARD (eds.), *Israelite Wisdom. Theological and Literary Essays*. In Honor of Samuel Terrien, New York, 1978, pp. 191-204. J. CRENSHAW, *Ecclesiastes. A Commentary* (OTL), Philadelphia, 1987, pp. 140f, ist ihm darin gefolgt. Bereits von F. DELITZSCH, *Hoheslied und Koheleth* (Anm. 11), p. 320, zurückgewiesen.

17. W.A. BRINDLE, *Righteousness and Wickedness in Ecclesiastes 7:15-18*, in *AUSS*, 23/3 (1985) 253-256. M. FOX, *Qohelet* (Anm. 12), pp. 233-235. TH. KRÜGER, *Theologische Gegenwartsdeutung im Kohelet-Buch* (Habil. Masch.), München, 1990, p. 339. R.E. MURPHY, *Ecclesiastes* (WBC, 23A), Dallas, Word Books, 1992, pp. 68.70.

18. W.A. BRINDLE, *Righteousness* (Anm. 17), pp. 243-251 klassifiziert ältere und neuere Interpretationen des Textes: (1) The Golden Mean; (2) Fanaticism and Legalism; (3) Overreaction to Truth; (4) Self-righteousness. Im Grunde lassen sich drei Interpretationstypen herausschälen: (1) Goldene Mitte; (2) Mischung aus Gut und Böse (M. Fox); (3) Selbstgerechtigkeit (R.N. Whybray).

19. F. DELITZSCH, *Hoheslied und Koheleth* (Anm. 11), p. 319: »... ein Allerlei..., welches durch 15[b] als ein Zweierlei bestimmt wird«. L. LEVY, *Das Buch Qoheleth. Ein Beitrag zur Geschichte des Sadduzäismus*, Leipzig, 1912, p. 108. So die meisten Kommentatoren. Cf. Koh 2,14; 3,19f.

20. So auch in Koh 2,14.

habe ich schon vorgegriffen. Ich kehre zurück zu V.15. V.15a leitet –
wie gesagt – eine Beobachtung ein.

V.15b teilt die Beobachtung mit. Es liegt ein Bikolon vor in Form eines antithetischen Parallelismus. Die im antithetischen Parallelismus
verwendeten Antonyme צַדִּיק und רָשָׁע können als kontradiktorisches,
aber auch als konträres Gegensatzpaar verstanden werden. Dies bleibt
zunächst offen. Die Unterscheidung ist wichtig, weil sie hilft, die
Argumentationsstrategie des Textes zu verstehen[21]. Sämtliche Texte des
Alten Testamentes, an denen das Gegensatzpaar צַדִּיק / רָשָׁע begegnet,
verstehen den Gegensatz implizit als einen *kontradiktorischen*: Unter
dem Gesichtspunkt von Sittlichkeit gibt es Gerechte und Frevler:
tertium non datur[22]:

V.15b kann aber auch als *konträrer Gegensatz* verstanden werden. In
diesem Verständnis nehmen die Bezeichnungen »Gerechter« und
»Frevler« die beiden einander gegenüberliegenden Pole einer Strecke«
ein. Zwischen ihnen gibt es ein Drittes:

Mit diesen beiden Verstehensmöglichkeiten arbeitet der Text. Ein
zeitgenössischer Leser konnte den hier vorausgesetzten Gegensatz im
Grunde nur als einen kontradiktorischen verstehen. Dies ergibt sich einfach aus allen uns bekannten alttestamentlichen Texten, in denen dieses
Gegensatzpaar begegnet. »Gerecht« entspricht »sittlich gut« und »frevlerisch« entspricht »sittlich schlecht«. Viele Exegeten setzen diese Bedeutung der Wörter צַדִּיק und רָשָׁע auch für ihre Verwendung in V.16
und V.17 voraus und kommen dann zu der eigenartigen Feststellung,
Kohelet würde ein gewisses Maß an frevlerischem Verhalten nahelegen,
worin sich sein eklatanter Widerspruch zur ethischen Tradition des Al-

21. Zum Begriff des konträren Gegensatzes im Rahmen ethischer Argumentation cf.
ARISTOTELES, *Eth. Nic.* 1108b.
22. Gen 18,23.25; Ex 9,27; 1 Kön 8,32; 2 Chr 6,23; Jes 5,23; Ez 13,22; 18,20.24;
21,8f; 33,12; Hab 1,4.13; Mal 3,18; Ps 1,5f; 7,10; 11,5; 34,22; 37,12.16f.21.32; 58,11;
68,3f; 75,11; 125,3; (129,4); Spr 3,33; 10,3.6f.11.16.20.24f.28.30.32; 11,8.10.23.31;
12,3.5.7.10.12.21.26; 13,5.9.25; 14,19.32; 15,6.28f; 17,15; 18,5; 21,12.18; 24,16.24;
25,26; 28,1.12.28; 29,2.7.16.27; Koh 3,17; 8,14; 9,2. Cf. Ex 23,7; Dtn 25,1; 2 Sam
4,11; 2 Chr 6,23; Neh 9,33.

ten Testaments zeige[23]. Ich möchte im folgenden zeigen, daß diese Interpretation falsch ist.

Sie scheint allerdings durch den folgenden V.16aα bestätigt zu werden, doch es *scheint* nur so. Denn der in V.16aα erteilte Ratschlag lautet nicht: אַל־תְּהִי צַדִּיק, sondern: אַל־תְּהִי צַדִּיק הַרְבֵּה, »sei nicht *über die Maßen* gerecht!«. Offensichtlich gibt es unterschiedliche Grade des Gerechtseins. Zumindest gibt es ein Zuviel, welches schädlich ist, wie die rhetorische Frage in V.16b unterstellt. Damit beginnt der Prozeß der Korrektur des beim Leser vorausgesetzten Vorverständnisses: der von ihm zunächst mit dem Wort »gerecht« verbundene semantische Gehalt beginnt sich zu verwandeln.

Der Ratschlag aus V.16aα wird durch V.16aβ weitergeführt. In herkömmlicher Terminologie ausgedrückt liegt ein synonymer Parallelismus vor. Die Parallelisierung von Gerechtigkeit und Weisheit und dann weiter von Frevel und Torheit in V.17a gehört zum Repertoire alttestamentlicher weisheitlicher Texte und dürfte für den zeitgenössischen Leser nichts Überraschendes beinhalten[24]. Für unsere Fragestellung ist zu-

---

23. So F. CRÜSEMANN, *Die unveränderbare Welt. Überlegungen zur »Krisis der Weisheit« beim Prediger (Kohelet)*, in W. SCHOTTROFF & W. STEGEMANN (eds.), *Der Gott der kleinen Leute. Sozialgeschichtliche Auslegungen* (Bd. I Altes Testament), München-Gelnhausen, ²1979, p. 99: »Da landet das radikale Denken auf dem mittleren Weg. Man soll, erstaunlich genug, an Gerechtigkeit und Frevel gleich stark partizipieren und nichts übertreiben, um nicht in Gefahr zu geraten. Und diese Haltung wird auch noch als Gottesfurcht bezeichnet... Nirgends ist der Bruch mit der israelitischen Tradition so deutlich: nicht zu sehr ein *ṣaddîq* soll man sein.« C.D. GINSBURG, *Coheleth, commonly called the book of Ecclesiastes. Translated from the Original Hebrew with a Commentary, Historical and Critical*, 1861, ed. by H.M. ORLINSKY (The Library of Biblical Studies), New York, 1970, pp. 379f. G.A. BARTON, *A Critical and Exegetical Commentary on the Book of Ecclesiastes* (ICC, 21), Edinburgh, 1908 (Repr. 1959), p. 144. So im Grunde auch M. FOX, *Qohelet* (Anm. 12), pp. 235f, wenn er schreibt: »... the term *rašaʿ*, »wicked«,... always denotes truly immoral behavior.« Er unterstellt diese Bedeutung auch in Koh 7,15-18. Ibid., p. 234: »Qohelet teaches us to accept in ourselves a mixture of good and bad«. Ähnlich D. MICHEL, *Untersuchungen zur Eigenart des Buches Qohelet*. Mit einem Anhang von R. G. Lehmann, Bibliographie zu Qohelet (BZAW, 183), Berlin-New York, W. de Gruyter, 1989, p. 260: »Es kommt darauf an, die richtige Mischung aus beiden [scil. Frevel und Torheit] zu finden!« Ich versuche zu zeigen, daß der Autor diese Bedeutung beim Leser zunächst voraussetzt (V.15), sie dann abbaut (VV.16.17) und schließlich durch einen neuen Begriff (»Gottesfurcht«) ersetzt (V.18).

24. R. GORDIS, *Koheleth* (Anm. 11), p. 276. R. MURPHY, *Ecclesiastes* (Anm. 17) p. 70. Allerdings hat mich Frau Dr. Ruth Scoralick darauf hingewiesen, daß im Buch der Sprichwörter צדיק und חכם nur dreimal parallel gesetzt sind: Spr 9,9; 11,30; 23,24. Zur Diskussion der Stellen cf. R. SCORALICK, *Einzelspruch und Sammlung. Komposition im Buch der Sprichwörter Kapitel 10-15* (BZAW, 232), Berlin-New York, W. de Gruyter, 1995, pp. 68-73. »רשעים / צדיקים werden nur in wenigen Einzelfällen mit weisheitlichen Ausdrücken... kontrastiert. Eine gängige Austauschbarkeit untereinander kann man daraus nicht folgern, allerdings auch keine vollständige Trennung der Terminologien« (*ibid.*, p. 72). An dieser Stelle möchte ich auf einen Einwand von M. FOX gegen die Interpretation des Textes als Empfehlung des goldenen Mittelweges eingehen. M. FOX, *Qohelet*

nächst wichtig, daß das Wort יוֹתֵר in V.16aβ wiederum signalisiert, daß sich die Diskussion auf die Erörterung eines konträren Gegensatzes zubewegt: So wie es ein Zuviel an Gerechtigkeit gibt, so gibt es auch ein Zuviel an Weisheit.

V.17aα macht nun vollends deutlich, daß hier im Rahmen eines konträren Gegensatzpaares diskutiert wird. Wiederum steht parallel zu V.16aα das Wort הַרְבֵּה: »Sei nicht *über die Maßen* frevlerisch!« Auch hier gibt es offensichtlich ein Zuviel. Von V.15b her gesehen kommt diese Aussage überraschend. Die Beobachtung von V.15b »Es kommt vor, daß ein Frevler trotz[25] seines Frevels lange lebt« läßt beim Leser die Frage aufkommen, ob nun der Ratschlag erteilt wird: »Sei ein Frevler!« Genau dieser Ratschlag aber wird nicht erteilt. Damit wird nun eindeutig die zunächst als kontradiktorischer Gegensatz verstandene Gegenüberstellung von צדיק und רשע auf ein konträres Verständnis hin geöffnet: Offensichtlich gibt es zwischen Gerechtigkeit und Ungerechtigkeit etwas Drittes. Was mag das sein?

So wie V.16a Gerechtigkeit und Weisheit parallelisiert, so V.17a Frevel und Torheit. Nun treffen die soeben genannten Beobachtungen auf V.17aβ nicht zu. Hier wird nicht einschränkend, sondern absolut formuliert: »Sei kein Tor!« Vor dem Hintergrund meiner bisherigen Argumentation müßte ich diese Ausdrucksweise als verkürzende Redeweise (Ellipse) deuten. Das Metrum könnte dafür den Ausschlag gegeben haben. Nach A. Lauha sind V.16 und V.17 in metrischer Hinsicht chiastisch angeordnet. Nach W.A. Brindle erstreckt sich die chiastische

---

(Anm. 12) p. 233, wendet ein: »... the passage does not counsel the Peripatetic ideal of the Golden Mean (contrary to Delitzsch, Hertzberg, Gordis etc.). According to that principle, wisdom is not one of the extremes to be avoided, but is rather the mid-point between two extremes...«. Kohelets Weisheitsbegriff entspricht in der Tat nicht dem des Aristoteles. Das gleiche gilt auch für den Begriff »Gerechtigkeit«. Gerechtigkeit (δικαιοσύνη) ist bei Aristoteles eine Mitte (μεσότης) (*Eth. Nic.* 1129a-1138b, besonders 1133b-1134a), »die vollkommene Tugend« (ἀρετὴ τελεία) (*Eth. Nic.* 1129b), kein zu meidendes Extrem wie in Koh 7,16aβ. Vergleichbar ist nicht der semantische Gehalt verschiedener Begriffe, sondern – wenn überhaupt – die Argumentationsform. Sie muß in Koh 7,15-18 zunächst von ihren alttestamentlich-jüdischen Voraussetzungen her verstanden werden. Mir geht es nicht um den Vergleich verschiedener Begriffe, sondern um das Verständnis der in Koh 7,15-18 vorliegenden Argumentationsform.

25. Mit den meisten Autoren nehme ich בְּ‎-adversativum an. Cf. G. Ogden, *Qoheleth* (Readings. A New Biblical Commentary), Sheffield, Sheffield Academic Press, 1987, p. 113, mit Hinweis auf Num 14,11; Jes 9,11. Ebenso K. Galling, *Die Fünf Megilloth* (HAT, 1,18), Tübingen, J.C.B. Mohr (P. Siebeck), ²1969, pp. 73-125, spec. p. 107. A. Lauha, *Koheleth* (Anm. 11), pp. 132f. J. Vilchez, *Ecclesiastes* (Anm. 11), p. 316. Cf. Dtn 1,32. Neuerdings plädiert R. Lux, *Lebenskompromiß* (Anm. 12), p. 273 im Anschluß an H.W. Hertzberg, *Der Prediger* (KAT, XVII, 4), Gütersloh, Mohn, 1963, wieder für בְּ‎-instrumentalis oder בְּ‎-pretii.

Anordnung auf die gesamte Texteinheit, so daß sich folgende metrische Form ergibt[26]:

V.15:	2 + 2 + 3 + 3
V.16:	3 + 2 + 2
V.17:	2 + 2 + 3
V.18:	3 + 3 + 2 + 2

Das Phänomen könnte aber auch noch anders interpretiert werden, und zwar als metasprachliche Aussage. Und dieser Interpretation gebe ich hier den Vorzug. »Sei nicht töricht!« hieße dann im vorliegenden Kontext: Sei nicht jemand, der die hier zur Diskussion stehende Alternative im Sinne einer Ausschließlichkeit (tertium non datur), also eines kontradiktorischen Gegensatzes versteht! Es läge also bereits eine Reflexion auf der Metaebene vor[27]. Bei einem solchen Verständnis würden der weitere Argumentationsgang und der positiv formulierte Ratschlag von V.18 vorbereitet. Und dieser zielt nun genau auf eine Überwindung der Alternative.

Was ist gut? »Gut ist, wenn du an dem einen festhältst, aber auch von dem anderen deine Hand nicht wegnimmst (ruhen läßt).« זֶה ... זֶה kann sich im vorliegenden Kontext nur auf die bisher genannten zwei Möglichkeiten beziehen: Gerechtigkeit und Frevel[28]. Der Angesprochene soll also durchaus an der Gerechtigkeit festhalten. Allerdings – so kann aus der bisherigen Argumentation gefolgert werden – nicht in übermäßiger Weise. Und das Gleiche gilt vom Frevel: Auch vom Frevel sollst du deine Hand nicht fernhalten.

Damit aber hat sich unter der Hand die Bedeutung der Wörter צדיק und רשע gewandelt. Das Wort צדיק ist nun nicht mehr – wie in der traditionellen Weisheit – synonym mit »sittlich gut« und das Wort רשע nicht mehr – wie in der traditionellen Weisheit – synonym mit »sittlich schlecht«. Beide Wörter bezeichnen in Koh 7,15-18 ein Verhalten, über dessen sittliche Güte bzw. sittliche Schlechtigkeit erst noch zu diskutie-

---

26. W.A. BRINDLE, *Rightousness* (Anm. 17), p. 254.

27. Cf. Hos 14,10, wo weise sein und klug sein Eigenschaften bezeichnen, die sich auf das Verständnis des vorangehenden Textes beziehen.

28. Eine bisher – soweit ich sehe – in der Forschung nicht vertretene Abgrenzung nimmt A. FISCHER, *Skepsis oder Furcht Gottes? Studien zur Komposition und Theologie des Buches Kohelet* (BZAW, 247), Berlin-New York, W. de Gruyter, 1997, pp. 97-102, vor. Er trennt die VV. 15-17 als selbständige Sprucheinheit von V.18 als davon unabhängige in sich stehende Maxime ab. Die doppelte Deixis זה ... זה von V.18 bezieht sich nach A. FISCHER nicht auf die Mahnungen in den VV. 16-17. Kohelet – so A. FISCHER - zitiert in V.18a eine sprichwörtliche Weisheitsregel und kombiniert sie in V.18b mit der Furcht Gottes. Dies ergibt meines Erachtens keinen Sinn. Zu der hier vorausgesetzten Abgrenzung cf. R LUX, *Lebenskompromiß* (Anm. 12), p. 270.

ren ist. Es liegt also – um mit J. Habermas zu sprechen – ein explikativer Diskurs vor, das heißt eine Form der Argumentation, in der die Bedeutung von Ausdrücken nicht mehr naiv unterstellt oder abgestritten, sondern als kontroverser Anspruch zum Thema gemacht wird[29]. Wodurch wird ein mit diesen Wörtern bezeichnetes Verhalten inhaltlich bestimmt? Es bieten sich zwei Möglichkeiten an: zum einen durch Bezug auf das traditionale weisheitliche Lebenswissen, zum anderen durch Bezug auf die Tora. Die Alternative muß hier nicht entschieden werden. Möglicherweise konnten von den Lesern – je nach lebensweltlicher Einbindung – sowohl die eine als auch die andere Verstehensmöglichkeit herausgehört werden. Ich vermute allerdings, daß unser Text bereits in einen Diskussionszusammenhang gehört, in dem die Bedeutung des Wortes צַדִּיק in Richtung »toragemäß« und die Bedeutung des Wortes רָשָׁע in Richtung »torawidrig« tendiert[30]. Ich kann das hier nicht beweisen, möchte aber auf zwei zeitgleiche Texte verweisen, in denen das ähnlich zu sein scheint: Ps 1 und Mal 3,13-21.22.

Mit Ps 1, der programmatischen Eröffnung des Psalters, kommen wir zeitlich in die Nähe Kohelets. Den Frevlern, Sündern und Spöttern von Ps 1 werden keine klassischen Verbrechen zugeschrieben wie Bestechung, Raub, Mord, Verfolgung der Unschuldigen usw. (vgl. Spr 1,10-19). Ihr Verhalten weist vielmehr einen kommunikativ-reflexiven Zug auf: sie verkehren in einem Rat, sie stehen am Wege, sie sitzen in einem Kreis (V.1). Den Frevlern gegenübergestellt wird der Mann, der »seine Lust hat an der Tora JHWHs, seine Tora rezitiert bei Tag und bei Nacht«. Durch die vorauslaufende, in negativer Abgrenzung vom »Mann der Tora« erfolgende Charakterisierung bekommt der Begriff des Frevlers eine inhaltliche Akzentuierung in Richtung eines reflektierten Ver-

---

29. J. HABERMAS, *Theorie des Kommunikativen Handelns. Handlungsrationalität und gesellschaftliche Rationalisierung* (Bd. 1). *Zur Kritik der funktionalistischen Vernunft* (Bd. 2), Frankfurt am Main, Suhrkamp, 1981, [4]1987, Tb 1995, pp. 44-71. Die Deutung von K. GALLING, *Kohelet-Studien* (Anm. 11) p. 291, unterstellt – um in obiger Terminologie zu bleiben – ein solch naives Verständnis: »Die Termini צַדִּיק und רָשָׁע, die der »jüdischen« Vätersphäre angehören,… sind… ihres existentiellen Anspruchs beraubt.« Ähnlich A. LAUHA, *Koheleth* (Anm. 11), p. 133: »Die kühne Ironie Kohelets geht gefährlich weit. Er scheint sich gewissermaßen auf Kosten der Begriffe צדיק und רשע lustig zu machen; beide braucht man nicht so ernst zu nehmen, als würden sie sich gegenseitig ausschließen.«

30. Ähnlich F. DELITZSCH, *Hoheslied und Koheleth* (Anm. 11), p. 320: »Also muß רשע hier ein von der Strenge des Gesetzes sich entbindendes Handeln sein«. Die Einheitsübersetzung legt ebenfalls dieses Verständnis zugrunde: »Es kommt vor, daß ein gesetzestreuer Mensch trotz seiner Gesetzestreue elend endet, und es kommt vor, daß einer, der sich nicht um das Gesetz kümmert, trotz seines bösen Tuns ein langes Leben hat.« N. LOHFINK, *Kohelet* (Anm. 12), p. 54, schreibt dazu: »Die EÜ trägt schon ein wenig jene Grundstimmung ein, die sich dann bald in der pharisäischen Bewegung mit den Wörtern verbinden sollte.«

haltens mit Wahrheitsanspruch. Mit den hier einander gegenübergestellten Gruppen, dem Mann (Mensch) der Tora (Sg.) und den Frevlern (Pl.), scheinen sich zwei unterschiedliche Verhaltensweisen bezüglich der Tora mit unterschiedlichem Legitimationsanspruch gegenüberzustehen. Vielleicht kann man den Gedanken sogar noch etwas präzisieren. Das reflexive Moment scheint bei den Frevlern etwas stärker zu sein als beim »Mann der Tora«. Dieser rezitiert sie einfach und hat seine Lust an ihr. Die Frevler treten in Gruppen auf und scheinen sich über die ihnen vorgegebene Tradition der Torarezitation hinwegzusetzen. Das Neue scheint also nicht zu sein, daß hier zur Torarezitation aufgerufen, sondern daß diese vorgegebene Tradition in Frage gestellt wird. Angesichts dieser Infragestellung allerdings wird die Tradition eindringlich bekräftigt und ihre Beachtung als höchst lohnenswert dargestellt.

Mal 3,13-21 geht von einer ähnlichen Beobachtung aus wie Koh 7,15: Gott zu dienen und seine Anordnungen zu beachten, hat keinen Sinn, die Frevler haben Erfolg (VV. 14-15). Die JHWH-Fürchtigen diskutieren über diese Erfahrung (V.16a), und JHWH antwortet ihnen. Er stellt ihnen in Aussicht, daß an einem von ihm selbst herbeigeführten Tag der Unterschied zwischen dem Gerechten und dem Frevler wieder sichtbar wird (V.18). O.H. Steck datiert den Text in die Zeit zwischen 240-220 v.Chr[31]. Es folgt in V.22 der Aufruf, der Tora des Mose zu gedenken. O.H. Steck datiert Mal 3,22-24 etwas später, zwischen 220 und 201 oder zwischen 198 und 190 v.Chr[32]. Wir kommen mit beiden Texten zeitlich in die Nähe Kohelets. Die Ausgangsbeobachtung entspricht Koh 7,15b, die Lösung des Problems ist eine gänzlich andere: Es wird in Aussicht gestellt, daß die beobachtete Diskrepanz zwischen Tun und Ergehen an einem zukünftigen Tag aufgehoben wird. Ferner wird zur Beachtung der Tora aufgerufen[33].

Was im Horizont einer traditional-weisheitlichen oder einer toraorientierten Ethik mit צדיק bezeichnet wird, versucht das Buch Kohelet mit den zwei Begriffen טוב »gut« und ירא אלהים »Gott fürchten« zu fassen. Beide Begriffe begegnen in V.18. »Gut« (טוב) bezeichnet hier das, was zu tun ist angesichts der zu verwerfenden Extreme von V.16 und V.17. Ist die bisherige Interpretation richtig, dann ist hiermit ein Handeln ge-

---

31. O.H. STECK, *Der Abschluß der Prophetie im Alten Testament. Ein Versuch zur Vorgeschichte des Kanons* (BThSt), Neukirchen-Vluyn, Neukirchen, 1991, pp. 43-60. 197. Cf. auch E. BOSSHARD / R.G. KRATZ, *Maleachi im Zwölfprophetenbuch*, in *BN* 52 (1990) 27-46. Die »Überarbeitungsschicht Mal II« datieren sie »ins 3.Jh. v.Chr. (Ptolemäerzeit)«. *Ibid.*, p. 45.

32. *Ibid.*, p. 198.

33. Weitere Texte, die in diesem Zusammenhang besprochen werden müßten, wären Ps 119; Spr 28,4; Hab 1,4.

meint, das sowohl durch Nähe wie durch Distanz zur traditionellen Ethik, sei es dem alten weisheitlichen Lebenswissen, sei es der Tora, bestimmt ist. Ist letzteres der Fall, wie ich vermute, dann ginge es in Koh 7,15-18 um eine Diskussion bezüglich des rechten Verhältnisses zur Tora. Es ginge um eine *Hermeneutik der Tora*. Daß dieser Diskussionspunkt im Koheletbuch eine ganz zentrale Rolle spielt, hat vor kurzem Thomas Krüger gezeigt[34].

Der Mensch, der sich gut verhält, und zwar so, wie V.18a sagt, dürfte derjenige sein, der in V.18b als der Gottesfürchtige bezeichnet wird. Damit ist nun die entscheidende dritte Gestalt, für die V.15b zunächst keinen Platz zu haben schien, für die aber die Diskussion von V.16 und V.17 einen Platz bereitet hat, genannt: der Gottesfürchtige. Das »Gute« aus V.18a, das sich formal als Mitte zwischen den beiden zu verwerfenden Extremen von V.16 und V.17 erweist, wird somit in V.18b mit dem Begriff der *Gottesfurcht* inhaltlich bestimmt. Schwierigkeiten bereitet die Wortverbindung יֵצֵא אֶת־כֻּלָּם. Zwei Möglichkeiten stehen zur Diskussion: 1. Vorausgesetzt wird das übliche Verständnis von יצא »herausgehen, entkommen«. So H.W. Hertzberg, W. Zimmerli, A. Barucq[35]. Zu übersetzen wäre dann: »Wer Gott fürchtet, entgeht beidem.« Gemeint wären dann die negativen Folgen der beiden zuvor genannten Verhaltensweisen, vor denen V.16 und V.17 warnt: übermäßige Gerechtigkeit und übermäßiger Frevel. Der Gottesfürchtige würde also der Selbstzerstörung (V.16aβ) und dem frühzeitigen Tod (V.17aβ) entgehen. Ob dieses Verständnis sprachlich möglich ist, sei dahingestellt[36]. Ich sehe ein inhaltliches Problem. Die Interpretation »Wer Gott fürchtet, entgeht der Selbstzerstörung und dem frühzeitigen Tod« unterstellt Kohelet eine Ansicht, die uns als Tun-Ergehen-Zusammenhang vertraut ist[37], von der sich allerdings schwerlich behaupten läßt, daß Kohelet sie teile. Im Gegenteil. In 8,12b-14 setzt er sich kritisch mit dieser Ansicht im Zusammenhang mit der Gottes-

---

34. TH. KRÜGER, *Die Rezeption der Tora im Buch Kohelet*, in L. SCHWIENHORST-SCHÖNBERGER (ed.), *Das Buch Kohelet. Studien zur Struktur, Geschichte, Rezeption und Theologie* (BZAW, 254), Berlin-New York, W. de Gruyter, 1997, pp. 303-322.

35. H.W. HERTZBERG, *Der Prediger* (Anm. 25), p. 141. W. ZIMMERLI, *Das Buch des Predigers Salomo* (ATD, 16/1,2), Göttingen, Vandenhoeck & Ruprecht, 1962, ³1980, p. 205. So auch HAL II, 407. A. BARUCQ, *Ecclésiaste* (Verbum Salutis), Paris, Beauchesne, 1968, pp. 129-133.

36. C.-L. SEOW, *Ecclesiastes* (AB 18C), New York, Doubleday, 1997, p. 255, hält diese Übersetzung unter Hinweis auf Gen 44,4; Ex 9,29.33; Dtn 14,22; Jer 10,20 und P. JOÜON – T. MURAOKA, *A Grammar of Biblical Hebrew*, Rome, Biblical Institute, 1991, §125n, für grammatikalisch möglich.

37. So z.B. Spr 10,27: »JHWH-Furcht verlängert die Tage, doch die Jahre der Frevler sind verkürzt.« Cf. ähnlich Spr 19,23; Ps 112.

furcht auseinander. Folglich legt sich die zweite Möglichkeit näher. Sie wird vertreten von F. Delitzsch, R. Gordis, C.F. Whitley, N. Lohfink, R. Murphy. Sie übersetzen יצא mit Hinweis auf Sirach und Mischna mit »durchkommen, seine Pflicht erfüllen, sich recht verhalten«[38]. כֻּלָּם bezieht sich dann nicht auf die negativen Folgen der einander gegenübergestellten Verhaltensweisen, sondern auf die Verhaltensweisen *selbst*. Demnach würde die Gottesfurcht in bezug auf die beiden zu verwerfenden Extreme übermäßiger Gerechtigkeit und übermäßigen Frevels das rechte Verhalten sein. Über die dabei zu erwartenden Folgen sagt der Text zumindest in V.18 nichts.

Man kann ernsthaft fragen, ob der Text nicht zunächst beide Verstehensmöglichkeiten offenläßt. V.16a und V.17a sprechen eine Warnung aus, und V.16b und V.17b begründen sie in Form einer rhetorischen Frage mit dem Hinweis auf die negativen Folgen des Verhaltens, vor dem gewarnt wird. Es liegt eine teleologische Argumentationsfigur vor. Angesichts der zu meidenden Extreme sagt nun V.18a positiv, was zu tun sei. Die Empfehlung wird in V.18b mit dem Begriff der Gottesfurcht expliziert. In Parallele zu den Versen 16 und 17 (Warnung + Begründung mit Hinweis auf die Folgen) kann der Leser auch V.18 als Empfehlung + Begründung mit Hinweis auf die Folgen verstehen, zumal in der Diskussion eine für die alttestamentliche Weisheitslehre selbstverständliche eudaimonistische Ethik vorausgesetzt wird. Von einem durch Gottesfurcht bestimmten Verhalten könnte man dann erwarten, daß es den in V.16 und V.17 genannten negativen Folgen der zu meidenden Extreme entgeht. Der Leser könnte den Text so verstehen. Liest er dann weiter, wird sein erstes Verständnis spätestens in 8,12b-14 korrigiert[39]. Bei einem zweiten Lesen sieht dann alles wieder ganz anders aus. Ist die bisherige Interpretation richtig, dann erweist sich der Begriff der Gottesfurcht als der hermeneutische Schlüssel für Kohelets Torainterpretation.

---

38. F. DELITZSCH, *Koheleth* (Anm. 11), p. 321. R. GORDIS, *Koheleth* (Anm. 11), pp. 277f: »he who reverences God will do his duty by both!« (p. 178). C.F. WHITLEY, *Koheleth. His Language and Thought* (BZAW, 148), Berlin, W. de Gruyter, 1979, pp. 66f, verweist u.a. auf Sir 38,17. N. LOHFINK, *Kohelet* (Anm. 12), p. 55: »Wer Gott fürchtet, wird sich in jedem Fall richtig verhalten«. R. MURPHY, *Ecclesiastes* (Anm. 17), pp. 68f: »But the one who fears God will come through with respect to both«. Angegeben werden Sir 38,17; mBer 2,1; bBer 8b; 20b; bPes 86b.

39. 8,12b-14 muß allerdings nicht notwendigerweise das hier skizzierte erste Verständnis von 7,15-18 aufheben. Wahrscheinlich setzt sich Kohelet in 8,12b-14 mit einem Verständnis von Gottesfurcht auseinander, welches dieses einfachhin mit Torabeachtung identifiziert. D.h. das Koheletsche Verständnis von Gottesfurcht (3,14b; 5,6b; 7,18b) unterscheidet sich von dem seiner Gesprächspartner (»Gegner«), die in 8,12b.13 zitiert werden. Cf. dazu L. SCHWIENHORST-SCHÖNBERGER, *Glück* (Anm. 1), pp. 189f.

Gottesfurcht ist das regulative Prinzip eines richtigen Verhältnisses zur Tora, das zu einem sittlich guten und im Kontext eudämonistischer Ethik zu einem erfolgreichen Verhalten führt. Ich breche den Gedankengang an dieser Stelle zunächst ab und komme zu folgender weiterführenden These:

In Koh 7,15-18 findet eine innerjüdische Diskussion statt über den Geltungsanspruch der traditionellen Ethik bzw. den Geltungsanspruch der Tora. Diese Diskussion wird mit Hilfe einer Argumentationsstrategie geführt, die mir im Rahmen der zeitgenössischen Literatur aus der griechischen Philosophie bekannt ist. Im Hintergrund scheinen analoge gesellschaftliche Entwicklungen zu stehen, die einander vergleichbare Reflexionsprozesse ausgelöst haben. Ein kurzer Blick auf die Nikomachische Ethik des Aristoteles kann dies verdeutlichen.

III. ARISTOTELES: NIKOMACHISCHE ETHIK

Bezüglich der Nikomachischen Ethik des Aristoteles möchte ich im Rahmen dieses Vortrages nur auf zwei Punkte eingehen: (1) den gesellschaftlichen Ort der ethischen Reflexion und (2) den Ausgangspunkt der Tugendlehre.

(1) In der Nikomachischen Ethik unternimmt Aristoteles den Versuch, eine Theorie des guten und gelingenden Lebens zu entwerfen. Dies geschieht unter dem Einfluß der durch die sophistische Kritik entstandenen Legitimationskrise von Sitte und Herkommen.

Seine Reflexionen bewegen sich im Spannungsfeld eines vorphilosophischen Ethos von Sitte und Herkommen (ἔθος) und der durch Aufklärung und Kritik vorphilosophischen Lebenswissens entstandenen Philosophie der sophistischen Intellektuellen (διάνοια). Es geht um die Frage: »Muß man seinem Vater oder den Intellektuellen folgen?«[40] Wissenssoziologisch und entwicklungspsychologisch gesehen ist es der Ort der fortgeschrittenen sekundären Sozialisation, der Ort also, an dem das im Elternhaus angeeignete und durch die Schule gefestigte Wissen plötzlich fraglich wird, weil in der durch Arbeitsteilung differenzierten Gesellschaft mit ihren unterschiedlichen Lebenswelten alternative Lebensweisen in den Blick kommen und somit deutlich wird, daß das bisher erworbene Wissen nicht das einzig mögliche und folglich nicht wirklich zwingend ist:

---

40. ARISTOT. *soph. el.* 173a.

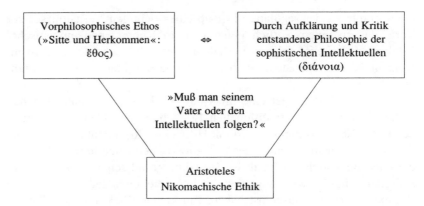

Die vorphilosophische Ethik der Griechen ist formal und inhaltlich vergleichbar mit der Ethik, wie sie uns im Alten Testament im Buch der Sprichwörter und Jesus Sirach überliefert ist. Sie ist »*formal gekennzeichnet* durch: 1. lockere Reihung der Vorschriften darüber, wie man sich im Kampf und Symposion, gegenüber Freund und Feind, Älteren und Jüngeren und dgl. zu verhalten habe.... 2. Begründung der Regeln durch Herkommen und allgemeiner Übereinstimmung und durch mahnende und warnende Beispiele aus der Geschichte, nicht aber durch Nachweis ihrer Richtigkeit. – 3. Vermischung sittlicher und gesellschaftlicher Gesichtspunkte.«[41]

(2) Bezüglich der Tugendlehre möchte ich darauf hinweisen, daß die von Aristoteles im 2. Buch der Nikomachischen Ethik mitgeteilte Beobachtung, von der die Bestimmung der Tugend ihren Ausgangspunkt nimmt, formal die gleiche ist, wie in Koh 7,15: der Mangel und das Übermaß. Beide Beobachtungen setzen eine eudämonistische Ethik (im Sinne Kants) voraus. Ziel des rechten Verhaltens ist ein langes und gesundes Leben. Das Gegenteil: ein frühzeitiges Zugrundegehen, so bei Aristoteles, so bei Kohelet. Aristoteles allerdings greift ein für die griechische Kultur typisches Paradigma auf: Heilkunst und Leibesübung, Kohelet hingegen artikuliert sich im jüdischen Paradigma der Toraausübung. Aristoteles schreibt:

41. O. GIGON, Art. *Ethik*, in *Lexikon der Alten Welt*, Augsburg, Weltbild Verlag, 1965, Nachdr. 1994, p. 880. Diese Form der Ethik ist uns vor allem überliefert im zweiten Teil von HESIODS *Werken und Tagen* 286ff, in Form von Merksprüchen und Mahnungen religiösen und moralischen Charakters. Hier werden hauptsächlich »Ratschläge für die praktische Lebensführung« erteilt, »ein Kodex von Verhaltensformen in kleinbäuerlicher Umgebung« entworfen. Cf. E. HEITSCH, *Hesiod*, in F. RICKEN (ed.), *Philosophen der Antike I*, Stuttgart u. a., Kohlhammer, 1996, pp. 17-37, spec. pp. 34f. Für die vorphilosophische Ethik der Griechen, deren Quellen uns nur spärlich überliefert sind, sind neben Hesiod vor allem Phokylides, Theognis, Demokrit, Antiphon und Isokrates zu nennen.

Zuerst kommt in Betracht, daß Dinge dieser Art ihrer Natur nach durch Mangel und Übermaß zugrunde gehen.... Übertriebene Körperübungen ebenso wie unzureichende führen den Verlust der Leibeskraft herbei. Desgleichen verdirbt ein Übermaß oder ein unzureichendes Maß von Speise und Trank die Gesundheit, während das rechte Maß (τὰ σύμμετρα) sie hervorbringt, stärkt und erhält. Ebenso ist es nun auch mit der Mäßigkeit, der Tapferkeit und den anderen Tugenden. Wer alles flieht und fürchtet und nichts erträgt, wird feig, dagegen wer gar nichts fürchtet und gegen alles angeht, tollkühn. Desgleichen wird, wer jede Lust genießt und sich keiner enthält, zügellos, wer aber jede Lust flieht, wie die sauertöpfischen Leute, verfällt in eine Art Stumpfsinn. Denn Mäßigkeit und Tapferkeit werden durch das Zuviel und Zuwenig aufgehoben, durch die rechte Mitte (μεσότης) erhalten. [42]

Nach Aristoteles gehören »das Übermaß und der Mangel dem Laster an, die Mitte aber der Tugend«[43]. Die Tugend als Mitte ist also nicht die auf Kompromiß bedachte Mittelmäßigkeit, wie oft im Zusammenhang mit Koh 7,15-18 behauptet wird. Aristoteles sagt im 2. Buch seiner Nikomachischen Ethik ausdrücklich, daß die Tugend als Mitte nicht »die Mitte nach dem arithmetischen Verhältnis ist« (1106a.b), also nicht das, was wir unter der auf Kompromiß bedachten Mittelmäßigkeit verstehen. »Ihrer Substanz und ihrem Wesensbegriff nach ist die Tugend Mitte; insofern sie aber das Beste ist und alles gut ausführt, ist sie Äußerstes und Ende«[44].

IV. KOH 7,15-18: REFLEXIVE ETHIK

Wie sind vor diesem Hintergrund die Verhältnisse in Koh 7,15-18 zu beurteilen? In V.15 wird das Konzept traditioneller Ethik, sei es das alte Ethos, sei es die der Tora, in Frage gestellt: Etwas Vorhandenes, etwas ungefragt in Geltung Stehendes, kurz: Tradition wird zum Gegenstand einer kritischen Reflexion gemacht. Deshalb spreche ich hier von einer reflexiven Ethik. Nebenbei bemerkt: Auch Aristoteles weist darauf hin, daß der Hörer seiner Nikomachischen Ethik ein gewisses Alter erreicht und eine durch eigene Lebenspraxis erworbene Vertrautheit mit dem bürgerlichen und tätigen Leben erlangt haben muß, um seinen Ausführungen mit Gewinn folgen zu können[45]. Vor einem ähnlichen Hinter-

---

42. ARISTOT., *Eth. Nic.* 1104a. Üb. nach E. ROLFES bzw. G. BIEN, Hamburg, Meiner, ⁴1985, mit kleiner Änderung.

43. ARISTOT., *Eth. Nic.* 1106b: »... τῆς μὲν κακίας ἡ ὑπερβολὴ καὶ ἡ ἔλλειψις, τῆς δ'ἀρετῆς ἡ μεσότης.

44. *Eth. Nic.* 1107a: »διὸ κατὰ μὲν τὴν οὐσίαν καὶ τὸν λόγον τὸν τὸ τί ἦν εἶναι λέγοντα μεσότης ἐστὶν ἡ ἀρετή, κατὰ δὲ τὸ ἄριστον καὶ τὸ εὖ ἀκρότης.

45. ARISTOT., *Eth. Nic.* 1095a. Cf. die Einleitung des Herausgebers der deutschen

grund scheint mir auch die sicherlich nicht zufällig gewählte Anrede
בָּחוּר »junger Mann« in Koh 11,9 zu verstehen zu sein, die sich von der
für das Buch der Sprichwörter signifikanten Anrede בְּנִי »mein Sohn«
unterscheidet. Die von der traditionellen Ethik behauptete Kohärenz von
Handlung und Handlungsfolge[46] wird durch die in V.15b mitgeteilte Beobachtung in Frage gestellt. Die Infragestellung geschieht im Rückgriff
auf die Empirie. In der Relativierung traditioneller Ethik durch Rekurs
auf die Empirie liegt eine methodologische Entsprechung zur Sophistik[47]. Erfahrungen der Inkohärenz von Handlung und Handlungsfolge
dürften auch im Rahmen traditioneller jüdischer Ethik nicht unbekannt
gewesen sein. Es ist meines Erachtens naiv zu behaupten, die der Erzie-
hung zugrundeliegende Vorstellung vom Tun-Ergehen-Zusammenhang
sei erst mit Ijob und Kohelet in die Krise geraten. Die Systemstörungen
waren bekannt, konnten aber in das System integriert werden[48]. Ja, man
kann sogar sagen, daß das System die Funktion hatte, solche Störungen
zu integrieren, im Hintergrund zu halten und dadurch kognitiv unschädlich zu machen. Die Sprache der weisheitlichen Tradition ist bei diesem
Thema weitgehend präskriptiv, nicht deskriptiv. In Koh 7,15 wird nun
der Hintergrund zum Vordergrund: Die Störung wird thematisiert, aber
nicht mehr in das überlieferte System integriert. Doch Kohelet bleibt
nicht bei der Thematisierung der Störung stehen. Er vertritt auch nicht –
wie oft behauptet wird – eine der traditionellen Ethik einfachhin wider-
sprechende Konzeption. Vor diesem Mißverständnis warnt eindeutig
V.17a. Ich hatte es bereits angedeutet: V.17 »sei nicht über die Maßen
frevlerisch und sei kein Tor! Warum willst du sterben vor deiner Zeit?«

Übersetzung der Nikomachischen Ethik im Meiner Verlag Günther Bien, *Vernunft und Ethos. Zum Ausgangsproblem der Aristotelischen Ethik*, pp. XXXVI; XLV.

46. Cf. Dtn 4,40; 5,16; Spr 3,1f; 4,10; 7,24-27; 10,2.27; 11,4-8.21; 12,12f.21; 14,32; 16,31; 21,21; Ps 1; 8,14; 34,22; 73,18; Jes 3,10f.

47. A. GRAESER, *Die Philosophie der Antike*, Bd. *2. Sophistik und Sokratik, Plato und Aristoteles* (Geschichte der Philosphie II, ed. W. RÖD), München, C.H. Beck, 1983, pp. 56-63, stellt die Sophisten Diagoras von Melos, Prodicus von Ceos und Critias unter dem Gesichtspunkt »Angriffe gegen die Religion« vor. Nach Sextus Empiricus, *Adversus Mathematicos* IX, 52, wurde Diagoras in dem Augenblick Atheist, »als einer seiner Antipoden einen Meineid leistete und ungestraft davonkam.« Ich verweise ferner auf die »*Dissoi Logoi*«, eine anonyme Schrift in dorischem Dialekt aus der Zeit um 400 v.Chr., in der im Stil einer Pro- und Contra-Diskussion u.a. Fragen bezüglich (I) Gut und Schlecht, (II) Schön und Schändlich, (III) Gerecht und Ungerecht, (IV) Wahr und Falsch abgehandelt werden. Cf. A. GRAESER, *ibid.*, pp. 63-69. Unter dem Gesichtspunkt »Kritik der konventionellen Moral« stellt A. GRAESER, *ibid*, pp. 69-80, die Sophisten Antiphon, Callicles und Thrasymachus vor.

48. Aus der Fülle der hier zu nennenden Texte verweise ich nur auf Jer 12,1; Hab 1,4.13; Ps 10; 73; Spr 3,11f; Weish 1-6,21. Aus dem griechischen Bereich sei hier nur verwiesen auf HESIOD, *Werke und Tage*, 264-274, wo sich folgende vier Schritte finden. (1) Tun-Ergehen-Zusammenhang, (2) Störung des Tun-Ergehen-Zusammenhangs, (3) Hoffnung auf Beseitigung der Störung, (4) Ermahnung, das Recht zu achten.

ist im Grunde nur als Antwort auf eine Schlußfolgerung zu verstehen, die man aus der Beobachtung von V.15b ziehen könnte, nämlich die, daß ein Leben jenseits des traditionellen Ethos bzw. ein Leben ohne Torabindung in jedem Fall gut gelingt. Eine solche Ansicht teilt Kohelet offensichtlich nicht. Weiterhin ist zu beachten, daß in V.15b keine universale Aussage bezüglich des Ergehens von Gerechten und Frevlern gemacht wird wie z.B. in den Klagen Ijobs und einigen Psalmen, sondern eine Einzelbeobachtung mitgeteilt wird. Also nicht: »Der Gerechte geht in seiner Gerechtigkeit früh zugrunde...«, sondern: *»Es kommt vor*, daß *ein* Gerechter *trotz* seiner Gerechtigkeit früh zugrunde geht...«. Die Einleitung einer Beobachtung mit Hilfe der Partikel יֵשׁ leitet im Buch der Sprichwörter oft die Mitteilung eines Paradoxons ein[49]. Ein solches Verständnis dürfte auch in Koh 7,15b mitschwingen: Etwas vom bisherigen Wissensbestand her Unerwartbares bzw. im Kontext des traditionellen Wissens kognitiv unschädlich Gemachtes wird offen ausgesprochen und nicht mehr in das traditionelle Paradigma integriert. Ferner ist die Argumentation nicht – wie A. Fischer behauptet – mit V.17 abgeschlossen. Vielmehr kommt Kohelet zu einer Integration seiner Beobachtung in ein neues Paradigma. Die Grundlegung, nicht die Ausführung dieses Paradigmas, findet sich in V.18. Es ist die Ethik des goldenen Mittelweges:

Koh 7,15-18

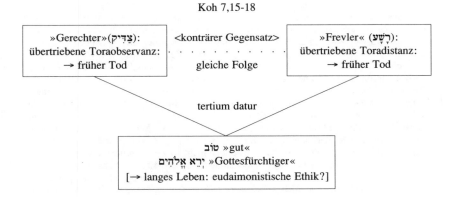

Wodurch mag dieser Prozeß des Plausibilitätsschwundes traditioneller Ethik angestoßen sein? Theoretisch könnte es sich um eine systemimmanente Entwicklung handeln. Herkömmlicherweise wird dies abgehandelt unter dem Stichwort »Krise der Weisheit«. Wer mit einem rein systemimmanenten Plausibilitätsschwund rechnet und Kohelet als Aus-

---

49. Spr 11,24; 13,7; 14,17; 16,25; 18,24; 20,15.

druck dieses Prozesses und als Reaktion darauf versteht, kann die Größe Hellenismus in diesem Zusammenhang außer Acht lassen. Doch Erkenntnisse der Wissenssoziologie machen die gegenteilige Annahme weitaus wahrscheinlicher[50]: Die Plausibilitätskrise traditionellen Wissens wird i.d.R. angestoßen und forciert von außen, durch die Begegnung mit alternativen Wissensbeständen. Dies gilt auch für die griechische Ethik: Der sophistische Relativismus ist völlig undenkbar ohne daß die Kenntnis nichtgriechischer Kulturen in die Köpfe einiger griechischer Intellektueller gelangt wäre. Die Ethnographie wurde herangezogen, um die Relativität moralischer Urteile zu beweisen[51].

Wenn ich nun die traditionelle Datierung des Buches Kohelet in die 2. Hälfte des 3. Jh.s voraussetze, und ich sehe gegenwärtig keinen Anlaß, davon Abstand zu nehmen, dann kommt zunächst die griechisch-hellenistische Kultur in Frage. Die für *unsere Fragestellung* relevante Begegnung jüdischer und griechischer Kultur darf man sich dabei nicht so vorstellen, wie man das im Rahmen einer sozialgeschichtlichen Fragestellung gerne tut, daß die eine Kultur von der anderen auf breiter Ebene, also auch im Bereich der sog. materiellen Kultur, durchdrungen sein müßte. Dies wäre möglicherweise schon ein weiter fortgeschrittener Prozeß. Wenn ich also die These vertrete, daß das Buch Kohelet nur angemessen verstanden werden kann, wenn man damit rechnet, daß das

---

50. N. LOHFINK, *Kohelet* (Anm. 12), p. 55, interpretiert den Text ebenfalls mit »wissenssoziologischen Kategorien«. Auch scheint sein Gesamtverständnis des Buches von der Wissenssoziologie angeregt zu sein. Ich halte diesen Ansatz für sehr fruchtbar und verdanke ihm viel. Kritisch zu N. LOHFINKS Interpretation äußert sich D. MICHEL, *Untersuchungen* (Anm. 23), pp. 260f. Zur Wissenssoziologie: P.L. BERGER / TH. LUCKMANN, *Die gesellschaftliche Konstruktion der Wirklichkeit. Eine Theorie der Wissenssoziologie* (engl. 1966), Frankfurt a.M., Fischer, 1987. – Nach Abschluß dieses Artikels stelle ich fest, daß offensichtlich C. R. HARRISON in seiner bei J.L. CRENSHAW angefertigten Dissertation *Qoheleth in Social-historical Perspective*, Diss. Duke University, Durham, NC, 1991, das Verhältnis von Kohelet und hellenistischer Kultur mit Hilfe der Wissens- und Religionssoziologie von P.L. BERGER zu fassen sucht. Aufgrund einer kursorischen Durchsicht der Arbeit vermute ich, daß unsere Positionen bezüglich der Verhältnisbestimmung von Kohelet und hellenistischer Kultur vielleicht doch nicht so weit auseinanderliegen. Ich teile sein Anliegen: »... this review has demonstrated the necessity of examining Qoheleth's similarity to philosophical systems rather than to isolated philosophical words, phrases, or concepts.« Ich habe mich ähnlich geäußert in: *Glück (Koh 2,24)* (Anm. 1), p. 246; und ich habe versucht, dieses Programm durchzuführen. Ein Hauptunterschied zwischen meiner und C.R. HARRISONS Position dürfte wohl im Gesamtverständnis des Buches liegen. Nach C.R. HARRISON vertritt Kohelet eine durch und durch pessimistische Position. So auch in seinem Aufsatz »*Qoheleth among the Sociologists*«, in *Biblical Interpretation* 5 (1997) 160-180. – Soweit eine vorläufige Stellungnahme. Zum Vergleich beider Positionen siehe R. BOHLEN, *Kohelet im Kontext hellenistischer Kultur*, in L. SCHWIENHORST-SCHÖNBERGER (ed.), *Das Buch Kohelet* (Anm. 34), pp. 262-268.

51. Cf. O. GIGON, *Ethik* (Anm. 42), p. 882. F. LASSERRE, Art. *Ethnographie*, in *Lexikon der Alten Welt*, Augsburg, Weltbild Verlag, 1965, Nachdr. 1994, pp. 886-890, spec. p. 888.

Wissen um die griechisch-hellenistische Kultur in das Bewußtsein eines jüdischen Gelehrten des 3. Jh. gelangte, dann heißt das keineswegs, daß die archäologisch nachweisbare materielle Kultur Palästinas bereits in dieser Zeit stark hellenistisch durchdrungen sei. Insofern widerlegen die archäologischen Untersuchungen von C.R. Harrison meine These nicht[52].

Unter Berücksichtigung der vorangehenden Textanalyse, wissenssoziologischen Überlegungen und auch im Rückgriff auf ein Gesamtverständnis des Buches, das ich an anderer Stelle dargelegt habe, möchte ich nun abschließend erläutern, wie ich das Buch Kohelet im Kontext jüdischer Tradition und in der Begegnung mit griechisch-hellenistischer Philosophie verstehe.

V. Kohelet und die griechisch-hellenistische Philosophie

Um sofort einem Mißverständnis entgegenzutreten: Kohelet überträgt nicht das jüdische Paradigma in das griechische. Das hat möglicherweise Philo von Alexandrien getan, zumindest wenn ich dem Urteil des Philospezialisten Jehoshua Amir folge. Das Buch Kohelet artikuliert sich in der jüdischen Tradition, aber es verhält sich zu beiden Lebenswelten reflexiv: zur jüdischen und griechischen, allerdings in unterschiedlicher Weise. Die Reflexivität zeigt sich literarisch darin, daß er das Selbstverständnis jüdischer und griechisch-hellenistischer Lebenswelt zur Sprache bringt, zitiert und kritisch kommentiert. Im kritischen Gespräch mit dem Selbstverständnis dieser Lebenswelten legt er einen eigenen Entwurf vor. Dieser wird aber nicht materialiter ausgefüllt, wie wir es vor allem von Sirach kennen, sondern nur im Ansatz entworfen. Wissenssoziologisch gesprochen gehörte Kohelet nicht zur Gruppe der Gelehrten, sondern der Intellektuellen. Ein Gelehrter war Jesus Sirach. Kohelet war ein Intellektueller, der sich aus einer gewissen Distanz zu dem in seiner Gesellschaft gültigen Wissensbestand reflexiv verhält. Diese Beobachtung wird auch durch die literarische Form des Buches unterstützt: Der Autor spricht nicht direkt zum Leser sondern mittels der von ihm eingeführten Figur des Kohelet. Vielleicht sollte die literarische Pseudonymität den Autor schützen[53]. Zeitgeschichtlich läßt sich das Buch am besten aus der frühen Phase jener innerjüdischen Auseinandersetzung verstehen, die uns vor allem aus den beiden Makkabäerbüchern bekannt ist: die Auseinandersetzung um den Geltungsanspruch der Tora und die

---

52. C.R. Harrison, *Qoheleth in Social-historical Perspective* (Anm. 50). Dazu R. Bohlen, *Kohelet* (Anm. 50), pp. 262-268.

53. Cf. M. Fox, *Frame Narrative and Composition in the Book of Qohelet*, in *HUCA* 48 (1977) 83-106.

Frage einer griechischen Interpretation der jüdischen Tradition. Soweit erkennbar, versteht Kohelet seinen Entwurf nicht als inhaltlichen Widerspruch zur jüdischen Tradition in ihrer Gesamtheit[54]. Er versucht, die Substanz jüdischer Tradition in einem alternativen Paradigma zur Sprache zu bringen. Hier spielt nun der Begriff der Gottesfurcht eine zentrale Rolle. Dieser Begriff – an wenigen, aber zentralen Stellen gesetzt – scheint mir aus der Sicht Kohelets die Essenz jüdischer Tradition im neuen Paradigma ins Wort zu fassen. So auch in unserem Text Koh 7,15-18. Der צַדִּיק und der רָשָׁע werden problematisiert, der יְרֵא אֱלֹהִים, der Gottesfürchtige, wird als der jene Alternativen überwindende Dritte etabliert, dessen Verhalten in jedem Fall gut (טוֹב) ist. Damit steht der Autor des Buches in kritischer Auseinandersetzung mit jener zeitgenössischen Tendenz, die die Gottesfurcht mit der Toraobservanz einfachhin identifizierte[55]. Kohelet scheint den Begriff der Gottesfurcht der Toraobservanz vorzuordnen. Ich kann diese These hier nicht argumentativ entfalten, möchte aber doch die Richtung andeuten, in die ich denke: Mit Gottesfurcht scheint jene Haltung gemeint zu sein, aus der heraus Tora überhaupt erst vernommen werden kann. Kohelet führt seinen Hörer/Leser gewissermaßen an den Sinai zurück, zu jenem Ort ursprünglichen Hörens, welches dem Opfern vorausging (Koh 4,17; Ex 19; 24). Der Begriff der Gottesfurcht wird bei Kohelet zu einem kritisch-regulativen Prinzip einer inhaltlich gefüllten Tora. Kohelet wirft Tradition nicht einfachhin über Bord, sondern er versucht, sie auf ihren Ur-sprung zurückzuführen und sie von dort her neu zu deuten. Damit korrespondiert eine gewisse Form von Gottunmittelbarkeit, die er vor allem in 3,10-15 entfaltet.

»Nach dem Verständnis der Antike will Philosophie lehren, worin das höchste Gut besteht und durch welches Verhalten wir es in unserem Leben verwirklichen können.« Mit diesem Satz leitet Friedo Ricken die von ihm herausgegebene zweibändige Darstellung antiker Philosophen ein[56]. In seiner Einführung erinnert er an den Praxisbezug antiker Philosophie. Ihrem Selbstverständnis nach will sie eine »Anweisung zum guten Leben« sein. In meinem Buch *»Nicht im Menschen gründet das Glück« (Koh 2,24). Kohelet im Spannungsfeld jüdischer Weisheit und hellenistischer Philosophie*, habe ich versucht zu zeigen, daß das Buch Kohelet von einer Leitfrage bestimmt ist, nämlich der Frage nach dem Inhalt und der Bedingung der Möglichkeit menschlichen Glücks (2,3→2,24; 3,12→3,22; 5,17-19; 8,15; 9,7-10; 11,7-8.9-12,7.8). Diese Frage wurde

---

54. Auch R. Lux, *Lebenskompromiß* (Anm. 12), pp. 272.275, kommt von einem anderen Ansatz her zu einem ähnlichen Ergebnis.
55. Cf. Sir 1,26f. L. SCHWIENHORST-SCHÖNBERGER, *Glück* (Anm. 1), pp. 320-324.
56. F. RICKEN , *Philosophen* (Anm. 41), p. 9.

in der jüdischen Tradition vor Kohelet *so* nicht gestellt. Natürlich kann die gesamte traditionelle Weisheit mit ihrer vorphilosophischen Güterlehre als Antwort auf diese Frage verstanden werden, aber die Art und Weise, *wie* sie im Koheletbuch gestellt und in kritischer Diskussion unterschiedlicher Lebenskonzepte beantwortet wird, zeugt von einem Grad an Reflexivität, welcher meines Erachtens nur angemessen als Sprung im Verhältnis zur Tradition zu bestimmen ist[57]. Meines Erachtens kam es zu diesem Sprung, weil die Plausibilität des traditionellen jüdischen Paradigmas durch die Begegnung mit griechisch-hellenistischer Kultur erschüttert worden ist. In der Begegnung mit der griechisch-hellenistischen Kultur dürfte jüdischen Gelehrten deutlich geworden sein: es geht auch anders, vielleicht sogar besser. Dabei konnte Kohelet die systemischen Widersprüche und Randunschärfen der eigenen Tradition zur Sprache bringen. Diese Widersprüche und Randunschärfen waren zwar immer bewußt, wurden aber im Hintergrund gehalten. Der Ansatz, Kohelet aus innerjüdischer Tradition zu verstehen, kann also bei dem hier entwickelten Verständnis integriert werden.

Nun war aber die Frage nach dem individuellen Glück auch die Kernfrage der hellenistischen Philosophien[58]. Diese wiederum sind nicht als völlig von der Gesellschaft abgetrennte akademische Schulbetriebe zu verstehen. Gerade in ihrer praktischen Ausrichtung gewannen sie Öffentlichkeitscharakter und in einigen Kreisen eine quasi-religiöse Dignität. Kurz: sie waren Bestandteil der Symbolwelt hellenistischer Kultur[59]. Im Rahmen seiner Leitfrage nach Inhalt und Bedingung der Möglichkeit menschlichen Glücks geht Kohelet im dritten Teil seines Buches (6,10-8,17) kritisch mit traditioneller jüdischer Ethik ins Gespräch. Im Rahmen der von mir vorausgesetzten Vierteilung des Buches[60], steht der dritte Teil

---

57. Ob dieser Sprung als *inhaltlicher* Bruch mit der Tradition zu verstehen ist, wie in der Koheletexegese häufig vertreten, ist eine andere Frage.

58. M. HOSSENFELDER, *Die Philosophie der Antike 3. Stoa, Epikureismus und Skepsis* (Geschichte der Philosophie III. ed. W. RÖD), München, C.H. Beck, 1985. M. FORSCHNER, *Über das Glück des Menschen. Aristoteles, Epikur, Stoa, Thomas von Aquin, Kant*, Darmstadt, Wiss. Buchgesellschaft, 1993. H. FLASHAR (ed.), *Die Philosophie der Antike: Die hellenistische Philosophie* (Bd. 4), Basel, Schwabe, 1994, (begründet von F. UEBERWEG, *Grundriss der Geschichte der Philosophie*, völlig neubearbeitete Ausgabe).

59. Diese These kann im Rahmen des Vortrages nicht weiter begründet werden, es müßte vor allem im Gespräch mit C.R. HARRISON (s.o. Anm. 50) geschehen. An dieser Stelle verweise ich nur auf P. STEINMETZ, *Philosophie*, in H.H. SCHMITT & E. VOGT (eds.), *Kleines Wörterbuch des Hellenismus*, Wiesbaden, Otto Harrassowitz, 1988, pp. 541-543.

60. F.J. BACKHAUS, *»... Denn Zeit und Zufall trifft sie alle...« Zu Komposition und Gottesbild im Buch Qohelet* (BBB, 83) Frankfurt a. M., 1993. L. SCHWIENHORST-SCHÖNBERGER, *Glück* (Anm. 1). Zur neueren Diskussion und Problemen der Abgrenzung ausführlich N. LOHFINK, *Das Koheletbuch: Strukturen und Struktur*, in L. SCHWIENHORST-SCHÖNBERGER (ed.), *Das Buch Kohelet* (Anm. 34), pp. 39-121.

im Dienst der Verteidigung (refutatio) seiner im ersten Teil (1,2.3-3,22) grundgelegten und im zweiten Teil (4,1-6,9) entfalteten These. Es geht um die Auseinandersetzung mit alternativen Glücksbestimmungen. Dabei geht er zweimal explizit auf den theologisch-ethischen Kernbestand der jüdischen Tradition ein: in 7,15-20 und 8,10-14. An beiden Stellen begegnet das Motiv der Gottesfurcht. Hier – und damit fasse ich meine These zusammen – findet eine kritische relecture der eigenen Tradition statt, die im Rahmen der Gesamtthematik des Buches zumindest *formal* angestoßen wurde durch griechisch-hellenistische Philosophie, insofern sie bereits zum Bestandteil des Alltagswissens hellenistischer Kultur geworden war.

An dieser Stelle kann dann auch noch einmal gefragt werden, ob Koh 7,15-18 *inhaltlich* von der in griechischer Literatur[61], insbesondere der Nikomachischen Ethik, anzutreffenden Idee der Mesotes angeregt wurde. R. Gordis weist darauf hin, daß diese Idee auf viele Juden im Mittelalter eine tiefe Faszination ausübte, insbesondere auf Maimonides, und er hält es für unbezweifelbar, daß Kohelet mit dieser, insbesondere in der aristotelischen Ethik vertretenen Idee vertraut war[62]. Gegen diese

---

61. Cf. HESIOD, *Werke und Tage* 693. THEOGNIS, 335: »Nichts betreibe zu sehr; halt immer die Mitte; nicht anders, Kyrnos, erreichst du das Ziel, schwer zu erlangenden Wert.« Üb. H. FRÄNKEL, *Dichtung und Philosophie des frühen Griechentums. Eine Geschichte der griechischen Epik, Lyrik und Prosa bis zur Mitte des fünften Jahrhunderts,* München, C.H. Beck, 1962, 4·1993, p. 477.

62. R. GORDIS, *Kohelet,* (Anm. 11) pp. 178, 275f. Es sei darauf hingewiesen, daß jüngst A. FISCHER, *Skepsis* (Anm. 28), pp. 208-210, in einem Exkurs auf die drei Lebensweisen in der Nikomachischen Ethik eingegangen ist und diese in Koh 1,12-2,26 unter der Leitfrage nach dem Glück wiederfindet: »Wir vermuten, daß hier die in hellenistischen Kreisen virulente Frage nach einem glücklichen Leben in Kohelets Erörterung eingeflossen ist« (*ibid.*, p. 209). »Ob Kohelet die drei βίοι als Topos gekannt oder sie im Spiegel der hellenistischen Zeit als typische Lebensweisen beobachtet hat, vermögen wir nicht zu sagen« (*ibid.*, p. 210, Anm. 122). – An dieser Stelle müßte dann auch eine sorgfältige Auseinandersetzung mit der Dissertation von M.R. STRANGE, *The Question of Moderation in Eccl 7:15-18* (Studies in Sacred Theology, Second Series, No. 199), Diss. Washington, D.C. 1969, The Catholic University of America (University Microfilms, Inc. Ann Arbor, Michigan, 69-19, 727) stattfinden, die mir leider erst nach Abschluß meines Artikels zukam. Der Autor geht von einer Bemerkung von P.W. SKEHAN, *CBQ* 12 (1950) 357, zu A. BEAS Kohelet-Kommentar aus: »Shekan wrote: »In common with most writers in modern times, Fr. Bea finds in Eccl the Greek concept of moderation (cited, v.g., in the exegesis of 7:15 as ne quid nimis); the reviewer is of the opinion that such a concept is foreign to the Book, and that reading it in sets up a handicap to full understanding of the author's thought.« *Ibid.*, p. IV. P.W. SHEKAN hatte sich 1938 auch im Sinne von »moderation« geäußert, aber später, 1968, im Gespräch mit dem Autor seine Ansicht geändert: »I would now say 'restraint' (instead of moderation) – which is different!« *Ibid.*, p. 124. M.R. STRANGE gesteht in einer Anmerkung (p. 124) ein, daß »in current English« die Tendenz bestehe, »moderation« und »restraint« gleichzusetzen. Er behauptet allerdings: »in the context of Greek moral philosophy, »moderation« is not the same as »restraint«. Das Ergebnis seiner Arbeit lautet (p. 127): »It is the concept of restraint which Bea and others have rightly seen in Eccl, while they mistakenly call it

These könnte man den Einwand erheben, daß sich das Motiv vom goldenen Mittelweg nicht nur in der griechischen Literatur findet. Es begegnet auch im Papyrus Insinger[63] und den Achikar-Sprüchen[64] und kann ebenso von dorther rezipiert worden sein. Dieser Einwand läßt sich generalisieren: Wissensbestände unterschiedlicher Kulturen waren in der 2. Hälfte des 3. Jh.s. in Jerusalem in gleicher Weise zugänglich. Es leuchtet nicht ein, der griechisch-hellenistischen Kultur in einem möglichen Rezeptionsvorgang Priorität einzuräumen[65].

Damit würde ich das Thema eines weiteren Vortrags angeben. Wir stoßen auf zentrale Fragen in der Verhältnisbestimmung von Literatur und Kultur in antiken Gesellschaften. Ohne nun dieses Thema angehen zu wollen, sei hier abschließend so viel gesagt: So wie man die Motive eines Buches letztlich nicht isoliert, sondern nur im Hinblick auf ihre Funktion im Gesamtkontext desselben angemessen verstehen kann, so muß man auch die gleichzeitig zur Verfügung stehenden Wissensbestände einer Gesellschaft, mögen sie auch unterschiedlicher Herkunft sein, im Hinblick auf ihre Verwendung bei jenen Theoretikern verstehen, die das Selbstverständnis einer Gesellschaft maßgeblich zur Sprache bringen. Und das waren in hellenistischer Zeit nicht nur, aber doch vor allem die Philosophen[66].

Katholische Theologische Fakultät   Ludger SCHWIENHORST-SCHÖNBERGER
Universität Passau
Michaeligasse 13
D-94032 Passau

moderation in the Greek sense. In the light of what has been said, all references to the Greek concept of moderation in connection with Eccl 7:15-18 are apt to be irrelevant and misleading. We began this study with the question: Is there a teaching on moderation in Eccl 7:15-18? Our search has led to a negative answer. The teaching contained in Eccl 7:15-18 is not moderation, but restraint. And it is Hebrew, not Greek.«

63. A. LAUHA, *Kohelet* (Anm. 11), p. 134.

64. R. GORDIS, *Koheleth* (Anm. 11), p. 277.

65. C. UEHLINGER, *Qohelet im Horizont mesopotamischer, levantinischer und ägyptischer Weisheitsliteratur der persischen und hellenistischen Zeit*, in L. SCHWIENHORST-SCHÖNBERGER (ed.), *Das Buch Kohelet* (Anm. 34), pp. 155-247, geht in diese Richtung.

66. Mit Frau DR. RUTH SCORALICK konnte ich die Thesen dieses Artikels diskutieren. Ihr danke ich für kritische Rückfragen und wertvolle Anregungen.

QOHELETH'S UNDERSTANDING OF
INTELLECTUAL INQUIRY

Consider two scholars of equal ability and accomplishment. The first externalizes her presuppositions, lays bare her particular concerns, discusses her methodological procedure, identifies her intended audience, and furnishes personal assessments of the data being explored. She consciously leaves nothing to chance, taking her readers by the hand and guiding them safely through difficult terrain. The second interpreter does not state the perspective from which he comes to the data, says nothing about his own personal interests, shuns any mention of theoretical issues guiding the analysis, seems oblivious to any specific audience, and maintains scholarly detachment from beginning to end. He trusts readers to enter into a dialogue with the text and to detect what the first scholar freely provided. Nevertheless, the second scholar reflected self-consciously about the things he left unstated and chose to challenge his audience intellectually rather than risk underestimating their ability to recognize perspective, personal agenda, method, reader, and authorial involvement.

Which of the two interpreters is more subjective, the one who leaves little to the imagination? Not necessarily, for the scholar who withholds data that he considers self-evident in order to involve readers more actively in an intellectual journey has made a conscious pedagogical decision. He has also acknowledged the intelligence of his audience. The first scholar, on the other hand, may have recognized that her readers lacked the experience and expertise necessary to sift through sophisticated arguments and to discern what does not lie on the surface. She, too, has chosen the pedagogy that she deems most appropriate to her subject and audience. In short, the mere articulation of ideological bias (e.g., form critic, feminist, social scientist, archaeologist, theologian) does not indicate a higher degree of ego-consciousness or subjectivism than silence about ideology does.

Qoheleth resembles the first of these two scholars, for in him an intrusive ego intervenes between the topic under exploration and the audience's perception of his discoveries[1]. He observes reality and reflects

---

1. Michael V. Fox, *Qohelet and His Contradictions* (JSOT SS, 71), Sheffield, 1989, p. 79-120. He writes that "Qohelet constantly interposes his consciousness between the reality observed and the reader" (p. 93). Fox's remarkable description of Qoheleth's epis-

introspectively on the experience. Indeed, he turns his own intellectual inquiry into the study of personal reflections. The impression he leaves approximates that of confession: then I saw, considered, knew, thought, pondered, said, and so forth. He was not the first, however, to interpose his subjective consciousness between experience and audience, nor was he the last. The unknown observer in Prov 7,6-27 who describes a fateful encounter between an adulteress and a young man opens the account with personal information concerning vantage point and then piles up verbs for observation: I looked out, saw, and perceived[2]. Similarly, the composer of the anecdote in Prov 24,30-34 consciously reflects on a personal journey of discovery: I passed by, saw, considered, looked, and learned[3]. The difference between these epistemologies and Qoheleth's may be measured in degrees; whether the latter thinker deserves the adjective "new" is doubtful. The same goes for "revolutionary." The later Ben Sira, the first Israelite sage to succumb to the temptation to claim authorship of a written text[4], allows his healthy ego[5] to manifest itself on several occasions. Similarly, the unknown author of Wisdom of Solomon considers the state of his soul and the details of his love life worthy information to convey to readers[6].

temology provides the understanding of intellectual inquiry that I shall be questioning in the remarks that follow. Although agreeing with him in many respects, I cannot concur in some essentials. At the same time, I consider his analysis of Qoheleth's epistemology indispensable reading.

2. The identification of the speaker as a woman who warns young men against a dangerous person of her own gender is hardly justified by appealing to the motif of a woman at the window or by conceding that women can criticize other women. The usual speaking voice in the book of Proverbs, the authorial persona, is masculine, an authoritative father, but he occasionally alludes to maternal instruction, one example of which appears in 31,1-9. Viewing the speaker of 7,6-27 as feminine has modern heuristic value, as Mieke HEIJERMAN demonstrates in *Who Would Blame Her? The 'Strange' Woman of Proverbs 7*, in Athalya BRENNER (ed.), *A Feminist Companion to Wisdom Literature*, Sheffield, 1995, pp. 100-109.

3. The verb עבר links the two accounts, 7,6-27 and 24,30-34 but in the former the young man in peril is the subject whereas the speaker passes by in the latter. The lesson derived from observation sometimes arises from what is missing from sight, as in Ps 37,25 (cf. R.N. WHYBRAY, *Proverbs*, Grand Rapids, 1994, p. 356).

4. My views about Ben Sira appear in *Sirach* (NIB), Nashville, 1997.

5. Peter HÖFFKEN, *Das Ego des Weisen*, in *TZ* 4 (1985) 121-135, focuses attention on sapiential self-consciousness, the extent to which the ego functioned as a criterion for assessing reality, particularly in Job and Qoheleth. Ben Sira refers to himself repeatedly (e.g., 24,30-34; 33,16-18; 34,9-12; 39,12, 32-35; 50,25-29; 51,13-30). Recognizing his place at the end of a long tradition, he lays claim to inspired utterance and to having labored on behalf of others.

6. Israelite sages did not rush to capitalize on erotic imagery for describing the intellectual quest, possibly because of the negative connotations of Wisdom's rival, Folly. Gradually, however, they embraced the idea of scholarly ardor. An acrostic poem in Sir 51,13-30 (vv. 13-20a of which appear on 11QPs^a) may represent such early daring, but the imagination threw off restraint in another poem from Qumran, 4Q184, which John

The extraordinary teaching attributed to Agur in Prov 30,1-14 throbs with personal introspection, all negative in character. He confesses his abyssmal ignorance, both about wisdom and about deity. Whatever the meaning of his initial observation, it seems to conclude with an acknowledgment of weakness, a perceived incapacity to measure up to the demands of existence. The language of this extraordinary wise man stands as a powerful warning against hasty assessments of vocabulary, for theistic sentiment (a twofold reference to El, allusion to the Holy One) is negated by powerful skepticism in vv. 1-4, which end on a mocking note familiar from the divine speech in Job 38,5[7].

Other factors also affect one's determination of a text's subjectivity, especially the author's selection of a particular mode of narration[8]. Omniscient narration may take place in first person or in third, and the author may opt to maintain distance by means of a persona, or even multiple personae[9]. Do these choices indicate different degrees of egocentricity? On the surface, it appears that first person dialogue signals heightened subjectivity, but a sentient self hovers over narration in the third person and makes its powerful presence felt at every step of the way. In a sense, such reticence increases the mystery and calls attention to the godlike presence behind the speaking voice. A persona, too, permits an author to remain in the shadows while focusing attention on an imaginary figure. Insofar as a persona replaces the actual author, the level of subjectivity recedes because it is once-removed.

Allegro entitled "The Wiles of the Wicked Woman." This text is informed by the description of the foreign/strange woman in the book of Proverbs, and erotic features, although exaggerated initially, are certainly discernible. Curiously, Qoheleth refused to spice up his teachings by emphasizing the sexual symbolism of intellectual pursuits, choosing rather to encourage actual sensual delights with one's lover (cf. Plato's erotic understanding of knowledge in *Symposium*).

7. CRENSHAW, *Clanging Symbols*, in *Urgent Advice and Probing Questions: Collected Writings on Old Testament Wisdom*, Macon, 1995, pp. 371-382 (originally published in D.A. KNIGHT & P.J. PARIS (eds.), *Justice and the Holy*, Philadelphia, 1989, pp. 51-64).

8. Current preoccupation with literary theory has rejuvenated biblical scholarship in many respects, despite hostile reception in some quarters. That hostility arises partly from a perception that the approach represents soft scholarship and partly from intrinsic notions that a historical method alone has legitimacy in the Academy. In some circles, the loss of a "single right answer" and the literary critic's substitution of "multiple possibilities" has eroded a perceived certainty in an era when all absolutes have come under attack.

9. FOX, *Qohelet and His Contradictions*, pp. 311-329, develops the notion of persona as a means of explaining the several voices in the book. In this view, an author projects a particular persona, perhaps fictional, and different voices address readers from various levels. Although a provocative interpretation, this approach overstresses the book's unity and downplays efforts to bring Qoheleth's teachings under the umbrella of traditional views about the central place of obedience to torah.

Both of these authorial decisions on Qoheleth's part further compli-
cate matters. On the one hand, he selected a narrative style in the first
person, giving the impression of total involvement in the learning process. The epilogues heighten the sense of immediacy by emphasizing the
achievements of the individual who speaks under the name Qoheleth[10].
Readers follow him through one experiment after another, watch him
agonize over injustice and life's utter futility, and sympathize with his
effort to salvage something from the daily treadmill-existence. On the
other hand, the author chose to speak through a fictional persona, King
Solomon. For some reason, Qoheleth abandoned this royal mode of address after the initial attempt in 1,12-2,26. Was this decision the result of
a desire for immediacy with his audience?

These ambiguities imply that, like most questions pertaining to
Qoheleth, his understanding of intellectual inquiry is multifaceted and
complex. In *The Gift of Asher Lev*, Chaim Potok has Picasso say to Lev:
"Truth has to be given in riddles. People can't take truth if it comes
charging at them like a bull. The bull is always killed, Lev. You have to
give the truth in a riddle, hide it so they go looking for it and find it
piece by piece; that way you can learn to live with it...."[11]. With this
warning in mind, we shall attempt to tease out some fundamental principles pertinent to a discussion of Qoheleth's epistemology, examine the
sapiential language for acquiring wisdom, and explore the sages' acknowledgment of limits imposed on the intellect.

I. ASKING PERTINENT QUESTIONS

A. *Prose, Poetry, and Philosophy.*

The scope of Qoheleth's own contribution to the book continues to
baffle the experts. An older way of dealing with this problem, the posit-
ing of voices in dialogue[12], has taken on a new wrinkle, the assumption
that Qoheleth's voice coincides with the prose components of the book,
which was subsequently challenged in various ways by additions in poetry. Whatever one thinks of the colometry lying behind Oswald

---

10. J.L. CRENSHAW, *Ecclesiastes*, Philadelphia, 1987, pp. 189-192.
11. I thank C. F. MELCHERT for calling my attention to this quotation (*Wise Teaching:
Biblical Wisdom and Educational Ministry*, Philadelphia, forthcoming).
12. In my survey of research on Qoheleth, four explanations for contradictions within
the book come to prominence: (1) redactional comments; (2) citations of traditional wisdom; (3) indications of life's ambiguities and time's passage; and (4) an endeavor to
embrace the entirety of experience (*Qoheleth in Current Research*, in *Urgent Advice and
Probing Questions*, pp. 520-529 [originally published in *HAR* 7 (1984) 41-56]).

Loretz's hypothesis[13], the effort to detect early forms of Jewish philosophy is surely salutary[14]. Critics have often commented on the extent of abstractions within the book, together with Qoheleth's striving to formulate a philosophy of existence.

Merely breaking away from traditional constraints of poetry does not constitute philosophy, although it may be an initial step in this direction. Clearly, Qoheleth's tenuous venture into allegory fails to grasp its vast potential for philosophizing[15]; for that advance one looks to Philo, whose fertile mind perceived the easy transition from sacred story to speculation about stages of intellectual and spiritual development. Likewise, the author of Wisdom of Solomon seized the idea of personified wisdom and formulated a philosophy of history that included an active governing principle, Wisdom, who participated in the divine essence. Both authors enjoyed the intellectual stimulation of an immediate environment steeped in Hellenism[16]; Qoheleth was further removed from the Greek cultural center, even if his expressions for human destiny approximate the Greek concept of fate[17]. Like Ben Sira, Qoheleth adopted traditional Jewish modes

---

13. O. LORETZ, *Poetry and Prose in the Book of Qoheleth (1:1-3:22; 7:23-8:1; 9:6-10; 12:8-14)*, in Johannes C. DE MOOR & Wilfred G. E. WATSON (eds.),*Verse in Ancient Near Eastern Prose*, Neukirchen/Vluyn, 1993, pp. 155-189; *Anfänge jüdischer Philosophie nach Qohelet 1, 1-11 und 3, 1-15*, in *UF* 23 (1991) 223-244; and *"Frau und griechisch-jüdische Philosophie im Buch Qohelet (Qoh 7, 23-8, 1 und 6, 6-10)*, in *UF* 23 (1991) 245-264. A. P. HAYMAN, *Qohelet and the Book of Creation*, in *JSOT* 50 (1991) 93-111, stresses the empirical methodology that attains philosophical character in subsequent reflection about creation in *Sefer Yeṣira*.

14. Robert GORDIS, *Koheleth – The Man and His World*, New York, 1968, pp. 88-94 remarks on Qoheleth's efforts to shape the Hebrew language in a form suitable for philosophical discourse. Gordis calls Qoheleth a linguistic pioneer (p. 88).

15. The debate over the appropriateness of labeling the imagery in Qoheleth's concluding description of old age and death (in Fox's view, a funeral) rages, with the extent of such symbolism dwindling more and more in recent commentaries. Daniel F. FREDERICKS thinks the imagery depicts a raging storm: *Life's Storms and Structural Unity in Qoheleth 11:1-12:8*, in *JSOT* 52 (1991), 95-114. On the scope of this poem, see Norbert LOHFINK, *Grenzen und Einbindung des Kohelet-Schlussgedichts*, in Peter MOMMER & Winfried THIEL (eds.), *Altes Testament Forschung und Wirkung*. Festschrift für Henning Graf Reventlow, Frankfurt am Main et. al., 1994, pp. 33-46.

16. Martin HENGEL, *Judaism and Hellenism*, Vols I-II, Philadelphia, 1974, remains the standard work on the relationship between the two cultures.

17. Peter MACHINIST, *Fate, miqreh, and Reason: Some Reflections on Qoheleth and Biblical Thought*, in Ziony ZEVIT, Seymour GITIN & Michael SOKOLOFF, *Solving Riddles and Untying Knots: Biblical, Epigraphic, and Semitic Studies in Honor of Jonas C. Greenfield*, Winona Lake, 1995, pp. 159-174. Machinist argues that Qoheleth moves toward a more explicit conceptualization and abstraction than earlier understandings of fate. He finds this tendency in three expressions for patterned time, חֶשְׁבּוֹן, מַעֲשֶׂה, and עוֹלָם, as well as in מִקְרֶה. He writes: "Put another way, what is significant in Qohelet is not simply the concern with the subject matter on which human reason focuses and the conclusions it yields, but an awareness of, a reflection on the reasoning process itself" (p. 173).

of presenting his teachings, although at times deeply touched by Hellenism[18].

This claim rests on a relatively late dating of the book of Ecclesiastes, now under attack from two directions. Daniel Fredericks' case rests on dubious grounds methodologically, for a demonstration that Qoheleth uses some early features of language does not offset the overwhelming evidence for late vocabulary and syntax[19]. Leong Seow's arguments, both linguistic and socio-economic, indicate the difficulty of establishing the date of any ancient text[20]. Tracing the detectable first appearance of a word or expression does not fix the time of its occurrence in another body of literature, even if one accepts Seow's view about the cessation of a given usage (e.g., שַׁלִּיט, which I question).

Equally unreliable is the attempt to postulate the exact socio-economic reality reflected in the book[21]. Apart from the problem presented by any literary work (i.e., does the author furnish accurate information about the actual context giving rise to the thoughts, or does one encounter an imaginary world?), how many eras of the past are distinctive enough to be recognizable millennia later? How do we know that Qoheleth's society alone experienced an excessive compulsion to "strike it rich," to climb the social ladder by whatever means, and to risk ruin in the process[22]? While Persian rulers may have presented an ideal situation for such preoccupations[23], so did the Ptolemaic ruling hierarchy[24].

18. Norbert LOHFINK, *Kohelet* (NEB), Stuttgart, 1980, has made a strong case for Greek influence on Qoheleth, even apart from his hypothesis that the structure of the book comprises a palindrome.

19. D. FREDERICKS, *Qoheleth's Language: Re-evaluating its Nature and Date* (ANETS, 3), Lewiston, 1988. An insightful assessment of this book has come from Antoon SCHOORS in *JBL* 108 (1989) 698-700 and *The Preacher Sought to Find Pleasing Words* (OLA, 41), Louvain, 1992, pp. 14-15.

20. C. L. SEOW, *Linguistic Evidence and the Dating of Qoheleth*, in *JBL* 115 (1996) 643-666.

21. SEOW, *The Socioeconomic Context of 'The Preacher's' Hermeneutic*, in *The Princeton Seminary Bulletin*, 1996, pp. 168-195, and *Ecclesiastes* (AB 18), New York, 1997.

22. Elias BICKERMANN, *Four Strange Books of the Bible*, New York, 1967, pp. 158-167, emphasizes Qoheleth's preoccupation with wealth; Frank CRÜSEMANN, *Die unveränderbare Welt. Überlegungen für 'Krisis der Weisheit' beim Prediger (Kohelet)*, in Willi SCHOTROFF & Wolfgang STEGEMANN (eds.) *Der Gott der kleinen Leute*, Munich, 1979, pp. 80-104 (ET, *The God of the Lowly*, Maryknoll, N.Y., 1984).

23. Seow's interpretation depends on the unique aspect of Persian rule, features that were not duplicated in the later Ptolemaic period. Such a claim is difficult, if not impossible, to substantiate.

24. C. Robert HARRISON, *Qoheleth in Social-historical Perspective*, Ph.D. Dissertation, Duke University, 1991, explores the Zenon papyri in placing Qoheleth within the period of the Ptolemies. Stephan DE JONG, *Qoheleth and the Ambitious Spirit of the Ptolemaic Period*, in *JSOT* 61 (1994) 85-96, concentrates on a psychological characteristic of the era.

Prophetic attacks on certain segments of eighth century Israel and Judah suggest that the drive to get rich, with its accompanying risks and privileges, did not originate with Persian hegemony, although the means of attaining wealth differed significantly.

B. *Embedded Tradition from Stoic Teachings*

A related issue concerns the nature of attitudes embedded within poetic sections of the book, specifically in the poem about times for everything in 3,2-8 and the reflection about cyclical events in 1,4-11. If Joe Blenkinsopp's reading of the facts can be sustained[25], namely that 3,1-8 is a citation from a Stoicizing Jewish sage or a Stoic composition translated into Hebrew, and that 3,9-22 constitutes idiosyncratic commentary, it follows that Qoheleth entered into dialogue with philosophical ideas about timely action (εὐκαιρία). In his view, no amount of studying the events that fill human experience enabled one to detect the right action for the occasion. Far too much randomness rendered the future uncertain. The circle of destiny trapped one and all, as the poem in 1,4-11 demonstrates so effectively.

The extent of polemic within Qoheleth's teachings, as well as the exact target of this attack, raise additional questions about the degree of subjectivism underlying his rhetoric. Such expressions as "crisis" and "bankruptcy of wisdom" served an important function as long as they were not generalized and absolutized[26]. Qoheleth's disillusionment with many traditional views does amount to a crisis arising from the sharp disparity between inherited beliefs and experienced reality, but his awareness of this gulf does not entirely invalidate the sapiential enterprise. He understands his own intellectual quest as a continuation of what earlier sages engaged in, and he insists that he is guided rationally. Regardless of whether or not his bold denial in 8,10-17 refers to another חָכָם or to his own deliberations, the final word rules out any claim to absolute truth.

One may justifiably speak of a personal crisis, a painful recognition that old answers no longer sufficed, but the experience enervated the

25. Joseph BLENKINSOPP, *Ecclesiastes 3.1-15: Another Interpretation*, in *JSOT* 66 (1995) 55-64. For a feminist reading of this text, see Athalya BRENNER, *M Text Authority in Biblical Love Lyrics: The Case of Qoheleth 3.1-9 and its Textual Relatives*, in A. BRENNER and Fokkelien VAN DIJK HEMMES, *On Gendering Texts: Female and Male Voices in the Hebrew Bible*, Leiden/New York/Köln, 1993, pp. 133-164.

26. Hartmut GESE, *Die Krisis der Weisheit bei Kohelet*, in *Les sagesses du Proche-Orient ancien: Colloque de Strasbourg, 1962*, Paris, 1963, pp. 139-151. Roland E. MURPHY, *The Tree of Life: An Exploration of Biblical Wisdom Literature*, 2nd edition, Grand Rapids, 1996, p. 212 and *Ecclesiastes*, Dallas, 1992, pp. 140-143, cautions against such language.

honest thinker rather than paralyzing him[27]. One could just as easily designate the personal event a creative moment leading to a revolutionary breakthrough[28], an acknowledgment that one cannot control human destiny through acts of virtue or piety. Living in accord with nature was not possible, regardless of what Stoics taught, nor could anyone conduct life in a manner that would guarantee longevity, health, wealth, and social esteem. Qoheleth resists a particular kind of wisdom in the same way the author of the book of Job undermines certainty[29], but neither author opposes wisdom as such.

C. *An Empirical Thinker?*

Much has been written about the empirical grounding of sapiential thinking, its thorough basis in experience. That claim applies to the book of Proverbs, with minor exceptions. Obviously, the speculation about Wisdom's role as witness during the creation of the world (Prov 8,22-36) did not arise from ordinary experience. Certain features of the book of Job also transcend empirical investigation, particularly the material in the Prologue and Epilogue, as well as the divine speeches from the whirlwind[30]. One could quibble about the latter point, insisting that encounter with the Holy belongs to human experience. In any event, few interpreters would deny the overwhelming experiential basis of Qoheleth's teaching. Michael Fox, who refuses to grant that wisdom literature is empirical, bestows that honor on Qoheleth alone[31].

That claim certainly applies to Qoheleth's method of study, but it obscures the extensive impact of non-experiential data on his thinking. Where, one asks, did he learn so much about the deity who, on

---

27. Rüdiger LUX, *Der 'Lebenskompromiss' – ein Wesenszug im Denken Kohelets? Zur Auslegung von Koh 7, 15-18*, in Jutta HAUSMANN & Hans-Jürgen ZOBEL (eds.), *Alttestamentlicher Glaube und Biblische Theologie*. FS H.D. Preuss, Stuttgart/Berlin/Köln, 1992, pp. 267-278, emphasizes the positive aspects of acknowledging conflicts between transmitted teachings and one's actual experiences.

28. Eric WEIL, *What Is a Breakthrough in History?*, in *Daedalus* (*Wisdom, Revelation, and Doubt: Perspectives on the First Millennium*), Spring, 1975, pp. 21-36, observes that the moments we consider breakthroughs are part of our own intellectual and political autobiography (p. 22), but breakthroughs imply breakdowns.

29. Carol A. NEWSOM, *The Book of Job* (NIB), Nashville, 1996, *passim*, throws dazzling light on the text's irony; from quite another perspective, so does Yair HOFFMAN, *A Blemished Perfection: The Book of Job in Context* (JSOT SS, 213), Sheffield, 1996.

30. Theophany occurs nowhere else in biblical wisdom; the presence of this genre in the book of Job is not easily explained (CRENSHAW, *When Form and Content Clash: The Theology of Job 38:1-40:5*, pp. 455-467 in ID., *Urgent Advice and Probing Questions* (originally published in R. J. CLIFFORD & J. J. COLLINS [eds.], *Creation in the Biblical Tradition*, [CBQ MS, 24], Washington D.C., 1992).

31. FOX, *Qohelet and His Contradictions*, pp. 85-100.

Qoheleth's own admission, remains hidden, thus concealing the essential character of divine activity? What empirical facts conveyed the following insights: that God has appointed a time for judgment, dislikes fools, will punish rash vows, created the world good/appropriate, dwells in heaven, creates the embryo within its mother's womb, chases the past, tests people in order to make them fear, gives human beings unpleasant business, keeps them preoccupied with joy[32], made men and women upright, has already approved one's actions, and rewards those who fear/worship the deity.

Such unsubstantiated assertions about God are not Qoheleth's only departure from an empirical base. How does he know what has been will recur, that people will not be remembered, that everything belongs within an ordered scheme, that the crooked cannot be straightened, that sadness makes the heart glad, that no righteous person exists? After all, he claims an active memory of all who preceded him on Jerusalem's throne. Did he, like Jeremiah, search high and low for a single righteous person? Has he not heard that in certain circumstances (educational, carpentry) the crooked can indeed be straightened, and vice versa, as Anii insisted to his son, Khonshotep?

The simple truth is that Qoheleth accepted an astonishing variety of transmitted teachings without submitting them to the test of experience. Occasionally, he uses emphatic language, e.g., "I know," when asserting something that none can confirm (3,14-15 and 8,12-13). One suspects that rhetoric aims at obscuring faulty logic in such moments. In light of overwhelming evidence of *a priori* knowledge in Qoheleth's teaching, it may be necessary to qualify the claim that a new era of empirical knowledge dawned when he appeared on the scene.

D. *Orality and Genre.*

Susan Niditch has brought the matter of orality into the forefront again[33], but without the assumptions accompanying previous discussion. In passing, she considers Qoheleth within the literacy end of a continuum, although her "trial runs" or "scenarios" necessarily belong to the realm of conjecture. My own independent study of Sirach emphasizes the primacy of orality in Ben Sira's pedagogy, his insistence that students attend to human discourse rather than written texts[34].

32. Norbert LOHFINK, *Qoheleth 5:17-19 – Revelation by Joy*, in *CBQ* 52 (1990) 625-635, thinks God uses joy as a medium of revelation. Otto KAISER, *Die Botschaft des Buches Kohelet*, in *ETL* 76 (1995) 48-70, also stresses the positive side of Qoheleth's message, as does Martin A. KLOPFENSTEIN, *Kohelet und die Freude am Dasein*, in *TZ* 47 (1991) 97-107.

33. Susan NIDITCH, *Oral World and Written Word*, Louisville, Ky., 1996.

34. CRENSHAW, *The Primacy of Listening in Ben Sira's Pedagogy*, in Michael L.

If one goes far enough back to the moment when individuals first perceived the insights presently embedded in the proverbial sayings within the biblical collections attributed to Solomon (Prov 10,1-22,16; 25-29), at least two things stand out. One, the discovery has nothing to do with literacy[35], and two, the mode of arriving at the new understanding is entirely empirical. At the later stage of transmission, Fox may be right that the saying reinforces ethos[36], but that admission does not rule out a prior discovery based on experience. Sages, like Qoheleth, may well have generalized on the basis of limited experience and they undoubtedly applied some insights to inappropriate categories. Nevertheless, they reached their conclusions by studying reality as they encountered it, and they tested these perceptions by observing patterns of behavior and repeatable events. In this respect, they functioned as pioneers in the search for knowledge; a later Qoheleth followed the same pathway.

Contemporary interpreters find it helpful to identify a text's genre, for this information provides a clue that assists in placing similar texts alongside one another and in this way to discover the unique features of each. Christian Klein's penetrating analysis of Ecclesiastes may say all that can rightfully be asserted, but calling a text *sui generis* amounts to an admission that every text is unique[37]. His useful observation that a מָשָׁל has parabolic and paradigmatic force helps readers appreciate

---

BARRÉ (ed.), *Wisdom, You Are My Sister. Studies in Honor of Roland E. Murphy, O. Carm., on the Occasion of His Eightieth Birthday* (CBQ MS, 29), Washington, D.C., 1997, pp. 172-187.

35. To understand the context within which such fresh insights first became one component among many in the process of transmission, one needs to learn more about the Israelite family. The recent publication edited by Leo G. PERDUE, *Families in Ancient Israel* (Louisville, 1997), contains valuable essays by Carol MEYERS (*The Family in Early Israel*), Joseph BLENKINSOPP (*The Family in First Temple Israel*), and John J. COLLINS (*Marriage, Divorce, and Family in Second Temple Judaism*), to which the editor adds a summary of their findings and theological reflections. The changes within society with respect to the family probably impacted heavily both on the content of sapiential instruction and on its form, but few traces of this adjustment have survived. The central role of parents in the small villages of the early period, the extraordinary demands on the whole family to survive in an agrarian economy of subsistence largely on grain, grapes, oil, and olives, and the importance of the clan began to slip during the monarchy, with its concerted effort to centralize power in the capital, its assertion of control over citizens' lives and possessions, and its usurpation of religious authority. The emerging disparity between the wealthy and the poor, with loss of land belonging to individual families and the exilic experience of being a resident alien, a feeling that continued in a sense during post-exilic times because of foreign rule, must surely have contributed to skeptical interpretations of reality. On the relevance of village life to the origin of the sayings in the book of Proverbs, see Claus WESTERMANN, *Roots of Wisdom: The Oldest Proverbs of Israel and Other Peoples*, Louisville, 1995.

36. FOX, *Qohelet and His Contradictions*, p. 91.

37. Christian KLEIN, *Kohelet und die Weisheit Israels: Eine formgeschichtliche Studie* (BWANT, 132), Stuttgart/Berlin/Köln, 1994.

Qoheleth's elusive appeal. Over the centuries, skeptics and orthodox, philosophers and neophytes, have been drawn to this book, and their fascination is rooted in its enigmatic quality, an open invitation to its use as a mirror.

Like genre, structure assists critics in their analysis of the book's message. Here, too, modern principles of investigation have proved ineffectual[38]. Some probabilities exist: poetic sections (1,4-11; 11,7-12,7) enclose the main body of teachings; a thematic statement precedes and follows these poems (1,2-3; 12,8); a pivotal section appears at the beginning of the main body (1,12-2,26; 3,1-22); certain refrains and repeated statements give an impression of unity despite frequent contradictions; and editorial additions provide orientation for readers (1,1; 12,8-14). Such indications of intentional arrangement do not offset the baffling effect of random sayings with no discernible relationship to the progress of Qoheleth's argument. Ingenuity has not been lacking in a modern attempt to crack the code, but it, too, has been *hebel*, futile.

II. THE ACQUISITION OF KNOWLEDGE

Although the sages never quite drew up a compendium of terms relating to learning, they did occasionally reflect on the pursuit of knowledge in ways that draw attention to specific verbs and nouns having to do with the intellectual process. In a few instances these teachers actually gather together several verbs that cover the entire scope of learning, and at other times they seem to discourage certain types of speculation. An examination of this vocabulary for intellectual achievement throws additional light on Qoheleth's epistemology[39].

Vocabulary for Teacher

Two expressions in Gen 12,6 and Judg 7,1 seem to reflect a period when Israel endeavored, through the assistance of trained technicians, to ascertain the divine plan for the future by means of divination. The teachers' terebinth

38. Otto KAISER, *Beiträge zur Kohelet-Forschung: Eine Nachlese*, in TR 60 (1995) 1-31 and 233-253. Two recent investigations of the book's structure are indicative: A. FISCHER, *Beobachtungen zur Komposition von Kohelet 1,3-3,15*, in ZAW 103 (1991) 72-86, and Stephan DE JONG, *A Book on Labour: The Structuring Principles and the Main Theme of the Book of Qohelet*, in JSOT 54 (1992) 107-116.

39. Nili SHUPAK, *Where Can Wisdom Be Found? The Sage's Language in the Bible and in Ancient Egyptian literature* (OBO, 130), Fribourg/Göttingen, 1993, approaches the topic from a different perspective than that employed here, but she reaches similar conclusions where our interests overlap. My fuller discussion is scheduled to appear in 1998 under the title *Education in Ancient Israel: Across the Deadening Silence:* (ABRL).

near Shechem (אֵלוֹן מוֹרֶה) and hill of instruction (גִּבְעַת הַמּוֹרֶה) respectively allude to the places of access to divine secrets. Belief in God as teacher occurs in several texts, but Job 35,11; Isa 28,26 and 30,20 stand out as particularly significant manifestations of this notion. Elihu describes Eloah as "one who gives songs during the night, who teaches us (מַלְפֵנוּ with missing א; the root is אלף and one expects מְאַלְפֵנוּ) more than the beasts of the earth and bestows more wisdom than the birds of the sky". The comparison appears to be between experiential observation, the basis of conclusions about reality in the sayings within the book of Proverbs, and revelation.

The two approaches to learning, the one horizontal, the other vertical, come together in Isa 28,23-29, for the farmer observes a certain rhythm in planting and sowing, but Isaiah insists that God also instructs him rightly, indeed that YHWH of hosts, the one who works wonders in counsel (הִפְלִיא עֵצָה) and excels in perspicacity, oversees this natural rhythm. The other text from the book of Isaiah, probably postexilic, concedes that YHWH will afflict Judah sorely, bestowing "bread of affliction and water of adversity," but promises that its teacher (מוֹרֶיךָ) will no longer hide, enabling eyes to behold the divine Instructor (מוֹרֶיךָ) and ears to discern a word from behind: "This is the way; walk in it," when the people veers either to the right or to the left. The divine enclosure of Judah, front and rear, is a noteworthy theological concept. In a text from the same general period, a personal name in I Chr 5,13, יוֹרַי, may be a short form of יוֹרִיָּה, with the probable meaning "whom YHWH teaches." Elihu sums up this theological conviction in the following words: "Look, El is sovereign in power; who is a teacher (מוֹרֶה) like him?" This religious conviction manifests its power in the Psalter (e.g., 94,12 with the Piel of יסר and למד, 119,108 with לַמְּדֵנִי) and in a hymnic text in Sirach (51,17, with מְלַמְּדַי cf. also 11Q Psa). This religious ideology shows signs of encountering skepticism over the effectiveness of divine instruction, given recalcitrant human nature. Accordingly, a text in Jer 32,33 places blame squarely on human shoulders. Even persistent effort on God's part, expressed by an infinitive absolute of למד, failed to overcome resistance.

Abstract qualities were also thought to possess the potential for instruction, not always for good. In Job 15,5 Eliphaz contends that Job's wickedness dictates his speech (יְאַלֵּף עֲוֹנְךָ פִּיךָ) with the result that his tongue chooses crafty retorts. Ben Sira notes that a person's mind (Greek ψυχή) informs him (יַגִּיד) more reliably than seven watchmen (37,14), a viewpoint at odds with the observation in Prov 28,26 that a fool relies on his own insights (לֵב) but the person who walks in wisdom will survive. Even the dead continue to function as teachers, according to Bildad, who in Job 8,8.10 urges Job to inquire about the reasoned conclusions they have bequeathed to society (חֵקֶר). This resorting to ancestral teaching is his way of compensating for life's ephemerality. Our remote ancestors teach us (ירה) across the centuries by reasoned utterances (מִלִּבָּם).

A list of living teachers within Israelite society would include virtually everyone, inasmuch as instruction is both positive and negative, intentional and unintentional. Sages, priests, parents, prophets, specialists of all kinds taught others both in word and in deed. Not always successfully, as a student confesses in Prov 5,13 ("I did not obey my teacher [מוֹרָי], did not incline my ear to my instructor [לִמְלַמְּדַי]"). Teachers did not necessarily escape a certain amount of pride in their ability to communicate effectively. Thus Elihu promises to teach Job rationality ("Be quiet, and I shall teach you wisdom" [הַחֲרֵשׁ אֲאַלֶּפְךָ], Job 33,33b).

From these texts one can discern the broad semantic range in Hebrew for teaching. The more frequently used verbs include Piel forms of למד אלף, and יסר, Hiphil forms of בין, שׂכל, and ירה, but various circumlocutions enrich this vocabulary (e.g., יוֹסִיף לֶקַח). A measure of reproof often characterized ancient instruction, graphically indicated in the Egyptian symbol for a teacher as a strong arm poised to strike with a cane. This predilection to punish uncooperative and dull students was given a theological basis in Prov 3,11-12 ("YHWH's discipline, [מוּסָר] my son, do not reject, nor loathe his teaching; for whom YHWH loves he instructs [יוֹכִיחַ] and afflicts [reading וִיכְאָב with LXX] the son in whom he delights"). This understanding of corrective discipline led to the use of the verb יכח in the sense of "to teach" and to circumlocutions such as "to receive תּוֹכָחוֹת."

Vocabulary for Students and their Activity

The considerably richer vocabulary designating students and their activity indicates the focus of countless aphorisms and Instructions. The familiar form of address, "my son" (Hebrew בְּנִי), occurs throughout the ancient Near East in Instructions; with a single exception, Egyptian Instructions limit this direct address of father to son to the Prologue, whereas Mesopotamian and Israelite texts intersperse it throughout the Instruction. Initially, this language actually indicated blood relationship, although it eventually came to signify a student, at least in Mesopotamia. Similarly, father (Hebrew אָב) at first referred to the head of a household, subsequently it may have taken on the extended meaning of "teacher." The word לִמּוּדִים

("those who are taught") connotes an acquired response that has become habitual – in animals as well as among human beings. One embarking on the task of acquiring such ingrained behavior bore the title תַּלְמִיד("pupil") in a late text, 1 Chr 25,8 ("Both small and large, teacher and pupil [מֵבִין עִם־תַּלְמִיד, assuming chiasm in the parallelism]).

The primary responsibility of students was to observe and listen, eye and ear uniting to convey knowledge to the mind for storage in the belly until released through the mouth. Such corporal imagery underlined the belief that the act of cognition involved more than the mental faculty, the heart (לֵב). Curiously, writing does not play a significant role in canonical wisdom literature. The verb כתב occurs only five times (Prov 3,3; 7,3; Job 13,26; 19,23; Qoh 12,10). The two occurrences in the book of Proverbs may echo Deuteronomic influence, the symbolic etching of divine teaching on the tablets of the heart (כָּתְבֵם עַל־לוּחַ לִבֶּךָ). The two occurrences in the book of Job mark emotional peaks in the struggle to maintain Job's integrity. In the first, he accuses God of writing bitter things about him, bringing to mind youthful indiscretions. The idea of God keeping a ledger is familiar from various texts in the Bible, as is the notion of YHWH writing on tablets of stone or on a wall. This idea, too, finds symbolic expression in Jer 31,33 ("...my teaching I will put within them, and I will write it on their hearts"). In the second text from the book of Job, the victim of God and friends expresses the wish that his words be written down, indeed inscribed in stone with an iron pen and lead as a perpetual testimony to his innocence, like the exploits of Darius recorded on the Behistun Rock.

The only use of כתב in Qoheleth occurs in the First Epilogue and presents a textual difficulty. The verb should be pointed as an infinitive absolute, וְכָתוֹב, in accord with Qoheleth's linguistic usage[40]. The words וְכָתוֹב יֹשֶׁר דִּבְרֵי אֱמֶת conclude an enumeration of activities that Qoheleth is said to have performed: "he wrote the most reliable words." This reluctance to use the verb כתב continues in Sirach, despite the obvious engagement of Ben Sira in literary activity (39,32). Nevertheless, he urges students to associate with learned people and to listen to their discourse. Nowhere does he tell them to read and write texts, but he assumes that they will become thoroughly familiar with traditional literature, possibly viewed as sacred by his time (cf. 48,10; 44,5). He does urge the keeping of careful records of income and expenses (42,7), and he refers to engraved gem stones and jewelry (45,11).

---

40. Despite the passive rendering in the Septuagint, strong textual evidence supports an active verb. One could object to an argument based on Qoheleth's linguistic practice, for the Epilogue derives from someone other than the author of the rest of the book.

The learning process began with observation. One looked carefully (שׂכל, חזה, ראה), exploring thoroughly (בקר, בקשׁ, דרשׁ, תור), assessing data by arranging them in an orderly way (תקן). Listening supplemented ocular discovery, (נתן לב, שׁמע, אזן). Reflecting on something and talking about it followed (שׂית לב and ספר). The actual discovery of an insight was expressed by verbs for finding and knowing, ידע, מצא; attaining a full grasp of an idea, by בין, מוסר לקח, קנה, and כון. Once an individual had acquired knowledge, he was obligated to hold on to it (חזק), guard it (נצר, שׁמר), love it (אהב), not abandon it (עזב), or neglect it (פרע), or despise it (שׂנא, בזה), or let it drop (רפה). The end product of this quest for learning went by many names, but one word, חָכְמָה, served as a supernym for all the rest (כִּשְׂרוֹן, עָרוּם, נָבוֹן, תּוֹכַחַת, תְּשִׁיָּה, עָרְמָה, תְּבוּנָה, בִּינָה, תּוֹרָה, מוּסָר, דַּעַת,). For Qoheleth that word חָכְמָה combined with the preposition ב designated rational inquiry, and חֶשְׁבּוֹן stood for the process of thinking and its result[41]. The person who possessed such knowledge was חָכָם, a sage.

The verbs for investigating the nature of things sometimes appear in clusters, probably in additive fashion, although the exact relationship in poetic parallelism cannot easily be determined. In Eccles 7,25, a context explosive with reflection about the nature of rational calculation, one finds the following sequence: תור, בקשׁ, ידע, and מצא, together with the result of this inquiry into things – חָכְמָה and חֶשְׁבּוֹן as the general conclusion, with specific manifestations involving the evil nature of folly and madness, and a certain type of woman, a femme fatale. Qoheleth refers to the process of drawing conclusions and associating them with one another to reach a total assessment of things ("one to one to find the sum [חֶשְׁבּוֹן], 7,27b), regrettably acknowledging that, despite all his effort, he has not found it (7,28a). He admits to having discovered one man among a thousand but not a woman, and also that God made humans morally upright but they have sought out numerous contrivances[42]. Perhaps this suggests that they have replaced the single absolute, the חֶשְׁבּוֹן, with multiple alternatives, חִשְׁבֹנוֹת.

Qoheleth's use of the infinitive לָתוּר with abstract qualities, wisdom and the sum of things, represents a shift from its usual application to tan-

---

41. P. MACHINIST, *art. cit.* (n. 17).

42. By understanding v. 26 as a quotation with which Qoheleth takes issue, several recent interpreters have endeavored to rid him of the charge of misogyny: Norbert LOHFINK, *War Kohelet ein Frauenfeind?*, in M. GILBERT (ed.), *La Sagesse de l'Ancien Testament* (BETL, 51), Gembloux 1979, pp. 259-287; A. SCHOORS, *Bitterder dan de dood is de vrouw (Koh 7, 26)*, in *Bijdragen* 54 (1993) 121-140; F.J. BACKHAUS, *"Denn Zeit und Zufall trifft sie alle": Studien zur Komposition und Gottesbild im Buch Qohelet* (BBB 83), Frankfurt, 1993. See also Thomas KRÜGER, *'Frau Weisheit' in Koh 7, 26?*, in *Bib* 73 (1992) 394-403, who introduces the notion of personified Wisdom here.

gible qualities like the land that spies explored. His modest findings are introduced by a concession in 7,23b that wisdom always retained its essence, which was so profound as to remain permanently hidden ("Far off...and deep, deep, who can find it?," 7,24). This admission that none can unravel life's mystery recurs in 8,1, often taken as a later gloss[43]. It reads: "Who is like the sage, and who knows the interpretation (פֵּשֶׁר) of a thing?" Usage demands that the rhetorical question be taken as a denial: "nobody knows the meaning of a matter (דָּבָר)"[44].

The epilogist who evaluated Qoheleth's contribution to society (הָעָם) as sage and teacher used a total of six verbs to characterize his intellectual approach (12,9-10). Qoheleth listened (וְאָזֵן), probed deeply (וְחִקֵּר), and arranged (תִּקֵּן) numerous sayings; he sought (בִּקֵּשׁ) to discover (לִמְצֹא) pleasing expressions, and he wrote (וְכָתוֹב) reliable things. The verb, "he listened," implies that people constituted the "texts" that he studied. The absence of a verb for reading at this late date, probably mid-third century, is noteworthy, although its effect is weakened by the further reference to writing. Presumably, Qoheleth expected someone to read his observations and to appreciate their form and substance.

An unusual verse in Sirach also juxtaposes six verbs to indicate the goal of students (6,27). Ben Sira urges them to seek (דרש), probe deeply (חקר), hunt for (בקש), discover (מצא), and having found the answer, to grasp it firmly (חזק) and not to let it fall (רפה). The second half of the verse echoes Prov 4,13, "Hold on to instruction; do not let it fall" (הַחֲזֵק בַּמּוּסָר אַל־תֶּרֶף).

The thoroughness implied in the verb חקר made it particularly appropriate as a description for divine exploration of human thoughts. In Ps 139,1-3 the Psalmist confesses that as a result of YHWH's penetrating search nothing lies hidden in a dark corner of the mind: "YHWH, you have searched me (חֲקַרְתַּנִי) and known me (וַתֵּדַע); you know my sitting and rising, you comprehend (בַּנְתָּה) my musings from afar; you measure (זֵרִיתָ) my path and couch; you are familiar with (הִסְכַּנְתָּה) all my ways." The same knowledge extends to speech prior to its utterance (v. 4). The psalmist's invitation to further divine scrutiny may resemble Cleanthes' famous prayer, "Teach me to do your will, O Zeus, for whether I want to do so or not I will do it," but the excitement over YHWH's extraordinary knowledge seems boundless. "Search me (חָקְרֵנִי), God, and know

---

43. The unusual word for interpretation, פֵּשֶׁר, may be an audial pun on the previous יָשָׁר. It would then indicate the meaning of searching for the sum of things, hence the verse would not be intrusive.

44. The rhetorical question, "Who knows?", implies that no one does, on which see my article entitled *The Expression* מִי יוֹדֵעַ *in the Hebrew Bible*, in *Urgent Advice and Probing Questions*, pp. 548-572 (originally published in *VT* 36 [1986] 274-288).

my mind (וְדַע לְבָבִי), test me (בְּחָנֵנִי) and ascertain (וְדַע) my anxious thoughts. See (וּרְאֵה) if any harmful way exists within me" (Ps 139,23-24).

An angry Job resented God's relentless searching for his sins despite the prior knowledge of his innocence ("that you seek [תְּבַקֵּשׁ] my sins and search for [תִדְרוֹשׁ] my transgressions," Job 10,6). Such inquiry on God's part placed the deity on the dubious level of humans, who by nature are of short duration. For modern readers there is something shocking about depicting God as having to search diligently to discover Job's wrongdoing, but the biblical YHWH cared about good and evil, and lacking omniscience, searched the human heart. This qualification explains why verbs for seeking were usually restricted to human subjects. Prov 18,15 is no real exception, for the human ear, the subject of the verb תְּבַקֵּשׁ, functions as *pars pro toto*. Seeking belongs to the essence of humankind, according to Eccles 3,6 (עֵת לְבַקֵּשׁ), along with its opposite, losing (וְעֵת לְאַבֵּד), possibly through a lapse of memory, or perhaps as a consequence of negligence and inattention. In one notoriously difficult text, Qoheleth characterizes God's activity as chasing the past (יְבַקֵּשׁ אֶת־נִרְדָּף), as if God attends to events that are present to human beings but were previously present reality to the deity (cf. Sir 5,3).

III. LIMITS TO KNOWLEDGE

In contrast to God's full knowledge as celebrated by the author of Ps 139, human discovery invariably came up against a teacher's tight fist, the restriction of knowledge. Qoheleth makes this point in opposition to anyone who insists that he has actually found knowledge, apparently of divine activity (8,17). The diligent toiling and seeking notwithstanding, one result follows – even a sage will be unable to discover that rare thing called knowledge. In 3,11 Qoheleth makes a similar point, at the same time granting that the deity created things beautiful and implanted something positive in the human mind. This unknown quality (הָעֹלָם in the MT, but it probably should be pointed הָעֶלֶם)[45] bestows a sense of the unknown and unknowable on all intellectual inquiry. Here, as well as in his notion of time, death, and rational inquiry, Qoheleth gives voice to his belief that all human endeavor comes up against absolute limits that affect the very nature of thought itself.

45. I examine this difficult verse at length in *The Eternal Gospel (Ecclesiastes 3:11)*, in *Urgent Advice and Probing Questions*, pp. 548-572 (originally published in J. L. CRENSHAW & J.T. WILLIS (eds.), *Essays in Old Testament Ethics*, New York, 1974, pp. 23-55).

When negated, the Niph'al form of the root חקר regularly connotes the unfathomable and immeasurable. Matitiahu Tsevat reads only one positive use in twelve Niph'al forms of חקר[46]. Seven have a negative particle, either אֵין or לֹא (Job 5,9; 9,10; 34,24; 36,26; Ps 145,3; Prov 25,3; Isa 40,28), two are objects of rhetorical questions and therefore negated (Job 11,7; 38,16), one appears in a corrupt text (Prov 25,27), and one is uncertain. The sole positive assertion occurs in Job 8,8 ("...and consider what their ancestors discovered"), unless Prov 25,27 also belongs to this usage ("nor the discovery of their honor, honorable"). The unfathomable usually refers to God's ways and deeds, although it can apply to extraordinary human beings such as kings (Prov 25,3, "the minds of kings are unsearchable").

The unfathomable nature of חָכְמָה comes to expression in the remarkable poem comprising the twenty-eighth chapter in the book of Job. Against the backdrop celebrating the extraordinary accomplishments of human beings in exploring the bowels of the earth in search of precious stones, the author remarks that even such ingenious effort cannot make a dent in the barrier separating humans from wisdom. The most anyone can do, even mythical Sheol and Abaddon, is eavesdrop on a rumor. Here these two locations for the realm of the dead are personified. Job will later discover how terribly unsatisfactory secondhand knowledge really is – when he comes face to face with the one who rebukes him from a whirlwind, prompting him to say: "By the hearing of an ear I heard about you, but now my eye sees you...." With regard to God's knowledge of Wisdom, the poet says: "God sees her way and knows her place, for he looks to the ends of the earth and sees under all the heavens" (28,23). The sovereign of wind and ocean, rain and lightning, saw wisdom, discussed it, established it, and probed it deeply (28,27).

This verse covers four distinct stages in the intellectual process. The first, observation, engages the eyes as they examine an observable phenomenon. It connotes immediate knowledge, firsthand experience, thus intimate knowledge. The second, discussion, involves the organ of speech as the agency through which an individual endeavors to articulate whatever conclusion he has reached in a way that communicates with others. This discussion also entails hearing with discernment. In this way private insights become public commodity, and the collective knowledge of a given community makes its contribution to private knowledge. The third stage, establishing hypotheses and reaching provisional conclusions, functions within the mind, for the discoverer ultimately bears

---

46. מֶחְקָר, חֵקֶר, חָקַר, in G.J. BOTTERWECK & H. RINGGREN (eds.), *Theological Dictionary of the Old Testament*, Vol. 5, Grand Rapids, 1986, p. 150.

sole responsibility for any new insight. The final stage, analytic assessment by exploring every facet of an idea, returns to the earlier image of probing the recesses of earth in search of precious gems, then examining them for possible flaws. The four verbs – ראה, ספר, כון, and חקר — nicely describe the cognitive analytic process as the poet understood it.

Ben Sira proceeds even farther than the author of Job 28 toward limiting intellectual inquiry. Whereas the poet responsible for the above description of indefatigable energy in the pursuit of the unknown grudgingly conceded that this effort ultimately aborted when wisdom was its object, Ben Sira considers some kinds of curiosity not only futile but also inappropriate. He writes:

> 3¹⁷My son, when prosperous comport yourself humbly and you will be appreciated more than those who are generous with gifts. ¹⁸Defer before the great ones of society and you will discover favor with God, ¹⁹for God's compassion is vast, and he reveals his secret thoughts to the lowly. ²¹Seek not unfathomable wonders, nor probe into things concealed from you. ²²Attend to what is entrusted to you; hidden things are not your business. ²³Do not talk about what exceeds your grasp, for more than you (understand) has been shown to you. ²⁴Indeed, human speculations are numerous, and evil conjectures lead one astray.⁴⁷

One naturally thinks of Am 3,7, "Surely the Lord YHWH does not do anything without revealing his secret counsel to his servants the prophets," but Ben Sira extends this divine generosity to the humble. Having said that, he stresses the sufficiency of such revelation. Not willing to let readers draw their own conclusions on the basis of this principle of disclosure, he presses the point that some sorts of rational inquiry have perverse consequences, echoing a similar viewpoint in Deut 29,29 [MT 28], "The secret things belong to YHWH our God, but the revealed things belong to us and to our posterity...." This attack on the very essence of rational inquiry, the desire to penetrate the unknown and make it comprehensible, does not automatically follow from humble acknowledgment that the intellect can never explain the mystery of life. The necessities of polemic have forced Ben Sira into an untenable position: some things are not subject to cognitive analysis. Regardless of whether this restriction of knowledge refers to Greek astrological and cosmological speculations or to Jewish variations of such efforts to control one's fate, it clearly expresses the view that certain types of intellectual endeavors bode ill for those with a curious mind.

By reading תאמר for the meaningless תמר in v. 23, one brings this discussion into line with a significant thrust in Ben Sira's apologetic. The

---

47. Author's translation.

formula of debate, introduced by אַל תֹּאמַר, normally appears in contexts dealing with theodicy[48]. He may reject certain kinds of speculation about divine justice within society, and in doing so he insists that Israel's wonder-worker, alluded to in v. 21, has conveyed sufficient information to enable those buffeted by life's waves to trust confidently in divine goodness.

Conclusion

With respect to subjectivity, or the amount of involvement of the ego in the learning process, Qoheleth differs from other biblical sages only in degree, and this difference may reflect varying pedagogical strategies. As for the empirical base of his insights, Qoheleth resembles earlier sages at the time of initial discovery. His attempt to forge philosophical concepts, while innovative and bold, never quite got off ground, but the failure may have little to do with the matter of poetry versus prose. In his understanding of the intellectual enterprise, he was quite at home with sages who preceded him and who came after him, if his choice of language and recognition of the outer limits of knowledge have any bearing on this issue. Perhaps Qoheleth was epistemologically less revolutionary than some critics have imagined.

The Divinity School   James L. CRENSHAW
Duke University
Durham, NC 27708-90967
U.S.A.

48. James L. CRENSHAW, *The Problem of Theodicy in Sirach: On Human Bondage*, in *Urgent Advice and Probing Questions*, pp. 155-174 (originally published in *JBL* 94 [1975] 49-64).

THE INNERSTRUCTURE OF QOHELET'S THOUGHT

I. INTRODUCTION

My basic thesis is that the central concern of the book of Qohelet is *meaning* – not transience, not work, not values, not mortality. These themes are there, but they are all ways of approaching the more fundamental issue, the meaning of life. What unites all of Qohelet's complaints is the collapse of meaning, which is revealed in the contradictions that pervade life. But the collapse, the tearing down, is only one aspect of his work; the other is building up, reconstructing and recovering meanings. I will try to describe the logic that underlies and generates his complaints and his affirmations.

The concept of "the meaning of life" is slippery but indispensable in discourse about values of greatest importance. In language, "meaning" is a predictable connection between signifier and signified. That which is signified must be something other than the signifier itself, whether in external reality, in thought, or in language. Transferring the concept of meaning to non-linguistic realities, we say that an action or quality is meaningful when it accomplishes something external to and appropriate to the action. To say that a person's *life* has meaning implies that the sum total of his deeds and experiences achieve or prove something beyond themselves. To take a phrase from Qohelet (2,2b), they *do* something.

A. *Contradictions*

The book of Qohelet is full of contradictions. From the beginning of Qohelet-interpretation[1], interpreters have recognized the contradictions in Qohelet, but they have almost always viewed them as a problem to be remedied. The remedies are arbitrary and ad hoc. They include finding clever harmonizations, identifying one of the propositions as an unmarked quote, and ascribing one of the propositions to an opinion that Qohelet is evaluating without embracing. None of these means provide

---

1. R. Judah ben Samuel says in Rab's name: "The sages wished to remove the book of Qohelet from circulation because its words are self-contradictory. Why didn't they remove it from circulation? Because it begins in words of Torah and ends in words of Torah". First of all, the contradictions are recognized; second, they are not eliminated; third, they are interpreted by being subsumed to a higher conceptual framework. My own approach follows these principles.

criteria for distancing one opinion from Qohelet rather than the other. Qohelet himself provides none. Some of these same techniques have been used by traditional or conservative commentators to make Qohelet fit the *conventional* mold. They identified the *skeptical* remarks with a fool or a callow student[2]. Currently the prevalent approach is to identify certain statements as words that Qohelet quotes in order to dispute or modify them. But this is too facile. I am not saying that there are no quotations in Qohelet, but that they don't matter. For, quoted or not, words an author speaks in his own voice are an expression of his own ideas, unless he shows us otherwise.

Another form of harmonization is to describe clashing views as instances of relativization or the *Zwar-Aber Aussage*[3]. Of course there are relativizations in Qohelet. Whenever we speak, one sentence constantly relativizes others. We cannot say everything in a single sentence. But this does not solve the problem in Qohelet. If I say: *zwar*, God protects the righteous, *aber* many righteous people perish, the "*aber*" is the problem, not the solution. If it were, Qohelet would not call this and similar anomalies הבל and רע.

In any case, the fact that so many commentators find it necessary to deal with contradictions demonstrates that Qohelet contains contradictions, or at least things that look like them. *Something* calls for harmonization. What? Why? Is Qohelet just unable to say what he means, or is he at least provoking the reader with "apparent" contradictions? If so, why?

Understanding Qohelet, as I have argued elsewhere, requires taking his contradictions seriously. He means them. They're what he calls הבל.

To be precise, Qohelet is not contradicting himself so much as *observing* contradictions. But underneath the tangle of inconsistencies, meanderings, and frustrations, there is an organizing logic – hidden premises and definitions that may be deduced from the bumpy and inconsistent surface of his explicit statements. On the deep level, Qohelet *is* consistent. Indeed, this consistency may be the source of what troubles him.

B. *The Absurd*

Qohelet does not have a way to say "meaningful", but he does have its antonym, absurd. To express this, he makes metaphorical use of the word הבל.

2. Eighteenth and nineteenth century commentators that took this approach were Heinemann, du Hamel, Herder, Eichhorn, and Nachtigal; see the summaries in C.D. GINSBURG, *Coheleth*, New York, Ktav, 1970 (first pub. 1861), pp. 84, 165, 184, 185, and 192, respectively. The understanding of "Qohelet" as referring to an "assembly" (קהילה) of individuals with different views is mentioned (and rejected) by Ibn Ezra (on 7,3).

3. This concept was developed by H.W. HERTZBERG, *Der Prediger* (KAT n.F. XVII, 4), Gütersloh, Mohn, 1963, pp. 29-31 and passim.

The absurd is a disjunction between two phenomena that are thought to be linked by a bond of harmony or causality, or that *should* be so linked. Such bonds are the *sine qua non* of rationality, and all deduction and explanation presuppose them. The essence of "absurd" is, as Camus says, *contradiction*[4]. Thus the absurd is irrational, an affront to reason. The quality of הבל infects life in its entirety.

The argument for glossing הבל as "absurd", which I have developed elsewhere[5], is basically that it works better than any other rendering. Qohelet's usage is not a complete innovation, since elsewhere in the Bible הבל sometimes means "deceitful" or "illusory"[6], which is one step from "absurd". Qohelet's innovation is in applying the word to facts or scenarios that violate reason, which is to say *Qohelet's* reason.

Qohelet is not complaining that things are not enduring or valuable or worthy or useful enough. What he is lamenting is the refractory, paradoxical, cussed quality of reality. Significance cannot be *read* out of events. And since the sages set their hearts on understanding and teaching the meaning of behavior and events, the senselessness of phenomena was, to the wise Qohelet, almost a personal insult.

Qohelet sees absurdities in a variety of phenomena belonging to three domains: work and pleasure, wisdom, and righteousness.

II. TEARING DOWN

Qohelet deconstructs meaning, or at least grand, universally valid meanings, by uncovering contradictions.

A. עמל and שמחה: *Labor and its Products*

Qohelet treats work and pleasure as a single theme, for work produces שמחות, that is, pleasant things.

שמחה in Qohelet does not mean joy or happiness. That misunderstanding has lead to the image of Qohelet as a "preacher of joy"[7]. There

---

4. Albert CAMUS, *The Myth of Sisyphus* (transl. Justin O'Brien), New York, Random House, 1955 (original publication in French: 1948), pp. 22f.

5. See further my article *The Meaning of* hebel *for Qohelet,* in *JBL* 105 (1986) 409-27; and my *Qohelet and His Contradictions*, (JSOT SS, 71) Sheffield, Sheffield Academic Press, 1987 (repr. 1989), pp. 29-51.

6. הבל can be used as a synonym of כזב, שקר, אָוֶן, and מעל and can connote "deceit", "lie". Examples are Zech 10,2; Ps 62,10; Prov 31,30; Job 21,34 (// מעל).

7. R.N. WHYBRAY, *Qoheleth, Preacher of Joy*, in *JSOT* 23 (1982) 87-98. Similarly N. LOHFINK, *Qoheleth 5:17-19 – Revelation by Joy*, in *CBQ* 52 (1990) 625-35.

would be little point in commending joy as a solution to life's joyless-
ness. That's like telling a chronically depressed person just to "cheer
up". Qohelet certainly has little joy. As often in the Bible, שמחה refers to
pleasure, whether trifling or significant[8].

Labor produces wealth, wealth buys pleasure, and pleasure is good. It
is man's portion in his toil, the *best* thing in life: "There is nothing better for a man <than> to eat and drink and show himself enjoyment [טוב]
through his toil" (2,24; 3,12). *And yet* there is no profit in toil, and the
pleasures it yields are absurd. "Of amusement I said, 'Inane!' and of
pleasure, 'What does this accomplish?'" (2,2).

The contradiction cannot be eliminated by drawing a distinction between the pleasures that Qohelet condemns – supposedly trivial and
trite ones – and the ones he commends – supposedly worthy and
deeper joys[9]. The pleasures Qohelet calls absurd and inane in chapter 2
are not trite or in any way illicit. They are qualitatively the same as the
exemplary ones – eating, drinking, and enjoying life – that he
commends elsewhere.

How then do work and its rewards fail? The one bad thing that
Qohelet says about wealth and the pleasures it yields is that the toiler
may – indeed *must* – lose the fruit of his toil, and someone may get it
who did not work for it. It is worse if the recipient is a fool, and it is
better if he is one's son, but nothing really soothes the sting of loss and
frustration. In the meantime, to be sure, one may be enjoying himself,
and that is good. But, for Qohelet, that's not enough to redeem labor
from absurdity.

At root, the problem with pleasure, and thus with the toil that produces the means for it, is not inherent in either of them. The problem is
what happens *to* them: God strips them of meaning by not guaranteeing
an exclusive and invariable causal connection between effort and reward. This, for Qohelet, proves the *meaninglessness* of human effort.

B. *Wisdom and its Advantages*

Wisdom is the greatest of human powers. It discovers truths and helps
one succeed in life and avoid harm. *And yet* it is vulnerable and disturbing and frustrated in its task, hence senseless.

8. Compare Isa 22,13, where the doomed revelers have a שמחה which is surely not
joy. שחוק, when it means merriment and not actual laughter, is a near-synonym of שמחה
and does not necessarily refer to trivial merriment – the שחוק of the returning exiles (Ps
126,2) is an expression of a joy as deep and worthy as any called שמחה.
9. According to C. D. GINSBURG, for example (*op. cit.*, p. 276), Qohelet is denouncing
"pleasure and mirth" while allowing "innocent cheerfulness and pleasure". W. ZIMMERLI
labels the deficient pleasures "das blinde Sich-Hingeben an die Freude" (*Das Buch des
Predigers Salomo* [ATD 16, 1], Göttingen, Vandenhoeck & Ruprecht, 1962, p. 157).

Both propositions in this contradiction are true. The problem is not an intrinsic failing of wisdom, but what happens *to* wisdom. This is not a logical contradiction, but it has the feel of one, because it violates what *should* be.

Qohelet has no doubt that wisdom is valuable. It is generally effective in achieving its goals, such as producing wealth. Qohelet believes that one who toils "in wisdom" will probably grow rich, as he himself did (2,9.19.21). In a variety of traditional-sounding maxims, he commends wisdom of various sorts: The wise man's speech is pleasant and careful (10,12), his face cheerful (8,1b). He has a grasp for the right time and correct behavior, particularly in the presence of the authorities (8,5). Indeed, wisdom is as superior to stupidity as light is to darkness (2,13). This is not an idea that Qohelet merely *quotes* or *examines*, but a fact that he *saw*, which is a way of affirming its truth[10].

In one way, Qohelet ascribes to wisdom a power that even surpasses the lofty claims made for it in Proverbs. For Qohelet, wisdom includes speculative intellect, the rational faculty which enables one to investigate the world and to derive new truths about life. Strangely, no other biblical author associates the exploratory intellect with חכמה, or, for that matter, even describes its operation (though the author of Job 28 is aware of it). Qohelet regards wisdom not only as a goal of seeking, as the substance of knowledge. He also sees it as a *means* of seeking, as a precondition of knowledge.

Qohelet has nothing bad to say about wisdom, but only about what happens *to* it: as great as wisdom is, it fails to achieve what it should. It is stymied in four ways.

(1) Wisdom does not provide *enough* knowledge, which is to say, all the knowledge that Qohelet wants, namely an understanding of the rationale of life's events. Qohelet determines "to investigate and to explore with wisdom all that occurs under the heavens" (1,13). Qohelet is the only sage who defines wisdom's goal so radically, and of course wisdom falls short, for not even the wise man can "find" or "grasp" מעשה האלהים, "what God does" (8,17). This is because God places barriers before wisdom, so that man cannot find out "what will happen afterwards" – in the future (3,22; 6,12; 7,14).

---

10. D. MICHEL, *Untersuchungen zur Eigenart des Buches Qohelet* (BZAW, 183), Berlin, de Gruyter, 1989, argues that ראה in 2,13 (as in 1,14.16; and 2,12) means "(prüfendes) betrachten" rather than "see" (pp. 25-30). He understands 2,13 as citing an opinion Qohelet examines rather than a conclusion he affirms. (Gordis too understands the verse as a quotation.) However, ראה with a "that"-clause always introduces a proposition the speaker accepts. ראה governing a noun, on the other hand, means "see", "look at", "consider"; and since the object of observation has no propositional content, there is no implication of truth or falsity.

(2) Wisdom is vulnerable to folly and fortune. A man who earns his wealth in "wisdom and knowledge and skill" (2,21) may lose it, and another, who may be a fool, may gain that same wealth (2,19). Both labor and wisdom are tainted by this flaw. Even when wisdom (or, we might say, intelligence) makes a man rich, it cannot *secure* sustenance, let alone wealth and favor (9,11.15 f.; 10,5-7). Though powerful (9,18a), wisdom is easily, and paradoxically, undermined by folly (9,18b).

(3) Wisdom hurts. Defined as the attempt to "investigate and to explore with wisdom all that occurs under the heavens" (1,13), wisdom is an ענין רע, a "miserable business" (1,13), not so much in its failure as in its success. In its very success it gives knowledge and so reveals the bitterness and absurdities of life. As Qohelet says on the grounds of his own experience: "in much wisdom there is much irritation, and whoever increases knowledge increases pain" (1,17b-18).

(4) Wisdom is wiped away by death. Fool and wise man alike die and are forgotten (2,15). This is not a failing of wisdom but an injustice done *to* wisdom, the ultimate insult: Wisdom's polar advantage over folly is erased by death's brutal egalitarianism.

Contrary to a common misreading, Qohelet is not a polemic against wisdom or Wisdom Literature or a Wisdom School or the "received wisdom"[11]. To differ is not to attack, especially when one is not even aware of the difference. Qohelet himself received the received wisdom and never repudiates it. Rather, he aligns himself with wisdom and complains bitterly about what life, which is to say, God, does to this worthy human power. And when life is done with it, death comes and wipes out all distinctions.

---

11. Many scholars view the book of Qohelet as a polemic against Wisdom (or the Wisdom "school"); e.g., W. ZIMMERLI, *op. cit.*, pp. 132-35. Joh. FICHTNER, *Die altorientalische Weisheit in ihrer israelitisch-jüdischen Ausprägung* (BZAW, 62), Giessen, 1933, p. 8, says that Qohelet undertakes "eine radikale Kritik an der Wert der Weisheit". According to G. VON RAD, "Dass sich Kohelet gegen die herrschenden Lehren wendet, ist nicht zu bezweifeln... (*Weisheit in Israel*, Neukirchen-Vluyn, Neukirchener Vlg., 1970, p. 301). Further, "... Diese Erklärung versagt aber deshalb, weil sich Kohelet ja nicht nur gegen Auswüchse der traditionellen Lehre wendet, sondern gegen das ganze Unternehmen" (*ibid.*). J.A. LOADER concludes that "... Qohelet is constantly polemizing [*sic*] against general *hokma* by turning its own topoi against it, by using its own forms and types with antichokmatic function and by categorically opposing the very heart of chokmatic optimism" (*Polar Structures in the Book of Qohelet* [BZAW, 152], Berlin, de Gruyter, 1979, p. 117). H. H. SCHMID says that it is generally granted that Qohelet takes a stance critical of wisdom (*Wesen und Geschichte der Weisheit* [BZAW, 101], Berlin, Töpelmann, 1966, p. 186).
    R. E. Murphy's assessment of Qohelet's ambivalent relation toward wisdom is more

C. צדק ומשפט: *Righteousness and its Rewards*

Human righteousness is rewarded in divine judgment and wickedness is punished. *And yet* God allows severe and irremediable inequities of fate, with the righteous sometimes suffering and the wicked prospering.

God's justice is probabilistic and its fulfillment often lies in the indefinite future. But for Qohelet, who requires that justice be absolute and immediate, the exceptions breach equity beyond resolution.

The contradiction is most blatant in 8,10b-14: Qohelet first says that he "knows" that it will go well with the God-fearing, while the wicked will die young. But

> (14) There is an absurdity that happens on the earth: there are righteous people who receive what is appropriate to the deeds of the wicked, and there are wicked people who receive what is appropriate to the deeds of the righteous. I said that this too is absurd.

This is, and is supposed to be, a contradiction. Neither proposition modifies nor relativizes the scope of the other. Proverbs uses as theodicy the belief that justice would *eventually* come and tidy up the exceptions[12]. Qohelet accepts this assumption but *evaluates* the process differently: a delay in justice is an irremediable injustice.

These violations are not simply rejoinders to "common" or "conventional" opinions, for they contradict Qohelet's own beliefs as well. Qohelet never sets himself across the divide from the more conventional beliefs, and he does not invoke the anomalies to undermine orthodox wisdom. He applies the הבל-judgment only after describing both the rule *and* its violation. Nor can we banish the anomalies simply by calling them anomalous, an approach suggested by Ibn Ezra and some recent commentators. The exceptional cases *are* the problem. For Qohelet, it is they, and not the weight of statistics, that are decisive and that undermine

---

nuanced (*Ecclesiastes* [WBC, 23A], Waco, Texas, Word, 1992, pp. lxi-lxiv). He describes the relation between Qohelet and the older wisdom as dialectical rather than polemical and summarizes Qohelet's relation to traditional wisdom as follows: "First, it is within this tradition that he thought and wrote; his work is intelligible only in this perspective. Second, even while he quarrels with views of traditional wisdom, his goal remains that of an Israelite sage: the discovery of what is good for humans to do (Eccl 2:3b). He does not simply jettison past teaching; he purifies and extends it. His grief against classical wisdom is its claim to security, not its methodology. Third, his argument is not theoretical; it is practical...." (p. lxiv). This characterization is mostly accurate, but I would disagree with the last point. Qohelet is trying hard to arrive at a theoretical and abstract (as well as practical) evaluation of all he surveys.

12. See R. VAN LEEUWEN, *Wealth and Poverty: System and Contradiction in Proverbs*, in *Hebrew Studies* 33 (1992) 25-36, pp. 33f. Examples are "The evil man has no future; the lamp of the wicked will be put out" (24,20). "He who closes his ear to the cry of the poor will himself cry out and not be heard" (21,13).

equity. How many unjust decisions would a *human* judge have to make before he "relativized" his fairness out of existence?

It is not only the anomalies that contradict divine justice. There is a systemic and invariable violation: death. It's not that death is so bad in itself that distresses Qohelet, but that it is *unfair*; it fails to recognize distinctions: "This is *the* worst thing [read זה הרע] in all that happens under the sun, that there is a single fate for everyone" (9,3; sim. 9,11f.).

It is very revealing that Qohelet does not call for *amelioration* of injustice. When he observes that the oppressed lack a comforter – *even* a comforter, let alone a helper – he just bemoans the lack, or, more precisely, the fact that he must *see* such unpleasantness (4,1-3). For better than the living or the dead is he who "never existed, who has not seen the evil events that occur under the sun" (4,3). Qohelet never calls upon the readers to offer *aid* or *comfort*. When he observes judicial corruption (3,16), he does not demand that justice be instituted in the courts. He doesn't even chastise the unjust judges. He merely reminds himself that God will eventually judge (3,17), then he goes on to say that it doesn't really matter, because everyone dies the same. How, then, should we respond if we see "the oppression of the poor and robbery of justice and right in the state" (5,7)? "Do not be surprised at the matter", he advises. That's just the way things are.

That's just the way the world is, and מעות לא יוכל לתקן (1,15), "nothing warped can be straightened out". For Qohelet, either something is just or it is unjust, and that is that. The cruel fact of time's irreversible arrow makes remediation of injustices impossible. What is is what will be. The moment becomes absolute. Each case becomes determinative for the nature of life.

III. BUILDING UP

As well as tearing down, Qohelet builds up, providing numerous maxims on how to live, how to make the best of the bad deal that is life. Often he tells us what is "good" or what is "better than" other things. These maxims, though appearing haphazardly and touching upon a mix of topics, also have a cohesion on the deep level.

Qohelet's counsels are not solutions; they are only *accommodations*. These come down to embracing the very activities that elsewhere he judges senseless: work and pleasure, wisdom, and righteousness. These are allowed value for the moment only, but the moment is all we have. These accommodations allow humans to create *little meanings*, local meanings, within the great absurd.

It will require less time to describe the reconstruction of meanings than the subversion of meaning, not because the reconstruction is less important but because it is easier to describe. This is because the basis for it in large part resides in the affirmation of behaviors whose meaning is undermined by contradiction. These were judged הבל, but their value was not eliminated. After all, if the negatives are not neutralized by the positives, then the positives too survive, even when judged ineffective and meaningless. In other words, they are "good portions" even if they fall short of being יתרונות, "profits".

Local meanings are recovered by the following principles:

(1) Pleasure is *good* during the moment it is experienced; this slight plus is enough to make life, with all its miseries, preferable to death (6,6).
(2) Pleasure *distracts* one from excessive awareness: A man who is allowed enjoyment "will not much call to mind the days of his life, since God is keeping him occupied [reading מעגהו] with his heart's pleasures" (5,19)[13].
(3) Wisdom – meaning simply know-how and good sense – works well in practical matters, especially in comparison to stupidity, which earns contempt and makes a mess of things.
(4) Work, pleasure, and intellect (חכמה and חשבון) are our חלק, our portion. Even if our portion is not a יתרון, it is what we have:

> All that you can manage to do[14], do in accordance with your strength [reading ככחך], for there is no activity or calculation or knowledge or wisdom in Sheol, where you are headed (9,10; cf. vv. 7-9).

Qohelet recommends not only pleasure and wisdom, which he has called good and beneficial, but also מעשה, activity, which is one of the terms he uses for labor. *Doing* and *thinking* are to be embraced simply because they too are our portion; they are *ours*. Instead of a meaningful life, we have glimmers of goodness in life. These flicker on and off like sparks in the infinite darkness.

---

13. Thus LXX and Syr. (It is also possible to regard the dir. obj. as elided, being implicit in 19a). העגה corresponds to Syriac *'a'niy*, "busy one (with)"; thus Syr can translate exactly *ma'ne' leh*. עגה in the qal means "be busy with" in 1,13 and 3,10, and in both cases it is said that God "gives" man an עגין "task" to be busy with. "Giving (נתן) an עגין" is equivalent to the hiphil causative העגה, which may be a denominative from that noun and is probably an Aramaism.

14. תמצא ידך: the hand "finding" or "reaching" signifies metaphorically the concept of *ability* (most clearly in Lev 12,8; 25,28; Isa 10,10). To be *able* to experience pleasure means being able to pay for it, to afford it.

What about righteousness? This, strangely, Qohelet advocates only occasionally, and without much vigor. He instructs us not to be "too wicked" or "very wicked", and not to act the fool, lest we die early (7,17) – a lukewarm moralization indeed! Possibly we can add 8,8, which in the MT is warning (also lukewarm) that "wickedness will not let its possessor escape", that is, from death[15]. He certainly does not repudiate righteousness just because its pay-off is uncertain. Perhaps he regards it as less problematic, or perhaps he is less convinced of the practical value of righteousness than of wisdom, and since when he offers counsel, it is guidance for practical management of life rather than moral exhortation, he gives less effort to inspiring righteous behavior. In any case, Qohelet is not primarily a moralizer, and in this regard he stands far from Proverbs and Ben Sira, who identify wisdom and righteousness.

IV. QOHELET'S LOGIC

How can Qohelet hold both sides of his contradictions? Early commentators had trouble believing that Solomon could deny the preeminent powers of wisdom or the certainty of divine justice. Modern commentators find it harder to credit him with affirmations of these values.

Qohelet does believe the dogmas we consider conventional, and it would be a greater cause for surprise if he did not. These dogmas belong to his inherited world construction. They are a model of reality, an indispensable means of filtering data and interpreting reality. From social inheritance and from the endless sifting of individual experience, all humans develop mental models that guide perception and thought and organize their world-view[16]. Input is accepted as long as it conforms to the models. We all have filters on our vision that in part determine what we see *and know* as real. Sometimes, however, our expectations are violated so frequently, or so inescapably, that we must modify or even replace our models. One *can* step away from inherited models, but it is difficult to do so, and it is no surprise when one does not do so.

Qohelet is truly at a crisis – a turning point – but he hasn't yet rounded the bend. Qohelet "knows" – presupposes – that the good will be rewarded and the wicked punished, and nothing he "sees" dislodges

15. We should probably emend רשע to עשר "wealth" (BHS), compare Prov 11,4 and Ezek 7,19. Deliverance from death does not mean immortality but preservation from a premature demise when disaster strikes.
16. Jerome BRUNER, *Actual Minds, Possible Worlds*, Cambridge, Mass., Harvard Univ., 1986, p. 47.

this presupposition. He believes in divine justice, he *knows* that God will judge, but he also *sees* the injustice of undeserved fates and delayed retribution. He states both these "facts" but, instead of getting rid of one, he lets them clash and calls the resulting discord הבל. This leaves the reader uncomfortable and dissatisfied – as it should, because Qohelet is describing an uncomfortable world. He stands on the boundary of two world-views, wavering uncomfortably but honestly between them. When inconsistency prevails, meaning collapses.

Why does Qohelet see contradictions where others saw rules and exceptions and found ways to modulate the clash? The root of what troubles Qohelet lies in his peculiar and idiosyncratic construction of reality. He expects strict consistency and so perceives contradictoriness everywhere. This is a *construction*. Neither the rules nor their violations nor the absurdity of the contradiction is "out there" in the form of an external reality waiting only to be recognized – as some interpreters suppose when they praise Qohelet for "realism", as if he saw realities the other sages were blind to.

Qohelet's construction of reality rests on a hidden structure of assumptions, a theoretical scaffolding, so to speak. We can discern the outlines of this structure by observing Qohelet's expectations, which are in turn revealed by what *violates* them.

Qohelet assumes that what is required to make the universe rational and meaningful is strict equity. All behavior must produce appropriate and commensurate results. This is what he *expects*. When, inevitably, he finds this principle violated, he does not simply discard the old models, which are still his way of seeing the world, and which are *supposed to* make sense of the world. He doesn't shrug his shoulders as an atheist might do and turn to develop new principles that make sense of his current observations. Instead, he despairs of meaning.

For Qohelet, meaningfulness in human affairs requires an invariable mutual entailment of behavior X and the appropriate consequence Y. To be appropriate, the consequence must be
(1) immediate (8,10-11) – it is absurd if justice is delayed;
(2) individual (2,18.26; 6,2) – it is absurd that someone who did not toil gets the toiler's earnings;
(3) visible (8,11) – if people do not see justice fulfilled, they become morally perverted (8,11b); and
(4) final and irreversible – If one finally loses what he earned, his efforts are senseless (5,14f.; 4,15f.). A man's wisdom should somehow extend its benefits beyond the grave.
Any infraction of these stipulations constitutes injustice.

Qohelet sees that labor, wisdom, and righteousness – the three great domains of human endeavor – do not *exclusively* entail appropriate rewards. It seems that only a consequence that met such strict stipulations would qualify as a יתרון, a "profit". This is true of the obverse: inactivity, folly, and wickedness do not exclusively entail their appropriate penalties, as defined by the stipulations mentioned earlier.

It is often assumed that didactic wisdom literature assumes the working of strict equity, but it does not, or at least not to such a degree. Proverbs, Ben Sira, and their foreign predecessors knew that justice can be delayed, that the righteous can lose their wealth and become impoverished and suffer in other ways, and that reward and punishment can be internal and invisible. But unlike Qohelet, the other sages find a way to compensate for or explain away such violations of justice.

Qohelet introduces many of the violations that he calls הבל by the particle יש, "there are". These are "Grenzfälle", borderline-cases, as D. Michel calls them[17], but as he observes, they are not marginal for *Qohelet* as they are for conventional wisdom[18]. Yet they are also not simply rejoinders to "common" or "conventional" opinions, for they contradict Qohelet's own beliefs as well. As said before, he never sets himself across the divide from the more conventional beliefs, and he does not invoke the anomalies to undermine orthodox wisdom. If that were his purpose, he would call the *conventional* idea הבל, but he never does. He does not place the הבל-judgment after, for example, "it will go well with God-fearing people, because they are afraid of him, and... it will not go well with the wicked man etc" (8,12b-13). He applies the הבל-judgment only *after* describing the violation. For Qohelet the anomalies do not undermine the rule but rather the world's rationality.

Beneath the entire structure lies Qohelet's belief in a deity who, in principle, guarantees the working of right causation. An absolute ruler with absolute powers can and *should* ensure invariant justice. Anomalies cannot be pushed to the periphery, because God's power reaches everywhere. *Everything* that happens is מעשה האלהים. Injustices cannot be explained away by promises of future rectification, because they are unjust *now*, and God could rectify them immediately. Wisdom need not fail, for God could guarantee its invariable success. Death need not wipe out differences, because it is God who decides lifespans and could even conquer death. If Qohelet contradicts himself in this regard, he does so no more than any believer in a just God who fails to execute justice. Qohelet, however, refuses to push the issue aside.

17. *Op. cit.*, chap. VII, esp. p. 199.
18. *Ibid.*, p. 199.

Qohelet has no way of extricating himself from the dilemma his own presuppositions have created. He presupposes a set of criteria so rigorous that nothing "under the sun" escapes the judgment of profitlessness and meaninglessness. These criteria, it must be stressed, are Qohelet's own. Most of his readers, I would imagine, are more flexible and, we may say, more *realistic*, less absolutistic in their assumptions than Qohelet. But exegesis cannot test Qohelet against external standards of reasonableness. To do so, and to bring him into conformity with these standards, is to miss the grim stringency of Qohelet's world view.

After all his tearing down, how can Qohelet build up? How can he say that *anything* is good? Yet he does. Though we have no "profits" we can have "portions", and they can be "good".

Qohelet's affirmations are based on a much more modest standard: something is "good" if it is better than its alternative. Profitability is an absolute, and it is unavailable. Goodness is relative. The relativization is often explicit, as in the טוב מן sayings. Even elsewhere, the second term of comparison is usually evident. In assessing things for goodness, stipulations for meaningfulness are set aside. Y need not be exclusively entailed by X, nor need it be final. Grand meanings are lost. The moment becomes absolute: ביום טובה היה בטוב (7,14). This is truly a relativization – of values, not of Qohelet's contraries.

Qohelet uses יתרון, "profit", in the strict sense of a surplus return on an investment of labor, whereas a חלק, in Qohelet and elsewhere, is simply a possession, something one gets out of something, regardless of whether it is adequate or satisfying or deserved or durable. Think of it this way: If somebody opens a store that provides him with sufficient take-home pay to keep going day-to-day *and no more*, never producing a surplus and putting the business in the black, Qohelet would call the take-home pay the man's "portion". He would even allow that the food and drink he bought with it were "good". Yet by Qohelet's severe accounting, the business realizes no *profit*. Someone else might say that even if there is no profit in the strict sense, the business *is* keeping its owners going and is by no means senseless. But Qohelet demands more.

When he doesn't get it, he seeks accommodations not solutions. Accommodations are obviously not enough to satisfy Qohelet's *will to meaning*, the sense that there is something important that needs doing and that he can do. The evaporation of this sense of meaning leaves an existential vacuum. And how better to say "existential vacuum" in Biblical Hebrew than הבל, literally "vapor"?

The best Qohelet can offer is a temporary, local tactic for coping with the vacuum: When you possess something good, enjoy it immediately.

Seize the moment, *experience* pleasure, because however inadequate pleasure may be, experiencing it, "seeing good", as he puts it, is in man's control. It is *his*, his portion, his choice, and it lies within, which is the only realm of human freedom.

The same is true of wisdom. Human wisdom is deficient, vulnerable, and sometimes irritating, but it *is* wisdom, and it is the greatest of human powers. It is as light versus darkness. Man is free to seek knowledge, and some knowledge he can attain. Qohelet not only advocates wisdom, he lives it. He chooses its path, amasses it from the past, and seeks more. He understands wisdom as the rational intellect whereby one can look at the world with an unflinching gaze and assay it by human measures. This too is man's portion, something he can say is *his* in a world where so much is alienated.

Even though man's effectiveness has been radically circumscribed and his wisdom hemmed in on all sides, he has not been deprived of freedom or hope of happiness. Freedom lies within, in the experiential realm. In this regard, as well as in his vision of absurdity, Qohelet is akin to Albert Camus and other existentialists.

Even if man cannot shape events, he can choose how to respond as they impinge upon him. Enjoyment of the moment, when this is allowed him, is one way. Wisdom – just seeing things lucidly and soberly – is another. Just to live is sweet, even when life is somber. The ability to taste this sweetness is ours, the living. These possibilities lie within.

God *wants* man to drink of life's sweetness. If you are doing this, it is not because you, like Sisyphus, have wrested a moment of respite from a hostile deity. It is what God wants you to do. Indeed, he must have *already* chosen this for you (9,7). Knowing this may turn pleasure into happiness.

1220 Linden Drive, room 1338   Michael V. Fox
University of Wisconsin
Madison, WI 53706
U.S.A.

QOHELETH AS A THEOLOGIAN

The use of the term "theologian" in the title of this paper requires an explanation. On one view it denotes a person learned in theological matters who, if he writes, does so primarily for his own satisfaction or in dialogue with other theologians as a purely academic exercise, offering his own reinterpretation of his faith – or of some aspect of it –, not expecting to be understood by the great majority of literate lay persons, and with no thought of grappling with the doubts and problems that may trouble the faith of the ordinary believer. Theologians of that sort are probably less numerous today than they once were. Most modern theologians, even though they may be aware that their writings will be studied only by a minority of educated people, are more inclined to address contemporary issues and to express their arguments as far as may be possible in plain language.

In this paper I maintain that Qoheleth was a theologian of the latter kind. I designate him as a theologian rather than as a philosopher, though that title would not be entirely inappropriate. It would also be proper to call him an apologist, since he was concerned to present the Jewish faith to his readers in a realistic way that would be acceptable to his contemporaries, who were living in a world in which many of the old traditional certainties seemed to have become untenable. He should thus be seen not as a destroyer but as a would-be defender of the Jewish faith.

That his book cannot be classified in conventional terms simply as an example of "Old Testament wisdom literature" is clear. In terms of the ancient Hebrew literary tradition it is unique, and can only be interpreted in its own terms. (This is not, of course, to deny or belittle its *origins* in the so-called "wisdom tradition" and its affinities with that tradition, or on the other hand to rule out the possibility that Qoheleth was influenced by external notions, whether Mesopotamian or Greek.) One of the most remarkable features of the book is its strongly personal tone. Only here in the Hebrew Old Testament do we find a writer who reveals his identity – albeit only by means of a *nom de plume* ("I, Qoheleth", 1,12) – and who fills his work with claims that he has made his own personal assessment of the state of the world: of the nature of God, human nature with its possibilities and limitations, society, religious duties, ethics and the practicalities of life.

These claims are made so frequently in the book that they may be seen as a *leitmotif*. First person verbs carrying this meaning are regularly placed by way of preface to a particular observation or at its conclusion. They constitute an emphatic declaration by Qoheleth that he is an independent observer and thinker. There are at least fifty of them in a book consisting of only 222 verses[1]. All these verbs attest to a deliberate purpose to observe, consider and draw conclusions from various phenomena and situations, an intention clearly set out in 1,13, where it is imaginatively attributed to Solomon: "I applied my mind to seek and search out by wisdom all that is done under heaven". The frequent use of the first person "I" (אני) draws strong emphasis to the fact that these are the mental activities of an individual thinker untrammeled by innate religious tradition or current philosophy.

The programmatic statement in 1,13 implies an intention also to carry out this wide-ranging programme systematically. Nowhere else in the Old Testament is there a statement of a comparable intention, not even in such books as Deuteronomy or Second Isaiah with regard to which it is customary to speak of a consistent theology. Qoheleth's claim to have made a *personal* investigation is also unique – and in this respect the book probably owes a great deal to the Hellenistic spirit. Qoheleth as a Jew did a very bold thing in making public his private thoughts and in attempting to order them systematically. Whether he can be said to have been successful in the latter intention is a matter that has been widely discussed.

The form in which his material is presented may suggest that the book was not the result of a single literary impulse. Efforts that have been made to discover in it the kind of single progressive logical argument that we find in, for example, a treatise by Aristotle have been unsuccessful. Rather, the *Pensées* of Pascal may provide a partial analogy: that work, which has been published in various arrangements many times, is not a finished product but consists of numerous notes later collected together, made in preparation for a great treatise that was never written. These notes are not arranged in any logical sequence; and every edition published since Pascal's death has presented them in a different order, each editor having arranged them in the way that has seemed to him to

---

1. ראיתי, "I saw", nineteen times (1,14; 2,13.24; 3,10.16.22; 4,4.15; 5,12.18; 6,1; 7,15; 8,9.10.14.17; 9,13; 10,5.7); "I thought" (2,2; 6,3; 9,16); אמרתי בלבי, "I thought to myself" (2,1.15; 3,17-18); דברתי אני עם לבי, "I said to myself" (1,16); נתתי את־לבי, "I applied my mind" (1,13.17; 8,16; 9,1); תרתי בלבי "I searched in my mind" (2,3); פניתי, "I turned to consider" (2,11.12); ידעתי, "I know/perceived" (2,14; 3,12.14; 8,12); שבתי אני ואראה, "Again I saw" (4,1.7; cf. 9,11); נסיתי, "I tested" (7,23); לא מצאתי/מצאתי/מוצא אני, "I found/did not find" (7,26-29).

correspond to Pascal's intentions, but which probably does not. Never-theless, the nature and content of the material are such that it is possible to form a reasonably clear impression of the mind of Pascal and to sur-mise with considerable probability what was his theology (for the *Pensées* are primarily theological in character). Admittedly a knowledge of his other, completed, works has to some extent served as a guide to this enterprise.

It would be unwise to carry this analogy too far. It is not probable that the book Qoheleth is a collection of notes for a theological treatise which was never written; nor do we have other works of his that we can consult. On the other hand, the disjointed character of Qoheleth's book, the reason for which is not clearly known, does not in my opinion pre-clude the reader from perceiving that it has a unity of thought – a per-ception that owes a good deal to Qoheleth's constant repetition of key phrases, but more than that: despite some contradictions, which may well point to tensions in Qoheleth's thought (and there are, it should be noted, such tensions also in the *Pensées*), there is sufficient consistency of thought displayed in Qoheleth's book to enable the reader to form a clear idea of his views.

I. QOHELETH AS A TEACHER

But we must enquire what Qoheleth was attempting to achieve in writing his book. It is reasonable to suppose that his purpose was to make his views known to others in order to persuade them of their truth: in other words, he was, in some sense of the word, a *teacher*, and one who wished to point out certain errors in the current beliefs and teaching of his day. That he was a "wise man" (חכם) who "taught the people" (למד־דעת את־העם, 12,9) in addition to (יתר) his literary activity of "weighing, examining and correcting" or "arranging" (אזן וחקר תקן) many (earlier) sayings (משלים) is affirmed by the epiloguist, and there is no reason to doubt the correctness of this statement, even though it is not quite certain what is meant by העם in the context[2].

That Qoheleth's purpose was an educative one is supported by stylis-tic considerations. Especially in the second half of the book he makes frequent use of the proverb style – that is, especially of the "sentence" (*Aussagewort*) which succinctly describes a key aspect of life, the admo-

---

2. It has been generally assumed that the reference is to the instruction of a wide pub-lic. עם is used in a variety of senses in the Old Testament, however. A. BARUCQ, *Ecclésiaste* (Verbum Salutis, 3), Paris, 1967, p. 10) suggested that it may mean "group" here, possibly in the sense of "school".

nition (*Mahnwort*) which equally succinctly gives advice, and the so-
called "'better'-proverb", which states what is preferable to something
else. These types of saying are especially characteristic of the book of
Proverbs. Some of those contained in his book were probably sayings
already current in Qoheleth's time, but others were almost certainly
composed by Qoheleth himself, indicating his continued attachment to
the methods of the traditional חכם[3]. The admonitions cover a wide range
of advice: behaviour in the temple (4,17-5,6), avoidance of anger (7,9),
disregard of gossip (7,21), obedience to the king (8,2), abstention from
dangerous thoughts and speech liable to be repeated by others (10,20)
and prudent business practice (11,1-2), in addition to general advice
about moral behaviour (7,16-17) and the enjoyment of life (9,7-10;
11,9-12,1). Some of these items are similar in theme to sayings in the
book of Proverbs. They show the extent to which Qoheleth regarded
himself as an heir to the literary tradition of the book of Proverbs, whose
purpose was also essentially educative.

But it is also clear that Qoheleth was not a schoolmaster or teacher of
young children. Children might have been capable of understanding and
profiting by some of the "proverbial" material in the book, but certainly
not the majority of Qoheleth's more extended reflections on God, the
world, man and society, for example 1,3-3,15. It is significant that
Qoheleth never uses the phrase "my son", which is a characteristic form
of address by a teacher to a young pupil occurring frequently in Proverbs, especially in chapters 1-9, and having its origins in some earlier
non-Israelite wisdom literature. Only once does he use a direct form of
address: in 11,9 his advice is addressed specifically to the young man,
the בחור (probably used here in a collective sense). This word here evidently denotes a person in early manhood, in the prime of life (compare
also ילדותך, 11,9; בחורותך, 11,9; שחרות, 11,10). It cannot of course be
shown incontrovertibly that this form of address, which occurs only
once in the book, proves that the entire book was written for such young
men, but this is extremely probable: this passage (11,9-12,8), which recommends the enjoyment of life in youth before the onset of old age and
death, is Qoheleth's final word to his readers, and constitutes the climax
of the whole work.

Apart from the useful but meagre notice by the epiloguist in 12,9-10,
the book contains no direct information either about the circumstances in
which Qoheleth's instruction was given, or about the period when the

---

3. See R.N. WHYBRAY, *The Identification and Use of Quotations in Ecclesiastes*, in
J.A. EMERTON (ed.), *Congress Volume, Vienna 1980* (SVT, 32), Leiden, 1981, pp. 435-
451.

book was written or where it was written. It is not the purpose of this article to participate in the learned debate on the book's date and place of composition which began already in the rabbinic period and has continued to be pursued up to the present day; however, if the place of the book in Israel's religious and theological history is to be correctly understood, it is necessary for me to declare a position on these matters for the purpose of my argument here. I shall assume the view of the majority of scholars – though not of all – that the place of composition was Jerusalem or its environs, and that the book was written during the period when Hellenistic culture had begun to spread its influence in Palestine. Some time during the third century B.C., therefore, and most plausibly the latter half of that century, appears to be the most probable solution to the question[4].

Without entering, then, into the discussion in detail it will be useful to summarise the arguments that have led to this conclusion. There are several of these: Qoheleth's mode of thought, hardly conceivable without some familiarity with a Greek-inspired mentality (though Greek influence on the contents of the book is another question); the personal style and (semi-) self-identification of the author; an apparent ignorance of the critical situation of the Jews of Palestine at the time of the Maccabean crisis in the second century B.C.; Qoheleth's familiarity with earlier Israelite wisdom thought and with at least some other Old Testament books; and, not least, the language of the book. Delitzsch's comment that if the book was written in the time of Solomon the Hebrew language has no history has been corroborated and extended to suggest a period many centuries later than that of Solomon[5].

A further argument for a third century date has been put forward which is less easy to assess: it has been alleged that the book unmistakably reflects a particular state of Palestinian Jewish society quite distinct from that of any other period, a period characterized by disorientation resulting from the invasion of an alien culture and way of life (so, e.g., Hengel)[6], a feeling of powerlessness and disillusion under an oppressing

---

4. Recent exceptions include C.F. WHITLEY, *Koheleth. His Language and Thought* (BZAW, 148), Berlin, 1979 (152-145 B.C.); D.C. FREDERICKS, *Qoheleth's Language. Reevaluating its Nature and Date* (Ancient Near Eastern Texts and Studies, 3), Lewiston (NY) – Queenston (Ont.), 1988 (probably pre-exilic).

5. The language of Qoheleth has recently been studied in detail by A. SCHOORS, *The Preacher Sought To Find Pleasing Words. A Study of the Language of Qoheleth* (OLA, 41), Leuven, 1992. This confirms the general consensus that the book is written in Late Biblical Hebrew. Schoors's work begins with a useful account of previous research on the topic, pp. 1-16.

6. M. HENGEL, *Judentum und Hellenismus*, Tübingen, 1969, pp. 210-237 (English translation: *Judaism and Hellenism* 1, London, 1974, pp. 115-128). See also R. KROEBER, *Der Prediger* (Schriften und Quellen der Alten Welt, 13), Berlin, 1963, pp. 26-27.

foreign regime unlike that of the Persians (so Lang)[7], a new materialism accompanied by an obsession on the part of the aristocracy to benefit from the new sources of wealth in the form of new technologies and commercial enterprise and to obtain lucrative positions in the administration of the country (de Jong)[8], leading to a sharp exacerbation of the inequalities between rich and poor (Lohfink)[9]. Some of these supposed social features may, at least at first, seem to be mutually contradictory; but it could be argued that these very contradictions are a reflection of a society undergoing violent change[10].

It would be generally agreed that the main topics of the book are God, the world that he has created, human society and the life of the individual in society. But it is necessary to enquire further what was Qoheleth's intention in teaching and writing about these matters. Several conflicting answers have been given to this question. One is that Qoheleth was, or was by intention, a philosopher who set out as systematically as possible his view of reality in order to convince his audience but with no specific religious or theological message to propound[11]. Such an intention would not necessarily exclude the giving of practical advice, which is undoubtedly one feature of the book. In pursuance of this view attempts have been made to demonstrate that Qoheleth was familiar with and influenced by one or more of the main Greek systems of philosophy or by the "popular philosophy" of his day[12]. Another view is that his purpose was essentially polemical: to undermine and demonstrate the falsity of the so-called "dogma of retribution" – that is, the view supposedly represented especially by the book of Proverbs and by Job's three interlocutors, that human actions, good or bad, inevitably reap their consequences in the moral form of reward or punishment in this life; or to demonstrate the irrationality of belief in a life after death in which retribution which had failed to take place in this world had

7. B. LANG, *Ist der Mensch hilflos? Zum Buch Kohelet* (Theologische Meditationen, 53), Einsiedeln, 1979, pp. 66-67.

8. S. DE JONG, *Qohelet and the Ambitious Spirit of the Ptolemaic Period*, in *JSOT* 61 (1994) 85-96.

9. N. LOHFINK, *Kohelet* (Die Neue Echter Bibel), Würzburg, 1980, pp. 6-9.

10. See also V. TCHERIKOVER, *Hellenistic Civilization and the Jews*, Philadelphia, 1961; M. ROSTOVTZEFF, *The Social and Economic History of the Hellenistic World*, Oxford, 1941.

11. J.L. CRENSHAW, for example, in *Ecclesiastes* (OTL), Philadelphia – London, 1987, though he probably would not accept the term "systematic" with regard to Qoheleth, holds a view of the book which does not admit the possibility of any positive message (e.g. p. 23).

12. This is an old question. Recently it has been discusssed by WHITLEY, *Koheleth* (n. 4), pp. 165-175 and R. BRAUN, *Kohelet und die frühhellenistische Popularphilosophie* (BZAW, 130), Berlin, 1973.

been postponed to the next. Yet others have seen in the book an attack on the Jewish religion itself, maintaining that the God (not Yahweh but Elohim) is not the God of the Old Testament but a remote God who, although he created the universe, is unconcerned with the fate of his human creatures and has abandoned them to the working of an impersonal and unpredictable fate[13]. Qoheleth has thus been dubbed a pessimist, a sceptic, a cynic and a nihilist. The book is thus, according to some critics, an anti-religious book, and Qoheleth was intent on destroying his readers' faith by demonstrating its irrationality and naivety.

It is my contention that Qoheleth was none of these things: that on the contrary he was a Jewish theologian-teacher whose purpose was, out of a genuine religious faith, to show a young but adult male audience how to maintain their faith in circumstances that militated powerfully against it. This indeed involved some modification of the faith in which they had been brought up: Qoheleth's theology was undoubtedly in some respects "unorthodox"; but it was designed to take into account the changing situation of Jewish society and to counter the new and exciting temptations of the Hellenistic world, yet remaining within the boundaries of the essential features of Judaism. To demonstrate this will involve looking at the book from a different standpoint from what has become customary in academic circles: as a religious and theological work concerned to defend rather than attack the Jewish faith.

II. CONSERVATISM AND RADICALISM

Qoheleth was, I submit, both conservative – in his attachment to the basic tenets of Judaism –, and radical – in that he put forward his own reinterpretation of some aspects of it. Before proceeding to a detailed investigation of the radical aspects of his teaching it is appropriate and important to examine the extent of his conservatism[14]. It is in my opinion quite clear that he was neither putting forward a new religion nor advocating the practice of an alien religion whether Greek or other; it is equally certain that he was not attacking religious belief altogether. The supposed influence on him of specific Greek philosophical systems has never been convincingly demonstrated; and if in certain respects his

13. Such views are represented by, e.g., H.-P. MÜLLER, *Wie sprach Qohälät von Gott?*, in *VT* 18 (1968) 507-521; A. LAUHA, *Kohelet* (BKAT, 19), Neukirchen, 1978, pp. 16-18; J.A. LOADER, *Ecclesiastes. A Practical Commentary* (Text and Interpretation), Grand Rapids, 1986, pp. 14-15; CRENSHAW, *Ecclesiastes* (n. 11), p. 24; H.W. HERTZBERG, *Der Prediger* (KAT, XVII,4), Gütersloh, 1963, pp. 225-227.

14. See R.N. WHYBRAY, *Conservatisme et radicalisme dans Qohelet*, in *Sagesse et Religion, Colloque de Strasbourg 1976*, Paris, 1979, pp. 65-81.

thought appears to run parallel with notions that are to be found in Greek literature, it should be borne in mind that, in the absence of any evidence of direct textual dependence, coincidences of this kind may reasonably be judged to be just that: parallels, conceivably prompted by the spirit of the age and by comparable social and intellectual backgrounds, rather than instances of direct borrowing.

Qoheleth and the Old Testament Faith

It is indubitable that the book can only have been written by a believing Jewish writer. Qoheleth's clearly stated belief in a sole, absolutely transcendent God who created the world as a good world (3,11), who made mankind from dust and animated them with the breath of life (3,19), but who reduces them again to dust when they die (3,20; 12,7) was to be found nowhere else in the ancient world of his time. Many aspects of his view of human life and destiny also correspond to Old Testament teaching in that he stresses the weakness and insignificance of mankind and their total dependence on their creator, and at the same time states that it is by its own actions that mankind has become corrupted (7,29). He constantly affirms that life is a gift from God, and that God's intention is that mankind should live it to the full and should find enjoyment in it whenever possible. When he acknowledges that human life is beset by evils, disappointments and injustices he is stating a fact of common experience, but also one which finds an echo in much of the Old Testament story. His reluctance to believe that there is a worthwhile life after death (3,21), together with his view of existence in Sheol as a miserable state devoid of positive qualities (9,10) – a view which may be directed against the contrary belief in a resurrection to life recently introduced into some Jewish circles – corresponds entirely to the "standard" teaching of the Old Testament. These elements of religious belief taken together constitute a solid corpus of orthodox faith.

This, however, is not the whole of Qoheleth's teaching. It is with regard to other aspects of his thought that he shows himself to be a radical thinker, and it is these that have elicited the judgement of many scholars that he held a pessimistic or sceptical view of reality that is incompatible with Jewish belief. This, it is argued, is especially true of his teaching about God: it has frequently been maintained that Qoheleth's God is not the God of the Old Testament. Here the main contention is that his God is an utterly remote and impersonal God who is indifferent to, and does not concern himself with, human sufferings or the fate of individuals:

that he has created a world devoid of morality[15] in which there is no correlation between human actions and their consequences, and that human life is therefore meaningless (הבל). These teachings, it is held, are totally contrary both to the teaching of the Old Testament and to the wisdom tradition.

It may, however, be argued that this judgement grossly overstates the gap between Qoheleth's teaching and that of the Old Testament in general, and also that it ignores the fact that the Old Testament is not a wholly consistent body of teaching: that there are many "Old Testament theologies". In fact, even if this judgement accurately portrays his thoughts, much of his teaching has Old Testament precedents. These things are a matter of degree. It is true that Qoheleth makes no direct reference to divine action in history, the so-called *Heilsgeschichte*, but this is also true of the earlier wisdom books of Proverbs and Job. The sense of human desolation – that God hides himself from human distress – is also a frequent theme in the psalms of lamentation, and also in such popular sayings as that cited by the woman of Tekoa, "We are like water spilled on the ground, that cannot be gathered up" (2 Sam 14,14). That men and women are left by God in a state of helplessness and frustration because God has his own hidden plans for them is clearly stated in the book of Proverbs in contradiction to that book's otherwise "optimistic" tone: while it is true on the one hand that "Whoever walks in integrity walks securely" and that "The fear of God prolongs life, but the years of the wicked will be short" (Prov 10,27), it is affirmed a few chapters later that "The human heart plans its course of action (דרכו), but it is Yahweh who directs his steps" (16,9) and that "The lot is cast into the lap, but every decision is from Yahweh" (16,33). The tension between these contrasting views of reality is no less palpable than some of the tensions within Qoheleth's book, where the author can speak on the one hand of the God who created a perfect (יפה) world (3,11) and yet maintain that "men are snared in an evil time when it suddenly falls upon them" (9,12).

Many more examples could be given of correspondences between the view of God entertained by Qoheleth and certain aspects of Old Testament teaching on that subject. Some of the most striking parallels are

---

15. Many critics speak of a breakdown of moral values in Qoheleth, especially H. GESE, *Die Krisis der Weisheit bei Kohelet*, in *Les sagesses du proche-orient ancien. Colloque de Strasbourg 1962*, Paris, 1963, pp. 139-151 (English translation: *The Crisis of Wisdom in Koheleth*, in J.L. CRENSHAW (ed.), *Theodicy in the Old Testament* (Issues in Religion and Theology, 4), Philadelphia, 1983, pp. 141-153; LAUHA, *Kohelet* (n. 13), pp. 14-16; MÜLLER, *Wie sprach Qohälät* (n. 13), p. 520; LANG, *Ist der Mensch hilflos?* (n. 7), p. 27; CRENSHAW, *Ecclesiastes* (n. 11), p. 23.

with parts of Gen 1-11, which reflect in general terms on the human condition in God's world[16]. These chapters, with the exception of the story of the Flood, where the total corruption of the human race (6,5.11-12) is countered by a new beginning accompanied by a divine promise (9,1-17), present a far from positive view of God's dealings with men and women. In Gen 3 and the story of the Tower of Babel (Gen 11,1-9) in particular, the human race is presented in extremely negative terms with regard both to its behaviour towards God and, especially, its alienation from God. Gen 3, although God is presented after the event as showing some concern for human welfare in providing the man and the woman with clothing (3,21), is a paradigm of the present unsatisfactory human condition, portraying mankind as left by God to make their way in the world by their own efforts, excluded from the environment that God had originally intended for them, doomed to suffer and to survive only through unending harsh labour in a world that God has cursed, until his human creatures return to the dust from which they have been taken (3,17-19). Again in 11,1-9, in a story that forms the climax of the series of stories that had begun with the creation of the world, the human race is made sharply aware of its limitations and helplessness before God; moreover, God sows the seeds of human conflict through his confusion of languages. Nor does their author shrink from a portrayal of God which is far from sympathetic. In two verses (3,22 and 11,6) he reveals God's inner thoughts in which he expresses his determination to ensure that mankind is frustrated in its ambitions and kept in its state of inferiority: reflecting on the fact that "the man has become like one of us" in acquiring the knowledge of good and evil, he determines to limit the damage to himself ("lest he take from the tree of life and eat, and live for ever", 3,22); similarly in 11,6 he reflects that if human beings are not thwarted, "nothing that they do will now be impossible for them". These chapters, then, express, though in mythological imagery that is alien to Qoheleth's style and mode of thought, a view of God and of his treatment of his human creatures that is as sombre as anything that Qoheleth himself presented to his readers.

One of the passages in Qoheleth which has been interpreted as teaching the futility of human life is 1,3-11[17]. But this passage has been generally misunderstood, partly owing to the misinterpretation of two words: דור (v. 4), generally held to refer to the successive periods in the history of mankind, and יגעים, usually rendered by "weary", or by an

16. See C.C. FORMAN, *Koheleth's Use of Genesis*, in *JJS* 5 (1960) 256-263.
17. On what follows see R.N. WHYBRAY, *Ecclesiastes 1,5-7 and the Wonders of Nature*, in *JSOT* 41 (1988) 105-112.

extension of meaning, "wearisome". The latter word occurs only in two other places in the Old Testament (Deut 25,18 and 2 Sam 17,2), where it does seem to mean "weary". But two instances are insufficient to determine meaning, and in the present context it is more likely to be linked in sense with the noun יְגִיעַ, which means either effort or the result of effort. So the phrase כָּל־הַדְּבָרִים יְגֵעִים probably means "all things are in constant activity". As for the phrase דוֹר הֹלֵךְ וְדוֹר בָּא in v. 4, there is no reason in the context to suppose that this refers to *human* generations. The word דוֹר is also used to denote time past and present (cf. Isa 41,4; 51,9). It is also significant for the understanding of the passage that the word הֶבֶל, so often rendered by "futility" in Qoheleth, does not occur in the passage: in the nearer context it occurs only in v. 2, which is not part of Qoheleth's discourse, and in v. 14, which belongs to a different section of the book.

1,3-11, then, is not a comment on the futility of human life. V. 3, though it speaks of the improbability that profit (יִתְרוֹן) can be derived from human toil (עָמָל), is probably not part of this passage but belongs to the introduction to the book (1,1-2)[18]. Vv. 4-11 are principally concerned with the processes of nature rather than having man as their centre of interest. Their purpose is to point out, on the basis of a variety of observations, that nature does not change but is essentially cyclical. V. 9b, "What has been *done* is what will be", may be intended to include human life within this general conclusion, but there is no reason to suppose that Qoheleth is saying that history repeats itself in endless circles. Whether he has God's actions or man's in mind here, he is pointing out the limitations within which man will do well to be content to live his life as an integral part of the "whole work of God". V. 11 is certainly a specific reference to human nature, but its point is only to note the fallibility of human memory. It is a response to the hypothetical comment of v. 10: people may claim that an event or situation is unprecedented, but this is only because we easily forget what has happened in former times. The "cosmological" argument of this passage includes thoughts that had not been expressed in quite the same way in earlier Hebrew literature, but it is not essentially innovative: the regularity of natural phenomena is attested elsewhere in the Old Testament, notably in Gen 1, in God's promise to Noah in Gen 8,22 and in Isa 28,23-26 and Job 38-41.

It has been further maintained that Qoheleth departs from the traditional religion of the Old Testament in that he taught a doctrine of impersonal fate, and that he denied that man possesses free will. The view

18. The commentators are divided on this point.

that he believed in the existence of impersonal fate, or that God himself
was perceived by him *as* impersonal fate, is based mainly on 9,11,
"Time and chance (פגע) happen to them all" (עת ופגע יקרה את־כלם) and
on his use in five places (2,14.15; 3,19; 9,2.3) of the word מקרה. פגע
occurs only twice in the Old Testament; the other place is 1 Kings 5,18,
where Solomon declares that God has given him rest on every side and
that in consequence he is faced neither by adversary nor by misfortune
(פגע רע). Here there is clearly no sense of impersonal fate: פֶּגַע is simply
what happens or what one encounters in life (פֶּגַע). מקרה is also a rare
word that occurs in only three other places in the Old Testament (1 Sam
6,9; 20,26; Ruth 2,3) and also denotes what happens to a person (קרה).
In Qoheleth it is used in every case of the inevitability of death, but with
no connotation that life and death are controlled by an impersonal fate:
on the contrary, for him life is a gift of God, and at death human beings
"return to God who gave it" (12,7).

On the question of determinism and free will it should be noted that
this is a perennial problem to which no consistent solution is to be found
in the Old Testament, and which Qoheleth – together with his theological successors – was unable to solve. Almost throughout the Old Testament human beings are regarded as responsible for their actions; yet in
some notable instances it is stated that these can be determined by God.
Thus according to Isa 6,10 God proposes to prevent the people of Jerusalem from understanding his message; and he similarly hardens the
heart of Pharaoh (Exod 7-10). Those passages make it clear that God is
able to dictate both human thoughts and actions. But no attempt was
made by Old Testament writers to face this paradox. It cannot be said
that there is an Old Testament doctrine either of determinism or of human free will: God's control of his human creatures is absolute, yet they
are free to choose and responsible for their actions. Qoheleth also makes
no attempt to resolve the paradox. He stresses, probably more strongly
than his predecessors, that the good or bad fortune and the span of life of
individuals are determined by God and not by themselves; yet his rhetorical questions in 7,16 ("Why should you destroy yourself?"; "Why
die before your time?") and much of the practical advice that he gives
show that he believed that to a limited extent man could influence his
destiny by changing his behaviour.

That Qoheleth's view of human expectations of happiness in this life
was on the whole a sombre one cannot be denied. This view was no
doubt partly the consequence of his observations of the social conditions
of his time: Qoheleth was above all a realist. But he was not a nihilist:
this is shown by his readiness to give practical advice which he obvi-

ously expected would be useful to his readers. Moreover, others before
him (for example, Job – especially in Job 3 – and Jeremiah in Jer. 20,14-
18) had expressed no less serious doubts about the meaningfulness of
their lives; and if Qoheleth was sometimes moved to say that he hated
life (2,17), or that he turned his heart to despair (שׁאי) over the results of
his labour (2,20), or even that all the days of one's life are "full of pain"
(2,23), these outbursts must be balanced by the evident sincerity of his
assertion that "Light is sweet, and it is pleasant to see the sun" (11,7)
and his recommendation that "Even those who live many years should
rejoice in them all", even though "the days of darkness will be many"
(11,8). In view of these considerations it would be wise to reconsider the
meaning of the word הבל as unlikely to imply a total rejection of everything in life as futile or valueless. (See the Appendix below.)

The view that Qoheleth did not uphold the importance of moral principles is a strange one. It is mainly based on an interpretation of 7,16,
אל־תהי צדיק הרבה, which is usually taken to mean "Do not be too righteous"[19]. This and the following verses are generally interpreted as showing that Qoheleth advocated a "golden mean" in morality: that he advised that to overdo upright conduct will lead to disaster as much as to
overdo wicked conduct. However, as I have argued elsewhere, the advice given in 7,16 probably means "Do not *pretend* to be a 'righteous
person'" or, "Do not be self-righteous". Apart from these misinter-
preted verses there is no evidence in the book that Qoheleth advocated
immorality or that he thought that moral behaviour was a matter of indifference. On the contrary, he regularly contrasts "the wicked" (רשׁע) and
the "righteous" (צדיק, 3,17; 7,15; 8,14; 9,2) and deplores the fact that
often they receive the opposite of what they respectively deserve. However, he affirms that the wicked will be judged for their deeds, even
though retribution may not always be speedy (3,17; 8,10). Its delay encourages the spread of evil in the hearts of men (8,12). It will not be well
with the wicked, but only with those who "fear God" (8,13). Qoheleth
also speaks of the "sinner" (חוטא), whom he evidently regards as
equivalent to the wicked (2,26; 7,26; 8,11; 9,2). One instance of wickedness particularly arouses his fierce indignation: oppression of the
weak by the powerful (4,1).

In all this Qoheleth was struggling with problems that had exercised
the minds of the authors of Proverbs. He did not accept the view that
people always get what they deserve in this life, and constantly points

---

19. On these verses see R.N. WHYBRAY, *Qoheleth the Immoralist? Qoh 7,16-17*, in
J.G. GAMMIE et al. (eds.), *Israelite Wisdom: Theological and Literary*. FS Samuel
Terrien, Missoula, 1978, pp. 191-204.

out that death levels all. Justice does not prevail, and this is due to human corruption (7,29). Qoheleth never blames God for this state of affairs, and there can be no doubt of his indignation at human wickedness. The references to God's judgement (3,17; 11,9; 8,12-13 etc.), thought by some to be so inconsistent with Qoheleth's main views as to be interpolations into the book by others or quotations of views that he rejected[20], can be explained by indications of his own admitted failure to understand reality in all its aspects – the relative failure of wisdom[21]. Positively, his commendation of those who "fear God" (3,14; 5,6; 8,12-13) and his assurances in 8,12-13 that it will be well with them attest to a confidence, albeit a puzzled one, in God's good intentions towards the human race. It certainly is not correct to say that he is morally indifferent or that for him it does not matter whether one does good or evil.

Finally it has been alleged that Qoheleth was indifferent to the kind of piety that was the mark of the Israelite faith[22]. By the latter is usually meant a belief in God as saviour and helper, as one who approaches and can be approached and with whom a personal communion can be established. Some observations are in order here.

1. References to the official cult are gathered in one section of the book: 4,17-5,6. Here Qoheleth refers to visits to the temple, sacrifice, listening to priestly instruction, prayer and the making of vows. It is significant that he assumes that his readers regularly engage in these activities. But his attitude towards them is one of caution: if they are performed thoughtlessly they may become an occasion for sin and cause God to be angry. It seems clear that worship was not a matter of indifference for Qoheleth. The prudential character of his advice has, however, led many commentators to conclude that his attitude towards it was entirely negative. This is an unwarranted conclusion. Qoheleth does not at-

20. This view was commonly held a century ago by critics who "discovered" multiple "sources" in the book: C.J. SIEGFRIED, *Prediger und Hoheslied* (HKAT), Göttingen, 1898; E. PODECHARD, *L'Ecclésiaste* (EB), Paris, 1912; G.A. BARTON, *The Book of Ecclesiastes* (ICC), Edinburgh, 1908. But individual interpolations (or in some cases quotations supposedly made by Qoheleth in order to refute them) on a modest scale have continued to be postulated, e.g. by R.B.Y. SCOTT, *Proverbs. Ecclesiastes* (AB), Garden City, 1965; W. ZIMMERLI, *Das Buch des Predigers Salomo* (ATD), Göttingen, 1967²; K. GALLING, *Der Prediger* (HAT), Tübingen, 1969²; LAUHA, *Kohelet* (n. 13); CRENSHAW, *Ecclesiastes* (n. 11).

21. More recent commentators (e.g. R. GORDIS, *Koheleth: The Man and His World*, New York, 1978³; R.E. MURPHY, *Ecclesiastes* (WBC), Dallas, 1992; LOHFINK, *Kohelet* (n. 9); LOADER, *Ecclesiastes* (n. 13)) have in various ways tended to regard these passages as integral to Qoheleth's own thought.

22. E.g. L.G. PERDUE, *Wisdom and Cult*, Missoula, 1977, pp. 180-188; HERTZBERG, *Der Prediger* (n. 13), pp. 224, 233; HENGEL, *Judentum und Hellenismus* (n. 6), pp. 117, 121; LAUHA, *Kohelet* (n. 13), pp. 16, 17.

tempt to dissuade his readers from performing their customary religious obligations; moreover, he devoted a sizeable section of his book to instructing them about the way in which they ought to perform them.

2. The commonly held view that Old Testament religion placed great emphasis on personal belief in God's loving care for individual human creatures and on a close personal relationship with him is probably a considerable overstatement. This is, of course, an important theme in many of the Psalms, though some – particularly Ps. 90 – present a much bleaker picture. The "historical" books of the Old Testament are more concerned with God's relations with the nation than with individuals, although there are exceptions, e.g. the story of Hannah in 1 Sam 1-2. The book of Proverbs has the lives of individuals as its subject, but makes few references to worship and almost none to prayer. In the book of Job, piety, goodness and the due performance of sacrifice (Job 1-2) count for nothing when God is persuaded to strike Job and cause him to suffer; and Job, unable until the end of the book to communicate with a silent God, regards him as an enemy rather than as a friend.

3. In fact we know surprisingly little about the "unofficial" religion of ordinary Israelites, either in the pre-exilic period or later[23]. But there can be no doubt that by Qoheleth's time the religious situation had greatly changed from that of pre-exilic times; it could hardly be otherwise. From the early post-exilic period onwards religious differences had proliferated within Judaism and within the Jerusalem community itself. Qoheleth's book has to a large extent a polemical character: he rejected, for example, the position of those who had begun to entertain a belief in afterlife, together with eschatological beliefs generally, and he made no mention of the supreme importance attached in other circles to the Law of Moses. It would seem also that he dissociated himself from certain other forms of private piety, possibly of a "popular" kind. It is also clear that the doctrine that he taught was, as had been the case with his predecessors such as the authors of Deuteronomy and the Second Isaiah, adapted to the special circumstances of his own time, when the optimism of the earlier wisdom teaching represented by the book of Proverbs had

23. The problem is the highly selective character of the presentation of Israelite beliefs and practices in the Old Testament. Thus R. ALBERTZ in his monumental *Religionsgeschichte Israels in alttestamentlicher Zeit*, Göttingen, 1992 (english translation: *A History of Israelite Religion in the Old Testament Period*, 2 vols., London, 1994) includes separate sections at various points on "personal piety", "family piety", "the subsidiary cult of the family", "the piety of the poor", etc., but candidly admits that in trying to enable readers to "re-experience the suffering and the joy, the struggle, the failure and the success of the Israelites down the generations", "no one who knows the state of the sources will be surprised that I often get to the very edge of the possibilities of reconstruction" (ET, p. viii).

been made unrealistic by drastic social changes and by the atmosphere of both disillusionment and frantic opportunism that had invaded especially the aristocracy and wealthy class of the Jerusalem of the Ptolemaic period. Qoheleth was a realist; but his teaching remained true to the essential faith of Judaism, and he was not an iconoclast but a theologian for his time.

A Theologian for his Time

It was not, however, Qoheleth's primary purpose to expound a systematic body of belief. Rather, his primary aim was a practical one: to impress on his readers the necessity to accept the world as it is with all its shortcomings and, as a teacher of wisdom, to counsel them to "fear God" (3,14; 5,6; 7,18; 8,12.13) in their actual situation, personal, social, economic, intellectual and political. He began his book (1,4-15) by putting things in perspective, telling them that the world is far from perfect and that they are not to expect fundamental changes: the world has been arranged in such a way that "what has been is what will be, and what has been done is what will be done; there is nothing new under the sun" (1,9). Eschatological hopes, then, among other things, are ruled out, and the world cannot be changed. He reinforces this assertion in 7,13: "Consider the work of God; who can make straight what he has made crooked?".

But experience also showed that life holds good things as well as bad. Although Qoheleth represents "Solomon" as declaring that he hates life because of the bad things that happen (2,17) and that he hates the labour (עמל) that he had undertaken because it might be dissipated by his heirs (2,18-21), and although in a passage about the victims of oppression he feels that death or non-existence could be preferable to life (4,1-3), he nevertheless communicates to his readers his own joy in being alive: just to enjoy the daylight and to see the sun is "sweet" and "good" (11,7). However bad things might be, Qoheleth never expressed the thought that suicide might be an option. In this he was completely Hebraic. He pointed out that enjoyment of life is possible (2,24; 3,12; 5,17; 9,7-10) and is a gift from God, and he earnestly advised his young readers to enjoy this gift to the full while they were still in the prime of life (11,8-12,1), though they ought always to remember that they are all mortal; and also that they should take warning that over-indulgence in the pursuit of pleasure can be folly (7,1-6).

Qoheleth did in fact lay great stress on human mortality – a necessary reminder to the young, who are particularly prone to put the thought of it from their minds. In 3,18-21 (and also 12,7) he may have been thinking of Gen 3,19 – "dust to dust" –, though that belief is not exclusive to that chapter. If God is the giver of life, that life has been ordained as a limited one by his design, and what he has given he will some day take back again. But in 3,22 Qoheleth draws from this consideration a positive recommendation, that a person should enjoy his work (מעשׂיו) within the limits (חלק) that have been allotted to him. In 5,14 he reinforces the observation of "Solomon" (2,21), pointing out that material possessions cannot be retained beyond the grave, and in 3,21 and 6,12 he is at one with traditional Israelite belief that there is no certainty about a meaningful life after death. In all this there is a realism, harsh perhaps, but salutary, especially for the young and ambitious.

Nothing that Qoheleth said about the insignificance of human beings in comparison with God conflicts with traditional Israelite belief. The unequivocal statement "God is in heaven and you on earth" (5,1), made as a warning to be circumspect in one's dealings with God in worship, would have been endorsed by any Jewish reader. Qoheleth's constant insistence on human ignorance of God's plan and God's deeds, however, was deliberately critical of the teaching of wisdom reflected – though with some exceptions already mentioned – in the book of Proverbs, which put great emphasis on human competence in most respects to deal with one's environment and on the individual's ability, through right conduct and conformity to one's teachers, to ensure prosperity and happiness. The reasons why Qoheleth, as a conscientious theological teacher, laid such stress on men's ignorance of their fate will be explored below. Briefly, these reasons, all of which were relevant to the particular situation of his readers, included an intention 1. to show the folly of overweening social and economic ambition, which was endemic to the Jewish society of his day; 2. to point out the folly of making the acquisition of material possessions one's principal goal in life; 3. to demonstrate that to take pride in one's own cleverness is pretentious nonsense; 4. to give a reason for the sudden reversions of fortune that characterized contemporary society.

Wealth

Qoheleth's teaching about wealth is to be found principally in 5,9-16. It makes best sense if both Qoheleth and his audience were aware of some specific cases, which he then used to illustrate his points, namely that wealth cannot by itself produce happiness and that its continued possession cannot in any case be guaranteed. He piles his observations one upon another, first pointing out that it is not the possession of wealth itself that corrupts a person but that it does so when those who possess it are never satisfied with what they have but are moved by an insatiable desire to increase it. This never-ending insatiability becomes an obsession (5,9). He points out that one reason why wealth is not ultimately satisfying is that it will attract a crowd of scroungers who will find means to "feed" on it for themselves, so that its possessor will do no more than glimpse it before it disappears (v. 10). It is also the cause of worry and sleeplessness from which the ordinary working person is free (v. 11); it can be quickly lost in an unwise business venture (vv. 12-13); it has to be relinquished at death (vv. 14-15); and it is often the cause of misery (v. 16). Qoheleth concludes this catalogue in vv. 17-19 with one of his recommendations to be content with one's lot: if we become rich, this is because God has bestowed wealth on us so that we may enjoy it while it lasts. The message of the whole passage is that wealth is good and can be enjoyed provided that it neither becomes an obsession nor is taken for granted. This is thus a thoroughly theological comment, and one which is intensely relevant to a particularly acute contemporary problem.

Wisdom

Jerusalem society in Qoheleth's day was one in which there was great scope for the clever and the ambitious. This was also a society that had inherited a reverence for "wisdom" as a means whereby a person could fulfil his ambitions. Qoheleth was himself a wisdom teacher, and consequently valued wisdom – but in its proper place. He of course found it infinitely preferable to folly or stupidity and esteemed it as enabling a person to "see where he was going" whereas "fools walk in darkness" (2,13-14). Several of his comments on wisdom are remarkably similar to the teaching of the book of Proverbs: it gives power or authority to those who possess it (7,19); as common sense it is essential to the performance of specific tasks (10,10); it is more effective than military strength (9,16.18), and can give success to the defenders of a city against its attackers (9,15).

In what he says about wisdom, however, Qoheleth characteristically sounds a theological note which has the effect of warning his readers against overestimating their own cleverness and so in fact laying claim to something that is an exclusive quality reserved to God alone. In these passages he is concerned with a much more elevated concept of wisdom than that exemplified in the preceding paragraph, though one that is even

more relevant to his readers, as it concerns the limitations set by God on
every member of the human race. Fundamentally this is discourse about
the way God made the world in which we live. It concentrates especially
on human *ignorance*, which affects the way in which human beings live
and must live their lives, and indeed their very existence. Basic to this
situation is the question of what God has permitted them to *know*.

It was, partly at least, in order to convince his audience of their own
ignorance that Qoheleth spoke so definitely of his own failure to penetrate the mind of God. He no doubt hoped that a confession that even
he, their revered teacher, who had devoted so much of his life to wrestling with the problem of human knowledge but now admitted the failure
of his self-imposed intellectual enquiries, would show them that they
could hardly expect to succeed where he had failed. He made it clear
that these enquiries were immense in their scope.

In 1,12-13, speaking in the guise of "Solomon", Qoheleth claimed to
have attempted the most comprehensive task that any philosopher could
attempt: "I applied my mind to seek and search out by wisdom all that
happens under heaven". Still in the guise of the great king who "had
acquired great wisdom, surpassing all who were over Jerusalem before
me" (1,16), he sadly concluded that "in much wisdom is much vexation,
and those who increase knowledge increase sorrow" (1,18). Although
wisdom is better than folly (2,14), the wise man suffers the same fate as
the fool (2,15-17). In 7,25, now speaking in his own person, Qoheleth
similarly informs his readers, "I turned my mind to know and to search
out and to seek wisdom and the sum of things (חשבון)"; but he is forced
to admit, "I thought, I will be wise; but it was beyond my grasp (רחוקה
ממני)". What happens (i.e., phenomena in general) is "beyond our
grasp" and is "deep, deep; who can discover it (מי ימצאנו)?" (7,23-24).
The verb מצא, "to find, to find out", here particularly "to grasp, to understand", is a key word in Qoheleth. It is used of the innate human inability to understand the ways of God, and is concerned especially with
the assertion that the reason for this inability is that it is God's deliberate
purpose that man should remain ignorant of them. Accordingly in 3,11
Qoheleth states that the Creator, who has "made everything good (or,
appropriate, יפה) in its time (בעתו), has placed the mysterious עלם in
men's hearts, yet so that (מבלי אשר) they cannot grasp (לא־ימצא) the
things (המעשה) that God has done from beginning to end". In 7,14 he
speaks in a similar way of human inability specifically to know whether
they will experience success or failure in the future, but significantly
links this statement with a piece of practical advice: "In times of prosperity be glad, and in times of misfortune consider this: it is God who

makes the one as well as the other, so that man cannot find out (‑על
דברת שלא ימצא) anything about his future (אחריו)". Finally 8,16-17 contains another frank avowal that however much wisdom a person may
possess, he is no more able than anyone else to understand God's activity: "When I applied my mind to acquire knowledge and wisdom, and to
observe the business (הענין) that is transacted in the world so that there is
no sleep for the eyes day or night, then I contemplated all God's activity
– that no one can find out (למצא) what is being done under the sun.
However much a man may labour in seeking it, he will not find it;
moreover, even if a wise man claims to know it, he cannot find it out."
The context of this assertion is interesting: the previous verse (8,15)
commends what Qoheleth believed to be a more suitable activity for human beings: "So I commend enjoyment, for there is nothing better for
men under the sun than to eat and drink, and enjoy themselves, for this
will go with them in their toil through the days of life that God gives
them under the sun."

In making these assertions about the limits of human knowledge
Qoheleth was not denying – nor was he specifically affirming – the traditional Israelite belief that God has revealed himself through his actions
in many ways: that is not the question with which he was dealing. He
was simply pointing out an obvious fact about human nature as it applies
to individuals, and tracing this back to God, who had created that human
nature. His intention was to dissuade his readers from a foolish illusion
especially characteristic of the young male, that one could plan one's
career as if one's success depended on one's own efforts. The point that
he was making, although it contradicts the anthropology of much of the
book of Proverbs, was in fact anticipated by other proverbs in that book
(e.g. Prov 16,9; 19,21) which emphasize Yahweh's total control over
human plans and the possibility that he may override them. Qoheleth's
aim was to show that it is folly to attempt to live one's life without taking God into account.

Knowing the "Time" [24]

The concept of the "time" (עת) and of "knowing the time" is a corol-
lary of this. "Everything under the heaven has its season (זמן) and its
time" (3,1; cf. 3,17; 8,6); and God "has made everything in its time
(בעתו)" (3,11). But this "time" is hidden from man, who "does not

---

24. For a "classical" discussion of this topic, see especially G. VON RAD, *Weisheit in
Israel*, Neukirchen-Vluyn, 1970, pp. 182-188, 295-296, 302-303 (english translation:
Wisdom in Israel, London, 1972, pp. 138-143, 228-229, 233-234).

know the time" (9,12). To a limited degree and in dealing with immediate problems such as the best way to deal with an autocratic monarch, Qoheleth accepts that human wisdom is capable of making a correct decision: "The wise mind will know both the appropriate time (עת) and the appropriate approach (משפט,"way") of speech or action" (8,1-5). A person's "time" is not, however, immutably predetermined by God, who can change his mind; and so a person can "die before his time if God disapproves of his behaviour: so, למה תמות בלא עתך (7,17). There are in fact many instances of this in the Old Testament. Man has, therefore, some freedom to determine his fate, but a very limited freedom; and God always remains the arbiter. God alone has control over every person's time of death (8,8) and also over what happens to him while he lives. It is in this context that the statement that"time (עת) and chance (פגע) happen to all"(9,11) should be understood (see above). Qoheleth's view, which is impeccably"orthodox"on this matter, can be summed up in the succinct and no doubt much needed reminder, made in connection with the proper approach to God in private worship, that"God is in heaven and you on earth"(5,1).

Qoheleth was well aware that the world is full of wickedness, and he made this clear to his readers. Probably some of his pupils were as yet not fully aware of the social evils that were being perpetrated in their society. He restated the belief that no one is perfectly righteous and without sin (7,20), and that this is not God's doing: God created man righteous (ישר), but they corrupted themselves (7,29). Their minds are full of wickedness (מלא־רע) and madness (הוללות; 9,3). Wickedness is prevalent where there ought to be justice (3,16; 9,3). There were instances of intolerable oppression of the powerless by the powerful which remained unremedied (4,1). Qoheleth drew attention to these evils, and described them in a way which shows that he hoped to persuade his audience to take them seriously and to elicit their sympathy with the victims of injustice when he commented, "there was no one to comfort them" (4,1). But, as has often been noted, he did not attempt to persuade his pupils to intervene in order to change the situation, nor is there any evidence that he himself tried to do so. He clearly regarded these evils as an inevitable symptom of the human situation that no human efforts could reform. He was far from being a social reformer, still less a denunciatory prophet. He was above all an observer and a commentator on the way of the world, though not a cynical one.

If Qoheleth was totally sceptical of any notion that the evils of society could or would be redressed by human agency, this was evidently not the case with divine agency. In a number of passages he speaks of God's

judgement. He follows his statement in 3,16 that wickedness (הרשע) is
to be found in the place of justice (מקום המשפט) and righteousness
(הצדק) with the declaration "I thought in my mind, God will judge
(ישפט) both the righteous and the wicked". In 11,9, addressing the
"young man" (בחור) directly, having encouraged him to enjoy life while
he is young and (ironically?) to follow his instincts and desires, he concludes with the warning, "but know that God will bring you to justice
(יביאך האלהים במשפט)". Again in 8,11-13, after speaking about the hon-
ours paid in the city to the wicked at their funerals, he strongly affirms
that while "it will be well (יהיה טוב) with those who fear God, it will *not*
be well with the wicked, even though they may live long lives". Whatever he may have meant by "judgement" and "being well" (or not),
Qoheleth is clearly not referring to a judgement after death; whatever he
means by the concept of judgement, it refers to the present life. In all
these passages he speaks as the teacher of young men, and his words
were intended to be a warning about the consequences of their future
conduct.

It has frequently been said that in speaking of a divine judgement both
of the righteous and the wicked, of those who fear God and those who
do not, Qoheleth was directly contradicting his own statements that we
cannot know what will happen to us in this life, because that depends on
the "time" which God determines for us and of which we are ignorant.
This view is not strictly correct. I do not intend to pursue this controversial question here in detail, but it might be better to speak of a paradox
or of a tension rather than of a contradiction. (It will not do, incidentally,
to adopt the easy (!) solution and to argue that these statements about
divine judgement have been inserted into the text by others to "correct"
Qoheleth's teaching.) Admittedly in so far as God's "time" is the time
that God chooses for our deaths, Qoheleth states the obvious fact (to
him) that we all undergo the same fate when we die, whatever our conduct may have been in life: "the same fate (מקרה) comes to all: the
righteous and the wicked, the good and the evil, the clean and the un-
clean, to him who sacrifices and him who does not" (9,2). But the recurring "times" of which he speaks in 3,2-8 – that is, the events which occur during our lives – are in a different category. Qoheleth's point here
is that we do not *know* when God will declare such "times", nor that
when he does, his decision will be immoral or haphazard. In 8,11 he admits that the punishment of the wicked may be delayed, and that this
may encourage wickedness in others. Unfortunately we remain ignorant;
but for Qoheleth (8,12-13) that judgement is assured. The lesson that
Qoheleth teaches is a moral and theological one.

This is equally true of Qoheleth's teaching about wealth. The "Solomonic" episode (1,12-2,11) has the characteristics of a moral tale – a common though minor genre of wisdom literature – in which a teacher tells, in the first person singular, of his own experiences, true or fictitious, in order to teach a moral lesson. In this case the narrator himself is, in one sense, fictitious: the author claims to have been "king over Israel in Jerusalem" (1,12) – that is, presumably, the famous Solomon (though the name "Solomon" does not occur in the text, and it was an editor who added the words "son of David" in 1,1). At the same time the author states that he is Qoheleth himself: "I Qoheleth was king..." (1,12). The purpose of this "Solomonic fiction", which may not have been intended to be taken seriously by the reader, was to present a dazzling picture, suitably embellished, of a famous king who surpassed everyone who had preceded him (1,16) both in wisdom and in wealth and luxury, and then to shatter the readers' illusion by portraying this idealized king as totally disenchanted: neither his wisdom nor his wealth was able to give him lasting satisfaction. The climax comes in 2,11, where Solomon looks back on his life and reflects that his grandiose schemes are הבל and a chasing after wind, and that in this life "under the sun" one cannot claim to have derived any lasting satisfaction (יתרון, "profit") from the efforts of a lifetime. The moral is obvious: what was true of the life of the world's most privileged person is bound *a fortiori* to be true of the lives of us all. This is a warning not to treat the acquisition of wealth and power as the most important goal in life. But the theological implication comes somewhat later, with the observation in 2,24-26 that all satisfaction in life comes as God's gift.

That wealth and pleasure are God's gifts is repeated in 5,17-19 – though they are ephemeral because they depend on his continuing good will (6,1-3). Elsewhere in the book the *love* of money is dismissed as ultimately useless (5,9). It is clear that Qoheleth's attitude to wealth was motivated by his religious and theological convictions.

Space does not allow a full treatment of a number of other topics; but some of these may be briefly discussed in which Qoheleth showed his concern in the advice that he gave in his role as a theological teacher. In 7,16-18, for example, he linked his advice to avoid self-righteousness with the comment that the fear of God will protect a person from disaster. Above all, he found divine sanction for his constantly reiterated recommendation to enjoy the good things of life (2,24-25; 3,12-13; 5,17; 8,15; 9,7-9; 11,8-12,1).

Joy and Pleasure

It was not that Qoheleth approved of pleasure when it was simply the result of self-indulgence. That had been the source of Solomon's pleasure: he says of himself, "Whatever my eyes desired I did not withhold from them; I did not deny myself any pleasure (שמחה)" (2,10). But he himself admitted that this proved to be ephemeral and unsatisfying (2,11). Qoheleth could also maintain that grief (כעס) is preferable to laughter (7,3) and that the heart of fools is to be found in the house of mirth (7,4); and he referred to the laughter of fools as being like the crackling of thorns under a pot (7,6) and held that it is better to hear the rebuke of the wise than to hear the song of fools (7,5). In these verses his concern was to castigate the thoughtlessness of those who behaved as if they were unaware of their mortality rather than to speak against pleasure as such.

In his commendations of joy and pleasure Qoheleth always stressed that true enjoyment in life comes as a gift from God. And it is significant that in his final advice to the young to enjoy life while they can, he stresses that they should remember their Creator (12,1). In fact this whole passage (12,1-7) is set within the context of the Israelite doctrine of the creation: the breath of life is itself a gift from God (12,7). That God created human beings to be mortal and to have only a comparatively short time to live is to be accepted, not regretted. For every person there is a time (עת) determined for him by God to be born, and a time for him to die (3,2). It is within those boundaries that he exists; and within them that he is *bidden* (not just permitted) to make the most of his capacity for enjoyment until his strength fails. Qoheleth is a realist who takes life as he finds it and advises his readers to do so, too. This final passage (12,1-7), which begins and ends with God, is characteristic of his thought and teaching. The final words of the book (apart from the editorial appendix) are "God who gave it" (האלהים אשר נתנה).

APPENDIX: HEBEL AND THE FEAR OF GOD

Two important questions remain to be discussed, on neither of which any consensus of opinion has emerged. These are 1. the meaning for Qoheleth of the word הבל, which occurs thirty-four times in the book (one half of the total number of occurrences in the Old Testament), together with the analogous phrases רעות רוח, often taken to mean "chasing after the wind", which occurs seven times, almost always immediately following הבל, and רעיון רוח, which occurs twice; and 2. the meaning for Qoheleth of the fear of God. The discussions will necessarily be brief.

1. In order to determine the meaning of הבל in Qoheleth it is first necessary to consider its meanings elsewhere in the Old Testament. There it has a range of meanings, all of which are related to a basic sense of "breath", either in a literal or in a variety of metaphorical senses. In its literal sense it always carries the connotation of something that is transitory or fleeting, making it a suitable image of human life in contrast with the divine nature and with the perspective of eternity. When the passages which employ the term in metaphorical senses are considered, there are nuances in its use, but these are only of limited value in assessing in what sense Qoheleth understood it. In about a third of those passages it denotes pagan idols or idolatry, seen as useless, with the further implication that to worship such idols is both stupid and dangerous. This is a sense in which it is certain that Qoheleth did *not* use the word. In a large number of cases it refers in other ways to what is useless or meaningless: help that does not materialize (Isa 30,7; Lam 4,17) or consolations that are ineffective (Zech 10,2); human effort or labour (Job 9,29; Isa 49,4); lies (Jer 16,19); female beauty (Prov 31,30); human activity in general (Ps 39,7). The common element in all these usages may perhaps be said to be insubstantiality.

הבל[25] is of course a key word in Qoheleth's vocabulary. Frequently he concludes a pericope with the comment that "this is הבל", or "הבל and רעות רוח". However, the words "הבל הבלים ..., all is הבל" in 1,2, repeated in 12,8, are not those of Qoheleth: they are an editorial interpretation of what was supposed to be the essence of Qoheleth's teaching, placed at the beginning and conclusion of his work to guide the reader to read it in a particular way. It should not be assumed that this is a correct interpretation of his thought. At the same time, it should not be taken for granted that he always employed the term הבל in the same sense.

In fact, Qoheleth uses the term with respect to a bewildering variety of matters: of wealth and the love of wealth (5,9; 6,2); of the fact that wisdom confers no advantage over folly when death occurs (2,15; cf. 3,19); of the deceptiveness of pleasure (2,1) and of the inane laughter of

---

25. Among recent interpretations of הבל in Qoheleth are those of BARUCQ, *L'Ecclésiaste* (n. 2); M.V. FOX, *The Meaning of Hebel for Qohelet*, in *JBL* 105 (1986) 409-427; CRENSHAW, *Ecclesiastes* (n. 11); MURPHY, *Ecclesiastes* (n. 21): (absurdity); LAUHA, *Kohelet* (n. 13): (human insignificance); O. KAISER, *Die Sinnkrise bei Kohelet*, in G. MÜLLER (ed.), *Rechtfertigung, Realismus, Universalismus in biblischer Sicht*. FS Adolf Köberle, Darmstadt, 1978, pp. 3-21 (= *Der Mensch unter dem Schicksal* (BZAW, 161), Göttingen, 1985, pp. 91-109): (futility, meaninglessness); G. OGDEN, *Qoheleth* (Readings – A New Bible Commentary), Sheffield, 1987.

fools (7,6); and, more generally, of life itself (7,15; 9,9) and in particular of youth (11,10); of toil (2,11; 4,4.8); of human ignorance of the future (2,19) and the inequitable distribution of rewards and punishments (2,26; 8,10.14); of the need to relinquish one's possessions at death (2,19-21); of the uncertainties of political power (4,13-16); and finally of "all that is done under the sun" (1,14; 2,17). In a few cases he supplements the word with phrases such as "and a great evil" (2,21) or "and a grave disorder" (חֳלִי רָע; 6,2).

There is no English equivalent for the term הבל as it was used by Qoheleth. Among those that have been proposed, "futility" is certainly inappropriate: Qoheleth would not have been a teacher giving practical advice to young men about the way they should live if he had thought that life was ultimately futile. "Absurd" does not carry the same implication, and probably comes nearer the mark: Qoheleth was an observer of human behaviour as well as an observer of human expectations and human fortunes, and shrewdly commented on many things that seemed to him to be absurd – that made no sense. He did not hesitate to affirm that there is much wickedness in the world and that there is evil in every person, but he went much further than that: the very conditions of life itself – mortality, toil, ignorance of God's intentions, the limited value of human wisdom and its frequent frustration by folly (10,1) – he could describe as evil (1,4; 2,17; 4,4.8; 6,2; 9,3) and so as senseless, absurd. Nevertheless his encouragement to his readers to enjoy good things when they came their way precludes the view that life is essentially futile. For him there were certainly aspects of reality that could properly be labelled futile or meaningless; but the meanings of the word הבל itself do not seem to be substantially different from its meanings elsewhere in the Old Testament: he sees human life as insubstantial, transitory, sometimes senseless or absurd, in the perspective of eternity.

2. The commonly held view that the "fear of God" that Qoheleth commended to his readers was fear – that is, terror – in the most literal sense[26] cannot be sustained: it has no basis in the text. Although there are, of course, passages in the Old Testament where Yahweh appears as a literally terrifying God, and Qoheleth can speak of God as having no pleasure in fools (5,3) or of his being angered by sin (5,5), there is no reason to suppose that for him the fear of God (האלהים) differed from

26. So LANG, *Ist der Mensch hilflos?* (n. 7), p. 45; LOADER, *Ecclesiastes* (n. 13), p. 41; CRENSHAW, *Ecclesiastes* (n. 11), p. 100. E. PFEIFFER, *Die Gottesfurcht im Buche Kohelet*, in H. GRAF REVENTLOW (ed.), *Gottes Wort und Gottes Land*. FS Hertzberg, Göttingen, 1965, pp. 133-158 argued that the term is used by Qoheleth in more than one sense and that at least in 3,14 he uses it in the literal sense of "fear".

that which is found in such texts as Deuteronomy: obedience, love, service, worship (e.g. Deut 10,12), conformity to God's moral commands (Lev 19,14), avoidance of sin (Job 1,9), honest conduct (Prov 14,2) – in short, the reverence for, and the worship of God, characteristic of sincere Yahwists (so, e.g., Prov 31,30 and many of the Psalms).

Qoheleth speaks of the fear of God in only four passages. In 5,6, the first part of which is probably corrupt, the final imperative "but fear God" refers to the warnings in the preceding verses about such matters as failure to implement vows made to God, which may lead to punishment. 8,12-13 are an assurance that those who fear God will be accepted by him, while the wicked will not be accepted by him because they do not fear him. 7,15-18 is a partly obscure passage; but it also ends with an assurance that the person who fears God will "escape" (or, possibly, succeed – יצא, literally, "come out" —) because he has followed Qoheleth's warning against certain kinds of foolish or wicked conduct that would lead to disaster. In 3,14 Qoheleth remarks that since God's actions, unlike those of human beings, are reliable and not subject to change, this ought to induce a proper awe and reverence (שיראו מלפניו). Of this handful of passages only 5,6 specifically mentions God's reactions to human behaviour; here it is interesting to note that this verse does *not* support the view that Qoheleth's God is a remote or indifferent God. But this verse, which speaks of God's anger, does not go beyond the belief, expressed in the wisdom literature as well as elsewhere in the Old Testament (cf. Prov 15,25) that God will punish the wicked. In none of these passages can it be maintained that for Qoheleth fearing God meant being in a constant state of terror. On the contrary, he would have agreed with Prov 14,26 that "In the fear of Yahweh one may have great confidence".

† R.N. WHYBRAY

PROBLÈMES D'INTERPRÉTATION DE
L'ÉPILOGUE DE *QOHÈLÈT**

Les cinq derniers versets du livre de *Qohèlèt* présentent des difficultés grammaticales et lexicales qui, bien que ponctuelles, engagent l'interprétation du passage tout entier. La comparaison de deux traductions prises au hasard suffit, à elle seule, à donner une idée de la variété des options possibles[1] (voir, à la p. 268, la traduction d'Antoine Guillaumont – très littérale, selon les principes de la *Bible de la Pléiade*[2] – mise en parallèle avec celle, plus explicite, de Norbert Lohfink[3]). Les pages qui suivent voudraient ouvrir le large éventail des interprétations défendables et présenter les arguments qui soutiennent chacune.

La traduction la plus naturelle du début du v. 9 est donnée par É. Osty[4]:

Outre que Qohèlèt fut un sage,
il a encore enseigné la science au peuple.

Le premier mot se prête déjà à diverses interprétations[5]: en donnant à יֹתֵר son sens fort de «surplus, surcroît», on peut traduire, comme le fait J.-J. Lavoie: «Et Qohèlèt fut plus qu'un philosophe, il a encore enseigné la connaissance au peuple»[6]. Les deux traductions qui viennent d'être

---

* Je tiens à exprimer ma gratitude, pour leur participation active et stimulante, aux membres du Séminaire francophone (J. Brière, A. de Pury, M. Gilbert, B. Gosse, R. Kuntzmann, N. Lohfink, J. Vermeylen, Fr. Vinel et A. Wénin) et en particulier au rapporteur, P.-M. Bogaert.
    1. L'exercice a été effectué, à partir de l'*Einheitsübersetzung* et de la traduction de W. M. L. de Wette, par Chr. Dohmen – M. Œming, *Biblischer Kanon, warum und wozu? Eine Kanontheologie* (QD, 137), Freiburg-Basel-Wien, 1992, pp. 38-39.
    2. *La Bible. Ancien Testament*, édition publiée sous la direction d'É. Dhorme (Bibliothèque de la Pléiade), vol. 2, Paris, 1959, pp. 1531-1532.
    3. N. Lohfink, *Les épilogues du livre de Qohélet et les débuts du canon*, in P. Bovati – R. Meynet (eds.), *«Ouvrir les Écritures». Mélanges offerts à Paul Beauchamp* (LD, 162), Paris, 1995, pp. 77-96.
    4. *La Bible*, traduction française par É. Osty avec la collaboration de J. Trinquet. Introductions et notes d'É. Osty et J. Trinquet, Paris, 1973, p. 1353.
    5. Voir la discussion détaillée dans A. Schoors, *The Preacher Sought to Find Pleasing Words: A Study of the Language of Qohelet* (OLA, 41), Leuven, 1992, pp. 115, 138-139 et dans N. Lohfink, *Zu einigen Satzeröffnungen im Epilog des Koheletbuches*, in A. A. Diesel – R. G. Lehmann – E. Otto – A. Wagner (eds.), *«Jedes Ding hat seine Zeit…» Studien zur israelitischen und altorientalischen Weisheit. FS D. Michel* (BZAW, 241), Berlin – New York, 1996, pp. 131-147, spéc. pp. 131-139.
    6. J.-J. Lavoie, *Un éloge à Qohélet: Étude de Qo 12,9-10*, in *Laval théologique et philosophique* 50 (1994) 145-170; cf. D. Lys, *L'Ecclésiaste ou que vaut la vie? Traduction, introduction générale, commentaire de 1/1 à 4/3*, Paris, 1977, p. 30.

Deux traductions de Qo 12, 9-14

A. Guillaumont (n. 2)	N. Lohfink (n. 3)
9 Outre que Qôhéléth fut un sage, il a encore enseigné la science au peuple; il a écouté et examiné, il a mis en ordre un grand nombre de proverbes.	9 Sans compter que Qohélet fut un maître, il a en outre enseigné publiquement le savoir, et, après les avoir rassemblés et examinés, il a corrigé beaucoup de proverbes.
10 Qôhéléth s'est appliqué à trouver des paroles plaisantes, et à écrire avec rectitude des paroles de vérité.	10 Qohélet a tenté de trouver des paroles bien frappées, ces paroles véritables ont été mises par écrit en bon ordre.
11 Les paroles des sages sont comme des aiguillons, et comme des clous plantés les auteurs de recueils; ils sont donnés par un pasteur unique.	11 Les paroles des maîtres sont comme des aiguillons, comme des piquets plantés, les paroles des auteurs de recueils n'importe quel berger les emploie tous deux.
12 Quant à faire plus que cela, mon fils, garde-t'en: faire des livres en grand nombre serait sans fin et beaucoup d'étude est une fatigue pour la chair.	12 Pour ce qui serait en plus d'elles, mon fils, sois sur tes gardes. Quand bien même on n'arrêterait jamais de faire toujours davantage de livres, et qu'on ruinât son corps en étudiant toujours plus,
13 Fin du discours: le tout entendu, crains Dieu et observe ses préceptes, car c'est là tout l'homme.	13 le mot de la fin, après avoir tout lu, serait seulement: crains Dieu et garde ses commandements. Car c'est le tout de l'homme.
14 Car Dieu fera venir toute œuvre en jugement, concernant tout ce qui est caché, que ce soit bon ou mauvais.	14 Car tout ce qui se fait, Dieu le traduit en jugement, jugement qui s'étend à tout ce qui est caché, soit le bien, soit le mal.

envisagées supposent que le texte distingue deux activités ou au moins
un état et une activité: d'une part, l'état ou l'activité du חָכָם et, d'autre
part, l'activité qui consiste à enseigner le peuple. On verra alors, dans le
חָכָם, soit simplement l'homme instruit, l'érudit[7] ou encore un philosophe en chambre retranché dans sa tour d'ivoire[8]; l'idée exprimée par le
texte serait que Qohèlèt ne s'est pas contenté d'être sage pour lui-même,
mais qu'il a aussi fait profiter les autres de son savoir. Mais le mot חָכָם
pourrait désigner ici le maître de sagesse qui enseigne, dans une école
instituée, à un cercle restreint de disciples. Dans ce cas, le texte suggére-
rait que Qohèlèt, à côté de son activité scolaire, a pris l'initiative de
s'adresser à de plus larges auditoires. N. Lohfink se demande si Qohèlèt
n'est pas ici assimilé aux philosophes itinérants de l'époque hellénistique, qui s'adressaient à qui voulait bien les écouter sur les places publi-
ques[9].

La distinction entre les deux activités est moins explicite dans la
TOB, qui propose:

> *Ce qui ajoute à la sagesse de Qohéleth,*
> *c'est qu'il a encore enseigné la science au peuple.*

Au siècle dernier, H. Ewald et F. Hitzig[10] défendaient une interprétation de וְיֹתֵר שֶׁ, qui a été reprise depuis par plusieurs auteurs: וְיֹתֵר, suivi
du relatif, aurait le sens de: «et il reste à dire que, et il faut ajouter
que»[11]. A. Lauha s'autorise à traduire: «Ein Nachtrag: Kohelet war ein
Weiser...»[12]. La deuxième partie du stique devient alors comme une ex-
plicitation de la première et précise en quoi a consisté la «sagesse» de
Qohèlèt. Dans ce cas, עוֹד n'est plus le simple pendant de וְיֹתֵר שֶׁ («non
seulement Qohèlèt a été un sage, *mais encore* il a enseigné la connaissance au peuple»), mais doit être interprété comme un adverbe de

---

7. Cf. *Einheitsübersetzung*: «ein Gelehrter».

8. Cf. F. J. BACKHAUS, *Der Weisheit letzter Schluß! Qoh. 12,9-14 im Kontext von Traditionsgeschichte und beginnender Kanonisierung*, in BN 72 (1994), 28-59, p. 34.

9. N. LOHFINK, *Kohelet* (Neue Echter Bibel, 1), Würzburg, 1980, p. 12.

10. H. EWALD, *Die poetischen Bücher des Alten Bundes*, vol. 4, Göttingen, 1837, pp. 225-226; F. HITZIG, *Der Prediger Salomo's* (Kurzgefasstes exegetisches Handbuch zum AT, VII), Leipzig, 1847, p. 216.

11. M. V. FOX, *Frame-Narrative and Composition in the Book of Qohelet*, in HUCA 48 (1977), 83-106, pp. 96-97: «now furthermore...»; cf. ID., *Qohelet and his Contradictions* (JSOT SS, 71), Sheffield, 1989, pp. 310 et 322: «furthermore...»; Chr. DOHMEN, *Der Weisheit letzter Schluß? Anmerkungen zur Übersetzung und Bedeutung von Koh 12,9-14*, in BN 63 (1992) 12-18: «es ist nachzutragen, daß...» (pp. 13-14); BACKHAUS, *Der Weisheit letzter Schluß!* (n. 8), p. 32: «nachzutragen ist, daß...».

12. A. LAUHA, *Kohelet* (BKAT, 19), Neukirchen, 1978, p. 217; de même: D. MICHEL, *Qohelet* (EdF, 258), Darmstadt, 1988, p. 168; cf. J. A. LOADER, *Prediker: een praktische bijbelverklaring*, Kampen, 1984, p. 152: «een bijvoegsel»; G. OGDEN, *Qoheleth* (Readings – A New Biblical Commentary), Sheffield, p. 208.

temps, ayant le sens de «continuellement»[13]. D'où, par exemple, la traduction de Chr. Dohmen[14]:

> *Est ist nachzutragen, daß Kohelet ein Weiser war, ständig lehrte er das
> Volk Einsicht.*

L'expression «enseigner le peuple» ne revient ailleurs dans la Bible
hébraïque qu'une seule fois, en 2 Chron 17,9, dans la notice sur l'instruction religieuse dispensée à la population judéenne par ordre du roi
Josaphat. En Qo 12,9, le mot עָם désigne sans doute, par opposition à
חָכָם, ceux qui n'ont pas étudié dans les écoles de sagesse[15].

Le stique suivant fait se succéder trois verbes. Le premier est וְאִזֵּן,
que les versions ont interprété comme une forme du verbe אזן «écouter»
ou du substantif de même racine, qui signifie «oreille»[16]. A.
Guillaumont traduit:

> *Il a écouté et examiné, il a mis en ordre un grand nombre de proverbes.*

Fr. J. Backhaus suppose qu'il s'agit ici d'une écoute critique, qui
cherche à évaluer les dits traditionnels[17]; N. Lohfink pense qu'il s'agit
plutôt d'une écoute attentive qui cherche à recueillir les proverbes[18].
Mais le substantif מֹאזְנַיִם «balance» suppose l'existence d'une racine
homonyme ayant le sens de «peser»[19]. On traduit donc habituellement,
comme le fait la TOB:

> *Il a pesé, examiné, ajusté un grand nombre de proverbes.*

L'opération concerne soit le contenu des מְשָׁלִים, que Qohèlèt aurait
soigneusement évalué, soit la formulation au niveau du rythme et du parallélisme[20].

וְחִקֵּר est l'unique forme de Piel attestée du verbe חקר. A. Lauha et M.
Tsevat renvoient tous deux à Si 44,5 pour justifier soit la traduction
ersinnen («inventer»)[21], soit la traduction «scander»[22]. Mais le sens de

---

13. Cf. H. W. HERTZBERG, *Der Prediger* (KAT XVII/4), Gütersloh, 1963, pp. 217-
218; K. GALLING, *Der Prediger*, in *Die Fünf Megilloth* (HAT XVIII), 2e éd., Tübingen,
1969, p. 124. Voir la discussion détaillée dans LOHFINK, *Zu einigen Satzeröffnungen*
(n. 5), pp. 143-147.
14. DOHMEN, *Der Weisheit letzter Schluß?* (n. 11), p. 13.
15. R. GORDIS, *Koheleth – the man and his world*, New York, 1955, p. 342.
16. Ainsi la LXX: οὖς ἐξιχνιάσεται κόσμιον παραβολῶν: «l'oreille dépistera la
beauté des paraboles».
17. BACKHAUS, *Der Weisheit letzter Schluß!* (n. 8), p. 35.
18. LOHFINK, *Les épilogues du livre de Qohélet* (n. 3), pp. 86-87. D'où sa traduction
de אזן par «rassembler».
19. *HAL* 27.
20. Voir l'inventaire des opinions dans GORDIS, *Kohelet* (n. 15), p. 342.
21. LAUHA, *Kohelet* (n. 12), p. 218; BACKHAUS, *Der Weisheit letzter Schluß!* (n. 8), p. 32.
22. חקר in *TWAT* III.159 (Tsevat).

«examiner, explorer, scruter» est bien attesté au Qal, et ce sens peut convenir ici[23].

Le troisième verbe, תִקֵּן, est en asyndète, ce qui a amené certains exégètes à penser que le mot était une glose[24]. Mais, pour N. Lohfink, l'asyndète est justifiée parce que l'action indiquée par le verbe est postérieure aux deux précédentes; d'où sa traduction[25]:

> après les avoir rassemblés et examinés, il a corrigé beaucoup de proverbes.

L. Di Fonzo considérait plutôt les deux premiers verbes comme des modalités de l'action décrite par le troisième[26]:

> e ponderando e ricercando compose molti proverbi.

Le verbe תקן apparaît en 1,15 à l'infinitif Qal avec le sens de «être droit» et en 7,13 au Piel, avec le sens causatif de «redresser». Il semble donc légitime de traduire: «il a rectifié un grand nombre de proverbes», c.-à-d. qu'il les a corrigés[27]. Mais plusieurs auteurs pensent qu'un rapprochement avec l'accad. *taqānu* «ordonner» autorise la traduction «formuler, composer»[28]. Selon A. Lauha, nous aurions ici un terme technique ayant le sens de *in gute Form bringen*[29].

Ces trois verbes décrivent l'activité littéraire de Qohèlèt. Selon les options prises, les différentes traductions aboutissent à présenter Qohèlèt soit comme un créateur original, soit, au contraire, comme un encyclopédiste critique. La traduction de Lohfink est très explicite; de même celle d'É. Glasser[30]:

> Il a pesé et examiné, en les rectifiant, nombre de proverbes.

---

23. *HAL* 334.

24. Ainsi F. HORST, dans l'apparat critique de la BHS.

25. LOHFINK, *Les épilogues du livre de Qohélet* (n. 3), p. 86; cf. ID., *Zu einigen Satzeröffnungen* (n. 5), pp. 141-142.

26. L. DI FONZO, *Ecclesiaste* (La Sacra Bibbia), Torino – Roma, 1967, pp. 328-330. De même: C.D. GINSBURG, *Coheleth, Commonly Called the Book of Ecclesiastes*, London, 1861 (reprint: New York, 1970), p. 472: «carefully and studiously composed many parables»; FOX, *Frame-Narrative and Composition* (n. 11), p. 96: «weighing and investigating he composed many sayings»; cf. ID., *Qohelet and his Contradictions* (n. 11), pp. 322-323.

27. Voir la discussion dans LAVOIE, *Un éloge à Qohélet* (n. 6), pp. 159-161.

28. DI FONZO, *Ecclesiaste* (n. 26), p. 330: «compose molti proverbi»; GALLING, *Der Prediger* (n. 13), p. 123 et LAUHA, *Kohelet* (n. 12), p. 217: «(er) formte viele Sprüche»; GORDIS, *Kohelet* (n. 15), p. 342; MICHEL, *Qohelet* (n. 12), p. 168: «er faßte viele Sprichwörter ab»; DOHMEN, *Der Weisheit letzter Schluß?* (n. 11), pp. 13-14: «viele Sprüche hat er formuliert»; BACKHAUS, *Der Weisheit letzter Schluß!* (n. 8), p. 33: «er faßte viele Sprüche/Reflexionen ab»; *HAL* 1642: «formen».

29. LAUHA, *Kohelet* (n. 12), p. 218.

30. É. GLASSER, *Le procès du bonheur par Qohelet* (LD, 61), Paris, 1970, p. 176.

Cette traduction présente l'entreprise de Qohèlèt comme un effort de révision critique et de correction du donné traditionnel[31]. À la limite, Qohèlèt pourrait n'être qu'un rédacteur ou un correcteur, travaillant sur une matière ou du moins d'après des données préexistantes[32].

Par contre, une traduction comme: «Il a pesé, scruté, ajusté beaucoup de proverbes» (É. Osty) peut s'accompagner du commentaire suivant: «le choix de ces trois termes («pesé, scruté, ajusté») souligne le soin que mettaient les maîtres de sagesse à forger leurs maximes, sentences et proverbes. Ce n'était pas une littérature populaire, mais savante, bien qu'elle fût destinée à instruire le peuple»[33].

Que représentent les «proverbes en grand nombre» que Qohèlèt est censé avoir corrigés ou composés? On s'attendrait à trouver ici une référence au livre de *Qohèlèt* lui-même. Mais certains auteurs estiment que celui-ci contient trop peu de מְשָׁלִים au sens strict du terme pour être visé[34]. Pour E. Podechard, il serait ici question d'une autre œuvre de Qohèlèt, par laquelle celui-ci aurait assis sa réputation de sagesse auprès du peuple; le but de l'épilogue ne serait pas de faire une apologie (assez mal placée selon Podechard) de l'écrit qui précède, mais de renseigner le lecteur sur une première œuvre du même auteur, qui «servirait de passeport et d'excuse à l'Ecclésiaste»[35]. Podechard se demandait même s'il ne fallait pas identifier cette œuvre avec tout ou partie du livre des *Proverbes*. Cette thèse, qui avait déjà été émise par F. Hitzig, D. G. Wildeboer et G. A. Barton[36], a été reprise depuis par G. H. Wilson[37]: les «proverbes en grand nombre» (v. 9), associés aux «dits de sages» (דִּבְרֵי חֲכָמִים) constitués en recueil (v. 10), renverraient au livre des *Proverbes*, lequel se donne d'ailleurs explicitement comme un recueil composé «pour comprendre proverbe (מָשָׁל) et allégorie, dits de sages (דִּבְרֵי חֲכָמִים)

---

31. Cf. B. S. CHILDS, *Introduction to the Old Testament as Scripture*, London, 1979, p. 585: «The emphasis does not fall on his writing activity, although this is included, but on his critical judgment in the collection of wisdom».

32. E. PODECHARD, *L'Ecclésiaste* (EB), Paris, 1912, p. 473.

33. OSTY - TRINQUET, *La Bible* (n. 4), p. 1353.

34. Voir par ex. R. E. MURPHY, *Qoheleth's «Quarrel» with the Fathers*, in D. Y. HADIDIAN (ed.), *From Faith to Faith*. FS D. G. Miller, Pittsburg, 1979, pp. 235-245 (p. 242).

35. PODECHARD, *L'Ecclésiaste* (n. 32), pp. 475-476.

36. HITZIG, *Der Prediger Salomo's* (n. 10), p. 217; D. G. WILDEBOER, *Der Prediger* (KHAT XVII), Tübingen, 1898, p. 166; G. A. BARTON, *The Book of Ecclesiastes* (ICC), Edinburgh, 1908, p. 197.

37. G. H. WILSON, *«The Words of the Wise». The Intent and Signification of Qohelet 12:9-14*, in *JBL* 103 (1984) 175-192. Voir la discussion dans G.T. SHEPPARD, *The Epilogue to Qoheleth as Theological Commentary*, in *CBQ* 39 (1977) 182-189 (pp. 183-184) ou ID., *Wisdom as a Hermeneutical Construct. A Study in the Sapientializing of the Old Testament* (BZAW, 151), Berlin – New York, 1980, pp. 122-123; V. D'ALARIO, *Il Libro del Qohelet. Struttura letteraria e retorica* (SupRivBib, 27), Bologna, 1992, pp. 171-172.

et énigmes» (Pr 1,6). Dans la lecture qu'en fait G. H. Wilson, Qo 12,9-14 cesse d'être l'épilogue du seul livre de *Qohèlèt*, pour devenir la conclusion de tout le recueil des *Ketuvîm*, ou, au moins, des *Proverbes* et de *Qohèlèt*, qui se trouvent ainsi placés sous l'autorité du même auteur: Qohèlèt *alias* Salomon; la finale du v. 11, quelle qu'en soit l'interprétation exacte, voudrait indiquer que ces écrits, dans leur diversité, ont même provenance, et les v. 12-14 proposeraient une clef de lecture valable pour tous[38].

Le v. 10 apprend au lecteur que Qohèlèt s'est appliqué à trouver des דִּבְרֵי־חֵפֶץ. L'expression est un *hapax* et son sens est difficile à préciser. On voit généralement ici un éloge de l'esthétique de la forme; c'est ce que suggèrent des traductions comme: «paroles plaisantes» (Lys[39], *TOB*), «paroles agréables» (Podechard, Segond), «paroles plaisantes» (Guillaumont), «dits agréables» (Osty), «propos savoureux» (Pautrel dans *BJ*), «Worte, dei Freude machen» (*HAL*, 326). S'il faut traduire «paroles de désir (amoureux)», l'expression pourrait faire référence au *Cantique des Cantiques*[40]. Mais חֵפֶץ peut aussi désigner l'activité humaine, les affaires, le négoce[41]; on pourrait donc comprendre, à la suite de la Vulgate: «des paroles utiles» (dans la vie courante); R. Braun risque un parallèle avec les χρηστοὶ λόγοι des philosophes cyniques[42]; Chr. Dohmen pense que l'expression est un terme technique désignant un genre littéraire: il s'agirait des paroles ou des proverbes qui ont trait aux situations de l'existence humaine[43].

L'interprétation de la forme כָּתוּב, au v. 10b, est décisive[44]. La LXX a interprété le participe passif Qal comme un complément de לִמְצֹא, coordonné à דִּבְרֵי־חֵפֶץ et juxtaposé à דִּבְרֵי אֱמֶת; le sens est alors celui qui est donné par Fr. Delitzsch[45]:

> *Es strebte Koheleth zu erreichen Worte der Anmut*
> *und Niedergeschriebenes in Aufrichtigkeit, Worte der Wahrheit.*

---

38. En faveur de cette thèse, Wilson tire argument du fait que le titre du livre des *Proverbes* et le titre du livre de *Qohèlèt* portent la marque d'un même éditeur: cf. Pr 1,1 et Qo 1,1.

39. Lys, *L'Ecclésiaste ou que vaut la vie?* (n. 6), p. 30.

40. Suggestion de A. DE PURY dans sa communication au colloque.

41. W.E. STAPLES, *The Meaning of ḥēpeṣ in Ecclesiastes*, in *JNES* 24 (1965) 110-112.

42. R. BRAUN, *Kohelet und die frühhellenistische Popularphilosophie* (BZAW, 130), Berlin – New York, 1973, p. 143.

43. DOHMEN, *Der Weisheit letzter Schluß?* (n. 11), pp. 14-15.

44. Voir la discussion dans SCHOORS, *The Preacher Sought* (n. 5), pp. 45-46.

45. Fr. DELITZSCH, *Biblischer Commentar über die poetischen Bücher des Alten Testaments*, t. 4 *Hoheslied un Koheleth* (Biblischer Commentar über das Alte Testament, 4/4), Leipzig, 1875, p. 415; cf. BRAUN, *Kohelet und die frühhellenistische Popularphilosophie* (n. 42), p. 143: «Kohelet suchte brauchbare Worte zu finden, treffend geschriebenes, Worte der Wahrheit».

Mais le participe peut être considéré comme l'attribut d'une proposition indépendante, dont דִּבְרֵי אֱמֶת serait le sujet. C'est l'option de Lohfink, dans une traduction qui rend explicite l'identification des דִּבְרֵי־חֵפֶץ du premier stique avec les דִּבְרֵי אֱמֶת du second stique[46]:

Qohèlet a tenté de trouver des paroles bien frappées,
ces paroles véritables ont été mises par écrit en bon ordre.

Quelques manuscrits hébreux ont la leçon וְכָתַב «et il a écrit», qui a l'appui de la Vulgate et du syriaque. «This reading, écrit A. Schoors, certainly makes a more fluent and meaningful sense»[47]. C'est l'option de A. Lauha[48]:

Kohelet war bemüht, defällige Worte zu finden,
und schrieb redlich Worte der Wahrheit.

On obtient un sens très proche en corrigeant la vocalisation du TM pour lire וְכָתוּב, dont on fait un infinitif consécutif soit après בִּקֵּשׁ, soit après לִמְצֹא[49]; cette option est celle de la plupart des commentateurs; on traduit alors:

Qohèlèt s'est appliqué à trouver des paroles agréables
et à écrire (ou et il a écrit) avec exactitude des paroles de vérité.

Selon que l'on considère le verbe comme un passif ou comme actif, le stique prend un sens tout différent. Dans le premier cas, c'est la fidélité de l'écrit à l'enseignement de Qohèlèt qui est mise en avant. Dans le second cas, la rectitude est mise au crédit de Qohèlèt: il n'a pas seulement cherché à plaire par des דִּבְרֵי־חֵפֶץ, il a écrit sans fard (יֹשֶׁר) ce qui était vrai (דִּבְרֵי אֱמֶת)[50].

Est-il possible de trancher? En fait, il n'y a aucune raison pour abandonner la *lectio difficilior* du TM, d'autant plus qu'elle a ici l'appui de la LXX. On interprétera donc le texte comme le font É. Glasser[51], N. Lohfink, ou encore la *TOB*, qui traduit de manière tout à fait explicite:

46. LOHFINK, *Les épilogues du livre de Qohélet* (n. 3), p. 86; cf. déjà EWALD, *Die poetischen Bücher des Alten Bundes* (n. 10), vol. 4, p. 225: «es suchte Kohélet gefällige Worte zu finden, doch aufgeschrieben sind redliche, treue Worte»; *Einheitsübersetzung*: «Hier sind diese wahren Worte sorgfältig aufgeschrieben».

47. SCHOORS, *The Preacher Sought* (n. 5), pp. 45-46.

48. LAUHA, *Kohelet* (n. 12), p. 217.

49. GINSBURG, *Coheleth* (n. 26), p. 473 prétend que le participe passif peut avoir une valeur consécutive, comme l'infinitif, et renvoie à Qo 8,9.

50. BARTON, *The Book of Ecclesiastes* (n. 36), p. 197 rend l'opposition très explicite: «Qoheleth sought to find pleasant words, but he wrote uprightly words of truth».

51. GLASSER, *Le procès du bonheur par Qohelet* (n. 30), p. 176: «L'écrit est exact; les paroles sont authentiques».

Qohéleth s'est appliqué à trouver des paroles plaisantes
dont la teneur exacte est ici transcrite: ce sont des paroles authentiques.

Le v. 11 se prête lui aussi à des interprétations différentes[52]. Le premier stique introduit une image empruntée à la vie agricole:

Les paroles des sages sont comme des aiguillons

Vient ensuite une deuxième comparaison, où, cette fois, le comparant précède le comparé:

וּכְמַשְׂמְרוֹת נְטוּעִים בַּעֲלֵי אֲסֻפּוֹת

L'expression בַּעֲלֵי אֲסֻפּוֹת se traduit littéralement «les maîtres (*ou* les détenteurs, *ou* les possesseurs) des choses amassées (*ou* assemblées)», éventuellement, «les maîtres des assemblées»[53]. La traduction «comme des clous solidement plantés (ainsi sont) les maîtres des assemblées»[54] donnerait un sens satisfaisant et trouverait, en Is 22,23, un parallèle intéressant, mais ce sens n'est pas appelé ici par le contexte. Aussi les interprètes préfèrent-ils voir dans «les choses amassées» des collections de sentences. Les «maîtres» des collections sont alors, soit leurs auteurs, soit ceux qui en possèdent à fond la connaissance[55]. On traduit donc habituellement:

Les auteurs de recueils sont comme des clous (bien) plantés.

Peut-être la règle du parallélisme (ici, avec דִּבְרֵי חֲכָמִים) invite-t-elle à suppléer le mot דִּבְרֵי et à supposer que l'expression désigne ici, par ellipse, les sentences des auteurs de recueils. D'où la traduction de Fr. J. Backhaus[56]:

Wie eingeschlagene Nägel sind die (Worte) der Sammlungen.

---

52. La construction même du verset est controversée. WILDEBOER, *Der Prediger* (n. 36), pp. 166-167 propose de couper ainsi: «Die Worte der Weisen sind wie Stacheln und wie eingeschlagene Nägel, die Sammler sind gegeben von demselben Hirten»; même construction de la phrase chez LAUHA, *Kohelet* (n. 12), p. 217: «Die Worte der Weisen sind wie Treibstacheln und wie eingeschlagene Nägel. Die Lehrmeister sind van ein und demselben Hirten gegeben».
53. Voir la discussion dans LAUHA, *Kohelet*, pp. 219-220.
54. Cf. GINSBURG, *Coheleth* (n. 26), p. 474; GALLING, *Der Prediger* (n. 13), p. 123.
55. R. B. Y. SCOTT, *Proverbs. Ecclesiastes* (AB, 18), Garden City (NY) 1965, p. 256: «those who master the collected sayings».
56. BACKHAUS, *Der Weisheit letzter Schluß!* (n. 8), p. 32; cf. FOX, *Frame-Narrative and Composition* (n. 11), p. 98; ID., *Qohelet and his Contradictions* (n. 11), p. 324; LOHFINK, *Les épilogues du livre de Qohélet* (n. 3), pp. 86 et 88; DOHMEN, *Der Weisheit letzter Schluß?* (n. 11), pp. 13 et 15-16. Cf. Qo 10,13, à propos du sot: «le début des paroles de sa bouche est folie, et la fin [des paroles] de sa bouche est démence furieuse»; cf. aussi Qo 10,12.

On traduira de la même manière si on suppose que בְּעַל a ici le sens de «élément constitutif de»: les «éléments» des recueils sont les sentences elles-mêmes[57].

Il y a lieu de rappeler ici, pour mémoire, la solution de Podechard, qui faisait de בַּעֲלֵי un apposé de מַשְׂמְרוֹת, ce qui lui permettait de traduire[58]:

> Les paroles des sages sont comme des aiguillons,
> et comme des clous plantés porteurs de provisions.

Cette interprétation, adoptée par É. Osty, a le désavantage de sortir de l'image agricole ou pastorale à laquelle ramène la fin du verset, qui parle d'un berger[59].

L'ambiguïté du verset tient à l'interprétation du mot מַשְׂמֵר (écrit partout ailleurs מַסְמֵר)[60]. Si le mot désigne la partie saillante de l'aiguillon, le parallélisme est alors rigoureusement synonymique[61]. Par contre, si le mot a ici le sens de «piquet», les deux premiers stiques du verset se complètent pour décrire l'un la fonction dynamique des dits de sagesse (qui stimulent, à la manière de l'aiguillon), l'autre leur fonction normative (ils servent de garde-fou, comme les piquets indiquent aux troupeaux les limites à ne pas franchir)[62]. Cette interprétation est celle de N. Lohfink[63] et de la *TOB*, qui traduit:

---

57. Cf. DELITZSCH, *Hoheslied und Koheleth* (n. 45), pp. 417-418; BARTON, *The Book of Ecclesiastes* (n. 36), pp. 197 et 200, qui renvoient à Gn 14,13; Ne 6,18; BRAUN, *Kohelet und die frühhellenistische Popularphilosophie* (n. 42), p. 143 traduit «die Leitsprüche der Sammlungen».

58. PODECHARD, *L'Ecclésiaste* (n. 32), p. 479, qui commente: «les fines sentences piquent l'esprit comme des aiguillons; mais aussi elles se fixent, restent fichées dans la mémoire comme les clous plantés dans les murs, portant avec elles des ressources multiples pour les difficultés éventuelles».

59. Je rappelle, pour mémoire, que A. ALLGEIER, *Das Buch des Predigers oder Koheleth* (Heilige Schrift des Alten Testamentes, VI/2), Bonn, 1925, pp. 53-54 voyait dans בַּעֲלֵי l'état construit pluriel du mot עָלֶה, précédé de la préposition בְּ; d'où sa traduction: «eingetrieben in die Blätter der Sammlung», la collection étant ici celle des Livres Saints.— La traduction «pour le bien des troupeaux» proposée par R. PAUTREL, *Data sunt a pastore uno*, in *RSR* 41 (1953) 406-410 repose sur une correction.

60. Voir F. BAUMGÄRTEL, *Die Ochsenstachel und die Nägel in Koh 12,11*, in *ZAW* 81 (1969) 98.

61. GORDIS, *Kohelet*, p. 343; DOHMEN, *Der Weisheit letzter Schluß?* (n. 11), p. 15; BACKHAUS, *Der Weisheit letzter Schluß!* (n. 8), p. 36; FOX, *Frame-Narrative and Composition* (n. 11), p. 102: «I suggest that the «nails» are identical with the «goads» and are «implanted» either in the sense that they are stuck in the flesh or in the sense that they are fixed in the end of the staff. In either case the *tertium comparationis* of the words of the wise and goads/nails is not that they are immovable nor even so much that they prod one on to better actions, but rather that they both prick and hurt you, that they are somewhat dangerous» (cf. ID., *Qohelet and his Contradictions* (n. 11), pp. 324-325).

62. Dans ce cas, la graphie de מַשְׂמֵר avec שׂ au lieu de ס pourrait avoir pour but de rapprocher le mot de la racine שׁמר. Ce ne serait qu'un jeu orthographique de plus dans un livre qui en compte déjà beaucoup. La première partie de ce même verset joue sur le rapprochement entre דָּבָר et דָּרְבָן. Voir Kl. KOENEN, *Zu den Epilogen des Buches Qohelet*, in *BN* 72 (1994) 24-27.

63. LOHFINK, *Les épilogues du livre de Qohélet* (n. 3), p. 89, n. 27.

Les paroles des sages sont comme des aiguillons,
les auteurs de recueils sont des jalons bien plantés.

La dernière partie du verset se prête elle aussi à plusieurs interprétations. La traduction littérale en est: «ils sont donnés par un (seul) pasteur» (מֵרֹעֶה אֶחָד). Ces quelques mots peuvent être considérés comme une proposition relative ou comme une proposition indépendante, sans que le sens s'en trouve affecté[64]; celui-ci paraît être que, malgré la diversité des formes littéraires, les dits des sages ont même origine. Si le pasteur doit être identifié à YHWH, le verset affirmerait l'origine divine de la littérature de sagesse (et donc, implicitement, du livre de *Qohèlèt*)[65]. Par contre, si l'image du berger renvoie à Salomon, la pointe du verset vise à mettre cette littérature en général (et *Qohèlèt* en particulier) sous le patronage du roi[66]. Enfin, si אֶחָד a ici la valeur d'un article indéfini, le sens pourrait être que n'importe quel berger utilise à la fois l'aiguillon (pour inciter ses brebis au mouvement) et des piquets (pour les empêcher de s'égarer)[67].

Le v. 12 pourrait se traduire littéralement comme suit:

Et en plus de ces choses, mon fils, sois averti:
faire beaucoup de livres n'a pas de fin
et beaucoup d'application studieuse est fatigue de la chair.

La première difficulté est de savoir ce que sont «ces choses» (מֵהֵמָּה) qui sont en excédent[68]. Le pronom démonstratif pourrait avoir une portée tout à fait générale, ce qui amènerait à traduire, avec D. Lys[69]:

En plus de tout cela, mon fils, laisse-toi instruire.

Dans ce cas, les trois derniers versets sont présentés comme une ultime recommandation ajoutée en dernière minute[70]. A. Lauha se risque même à traduire: «Ein zusätzlicher Nachtrag: Mein Sohn, laß dich warnen!»[71].

---

64. Voir la discussion dans SCHOORS, *The Preacher Sought* (n. 5), p. 210.

65. Voir R.E. MURPHY, *Ecclesiastes* (WBC, 23A), Dallas, 1992, p. 125.

66. Voir récemment BACKHAUS, *Der Weisheit letzter Schluß!* (n. 8), p. 36.

67. LOHFINK, *Les épilogues du livre de Qohélet* (n. 3), p. 89; cf. FOX, *Frame-Narrative and Composition* (n. 11), pp. 102-103; ID., *Qohelet and his Contradictions* (n. 11), p. 325.

68. Voir la discussion détaillée dans GINSBURG, *Coheleth* (n. 26), pp. 475-476 et dans LOHFINK, *Zu einigen Satzeröffnungen* (n. 5), pp. 131-139.

69. LYS, *L'Ecclésiaste ou que vaut la vie?* (n. 6), p. 31; cf. GORDIS, *Kohelet* (n. 15), p. 344; BACKHAUS, *Der Weisheit letzter Schluß!* (n. 8), p. 33: «Und mehr als vor diesen, mein Sohn, laß dich warnen».

70. GALLING, *Der Prediger* (n. 13), p. 123: «Nachzutragen ist darüber hinaus: Laß dich warnen, mein Sohn».

71. LAUHA, *Kohelet* (n. 12), p. 221; cf. MICHEL, *Qohelet* (n. 12), p. 168: «Ein Nachtrag darüber hinaus...».

Pour M. Fox, מֵהֵמָּה annonce ce qui suit[72]:

At the same time, my son, of these things be wary: Making...

Mais, pour beaucoup d'interprètes, מֵהֵמָּה renvoie aux «paroles des sages» et aux recueils dont il a été question au v. 11. Le sens est alors[73]:

Et quant à plus de paroles que celles-ci, mon fils, sois averti...

Un empêcheur de tourner en rond demandera en quoi l'étude des paroles des sages ménage davantage le corps que l'étude d'autres livres.
Mais sans doute הִזָּהֵר introduit-il ici un dit traditionnel.

Au v. 13, סוֹף דָּבָר a été diversement traduit: «conclusion» (E.
Podechard, Crampon, É. Osty), «fin du discours» (L. Segond, A. Guillau-
mont, *TOB*), «point final du discours» (D. Lys), «le mot de la fin» (N.
Lohfink), «en fin de compte» (A. Barucq), «trêve de discours» (É.
Glasser) et même «letzter Nachtrag» (H. W. Hertzberg)[74].
Chr. Dohmen rattache סוֹף דָּבָר à ce qui précède[75]:

...mit dem Ergebnis: Man hat alles verstanden.

N. Lohfink va plus loin dans ce sens et considère les deux phrases no-
minales du v. 12b comme deux circonstancielles d'une proposition dont
le v. 13b serait le sujet et סוֹף דָּבָר, le prédicat; הַכֹּל נִשְׁמָע serait une tem-
porelle. D'où une traduction suggestive, qui met en évidence l'articulation du discours (voir p. 268).

נִשְׁמָע doit probablement être considéré comme un participe ou un parfait Nifal: «tout ayant été entendu» ou «tout a été entendu». La traduction de F. J. Backhaus[76]: «Als Schlußwort laßt uns folgendes Beides
hören/beachten: Fürchte Gott...» est plutôt inattendue, même si on ad-
met que l'auteur s'adresse ici, non seulement à son disciple (qu'au v.
précédent il appelle «mon fils»), mais aussi à son lecteur.

Cela dit, comment comprendre le verset? הַכֹּל désigne-t-il l'ensemble
du «discours» de Qohèlèt, auquel cas nous aurions ici la conclusion propre au livre. – Ou bien הַכֹּל renvoie-t-il aux livres dont il est inutile de
multiplier le nombre: qu'on en lise un ou qu'on les lise tous[77], le profit

---

72. Fox, *Qohelet and his Contradictions* (n. 11), pp. 310 et 326; cf. ID., *Frame-Narrative and Composition* (n. 11), p. 98.
73. Podechard, *L'Ecclésiaste* (n. 32), p. 481.
74. Hertzberg, *Der Prediger* (n. 13), p. 216.
75. Dohmen, *Der Weisheit letzter Schluß?* (n. 11), pp. 13 et 16-17.
76. Backhaus, *Der Weisheit letzter Schluß!* (n. 8), p. 33. Voir aussi Galling, *Der
Prediger* (n. 13), p. 123: «Als Schluß das Ganze wollen wir hören»; Lauha, *Kohelet*
(n. 12), p. 221: «Zu guter Letzt laßt uns die Summe hören».
77. Ou qu'on se les fasse lire, ce qui justifie l'emploi du verbe שמע.

est le même; ils enseignent tous la même chose. – Ou bien encore faut-il considérer וְשָׁמַע comme un accompli, indiquant le résultat lui-même: écrire des livres est sans fin, les étudier est épuisant, et tant d'effort aboutit à cette conclusion que tout a déjà été dit et redit, entendu et réentendu[78]. La suite du verset serait alors non pas la conclusion tirée des livres eux-mêmes, mais la conclusion que l'auteur tire de l'inutilité qu'il y a à multiplier les livres et les lectures: puisque tout a déjà été entendu, il ne reste qu'à craindre Dieu et à garder ses commandements; cela suffit, c'est tout l'homme. On retrouverait ici le thème du «rien de nouveau sous le soleil» et une interprétation possible de 1,8[79]:

> *Toutes les paroles sont lassantes; on ne peut dire à quel point.*

— Ou bien encore le v. 13 est-il une conclusion que l'épiloguiste tire *a contrario* des propos sceptiques et désabusés de Qohèlèt? Pour ne pas laisser son lecteur perplexe, l'épiloguiste s'attribuerait le dernier mot pour réaffirmer l'importance de la pratique des commandements[80].

S'il faut «craindre Dieu et garder ses commandements», c'est parce que זֶה כָּל־הָאָדָם. L'hébreu juxtapose un sujet et un substantif, en laissant au lecteur le soin d'établir entre les deux le rapport qui convient[81]. כָּל־הָאָדָם pourrait signifier «l'homme tout entier», «tout l'homme»; pour N. Lohfink, la crainte de Dieu serait le tout de l'homme, en ce sens que «sur l'existence et l'éthos de l'homme on ne peut en dire plus; tout ce qu'on pourrait ajouter revient au même»[82]. Mais, ailleurs dans le livre, כָּל־הָאָדָם a le sens de «tout homme», «tous les hommes». Par exemple en 3,13:

> *Car tout homme qui mange, boit et goûte le bonheur dans tout le mal qu'il se donne, c'est un don de Dieu* (voir aussi 5,18 et 7,2).

---

78. Ainsi GLASSER, *Le procès du bonheur par Qohelet* (n. 30), p. 176: «Trêve de discours, tout a été entendu».

79. Inteprétation de LOADER, *Prediker* (n. 12), p. 24: «Alle woorden zijn vermoeiend; geen mens kan het uitspreken» (cf. aussi p. 26); MURPHY, *Ecclesiastes* (n. 65), p. 8; voir la discussion dans F. ELLERMEIER, *Qohelet. Teil I. Abschnitt 1: Untersuchungen zum Buche Qohelet*, Herzberg am Harz, 1967, pp. 201-208.

80. J. COPPENS, *La structure de l'Ecclésiaste*, in M. GILBERT (ed.), *La sagesse de l'Ancien Testament* (BETL, 51), Gembloux—Leuven, 1979, pp. 288-292 voyait dans *Qohèlèt* «un exercice de réflexion personnelle tendant à montrer les limites d'une pensée simplement humaine et à dévoiler les conclusions paradoxales, voire absurdes auxquelles elle aboutit nécessairement quand elle se prive des lumières de la révélation divine». *Qohèlèt* devenait ainsi «un plaidoyer pour la nécessité de recourir à la Torah pour une règle de vie valable» (pp. 291-292).

81. Voir la discussion détaillée dans la contribution de A. SCHOORS (ci-dessus, p. 18-19).

82. LOHFINK, *Les épilogues du livre de Qohélet* (n. 3), p. 92.

On serait alors autorisé à gloser, comme le font Pautrel (*BJ*) et
l'*Einheitsübersetzung*[83]:

> *C'est là le devoir de tout homme.*
> *Das allein hat jeder Mensch nötig.*

En reprenant la phraséologie de 11,9, le v. 14 apporte une motivation
complémentaire au précepte donné au verset précédent de craindre Dieu
et d'observer ses commandements: c'est le fait du jugement divin. La
syntaxe de la phrase est claire; le seul point qui prête à discussion est de
savoir si c'est du jugement d'outre-tombe qu'il est ici question, ou d'une
rétribution terrestre[84].

Contrairement à ce que le titre de cette contribution permettait peut-
être d'espérer, on n'abordera pas ici l'interprétation d'ensemble de l'épilogue, mais on espère au moins avoir montré que, dans le cas de l'épilogue de *Qohèlet* comme ailleurs, le travail de l'interprète consiste à frayer
un chemin au lecteur parmi un foisonnement de sens possibles et à trancher dans l'interprétation pour bâtir une cohérence.

Ici se pose également la question de la cohérence des derniers versets
du livre avec le reste de l'écrit. Dans quelle mesure le portrait de
Qohèlèt et la description de sa technique de travail (v. 9-10) correspon-
dent-ils à l'idée que le lecteur a pu se faire de l'auteur et de ses métho-
des? Les informations qui sont ici données sont-elles purement anecdo-
tiques ou changent-elles quelque chose à la lecture de l'opuscule? En
s'efforçant de situer l'entreprise de Qohèlèt dans la tradition sapientiale,
les v. 10-11 veulent-ils implicitement prendre la défense d'un livre contesté?

Une solution classique consiste à distinguer les v. 9-11, qui font
l'éloge de l'auteur, des v. 12-14, qui corrigeraient la théologie du livre
en lui donnant une conclusion (סוֹף דָּבָר) entièrement assimilable par la
foi juive traditionnelle[85]. Pour prendre la défense d'un livre contesté et

---

83. Cf. GALLING, *Der Prediger* (n. 13), p. 123 et LAUHA, *Kohelet* (n. 12), p. 221: «das
gilt für jeden Menschen»; A. MAILLOT, *Qohélet ou Ecclésiaste ou la contestation*, 2e éd.,
Paris, 1987, p. 167: «Ça vaut pour tout homme».
84. Voir Th. KRÜGER, *Dekonstruktion und Rekonstruktion prophetischer Eschatologie
im Qohelet-Buch*, in *«Jedes Ding hat seine Zeit...»* (n. 5), pp. 107-129 (p. 127).
85. Sur l'unité littéraire de Qo 12,9-14, voir l'état de la question dans MURPHY,
Ecclesiastes (n. 65), pp. 127-128. Fr. J. BACKHAUS, *«Denn Zeit und Zufall trifft sie alle»*.
Studien zur Komposition und zum Gottesbild im Buch Qohelet (BBB 83), Frankfurt am
Main, 1993, pp. 344-351 a ramassé les arguments qui invitent à dissocier les v. 9-11 des
v. 12-14; ces arguments sont admis par la plupart des interprètes: voir récemment L.
SCHWIENHORST-SCHÖNBERGER, *Kohelet: Stand und Perspektiven der Forschung*, in ID.
(ed.), *Das Buch Kohelet. Studien zur Struktur, Geschichte, Rezeption und Theologie*

lui assurer sa place parmi les écrits de sages, voire son statut d'Écriture, un glossateur l'aurait résumé dans les termes de la piété légaliste[86]. Cette solution fait difficulté, car elle oblige à penser que soit le disciple n'a pas compris le fond de la pensée du maître[87] – ce qui ne ferait honneur ni à l'un ni à l'autre –, soit qu'il était prêt à renier l'originalité même de la pensée de Qohèlèt pour autant que son écrit soit accueilli parmi les livres qui souillent les mains – ce qui est payer fort cher le prix d'une place dans le canon. Un scribe qui pensait, avec le *Siracide*, que la sagesse commence dans la crainte de Dieu et culmine dans la pratique des commandements n'aurait-il pas dû chercher à combattre le livre de *Qohèlèt* pour l'exclure du canon (où sa place était encore controversée à la fin du Ier s. de notre ère) plutôt que de consentir à toutes les concessions pour l'y maintenir?

Une dernière observation: s'il y a lieu, au v. 11, de conserver la *lectio difficilior* כָּתוּב du TM, il faut considérer que l'épiloguiste se présente

(BZAW, 130), Berlin – New York, 1997, pp. 5-38 (pp. 14-15). Il faut toutefois noter que l'interprétation de וְיֹתֵר comme étant l'annonce explicite d'un ajout (avec le sens de «et il faut ajouter que») n'est qu'une interprétation parmi d'autres possibles. Dans *Der Weisheit letzter Schluß!* (n. 8), pp. 30-31, le même BACKHAUS s'est efforcé de montrer que le v. 11 devait être dissocié des deux précédents; les raisons qu'il invoque ne sont pas contraignantes; comme l'écrivait déjà PODECHARD, *L'Ecclésiaste* (n. 32), p. 159: «faire l'éloge des sages (11) après que Qohéleth a été rangé en leur compagnie (9a) et représenté comme se livrant aux mêmes travaux (9b-10), c'est faire encore l'éloge de Qohéleth». HERTZBERG, *Der Prediger* (n. 13), pp. 217-221, reconnaissait lui aussi trois mains différentes dans l'épilogue, mais il leur attribuait respectivement les v. 9-11, 12, 13-14. BARTON, *The Book of Ecclesiastes* (n. 36), pp. 45 et 199, qui interprète סוֹף דָּבָר au sens de «End of discours», pense que le livre se terminait primitivement au v. 13a; les v. 13b-14 seraient une glose pieuse ajoutée par le Ḥasîd; dans le même sens: MAILLOT, *Qohélet* (n. 83), pp. 167-168.

86. Le v. 14 reprend la phraséologie de 11,9, mais avec un déplacement de sens possible: voir MURPHY, *Ecclesiastes* (n. 65), p. 128. Le thème de la «crainte de Dieu» (12, 13) est déjà apparu en 3,14; 5,6; 7,18; 8,12bis. 13. Mais BACKHAUS, *«Denn Zeit und Zufall trifft sie alle»* (n. 85), p. 349 fait remarquer que, dans le corps du livre, la crainte de Dieu est une attitude d'humble résignation devant un dieu inaccessible et lointain, alors que, dans l'épilogue, elle devient une forme de piété légaliste, le fossé qui sépare l'homme de Dieu étant ici comblé par les commandements qui expriment la volonté divine. L'art de l'épiloguiste serait alors de parler comme Qohèlèt, mais pour lui faire dire tout autre chose.

87. GLASSER, *Le procès du bonheur par Qohelet* (n. 30), p. 178: «Dans les v. 11-12, il (= l'épiloguiste) a noyé l'œuvre si originale de Qohelet dans l'ensemble des écrits de sagesse. Ici (= aux v. 13-14), il expose ce qui constitue un leit-motiv de la tradition: la sagesse commence et culmine dans la crainte de Dieu, vue dans sa double dimension religieuse et morale... Qohelet a été édité par un homme qui lui vouait sympathie et respect, mais qui n'a peut-être pas compris le fond de sa pensée, ou en tout cas ne s'y est pas rallié. Nous le soupçonnons d'avoir été un conciliateur à tout prix, effarouché quelque peu par les affrontements et par les mises en question; vaguement troublé, il s'empresse de dire: «De toute façon, nous nous accordons sur l'essentiel: être sage consistera toujours à craindre Dieu; c'est la fin de tout discours, le dernier mot de toute sagesse.» Seule une lecture superficielle de Qohelet permettrait de l'annexer ainsi au courant sapientiel traditionnel!»

explicitement comme l'éditeur du livre et déclare s'être acquitté cons-
ciencieusement de la tâche qu'il s'était fixée, à savoir mettre par écrit
l'enseignement du maître. Dans ce cas, il faut conclure qu'il n'y a jamais
eu de livre de *Qohèlèt* avant que l'épiloguiste ne l'édite: en effet, si le
livre de *Qohèlèt* circulait déjà à l'époque où l'épilogue lui a été ajouté, il
n'y avait plus guère de raisons de préciser que l'écrit était conforme aux
paroles du sage. Contrairement à l'opinion reçue, le livre de *Qohèlèt* n'a
donc jamais circulé sans son épilogue (au moins sans les v. 9-11). En
d'autres termes, nous n'avons accès à la pensée de Qohèlèt qu'à travers
l'œuvre de son éditeur, ou, si l'on préfère, à travers la longue citation qui
en est faite par celui qui a rédigé (la première partie de) l'épilogue.

À la limite, l'épiloguiste pourrait être l'auteur réel de tout le livre et
Qohèlèt, un personnage purement fictif relégué dans un passé mal défini,
un être de plume que l'auteur métamorphoserait à son gré (l'identifiant
tantôt à Salomon, abandonnant ensuite ce travestissement pour dire, fi-
nalement, que «Qohèlèt fut un sage»), un simple «narrateur» à qui
l'auteur ferait endosser la responsabilité d'une pensée audacieuse[88].
L'épilogue jouerait le rôle de dénégation: Qohèlèt confesse que la sagesse est restée hors de sa portée (7, 23), et pourtant l'épilogue déclare
qu'il a été un sage; Qohèlèt affirme qu'on ne peut redresser ce qui a été
courbé (1, 15), et pourtant l'épilogue déclare qu'il s'est employé à «redresser» les proverbes; Qohèlèt proclame l'impossibilité de trouver (8,
17), et pourtant l'épilogue déclare qu'il s'est appliqué à «trouver» des
dits agréables. Ce ne serait pas la seule preuve de l'ironie de l'auteur du
livre de *Qohèlèt*.

Grand-Place, 45   J.-M. AUWERS
B-1348 Louvain-la-Neuve   Chercheur qualifié au F.N.R.S.

---

88. Cf. Fox, *Frame-Narrative and Composition* (n. 11); ID., *Qohelet and his Contradictions* (n. 11), pp. 311-321; J.-M. AUWERS, *La condition humaine entre sens et non-
sens. Le bilan de Qohèlèth*, in A. THÉODORIDÈS, P. NASTER, A. VAN TONGERLOO (eds.),
Humana condicio. La condition humaine (Acta Orientalia Belgica, 6), Bruxelles – Louvain-la-Neuve – Leuven, 1991, pp. 193-211 (pp. 209-210); LAVOIE, *Un éloge à Qohélet*
(n. 6), pp. 169-170.

LE TEXTE GREC DE L'*ECCLÉSIASTE*
ET SES CARACTÉRISTIQUES
UNE RELECTURE CRITIQUE DE L'HISTOIRE DE LA ROYAUTÉ

I. INTRODUCTION

En 1963, Dominique Barthélemy consacrait dix pages à la «Septante de l'Ecclésiaste» dans son ouvrage Les *devanciers d'Aquila*[1]. Il donnait ainsi une impulsion décisive à l'étude des réviseurs de la LXX, et plus particulièrement du groupe désormais appelé *kaige*, d'après l'habitude caractéristique de traduire וגם par καί γε. En accord avec les témoignages de plusieurs auteurs anciens, il attribuait la version grecque de *Qohélet* à Aquila, juif du début du IIème siècle de notre ère. Cette traduction, signée donc, ce qui est déjà remarquable, aurait été intégrée à la Septante, rendant par là même problématique l'identification de la colonne «Aquila» des Hexaples origéniens[2] pour l'*Ecclésiaste*: sur ce dernier point, là où Jérôme (qui pour sa part nous laisse plusieurs versions latines de ce livre biblique[3]) proposait de voir la marque d'une révision par Aquila de sa propre traduction – l'*Ecclésiaste* constituerait son premier travail –, Barthélemy récuse la possiblité d'attribuer à Aquila ces leçons hexaplaires et y voit plutôt la marque de Symmaque. Concernant Aquila, il montre, à partir de quelques traductions-types, comment il «perfectionne l'oeuvre du groupe *kaige*»[4].

Mais c'est d'abord le caractère tardif de cette traduction qu'il faut souligner: au début du IIè siècle de notre ère, sans doute en Palestine, l'*Ecclésiaste* est le dernier livre biblique à être traduit et les textes grecs contemporains sont, il est à peine utile de le rappeler, ceux du Nouveau

---

Abréviations utilisées : *Qo* pour le texte hébraïque et *Eccl* pour le texte grec (sauf indication contraire, les traductions proposées de versets de l'*Ecclésiaste* sont des traductions du texte grec); Aq. = Aquila; Hex. = Hexaples; 1-4 Rg = 1-4 Règnes (LXX); BA = *Bible d'Alexandrie* (traduction française de la LXX, vol.1 à 6, Paris); PGL = G.W.H. Lampe, *A Patristic Greek Lexicon*, Oxford, 1961.

1. D. BARTHÉLEMY, *Les devanciers d'Aquila*, Leiden, 1963 — sur la «Septante» de l'Ecclésiaste et Aquila: pp. 21-33; sur les liens entre Aquila et le groupe *kaige*, pp. 81-88.

2. Voir F. FIELD (ed.), *Origenis Hexaplorum quae supersunt; sive veterum interpretum graecorum in totum vetus testamentum fragmenta*, reimpr., Hildesheim, 1964.

3. Le Professeur Sandro Leanza, éditeur de chaînes patristiques sur l'Ecclésiaste, a étudié ces divers états de la traduction de Jérôme (S. LEANZA, *Le tre versioni geronimiane dell'Ecclesiaste*, in *Annali di Storia dell'Esegesi* 4 (1987) 87-108).

4. BARTHÉLEMY, *Les devanciers d'Aquila* (n. 1), p. 81.

Testament et certains apocryphes; dans la littérature juive, les oeuvres
de Philon et Flavius Josèphe la précèdent et dans la littérature grecque
profane, nous sommes à l'époque de Plutarque, Marc-Aurèle, Galien.

Il est, sur le plan chronologique et historico-théologique, un second
point qu'il importe de mettre en relief: le moment de la traduction de
Qohélet correspond à la date de fixation du canon juif, au moment de
l'assemblée de Jabné. Dans l'article qu'il a consacré en 1984 à l'état de
la Bible juive depuis le début de notre ère jusqu'à la deuxième révolte
contre Rome[5], D. Barthélemy établit un rapport direct entre la décision
de la traduction et la confirmation du maintien du livre dans le groupe
des Ecrits. Il souligne en effet: «...*Qohélet* fut traduit en grec et diffusé
dans la diaspora comme lecture liturgique pour la fête des Tentes, juste
après la décision de l'assemblée de Jabné. C'est ce que suggère le fait
que la 'Septante' de *Qohélet* semble bien être une oeuvre de jeunesse
d'Aquila»[6]. Le point de vue important, ici, est la perspective ouverte par
le fait de traduire un texte problématique, aux affirmations iconoclastes,
mais qui fait désormais partie d'un tout clos et sacré.

Dès l'antiquité, le grec d'Aquila a eu mauvaise réputation: traducteur
servile[7], il pèche par un littéralisme excessif, à force de respecter scrupu-
leusement l'ordre et le nombre des mots de l'hébreu – la traduction de la
particule d'accusatif את par la préposition σύν (suivie de l'accusatif!) en
étant l'exemple le plus évident, qui le relie aux réviseurs du groupe
kaige. Un tel littéralisme aurait pour raison d'être le respect des règles
exégétiques enseignées par Rabbi Aquiba. Mais plus récemment, différents articles[8] ont remis en question ce lien de filiation, dont Barthélemy
avait fait sa thèse. Cet aspect des discussions autour d'Aquila nous
amène au deuxième angle d'approche de la version grecque de l'*Ecclésiaste*: répond-elle à des présupposés théologiques, porte-t-elle la marque du premier rabbinisme? C'est se placer du côté de l'intention du tra-

5. D. BARTHÉLEMY, *L'état de la Bible juive depuis le début de notre ère jusqu'à la
deuxième révolte contre Rome (131-135)* in J.N. KAESTLI — O. WERMELINGER (eds.), *Le
canon de l'Ancien Testament, sa formation et son histoire*, Genève, 1984, pp. 9-45.
6. BARTHÉLEMY, *L'état de la Bible juive* (n. 5), p.29.
7. C'est le terme employé par Origène à propos de Dn 3,24: «.. C'est ainsi que tradui-
sit Aquila, esclave du texte hébraïque littéral — δουλεύων τῇ ἑβραικῇ λέξει, lui qui est
considéré chez les Juifs comme ayant traduit l'Ecriture avec beaucoup de zèle...»
(ORIGÈNE [M. HARL — N. DE LANGE (eds.)], *Philocalie 1-20: Sur les Écritures et la lettre à Africanus sur l'histoire de Suzanne* (SC, 302), Paris, 1983, p. 527).
8. L.L. GRABBE, *Aquila's Translation and Rabbinic Exegesis*, in *JJS* 33 (1982) 527-
536; O. MUNNICH, *Contribution à l'étude de la première révision de la LXX*, in W.
HAASSE (ed.), *Religion. Hellenistisches Judentum in römischer Zeit, ausgenommen Philon
und Josephus* (ANRW II, 20/1), Berlin - New York, 1987, pp. 190-220; L.J. GREENSPOON,
*Recensions, Revisions, Rabbinics. Dominique Barthélemy and Early Developments in the
Greek Traditions*, in *Textus* 15 (1990) 153-167.

ducteur, notion difficilement acceptable, comme on le soulignera plus loin. Mais ce n'est cependant pas une fausse question, une question inexistante: l'enjeu est bien en effet la constitution d'Ecritures juives en grec qui seraient distinctes de la *Septante*, Bible grecque de l'Eglise naissante. On sait en effet que l'empereur Justinien autorisa (*Novella* 146) l'utilisation liturgique de la «Bible d'Aquila»[9] par la diaspora juive hellénisée, et les témoignages médiévaux, tels les documents de la Genizah du Caire publiés par Nicholas de Lange[10], montrent l'importance de cette version et sa diffusion.

Avant d'aborder l'examen de quelques aspects de la version grecque de l'*Ecclésiaste*, un bref détour herméneutique n'est pas inutile et trois articles récents pourront nous en fournir le moyen. Lors du colloque de l'*IOSCS* de 1989, le professeur Aejmelaeus[11], aujourd'hui responsable de l'entreprise d'édition critique de la Septante à l'université de Göttingen, abordait, en se référant à l'étude de James Barr sur la «typologie du littéralisme»[12], la question de l'opposition entre ce qui serait technique de traduction et ce qui relèverait d'une véritable «intention du traducteur»; elle dit son accord avec l'idée que le littéralisme est davantage, selon l'expression de J. Barr, «une technique facile» c'est-à-dire la recherche d'équivalents en quelque sorte obvies et donc pouvant donner lieu à un usage systématique – qu'une volonté de littéralisme puis elle ajoute: «It was only later, in the times of the recensions and of Aquila, that literalism became a conscious method of translation, which was believed to produce good and accurate translation» (p. 68).

De leur côté, S. Brock, dans des réflexions sur les règles de traduction mises en oeuvre dans la LXX, et Lester Grabbe[13] à propos des versions grecques postérieures à la LXX, c'est-à-dire Aquila, Symmaque et

---

9. A. PAUL, *La Bible grecque d'Aquila et l'idéologie du judaïsme ancien*, in W. HAASSE (ed.), *Religion* (n. 8), pp. 221-245. — JUSTINIEN, *Novellae, Corpus Juris Civilis* III/2.

10. N. DE LANGE, *Greek Jewish Texts from the Cairo Genizah*, Tübingen, 1996, en particulier chap. 9: *A Greek Translation of Kohelet (Ecclesiastes)*, pp. 71-78.

11. A. AEJMELAEUS, *Translation Technique and the Intention of the Translator*, in C.E. COX (ed.), *VIIth Congress of the IOSCS Leuven 1989* (SBL SCS, 31), Atlanta (GA), 1991, pp. 23-36; repris in Id., *On the Trail of the LXX Translators. Collected Essays*, Kampen, 1993, pp. 65-76.

12. J. BARR, *The Typology of Literalism in Ancient Biblical Translations*, Göttingen, 1979.

13. Voir: S. BROCK, *To Revise or Not to Revise. Attitudes to Jewish Biblical Translation*, in G. BROOKE – B. LINDARS (eds.), *Septuagint, Scrolls and Cognate Writings. Papers Presented to the International Symposium on the Septuagint and its Relation to the Dead Sea Scrolls and Other Writings (Manchester, 1990)* (SBL SCS, 33), Atlanta, 1992, pp. 301-338; L. GRABBE, *The Translation Technique of the Greek Minor Versions. Translations or Revisions?*, in G. BROOKE – B. LINDARS (eds.), *op.cit.*, pp. 505-556.

Théodotion, soulignaient que, pour le dire simplement, l'intention propre du traducteur était – et reste encore aujourd'hui! –, comme par définition, de bien traduire; et qu'ainsi les révisions (plutôt peut-être que retraductions) de la LXX visaient d'abord une amélioration, c'est-à-dire une plus grande proximité, un plus grand respect de l'original, une plus grande homogénéité aussi par rapport à une traduction entreprise plusieurs siècles auparavant, et faite en plusieurs lieux, c'est-à-dire dans des aires culturelles différentes.

Ces deux dernières séries de remarques vont nous fournir un cadre de présentation à la version grecque de l'*Ecclésiaste*. Plutôt que de nous heurter à la question, insoluble sans doute, de l'intention d'Aquila, le traducteur, on se placera du point de vue de la réception du texte, d'un texte partie de l'ensemble LXX (en tenant compte également des leçons hexaplaires attribuées à Aquila pour les autres livres bibliques): une enquête de type lexical nous amènera d'abord à caractériser le travail du traducteur comme un travail unifiant, uniformisant par rapport au TM.

Mais cette uniformisation produit des effets qui ne peuvent être que des effets de sens; elle est elle-même interprétative, et c'est là que l'*Ecclésiaste* grec, plus que l'hébreu, nous invite par ses choix sémantiques à une relecture de l'histoire de la royauté en Israël – c'est du moins ce qu'on essaiera de voir dans un second temps.

II. Enquête lexicale

Précisons d'emblée qu'elle ne vise pas à l'exhaustivité que permet une méthode statistique mais la classification qui va être proposée vise à une description du mode de traduction – la question sous-jacente reste donc: qu'en est-il, du point de vue du lexique, du littéralisme imputé à Aquila ?

Concordances et dictionnaires des deux langues, l'hébreu et le grec, sont bien sûr à la base de cette étude, et deux instruments de travail plus spécifiques sont à signaler, en partie pour une mise en garde. Reider et Turner[14] ont publié en 1973 un *Index to Aquila* sur la base de la concordance de la LXX publiée par Hatch et Redpath en 1897[15] et de textes et fragments publiés postérieurement[16]. Tov[17] a signalé les imperfections

---

14. J. REIDER – N. TURNER, *An Index to Aquila* (SVT, 12), Leiden, 1966.
15. E. HATCH – H.A. REDPATH, *A Concordance to the Septuagint and the Other Greek Versions of the Old Testament*, 2 vols., Oxford, 1897.
16. Ce sont essentiellement des fragments des livres des *Règnes* publiés par F. BURKITT (ed.), *Fragments of the Books of Kings According to the Translation of Aquila ...*, Cambridge, 1897 puis par C. TAYLOR (ed.), *Hebrew-Greek Cairo Genizah Palimpsests*

d'un tel lexique. Mais concernant notre *Ecclésiaste*, il faut ajouter un inconvénient majeur pour notre analyse: le texte LXX de l'*Ecclésiaste* n'est pas pris en compte comme étant d'Aquila; le vocabulaire de l'*Ecclésiaste* retenu par Reider-Turner est donc, pour Aquila, uniquement celui de la colonne hexaplaire mise sous ce nom (notre hypothèse de départ est autre, et cela a limité le recours à cet *Index*). J. Jarick[18], de son côté, a publié en 1989 une concordance des textes hébreu et grec de l'*Ecclésiaste*, avec le souci principal de montrer, statistiques à l'appui, l'étroite équivalence de termes d'un texte à l'autre, la très large majorité de ce qu'on a pu appeler des équivalents standards, donc l'existence d'une conception en quelque sorte univoque de la traduction. Et en cela la traduction de l'*Ecclésiaste*, notons-le au passage, est aux antipodes de celle des *Proverbes* ou du *Siracide*. Ces équivalents standards eux-mêmes demanderaient d'ailleurs réflexion, en particulier dans le cas des formes verbales et de leur variation quand on passe d'une langue à l'autre; l'étude de B. Isaksson[19] sur le système verbal dans Qo fournit dans ce domaine des analyses rigoureuses pour l'hébreu.

On peut signaler enfin, parmi les travaux récents de lexicographie de la LXX, l'index du *Dodékaprophéton* publié par T. Muraoka[20] et les deux volumes publiés par J. Lust, E. Eynikel et K. Hauspie[21].

Pour présenter les résultats de notre enquête lexicale, les mots analysés ont été classés en trois groupes. Mais d'abord, quels mots ont été retenus? Dans le vocabulaire largement répétitif du livre, à l'évidence, la littéralité de la traduction met pleinement en oeuvre pour les mots les plus fréquents le jeu des «équivalents standards» pour le passage de l'hébreu au grec; laissant de côté cet ensemble de termes, on a constitué la liste des «mots rares» – rares, voire uniques dans ce livre, mais surtout dans la LXX elle-même. Cette catégorie, «mots rares», peut paraî-

from the TAYLOR-SCHECHTER *Collection*, Cambridge, 1900; mais en appendice de HATCH—REDPATH figure également la concordance établie pour le Siracide après la découverte de l'original hébreu (E. HATCH – H. REDPATH, *A Concordance to the Septuagint. Supplement*, Graz, 1954, pp. 163-196.)

17. E. TOV, *Some Corrections to Reider-Turner's Index to Aquila, in Textus* 8 (1973) 164-174.

18. J. JARICK (ed.), *A Comprehensive Bilingual Concordance of the Hebrew and Greek Texts of Ecclesiastes* (SBL SCS, 36), Atlanta (GA), 1993.

19. B. ISAKSSON, *Studies in the Language of Qoheleth, with a Special Emphasis on the Verbal System*, Uppsala, 1987, spéc. chap. 6 : *Investigations of some current verbs in Qoheleth.*

20. T. MURAOKA, *A Greek-English Lexicon of the Septuagint. (Twelve Prophets)*, Leuven, 1993.

21. J. LUST – E. EYNIKEL – K. HAUSPIE, *A Greek-English Lexicon of the Septuagint*, 2 vols., Stuttgart, 1992, 1996.

tre bien floue, mais la notion d'*hapax legomenon* est quant à elle problématique (les études de Greenspahn et Muraoka[22], entre autres abordent
la complexité de sens du phénomène pour l'hébreu et le grec). Avec la
définition d'hapax pour une langue et un texte donnés, on présuppose
connu tout le système lexical d'une langue; pour plusieurs des termes
présentés ci-dessous, le statut d'hapax passe par exemple par un changement de catégorie grammaticale entre le terme hébreu et son correspondant grec. Par ailleurs, certains hapax, dont la rareté n'est que le résultat
de la rareté de l'objet qu'ils désignent, sont, de fait, moins probants que
des mots ayant un petit nombre d'occurrences (cinq au plus, selon la limite choisie) — c'est le cas par ex. pour κάππαρις, le caprier, en Eccl
12,5.

Pour chaque mot, l'analyse est présentée sous trois rubriques: les occurrences du mot, une caractérisation du type de traduction, les attestations du mot dans la langue grecque. Malgré les différences d'une catégorie à l'autre, qu'on commentera, cet ensemble de 37 termes permet de
mettre en évidence l'effet d'uniformisation produit par les choix
d'Aquila[23], et la grécité de son lexique — à l'inverse des rudesses de sa
syntaxe, et le contraste n'est pas sans poser de questions quant à
l'«auteur» et/ou à l'histoire textuelle de la traduction de l'*Ecclésiaste*.
Les trois catégories utilisées sont :

1. Cas où, à un mot rare du TM correspond un mot rare dans le grec —
   mais l'attestation du terme grec dans la langue profane ou du NT
   montre que la traduction atténuée, sinon supprime, l'étrangeté d'un tel
   terme (mais il est vrai que, du côté de l'hébreu, des rapprochements
   ont pu être faits avec les autres langues sémitiques, les sources
   cananéenes du langage de *Qohélet* par exemple, qui relativisent également la notion d'*hapax*).
2. Cas où, à un mot rare de *Qohélet* correspond un mot bien attesté dans
   la LXX et la langue grecque. L'effet d'uniformisation joue pleinement dans ce cas. Mais le principe de littéralité de la traduction limite
   le nombre de mots entrant dans ce groupe.
3. Cas où, à un mot sans surprise de *Qohélet*, bien attesté dans les autres
   livres, correspond au contraire un mot rare dans le grec — mais là en-

---

22. F.E. GREENSPAHN, *Hapax Legomena in Biblical Hebrew. A Study of the
Phenomenon and its Treatment since Antiquity with Special Reference to Verbal Forms*,
Chico, 1984; T. MURAOKA, *Hebrew Hapax Legomena and LXX Lexicography*, in C.E.
COX (ed.), *VIIth Congress of the IOSCS Leuven 1989* (SBL SCS, 31), Atlanta, 1991,
pp. 205-222.
23. Le terme hébreu est présenté entre parenthèses lorsque la correspondance entre
hébreu et grec fait difficulté et suggère une divergence textuelle, une confusion de lettre,
une corruption des mss., etc.

core la comparaison avec l'intertexte[24] (des textes littéraires aux recueils d'inscriptions et aux données papyrologiques) atténue cela et
on pourrait dire que cela «date» en quelque sorte la traduction, même
si l'étiquette de «néologisme» reste aléatoire. Le parallèle avec le
lexique du NT est là encore significatif.

On s'arrêtera seulement à l'étude de quelques cas pour chacun des
trois groupes de termes.

1. *Groupe 1: TM: mot rare ⇒ «LXX»: mot rare*

    Qo TM   *Eccl. «LXX»*

(1) פתגם   ἀντίρρησις
- Eccl 8,11 / TM: une seule autre occ.: Est 1,20
- terme de rhétorique bien attesté; 1 occ. chez Philon, *De aeternitate mundi*, 132

(2) דרבן   βούκεντρον
- Eccl 12,11 / TM: une seule autre occ.: 1 S 13,21. Vulgate: «stimuli»
- mot composé: voir en parallèle κέντρον ὄνῳ (Pr 26,3)
- attestation: un emploi signalé chez Grégoire de Nazianze; mais le nom simple κέντρον appartient à la langue classique.

(3) קֹהֶלֶת   ἐκκλησιαστής
- mot propre à Eccl / Qo
- trad. étymologique (קהל)
- attestation: langue classique (membre de l'assemblée); Philon, *De specialibus legibus* I,55: liste des fonctions du peuple dans l'exercice de la justice et du châtiment des impies.

(4) נֵפֶל   ἔκτρωμα
- Eccl 6,3 et Nb 12,12; Jb 3,16 (+ Hex.Aq. Ps 57,8) / TM נפל
- harmonisation: Aq. traduit par ἔκτρωμα les 3 occ. de נפל.
- attestation: Aristote ; NT : 1 C 15,8

(5) תקן   ἐπικοσμεῖν
- Eccl 1,15. Le ms A donne le verbe simple κοσμεῖν, employé en 7, 14. Voir aussi l'emploi de κόσμιον (9) en 12,9
- attestation : langue classique; Philon

(6) תקף   ἐπικραταιοῦν
- hapax Eccl 4,12 / TM: 2 autres occ.: Jb 14,20 et 15,24. Symm.: ὑπερισχύσῃ
- traduction par différenciation de κρατεῖν (Eccl 2,3 / TM: אחז)
- pas d'autre attestation; mais κραταιοῦν courant, y compris dans la

---

24. Sur l'intertextualité dans la LXX, voir G. DORIVAL, *Les phénomènes d'inter-textualité dans le livre grec des Nombres*, in G. DORIVAL – O. MUNNICH (eds.), «*Selon les Septante*». FS M. HARL, Paris, 1995, pp. 253-286. Mais la notion d'intertexte est prise ici dans un sens beaucoup plus large, celui des textes grecs connus. Cf. C. SPICQ, *Notes de lexicographie néo-testamentaire* (OBO, 22), 3 vols., Göttingen, 1978, p. 442.

LXX; plusieurs occ. du substantif ἐπικράτεια (class. de même qu'
ἐπικρατεῖν) en 4 M.

(7) אֲבִיּוֹנָה   κάππαρις
 - hapax Eccl 12,5 (Hex. Aq. = id.)
 - attesté chez Aristote, Théophraste

(8) יְגֵעָה   κόπωσις
 - hapax Eccl 12,12
 - trad.étymologique (יגע = κοποῦν en 10,15) et grammaticale (suffixe fé-
 minin) - pas d'autre attestation; mais κόπος et κοπιᾶν fréquents dans
 LXX et NT.

(9) תקן   κόσμιον
 - hapax Eccl 12,9
 - traduction: changement de catégorie grammaticale
 - attestation: substantif chez Plutarque. (diminutif de κόσμος); κόσμιος
 adj., désignant une des qualités du sage.

(10) (שִׁדָּה)   οἰνοχόη
 - hapax Eccl 2,8 mais bien attesté en grec
 - changement de sens? «coupes de vin» (Hex. Aq. = κυλίκια, «petites
 coupes»)
 - attestation: terme classique

(11) יִתְרוֹן   περισσεία
 - mot propre à l'Eccl., 11 occ.(Hex. Aq.:Lv 8,25)
 - trad. étymologique (יותר = περισσός)
 - attestation: LXX; NT : 4 occ.; Pères (PGL)

(12) הוֹלֵלוֹת   περιφέρεια
 - Eccl 9,3; 10,13 (Hex. Aq. et Symm.: Ps 90,4)
 - trad. étymologique (הלל = περιφέρειν 7,7)
 - attestation: à côté du sens class. de circonférence, le sens d'«égarement»
 est donné comme propre à la LXX; mais cf NT, Ep 4,14 «égarés à tout
 vent de doctrine».

(13) כשר   στοιχεῖν
 - Eccl 11,6 / TM : 2 autres occ. Qo 10,10 et Est 8,5
 - attestation : Xénophon, Polybe; NT : 4 occ.

Ce groupe comprend 13 termes, et on s'arrêtera à 4 d'entre eux.

Le mot κάππαρις (7) nous fournit d'abord le cas de ces «hapax
legomena» justifiés par la rareté de l'objet qu'ils désignent, en l'occurrence la câpre ou le câprier. Mais l'attestation du mot dans la langue savante d'Aristote ou de Théophraste atténue l'étrangeté.

Avec κόπωσις (8), employé dans l'expression κόπωσις σαρκός, «la
fatigue de la chair», et περισσεία (11), mot propre à l'Eccl, on voit
comment des traductions de type étymologique constituent dans le texte
même et dans l'ensemble de la collection biblique des familles de mots
et donc des réseaux de sens, qui font perdre son étrangeté au terme à

occurrence unique. A κόπωσις en effet il faut ajouter deux termes présentés dans le groupe 3, l'adjectif ἔγκοπος (22), «fatigant» et le verbe κοποῦν (27). Le terme περισσεία (11) quant à lui est dérivé de l'adjectif περισσός, employé 5 fois dans l'*Ecclésiaste* et déjà attesté dans le Pentateuque (Ex 10,5 et Nb 4,26). L'analyse étymologique conduit à une traduction qui fait appel au procédé de dérivation et par là, c'est à la fois l'histoire de la langue qui s'écrit — et les emplois de περισσεία sont attestés bien au-delà du IIème s. — et l'unité du texte biblique qui se fortifie.

L'emploi de οἰνοχόη (10) en Eccl 2,8 nous montre une traduction créatrice d'un sens original, divergeant en tout cas de l'hébreu. Cependant le sens de l'expression שִׁדָּה וְשִׁדּוֹת est discuté[25], comme l'atteste la diversité des traductions proposées (à titre d'exemple: *TOB*: «un échanson et des sommelières»; *BJ*: «coffret par coffret»; Guillaumont (*Pléiade*): «une dame, des dames»). Pour le grec, la traduction des trois derniers stiques du v.8 pourrait être: «Je me suis procuré chanteurs et chanteuses / et les délices des fils de l'homme, / pour le vin un échanson et des coupes». Le parallélisme des termes (ᾄδοντας καὶ ᾀδούσας et au dernier stique οἰνοχόον καὶ οἰνοχόας) apparaît comme une sorte de trompe-l'oeil. Le mot οἰνοχόη en effet est un terme tout à fait classique, désignant non pas une personne (la sommelière, l'échansonne), mais un type de vase à boire, en forme de coupe, bien connu des archéologues. La leçon hexaplaire attribuée à Aquila, κυλίκιον καὶ κυλίκια désigne aussi, à l'aide du diminutif, des petites coupes.

Le dernier mot du groupe, στοιχεῖν (13) appelle un bref commentaire: là où Qo utilise deux mots de même famille כָּשֵׁר et כִּשְׁרוֹן, le grec a deux mots différents, le verbe στοιχεῖν, «rendre, réussir», et le substantif ἀνδρεία (Eccl 2,21; 4,4; 5,10), «courage», pour כשרון. Si cela constitue une entorse à la traduction selon l'étymologie, l'introduction de la notion de courage, une des vertus du sage, est particulièrement intéressante dans le contexte hellénistique.

2. *Groupe 2: TM: mot rare ⟹«LXX»: mot bien attesté*

Qo TM	Eccl. «LXX»
(14) גּוּמָץ	βόθρος

  – Eccl 10,8: hapax TM / grec fréquent
  – effet de citation en grec: cf. Pr 26,27 et Ps 7,15
  – attestation: classique; Philon

---

25. Outre les discussions sur cette expression présentes dans les commentaires suivis de *Qohélet*, voir E. BONS, Šiddā wᵉ-šiddôt: *Überlegungen zum Verständnis eines Hapaxlegomenon*, in *BN* 36 (1987) 12-16.

(15) כְּבָר   ἤδη
   – terme hébreu propre à Qo (8 occ.)
   – attestation: terme classique

(16) מַשְׂמְרוֹת   ἧλος
   – Eccl 12, 11: hapax TM/ 8 emplois LXX
   – attestation: terme class.; NT: Jn 20,25

(17) תַּקִּיף   ἰσχυρός
   – Eccl 6,10: hapax TM / LXX: mot courant
   – trad. étymologique (תקף = ἰσχύειν); Hex. Aq.: multiples emplois, pour
     des termes hébreux très divers (trad. uniformisante?)
   – attestation: terme classique

(18) פֵּשֶׁר   λύσις
   – Eccl 8,1 / hapax TM
   – 3 occ. LXX (Eccl; Sg 8,8; DnLXX 12,8)
   – attestation: terme classique (rhétorique); NT: 1 Co 7, 27 au sens de «sé-
     paration, divorce»

Il n'est guère étonnant que ce groupe soit, avec 5 termes, le moins représenté puisque, mis à part le mot ἰσχυρός (17) qui répond à une traduction de type étymologique, le choix de termes courants pour traduire
des mots rares rompt avec le principe de littéralité de la traduction. Définir le mode de traduction est ici plus difficile, à moins de parler de traduction contextuelle ou *ad sensum*. C'est le cas, sans doute, pour ἤδη
(15), mot évidemment banal, pour traduire un terme propre à Qo: la
proximité d'un verbe au passé justifie dans les différentes occurrences le
choix de l'adverbe grec.

Avec βόθρος (14), qui traduit en Eccl 10,8 un hapax de l'hébreu,
גומץ, n'est-ce pas l'effet de citation qui est privilégié, recherché? L'expression peut se traduire: «celui qui creuse une fosse y tombera».
βόθρος est un terme courant, et l'expression ὀρύσσειν βόθρον est elle
aussi récurrente; mais le substantif grec correspond à des termes hébreux divers et le choix du mot en Eccl 10,8 souligne le parallèle avec
les propositions identiques de Pr 26,27 («celui qui creuse un trou – TM
שַׁחַת – pour son voisin y tombera») et du Ps 7,16 («il a creusé une ci-
terne ... et il tombera dans le trou – TM שַׁחַת – qu'il a préparé»). Ici encore l'uniformisation du texte biblique est à l'oeuvre.

3. *Groupe 3: TM: mot bien attesté ⇒ «LXX»: mot rare*

Qo TM   *Eccl. «LXX»*
(19) גֻּלָּה   ἀνθέμιον
   – hapax Eccl 12,6 / TM: 9 occ. (traduit par στρεπτός en 3 Rg 7,41-42 et
     translittéré en 2 Ch 4,12-13)

- intertextualité: en Ex 38,16, la tradition ms. hésite entre ἀνθέμιον et ἐνθέμιον pour désigner un des éléments du chandelier (cf *BA* 2, *ad loc.*)
- attestation: classique, au sens d'ornement floral (Xénophon, pap.)

(20) עצב   διαπονεῖσθαι
- Eccl 10,9; seule autre attestation LXX: 2 M 2,28; Hex. Aq.: 4 occ. (dont Eccl 10,9) / TM: nombreux emplois
- traduction uniformisante (Aq.: même verbe en Gn 6,7; 34,7; 1 Rg 20,3.34)
- attestation : Philon; NT : Ac 4,2; 16,18

(21) גבר   δυναμοῦν
- Eccl 10,10 (TM: seul autre emploi au piel en Za 10,6.12). Hex. Aq.: 4 occ. pour d'autres formes de גבר.
- attestation: LXX, NT et Pères (cf *PGL* s.v.)

(22) יגע   ἔγκοπος
- Eccl 1,8 (et Jb 19,2; Is 43,23)
- trad. étymologique (cf κοποῦν)
- pas d'autre attestation connue; néologisme?

(23) שלש   ἔντριτος
- Eccl 4,12 – cf emploi de τρισσεύειν en 1 Rg 20,20 (TM שלש; Hex. Aq. id.)
- trad. étymologique; changement de catégorie grammaticale (TM part. pual).
- seule attestation connue.

(24) תַּעֲנוּג   ἐντρύφημα
- Eccl 2,8: hapax LXX / TM bien attesté
- trad. grammaticale: préfixe + nom; le mot simple τρυφή est donné par plusieurs mss. et par Hex. Aq.
- une attestation chez Philon, *De somniis* II,242 (commentaire du nom Eden en Gen 2,8)

(25) (לְבַעַל הַלָּשׁוֹן)   ἐπᾴδειν
- Eccl 10,11 (+3 occ.LXX); Hex. Aq. Ps 57,6
- traduction *ad sensum*
- attestation: class. au sens de «charmer par des incantations» (Platon, Tragiques)

(26) מַתָּנָה   εὐτονία
- Eccl 7,7 (Hex. Aq. et Théodotion ibid.)
- changement de sens?
- attestation: vocabulaire philosophique et médical.

(27) יגע   κοποῦν
- Eccl 10,15 (et Jg 13,1); doublet de κοπιᾶν (Eccl 2, 18 ms.B); Hex.Aq. pour Eccl 1,3 (κοπῷ κοπιᾶν).
- attestation: Plutarque; Fl. Josèphe

(28) יקש   παγιδεύειν
- Eccl 9,12d (et 1 Rg 28,9)
- jeu étymologique absent du TM: en 12c, emploi de παγίς (TM פַּח), face aux 2 occ. de θηρεύειν au participe (TM אחז)
- attestation: LXX, *TJos*, NT: Mt 22,15

(29) חבק   περίληψις
  – hapax Eccl 3,5 / TM forme piel
  – traduction étymologique (περιλαμβάνειν/חבק dans le même verset)
  – attesté au sens de «compréhension»; ici au sens propre: action d'entou-
    rer (cf Ct 2,6)

(30) סְגֻלָּה   περιουσιασμός
  – Eccl 2,8 et Ps 134,4 / TM: terme bien attesté, traduit dans le Pentateuque
    (5 occ.) par l'adjectif περιούσιος
  – traduction étymologique
  – pas d'autre attestation connue

(31) מָלֵא   πληροφορεῖσθαι
  – hapax Eccl 8,11. מלא habituellement traduit par πληροῦν dans l'Eccl (4
    occ.; de même pour Hex. Aq.)
  – attestation: NT: 6 occ.; Pères (voir PGL, s.v.)

(32) (יָבִיעַ)   σκευασία
  – hapax Eccl 10,1 / TM problématique
  – traduction par approximation
  – attesté dans la langue classique

(33) חסר   στερίσκω
  – hapax Eccl 4,8 / TM seul autre emploi au piel en Ps 8,6
  – le même mot est traduit par ὑστερεῖν en 6,2; 9,8; 10,3 (+ emploi du
    subst. ὑστέρημα en 1,15)
  – attesté dans la langue classique

(34) לוה   συμπροσεῖναι
  – Eccl 8,15 (et Ps 93,20). Hex.Aq.: συνεισέρχεται
  – attestation papyrologique (IIIe s. av.J.C.)

(35) מַדָּע   συνείδησις
  – Eccl 10,20 (2 autres occ. Sg 17,11; Si 42,18)
  – langue philosophique; NT; Spicq (s.v.) signale la première attestation
    papyrologique (datée de 59 ap. J.C.)

(36) רצץ   συνθλίβειν, συντροχάζειν
  – Eccl 12,6 (mss AS συνθλίβειν / ms B συντρίβειν)
  – 2 hapax LXX pour traduire le même verbe dans le même verset: jeu éty-
    mologique différent du TM (en grec τροχὸς συντροχάζειν)
  – attestation: langue hellénistique; NT Mc 5,24 pour συνθλίβειν.

(37) לַחַשׁ   ψιθυρισμός
  – Eccl 10,11. Hex.Aq. Is 3,3
  – trad. étymologique (2 occ. du verbe ψιθυρίζειν = לחשׁ)
  – attestation: Plutarque, Lucien; NT: 2 Co 12, 20

Ce groupe est le plus nombreux, avec 20 termes, et on peut noter
d'abord l'abondance de termes qui semblent constituer des néologismes
et donc attester une date tardive de la traduction. Le procédé de composition, avec les préverbes prépositionnels par exemple, voire de surcompo-
sition (ex. συμπροσεῖναι (34) en 8,15) est à l'oeuvre.

Le mot περίληψις (29) relève de la traduction étymologique, le verbe correspondant περιλαμβάνειν apparaissant au début du verset, mais alors que dans la langue classique, le mot est surtout attesté au sens abstrait de «compréhension», son emploi en Eccl 3,5 marque un retour au sens propre, au sens étymologique: le fait d'entourer. La signification affective de l'expression («moment pour embrasser et moment pour s'abstenir d'embrassement») fait écho à l'emploi du verbe περιλαμβάνειν en Ct 2,6 (mais voir aussi Laban embrassant Jacob en Gn 29,13; Jacob embrassant les fils de Joseph en Gn 48,10).

Il faut enfin souligner la présence dans notre texte du mot συνείδησις (35), appartenant au vocabulaire philosophique hellénistique (l'expression σύνοιδά μοι, «j'ai conscience», est déjà classique); les attestations papyrologiques, en particulier du début du premier siècle de notre ère, signalées par Spicq, sont un indice que le mot est entré dans la langue commune. Il est remarquable que la notion de «conscience morale», par ce terme, figure conjointement dans l'*Ecclésiaste*, le livre de la *Sagesse* et le *Siracide*[26].

Deux mots de ce groupe nous confrontent encore au manque d'édition critique : l'hapax ἐντρύφημα (24) en 2,8 est concurrencé dans plusieurs manuscrits par le mot simple τρυφή; et dans le cas d'ἀνθέμιον (19), on peut se demander si on retrouverait selon les mss la même divergence qu'en Ex 38,16 (= TM Ex 37,17) où les deux termes ἀνθέμιον, décor floral, et ἐνθέμιον, bobèche, sont employés selon les manuscrits dans la description du chandelier. La même divergence en Eccl ne signalerait-elle pas un rapprochement entre les deux textes?

4. *Quelques conclusions pour ces remarques lexicales*

Le lexique grec de l'*Ecclésiaste* ne peut nous surprendre – à la différence de celui des *Proverbes* ou de *Job*. De trois points de vue:

– on a pu constater l'uniformisation produite par rapport aux autres livres. La référence aux données hexaplaires sous le nom d'Aquila dans les autres livres confirme cela.
– le travail d'uniformisation passe très souvent par une traduction de type étymologique. Littéralité plutôt que littéralisme, pourrait-on dire pour éviter toute connotation négative. — Plusieurs exemples manifestent d'ailleurs une traduction *ad sensum* (οἰνοχόη, σκευασία).

---

26. Sur l'emploi et la signification du terme en Sg 17 voir L. MAZZINGHI, *Notte di paura e di luce. Esegesi di Sp 17,1 - 18,4* (AnBib, 134), Rome, 1995, pp. 79-89 (je remercie le Père M. Gilbert de m'avoir signalé cette étude).

– l'élargissement de l'intertexte aux données des dictionnaires pour
l'ensemble de la littérature grecque montre enfin combien le lexique
d'Aquila est homogène à celle-ci. Grécité du lexique, donc, à côté des
rudesses syntaxiques: le mélange est étrange!

La partie thématique qu'on va aborder n'est pas sans lien avec les remarques lexicales qui précèdent. En effet, comme on le signalait dans l'introduction, l'homogénéité du lexique d'Aquila, l'uniformisation induisent une
interprétation par le seul fait des rapprochements qu'elles rendent possibles.

III. L'ECCLÉSIASTE GREC COMME INVITATION
À UNE RELECTURE CRITIQUE DE L'HISTOIRE DE LA ROYAUTÉ

Le jeu des rapports des livres sapientiaux entre eux et de chaque livre
sapiential aux autres livres, et à la Torah en priorité, est complexe et
passe par allusions et citations. Les commentateurs modernes de Qohélet
mais déjà les Pères signalent le phénomène, et le texte grec reproduit fidèlement ces allusions et citations; ainsi pour les références au livre de
la *Genèse* (Eccl 3,20 — «tout est né de la poussière et tout retourne à la
poussière» — évoquant Gn 2,7) ou à l'un des préceptes du *Lévitique*
(Eccl 5,3-4 — «voues-tu un voeu à Dieu, ne tarde pas à t'en acquit-
ter»— évoquant Lv 27,2). — Signalons cependant une correspondance
autrement troublante en Eccl 2,15ef: «...(e) alors moi, j'ai parlé à l'excès dans mon coeur, (f) parce qu'un insensé parle à l'excès». Les stiques
e et f se redoublent et si le stique f est un «+» généralement présenté
comme un proverbe, il est notable qu'il a des parallèles dans le NT (Mt
12,34 et Lc 6,43) ainsi que dans le *Logion* 45 de l'Evangile de Thomas.
On peut s'interroger sur l'origine et le rôle d'un tel doublet.
  Mais c'est au lien avec l'histoire de la royauté en Israël qu'on voudrait s'intéresser ici, parce que le contexte historico-théologique de la
traduction grecque, le contexte de formation du canon, rappelé dans l'introduction, y invitent. Tel a été l'axe de réflexion de cette seconde partie: si *Qohélet*, même déjà lu à Qûmran comme l'attestent les fragments
trouvés dans une des grottes, a dû à la pseudépigraphie salomonienne
d'être confirmé dans le corpus des Ecrits, la version grecque ne vient-
elle pas confirmer ce lien avec l'histoire de la royauté? La traduction
produirait ici deux effets convergents: 1. l'uniformisation multiplie les
phénomènes d'intertextualité; 2. et par là même, le texte se charge d'une
autre signification, ou du moins de références plus explicites, alors
même que les noms propres, de personnes et de lieux, inscrits dans le
récit historique, sont absents du texte sapientiel.

Le thème royal est introduit dès le premier verset: «Paroles de l'ecclésiaste, fils de David, roi d'Israël à Jérusalem», mais il est développé plus précisément par le biais de la question de la succession, comme l'atteste la récurrence d'une expression comme «celui qui viendra après» et la comparaison avec ceux qui ont régné avant «l'ecclésiaste» (Eccl 1,10.16; 2,7.9; 4,15).

En considérant attentivement les différents passages où apparaît le mot roi, βασιλεύς, où le thème royal, donc, passe au premier plan[27], on peut essayer de définir ce que modifie la version grecque. Dans plusieurs cas, les termes, les expressions ou les propositions entières utilisées appellent en écho des épisodes de la royauté de Saül, David, Salomon et ses successeurs. Les versets étudiés sont pris selon l'ordre du livre; mais c'est d'abord le terme-clef du livre, הבל / ματαιότης qui retiendra notre attention.

a. Eccl 1,2 et parallèles: Ματαιότης ματαιοτήτων, εἶπεν ὁ ἐκκλησιαστής, τὰ πάντα ματαιότης. Le substantif ματαιότης traduit systématiquement l'hébreu הבל mais si l'on regarde, du côté du grec, l'emploi des mots de même famille (le substantif n'apparaît pas avant les Psaumes), on découvre que le verbe ματαιοῦν, au parfait passif, qualifie à quatre reprises l'attitude du roi:

– 1 Rg 13,13: Samuel s'adresse à Saül qui a accompli les rites de sacrifice sans l'attendre: Μεματαίωταί σοι, ὅτι οὐκ ἐφύλαξας τὴν ἐντολήν μου ... (TM: verbe סכל).
– 1 Rg 26, 21: Saül reconnaît ses torts devant David: ....μεματαίωμαι καὶ ἠγνόηκα πολλὰ σφόδρα (TM: verbe סכל).
– 4 Rg 17, 15: accusation collective portée contre Israël et Juda après la chute du royaume du Nord: .... ἐπορεύθησαν ὀπίσω τῶν ματαίων καὶ ἐματαιώθησαν ... (TM: verbe הבל).
– 1 Ch 21, 8: David reconnaît son péché devant Dieu: ....ἐματαιώθην σφόδρα (TM: verbe סכל).

L'accusation de ματαιότης, donnée en tête de l'*Ecclésiaste* comme parole du roi, et récurrente tout au long du livre, fait dans le texte grec écho à ces différents épisodes; l'attribution de ces paroles à un roi et l'identité de lexique ont un effet convergent. L'accusation de «vanité»

---

27. La sélection de ces passages laisse entière la redoutable question de la structure de l'ensemble du livre qui continue de susciter maintes questions et publications. Voir en particulier A. SCHOORS, *La structure littéraire de Qohélet*, in *OLP* 13 (1982) 91-116 et V. D'ALARIO, *Il libro del Qohelet. Struttura letteraria e retorica* (SupRivBib, 27), Bologna, 1993, chap. 2.

apparaît alors d'abord comme le jugement porté sur les rois successifs d'Israël et de Juda, un jugement prêté à Salomon. On peut se demander en outre si cela ne donne pas à lire dans les deux premiers mots du livre «Paroles de l'ecclésiaste, fils de David» un écho de 3 Rg 11,41: «Le reste des paroles de Salomon, tout ce qu'il a fait, et toute sa sagesse, cela n'a-t-il pas été écrit dans le livre des paroles de Salomon – ἐν βιβλίῳ ῥημάτων Σαλωμων…» Podechard[28] dans son commentaire suggérait la possibilité du rapprochement. Dans le TM comme dans la version grecque est en tout cas soulignée de cette façon l'intention du pseudépigraphe.

b. Eccl 5,5: Μὴ δῷς τὸ στόμα σου τοῦ ἐξαμαρτῆσαι τὴν σάρκα σου καὶ μὴ εἴπῃς πρὸ προσώπου τοῦ θεοῦ Ἄγνοιά ἐστι, ἵνα μὴ ὀργισθῇ ὁ θεὸς ἐπὶ φωνῇ σου καὶ διαφθείρῃ τὰ ποιήματα χειρῶν σου. — Ne laisse pas ta bouche faire pécher ta chair, et ne dis pas devant la face de Dieu que «c'est une erreur», pour que Dieu ne se mette pas en colère à ta voix et qu'il ne détruise pas les oeuvres de tes mains.

Le *Lévitique* reconnaît la possibilité de l'erreur ou de la faute involontaire (voir Lv 5, 18: TM שָׁגְגָה / LXX ἄγνοια; en Lv 4, 2.22 et 5,15, emploi du même substantif ἄγνοια par Aquila, là où la LXX a recours à l'adverbe ἀκουσίως). Ce serait un exemple supplémentaire du travail de révision et d'uniformisation du texte grec accompli par Aquila, l'équivalence שגגה = ἄγνοια jouant aussi dans notre verset d'Eccl. Mais Eccl 5,5 offre aussi un parallèle avec 1 Règnes 14, 24, verset pour lequel il y a divergence entre TM et grec; et seul le grec permet le rapprochement entre les deux passages. Dans le récit, Saül, au moment de livrer combat, interdit au peuple de manger, et la défaite qui s'ensuit montre qu'il s'agissait d'un respect mal compris, inopportun, de la Loi. Au v. 24, là où le TM dit: «les hommes d'Israël avaient souffert ce jour-là», la LXX écrit (traduit?): «Καὶ Σαουλ ἠγνόησεν ἄγνοιαν μεγάλην ἐν τῇ ἡμέρᾳ ἐκείνῃ — et Saül commit ce jour-là une grave erreur». Si le premier stique d'Eccl 5,5 peut évoquer un interdit alimentaire, n'a-t-on pas un effet de citation ou au moins d'allusion qui, au-delà de l'uniformisation lexicale, invite à lire l'histoire des rois — et de leurs fautes — sous l'expression abstraite?

c. Eccl 5,7-8: Ἐὰν συκοφαντίαν πένητος καὶ ἁρπαγὴν κρίματος καὶ δικαιοσύνης ἴδῃς ἐν χώρᾳ, μὴ θαυμάσῃς ἐπὶ τῷ πράγματι· ὅτι ἐπάνω ὑψηλοῦ φυλάξαι καὶ ὑψηλοὶ ἐπ' αὐτούς. 8. Καὶ περισσεία γῆς ἐν παντί ἐστιν, βασιλεὺς τοῦ ἀγροῦ εἰργασμένου.

---

28. E. PODECHARD, *L'Ecclésiaste*, Paris, 1912, *ad loc.*

Le sens de ces versets est difficile, particulièrement pour la fin du v.8. Dans la logique de notre hypothèse de travail cependant, un parallélisme lexical, qui existe aussi dans l'hébreu, peut faire lire dans ces versets un écho de l'histoire de Mephibosheth, le fils infirme de Jonathan. 2 Rg 8, 15 fait l'éloge du règne de David: «David régna sur tout Israël. David faisait droit et justice à tout son peuple» (LXX: κρίμα καὶ δικαιοσύνην / TM: משפט וצדקה — l'emploi des deux termes au singulier et coordonnés n'est pas fréquent). Puis au chapitre 9, vv.7-8, David s'informe des descendants de Saül et fait venir Mephibosheth auquel il promet: «je te restituerai toutes les terres (LXX : πάντα ἀγρόν / TM שָׂדֶה) de ton père Saül» (v.7); puis il ordonne à son serviteur Civa: «... travaille pour lui la terre» (LXX : καὶ ἐργᾷ αὐτῷ τὴν γῆν). L'attitude de David n'est pas sans ambiguïté puisqu'en fait il trouve ainsi une occasion de faire surveiller Mephibosheth, selon l'interprétation habituellement donnée de l'épisode. Et si l'on s'accorde sur le jeu de l'intertextualité pour ces deux passages, l'expression finale du v.8 serait la traduction par approximation de l'expression hébraïque, le parallèle avec l'épisode de 2 Rg éclairant le sens du verset sapientiel. Mais la caractéristique du texte de sagesse est de marquer nettement sa critique de l'attitude royale avec la série des termes connotés négativement (oppression, saisie, profit).

d. Eccl 8, 2-4: Στόμα βασιλέως φύλαξον καὶ περὶ λόγου ὅρκου θεοῦ μὴ σπουδάσῃς· 3 ἀπὸ προσώπου αὐτοῦ πορεύσῃ, μὴ στῇ ἐν λόγῳ πονηρῷ ὅτι πᾶν, ὃ ἐὰν θελήσῃ, 4 καθὼς λαλεῖ βασιλεὺς ἐξουσιάζων, καὶ τίς ἐρεῖ αὐτῷ· Τί ποιήσεις;

Le verset 2 appellerait sans doute un commentaire mais c'est la mention de la domination royale au v.4 («comme parle un roi puissant et qui lui dira: 'Que feras-tu?'») qui nous retiendra ici. Une expression identique (sans autre parallèle) définit en effet le pouvoir de Salomon en 3 Rg 4, 21 (= TM 1 R 5, 1): καὶ Σαλωμων ... ἦν ἐξουσιάζων ἐν πᾶσιν τοῖς βασιλείοις. Le choix d'ἐξουσιάζειν correspond aussi à la leçon hexaplaire attribuée à Aquila en 3 Rg 4,21; à l'inverse, pas d'identité lexicale en hébreu: le verbe משל est employé à propos de Salomon en 1 R 5,1 face à l'adjectif שַׁלְטוֹן en Qo 8,4. Avec ce parallélisme textuel propre au grec, la conjonction καθώς, qui marque la comparaison en tête du verset, peut alors s'interpréter comme introduisant une citation, ou au moins une allusion au texte de 3 Rg (et pas seulement comme le résultat de la confusion fréquente entre bèth et kaph – באשר / כאשר).

On voit bien avec cet exemple le double effet de la traduction: שִׁלְטוֹן et toujours traduit par ἐξουσιάζειν dans l'Eccl — la littéralité est donc respectée — et en même temps, cela ouvre la possibilité d'un rapprochement avec le récit de la royauté salomonienne.

e. Eccl. 9,14: Πόλις μικρὰ καὶ ἄνδρες ἐν αὐτῇ ὀλίγοι, καὶ ἔλθῃ ἐπ' αὐτῆς βασιλεὺς μέγας καὶ κυκλώσῃ αὐτὴν καὶ οἰκοδομήσῃ ἐπ αὐτὴν χάρακας μεγάλους... — une ville petite et des hommes peu nombreux en elle, et qu'un grand roi vienne contre elle, l'encercle et établisse contre elle des retranchements...

On peut d'abord remarquer que, sans doute par suite d'une différence de vocalisation, le substantif χάραξ traduit dans ce verset l'hébreu מָצוֹד, alors que ce terme a été traduit par θήρευμα en Eccl 7,27 (et cela correspond à la traduction selon l'étymologie, le verbe θηρεύειν traduisant régulièrement צוד). Mais l'expression οἰκοδομεῖν χάρακας, employée seulement ici et en 3 Rg 12, 24f et 21, 12 nous met sur la voie d'un autre rapprochement: elle peut se lire comme un écho de l'histoire de Jéroboam. On trouve en effet en 3 Rgn 12, 24f: «Et Jéroboam construisit là un retranchement»; or les vv. 24a-z sont absents de l'hébreu[29] et sont une relecture du règne de Jéroboam.

Mais on peut ajouter un autre parallèle, propre au grec lui aussi, qui nous permet de ne pas lire dans le verset de l'Eccl une simple allusion historique, mais davantage une réflexion sur l'action des rois: en Is 37, 33-35, il s'agit de marquer les limites du pouvoir de Sennachérib face à Jérusalem. Au v. 33 («il ne l'entourera pas d'un retranchement»), l'expression κυκλοῦν χάρακα est elle aussi homogène au vocabulaire d'Eccl 9,14, alors que le TM utilise une expression différente (v. 33 שָׁפֵךְ סֹלְלָה).

f. Eccl 10,20: Καί γε ἐν συνειδήσει σου βασιλέα μὴ καταράσῃ — et vraiment, dans ta conscience, ne maudis pas le roi.

Pour ce verset, notons d'emblée que l'intertextualité fonctionne également en hébreu et en grec. L'interdiction de maudire le roi ne serait-elle pas en effet le rappel de ce qu'il en a coûté à Shiméï d'avoir maudit David (2 Rg 16,5-13)? Les malédictions lancées par Shiméï (grec καταρᾶσθαι / TM קלל) sont mentionnées avec insistance dans ces versets (6

---

29. Sur les problèmes textuels et d'interprétation liés à ce double récit du règne de Jéroboam, voir en particulier R.P. GORDON, *Source Study in 1 Kings XII 24a-na*, in *Transactions* 25 (1973-74) 59-70; ID., *The Second LXX Account of Jeroboam. History or Midrash?*, in *VT* 25 (1975) 368-393. Et plus récemment, un important article d'A. SCHENKER, *Jéroboam et la division du royaume dans la LXX ancienne. LXX 1R 12, 24a-z, TM 11-12;14 et l'histoire deutéronomiste*, in A. DE PURY – T. RÖMER – J.D. MACCHI (eds.), *Israël construit son histoire. L'historiographie deutéronomiste à la lumière des recherches récentes*, Genève, 1996, pp. 193-236, que m'a signalé Ph. Lefebvre.

emplois du verbe); et Salomon punit ensuite Shiméï d'avoir ainsi of-
fensé David (3 Rg 2, 8 et 43-46). Faire porter l'interdiction sur ce qui
se passe au for intérieur, dans la conscience, constitue la réflexion propre du sage, alors que le récit de 2 Rg insiste sur le fait que Shiméï
exprime bruyamment ses malédictions : il invective et lance même des
pierres.

La convergence de ces quelques exemples est sans doute plus pro-
bante que chacun pris séparément et on a pu voir en outre que les cas où
le grec se calquait sur l'hébreu étaient renforcés des versets où l'on a au
contraire une spécificité du grec. Le thème de la royauté, s'il est dissé-
miné dans le texte, a une place privilégiée du fait de la fiction
salomonienne — bien sûr, cela ne résout pas le problème de la composition, de la structure du livre! Les allusions à différents épisodes de l'histoire de la royauté donnent lieu, dans les versets que nous venons d'examiner, à un jugement qui s'exprime, soit par des termes à connotation
péjorative (par ex. pour ματαιότης et en Eccl 5,7-8), soit par la formulation de défenses (Eccl 5,5; 8,2-4; 10,20). Ainsi s'élabore la réflexion du
sage, mais le cas du roi n'est peut-être qu'un cas particulier et il y aurait
lieu, pour mener à terme cette étude, de voir comment les références à
l'histoire royale d'Israël s'insèrent dans tout un ensemble de références,
et surtout à la *Genèse* et à la Loi comme on le signalait précédemment;
un des effets de la traduction grecque de l'*Ecclésiaste* est peut-être de
souligner, par le biais de ses choix lexicaux, cette intertextualité généra-
lisée. Et cela, n'est-ce pas une façon, pour qui lit le texte, de le reconnaître comme partie d'un corpus, d'un corpus canonique?

IV. QUELQUES REMARQUES CONCLUSIVES

Il revient au traducteur de la LXX, ici de l'*Ecclésiaste*, de mettre en
évidence ces parallèles textuels; tâche difficile, mais qui d'une certaine
façon rejoint celle d'Aquila traduisant pour la première fois *Qohélet*!
Avec l'oeuvre d'Aquila, traduction de l'Eccl et révision de la LXX, on
peut dire que la Bible grecque est achevée. Et cela donne sans doute une
place privilégiée à notre texte de l'Eccl. En lien peut-être avec un autre
achèvement, celui du processus de canonisation, la traduction dans la
littéralité (et c'est le travail pour l'ensemble des livres bibliques qu'il
faut ici prendre en compte) va dans le sens d'une unification du texte
biblique même pour des termes rares, essentiellement grâce à des traductions de type étymologique. Cela est bien sûr encore plus vérifiable pour

les termes courants de *Qohélet* et leurs équivalents standard. — Ce sont ainsi des champs lexicaux qui se constituent et se renforcent, multipliant pour le lecteur les possibilités de parallèles d'un livre à l'autre.

Si, en outre, le texte grec souligne davantage que l'hébreu, comme nous avons essayé de le montrer, le lien avec l'histoire de la royauté, cela peut encore se comprendre comme une pratique de la traduction, faut-il dire de type targumique pour reprendre le titre d'un article de Le Déaut[30], visant à souligner la signature salomonienne de l'*Ecclésiaste*. Et dans le contexte d'un livre sapientiel, les allusions à différents épisodes historiques se complètent d'un jugement critique attribué à l'«ecclésiaste», qui est à la fois roi et sage (Eccl 1,1.12 et 12,9).

Il reste à souhaiter, pour enrichir et confirmer ces approches, la parution d'une édition critique de l'*Ecclésiaste* dans la collection de la LXX de Göttingen et plus encore celle, qui relève sans doute d'un projet plus ambitieux mais déjà amorcé, d'une réédition des Hexaples. La spécificité de la version grecque de *Qohélet* sortirait alors davantage du domaine de la conjecture.

10, rue d'Arras   Françoise VINEL
F-67000 Strasbourg

---

30. R. LE DÉAUT, *La Septante, un Targum?*, in R. KUNTZMANN – J. SCHLOSSER (eds.), *Études sur le judaïsme hellénistique. Congrès de Strasbourg, 1983* (LD, 119), Paris, 1984, pp. 147-195.

"WHO IS LIKE THE WISE?"
SOME NOTES ON QOHELET 8,1-15

Last year, A.A. Fischer published a monograph in which he holds the view that it is impossible to regard the Book of Qohelet as a literary work of art out of one piece[1]. It should, on the contrary, be considered as a composite work, of which 1,3-3,15, the so-called 'Grundschrift'[2], has been composed by Qohelet himself. Because of its fine composition, this 'Grundschrift' should be distinguished from the remainder of the Book (3,16-12,7). According to Fischer's analysis, Qoh 3,16-12,7 is to be characterized as a collection of school texts, that has been connected to the 'Grundschrift' by a redactor, who is identified by Fischer with 'the first epilogist', who is the author of Qoh 12,9-11. After a thorough investigation[3], three substantial literary units from that first redaction (Qoh 5,9-6,9; 9,1-12; 11,1-12,7) are qualified as an "in sich geschlossene thematische und argumentative Einheit"[4], that on the one hand is prior to the 'Grundschrift', and on the other hand, has come from Qohelet himself. According to Fischer, also Qoh 4,17-5,6; 7,1-22, and 9,13-10,13, which are composite and glossed *school texts*, must derive from Qohelet himself[5].

Although Qoh 8,1-8 and 8,10-15 prove, according to Fischer, to be coherent texts on their own[6], Chapter 8 of the Book of Qohelet as a

I like to thank all participants of the Seminar on Qohelet 8 during the Colloquium for their stimulating contributions, and my colleague Dr. J.A. Wagenaar for his advice.

1. A. A. FISCHER, *Skepsis oder Furcht Gottes? Studien zur Komposition und Theologie des Buches Kohelet* (BZAW, 247), Berlin-New York, Walter de Gruyter, 1997, p. 20.

2. This term seems to be coined by Carl SIEGFRIED, *Prediger und Hoheslied* (HK, II 3,2), Göttingen, 1898, pp. 5ff. During the last decade or two, this view has been reintroduced by several scholars: H.-P. MÜLLER, *Theonome Skepsis und Lebensfreude. Zu Koh 1,2-3,15*, in *BZ* 30 (1986) 1-19; D. MICHEL, *Untersuchungen zur Eigenart des Buches Qohelet* (BZAW, 183), Berlin-New York, 1989, p. 269: "Der Abschnitt 1,3-3,15... bildet eine in sich geschlossene Abhandlung, die eigentlich von ihrem Thema her keiner Fortsetzung bedarf"; A. FISCHER, *Beobachtungen zur Komposition von Koh 1,3-3,15*, in *ZAW* 103 (1991) 71-86; N. LOHFINK, *Kohelet* (NEB), Würzburg, ²1980, p. 23 characterizes Qoh 1,12-3,15 as "die grundlegendste und zusammenhängendste Darlegung des ganzen Buches". Recently, the view has been defended that Qoh 1,3-3,22 "eine wohldurchdachte Gesamtstruktur ausbilden": F.J. BACKHAUS, *»Denn Zeit und Zufall trifft sie«. Studien zur Komposition und zum Gottesbild im Buch Qohelet* (BBB, 83), Bodenheim, Anton Hain, 1993, p. 143.

3. FISCHER, *Skepsis* (n. 1), pp. 56-182.

4. *Ibid.*, p. 182.

5. *Ibid.*, p. 50. Cf. J. COPPENS, *La structure de l'Ecclésiaste*, in M. GILBERT (ed.), *La Sagesse de l'Ancien Testament* (BETL, 51), Louvain, University Press – Peeters, ²1990, pp. 288-292.

6. FISCHER, *Skepsis* (n. 1), p. 19: "... erweisen sich 8,1-8; 8,10-15 als kohärente

whole is characterized by him as obviously a secondary composition by the first epilogist made up from the inheritance of the wise[7]. Whether such a judgement is correct or not, Chapter 8 nowadays belongs to the canonical Biblical text that is to be studied and read as such. I will therefore offer some notes on Qoh 8,1-15, which is no doubt a complicated text.

The present text forms part of a larger section (Qoh 6,10-8,17), for which Ludger Schwienhorst-Schönberger proposed a fine overall structure, viz. three traditional wisdom clusters (anthropology, wisdom, and theology/ethics) are subjected to a critical investigation by Qohelet[8]:

6,10-12	introduction
7,1-10	anthropology (death/humankind)
7,11-14	wisdom
7,15-20	theology/ethics (righteous – wicked)
7,21-22	provisional conclusion
7,23-25	introduction
7,26-29	anthropology (death/man-woman)[9]
8,1-9	wisdom in social context
8,10-15	theology/ethics (righteous – wicked)
8,16-17	final conclusion

QOHELET 8,1-9[10]

First of all, scholars hold different opinions regarding the literary status of Qoh 8,1. Quite a few commentators believe that either Qoh 8,1a

Einzeltexte...". On his assumptions ("vermuten wir...") with regard to the function of 8,9, see pp. 14-15.

7. *Ibid.*, p. 50: "Dagegen ist Kapitel 8 offensichtlich als eine aus der Hinterlassenschaft des Weisen durch den ersten Epilogisten zusammengestellte sekundäre Komposition zu betrachten".

8. L. Schwienhorst-Schönberger, *"Nicht im Menschen gründet das Glück" (Koh 2,24). Kohelet im Spannungsfeld jüdischer Weisheit und hellenistischer Philosophie* (HBS, 2), Freiburg, Herder, ²1996, p. 6.

9. Recently, Ingrid Riesener has published a very fine and stimulating article dealing with the structure and meaning of Qoh 7,25-29; I. Riesener, *Frauenfeindschaft im Alten Testament? Zum Verständnis von Qoh 7,25-29*, in Anja A. Diesel, Reinhard G. Lehmann, Eckart Otto und Andreas Wagner (eds.), *"Jedes Ding hat seine Zeit..."*. *Studien zur israelitischen und altorientalischen Weisheit. Diethelm Michel zum 65. Geburtstag* (BZAW, 241), Berlin-New York, Walter de Gruyter, 1996, pp. 193-207.

10. Literature on Qoh 8,1-9: J.L. Crenshaw, *The Expression* mî yôdēaʻ *in the Hebrew Bible*, in *VT* 16 (1986) 274-288; W.A. Irwin, *Ecclesiastes 8:2-9*, in *JNES* 4 (1945) 130-131; N.W. Waldman, *The DABAR RAʻ of Eccl 8:3*, in *JBL* 98 (1979) 407-408; Avi Hurvitz, *The History of a Legal Formula*, kōl ʼăšer ḥāpēṣ ʻāśāh, in *VT* 32 (1982) 257-267. Not available to me: D.A. Garrett, *Qoheleth on the Use and Abuse of Political Power*, in *Trinity Journal* 8 (1987) 159-177.

(דבר......מי) or the entire verse (מי.....ישׂנא)[11] should be considered as the *conclusion* of the previous section (Qoh 7,23-8,1)[12]. In recent studies, however, more than once the *kataphoric* function of Qoh 8,1a has been emphasized; Qoh 8,1a is composed of six words, five of which are repeated in the subsequent verses[13]: חכמה (8,1b); חכם (8,5b); מי (8,4.7); דבר (8,3.4.5); ידע (8,5a.5b.7).

One should keep in mind that in the present section two rhetorical questions have been incorporated (Qoh 8,4b: ומי יאמר־לו מה; Qoh 8,7b: מי יגיד לו), whereas Qoh 8,7a (ידע כי איננו) seems to be a kind of an echo of Qoh 8,1a.

With respect to Qoh 8,1a, however, I would like to discuss whether we have a *rhetorical* question here. For it is striking that the question מי כהחכם is followed by a second question (מי יודע), a pattern that is rarely found in the Book of Qohelet[14]. Moreover this second question is followed by an explicit description of its content (ישׂנא.........חכמת). Precisely this second question refrains from putting מי יודע in Qoh 8,1a on a par with the same formula elsewhere in the Book of Qohelet (2,19; 3,21; 6,12), as Crenshaw does, characterizing it as 'A Closed Door' type[15]. The

11. The text-critical apparatus of *BHS* has a small failure at 8,1c. The Greek text of the Septuagint has *not* μισθήσεται, but μισηθήσεται. The identical failure is also found in A. SCHOORS, *The Preacher Sought to Find Pleasing Words* (OLA, 41), Louvain, Peeters, 1992, p. 27.

12. G.Ch. AALDERS, *Het boek Prediker vertaald en toegelicht* (COT), Kampen, Kok, 1948, pp. 171-175; H.W. HERTZBERG, *Der Prediger* (KAT XVII,4), Gütersloh, Gerd Mohn, 1963, pp. 156-163; K. GALLING, *Der Prediger (Die Fünf Megilloth)* (HAT I/18), Tübingen, J.C.B. Mohr (Paul Siebeck), ²1969, pp. 108-110; R.B.Y. SCOTT, *Proverbs-Ecclesiastes* (AB 18), New York, Doubleday, 1965, pp. 238-239; LOHFINK, *Kohelet* (n. 2), pp. 56-59; N. LOHFINK, *War Kohelet ein Frauenfeind? Ein Versuch, die Logik und den Gegenstand von Koh. 7,23-8,1a herauszufinden*, in M. GILBERT (ed.), *La Sagessse de l'Ancien Testament*, pp. 259-287; J.A. LOADER, *Polar Structures in the Book of Qohelet* (BZAW, 152), Berlin-New York, Walter de Gruyter, 1979, pp. 50-54; A. LAUHA, *Kohelet* (BK XIX) Neukirchen-Vluyn, Neukirchener Verlag, 1978, pp. 140-147 defines Qoh 7,25-8,1 as a literary unit. Cf. M. FOX, *Wisdom in Qoheleth*, in L. PERDUE et al. (eds.), *In Search of Wisdom. Essays in Memory of J.G. Gammie*, Louisville, 1993, p. 118: "8,1a is a wry exclamation of despair at the possibility of ever understanding women (7:27-29)"; "Verse 1b begins a new unit" (*Ibid.*, 118 note 7). M.V. FOX – B. PORTEN, *Unsought Discoveries: Qoheleth 7:23-8:1a*, in *Hebrew Studies* 19 (1978) 26-38. J.L. CRENSHAW, *Mî yôdēa'*, p. 283 is typifying Qoh 8,1 as "unrelated to its context, unless it isolates a specific form of human machinations mentioned in the previous verse". In his commentary, however, he has defined Qoh 8,1-9 as a literary unit; J.L. CRENSHAW, *Ecclesiastes* (OTL), London, SCM, 1988, pp. 148-153. Also the Vulgate takes Qoh 8,1 to the previous passage.

13. E.g. BACKHAUS, *»Denn Zeit und Zufall trifft sie«* (n. 2), p. 245; SCHWIENHORST-SCHÖNBERGER, *"Nicht im Menschen..."* (n. 8), p. 181; J.L. CRENSHAW, *Ecclesiastes* (n. 12), p. 149; Chr. KLEIN, *Kohelet und die Weisheit Israels* (BWANT, 132), Stuttgart, Kohlhammer, 1994, p. 75.

14. Qoh 2,25.

15. CRENSHAW, *Mî yôdēa'* (n. 10), pp. 278-288.

fact is, that the twofold question in Qoh 8,1a is given a special answer. For אני at the opening of Qoh 8,2 should not, in fact, be precluded from being the answer to both questions that are posed in 8,1ab. "Who is like the wise, and who knows the explanation of the word[16]: "The wisdom of the sage........"?" is given the answer: "I (Qohelet) do". This solution has, first of all, the advantage of preserving the Hebrew text as we have it. Secondly, by assigning אני a place of its own, the internal (syntactical) structure of Qoh 8,2-3 gets more balanced: 8,2 imperative (שמור); 8,3a אל + prohibitive (תבהל); 8,3b imperative (תלך); 8,3c אל + prohibitive (תעמד); 8,3d evidence (כי).

As the author, at the opening of the Book, assumed "the persona of royalty"[17], claiming to be a king: "I, Qohelet, was king over Israel in Jerusalem" (Qoh 1,12), the personal pronoun אני may be connected to that earlier 'Königsfiktion' or 'Königstravestie'[18]. And is it a coincidence that אני in Qoh 8,2 is immediately followed by a number of verses in which a person's attitude towards the king, as well as the king's temper, are at the center of attention? Within such a fictional framework, the vocabulary of Qoh 8,2-5 could be considered as an echo of, or an allusion to, 1 Kgs 2,43, which is part of a narrative in which king Solomon is given prominence[19].

My proposal regarding אני does not interfere with Diethelm Michel's thesis that Qoh 8,2-5 is a quotation of an extant wisdom text that is commented upon, corrected and criticized in Qoh 8,6-9[20]. Michel's idea that Qohelet adopted an extant text in its entirety is favoured by the fact that from Near Eastern collections of wisdom literature several striking parallels to Qoh 8,2-5 can be adduced. Qohelet seems to quote wide spread and well-known material:

16. The Hebrew phrase פשר דבר is easily taken as an introduction to the subsequent bicolon, as the Old Versions do: Gr.: λύσιν ῥήματος; V.: 'solutionem verbi'; Syr.: pšrh dmlt'. Cf. D. MICHEL, Qohelet (EdF, 258), Darmstadt, Wissenschaftliche Buchgesellschaft, 1988, p.·153: "Deutung des Wortes"; HERTZBERG, Der Prediger (n. 12), p. 138: "Und wer kennt die Deutung des Satzes:"; SCHWIENHORST-SCHÖNBERGER, "Nicht im Menschen..." (n. 8), p. 181: "Mann könnte 8,1a folgendermassen umschreiben: '... wer kann den folgenden Text deuten/interpretieren?'".

17. CRENSHAW, Ecclesiastes (n. 12), p. 70. His comment on Qoh 1,12-2,26 is entitled 'The Royal Experiment'.

18. MICHEL, Qohelet (n. 16), pp. 76-78.

19. Cf. שמר, שבעת יהוה, מצוה in 1 Kgs 2,43; ידע and הרעה in 1 Kgs 2,44.

20. D. MICHEL, Qoheletprobleme. Überlegungen zu Qoh 8,2-9 und 7,11-14, in ThViat 15 (1979/1980) 1982, 81-103 (= D. MICHEL, Untersuchungen (n. 2), pp. 84-102). Most recently, Michel's hypothesis has been adopted by SCHWIENHORST-SCHÖNBERGER, "Nicht im Menschen..." (n. 8), pp. 181-186 with some small adjustments.

1) Aramaic *Ahiqar*:

    6.   Nicht lösche das Wort des Königs / heiß möge es dein[em Herzen] sein!
Sanft ist die Rede des Königs, (zugleich aber auch) schneidender und machtvoller als ein zweischneidi[ges] Messer.

    7.   Siehe, vor dir ist etwas Widerborstiges [ge]gen den Kö[nig]: Tritt du nicht in Erscheinung! Heftiger als ein Blitz ist sein Zor[n]! Hüte dich,

    8.   daß er ihn nicht über deinen G[lie]dern entb[re]nnen läßt und du dahingehst vor deiner Zeit.

    9.   [So ist der Zor]n des Königs: Wenn dir etwas befohlen ist, ist er ein loderndes [F]euer. Schnell, tu e[s, da]mit es nicht [ü]ber dir entfacht werde, so daß du deine Hände verbergen mußt.

    10. [Voll]ende das Wort des Königs mit Herzenlust. / [W]as rechten Hölzer mit Feuer, Fleisch mit einem Messer, ein Mensch mit einem [König?]]²¹.

2) The second maxim from the instructions of *Ptahhotep*:

    If you meet a disputant in action,
    A powerful man, superior to you,
    Fold your arms, bend your back,
    To flout him will not make him agree with you.
    Make little of the evil speech
    By not opposing him while he's in action;
    He will be called an ignoramus,
    Your self-control will match his pile (of words)²².

3) Demotic *Phibis* (Papyrus Insinger):

    Do not draw near,
    if it is not time for it,
    else your lord will hate you;
    (but also) do not be far removed,
    lest one must seek you
    and you cause stink in the heart of your lord²³.

Though some scholars regard Qoh 8,2-5 as a literary unit, because of the *inclusio* of שמור (Qoh 8,2) and שומר (Qoh 8,5), they nevertheless re-

---

21. I. KOTTSIEPER, *Die Geschichte und die Sprüche des weisen Achiqar*, in O. KAISER (Hrsg.), *Weisheitstexte, Mythen und Epen* (TUAT III/2: Weisheitstexte II) Gütersloh, Gerd Mohn, 1991, pp. 336-337 [X,6-10]. MICHEL, *Untersuchungen* (n. 2), pp. 94-95. Variant numberings are in circulation: Cowley 100-104; Sachau 54; Kottsieper X, 6-10.

22. M. LICHTHEIM, *Ancient Egyptian Literature* I, Berkeley-Los Angeles, 1973, p. 63; quotation from MICHEL, *Untersuchungen* (n. 2), p. 95.

23. J.T. SANDERS, *Ben Sira and Demotic Wisdom*, Chico CA, Scholars Press, 1983, p. 92. Cf. Fr. W. FREIHERR VON BISSING, *Altägyptische Lebensweisheit*, Zürich, Artemis, 1955, p. 99. There is a striking resemblance with Sir 13,9-10.

ject Michel's idea that Qoh 8,2-5 is adopted from another source as a whole, because of a large number of words and expressions typical of Qohelet (e.g. שלט, על דברת). However they do not exclude the possibility that Qoh 8,2-5 is a compilation of a number of 'loose' quotations[24]. That Qoh 8,2-5, in one way or the other, has indeed adopted current material is confirmed by the words ומי יאמר לו מה תעשׂה (Qoh 8,4b). It is a set phrase emphasizing someone's absolute power and superiority, which is used several times in the Old Testament (Job 9,12; Isa 45,9; Sir 36,8 [Gr. 33,10], Wisd 12,12) with regard to God[25]. In Dan 4,32, the phrase ויאמר לה מה עבדת is used with reference to *king* Nebukadnessar.

Qoh 8,2-5, in one way or another adopted from topoi-like material, can in fact clarify the position and function of Qoh 8,1b. For it is conspicuous that it contains a bicolon in which a person's wisdom is characterized in a positive way; such a view can hardly be Qohelet's! According to Christian Klein, who published a very stimulating study on Qohelet and wisdom literature, Qoh 8,1b is the *only* maxim in the entire Book of Qohelet that can be defined as a synthetic parallelismus membrorum[26]. If this is true[27], it might be adduced as supplementary evidence that the author already in 8,1b harks back to existing tradition(s). The חכמת אדם (8,1b), then, is in violent contrast with Qohelet's own view and criticism which is reflected in the רעת האדם (Qoh 8,6b; cf. 8,9b).

The first part of Qoh 8,1-9, viz. vv. 1b-5, appears to be dominated by the *positive* concept of wisdom, reflecting traditional views:

8,1a   מי כהחכם
8,1b   חכמת אדם
8,5b   לב חכם[28].

---

24. Most recently BACKHAUS, »Denn Zeit und Zufall trifft sie« (n. 2), pp. 61-62. LOHFINK, *Kohelet* (n. 2), pp. 59ff considers Qoh 8,1b-4 to be an extant proverb, Qoh 8,5-15 to be a renewed continuation of the problem of "Tun-Ergehen-Zusammenhang". In his opinion, Qoh 8,5 and 8,12b-13 are quotations, whereas Qoh 8,6-12a and 8,14-15 express a twofold criticism on these quotations.

25. Cf. P.C. BEENTJES, *Jesus Sirach en Tenach*, Nieuwegein, 1981, pp. 34-36. In literature on Qoh 8,4b a reference to Isa 45,9 is seldom given; CRENSHAW, *Ecclesiastes* (n. 12), p. 151, seems to be the only one to mention it.

26. KLEIN, *Kohelet und die Weisheit Israels* (n. 13), p. 75.

27. I am aware of some criticism on Robert Lowth's definition of synthetic parallelism; see e.g. A. BERLIN, *Parallelism*, in D.N. FREEDMAN (ed.), *The Anchor Bible Dictionary*, vol. V, New York, Doubleday, 1992, 155-162, esp. p. 156. Cf. LAUHA, *Kohelet* (n. 11), p. 144: "die beiden Stichoi... sind also synonym parallel".

28. Strikingly, SCHWIENHORST-SCHÖNBERGER, *"Nicht im Menschen..."* (n. 8), pp. 181-182, is both in 8,1a and in 8,5 referring to חכמה, whereas it is the verb חכם in 8,1a, and the adjective חכם in 8,5!

However in the second part of Qoh 8,1-9, viz. vv. 6-9, Qohelet is questioning this concept, using a number of central notions and motifs that were already used in 8,2-5:

עת ומשפט	8,6a	(8,5b)
ידע	8,7a	(8,5a)
רע/רעה	8,6b; 9,9b	(8,2d; 8,5a)
שלט	8,8a; 8,9a	(8,4a)

It can be no coincidence that Qohelet with the help of all these notions arrives at very *negative* conclusions:

איננו	8,7a
אין	8,8a
ואין	8,8b
ואין	8,8c
ולא	8,8d.

This pattern is solid proof enough that in 8,8d an emendation from רשע ('injustice/guilt') into עשר ('wealth')[29] is undesirable. In the first place, because the Hebrew text is meaningful as it is; there is no textual evidence whatsoever in the Hebrew MSS nor in the Old Versions to alter the text. Secondly, the Masoretic text must be maintained, because רשע was used in the previous section (Qoh 7,25). Thirdly, the adjective רשע will be one of the central themes in the subsequent section (Qoh 8,10-15)[30] and, in the fourth place, it resumes this theme from 7,15-20[31], a section that like a diptych makes a pair with 8,10-15.

In Qohelet research, the function of Qoh 8,9 is disputed. Galling, for example, considers 8,9 to be the introduction to the subsequent pericope, since the concrete observation in 8,10 needs an introduction[32]. But in what way, then, is Qoh 8,10ff. supposed to be a concrete elaboration of a general principle as formulated in Qoh 8,9? Power is in no way the theme of Qoh 8,10-15!

29. *BHS*; W. ZIMMERLI, *Das Buch des Predigers Salomo* (ATD 16/1) Göttingen, Vandenhoeck & Ruprecht, 1962, p. 216. Cf. *NEB*; *REB*.
30. Qoh 8,10. 13. 14 (2x).
31. SCHWIENHORST-SCHÖNBERGER, *"Nicht im Menschen..."* (n. 8), p. 185.
32. GALLING, *Der Prediger* (n. 12), p. 111: "Verschiedentlich wird 9 noch zur vorangehenden Sentenz gerechnet, aber die konkrete Beobachtung in 10 bedarf eine Einleitung, die zunächst auf die Grundfrage nach dem gebrauch der Macht hinleitet (cf 10s) (sic!)". E.W. HENGSTENBERG, *Der Prediger Salomo ausgelegt*, Berlin, Oehmigste's Verlag, 1859, pp. 200-204 regards Qoh 8,9-13 as a unit. Scholars in favour of Qoh 8,9 as the opening of 8,9-15 are listed in A. SCHOORS, *The verb* ראה *in the Book of Qoheleth*, in Anja A. DIESEL a.o. (eds.), *"Jedes Ding hat seine Zeit..."* (n. 9), p. 237, note 65; to be added: W.J. FUERST, *The Five Scrolls* (CBC), Cambridge, Cambridge UP, 1975, pp. 135-138.

Stephan de Jong, in his article on the structuring principles and the main theme of the Book of Qohelet, typified Qoh 8,9 as a "blurred borderline", and continues: "This verse shows a connection with the preceding verses, in which instructions are given about how to deal with authorities. However, it is also possible to consider 8.9 as an introduction to 8.10, which carries on with the word *ûbᵉkēn* and obviously presupposes 8.9"[33].

A. Fischer, too, characterizes Qoh 8,9 as a seam ("Nahtstelle"). On the one hand, it is a summary and a conclusion of 8,1-8; on the other hand, one should regard 8,9 as an introduction to a new reflection, the theme of which is briefly stated in 8,9b. The problem, however, is that this theme is *not* picked up in the subsequent verses (8,10 ff.). Fischer therefore supposes that Qoh 8,9 once was the introduction to an independent reflection on power, but that its continuation has been lost and therefore lacked in the Redactor's "Vorlage". Fischer conjectures that the redactor has filled that gap with another text originating from Qohelet, viz. 8,10-15, in which רעה was a central issue[34].

In my opinion, Fischer's assumption not only is very complicated, but also has some weak points. In the first place, precisely in Qoh 8,10, which constitutes the link, the רע/רעה theme is missing. So, there is no direct link with Qoh 8,9. And, moreover, one wonders if רע/רעה is indeed the central theme of Qoh 8,10-15. Is the צדיקים/רשעים complex not more likely to be the topic of these verses?

To sum up, with regard to עת, שלט, and רע in Qoh 8,9b, the most satisfying solution for Qoh 8,9 would be to consider this verse with most scholars as the conclusion of the preceding pericope[35]. In accordance with this view, ראיתי should be translated as "I examined", as was recently proposed by A. Schoors: "...the meaning of ראה can only be "to examine", since it is explained by the continuation of the verse:ונתון את־ לבי לכל־מעשה אשר נעשה תחת השמש"[36].

_____

33. S. DE JONG, *A Book on Labour: The Structuring Principles and the Main Theme of the Book of Qohelet*, in *JSOT* 54 (1992) 107-116; quotation p. 111. According to him, Qoh 5,8; 6,10-12, and 9,13-18 are also such "blurred borderlines".

34. FISCHER, *Skepsis* (n. 1), p. 14; he only mentiones רעה in 8,11a, whereas רע shows up in 8,11b, and 8,12a.

35. LOADER, *Polar Structures* (n. 12), pp. 69-73; SCHWIENHORST-SCHÖNBERG, *"Nicht im Menschen..."* (n. 8), pp. 185-186. Other scholars in favour of Qoh 8,9 as the conclusion of 8,1-9 are listed in A. SCHOORS, *The verb* ראה ..., (n. 32), p. 237, note 64.

36. SCHOORS, *The Verb* ראה ...(n. 32), p. 237. Schoors here adopts the view of Michel as expressed in 1982; cf. MICHEL, *Untersuchungen* (n. 2), p. 98.

QOHELET 8,10-15[37]

For the first time since Qoh 7,6b, in 8,10 a הבל-utterance is found.
Qoh 8,10 discusses an observation that is characterized as הבל and is
elaborated in the subsequent lines. Quite a number of Bible translations[38], commentaries[39], monographs[40], and articles[41] take the view that
Qoh 8,10 expresses an opposition between the רשעים and 'others', i.e. a
group contrary to them. The point where the Hebrew text of 8,10 skips
from one party to the other should be somewhere about ובאו. This view,
however, presents us with some difficulties:

– The Book of Qohelet, when discussing the (רשע(ים in opposition to
  other people, always defines that other party in a *concrete* way: צדיק /
  חכם (cf. 3,16-17; 7,15-18; 8,8; 8,12-14; 9,1-6). It is, therefore, not
  self-evident that Qoh 8,10 forms an exception, assuming that only in
  this instance an opposite group comes into play that is not explicitly
  mentioned.

– The connection and content of Qoh 8,11-12a, too, make it plausible
  that in 8,10 as a whole only the רשעים are at the centre of attention.
  For in 8,11-12a, that can (or must) be considered as a further elaboration and explanation of v. 10, only הרעה, רע, and חטא are discussed,
  all qualifications closely related to the רשעים. Not before Qoh 8,14,
  which follows on a kind of formula that frames the classical doctrine
  of retribution ("It will be well with those who fear God... But it will
  not be well with the evildoer..."), the opposition between ירא האלהים
  צדיק / versus רשע is introduced.

If רשעים in Qoh 8,10 is indeed the subject of the entire verse, then
some further questions arise. For how is it possible that those רשעים, af-

37. Literature on Qoh 8,10-15: C.W. REINES, *Koheleth viii,10*, in *JJS* 5 (1954) 86-87;
M.J.H. van NIEKERK, *Response to J.A. Loader's 'Different reactions of Job and Qoheleth
to the doctrine of retribution'*, in *OTE* 4 (1991) 97-105; J.J. SERRANO, *I Saw the Wicked
Buried (Eccl 8,10)*, in *CBQ* 16 (1954) 168-170; M.O. WISE, *A Calque from Aramaic in
Qoheleth 6:12; 7:12; and 8:13*, in *JBL* 109 (1990) 249-257; M.A. KLOPFENSTEIN,
Kohelet und die Freude am Dasein, in *TZ* 47 (1991) 97-107; R.N. WHYBRAY, *Qoheleth,
Preacher of Joy*, in *JSOT* 23 (1982) 87-98. Not available to me: Wojciech PAZERA,
Bojazn Boza jako kult religijny w ksiedze Koheleta ["The Fear of God" as Worship in the
Book of Qoheleth]", in *Ruch Biblijny i Liturgiczny* 41 (1988) 307-313.
38. *NEB*; *Einheitsübersetzung*; *Revidierte Elberfelder Bibel*; Dutch Catholic
Willibrord Translation 1995; Dutch Protestant Translation ('*Nieuwe Vertaling*' 1951).
39. GALLING, *Der Prediger* (n. 12), p. 111; ZIMMERLI, *Das Buch des Predigers
Salomo* (n. 29), pp. 219-220; HERTZBERG, *Der Prediger* (n. 12), pp. 167. 173-174.
40. LOADER, *Polar Structures* (n. 12), pp. 99-101; SCHWIENHORST-SCHÖNBERG, *"Nicht
im Menschen..."* (n. 8), pp. 186-190.
41. VAN NIEKERK, *Response to J.A. Loader* (n. 37), p. 100.

ter their burial, enter (בוא) and go (הלך)? People who are buried are unable to take upon themselves further activities. In other words: is it a question of 'being burried' or is there a Hebrew verb in this case that can be linked with a verb of motion like בוא, and הלך? All the Old Versions give something like 'being burried' or 'grave'. From a text-critical point of view there is no way that the participle קברים can be linked with a verb expressing some kind of motion. Nevertheless, one might wonder whether קברים, as a result of *beth – resh* interchange, could not be read as קרבים and considered as a very special verb of motion: 'to approach'[42]. For it is beyond doubt that the verb קרב, even in the Book of Qohelet[43], can have a cultic meaning, viz. to visit the house of God[44].

If the Hebrew verb קרב indeed played a role here, it could at the same time clarify the much debated expression מקום קדוש[45]. Qoh 8,10, then, is discussing all kinds of motion to and fro the *temple* by a group of persons, who are characterized by the author as רשעים, doing things to which a 'destructive judgment'[46] is added: "this too is הבל".

One more problem remains, i.e. the verbal form וישתכחו: "they were forgotten" (Qoh 8,10c), a statement that is incomprehensible within the present context. Why should Qohelet be firmly opposed to the fact that the wicked be forgotten? It is striking, however, that almost all Old Versions apparently did not read וישכחו, but seemingly had another verb in front of them: LXX καὶ ἐπῃνέθησαν, Aquila/Theodotion ἐκαυχήσαντο, Symmachus ἐπαινούμενοι, Vulgata *laudabantur*, Hieronymus *laudati sunt*.

This reading is confirmed by about a dozen or so Hebrew Manuscripts that have read the verbal form וישתבחו. In other words, it is not the verb שכח of the Masoretic text, but the verb שבח that makes sense here[47].

In my view, it is an important element with regard to the structure of this passage, that the verb שבח is also used at the *end* of this pericope

42. As far as I am aware, this emendation has been proposed for the first time by F.C. BURKITT, *Is Ecclesiastes a Translation?*, in *JTS* 23 (1922) 22-26; ID., *Ecclesiastes Rendered into English Verse*, London, ²1922. Cf. SERRANO, *I Saw the wicked burried* (n. 37), pp. 168-170; G.R. DRIVER, *Problems and Solutions*, in *VT* 4 (1954) 230-231.

43. Qoh 4,17 (5,1 *REB*). LOADER, *Polar Structures* (n. 12), p. 98 (note 82) erroneously refers to Qoh 4,7.

44. J.KÜHLEWEIN, קרב / *sich nähern*, in *THAT* II, ed. E. JENNI – CL. WESTERMANN, München, Chr. Kaiser Verlag, 1976, 674-681, esp. 678-681.

45. O. LORETZ, *Qohelet und der alte Orient. Untersuchungen zu Stil und theologischer Thematik des Buches Qohelet*, Freiburg-Basel-Wien, Herder, 1964, pp. 75-78. MICHEL, *Untersuchungen* (n. 2), pp. 217-221, esp. p. 220.

46. K. SEYBOLD, הֶבֶל *hebhel*, *TDOT* III, ed. G.J. BOTTERWECK – H. RINGGREN, Grand Rapids. MI, Eerdmans, 1988, pp. 313-320; quotation from p. 320.

47. In the Hebrew Bible, a *kaph – beth* interchange is documented several times: Josh 4,18; 1 Sam 30,30; 1 Kings 22,20; 2 Kings 3,24; Ps 49,12; 2 Chron 18,19. Cf. E. Tov, *Textual Criticism of the Hebrew Bible*, Assen, Van Gorcum, 1992, pp. 130 and 248.

(Qoh 8,15). For this concluding verse has וְשִׁבַּחְתִּי, which is rendered ἐπήνεσα in the LXX, which is the same verb as the verb used in Qoh 8,10c[48]. Strikingly, this important structural aspect of the *inclusio* between Qoh 8,10 and 8,15 is completely absent in Qohelet literature dealing with the text critical problem of Qoh 8,10.

However if the emendation וישתבחו, favoured by many scholars[49], is accepted, the subsequent subordinate clause (אשר כן־עשו) also becomes more clear: "priding themselves on having done so". As כן in the Hebrew Bible is often used in the sense of "correct" or "rightful"[50], a more adequate rendering would be: "priding themselves on having acted rightfully". Such a case, Qohelet is condemning as "This too is הבל".

Within the Book of Qohelet, subordinate clauses are a major issue[51]. Therefore it is not my intention to discuss this phenomenon in full, not even only as far as Qoh 8,1-15 is concerned. However there are a few points I would like to touch on. First of all, the syntax of Qoh 8,11-12a is problematic. A protasis introduced by אשר which is followed by an apodosis introduced by על־כן, is unprecedented in the Hebrew Bible[52]. Moreover, it presents a rather odd syntactical construction with regard to the opening of v. 12a: "Because..., therefore..., because...". A. Schoors holds the view that אשר at the opening of Qoh 8,11 has a *causal* function that is "reinforced by על־כן introducing the apodosis"; and he continues: "The אשר of vs. 12 undoubtedly has the same function: it introduces a causal clause that resumes 11a, thus forming an *inclusio* around the main clause in 11b"[53]. However if my aforementioned view is correct that Qoh 8,10 entirely deals with the רשעים, then vv. 11-12a must be considered as a further *explication* of the particular observation(s) made in v. 10, whereas the phrase כי גם־יודע אני marks the transition to the classical doctrine of retribution as is reflected in 8,12b-13. Both sections (vv. 11-12a; 12b-13), consisting of three lines each, are strongly linked, not only by כי גם־יודע אני in their centre, but also by the verb ארך *hiph.*, viz. מאריך (v. 12a) and its opposite לא־יאריך (v. 13b). The formulation of the classical doctrine of retribution (vv. 12b-13) is

48. Cf. Qoh 4,2, where the verb שבח is rendered ἐπήνεσα too.

49. SERRANO, *I saw the wicked burried* (n. 37), p. 170; DRIVER, *Problems and Solutions* (n. 41), p. 230; CRENSHAW, *Ecclesiastes* (n. 12), pp. 153-154; SCHOORS, *The verb* ראה ... (n. 32), p. 237, note 68.

50. E.g. Num 27,7; Jer 8,6; Amos 5,14. HAL³, p. 459 has listed 23 instances where such a meaning of כן is attested.

51. Cf. especially SCHOORS, *The Preacher* (n. 11), pp. 124-149.204-213; MICHEL, *Untersuchungen* (n. 2), pp. 200-244.

52. The combination אשר על־כן is known from Job 34,27. BDB ¹1906, p. 83 has rendered it 'forasmuch as'.

53. SCHOORS, *The Preacher* (n. 11), pp. 140-141.

followed by a strong statement (v. 14) that harks back to vv. 10-12a. It picks up הבל from v. 10, creating an *inclusio* both at the opening and at the end of v. 14. This structure, with Qohelet's own observations at the beginning and at the end, and the classical doctrine of retribution at the centre[54], is proof enough to fully disagree with those scholars who consider just that traditional point of view (8,12b-13) as a *gloss*[55].

Although Qoh 8,12b-13 is a reflection of the traditional doctrine of retribution, there are some aspects that should be paid attention to. Again, it is the use of אשר at the end of 8,12 that raises some problems. The parallel structure of

(יהיה־טוב ליראי האלהים אשר ייראו מלפניו) 8,12b and

(טוב לא־יהיה לרשע (...) אשר איננו ירא מלפני אלהים) 8,13 on the one hand, and the obvious causal meaning of אשר in 8,13, on the other hand, seem to limit the function of אשר in 8,12b to just a causal one: "In vs. 13, אשר איננו ירא is a causal clause, which forces us to accept the same meaning of the third אשר-clause in vs. 12"[56]

However a number of scholars agree with Delitzsch, that the notion יראי האלהים in Qoh 8,12 is not used in a normative way as, for example, is the case in Qoh 7,18, but descriptively, indicating a religious group[57]. The final אשר-clause of 8,12b is needed to give this saying a normative impact: "when they really fear before him"[58]. In Qoh 8,13, אשר, it is true, has a causal function, since its structure differs from that of Qoh 8,12b. For in 8,13 there is an extra clause (ולא־יאריך ימים כצל) between לרשע and the אשר-clause. I do agree with Backhaus that both the אשר-clause of 8,12b and that of 8,13b, as well as the 'extra clause' of 8,13a

54. "Its strategic position, between two contradictory flanks..."; VAN NIEKERK, *Response to J.A. Loader* (n. 37), p. 101.

55. E. Podechard, *L'Ecclésiaste* (EB) Paris 1912; A.M. Dubarle, *Les Sages d'Israel*, Paris 1946, pp. 95-128; GALLING, *Der Prediger* (n. 12), p. 112: "So muss man in 12b. 13 eine Glosse von QR² sehen, der die ihm frivol erscheinende Aussage in 12 bestreitet und damit dann freilich 14 desavouiert"; *Ibid.*, p. 154: "dogmatischer Zusatz von R²"; LAUHA, *Kohelet* (n. 12), p. 155: "Zusatz typisch für R²"; CRENSHAW, *Ecclesiastes* (n. 12), p. 155: "... the verdict "gloss" seems justified". KLEIN, *Qohelet und die Weisheit* (n. 13), p. 115, note 10: "8,12b.13... ist eine 8,12a korrigierende Glosse".

56. SCHOORS, *The Preacher* (n. 11), p. 141.

57. FRANZ DELITZSCH, *Hoheslied und Koheleth* mit Excursen von Consul D. Wetzstein (BC IV,4) Leipzig, 1875, p. 342. The quotation from Delitzsch as given by SCHOORS, *The Preacher* (n. 11), p. 141, note 693 is not correct; one should read: "... die auch wirklich *sind* was sie heißen'..

58. W. ZIMMERLI, *Das Buch des Predigers Salomo* (n. 29), 219: 'daß es den Gottesfürchtigen gut gehen wird, wenn sie sich vor ihm fürchten'. O. KAISER, *Dike und Sedaqa. Zur Frage nach der Sittlichen Weltordnung*, in NZSTh 7 (1965) 251-273, p. 262 [= ID., *Der Mensch unter dem Schicksal* (BZAW, 161) Berlin 1985, pp. 1-23, p. 12]: 'Wohl ergehen wird es den Gottesfürchtigen, wenn sie sich vor ihm fürchten'. BACKHAUS, *»Denn Zeit und Zufall trifft sie«* (n. 2), pp. 254-255.

can be considered the work of Qohelet, adding these three items to the core of the classical doctrine of retribution[59]:

יהיה־טוב ליראי האלהים

וטוב לא־יהיה לרשע.

However, there is one more point that deserves attention. Within this parallelism, 8,12 has a plural (ליראי האלהים), whereas 8,13 is in the singular (לרשע). Strikingly, this is the *only* occurrence in the entire Book of Qohelet where such a distinction is found. All other instances in the Book of Qohelet, dealing with the opposition of the wicked and the righteous, always have parallel pairs, either in the singular (Qoh 3,16-17; 7,15-18; 9,2) or in the plural (Qoh 8,14bc)[60]. The explanation I would like to give with respect to the deviant pattern of Qoh 8,12b-13 is, that by inserting a plural form in 8,12b, the author gives himself the opportunity to quote from an earlier passage in his work, viz. Qoh 3,14, which is part of the conclusion of the "founding tractate". And would it be a coincidence that Qoh 3,14 is preceded by the *carpe diem* motif (Qoh 3,12-13) that forms the conclusion of our pericope in Qoh 8,15?

Preludelaantje 6   Panc BEENTJES
NL-3438 TT Nieuwegein

---

59. BACKHAUS, *»Denn Zeit und Zufall trifft sie«* (n. 2), p. 255.

60. In other Old Testament Books, the alternation of singular and plural is very common, for example, רשעים / צדיק (Pss 7,10; 75,11) or its reverse צדיק / רשעים (Ps 37,16; Prov 10,6.7.11.20.32); רשע / צדיקים (Prov 10,24; 12,12).

OFFERED PAPERS

WIE HAST DU'S MIT DER RELIGION?
SPRECHHANDLUNGEN UND WIRKINTENTIONEN
IN KOHELET 4,17-5,6

»Gott sei mit dir, wenn du ihn findest. Mit mir ist er nicht ... Leb wohl!« So antwortet Kohelet dem kleinen schwarzen Mädchen, das auf der Suche nach Gott ist. Ob Bernard Shaw, der diese Geschichte erzählt, die Gottesvorstellung Kohelets richtig getroffen hat?[1] Wie es der ungewöhnliche Weisheitslehrer Kohelet mit Gott und mit der Religion hält, zeigt sich in 4,17-5,6, wo er ausdrücklich und konkret über religiöse Handlungen spricht[2]. Wie ist dieser Abschnitt im Gesamtaufriß des Buches verankert? Neben dieser Frage diskutiert die Forschung wichtige Einzelprobleme, für die als Voraussetzung zur weiteren Analyse eine Lösung versucht wird. Was in der Sekundärliteratur nicht angesprochen wird, ist die Frage, auf welche Weise der Text Ausdruck des (Sprech–) Handelns einer Person (des Verfassers) ist, was er bei den Hörenden und/oder Lesenden bewirken will und wie der Text dazu gestaltet wird. Die Untersuchungen der Sprechhandlungsabfolge und des Wirkgehalts werden auch die besonderen Akzente Kohelets zeigen: Die wenigen Stellen innerhalb der Weisheitsliteratur, die sich mit kultischen Aktivitäten befassen, sprechen wie Koh 4,17-5,6 über Gelübde, Gebete und die

---

1. B. SHAW, *The Black Girl in Search of God and Some Lesser Tales* (Erstveröffentlichung 1932), Harmondsworth, 1946, p. 33; vgl. B. LANG, *Ist der Mensch hilflos? Zum Buch Kohelet*, Zürich/Einsiedeln/Köln, 1979, p. 12.
    2. Literaturauswahl zu diesem Abschnitt: F. BACKHAUS, *Denn Zeit und Zufall trifft sie alle. Zu Komposition und Gottesbild im Buch Qohelet* (BBB, 83), Frankfurt am Main, 1993, pp. 174-184; V. D'ALARIO, *Il libro del Qohelet. Struttura letteraria e retorica*, Bologna, 1993, pp.121-125; A.A. FISCHER, *Skepsis oder Furcht Gottes? Studien zur Komposition und Theologie des Buches Kohelet* (BZAW, 1997), Berlin/New York, 1997; T. KRÜGER, *Theologische Gegenwartsdeutung im Kohelet-Buch*, Habilitationsschrift, München, 1990, pp. 373-391; N. LOHFINK, *Warum ist der Tor unfähig, böse zu handeln? (Koh 4,17-5,6)*, in *ZDMG.S* 5 (1983) 113-120; D. MICHEL, *Vom Gott, der im Himmel ist. Reden von Gott bei Qohelet*, in *Theologia Viatorum* 12 (1973-74) 87-100; ID., *Untersuchungen zur Eigenart des Buches Qohelet* (BZAW, 183), Berlin/New York, 1989, pp. 253-258; H.-P. MÜLLER, *Wie sprach Qohälät von Gott?*, in *VT* 18 (1968) 507-521; G.S. OGDEN, *The »Better«-Proverb (tôb-Spruch), Rhetorical Criticism, and Qoheleth*, in *JBL* 96 (1977) 489-505; R.B. SALTERS, *Notes on the History of the Interpretation of Koh 5,5*, in *ZAW* 90 (1978) 95-100; L. SCHWIENHORST-SCHÖNBERGER, *Nicht im Menschen gründet das Glück (Koh 2,24). Kohelet im Spannungsfeld jüdischer Weisheit und hellenistischer Philosophie* (HBS, 2), Freiburg u.a. 1994, 136-138; H. TITA, *Ist die thematische Einheit Koh 4,17-5,6 eine Anspielung auf die Salomoerzählung? Aporien der religionskritischen Interpretation*, in *BN* 84 (1996) 87-102.

Opferpraxis[3]. Kohelet teilt mit diesen Äußerungen den Grundakkord, daß es um die innere Einstellung und die ethische Aufrichtigkeit geht, bringt aber darüber hinaus eine unverwechselbare eigene Note ein.

DIE VERANKERUNG VON 4,17-5,6 IM BUCH KOHELET

Daß der Abschnitt Koh 4,17-5,6[4] zum Grundbestand des Buches gehört, wird heute nicht mehr bestritten[5]. Schon auf lexematischer Ebene sind eine Reihe von Wörtern zu nennen, die auch sonst häufig bei Kohelet belegt sind (u.a. עשׂה, טוב, ידע)[6]. Wie in 5,1a warnt in 7,9 und 8,3 die Wendung אַל־תְּבַהֵל vor überstürztem Handeln und ist mit dem Tun von Toren verbunden. Die Begriffe »Tor«, »Mund« und »Reden« (5,1-2.5) kommen außerdem in 10,12-15 vor, wo das endlose Gerede der Toren abqualifiziert wird. Daß bei vielen Worten nur Torenrede und

3. Spr 15,8.29; 20,25; 21,3.27; 28,9; Sir 7,10.14; 18,22-23; 34,21-35,22; vgl. G.S. OGDEN, *The ṭōb-Spruch in Qoheleth*, Th.D. diss., Princeton Theological Seminary, 1975, p. 217; siehe auch A. LANGE, *Weisheit und Torheit bei Kohelet und in seiner Umwelt*, Frankfurt/M. u.a., 1991, pp. 130-131; BACKHAUS, *Zeit und Zufall* (n. 2), p. 184; FISCHER, *Skepsis* (n. 2), p. 48.

4. 4,16c-d (»denn auch das ist Windhauch...«) scheint Schlußmarke eines größeren Zusammenhangs zu sein, während 4,17-5,6 einen formalen und sachlichen Neueinsatz bietet; vgl. FISCHER, *Skepsis* (n. 2), p. 12. 5,7-8 steht zwar inhaltlich isoliert, setzt aber mit dem Vetitiv in 5,7 formal die Mahnsprüche fort und bietet in 5,8 mit יְתְרוֹן ein verbindendes Stichwort zum folgenden Abschnitt (5,15). FISCHER, *Skepsis* (n. 2), p. 18, sieht daher 5,7-8 als redaktionelle Brücke zwischen den Textblöcken 4,17-5,6 und 5,9-6,9 an. 4,17-5,6 ist eine ursprüngliche Einheit (p. 19).

5. Frühere Kommentatoren (z.B. D.C. SIEGFRIED, *Prediger und Hoheslied* (HKAT), Göttingen, 1898, p. 11-12; 49-50 oder A.H. MCNEILE, *An Introduction to Ecclesiastes*, Cambridge, 1904, p. 25) führen an, die Stelle decke sich nicht mit dem sonst im Buch zu findenden Skeptizismus und unterbreche Kohelets Reflexionen über öffentliche Angelegenheiten. Diese These wird u.a. von G.A. BARTON, *A Critical and Exegetical Commentary on the Book of Ecclesiastes* (ICC, 21), Edinburgh, 1908, p. 45, und R. GORDIS, *Koheleth–The Man and His World* (TSJTSA, 19), New York, 1951, p. 236, zurückgewiesen. Eine strenge Systematik der Sentenzen ist auch sonst nicht durchgängig zu beobachten, daher kann ihr Fehlen hier kein Argument für einen literarkritischen Bruch sein. BARTON hält 5,2 und 5,6a (bis הַרְבֵּה) aufgrund ihrer weisheitlichen Spruchform für Glossen eines »Hokma-Bearbeiters« (p. 123). Derartige Bearbeitungen lassen sich jedoch nicht stringent genug nachweisen. Mit MICHEL ist zu konstatieren: »Der Versuch, mit Hilfe der Literarkritik die Schwierigkeiten des Buches Qohelet zu lösen, hat sich totgelaufen.« (D. MICHEL, *Qohelet* [EdF, 258], Darmstadt, 1988, p. 20). Zur Diskussion vgl. auch D'ALARIO, *Qohelet* (n. 2), p. 122.

6. O. LORETZ, *Qohelet und der alte Orient*, Freiburg, 1964, p. 166-178, hat die Vorzugsvokabeln Kohelets nach ihrer Häufigkeit geordnet. Folgende Wörter treffen auf 4,17-5,6 zu (in Klammern stehen Rang und Vorkommen): עשׂה »tun, das Tun, Werk« (häufigstes Wort bei Kohelet: 4,17d; 5,5e), טוב »gut, das Gute« (3.: 5,4a), ידע „wissen, das Wissen« (5.: 4,17d), רעה »böse, Unheil« (von רעע) (8.: 4,17d), הבל »Windhauch« (9.: 5,6), כס(י)ל »Tor, Torheit« (10.: 4,17c; 5,2b; 5,3c), חפץ »Gefallen finden, Angelegenheit« (25.: 5,3c).

Nichtigkeiten herauskommen (vgl. 5,2.6), greift Kohelet in 6,11 auf: »Es gibt viele Worte, die den Windhauch vermehren«[7]. Das Wort שְׁגָגָה (5,5) hebt Kohelet in 10,5 aus dem kultisch-gesetzlichen Bereich heraus und weitet die Bedeutung zu »Fehler aus Gedankenlosigkeit« aus. Die in 5,6 als abschließende Mahnung angeführte »Gottesfurcht« entspricht dem Ideal der »Goldenen Mitte« in 7,15-18 zwischen extremer Gesetzeserfüllung und Gesetzesmißachtung. Auch hier beschließt der Rat zur Gottesfurcht den Abschnitt. Sie ist (in 5,6 ebenso wie in 7,18) die vorsichtige Zurückhaltung angesichts eines ebenso undurchschaubaren wie wirkmächtigen Gottes[8]. Thematisch aufgegriffen und untermauert wird 4,17-5,6 in 9,2: Vor dem Tod ist aller Schicksal gleich, und auch der religiös Emsige kann durch seine kultische Geschäftigkeit sein Leben nicht verlängern. Die vielzitierte »Nichtigkeitsaussage« (vgl. 1,2 und 12,8) ist auch in 5,6 vertreten (הַבְלִים).

Der Text 4,17-5,6 ist damit sehr gut mit dem gesamten Buch vernetzt[9]. Daher ist nach dem kompositionellen Ort in der Gesamtkonzeption des Buches zu fragen[10]. Als plausibel erscheint bisher die Analyse von Lohfink, der eine palindromische Ringkomposition annimmt[11]. In deren Mitte steht 4,17-5,6 und unterbricht damit die »Gesellschaftskritik« (3,16-4,16; 5,7-6,10). Zeigt sich hier (mit Lohfink) die »Theozentrik« und damit auch das »Zentrum« der Wirkabsicht? Die Themen und Formulierungen vor allem in der zweiten Hälfte des Buches sind kaum auf einen gemeinsamen Nenner zu bringen, ferner kennt das Buch mehrere (andere) Höhepunkte[12]. Aus diesen Überlegungen heraus sollte die »Ringkomposition« nicht überbewertet werden. Auffällig bleibt der Befund der Mittelstellung[13] und die Beobachtung, daß der Im-

---

7. Vgl. FISCHER, Skepsis (n. 2), p. 8.

8. Vgl. u.a. C. KLEIN, Kohelet und die Weisheit Israels. Eine formgeschichtliche Studie (BWANT, 132), Stuttgart/Berlin/Köln, 1994, p. 112; FISCHER, Skepsis (n. 2), p. 244.

9. Diese Beobachtung relativiert das Problem, das TITA, Thematische Einheit (n. 2), pp. 87-89, anführt: Koh 4,17-5,6 falle derart aus dem Rahmen des Buches, daß man eine Anspielung auf andere alttestamentliche Traditionen vermuten müsse. Es ist nicht zwingend notwendig, zur Erklärung von 4,17-5,6 andere Texte und Traditionen heranzuziehen.

10. MICHEL, Qohelet (n. 5), pp. 33-45, stellt die wichtigsten Gliederungsversuche vor.

11. Vgl. N. LOHFINK, War Kohelet ein Frauenfeind? Ein Versuch, die Logik und den Gegenstand von Koh., 7,23-8,1a herauszufinden, in M. GILBERT (ed.), La Sagesse de l'Ancien Testament (BETL, 51), Leuven, 1979, pp. 267-269; ID., Kohelet (NEB), Würzburg, 1980, ⁴1993, p. 10 (vgl. die Würdigung durch MICHEL, Qohelet [n. 5], p. 42, und A. BONORA, Il libro di Qoèlet, Rom, 1992, p. 15). Problematisch ist an Lohfinks Ansatz die starke Systematisierung, die vor allem der Textvielfalt in 9,7-12,7 kaum mehr gerecht werden kann.

12. Vgl. etwa 1,12-18 (die Königstravestie); 3,1-15 (das Gedicht von der bestimmten Zeit).

13. Die Mittelstellung wird vielleicht auch durch die Verwendung des Plurals הַבְלִים, der sonst nur noch in Koh 1,2 und 12,8 auftaucht, signalisiert; vgl. LOHFINK, Warum ist der Tor unfähig (n. 2), p. 117.

perativ in 4,17 die erste explizite Mahnung Kohelets an die zweite Person ist[14] (nach 4,17 folgen weitere Imperative).

KLÄRUNG WICHTIGER EINZELPROBLEME IN 4,17-5,6

Die Analyse der Sprechhandlungsfolge und der Wirkintentionen setzt voraus, in wichtigen Einzelproblemen syntaktischer und semantischer Art begründete Entscheidungen zu treffen sowie eine knappe Strukturübersicht zu geben.

In 4,17 wird oft das Wort טוֹב ergänzt, um das מִן in מִתֵּת eindeutig als komparativisch auffassen zu können[15]. Ein derartiger Eingriff ist jedoch nicht nötig, da auch ohne טוֹב die Gegenüberstellung von »hören« und »(Opfer) geben« mit Hilfe der Präposition מִן erkennbar ist. Damit ist es auch möglich, den Infinitivus absolutus קָרוֹב als Fortführung des Imperativs שְׁמֹר anzusetzen[16]: Die erste Anweisung (»Achte auf deinen Fuß«[17]) wird von einem Umstandssatz mit כַּאֲשֶׁר (»wenn du zum Haus Gottes gehst«) gefolgt. Daran schließt sich syndetisch eine zweite Anweisung an, bei der der Infinitivus absolutus den Imperativ ersetzt (»und nähere dich...«) und zwei verschiedene finale Infinitivus-constructus-Angaben gegenübergestellt werden (»...um zu hören, anders als die Toren, die Opfer bringen«)[18]. Das zweite

14. Vgl. dazu (Neueinsatz in 4,17 und relative Eigenständigkeit von 4,17-5,6) KRÜGER, *Gegenwartsdeutung* (n. 2), p. 375.

15. Vgl. z.B. OGDEN, *»Better«-Proverb* (n. 2), p. 499; G.S. OGDEN, *Qoheleth*, Sheffield, 1987, p. 76; J.L. CRENSHAW, *Ecclesiastes* (OTL, 26), London, 1988, p. 115; BONORA, *Qoèlet* (n. 11), p. 85; BACKHAUS, *Zeit und Zufall* (n. 2), p. 175; D'ALARIO, *Qohelet* (n. 2), p. 123; SCHWIENHORST-SCHÖNBERGER, *Nicht im Menschen* (n. 2), p. 136, Anm. 51.

16. Vgl. GORDIS, *Koheleth* (n. 5), p. 237; MICHEL, *Qohelet* (n. 5), p. 141; KRÜGER, *Gegenwartsdeutung* (n. 2), p. 374.

17. Im Blick auf Spr 25,17 (הֹקַר רַגְלְךָ מִבֵּית רֵעֶךָ) ist der Singular (Qere, viele Manuskripte, LXX) vorzuziehen, auch wenn die Frage nicht eindeutig zu entscheiden ist und die Entscheidung auf die Bedeutung keine Auswirkung hat (vgl. A. SCHOORS, *The Preacher Sought To Find Pleasing Words. A Study of the Language of Qoheleth*, Leuven, 1992, p. 34).

18. Der Vorschlag von TITA, *Thematische Einheit* (n. 2), pp. 90-92, das מִן auf שְׁמֹר zu beziehen (»Bewahre deinen Fuß davor, ein Opfer von Toren zu geben...«), wirft eine Reihe erheblicher Probleme auf: In sämtlichen Parallelbelegen, die Tita anführt, folgt das מִן nahezu unmittelbar auf das Verb, während in Koh 4,17 eine lange Parenthese (von כַּאֲשֶׁר bis לִשְׁמֹעַ) anzusetzen wäre. Semantisch ist die Kombination, den *Fuß* vor dem *Opfern* zu bewahren, problematisch, während in den Parallelen Spr 3,26 (der Fuß wird vor dem Fang bewahrt) und Jes 56,2 (die Hand davor bewahren, Böses zu tun) das Bild eindeutig ist. Auch die Interpretation »Opfer geben nach Torenart« entfernt sich zu weit vom Text: Die Constructus-Verbindung besteht zwischen dem Geben und den Toren, d.h. es geht um die Tatsache, *daß* die Toren (Opfer) geben, nicht jedoch um eine Näherbestimmung des Opfers (זֶבַח) als Torenopfer oder törichte Opfer. Damit überzeugt weder

Problem dieses Verses ist der Begründungssatz, der nicht anders als mit »denn sie (die Toren) verstehen sich nicht darauf, Böses zu tun« zu übersetzen ist. Am plausibelsten erscheint es, mit Lohfink eine Verbindung zu 5,5 herzustellen[19]: Kohelet nimmt ironischerweise das Reden der Toren ernst, die in ihren Augen nur »versehentliche Irrtümer« (שְׁגָגָה) begehen und nichts Böses tun. Diese halbbewußte, jede Verantwortlichkeit zurückweisende Einstellung meint Kohelet in 4,17d, und er mahnt den Weisen in 5,5b-c, nicht in das Fahrwasser der Toren zu geraten und Verfehlungen als »Versehen« zu entschuldigen.

5,1-2 ist gegenüber 4,17 durch die neue Thematik (»ein Wort vor Gott hervorbringen«) als eigener Abschnitt ausgewiesen, der sich mit dem Gebet befaßt, auch wenn die spezifischen Termini (תהלה, תפלה) nicht vorkommen[20]. In 5,3 wird durch einen כַּאֲשֶׁר-Satz eine neue Situation angegeben (»Gelübde«), so daß 5,1-2 nicht lediglich den »Rahmen« zu 5,3-4 abgeben[21], sondern sich mit der Praxis wortreichen Betens auseinandersetzen.

Der Aussagespruch (Sentenz) 5,2 ist nach einem geprägten Typ gestaltet, wie er auch in Spr 25,23; 26,20; 27,17-18 u.ö. auftritt. Die Mitteilung der zweiten Hälfte des nach dem synonymen *parallelismus membrorum* gebauten Spruches wird jeweils durch eine Analogie (z.B. aus der Natur) anschaulich gemacht: »Ist kein Holz mehr da, erlischt das Feuer; wo kein Verleumder ist, legt sich der Streit.« (Spr 26,20). Die Analogie hat mit dem Thema an sich nichts zu tun, weckt aber erfahrungsgestützte Aufgeschlossenheit für die Lehre in der zweiten

---

die Übersetzung Titas noch seine Interpretation, hinter 4,17 stehe gar keine Opferkritik. An der Gegenüberstellung von »Hören« und dem Tun der Toren (»Opfer geben«) muß festgehalten werden. KRÜGER, *Gegenwartsdeutung* (n. 2), p. 374, faßt מתת als מַתַּת »Gabe« auf und übersetzt: »Eine Gabe der Toren ist ein Schlachtopfer«.

19. Vgl. LOHFINK, *Warum ist der Tor unfähig* (n. 2), pp. 119-120; so auch BACKHAUS, *Zeit und Zufall* (n. 2), p. 176; SCHWIENHORST-SCHÖNBERGER, *Nicht im Menschen* (n. 2), p. 138; anders MICHEL, *Untersuchungen* (n. 2), p. 254: Die Toren sind unwissend, so daß sie Schlechtes tun. GORDIS, *Koheleth* (n. 5), p. 238, interpretiert die wörtliche Übersetzung so: »They [die Toren] are good – because they lack the brains to do evil!«. SCHOORS, *The Preacher* (n. 17), p. 183, bezweifelt die Übersetzung Lohfinks und nimmt mit A. LAUHA, *Kohelet* (BK, 19), Neukirchen-Vluyn, 1978, p. 96-98, eine »gerundial function« (»begleitender Umstand«) des Infinitivs לַעֲשׂות an: »they are ignorant in connection with doing evil, i.e. they are ignorant so that they do evil«; in diesem Sinne auch LANGE, *Weisheit* (n. 3), p. 127-128.

20. Gegen TITA, *Thematische Einheit* (n. 2), p. 95.

21. So TITA, *Thematische Einheit* (n. 2), p. 102. Richtig sind Titas Beobachtungen hinsichtlich der Korrelation von 5,1-2 und 5,5. Allerdings handelt es sich nicht nur um einen Rahmen um 5,3-4, sondern um parallele Strophenteile, die sich ebenso wie 4,17 und 5,3-4 sowie 5,2 und 5,6 entsprechen. Zum formal parallelen Aufbau von 4,17-5,6 aus zwei »Strophen« vgl. LOHFINK, *Warum ist der Tor unfähig* (n. 2), pp. 118-119.

Hälfte[22]. Diesen Typ, den man auch als Vergleichsspruch[23] bezeichnen kann, hat der Verfasser von Koh 5,2 herangezogen: Daß der »Alptraum« auf »Geschäftigkeit« folgt, spielt eine untergeordnete Rolle[24], bildet aber die Analogie zu der Lehre, daß bei vielen Worten Torengeschwätz herauskommt. Wahrscheinlich zitiert Kohelet hier nur den Typ des Sprichworts und nicht einen vorgegebenen Merksatz. Er schafft damit eine Anspielung auf 2,23 (עִנְיָן)[25].

Auch in 5,5 verwendet Kohelet keine kultterminologisch eindeutigen Fachbegriffe. Dennoch ist anzunehmen, daß in 5,5b-c auf eine bestimmte Kultpraxis angespielt ist[26]. הַמַּלְאָךְ ist hier kein himmlisches Mittlerwesen[27], sondern ein offizieller Amtsträger im Tempelbereich (vgl. Mal 2,7). Es ist der Priester gemeint, der im Kontext der Sühnopfer für Sünden ohne Vorsatz (חטא בִּשְׁגָגָה, vgl. Lev 4,2.27; Num 15,27-31) auftritt[28]. Auf diese Opferpraxis für »unwissentliche« Sünden bezieht sich Kohelet[29] und brandmarkt Mißbrauch und Gedankenlosigkeit im Umgang mit diesen Vorschriften, sei es, daß tatsächliche Vergehen (unsoziales Verhal-

22. Vgl. dazu R.N. WHYBRAY, *Ecclesiastes*, London/Grand Rapids, MI, 1989, p. 94.
23. Vgl. KLEIN, *Kohelet* (n. 8), p. 70.
24. Der »Traum« steht in Parallelismus zur »Torenrede« und ist damit eindeutig negativ konnotiert, ebenso in 5,6, wo »Traum« in einer Reihe mit »Nichtigkeiten« und »vielen Worten« steht. Damit erscheinen die Bezüge, die TITA, *Thematische Einheit* (n. 2), p. 93; 100f., zwischen dem »Traum« hier und in der Salomotradition 1 Kön 3-11, in der der Traum als positiv konnotiertes Offenbarungsmittel fungiert, als sehr gezwungen.—Die negative Wertung von Träumen teilt Kohelet mit Sir 34,1-7.
25. Vielleicht könnte man חֲלוֹם »Traum« als »Illusion« interpretieren, die bei zuviel Geschäftigkeit (עִנְיָן) entsteht. Hier würde es sich dann um die Illusion handeln, Gott durch kultisch-religiöse Geschäftigkeit für sich vereinnahmen zu können. Dem setzt Kohelet in 5,6 sein spezifisches Verständnis von Gottesfurcht entgegen (Hinweis von A. Vonach).—Die Vermutung von LANGE, *Weisheit* (n. 3), pp. 128-129, bei 5,2 handle es sich aufgrund eines »schroffen« Parallelismus und des bei Kohelet nur zweimal (5,2 und 5,6) vorkommenden Wortes הַחֲלוֹם um ein Sprichwort aus der weisheitlichen Tradition, überzeugt nicht. Der Terminus עִנְיָן kommt nur bei Kohelet vor (acht Belege). Dies spricht sehr für eine Bildung des Wortlauts von 5,2 durch Kohelet selbst, während die Form des Spruchs sehr wohl aus der Tradition stammt.
26. Der Terminus שְׁגָגָה ist zunächst »ein juristischer Fachausdruck für eine unwissentliche Verfehlung, für deren Sühung das Gesetz eingehende Vorschriften erläßt (Lev 4,2ff.; Num 15,22ff.)« (LAUHA, *Kohelet* [n. 19], p. 100). Die Sühnung war mit einem bestimmten Opfer verbunden; vgl. LOHFINK, *Warum ist der Tor unfähig* (n. 2), p. 119; ID., *Kohelet* (n. 11), p. 39. Vgl. auch C. VAN DAM, *The Meaning of* שְׁגָגָה, in R. FABER (ed.), *Unity in Diversity. Studies presented to Prof. Dr. Jelle Faber*, Hamilton, Ontario: Senate of the Theological College of the Canadian Reformed Churches, 1989, pp. 13-24, hier p. 10. Van Dam vertritt die Ansicht, daß es sich (v.a. in Numeri) nicht nur um »unwissentliche« Verfehlungen handele, sondern grundsätzlich um alle vergebbaren Sünden, die aufgrund menschlicher Schwachheit ein Abweichen (שׁגה) von der Norm darstellen.
27. So erst in der Vulgata, vgl. SALTERS, *Interpretation of Koh 5,5* (n. 2), p. 99.
28. Vgl. GORDIS, *Koheleth* (n. 5), p. 239; SALTERS, *Interpretation of Koh 5,5* (n. 2), p. 100.
29. Vgl. LOHFINK, *Warum ist der Tor unfähig* (n. 2), p. 119.

ten) als »Versehen« kaschiert wurden, oder daß unbedachte Gebete und Gelübde mit der Bezeichnung שְׁגָגָה zurückgenommen wurden.

5,6 wird syntaktisch als eine einzige Prädikation aufgefaßt, wobei das erste כִּי adversativ anschließt (»vielmehr«)[30]. Eine Umstandsbestimmung (Präpositionalverbindung mit -בְּ) faßt drei wertlose Tätigkeiten[31] (Träume, Nichtigkeiten, viele Worte) zusammen, denen mit emphatischem כִּי die abschließende Empfehlung Kohelets (»wahrhaftig, den Gott fürchte!«) gegenübergestellt wird[32].

Für das weitere Verständnis ist ebenfalls ausschlaggebend, wie der Abschnitt 4,17-5,6 struktural aufgebaut ist. Zwischen zwei allgemeinen Mahnungen stehen zwei annähernd parallel gebaute »Strophen«[33]:

4,17		Eröffnende Mahnung: »Achte auf deinen Fuß!«
4,17	5,3-4	Mit כַּאֲשֶׁר wird jeweils die »Situation« angegeben. Imperative und Vetitive mahnen zu Zurückhaltung im kultischen Bereich. Zu den Toren (הַכְּסִילִים) wird ein Kontrast aufgebaut (vgl. auch die Verwendung von כִּי־אֵין). Mit מִן werden jeweils zwei Alternativen (hören/opfern und nicht geloben/geloben und nicht erfüllen) gegenübergestellt, wobei nach מִן die schlechtere steht.
5,1	5,5	Gemeinsam ist die Konstruktion mit je zwei Vetitiven und mit der Präposition לִפְנֵי. Vor dem Gott (הָאֱלֹהִים), der im Himmel ist und das Werk der Menschen zerstören kann, wird gewarnt: Der eigene Mund (5,1a/5,5a: פִּיךָ) kann durch unüberlegtes Gerede (5,1e/5,5d: דְּבָרֶיךָ / קוֹלֶךָ) vor (לִפְנֵי) Gott (bzw. dem „Boten«) Unheil bringen.
5,2	5,6	Entsprechungen auf Wortebene: חֲלוֹם, דְּבָרִים, הַרְבֵּה, כִּי / בְּרֹב.
	5,6	Abschließender Rat: „Fürchte Gott!«

Dem formal parallelen Aufbau entspricht die inhaltsorientierte Textstruktur: Es handelt sich um vier thematische Einheiten (Verhalten im Gotteshaus, Gebet, Gelübde, שְׁגָגָה-Praxis), die durch allgemeine Mah-

---

30. So auch KRÜGER, *Gegenwartsdeutung* (n. 2), p. 375.

31. Vgl. OGDEN, *Qoheleth* (n. 15), p. 79.

32. Vgl. GORDIS, *Koheleth* (n. 5), p. 240. SCHOORS, *The Preacher* (n. 17), pp. 103-104 betont die inhaltliche Nähe von adversativem und emphatischem כִּי hier und nimmt für das erste כִּי eine »emphatic force« (»in spite of...«) an, während er das zweite für eine Wiederholung (Dittographie?) hält. Gegen die Meinung einer Reihe von Forschern, die bei וּדְבָרִים von einem emphatischen -וּ ausgehen und zwei Sätze in 5,6 annehmen, hält SCHOORS (p. 126) mit GORDIS an der alten Lesart des MT und der wörtlichen Übersetzung der LXX fest (ein Satz).

33. Vgl.. LOHFINK, *Warum ist der Tor unfähig* (n. 2), pp. 118-119; anders BACKHAUS, *Zeit und Zufall* (n. 2), p. 179, der von einer chiastischen Struktur ausgeht (4,17 entspreche 5,5-6, 5,1-2 entspreche 5,3-4), dabei aber 5,6'b' (Mahnung zur Gottesfurcht) als formal überschüssiges Glied bezeichnen muß (abschließende Unterschrift).

nungen gerahmt werden[34]. Die ersten zwei Einheiten werden durch eine allgemeine Sentenz (5,2) abgeschlossen, die die sich aufdrängende Schlußfolgerung den Lesenden selbst überläßt. Die schon auf der syntaktischen Ebene feststellbare Häufung von Imperativen und Vetitiven sowie die beschriebene verdichtete Gestaltung in zwei parallelen Strophen sind Anzeichen dafür, daß dieser Text »aktiv« ist und in hohem Grade bei den Adressaten etwas bewirken will. Daher führt die Untersuchung der Sprechhandlungsabfolge und des Wirkgehalts näher an die Spur Kohelets und das Verständnis des Textes heran.

Erläuterungen zu Tabelle 1:

In der folgenden Tabelle 1 werden die Satzabgrenzung (mit übergreifenden Satzformen) und der Sprechhandlungsverlauf auf syntaktischer, satzsemantischer und kontextsemantisch-redesituativer Ebene dargestellt. Folgende Sigla bezeichnen die übergreifenden Satzformen (Spalte »Satzbindung«): I-förmige Klammern stehen für »Satzgefüge«. Als Satzgefüge sind Verknüpfungen von Sätzen durch syntaktische Unterordnung (Subordination) zu bezeichnen. In der graphischen Darstellung zeigt der dickere Balken den übergeordneten Satz (»Hauptsatz«) an. [-förmige Klammern markieren den »Erweiterten Satz«: Es handelt sich dabei um einen vollständigen Satz (z.B. 5,2a), der durch einen elliptischen Satz ohne Subjekt und/oder Prädikat erweitert wurde. Der elliptische Satz wird deshalb als eigener Satz (mit eigenem Kleinbuchstaben) abgegrenzt, weil er eine eigene Aussage (Prädikation) macht (5,2b: ohne Prädikat; בָּא aus 5,2a ist zu ergänzen).

Pfeile stehen für den »Satzbund«. Unter Satzbund ist die gleichgeordnete (koordinierte) Bindung von Sätzen durch gemeinsame Benutzung eines nur einmal ausgedrückten Satzelements zu verstehen. Bei einem Satzbund ist also ein syntaktisches Element (z.B. die satzeinleitende Konjunktion כִּי in 5,1c) nur einmal vorhanden, in dem oder den zugeordneten Satz (Sätzen) jedoch erspart (5,1d)[35]. Die Kennzeichnung der übergreifenden Satzformen (der Satzbindung) ist für die Sprechhandlungsanalyse unerläßlich, damit erkennbar wird, welche syntaktisch abgegrenzten Einzelsätze so gebunden sind, daß sie einen komplexen Sprechakt ausdrücken.

---

34. KRÜGER, *Gegenwartsdeutung* (n. 2), p. 387, spricht von einer chiastischen Klammer um 4,17-5,6. Die Einheit beginnt und endet mit einander struktural und semantisch entsprechenden Imperativen.

35. Zu Terminologie und Methodik der Beschreibung übergreifender Satzformen vgl. H. IRSIGLER, *Großsatzformen im Althebräischen und die syntaktische Struktur der Inschrift des Königs Mescha von Moab*, in H. IRSIGLER (ed.), *Syntax und Text* (ATSAT, 40), St. Ottilien, 1993, pp. 81-121; angewandt u.a. von T. HIEKE, *Psalm 80 – Praxis eines Methodenprogramms* (ATSAT, 55), St. Ottilien, 1997, pp. 56-64.

DER SPRECHHANDLUNGSABLAUF IN KOH 4,17-5,6
(vgl. Tabelle 1)

Sprache ist Handeln. Die Grundeinheit sprachlicher Kommunikation ist nicht das Symbol, das Wort oder der Satz, sondern die Produktion des Symbols, des Wortes oder Satzes im Vollzug des Sprechaktes[36]. Das Handeln durch Sprechen unterliegt (wie jedes zweckgerichtete Handeln) gewissen Regeln und Regelmäßigkeiten. Die Analyse der in einem Text regelhaft angewendeten Sprechhandlungsfunktionen und deren Abfolge fördert den Handlungscharakter und die Wirkweise eines Textes zutage und läßt ferner die Gestaltungsschwerpunkte und die Wirkabsichten des Verfassenden erkennen. Die Untersuchung erfolgt in drei Stufen: orientiert an der Syntax und ihren Indikatoren für Sprechakte (z.B. Imperative), an der Satzsemantik (Auswirkungen des Satzinhalts auf den Sprechakt) sowie an der Redesituation (Auswirkungen des gesamten Kontexts auf den einzelnen Sprechakt bzw. satzübergreifende, komplexe Sprechhandlungen)[37].

Auf syntaktischer Ebene (Spalte 2 nach dem hebräischen Text) dienen vor allem die Verbformationen als Indikatoren von Sprechhandlungen: So sind z.B. Imperative und Vetitive von der Ausdrucksseite her als DIREKTIVE Sprechakte zu klassifizieren. Auffällig ist in Koh 4,17-5,6, daß der Abschnitt von zwei positiven Aufforderungen gerahmt ist (4,17a/5,6), während innerhalb des Rahmens die negativen Warnungen (Vetitive) überwiegen. Die Tendenz des Textes geht also dahin, verstärkt zu ermahnen, gewisse Dinge zu unterlassen, während die Ermutigung zu bestimmten Handlungen deutlich in der Minderheit ist. So zeigt sich schon durch die quantitative Gewichtung der kritisierende Charakter des Textes.

Auf satzsemantischer Ebene (Spalte 3) präzisiert der Aussagegehalt den Charakter der Sprechhandlung. Folgerungs- und Begründungszusammenhänge werden erkennbar, Feststellungen und Warnungen erweisen sich als eigentlich positiv gemeinte Ratschläge. So ist z.B. die Feststellung, daß Gott im Himmel (und der Mensch auf der Erde) ist (5,1c-d), eine anaphorisch-KONNEKTIVE Begründung für die Warnung vor übereiltem Gebet (5,1a-b)[38]. Kataphorisch löst 5,1c-d die Folgerung

---

36. Vgl. J.R. SEARLE, *Sprechakte. Ein sprachphilosophischer Essay*, Frankfurt am Main, [4]1990, p. 30.

37. Die Vorgehensweise orientiert sich an der von H. Irsigler erarbeiteten Methodik, insbesondere dessen Skizze einer Klassifikation von Sprechakten; vgl. IRSIGLER, *Psalm-Rede* (n. 35), pp. 91-92. Weitere Hinweise auch bei HIEKE, *Psalm 80* (n. 40), pp. 172-176.

38. Gattungstypisch liegt hier (wie in Koh 4,17; 5,3.5-6) der »weisheitliche Mahnspruch« vor, der aus Mahnung (Imperativ) oder Warnung (Vetitiv) und einer Begründung (mit כִּי) besteht; vgl. dazu W. RICHTER, *Recht und Ethos. Versuch einer Ortung des weisheitlichen Mahnspruches* (StANT, 15), München, 1966, besonders pp. 37-39.—Warnungen vor Hast sind ein Topos der biblischen Weisheitsliteratur, vgl. Spr 19,2; 29,20; Sir 11,10.

Tabelle 1 | **Sprechhandlungsablauf**

		Satzbindung		*syntaktisch*[39]
4,17	a	שְׁמֹ֤ר רַגְלְךָ	⌐	/auffordern/: DIREKTIV-positiv
	b	כַּאֲשֶׁ֬ר תֵּלֵ֨ךְ אֶל־בֵּ֪ית הָאֱלֹהִ֡ים		
	c	וְקָר֣וֹב לִשְׁמֹ֑עַ		/auffordern/ bzw. /feststellen/[40]
		מִתֵּ֖ת הַכְּסִילִ֣ים זָ֑בַח		
	d	כִּֽי־אֵינָ֥ם יוֹדְעִ֖ים לַעֲשׂ֣וֹת רָֽע:		/feststellen/: ASSERTIV-konstativ
5,1	a	אַל־תְּבַהֵ֨ל עַל־פִּ֜יךָ	▲	/warnen/: DIREKTIV-negativ
	b	וְלִבְּךָ֧ אַל־יְמַהֵ֣ר		
		לְהוֹצִ֣יא דָבָ֗ר לִפְנֵ֣י הָאֱלֹהִ֑ים		
	c	כִּ֤י הָאֱלֹהִ֣ים בַּשָּׁמַ֔יִם		/feststellen/: ASSERTIV-konstativ
	d	וְאַתָּ֖ה עַל־הָאָ֑רֶץ	▼	
	e	עַל־כֵּ֛ן יִהְי֥וּ דְבָרֶ֖יךָ מְעַטִּֽים:		/feststellen/: ASSERTIV-prädiktiv
5,2	a	כִּ֣י בָּ֤א הַחֲלוֹם֙ בְּרֹ֣ב עִנְיָ֔ן	⌐	/feststellen/: ASSERTIV-konstativ
	b	וְק֥וֹל כְּסִ֖יל בְּרֹ֥ב דְּבָרִֽים:		
5,3	a	כַּאֲשֶׁר֩ תִּדֹּ֨ר נֶ֜דֶר לֵֽאלֹהִ֗ים	⌐	
	b	אַל־תְּאַחֵר֙ לְשַׁלְּמ֔וֹ	—	/warnen/: DIREKTIV-negativ
	c	כִּ֣י אֵ֥ין חֵ֖פֶץ בַּכְּסִילִ֑ים		/feststellen/: ASSERTIV-konstativ
	d	אֵ֥ת אֲשֶׁר־תִּדֹּ֖ר		
	e	שַׁלֵּֽם:	—	/auffordern/: DIREKTIV-positiv
5,4	a	ט֖וֹב	⌐	/feststellen/: ASSERTIV-konstativ
	b	אֲשֶׁ֣ר לֹֽא־תִדֹּ֑ר		
	c	מִשֶּׁתִּדּ֖וֹר		
	d	וְלֹ֥א תְשַׁלֵּֽם:		
5,5	a	אַל־תִּתֵּ֤ן אֶת־פִּ֨יךָ֙		/warnen/: DIREKTIV-negativ
		לַחֲטִ֣יא אֶת־בְּשָׂרֶ֔ךָ		
	b	וְאַל־תֹּאמַר֙ לִפְנֵ֣י הַמַּלְאָ֔ךְ	⌐	/warnen/: DIREKTIV-negativ
	c	כִּ֥י שְׁגָגָ֖ה הִ֑יא		
	d	לָ֣מָּה יִקְצֹ֤ף הָֽאֱלֹהִים֙ עַל־ק֣וֹלֶ֔ךָ	↓	/fragen/: INTERROGATIV
	e	וְחִבֵּ֖ל אֶת־מַעֲשֵׂ֥ה יָדֶֽיךָ:	▼	
5,6		כִּ֣י בְרֹ֤ב חֲלֹמוֹת֙		/auffordern/: DIREKTIV-positiv
		וַהֲבָלִ֔ים וּדְבָרִ֖ים הַרְבֵּ֑ה		
		כִּ֥י אֶת־הָאֱלֹהִ֖ים יְרָֽא:		

---

39. Die Klassifizierung der Sprechakte (ASSERTIV, DIREKTIV usw.) orientiert sich an den Bezeichnungs-weisen bei H. IRSIGLER, *Psalm-Rede als Handlungs-, Wirk- und Aussageprozeß. Sprechaktanalyse und Psalmeninterpretation am Beispiel von Psalm 13*, in K. SEYBOLD/E. ZENGER (eds.), *Neue Wege der Psalmenforschung*. FS W. Beyerlin (HBS, 1), Freiburg u.a. 1994, pp. 91-92.

40. Restituiert man einen *ṭōb-min*-Spruch, handelt es sich um eine Feststellung: „(Besser) ist es, sich zu nähern, um zu hören…«. Ohne Texteingriff ist der Infinitivus absolutus als Imperativ aufzufassen: »Nähere dich, um zu hören…«.

Sprechhandlungsablauf

satzsemantisch   *kontextsemantisch-redesituativ*

4,17 a /zur Vorsicht raten/:   (/eröffnen/: KOMMUNIKATIV)

b DIREKTIV-positiv   *Situationsangabe: Gang zum Gotteshaus*

c /zum Hören raten/   /gegenüberstellen/: EVALUATIV-positiv: »hören«

(Abgrenzung von den Toren)   EVALUATIV-negativ: »opfern«

d /begründen/: KONNEKTIV   /disqualifizieren/ (der כְּסִילִים): EVALUATIV-negativ

5,1 a /zur Vorsicht raten/:   /gegenüberstellen/: (EVALUATIV-positiv: besonnen)[41]

b DIREKTIV-negativ   EVALUATIV-negativ: »hastig«

    Situationsangabe: Gebet

c /begründen/: KONNEKTIV   /betonen/ der Distanz zwischen Gott und Mensch:

d   DIREKTIV-positiv (=zum Bedenken auffordern!)

e /folgern/: DIREKTIV-pos.   /einschärfen/ (durch Wiederholung): DIREKTIV-positiv

5,2 a /begründen/: KONNEKTIV   /auffordern zur Schlußfolgerung/: DIREKTIV-positiv

b   (Schwerpunkt der Sentenz auf Teil b!)

5,3 a   *Situationsangabe: Gelübde*

b /raten/: DIREKTIV-positiv   a+b+c: /gegenüberstellen/[42]

c /begründen/: KONNEKTIV   /disqualifizieren/ (der כְּסִילִים): EVALUATIV-negativ

d /folgern/:   /einschärfen/ (durch Wiederholung): DIREKTIV-positiv

e DIREKTIV-positiv

5,4 a /raten/: DIREKTIV-positiv   /qualifizieren/: EVALUATIV-positiv

b   a-d: /gegenüberstellen/:

c   EVALUATIV-positiv: »nicht geloben«

d   EVALUATIV-negativ: »geloben und nicht erfüllen«

5,5 a /zur Vorsicht raten/:   a-c: /gegenüberstellen/:

DIREKTIV-negativ   (EVALUATIV-positiv: Vorsicht, Zurückhaltung)

b   EVALUATIV-negativ: »leichtfertiges Reden vor

c   Gott, Mißbrauch des שְׁגָגָה-Opfers«[43]

d /begründen/: KONNEKTIV   /argumentieren/: Es ist unnötig, sich durch unbedachtes

e +/warnen/: DIREKTIV-neg.   Reden im religiösen Bereich den Zorn Gottes zuzuziehen.

5,6 /raten/: DIREKTIV-positiv   /gegenüberstellen/:

    EVALUATIV-negativ: Träume, Nichtigkeiten...

    EVALUATIV-positiv: »Fürchte Gott!«

---

41. Der gegenübergestellte Gegensatz ist durch die Negation implizit vorhanden: Verurteilt werden Hast und Unüberlegtheit beim Beten, nicht jedoch das Gebet selbst. Damit ist indirekt ein Rat zu besonnenem Sprechen vor Gott verbunden.

42. Wie in 5,1ab wird durch die Negation eine Verhaltensweise (hier implizit das Erfüllen des Gelübdes) einer anderen (hier das verzögerte oder nicht durchgeführte Erfüllen) vorgezogen (EVALUATIV-negativ: das Verhalten der Toren, die weder vor Gott noch vor den Menschen Gefallen finden; EVALUATIV-positiv (implizit): das Erfüllen der Gelübde ohne Verzögerung).

43. Zum שְׁגָגָה-Opfer vgl. LOHFINK, *Warum ist der Tor unfähig* (n. 2), p. 119.

5,1e aus: »Mach wenig Worte!« (DIREKTIV-positiv). Da hier semantisch eine leichte Verschiebung auftritt (zuerst: »keine Hast«, dann: »wenig Worte«), schließt sich mit der Sentenz in 5,2 eine Begründung für 5,1e (»wenig Worte«) an: Viele Worte sind Torengeschwätz.

Im Blick auf die Gelübde ist die Warnung »Zögere nicht...« (5,3b)[44] semantisch dem Rat »Erfülle rasch...« (DIREKTIV-positiv) äquivalent. Dieser positive Rat folgt dann auch in 5,3d-e auf die Begründung 5,3c: Die Aussage, daß an den Toren kein Gefallen besteht, dient anaphorisch-KONNEKTIV als Untermauerung der Aufforderung, bei der Gelübdeerfüllung nicht zu zögern. Implizit ist vorausgesetzt, daß ein solches Zögern als törichtes Verhalten gilt, das vor Gott wie vor den Menschen keinen Gefallen findet. Kataphorisch-KONNEKTIV löst 5,3c die Folgerung aus: »Was immer du gelobst, erfülle es!« (5,3d-e).

Der ṭōb-min-Spruch[45] in 5,4 ist, syntaktisch gesehen, eine Feststellung. Satzsemantisch steckt der Rat dahinter, keine unüberlegten Gelübde abzulegen, die man nicht erfüllen kann (DIREKTIV-positiv)[46]. In 5,5d-e begründet die rhetorische Frage den Rat zur Vorsicht mit dem Reden vor Gott mit dem Hinweis auf Gottes zerstörende Wirkmacht, die implizit selbst eine Warnung darstellt[47].

Die Abwechslung zwischen Warnungen, Ratschlägen und begründenden Feststellungen zeigt, daß der Text keine Liste von Geboten und Verboten sein will, sondern argumentativ zu überzeugen versucht. Das zeigt sich noch mehr bei Einbezug des Kontextes und der Redesituation (Spalte 4). Der einleitende Imperativ in 4,17a impliziert eine Anrede an ein »Du« und eröffnet damit einen explizit an jemanden gerichteten Kommuni-

---

44. Kohelet übernimmt Dtn 23,22 nahezu wörtlich, allerdings macht er aus dem einleitenden כִּי in Dtn 23,22 hier ein כַּאֲשֶׁר und damit aus dem Rechtssatz einen »sicherlich weniger gewichtigen und alltäglicheren ... Temporalsatz« (MICHEL, Untersuchungen [n. 2], p. 256). Zur Begründung greift Kohelet nicht auf die Sanktionierung durch יהוה (Dtn 23,22: Bestrafung der »Sünde« des Nicht-Erfüllens) zurück, sondern darauf, daß an den Toren, die ihre Gelübde nicht erfüllen, keiner Gefallen hat (ein argumentum ad hominem). Während die Kategorien in Dtn »Sünde« und »Nicht-Sünde« sind (vgl. ähnlich apodiktisch in Num 30,3), wägt Kohelet als »Weiser« zwischen »besser« und »schlechter« ab (vgl. Spr 20,25; Sir 18,22-23).

45. Zu dieser Sprichwort-Gattung vgl. J. WEHRLE, Sprichwort und Weisheit. Studien zu Syntax und Semantik der ṭōb...min-Sprüche im Buch der Sprichwörter (ATSAT, 38), St. Ottilien, 1993. Den ṭōb-min-Spruch speziell bei Kohelet untersucht OGDEN, »Better«-Proverb (n. 2), 489-505; ID., ṭōb-Spruch (n. 3), passim.—Der Gebrauch der Gattungen »weisheitlicher Mahnspruch«, »Sentenz« und »ṭōb-min-Spruch« zeigt, daß Kohelet in der traditionellen Weisheit(stradition) wurzelt.

46. »Ausdrücken beschreibt die Beziehung des Menschen zu den im ṭōb-Spruch genannten Teilbereichen der Wirklichkeit jedoch nicht genau genug. Indem er sagt, was besser ist, fordert er gleichzeitig ein bestimmtes Verhalten.« (KLEIN, Kohelet [n. 8], p. 96).

47. FISCHER, Skepsis (n. 2), p. 43, Anm. 184, spricht daher (wie im Falle von 7,16-17) nicht von rhetorischen Fragen, sondern von negativen Absichtssätzen.

kationsprozeß. Dies gilt im übrigen für das gesamte Buch, da erst ab dieser Stelle die zweite Person auftritt. Deutlicher als vor 4,17 bündelt Kohelet jetzt seine Absichten auf ein Gegenüber.

Kontextsemantisch wird 4,17-5,6 beherrscht von der Sprechhandlung der wertenden Gegenüberstellung. Kohelet stellt zwei Handlungsweisen gegenüber und bewertet eine von ihnen als positiv, die andere negativ, wobei nicht immer beide Glieder explizit ausgeführt sein müssen. Er reagiert auf eine vorfindliche Praxis und hält seine Alternative dagegen. Ausführlich ist dies in 4,17; 5,4 und 5,6 der Fall: In 4,17 wird das Hören (im Sinne von »zuhören«[48] und »begreifen«[49]) dadurch vorgezogen (EVALUATIV-positiv), daß das Geben von Opfern als Tätigkeit der Toren abqualifiziert wird (EVALUATIV-negativ)[50]. Zudem werden die Toren als halbbewußt und unverantwortlich dahinlebende Unverständige disqualifiziert (4,17d), für die alles Tun im Zweifelsfalle »ein Versehen« (שְׁגָגָה) ist. In 5,4 ist die Gegenüberstellung sogar mit ṭōb-min, »besser... als...« ausgeführt. Eher elliptisch dagegen stehen sich in 5,6 drei negativ qualifizierte Dinge (Träume, Nichtigkeiten, viele Worte) und der Rat zur Gottesfurcht gegenüber.

Durch das Übergewicht der Warnungen (DIREKTIV-negativ) überwiegen auch die explizit ausgeführten Abwertungen (EVALUATIV-negativ), die jedoch durch den Kontext und ihre Gestaltung auch eine positive Haltung implizieren. So steht der Warnung vor einem übereilten Gebet in 5,1 indirekt die positive Wertung besonnener, weniger Worte gegenüber, ebenso wird sicher in 5,3 gegenüber der Warnung vor verzögertem Gelübdeerfüllen das rasche Erfüllen als positiv gewertet. Auch in 5,5 steht dem unüberlegten Gerede und der שְׁגָגָה-Praxis als positiv die verbale Zurückhaltung im Kult und der Verzicht auf kultische Ausflüchte (»Sühnopfer für versehentlich begangene Sünden«) gegenüber.

FOLGERUNGEN AUS DEM SPRECHHANDLUNGSABLAUF

Aus den Aussagen und Sprechhandlungen Kohelets lassen sich sowohl die Praxis seiner Zeitgenossen rekonstruieren als auch Kohelets Reaktion darauf beschreiben. Der rege Opferbetrieb am nachexilischen Tempel mit dem Schwergewicht auf Sühn- und Sündopfer führte nicht

---

48. Vgl. LAUHA, *Kohelet* (n. 19), p. 98.
49. Vgl. GORDIS, *Koheleth* (n. 5), p. 237; zu dieser Bedeutung von שמע vgl. auch Gen 11,7; 42,23; Dtn 28,49; 2 Kön 18,26 usw. Die Einordnung von שמע in Koh 4,17 unter »Gehorsam« bei J. ARAMBARRI, *Der Wortstamm 'hören' im Alten Testament* (SBB, 20), Stuttgart, 1990, p. 265, erscheint unzutreffend.
50. Vgl. KRÜGER, *Gegenwartsdeutung* (n. 2), p. 377, präzisiert die Gegenüberstellung dahingehend, daß die Schlachtopfer deshalb als töricht abzulehnen sind, weil sie als gemeinsame Mahlzeiten von Gott und Mensch die Distanz zwischen Gott und Mensch nicht respektieren.

Tabelle 2	**Wirkgehalt**

im Redeablauf

4,17	a	Achte auf deinen Fuß	*allgemeine* Mahnung zu Vorsicht
	b	wenn du zum Haus des Gottes gehst	und Überlegtheit → 5,6
	c	und nähere dich, um zu hören,	*konkrete* Mahnung zu intellektuel-
		anders als die Toren, die Opfer bringen,	lem Hören statt rituellem Opfern
	d	denn sie verstehen sich nicht darauf,	Begründung durch ironische
		Böses zu tun.	Verfremdung[51]
5,1	a	Übereile dich nicht mit deinem Mund	*konkrete* Mahnung zur Zurück-
	b	und dein Herz eile nicht,	haltung beim Gebet (hinsichtlich
		um ein Wort vor dem Gott hervorzubringen,	Reden und innerer Einstellung)
	c	denn der Gott (ist) im Himmel,	*allgemeine* Feststellung
	d	und du (bist) auf der Erde,	und
	e	deshalb seien deine Worte wenige.	*konkrete* Handlungsanweisung
5,2	a	Denn der Traum kommt bei viel Getue	*allgemeine,* negative Schlußbilanz
	b	und die Rede eines Toren bei vielen Worten.	mit einer sentenzhaften Merkregel
5,3	a	Wenn du ein Gelübde für den Gott ablegst,	*konkrete* Anweisung zum Gelübde:
	b	zögere nicht, es zu erfüllen,	Die Pflicht, Gelübde zu erfüllen,
	c	denn es besteht kein Gefallen an den Toren.	wird zweimal (5,3b.d-e) ein-
	d	Was (immer) du gelobst,	geschärft (1. Stufe).
	e	erfülle es.	
5,4	a	Besser (ist es),	*Steigerung* durch den *ṭōb-min-*
	b	daß du nicht gelobst,	Spruch (2. Stufe): Angesichts der
	c	als daß du gelobst,	Erfüllungspflicht ist es besser,
	d	und nicht erfüllst.	kein Gelübde abzulegen.
5,5	a	Erlaube deinem Mund nicht,	*allgemeine* Mahnung zur Vorsicht
		daß er dein Fleisch in Schuld stürzt,	bei Reden im religiösen Bereich[52]
	b	und sage nicht vor dem Boten,	*konkrete* Ablehnung der Opfer für
	c	daß es ein Versehen (war).	versehentlich begangene Sünden
	d	Warum soll der Gott zürnen über deine Rede	Die *rhetorische Frage* greift argu-
	e	und das Werk deiner Hände zerstören?	mentativ 5,1-2.5a-c auf.
5,6		Vielmehr angesichts der vielen Träume	*allgemeine* Mahnung zu Vorsicht
		und Nichtigkeiten und Worten in Fülle -	und Überlegtheit in religiösen
		wahrhaftig: den Gott fürchte!	Bereichen → 4,17

---

51. Vgl. dazu die Deutung von Lohfink, *Warum ist der Tor unfähig* (n. 2), passim.
52. Der Satz wirkt durch eine versteckte Metaphorik und einen Schluß vom Kleineren auf das Größere: Der Mund steht für das Reden als das Kleinere, und dies soll nicht das Größere, den Körper, der für die ganze Person steht, in Sünde stürzen.

Wirkgehalt

Bewirkungsversuche	*Intention*
4,17 a *Bewußtseinsbildung* für ange- b messenes religiöses Handeln c *Identitätsstiftung* beim Adressaten durch Abgrenzung d von den »Toren«	Zu diesem adäquaten Verhalten soll angeleitet werden: Auch in der Religion ist das Hören und Verstehen wichtiger als das Vollziehen traditioneller oder ritueller Handlungen. Das Verhalten anderer (der »Toren«) ist dabei kein relevanter Maßstab.
5,1 a *Anleitung* zu angemessenem b Gebet: nicht unüberlegt, sondern – aufgrund der c *Bewußtwerdung* d. Abstandes d zwischen Gott und Mensch - e mit wenigen Worten;	Die Art des Gebets soll authentisch das Bewußtsein des wahren Verhältnisses zwischen Transzendenz und Menschheit wiedergeben: Der Mensch kann Gott nicht erreichen, geschweige denn mit wortreichen Gebeten manipulieren.
5,2 a *Zustimmung* aufgrund der vertrauten b Sentenzstruktur.	Die Schlußfolgerung liegt auf der Hand: Hastiges, wortreiches Reden vor Gott ist Torengeschwätz.
5,3 a *Mahnung* zum Erfüllen b der abgelegten Gelübde; c *Identitätsstiftung* durch d Abgrenzung von den Toren. e	Die erste Stufe betont das Gewicht des gelobenden Wortes vor Gott und schärft die Ernsthaftigkeit ein. Töricht ist es, leichtfertig mit Gelübden umzugehen. Die zweite Stufe erweitert den Horizont des Problems:
5,4 a Weitere *Bewußtseinsbildung* b durch die »Besser«-Qualifizierung c zierung der Entscheidung, d kein Gelübde abzulegen.	Der religiöse Bewußtseins- und Entscheidungsprozeß rationaler Prägung soll *vor* jeglichem religiösem Handeln, insbesondere vor starken Selbstverpflichtungen (Gelübde), stattfinden.
5,5 a *Bewußtwerdung* der Gefahren unbedachten Redens; b *Ausschluß* falscher Hintergec danken[53]; d *Bewußtseinsbildung*: Gott e kann strafend eingreifen.	Das Gewicht des eigenen Wortes vor Gott (hier: Gelübde; in 5,1: Gebet) soll gewahrt werden. Die Ernsthaftigkeit des religiösen Tuns soll nicht durch kultische Ausflüchte verwässert werden. Die rhetorische Frage wirbt darum, den zweifellos wirksamen Zorn Gottes zu vermeiden!
5,6 *Internalisierung* des erreichten Bewußtseinsstandes durch die Kategorie 'Gottesfurcht'	»Gottesfurcht« ist die Folgerung aus der angemahnten Ernsthaftigkeit bei religiösen Vollzügen: Zurückhaltung bei Reden und Tun, Bewußtwerdung des Abstands zwischen Mensch und Gott, aber auch der Wirkmächtigkeit und Unberechenbarkeit (und damit Unverfügbarkeit) Gottes.

---

53. Durch die Ablehnung des שְׁגָגָה-Opfers wird offenbar eine bei den Zeitgenossen Kohelets beliebte Praxis ausgeschlossen: der Mißstand, daß mit einem (billigen) Opfer für »versehentlich begangene Sünden« echtes Fehlverhalten kaschiert wurde. Kohelet betont, daß keine (religiöse oder profane) Handlung mit dem Hintergedanken begangen werden darf, man könne wieder alles rückgängig machen.

selten zur Veräußerlichung und zum Mißbrauch der Riten. Fehlende innere Einstellung und Sinnentleerung der Opfer waren die Folge. In für die Adressaten schockierender Weise verbindet Kohelet das Opfern mit dem Tun der Toren und akzentuiert demgegenüber das verstehende Hören, das auch als Gegenpol zum Reden Zurückhaltung impliziert.

Der poetischen Breite und dem Wortreichtum der Gebete seiner Zeitgenossen scheint Kohelet zu unterstellen, damit solle Gott manipulativ beeinflußt werden. Hier betont Kohelet den Abstand zwischen Gott und Mensch und damit die Unverfügbarkeit Gottes. Auch die nicht seltene Gelübdepraxis konnte dazu ausarten, Gott manipulieren zu wollen. Kohelet ist diese Ansicht peinlich, daher referiert er nur kurz die Rechtslage (mit Hilfe von Dtn 23,22-24 mit charakteristischen Änderungen[54]), betont das Erfüllen (5,3d-e) und unterbreitet dann seinen Rat, auf unüberlegte Selbstverpflichtungen ganz zu verzichten.

In 5,5b-c bezieht sich Kohelet auf einen religiösen Trick seiner Zeitgenossen: Durch die Deklaration eines Vergehens als »ein Versehen« (שְׁגָגָה) konnte es durch eine entsprechende Opfergabe gesühnt werden. Einer Verharmlosung der Schuld und des Unrechts war Tür und Tor geöffnet. Kohelet betont demgegenüber, daß die Lüge nicht unbestraft bleiben wird, denn Gott kann durch den Entzug des Wohlstandes (»...das Werk deiner Hände zerstören«) empfindlich strafend eingreifen. Gott ist »im Himmel«, also unberechenbar und kann daher auch nicht durch kultische Praktiken (Gebete, Gelübde, Opfer) gefügig gemacht werden. Was bleibt, sind kluge Zurückhaltung und Vorsicht, zusammengefaßt in der Chiffre »Gottesfurcht«[55] – damit nicht Alpträume (bzw. Illusionen) durch törichte Geschäftigkeit, Nichtigkeiten und eine Menge leerer Worte die Überhand gewinnen.

Die Beschreibung dessen, was der Sprecher Kohelet mit dem Text 4,17-5,6 *tut*, machte bereits deutlich, was er mit dem Text *will*. Daher wird nun der Wirkgehalt im Blick auf die Intention(en) des Textes bzw. seines Verfassers untersucht.

In der Tabelle 2 wird neben einer Übersetzung der Wirkgehalt dargestellt. Dabei wird zunächst der Blick auf den Redeablauf gelenkt. Darüberhinaus werden dann die Bewirkungsversuche herausgearbeitet und die einzelnen Wirkintentionen zu beschreiben versucht.

---

54. Siehe oben, n. 44; vgl. MICHEL, *Untersuchungen* (n. 2), p. 255-258.

55. Wie in 3,14 ist die Gottesfurcht die der absoluten Macht Gottes geschuldete und einzig mögliche praktische Verhaltensweise des Menschen. Gottesfurcht ist eine Haltung, die darauf bedacht ist, Gottes Zorn nicht herauszufordern und besonnen und verantwortlich zu handeln; vgl. FISCHER, *Skepsis* (n. 2), p. 244.

DER WIRKGEHALT IN KOH 4,17-5,6
(vgl. Tabelle 2)

Im Blick auf den *Redeablauf* (Spalte 2 nach der Übersetzung) fällt auf, daß der Text zwischen *allgemeinen* Mahnungen und *konkreten* Handlungsanweisungen abwechselt. Im Rahmen stehen *allgemein* gehaltene Weisungen: In 4,17a ist das »Achten auf den Fuß« ein bildlicher Ausdruck für die generelle Forderung, sich in acht zu nehmen[56]. In 5,6 ist die Gottesfurcht ein summarischer Begriff dessen, was Kohelet vorher konkret dargelegt hat[57]. Mehrfach ist eine Bewegung vom Allgemeinen zum Konkreten festzustellen: 4,17a-b werden von der konkreten Aufforderung zum verstehenden Hören präzisiert; aus der allgemeinen Feststellung 5,1c-d wird in 5,1e die konkrete Folgerung gezogen.

Ein weiteres Gestaltungsmittel, das die Wirksamkeit des Textes erhöht, ist die Steigerung: Im Bereich der Gelübde (5,3-4) wird zunächst die Erfüllungspflicht eingeschärft, dann aber durch den *ṭōb-min*-Spruch überboten, wobei die apodiktisch-knappe Anordnung in 5,3d-e ebenso wie der disqualifizierende Hinweis auf die Toren bereits den Boden für die »bessere« Alternative, nämlich nicht unüberlegt zu geloben, bereitet. Schließlich sind die argumentativ wirkenden »Abschlüsse« in 5,2 und 5,5d-e zu nennen: Die Sentenz mit sich aufdrängender Schlußfolgerung (5,2) schließt das Thema »Gebet« (»viele Worte sind Torenrede«) und vielleicht auch mit dem negativen Terminus »Getue« (עִנְיָן) das Thema »Opfern« ab. Die rhetorische Frage in 5,5d-e greift mit dem Stichwort »deine Rede« sowohl das Thema »Gebet« als auch die Warnung vor unbedachten Gelübden und dem Mißbrauch der שְׁגָגָה-Erklärung (5,5a-c) auf: Sie wirbt um die Einsicht, daß man doch das Wenige an Freude, was der eigenen Hände Tun einbringt (vgl. 3,22), nicht durch unvorsichtiges Reden vor dem unberechenbaren Gott aufs Spiel setzen soll.

Welche Versuche unternimmt nun Kohelet, um bei seinem Gegenüber etwas zu erreichen (Bewirkungsversuche, Spalte 3)? Es geht ihm zunächst um Bewußtseinsbildung: Die Zuhörenden bzw. Lesenden

---

56. Vgl. OGDEN, *Qoheleth* (n. 15), p. 76. KRÜGER, *Gegenwartsdeutung* (n. 2), p. 377, bezeichnet 4,17a als »Überschrift der ganzen Einheit«.

57. LOHFINK, *Kohelet* (n. 11), p. 40. Die Gottesfurcht hier entspricht keinesfalls dem vom zweiten Epilogisten in Koh 12,13 geforderten Tora-Gehorsam. Deswegen und weil in 5,6 keine literarkritischen Scheidungen möglich sind, trifft Michels Vermutung, 5,6b sei dem zweiten Epilogisten zuzurechnen (MICHEL, *Qohelet* [n. 5], p. 143), nicht zu.

sollen einsehen und verstehen, daß bei religiösem Handeln Vorsicht angebracht ist, daß ein unendlicher Abstand zwischen Mensch und Gott besteht, daß aber Gott dennoch unergründbar eingreifen kann und unbedachtes Reden zu Unheil führen wird. Man soll wissen, was man tut. Mit dieser Wachheit des Geistes will Kohelet unter seinen Adressaten eine Identität stiften, die sich von den »Toren«, den Ungebildeten und unbewußt daherlebenden Leuten abgrenzt. Diese Leute opfern, ohne dabei viel zu denken (oder »zuzuhören«), sie reden viel (auch beim Gebet), sie machen dauernd Gelübde und erfüllen sie dann nicht, sie haben kein Unrechtsbewußtsein. Sie sind das Gegenbild zum bewußt und überlegt (und daher zurückhaltend) lebenden Weisen. Kohelet versucht, durch die Disqualifikation bestimmter Handlungsweisen und der dahinterstehenden Personengruppe bei seinen Adressaten eine spontane Abwehrhaltung zu erreichen: Wer will schon so handeln wie die Toren! Als Lehrer bleibt Kohelet nicht bei allgemeinen Bemerkungen stehen, sondern gibt auch konkrete Anleitung zu sinnvollem religiösen Tun, wenn auch der Rat zum Unterlassen bestimmter Praktiken überwiegt. In 5,6 steigert sich Kohelets Strategie nochmals, indem er den erreichten Bewußtseinsstand als die wahre Gottesfurcht deklariert. Seine Anweisungen und seine Gottesvorstellung werden gleichsam theologisch internalisiert, indem implizit ausgesagt wird: Wer so handelt, fürchtet Gott!

Der Anlaß für Kohelet, den Text 4,17–5,6 zu schreiben, ist sicher weniger das innere Bedürfnis, etwas über Religion zu sagen, sondern die notwendige Reaktion auf das Verhalten seiner Zeitgenossen, der Zwang zur Stellungnahme[58]. Das ist aus dem Übergewicht der Abwehrhaltung und der Abqualifikation zu vermuten. Kohelet kritisiert die religiöse Praxis[59] und die dahinterstehenden Einstellungen seiner Adressaten.

Die leitenden Intentionen Kohelets (Spalte 4) gehen gleichwohl tiefer: Es geht ihm darum, die »richtige« Gottesvorstellung zu vermitteln und daraus die »richtige« Umgangsweise mit diesem Gott zu folgern. Kohelet stellt die Existenz Gottes an keiner Stelle in Frage, dennoch ist sie ein Problem für ihn: Gott ist einerseits unverfügbar und unerreichbar

---

58. Vgl. FISCHER, *Skepsis* (n. 2), p. 248: »Es handelt sich also bei den Lehren nicht um Philosophie, sondern um Einweisungen in das konkrete Leben.«

59. LOHFINK, *Kohelet* (n. 11), p. 10, nennt daher den Abschnitt Koh 4,17–5,6 »Religionskritik«. Da jedoch dieser Terminus von anderen Zusammenhängen her semantisch bereits besetzt ist, wirkt seine Anwendung hier problematisch. Alternativen wären »Anmerkungen zur religiösen Praxis« (MICHEL, *Kohelet* [n. 5], p. 141); »Infragestellung religiöser Praktiken« (Hinweis von A. Vonach) oder »Über die richtige Einstellung zur Religionsausübung«.

(»Gott ist im Himmel, und du bist auf der Erde«, 5,1c-d), andererseits ist dadurch seine Wirkmacht nicht beeinträchtigt (5,5d-e). Wenn aber Gott vom Menschen nicht erreicht oder gar berechnet werden kann, sind aufwendige religiöse Handlungen unangebracht. Sie können sogar kontraproduktiv sein, wenn sie aus einer falschen oder unklaren (unbewußten) inneren Haltung heraus getan werden. Gottes Wirkmacht steht hier (wie auch an anderen Stellen, vgl. 2,26; 3,11.14.17; 5,18-19; 6,2) außer Zweifel, sie kann aber vom Menschen nicht durchschaut werden (vgl. 3,11). Daher ist bei jeglicher Interaktion zwischen Mensch und Gott seitens des Menschen einerseits große Vorsicht und Zurückhaltung, andererseits große Ernsthaftigkeit angebracht. So betont Kohelet auch das Gewicht des gesprochenen Wortes und lehnt kultische Ausweichmanöver ab.

WIE HAST DU'S MIT DER RELIGION?

Das schwarze Mädchen in B. Shaws Geschichte lernt von Kohelet, daß Gott zu erkennen heißt, Gott zu sein. Gott kann nicht in dem Sinne gefunden werden, daß der Mensch ihn ergreifen oder begreifen würde. Kohelet meint, daß man sich darüber nicht beunruhigen sollte. Der biblische Prediger würde nicht so wortreich und zugleich pantheistisch und agnostisch auf die »Gretchenfrage« eingehen wie Goethes Heinrich Faust. Kohelet weist auf das Dilemma hin: Ein ferner, vom Menschen unergründbarer Gott wirkt unverfügbar im Schicksal aller. Sehr realistisch rät Kohelet daher zu angemessener Zurückhaltung: »Gott ist im Himmel, und du bist auf der Erde—also mach' wenig Worte!«

Für Kohelet müssen das religiöse Tun und die innere Gottesvorstellung einander entsprechen[60]. In religiösen Belangen soll sich ein weiser Mensch nicht anders verhalten als im Alltag, wo er sich auch von seinen Überlegungen, Erfahrungen und Weltvorstellungen leiten läßt[61]. Kohelet durchdenkt den religiösen Bereich ebenso konsequent wie die Alltagsphänomene an anderen Stellen des Buches. Seine realistische

---

60. Die differenzierte Stellungnahme Kohelets zum religiösen Tun zeigt sich z.B. beim Thema »Opfer«: Kohelet geht es nicht um eine allgemeine Abschaffung, vielmehr fordert er den einzelnen zum Verzicht darauf in seiner privaten Frömmigkeit auf. Törichte Kultpraktiken sind kein Hinderungsgrund für den Weisen, als Hörender zum Tempel zu gehen; vgl. KRÜGER, *Gegenwartsdeutung* (n. 2), p. 378. Kohelets Grundposition könnte auf die Formel gebracht werden: »praktische Anerkennung der Majestät Gottes«; vgl. FISCHER, *Skepsis* (n. 2), p. 248.

61. KRÜGER, *Gegenwartsdeutung* (n. 2), p. 389, sieht hinter 4,17-5,6 das »Ideal eines 'vernünftigen Gottes-Dienstes'«.

Schlußfolgerung zeigt sich in den *ṭōb-min*-Sprüchen, hier besonders in
5,3-4: Es ist besser, *vor* jeglicher religiöser Selbstverpflichtung genaue
Überlegungen anzustellen—die letztlich dann etwa von Gelübden abra-
ten, da die Gefahr besteht, das Gelübde nicht erfüllen zu können.
Kohelet denkt—wie so oft—einen (oder mehrere) Schritt(e) weiter als
seine Zeitgenossen.*

Sägmühle 7   Thomas HIEKE
D-91275 Auerbach-Michelfeld

* Ein herzlicher Dank gebührt den Kollegen Andreas Vonach, Innsbruck, und Dr. Georg
Steins, Bamberg, für ihre kritischen und hilfreichen Anmerkungen und die vielen guten
Gespräche.

KOHELET UND DIE FRÜHE APOKALYPTIK

EINE AUSLEGUNG VON KOH 3,16-21

Schlechterdings von zentraler Bedeutung für das Verständnis des Buches Kohelet ist die sich darin aussprechende Gewißheit des unentrinnbaren Todesgeschicks und die damit verbundene Einsicht in die Endlichkeit des Menschen. Wo immer die Todesverfallenheit in den Horizont des Nachdenkens Kohelets tritt, erweisen sich Weisheit und Gerechtigkeit, Besitz und Nachkommenschaft als relative und vergängliche Güter[1]. Ein über den Tod hinaus bleibender Gewinn seiner Mühen vermag der Mensch grundsätzlich nicht zu erzielen. Angesichts dieser Problematik stellt sich die Frage nach dem Verhältnis Kohelets zu den seit der fortgeschrittenen und späten Perserzeit in den Kreisen der eschatologisch und gesetzestreu gesinnten Chasidim aufkommenden apokalyptischen Erwartungen[2]. Dazu hat D. Michel in seinen *Untersuchungen zur Eigenart des Buches Qohelet* den weitestgehenden Versuch vorgelegt, indem er neben den gegen eine optimistische Weisheit gerichteten Reflexionen eine zweite Gruppe von Texten ausmachen zu können meinte, die gegen eine Haltung der Askese, des Leidens an der Welt und der Hoffnung auf eine Vergeltung nach dem Tode polemisiere[3]. Aus der Zusammenstellung der für seine These in Anspruch genommenen Texte 3,16-22; 5,10-19; 6,1-12; 7,1-10; 9,1-10 ergibt sich für ihn ein stimmiges Bild der einschlägigen Gesprächspartner Kohelets, die man sich am ehesten als Vertreter einer Anfangsphase der Apokalyptik vorzustellen habe.

In unserer eigenen Untersuchung *Skepsis oder Furcht Gottes?* haben wir die im Buch Kohelet vereinigten Lehren näherhin in einer Schule der Weisheit verortet und die darin enthaltenen tatsächlichen und fiktiven Einwände als Stilmittel des Unterrichts erklärt[4]. Daraus ergab sich

---

1. Cf. M. HENGEL, *Judentum und Hellenismus* (WUNT, 10), Tübingen, ³1988, p. 219. Zur Problematik des Todes bei Kohelet cf. M. SCHUBERT, *Schöpfungstheologie bei Kohelet* (BEATAJ, 15), Frankfurt a. M. - Berlin - New York - Paris, 1989, pp. 163-171; F. J. BACKHAUS, *»Denn Zeit und Zufall trifft sie alle«. Studien zur Komposition und zum Gottesbild im Buch Qohelet* (BBB, 83), Bonn, 1993, pp. 390-398.

2. Cf. HENGEL, *op. cit.*, pp. 319-381; O. KAISER, *Der Gott des Alten Testaments. Theologie des Alten Testaments I: Grundlegung*, Göttingen, 1993, pp. 141-146.

3. Cf. D. MICHEL, *Untersuchungen zur Eigenart des Buches Qohelet* (BZAW, 183), Berlin - New York, 1989, pp. 269-273.

4. Cf. A. A. FISCHER, *Skepsis oder Furcht Gottes? Studien zur Komposition und Theologie des Buches Kohelet* (BZAW, 247), Berlin - New York, 1997, pp. 35-43.

uns die Frage, ob aus solchen Einwänden zusammen mit der gegen sie gerichteten Polemik Kohelets überhaupt Positionen der frühen Apokalyptik erschlossen werden können. Für die Kompositionen 5,9-6,9; 7,1-22; 9,1-12 haben wir nachgewiesen, daß sie insgesamt als ein Spiegel der von Kohelet geführten Lehrgespräche gelesen werden können und über die Schuldebatte hinaus keine Hinweise enthalten, die eine Gruppe externer und apokalyptisch gesinnter Gegner Kohelets zu erkennen geben[5]. Mithin verbleibt in unserer Auseinandersetzung mit D. Michel die Einheit 3,16-4,3. Wir konzentrieren uns auf die Verse 3,16-21, da sie in der Geschichte ihrer Auslegung stets den Verdacht genährt haben, daß sich Kohelet hier gegen eine zu seiner Zeit aufkommende neue Lehre wende, die ein Aufsteigen des menschlichen Geistes zu Gott und damit ein Fortleben nach dem Tod in einer wie auch immer gearteten Weise vertreten habe[6]. Bevor wir uns jedoch dem Problem zuwenden können, ob Kohelet apokalyptische Erwartungen bereits kannte und ob er gegen sie offen polemisiert oder sie bewußt ausgeblendet hat, müssen wir das Teilstück 3,16-21 einer gründlichen Analyse unterziehen.

I. DER TEXT UND SEINE ZUSÄTZE IN 3,17f

Heftig umstritten und für die Auslegung von grundsätzlicher Bedeutung ist zunächst die Frage, ob das Teilstück 3,16-21 einheitlich ist oder eine spätere Bearbeitung erfahren hat[7]. Wir beginnen mit einer methodi-

---

5. Cf. in unserer Untersuchung die folgenden Abschnitte *Die Unverfügbarkeit des Glücks* (5,9-6,9), pp. 56-86; *Ein Schultext par excellence* (7,1-22), pp. 86-114; *Ein Geschick trifft sie alle* (9,1-12), pp. 115-148. Zur Diskussion der Bedeutung von חלק cf. pp. 74-81.

6. Cf. z. B. L. BERTHOLDT, *Historischkritische Einleitung in sämmtliche kanonische und apokryphe Schriften des alten und neuen Testaments*, Vol. V, Erlangen, 1815, p. 2235; L. LEVY, *Das Buch Qoheleth. Ein Beitrag zur Geschichte des Sadduzäismus*, Leipzig, 1912, p. 20 und 27; U. KELLERMANN, *Überwindung des Todesgeschicks in der alttestamentlichen Frömmigkeit vor und neben dem Auferstehungsglauben*, in ZTK 73 (1976) 259-282, pp. 278-281; H. N. BREAM, *Life without Resurrection: Two Perspectives from Qoheleth*, in *A Light unto My Path. Old Testament Studies in Honor of J. M. Myers* (Gettysburg Theological Studies, 4), Philadelphia, 1974, pp. 49-65, esp. 53-57; A. SCHOORS, *Koheleth. A Perspective of Life after Death?*, in ETL 61 (1985) 295-303, pp. 300-303. Zur Sache cf. H.-P. MÜLLER, *Weisheitliche Deutungen der Sterblichkeit: Gen 3,19 und Pred 3,21; 12,7 im Lichte antiker Parallelen*, in ID., *Mensch – Umwelt – Eigenwelt. Gesammelte Aufsätze zur Weisheit Israels*, Stuttgart - Berlin - Köln, 1992, pp. 69-100.

7. Cf. einerseits z. B. H. W. HERTZBERG, *Der Prediger* (²KAT, XVII/4), Gütersloh, 1963, p. 110; J. A. LOADER, *Polar Structures in the Book of Qohelet* (BZAW, 152), Berlin - New York, 1979, p. 95; R. N. WHYBRAY, *Ecclesiastes* (NCBC), Grand Rapids, London, 1989, p. 77; R. MURPHY, *Ecclesiastes* (WBC, 23 A), Dallas, Texas 1992, p. 36; und andererseits G. A. BARTON, *A Critical and Exegetical Commentary on the Book of Ecclesiastes* (ICC, 21), Edinburgh, 1908 (Reprinted 1959), p. 108; K. GALLING, *Der Pre-*

schen Vorbemerkung. Denn in der Debatte begegnet beiläufig immer wieder das Argument, daß man mit dem vorgegebenen Text auskommen könne und daher nicht zu der Annahme späterer Eintragungen gezwungen sei. Dahinter steht vermutlich eine gewisse Zurückhaltung gegenüber Eingriffen und Ausscheidungen im Text. Diesen Bedenken setzen wir entgegen, daß es bei einer redaktionsgeschichtlichen Beurteilung gar nicht um Prozeduren solcher Art geht, sondern um die dem Text insgesamt angemessene Erklärung seiner Entstehung und seines Zusammenhangs. Vor dem Hintergrund, daß in der gegenwärtigen Forschung die Einsicht in die Redaktionsprozesse weisheitlicher Literatur langsam wächst[8], wäre also nicht zu fragen, ob man das Textstück 3,16-21 irgendwie als Einheit sinnvoll lesen kann. Denn das läge zweifellos auch im Interesse seines Bearbeiters! Die Frage lautet vielmehr: Welche Interpretation vermag sämtliche im Text enthaltenen und seinem Verständnis entgegenstehenden Schwierigkeiten zu erfassen und bietet dafür die plausibelste Erklärung?

Kommen wir zur Auslegung zurück, können wir in der Tat eine erdrückende Zahl von Argumenten dafür nennen, daß der Vers 3,17 Kohelet abzusprechen und einer späteren Hand zuzuweisen ist. Einen ersten Hinweis gibt uns bereits die Doppelung der Formel אמרתי אני בלבי in v. 17 und 18. Sie ist insofern auffällig, als an keiner Stelle im Koheletbuch zwei offensichtlich zusammenhangslose Überlegungen Kohelets unmittelbar aufeinander folgen und mit derselben Formel eingeleitet werden[9]. Zweitens benutzt Kohelet die genannte Formel stets zur Einführung einer eigenen Überlegung oder eines Vorhabens[10]. Dem widerspricht, daß sie in v. 17 erkennbar eine traditionelle Anschauung

diger, in *Die Fünf Megilloth* (HAT, I/18), Tübingen, [2]1969, p. 96s; A. LAUHA, *Kohelet* (BK, XIX), Neukirchen-Vluyn, 1978, p. 74; J. L. CRENSHAW, *Ecclesiastes* (OTL), Philadelphia, 1989, p. 102; MICHEL, *op. cit.*, p. 250.

8. Zum Hiobbuch cf. M. WITTE, *Vom Leiden zur Lehre. Der dritte Redegang (Hiob 21-27) und die Redaktionsgeschichte des Hiobbuches* (BZAW, 230), Berlin - New York, 1994; zum Sprüchebuch cf. R. N. WHYBRAY, *Thoughts on the Composition of Proverbs 10-29*, in *Priests, Prophets and Scribes*. Festschrift J. Blenkinsopp (JSOT SS, 149), Sheffield, 1992, pp. 102-114; ferner Ruth SCORALICK, *Die Spruchanordnung im Buch der Sprichwörter Kapitel 10-15* (BZAW, 232), Berlin - New York, 1995. Für die Psalmen verweisen wir auf CH. LEVIN, *Das Gebetbuch der Gerechten. Literargeschichtliche Beobachtungen am Psalter*, in *ZTK* 90 (1993), pp. 355-381.

9. Cf. MICHEL, *op. cit.*, p. 250. Der Versuch, die Verbindung von v. 17 und 18 mittels der Zwar-Aber-Tatsache zu erklären, ist mit F. ELLERMEIER, *Qohelet I,1. Untersuchungen zum Buche Qohelet*, Herzberg, 1967, p. 127, zurückzuweisen, da der Gerichtsgedanke keinen relativen Wert repräsentieren kann. Selbst W. ZIMMERLI, *Das Buch des Predigers Salomo* (ATD, 16/1), Göttingen, [3]1980, p. 171s, äußert sich auffällig zurückhaltend.

10. Cf. Koh 2,1; 2,15; 3,18; ferner 7,23; und dazu MICHEL, *op. cit.*, p. 250. Bei den restlichen Belegstellen von אמרתי folgt stets eine *eigene* Bewertung, cf. 2,2; 6,3; 8,14; und 9,16, hier in Form eines durch Kohelet kommentierten Spruchs.

einleitet[11]. Drittens kommt der Hinweis auf Gottes Tun in v. 17 zu früh; denn Kohelet entwickelt seine Argumentation stets von der menschlichen Erfahrung aus, bevor er Gott ins Gespräch bringt und ein theologisches Ergebnis formuliert[12]. Viertens ist festzuhalten, daß es für das Verb שפט keinen weiteren Beleg im Buche Kohelet gibt. Das berechtigt uns fünftens zu der Frage, ob Kohelet überhaupt ein richterliches Handeln Gottes in Betracht gezogen hat. Die Vorstellung eines endzeitlichen Gerichts können wir jedenfalls von vorne herein Kohelet absprechen[13]. Wie sonst hätte er sein Verständnis des Todes als des großen Gleichmachers in dieser Schärfe herausstellen können[14]? Ob er hingegen mit einer gerechten Vergeltung auf Erden gerechnet hat, verlangt eine differenzierte Betrachtung. Denn dafür lassen sich immerhin die unverdächtigen Stellen 5,5 und 7,17 anführen, die ein göttliches Eingreifen für den Fall androhen, daß der Frevler Gottes Zorn durch sein ruchloses Tun herausfordert[15]. Wenn Kohelet darüber hinaus in 8,12b-13 den Grundsatz göttlicher Vergeltung zitiert, kann er dem Tun-Ergehen-Zusammenhang nicht prinzipiell widersprochen haben. Umgekehrt beweist die in 8,14 angefügte Ausnahme, daß nicht in jedem Fall dem Gerechten und dem Frevler sein Tun auf Erden vergolten wird. Dadurch bleibt der Tun-Ergehen-Zusammenhang dem verborgenen Willen Gottes untergeordnet und menschlicher Berechnung entzogen. Vor diesem Hintergrund ist es unwahrscheinlich, daß Kohelet in 3,17 den vor Gericht unschuldig Verurteilten einen gerechten Ausgleich sowie eine Bestrafung der Täter in Aussicht stellt und damit den Grundsatz göttlicher Vergeltung auf Erden einführt, dessen absolute Gültigkeit er selbst in Zweifel zieht. Berücksichtigt man, welches Gewicht er den Grenzfällen beilegt, kann v. 17 nicht seine eigene Meinung wiederge-

---

11. Cf. LEVY, *op. cit.*, p. 84; R. B. Y. SCOTT, *Proverbs. Ecclesiastes. Introduction, Translation, and Notes* (AB, 18), New York, 1965, p. 223; HERTZBERG, *op. cit.*, p. 110; G. OGDEN, *Qoheleth, Readings. A New Biblical Commentary*, Sheffield, 1987, p. 59s. Demgegenüber betrachtet L. SCHWIENHORST-SCHÖNBERGER, *»Nicht im Menschen gründet das Glück« (Koh 2,24). Kohelet im Spannungsfeld jüdischer Weisheit und hellenistischer Philosophie* (HBS, 2), Freiburg, 1994, p. 116s, bereits v. 16b als Zitat der Tradition, dem Kohelet in v. 17 einen kritischen Kommentar folgen lasse. Gegen seine Annahme, daß sich v. 16b auf das Endgericht beziehe, spricht aber nicht nur die Formel תחת השמש, sondern auch der sachliche Zusammenhang mit dem Abschnitt 4,1-3, der ebenfalls auf Erden geschehenes Unrecht reflektiert; cf. auch 5,7f.

12. Cf. z. B. 2,24-26; 3,10-15; 3,22; 5,17-19; 7,29; 9,7-10. Zur Sache cf. MICHEL, *op. cit.*, p. 35, 38, 282, ohne dessen Hypothese vom Urhebergott zu übernehmen. Mit ihr hat sich BACKHAUS, *op. cit.*, pp. 385-389, kritisch auseinandergesetzt.

13. Das völlige Fehlen einer Jenseitserwartung wird außerdem durch 4,1-3 bestätigt; cf. HERTZBERG, *op. cit.*, p. 113.

14. Cf. 2,14-16; 5,14f; 6,6; 8,10; 9,2f; 9,10.

15. Cf. FISCHER, *op. cit.*, p. 215 und 247.

ben. Schließlich können wir gegen die Ursprünglichkeit des Verses zusätzlich anführen, daß im folgenden weder auf das traditionelle Gegensatzpaar des Gerechten und des Frevlers noch auf den Gedanken einer immanten Vergeltung oder einer endzeitlichen Bestrafung zurückgegriffen wird. Statt dessen gedenken wir zu zeigen, daß die in v. 19-21 entwickelte Argumentation ausschließlich an v. 18bβ anknüpft und daher die Überlegung der Gleichheit von Mensch und Vieh als die einzige und ursprüngliche Kohelets erweist.

Fragen wir nun umgekehrt nach einer positiven Erklärung für die spätere Eintragung, können wir nicht nur die hinter v. 17 erkennbare Absicht der Redaktion erhellen, sondern seine Einfügung auch einer konkreten Hand zuweisen. Ausgangspunkt hierfür ist die Beobachtung, daß in 11,9b und 12,14 mit dem Ausdruck »ins Gericht bringen« eine 3,17 entsprechende Umschreibung der richterlichen Tätigkeit Gottes vorliegt[16]. Da die beiden genannten Verse auf den zweiten Epilogisten zurückgehen und das Gericht auf die Gesamtheit menschlichen Tuns beziehen, denkt er zweifellos an ein endgültiges Gericht[17]. Denn eine derart generelle Beurteilung, in der sogar die verborgenen bösen und guten Taten offenbar werden, cf. 12,13, kann erst nach dem Tod erfolgen. Daß 3,17 ganz auf dieser Linie liegt, ist mit Händen zu greifen, wird doch Gott hier nicht nur als unumschränkter Richter über Fromme und Gottlose eingeführt, sondern auch sein Urteilsspruch durch die gegenüber 3,1 auffällige Ergänzung על כל־המעשה über die Gesamtheit ihres Tuns verhängt. Demgemäß unterteilen wir v. 17b unter Berücksichtigung des masoretischen Trenners *Zaqeph parvum* in zwei Nominalsätze: Der erste greift auf 3,1 zurück, während der zweite den Gedanken im Sinne von 11,9b und 12,14 fortsetzt. Durch die sich chiastisch entsprechenden Glieder עת und שם hat der Bearbeiter offenbar den von Kohelet übernommenen Topos der qualifizierten Zeit zu einem im Jenseits[18] festge-

---

16. An allen drei Stellen ist האלהים das Subjekt und על כל־המעשה bzw. על־כל־אלה wird das Urteil gefällt. Aus sprachlichen und sachlichen Gründen können wir daher den Einwand von BACKHAUS, *op. cit.*, p. 135 n. 156, nicht gelten lassen, daß eine solche Interpretation in unerlaubter Weise [sic!] von 12,14 und 11,9b her argumentiere.

17. Cf. bereits F. DELITZSCH, *Hohes Lied und Koheleth* (BC, IV/4), Leipzig, 1875, p. 191 und 386s: »Aber angesichts der leidigen Erfahrungsthatsache, daß die gerechte göttliche Vergeltung sich diesseits nur zu häufig vermissen läßt 8,14., postulirt der Verf. hier und 3,17. 12,14 ein schließliches Gericht, welches die diesseitigen Widersprüche aufhebt und also ein jenseitiges sein muß; er hat keine klare Vorstellung von Zeit und Weise dieses Gerichtsvollzugs, aber die Unausbleiblichkeit desselben setzt ihm sein Gottesglaube außer allen Zweifel«.

18. Gegenüber den verschiedenen textkritischen Korekturen, cf. die Übersicht bei CH. F. WHITLEY, *Koheleth. His Language and Thought* (BZAW, 148), Berlin - New York, 1979, p. 34, halten wir an der Lesart des Ortsadverbs שם fest. Sein Bezug bestimmt sich lediglich durch den Kontext und dessen jeweiliger Interpretation. Da wir v. 17a auf das göttliche Endgericht deuteten, geht שם auf die endzeitliche Gerichtsstätte.

setzten Gerichtstermin im Sinne eines מועד משפט[19] umgedeutet. Mithin hat der zweite Epilogist angesichts des in v. 16 beobachteten und den Gerichtsbehörden angelasteten Unrechts an das dort über alles Tun verhängte Gottesgericht erinnert, bevor er Kohelet selbst zu Wort kommen und seine These über die Gleichheit von Mensch und Tier entfalten ließ. Daß er sich hier genötigt sah, selbst zur Feder zu greifen und den Gerichtsgedanken einzutragen, bestätigen auch unsere Beobachtungen zu 6,10; 8,8b; 9,3b und 11,9b. Denn seine Glossen beschränken sich auf die Stellen, die seiner Ansicht nach den nötigen Hinweis auf Gottes gerechte Vergeltung vermissen lassen[20]. Indem er 3,17aα.18aβ aufsprengte und v. 17aβb.18aα einfügte, hat er damit seine Erwartung eines göttlichen Endgerichts Kohelet als dessen eigene Meinung untergeschoben. Darüber hinaus können wir sogar plausibel machen, wie es zu dem Rückgriff auf 3,1 kam. Wenn wir uns vorstellen, daß dem Bearbeiter eine ähnliche Buchrolle zur Verfügung stand, wie sie uns in mehreren Fragmenten aus Qumran überliefert ist[21], fand er den Gedanken der qualifizierten Zeit in der unmittelbar benachbarten Kolumne auf etwa gleicher Höhe und hat ihn – darüber nachdenkend – seinen Zwecken adaptiert. Ein ähnliches Redaktionsverfahren ist ebenso für 9,3b mit Blick auf 8,11b anzunehmen[22].

Mit unserem Nachweis, daß es sich bei 3,17 um eine orthodoxe Korrektur des zweiten Epilogisten handelt, eröffnet sich uns eine exegetische Lösung für das gemeinhin als *crux interpretum* empfundene Textproblem in der ersten Hälfte von v. 18. Denn die drei Wörter לברם האלהים ולראות bereiten der Auslegung besondere Schwierigkeiten erstens wegen der Deutung von ברר, zweitens wegen des Fehlens eines finiten Verbs und drittens wegen des erzwungenen Subjektwechsels zwischen den koordinierten Infinitiven[23]. Verschiedene Textkonjekturen haben diese sprachlichen Schwierigkeiten zu bereinigen versucht[24], keine

---

19. Cf. 1QS IV,20 und dazu Ps 75,3!
20. Cf. FISCHER, *op. cit.*, p. 160, n. 558.
21. Cf. die Publikation von 4QQoh[a] durch J. MUILENBURG, *A Qoheleth Scroll from Qumran*, in *BASOR* 135 (1954), pp. 20-28; und zuletzt durch E. ULRICH, *Ezra and Qoheleth Manuscripts from Qumran (4QEzra and 4QQoh[a,b])*, in *Priests, Prophets and Scribes* (Anm. 8), pp. 142-150.
22. Cf. FISCHER, *op. cit.*, p. 127s.
23. Cf. HERTZBERG, *op. cit.*, p. 101. Dagegen möchte R. GORDIS, *Koheleth – The Man and His World* (TSJTSA, 19), New York, ³1968, p. 236, das Wort לברם als eine suffigierte Perfektform mit *Lamed emphaticum* deuten, um dadurch ein finites Verb zu erhalten; cf. dazu auch WHITLEY, *op. cit.*, p. 36s.
24. Cf. z. B. A. B. EHRLICH, *Randglossen zur Hebräischen Bibel*, Vol.7, Leipzig, 1914 (Nachdruck 1968), p. 67; D. MICHEL, *Qohelet* (EdF, 258), Darmstadt, 1988, p. 138: לא ברם; A. ALLGEIER, *Das Buch des Predigers oder Koheleth* (HSAT, VI/2), Bonn, 1925, p. 32; W. A. IRWIN, *Ecclesiastes 3,18*, in *AJSL* 56 (1939), p. 298s: לבראם. Dagegen ver-

der vorgeschlagenen Änderungen vermochte jedoch ganz zu überzeugen. Dies erhärtet unsere Vermutung, daß sämtliche Bemühungen um eine angemessene Erklärung erfolglos blieben, weil sie von einem falschen Lösungsansatz ausgegangen sind: v. 18 ist nicht textkritisch, sondern redaktionsgeschichtlich zu behandeln. Denn es ist leicht einzusehen, daß es der zweite Epilogist nicht bei der Einführung des göttlichen Vergeltungsgerichts bewenden ließ, sondern durch eine weitere Eintragung in v. 18 um den Ausgleich zwischen seiner eigenen und der folgenden Überlegung Kohelets bemüht gewesen ist.

Nehmen wir versuchsweise an, daß der zweite Epilogist im Zuge seiner Ergänzung auch die Infinitivkonstruktion in v. 18 eingetragen habe (kursiv)[25], hätte die ursprüngliche Überlegung Kohelets einmal gelautet:

> (18) Ich überlegte mir, was die Menschen betrifft: *damit Gott sie aussondere und sie erkennen müssen:* Dem Vieh sind sie gleich!

Unter dieser Voraussetzung erklären sich die bestehenden grammatischen Schwierigkeiten mühelos: Das finite Verb fehlt in der Ergänzung, weil der Bearbeiter die ursprüngliche Überlegung Kohelets nicht verdrängen, sondern mittels der finalen Infinitivkonstruktion lediglich einem Zweck Gottes unterstellen wollte. Konnte er dadurch einen Eingriff in den ursprünglichen Wortlaut geschickt umgehen, mußte er wegen der Einführung Gottes in v. 18aβ den Subjektwechsel innerhalb der koordinierten Infinitive wenigstens in Kauf nehmen. Unseren Lösungsversuch erhärtet die Tatsache, daß ברר als Gerichtsterminus bekannt ist und in Verbindung mit seinem Subjekt אלהים sachlich der Einfügung von v. 17 nahesteht[26]. In diesem Zusammenhang ermitteln wir für das Verb ברר die Bedeutung »aussondern«, wie sie im Alten Testament, in Qumran und besonders im Mittelhebräischen und Aramäischen bezeugt ist[27]. Daß ברר im juridischen Sinn gebraucht wird und ein zum festgesetzten Termin erfolgendes Gottesgericht beschreiben kann, bestätigt überdies ein Text aus Qumran. Dabei dient uns dieser als Annex zur Gemeinderegel

---

setzen K. BUDDE, *Der Prediger* (HSAT(K) II), Tübingen, ⁴1923, p. 429; HERTZBERG, *op. cit.*, p. 101; GALLING, *op. cit.*, p. 96, das Adverb שָׁם aus v. 17 nach v. 18 und deuten es als Perf. 3. sg. m. von שִׂים.

25. Cf. ferner WHITLEY, *op. cit.*, p. 37: »לברם האלהים would then be in the nature of a parenthesis, and may not even be original«.

26. Cf. HERTZBERG, *op. cit.*, p. 110, der diese inhaltliche Beziehung deutlich gesehen hat.

27. Cf. V. HAMP, Art. ברר, in *TWAT* I, c. 842; dazu Jer 4,11; Ez 20,38; Dan 11,35 (12,10). Die in W. GESENIUS, *Hebräisches und Aramäisches Handwörterbuch über das Alte Testament*, 17. Aufl., c. 119b, verzeichnete Bedeutung »sichten, prüfen« ist in der 18. Aufl., c. 181b, aufgegeben; cf. aber die Wurzel בור zu Koh 9,1, in der 18. Aufl., c. 133a. In der Bedeutung »Ausgesonderte« begegnet schließlich das Partizip in Neh 5,18; 1 Chr 7,40; 9,22; 16,41; CD 10,4.

beurteilte Abschnitt 1QS III,13-IV,26 insofern zur Absicherung unserer
Hypothese, als er ein dem zweiten Epilogisten entsprechendes Interesse
am endzeitlichen Richten Gottes zu erkennen gibt: nämlich daß Gott
zwar aktuell nicht in die Welt eingreift, aber schließlich zum festgesetzten Zeitpunkt sein richterliches Fazit ziehen wird[28]. Daher kommen wir
zu dem Schluß: *Über v. 17 hinaus hat der zweite Epilogist die Vorstellung in v. 18 eingetragen, daß Gott in seinem Gericht die Menschen
nach ihren Taten aussondere und sie angesichts des allerorts begange-
nen Unrechts erkennen müssen, daß sie nicht besser sind als das Vieh.*
Offenbar begründete sich für ihn die Gleichstellung der Menschen mit
dem Vieh durch den völligen Mangel an Sittlichkeit, den das Gottesgericht aufdecken werde. Daß wir es auch hier mit der Auffassung des
zweiten Epilogisten zu tun haben, bestätigt abschließend seine Einfügung in 9,3b, die unverkennbar die Bosheit und Verblendung der Menschen zur Begründung des Todesgeschicks bemüht.

Überprüfen wir das redaktionsgeschichtliche Ergebnis am Text, gewinnen wir ein außergewöhnlich klares Bild über seinen literarischen
Befund. Nach Abzug der Gerichtsbearbeitung verbleibt ein typischer
Schultext, der in seiner Struktur den im übrigen Buch versammelten
Lehren Kohelets ausgesprochen ähnlich ist: Beobachtung unter der Sonne (v. 16), Überlegung (v. 18*), Begründung (v. 19) und Beweisführung
(v. 20f). Gegen unsere Auffassung könnte man vielleicht einwenden,
daß der Übergang zwischen v. 16 und 18 sprunghaft sei. Doch zeigt der
Vergleich mit 4,1, daß Kohelet die soziale Frage nicht als ein selbständi-
ges Problem behandelt hat, sondern lediglich zum Ausgangspunkt seines
Nachdenkens nahm[29]. Aus beiden Beobachtungen 3,16 und 4,1 ergibt
sich als der verbindende Gedanke das Ausgeliefertsein des Menschen an
sein Schicksal, einerseits Unschuldiger durch ihre Verurteilung vor Gericht, andererseits Elender durch die Gewalt ihrer Bedrücker[30]. Damit
haben wir den Übergang und Anknüpfungspunkt für die Überlegung
Kohelets gefunden, die Menschen und Tiere gleichstellt: nämlich dem
Tod sind jene ebenso wehrlos ausgeliefert wie diese[31]. Daß Kohelet sein

---

28. Cf. dazu H. STEGEMANN, *Textbestand und Grundgedanken von 1 QS III,13-IV,26*,
in *RQ* 13 (1988) 95-131, p. 114s.

29. Cf. HENGEL, *op. cit.*, p. 99 und 216.

30. Die Zusammengehörigkeit beider Beobachtungen beweist einerseits die Einleitungsformel in 4,1, die das Thema der voranstehenden Reflexion aufnimmt und unter
einem neuen Blickwinkel fortführt; cf. 4,7; 9,11; dazu MICHEL, *op. cit.*, p. 251. Andererseits entsprechen sie sich auch formal, indem beide als repetitiver Parallelismus mit wört-
licher Wiederholung des zweiten Glieds ausgeführt sind; cf. DELITZSCH, *op. cit.*, p. 267.

31. Cf. 3,19 und dazu M. V. Fox, *Qohelet and his Contradictions* (JSOT SS, 71),
Sheffield, 1989, p. 197: »Observation of injustice – like others of Qohelet's unhappy
observations – brings him to thoughts of death«.

Thema durch das kunstvoll gestaltete phonetische Wortspiel[32] הַם־בְּהֵמָה הֵמָּה לָהֶם[33] zunächst verdeckt einführt, spricht wiederum für eine Unterweisung im Schulunterricht. Denn es ist leicht einzusehen, daß die änigmatische Form des Wortspiels seine Auslegung durch einen Lehrer der Weisheit geradezu herausfordert. Und wer als Kohelet selbst hätte es trefflicher vermocht?

II. ARGUMENTATION UND INTENTION VON 3,18-21

Nachdem wir den Text und seine Zusätze in v. 17 und 18* festgestellt haben, können wir nun die weisheitliche Argumentation nachzeichnen und bieten dazu eine Übersetzung des ursprünglichen Schultextes:

> (16) Noch dazu[34]: Ich beobachtete unter der Sonne: An den Ort des Rechts, dorthin ist das Unrecht gedrungen / und an den Ort der Gerechtigkeit, dorthin ist das Unrecht gedrungen[35]. (18*) Da überlegte ich mir, was die Menschen betrifft: Dem Vieh sind sie gleich[36]! (19) Denn das Geschick der Menschen und das Geschick des Viehs[37]: ein einziges Geschick besitzen sie beide, wie der Tod des einen, so ist der Tod des andern. Und einen einzigen Odem besitzen alle beide, und einen Vorzug des Menschen vor dem Vieh gibt es nicht. Denn alles ist vergänglich! (20) Alle beide gehen an einen einzigen Ort: »Alle sind aus Staub geworden und alle kehren zum Staub zurück.« (21) Wer kann wissen, ob der Odem der Menschen nach oben steigt, hingegen der Odem des Viehs nach unten zur Erde sinkt?

32. Der Gleichklang der Wörter unterstreicht die Gleichheit von Mensch und Vieh; cf. DELITZSCH, *op. cit.*, p. 270.

33. Da erst das Personalpronomen הֵמָּה den Anklang zu בְּהֵמָה herstellt, mußte Kohelet das eigentliche Subjekt בְּנֵי אָדָם in die Einleitungsformel nach vorne ziehen. Zu עַל־דִּבְרַת cf. Koh 8,2; Ps 110,4 und B. ISAKSSON, *Studies in Language of Qoheleth. With Special Emphasis on the Verbal System* (SSU, 10), Uppsala, 1987, p. 195, der eine Verwendung dieses Ausdrucks im mündlichen Vortrag für möglich hält.

34. Durch וְעוֹד wird der redaktionelle Anschluß an den Traktat 1,3-3,15 hergestellt; cf. FISCHER, *op. cit.*, p. 11s mit n. 38.

35. Zur Übersetzung cf. jetzt N. LOHFINK, *Das Koheletbuch: Strukturen und Struktur*, in L. SCHWIENHORST-SCHÖNBERGER (ed.), *Das Buch Kohelet. Studien zur Struktur, Geschichte, Rezeption und Theologie* (BZAW, 254), Berlin - New York 1997, p. 70 mit n. 115.

36. Eine den hebräischen Wortlaut wiedergebende Übersetzung ist im Deutschen nicht möglich. Was die einzelnen Elemente des lautmalerischen Satzes betrifft, bestimmen wir הֵם als Kopula im Nominalsatz und הֵמָּה als rückverweisendes Personalpronomen. Über die Deutung von לָהֶם als Reflexivum kann man streiten; cf. dazu GK §135i mit Hinweis auf לָהֶם in Jes 3,9; GORDIS, *op. cit.*, p. 237 mit Hinweis auf בָּהֶם in Ps 90,10. Eine Streichung des לָהֶם als Dittographie oder als aus v. 19 eingedrungenes Wort empfiehlt sich allerdings nicht.

37. Zur Vokalisation cf. den Apparat der *BHS*. Grammatisch haben wir es bei v. 19aα mit einem zusammengesetzten Satz zu tun, dessen Nachsatz durch ein *Waw apodosis* eingeleitet wird; cf. E. KÖNIG, *Historisch-kritisches Lehrgebäude der Hebräischen Sprache*, Vol. II/2, Leipzig, 1897, §415z; GK §143d. In der Übersetzung kennzeichnet der Doppelpunkt die Hervorhebung des Hauptsubjekts.

Wir setzen nochmals ein bei der Überlegung Kohelets, daß die Menschen dem Vieh gleich sind. V. 19 liefert dafür eine doppelte Begründung. Da bei seiner Auslegung bereits Entscheidungen für das Verständnis der Argumentationsstruktur fallen, ist eine genauere Untersuchung angebracht. Wir müssen dazu auf das Leitwort אחד achten. In der ersten Begründung (v. 19aαβ) kennzeichnet es das Todesgeschick, das Menschen und Tiere in gleicher Weise trifft. Viermal verbindet sich bei Kohelet אחד mit dem Schicksalsbegriff מקרה, und zwar stets, um den Gedanken auszudrücken, daß der Tod alle Unterschiede beseitigt[38]. Daran können wir seine fundamentale Bedeutung für das Denken Kohelets ablesen. Wie fest er davon überzeugt war, bestätigt zumal der Nachsatz in v. 19aβ, der den Tod des Menschen und des Viehs deiktisch miteinander identifiziert[39]. In der zweiten Begründung (v. 19aγbα) unterstreicht das Leitwort אחד die Wesensgleichheit des Geistes von Mensch und Vieh. Trotz der Bedeutungsbreite von רוח stimmen die Kommentare in seltener Geschlossenheit darin überein, daß unter dem Geist hier wie in 12,7b der Lebensodem zu verstehen ist, durch den Gott alle Kreatur zum Leben erweckt und am Leben erhält[40]. Dafür spricht auch die Zusammenstellung von אדם und בהמה, die im Alten Testament die Schöpfungs- und Schicksalsgemeinschaft von Mensch und Tier zum Ausdruck bringt[41]. Werden beide durch denselben Lebensodem als Geschöpfe Gottes ausgewiesen, kann es auch in dieser Hinsicht keinen Vorzug des Menschen vor dem Vieh geben.

Indem wir dem Leitwort אחד in v. 19 nachgingen, erwies sich uns die Identität des Todesgeschicks und des Lebensprinzips als doppelte Begründung für die Gleichstellung von Mensch und Vieh. In der weiteren Argumentation untermauert Kohelet nun seine These damit, daß er einerseits in v. 20 die Todesverfallenheit beider durch ein Zitat aus der Tradition *be*weist und andererseits in v. 21 den Vorzug des Menschen vor dem Vieh durch eine rhetorische Frage *ab*weist. Wir erhalten die parallele Begründungsstruktur[42]:

38. Cf. 2,14 (Weiser und Tor); 3,19 (Mensch und Vieh); 9,2f (Gerechter und Frevler, Reiner und Unreiner, etc.).

39. Zu der Aussage כמות זה כן מות זה cf. K. EHLICH, *Verwendungen der Deixis beim sprachlichen Handeln. Linguistisch-philologische Untersuchung zum hebräischen deiktischen System. Teil 2* (Forum linguisticum, 24), Frankfurt a. M. 1979, p. 852s.

40. Cf. z. B. DELITZSCH, *op. cit.*, p. 271; BARTON, *op. cit.*, p. 109; HERTZBERG, *op. cit.*, p. 111; SCOTT, *op. cit.*, p. 223; LAUHA, *op. cit.*, p. 76; OGDEN, *op. cit.*, p. 61; WHYBRAY, *op. cit.*, p. 79; MURPHY, *op. cit.*, p. 37.

41. Cf. J. BOTTERWECK, *Art.* בהמה, in *TWAT* I, 1973, c. 531s. Zu den weisheitlichen Texten cf. R. BARTELMUS, *Die Tierwelt in der Bibel. Exegetische Beobachtungen zu einem Teilaspekt der Diskussion um die Theologie der Natur*, in *BN* 37 (1987) 11-37, pp. 26-35.

42. Cf. GORDIS, *op. cit.*, p. 110 mit n. 14: »Koheleth also uses this alternate structure,

a	v. 19aαβ	Begründung: ein einziges Todesgeschick
b	v. 19aγbα	Begründung: ein einziger Lebensodem
	v. 19bβ	הבל-Formel
a'	v. 20	Beweis für v. 19aαβ: Zitat der Tradition
b'	v. 21	Beweis für v. 19aγbα: rhetorische Frage

Es ist sicher kein Zufall, daß im Eröffnungssatz der Beweisführung zum dritten Mal das Leitwort אחד erscheint und jetzt den gemeinsamen Ort kennzeichnet, an den alle Lebewesen im Tode gehen müssen. Obwohl der Ausdruck מקום אחד im Alten Testament nur hier in 3,20 und 6,6 begegnet, geht aus dem Zusammenhang beider Belege hervor, daß darunter der gemeinsame Versammlungsort der Toten und mithin die Scheol zu verstehen ist[43]. Im Gegensatz zu dem Bemühen der apokalyptischen Literatur, das Schattenreich zum Straf- und Aufbewahrungsort der Toten umzudeuten[44], bleibt Kohelet hier ganz im Rahmen alttestamentlicher Unterweltsvorstellungen[45]. Für ihn ist die Scheol der Ort, an dem alle Lebensregungen aufhören und sämtliche sozialen und sittlichen Unterschiede eingeebnet sind; cf. Jes 14,9-11; Hi 3,17-19; 21,23-26. Einen gerechten Ausgleich gibt es dort nicht!

Für die weitere Argumentation Kohelets ist das folgende Zitat von besonderer Bedeutung. Wie der Blick in die hebräische Bibel beweist, wird hier Gen 3,19 nicht wörtlich wiedergegeben, sondern sachlich die im jüdischen Denken weit verbreitete Vorstellung zitiert, daß der Mensch im Tod zum Staub zurückkehrt[46]. Auffällig genug hat Kohelet in v. 20b das traditionelle Zitat durch zweimaliges und betont an den Anfang gesetztes כל seinem Kontext angeglichen und dadurch hervorgehoben, daß der Weg der Vergänglichkeit von Mensch und Vieh ein und derselbe ist:

(20b) »*Alle* sind aus Staub geworden und *alle* kehren zum Staub zurück.«

Welche argumentative Strategie verfolgt er damit? Um sie näher ins Auge zu fassen, machen wir einen Umweg, indem wir die Art und Weise der Zitation im Buch Kohelet betrachten. R. Gordis hat sich als erster um ihre systematische Klärung des Problems der Zitate bemüht und sie als Stileigentümlichkeit Kohelets beschrieben[47]. Unter den verschiede-

with *c* giving reason for *a*, and *d* for *b*«.

43. Cf. dazu die Bezeichnung בית מועד als das mit der Totenwelt gleichzusetzende Versammlungshaus aller Lebenden in Hi 30,23.

44. Cf. z. B. Jub 7,29; 22,22; 1 Hen 22,3f; 102,5; 103,7f.

45. Zur Scheol im Buch Kohelet cf. FISCHER, *op. cit.*, pp. 146-148.

46. Cf. Gen 3,19; Ps 90,3; Hi 10,9; Sir 17,1; 1 QH X,3f; XII,26f; 1 QS XII,21f. Zur Sache cf. SCHOORS, *op. cit.*, p. 300s.

47. Cf. GORDIS, *op. cit.*, pp. 95-108. Zur Verwendung von Zitaten cf. weiter R. N. WHYBRAY, *The Identification and Use of Quotations in Ecclesiastes*, in *Congress Volume*

nen Verwendungsweisen bespricht er den Fall, daß Kohelet einen
Spruch vollständig zitiert, obwohl nur eine Hälfte für seine Argumentati-
on bedeutsam ist[48]. Genau den umgekehrten Fall vermuten wir in v. 20b.
Hier zitiert Kohelet nur die eine Hälfte der Tradition, meint aber den gesamten Vorstellungszusammenhang: nämlich daß alle Lebewesen zur
Erde zurückkehren, wenn Gott ihren Lebensodem zu sich nimmt. Dabei
lassen sich für den traditionsgeschichtlichen Zusammenhang der beiden
Motive von der Rückkehr zum Staube und von der Rücknahme des
Odems nicht nur biblische Belege anführen[49], sondern auch Kohelets eigene Vergänglichkeitsaussage in 12,7, mit der er sein Gedicht über Alter
und Tod beschließt. Da der Hörer- und Leserkreis Kohelets durch den
für das Verständnis der biblischen Bücher erforderlichen Unterricht in
der hebräischen Sprache mit der Tradition vertraut gewesen sein dürfte,
können wir diese zumal weisheitlich geprägte Vorstellung bei seinen
Rezipienten als bekannt voraussetzen. Darüber hinaus scheint Kohelet
diesen Zusammenhang ausdrücklich vorbereitet zu haben, indem er bereits in 3,19 die רוח als den Mensch und Vieh gemeinsamen Lebensodem einführte. Die in v. 21 folgende rhetorische Frage sollte von diesem biblischen Hintergrund her verstanden werden.

Warum hat Kohelet dann nur die eine Hälfte und nicht die vollständige Tradition zitiert? Genau darin zeigt sich die Gewandtheit seiner Argumentation: Die Vorstellung von der Rückkehr des Odems zu Gott
wird nicht zitiert, sondern als selbstverständlich vorausgesetzt und un-
ausgesprochen in die Beweisführung einbezogen. Denn wer sie kennt,
muß bezweifeln, daß der Odem des Menschen und der Odem des Viehs
im Tode in entgegengesetzte Richtungen gehen. Statt dessen wird er
Kohelet beipflichten, der durch die rhetorische Frage diese Möglichkeit
grundsätzlich verneint. *v. 21 richtet sich also nicht gegen die biblische
Vorstellung, sondern bestätigt sie und sichert sich dadurch die Zustimmung dafür, daß es nach dem Tod keine Bevorzugung des Menschen gegenüber dem Vieh gibt.*

Vor dem Hintergrund der von uns vorausgesetzten Schulsituation[50]
tritt die rhetorische Strategie Kohelets noch deutlicher hervor. Hätte
nämlich einer seiner Schüler dieser Beweisführung widersprochen, hätte
er nicht nur den Vorwurf des Lehrers fürchten müssen, daß er offensichtlich die biblische Lehre von der Rückkehr des Odems zu Gott nicht

Vienna (SVT, 32), Leiden, 1981, pp. 435-451; D. MICHEL, *Qoheleth* (EdF, 258), Darmstadt, 1988, pp. 27-33; *Untersuchungen, op. cit.*, pp. 84-115.
    48. Cf. GORDIS, *op. cit.*, pp. 101-103, der 5,1f und 11,3f als Beispiele anführt.
    49. Cf. Ps 104,29f; 146,4; Hi 34,14f; Sir 40,11; ferner Tob 3,6.
    50. Cf. FISCHER, *op. cit.*, pp. 35-50.

kenne, sondern auch Rede und Antwort stehen müssen, ob er ihr etwa nicht folgen wolle. Bei der rhetorischen Frage in v. 21 handelt es sich also um den Schlußstein der Argumentation. Ihre affirmative Funktion entspricht auch sonst dem Gebrauch rhetorischer Fragen bei Kohelet, der durch ihre strenge Verneinung vorausgegangene Thesen bekräftigt und dadurch die Meinung des Lehrers nachdrücklich unterstreicht[51].

Das führt zu dem Schluß, daß es in v. 21 gar nicht um die skeptische Zurückweisung der Frage geht, ob der menschliche Geist etwa nach dem Tode zu seiner himmlischen Wohnung aufsteige und dadurch Unsterblichkeit erlange, sondern um die abschließende Bestätigung, daß bei der Rückkehr des Odems zu Gott kein Unterschied zwischen Mensch und Tier besteht. Dieses Ergebnis läßt sich durch die grammatische Analyse erhärten. Denn in v. 21 liegt keine abhängige disjunktive Frage vor[52], sondern zwei koordinierte indirekte Satzfragen[53], die durch ihren sachlichen Kontrast in ein adversatives Verhältnis gesetzt sind:

(21) Wer kann wissen, ob der Odem der Menschen nach oben steigt, *hingegen* der Odem des Viehs nach unten zur Erde sinkt?

Eben dieser Gegensatz zwischen dem Weg des menschlichen Geists nach oben einerseits und dem Weg des tierischen Geists nach unten andererseits wird von Kohelet ausgeschlossen[54]. Bleiben wir bei der Deutung von רוח als Lebensodem, stimmt die zuerst genannte Vorstellung mit der biblischen Anschauung überein, während ihr die zweite widerspricht. Daher läßt sich die Möglichkeit nicht von der Hand weisen, daß Kohelet die Vorstellung vom Hinabfahren des tierischen Odems als Ge-

---

51. Cf. z. B. 2,15aβ; 2,19aα; 2,22; 2,25; 3,9; 4,8bα; 5,15b; 6,6b. Zur Sache cf. R. E. JOHNSON, *The Rhetorical Question as a Literary Device in Ecclesiastes*, The Southern Baptist Theological Seminary, 1986 (Diss.), pp. 205-207; FISCHER, *op. cit.*, p. 42s.

52. Die abhängige disjunktive Frage wird im zweiten Glied gewöhnlich durch אם oder או eingeführt; cf. z. B. Koh 2,19. Dabei vermerken die Grammatiker den seltenen Fall einer einfachen Wiederholung der Fragepartikel הֲ in Num 13,18; cf. KÖNIG, *op. cit.*, §379b; GK §150i; C. BROCKELMANN, *Hebräische Syntax*, Neukirchen, Glückstadt, 1956, §169c; R. MEYER, *Hebräische Grammatik I-IV*, Berlin, ³1969-1982 (Nachdruck 1992), §114,4c. Jedoch ist Num 13,18 nicht zu vergleichen, weil den beiden durch Waw verbundenen Fragen in Koh 3,21 weder Subjekt noch Prädikat gemeinsam sind.

53. Bei beiden indirekten Fragen handelt es sich um zusammengesetzte Sätze, deren Subjekt vorangestellt ist; cf. GK §143a. Daß das ה entgegen der masoretischen Punktation als Fragepartikel aufzufassen ist, beweist schon die Wortstellung von Partizip und folgendem Personalpronomen; cf. z. B. Gen 4,9. Zur Diskussion cf. A. SCHOORS, *The Preacher Sought to Find Pleasing Words. A Study of the Language of Qoheleth* (OLA, 41), Leuven 1992, p. 213s.

54. Die beiden Pronomina separata היא betonen die Ausschließlichkeit und verstärken damit den entscheidenden Gegensatz: Wer kann wissen, ob der Odem der Menschen, dieser und nur dieser nach oben steigt, *hingegen* der Odem des Viehs, dieser und nur dieser nach unten zur Erde sinkt?

genteil zum Aufsteigen des menschlichen Odems selbständig formuliert
hat. Mithin gibt sich die zweite Satzfrage als hyperbolische Rede zu erkennen, die durch ihren Widersinn die Antwort der Tradition unterstreicht, daß natürlich der Odem beider nach oben zu Gott zurückkehrt.
Warum sollte nicht auch für den Lebensodem gelten, was in v. 20a bereits für das Todesgeschick von Mensch und Tier festgestellt war: Alle
beide gehen an einen einzigen Ort? *Ist aber v. 21 als rhetorischer Einwand erkannt, erweisen sich alle religionsgeschichtlichen Erklärungs-
versuche, die hier eine inhaltliche Polemik vermuten, als nicht text-
gemäß.*

Unsere Auslegung besitzt einen gewissen Vorläufer in der forschungs-
geschichtlich interessanten und doch eigenwilligen Arbeit des aus
Dorpat stammenden Gelehrten R. Bidder, *Ueber Koheleths Stellung zum
Unsterblichkeitsglauben*[55]. Denn sie scheint buchstäblich das Gegenteil
von dem zu beweisen, was sie zu beweisen sucht. Bidder behauptet
nämlich, daß Kohelet an eine Unsterblichkeit des Menschen geglaubt
habe und sich dieser Glauben *indirekt* aus dem Gerichtsgedanken er-
schließe, er zeigt aber, daß man dafür keinen einzigen *direkten* Hinweis
aus dem Buch Koheleth beibringen kann[56]. In einer ausholenden
Exegese von 3,18-21 führt er geradezu akribisch den Beweis, daß hier
und in 12,7 die Lehre von der Unsterblichkeit des Menschen weder angezweifelt noch vertreten werde. »Das gewonnene Resultat aber ist
bloss ein negatives: wir wissen nicht, wie Koheleth zum Glauben an die
Unsterblichkeit steht«[57]. Im Anschluß an Bidder nennen wir nochmals
die wesentlichen Argumente, die unsere oben gegebene Auslegung un-
termauern: Erstens können wir für רוח in v. 19 und 21 folgerichtig die-
selbe Bedeutung »Lebensodem« ansetzen; denn es ist unwahrscheinlich, daß die Bedeutung von רוח im selben Argumentationszusammen-
hang wechselt und in v. 21 entgegen der alttestamentlichen Vorstellung
und in Abwehr einer fremden Lehre jetzt den individuellen Totengeist
oder die menschliche Seele bezeichne. Zweitens erweist sich v. 21 als
Schlußstein der Argumentation und bestätigt dadurch die affirmative
Funktion der rhetorischen Frage im Buch Kohelet und insbesondere in
der Schuldiskussion. Drittens lassen sich sowohl 3,21 als auch 12,7 in
Einklang mit der alttestamentlichen Überlieferung erklären. Damit erweisen sich sämtliche Versuche, die 12,7b als orthodoxe Glosse beurteilen oder einen Selbstwiderspruch zwischen 3,21 und 12,7 im Denken

---

55. R. BIDDER, *Ueber Koheleths Stellung zum Unsterblichkeitsglauben. Ein Beitrag
zur gerechten Beurtheilung des Buches Koheleth*, Erlangen, 1875.
56. Cf. p. 31, 45 und 52.
57. Cf. p. 18, 37s, und das Zitat p. 42.

Kohelets verankern, als überflüssig und gegenstandslos. Viertens bietet 3,18-21 eine in sich schlüssige Beweisführung, so daß der Text aus sich heraus verständlich ist und keiner zusätzlichen Hypothesen bedarf. Nach allem bewährt sich eine die Schulsituation voraussetzende Auslegung, die nicht zuletzt durch die rhetorische Formel מִי יוֹדֵעַ bestätigt wird[58].

III. DOCH EIN APOKALYPTISCHER HINTERGRUND IN 3,21?

Trotzdem hat gerade diese Einleitung immer wieder den Verdacht genährt, als wende sich Kohelet gegen eine bestimmte Gruppe, die für sich ein Wissen über das Jenseits beanspruche. Offenbar hat der Gedanke besonders fasziniert, daß Kohelet hier mit kalter und skeptischer Ironie die Phantasterei der Neugläubigen bekämpfe und dadurch ein frühes, wenn auch indirektes Zeugnis für die Jenseitshoffnung gefunden sei[59]. Allerdings belegen die vorsichtigen Äußerungen in der Kommentarliteratur, daß die Forschung hier über vage Vermutungen nicht hinausgekommen ist[60]. Das ist auch nicht verwunderlich; denn mit der rhetorischen Frage liegt weder ein Fremdzitat vor noch wird in ihr ein apologetischer Kontext vorausgesetzt. Für die Begründung der gegenteiligen Ansicht müßten methodisch wenigstens zwei Forderungen erfüllt sein: Erstens müßte die erschlossene Vorstellung religionsgeschichtlich nachweisbar sein und zweitens müßte die Gruppe näher beschrieben werden können, die als Gegner Kohelets in Erscheinung getreten wären und ihn zu seiner polemischen Spitze herausgefordert hätten[61]. Beiden Postulaten zu genügen, hat sich D. Michel in der eingangs erwähnten Untersuchung bemüht und Kohelets Gegner in Kreisen der frühen Apokalyptik aufgespürt[62]. Von seiner erkenntnistheoretischen Skepsis her polemisiere

---

58. Cf. JOHNSON, *op. cit.*, p. 155: »Like the question of Ecclesiastes 2:19, this question is composed of the מי יודע formula followed by the interrogative ה, and like 2:19, it (Ecc. 3:21) augments a preceding assertion. In 3:18-20, that assertation is the notion that humankind and the beasts are equal«. Cf. ferner CH. KLEIN, *Kohelet und die Weisheit Israels* (BWANT, 132), Stuttgart - Berlin - Köln, 1993, p. 118s.

59. Cf. W. BOUSSET, *Die Religion des Judentums im späthellenistischen Zeitalter* (HNT, 21), Tübingen ³1926, p. 273; und die oben unter n. 6 genannte Literatur.

60. Cf. z. B. HERTZBERG, *op. cit.*, p. 112, 232; N. LOHFINK, *Kohelet* (NEB, 1), Würzburg, 1980, p. 35; WHYBRAY, *op. cit.*, p. 80; CRENSHAW, *op. cit.*, p. 104; FOX, *op. cit.*, p. 197; MURPHY, *op. cit.*, p. 37.

61. Cf. dazu K. BERGER, *Die impliziten Gegner. Zur Methode des Erschließens von »Gegnern« in neutestamentlichen Texten*, in D. LÜHRMANN & G. STRECKER (eds.), *Kirche. Festschrift G. Bornkamm*, Tübingen, 1980, pp. 373-400.

62. In andere Richtung gehen die Überlegungen von KELLERMANN, *op. cit.*, pp. 279-281, der die Gegner Kohelets in hellenistisch beeinflußten Kreisen der klassischen Weis-

Kohelet gegen ihre Behauptung, daß die Seelen (Geister) der Menschen zu Gott aufstiegen und dort in einem von Gott ausgeübtes Jenseitsgericht geschieden würden[63].

Um unsere oben begründete Auslegung auch in diese Richtung abzusichern, überprüfen wir, ob sich die von Michel beschriebene Position der Gegner Kohelets aus der Frage von 3,21 herleiten läßt. Wir beginnen mit einer terminologischen Beobachtung und erinnern dabei vorerst an unsere Feststellung, daß die רוח beim lebendigen Menschen gemeinhin den Odem als die von Gott verliehene Lebenskraft bezeichnet. Wenn sie den Menschen im Tode verläßt, wandelt sich der Verstorbene zu einem in die Scheol eingehenden Totengeist[64]. Während nun die Totengeister im alttestamentlichen Sprachgebrauch רפאים heißen[65], wird erstmals in apokalyptischen Texten die רוח zur Bezeichnung der Verstorbenen individualisiert und personalisiert. Gleichzeitig verschiebt sich die Bedeutung dahingehend, daß die neue Benennung weniger das kraftlose Schattenwesen der Totengeister als vielmehr deren individuelle Fortexistenz betont. Aus dieser Entwicklung ergibt sich als typisch apokalyptischer Sprachgebrauch, daß von den Totengeister als den רוחות bzw. נפשת im Plural und nicht im Kollektiv gesprochen wird[66]. Hätte Kohelet

---

heit sucht. HENGEL, *op. cit.*, p. 228s; SCHWIENHORST-SCHÖNBERGER, *op. cit.*, p. 120; denken an die Auseinandersetzung Kohelets mit einer volkstümlichen, vielleicht unter hellenistischem Einfluß entstandenen Vorstellung vom Weiterleben der individuellen menschlichen Seele nach dem Tod. Zu den dafür in Anspruch genommenen griechischen Texten und Grabinschriften cf. P. HOFFMANN, *Die Toten in Christus* (Neutestamentliche Abhandlungen, N. F. 2), Münster, 1966, pp. 44-57; H.-P. MÜLLER, *op. cit.*, pp. 86-95. Allerdings gab schon E. RHODE, *Psyche. Seelencult und Unsterblichkeitsglaube der Griechen*, Freiburg - Leipzig - Tübingen, ²1898 (Nachdruck 1991), p. 385, zu bedenken, daß die Grabinschriften zwar in einigen Fällen der Hoffnung des Aufsteigens der Seele in himmlische Regionen Ausdruck verleihen, aber selten über den poetischen Aufschwung der Betrachtung hinausgehen. Ob sie über neue Glaubensvorstellungen und deren Verbreitung in hellenistischen Kreisen Jerusalems Auskunft geben können, ist zweifelhaft.

63. Cf. MICHEL, *op. cit.*, p. 118.

64. Zutreffend bemerkt HOFFMANN, *op. cit.*, p. 103 n. 30, daß diese Vorstellung eine Entsprechung im homerischen ψυχή-Verständnis findet. Cf. dazu A. SCHNAUFER, *Frühgriechischer Totenglaube. Untersuchungen zum Totenglauben der mykenischen und homerischen Zeit* (Spudasmata, 20), Hildesheim - New York, 1970, pp. 58-70; W. F. OTTO, *Die Manen oder Von den Urformen des Totenglaubens* (Sonderausgabe, WBG), Darmstadt, 1983, pp. 31-36 und 45-54.

65. Cf. Ps 88,11; Hi 26,5; Spr 2,18; 9,18; 21,16; Jes 14,9; 26,14.19.

66. In den aramäischen Fragmenten des Henochbuchs sind die נפשת in 1 Hen 13,6; 22,3 belegt, während in 1 Hen 22,5 die רוח מת אנש einen individuellen Totengeist bezeichnet, der durch den Engel mit dem Geist Abels identifiziert wird; cf. K. BEYER, *Die aramäischen Texte vom Toten Meer*, Göttingen 1984, p. 237-241. Für die Sprachentwicklung ist mit O. KAISER, in ID. & E. LOHSE, *Tod und Leben* (Biblische Konfrontationen, 1001), Stuttgart, 1977, p. 35, auf 4 Esr 7,78-80 hinzuweisen. Hier wird Koh 12,7 zitiert, der Odem des Menschen in seiner Rückkehr zu Gott personal verstanden und den Seelengeistern der Verächter bei ihrem Erscheinen vor dem Höchsten ein qualvolles Los beschieden.

in 3,21 die apokalyptische Terminologie übernommen und demgemäß von den Geistern der Menschen im Plural gesprochen, besäßen wir einen eindeutigen Hinweis auf die von ihm bekämpfte Lehre. Da er es nicht getan und sich mithin nicht vom traditionellen Sprachgebrauch abgesetzt hat, bleibt die Beziehung von רוח auf die Totengeister eine bloße, durch nichts zu beweisende Vermutung.

Was nun die inhaltlichen Aspekten der von Michel erhobenen Gegenposition anlangt, schicken wir voraus, daß sich in der apokalyptischen Literatur die Vorstellung, daß in den letzten Tagen die Seelen der Gerechten in den Himmel entrückt werden[67] mit der Erwartung einer endzeitlichen Auferweckung verbindet, sei es zum Heil für die Frommen oder sei es zur Vorbereitung des Gerichts an den Frevlern[68]. Dabei belegen die einschlägigen Texte zu beiden Vorstellungen, daß die Apokalyptik nicht am Weiterleben der Menschen nach dem Tod an sich interessiert gewesen ist, sondern am Los der verstorbenen Gerechten; cf. 1 Hen 103,3f. Wenn nun die Gesprächspartner Kohelets ein allen Menschen bestimmtes Aufsteigen ihrer Geister behauptet hätten, müßten sie 3,21 gemäß eine dort erfolgende Verurteilung der Frevler voraussetzen. Ein solches Vergeltungsgericht in der Höhe wird aber in 3,21 weder angedeutet noch gibt es dafür im Jubiläen- und Henochbuch frühapokalyptische Belege. Vielmehr werden nach 1 Hen 22 die Totengeister in der Unterwelt gemäß ihrer sittlich-religiösen Qualität geschieden[69]. Von dort werden später die Seelen der Frommen in die himmlische Lichtwelt entrückt, während die bereits zu Lebzeiten Gerichteten in der Unterwelt verbleiben. Lediglich die Totengeister der noch nicht Gerichteten werden in der Endzeit zusammen mit den lebenden Frevlern verurteilt[70]. Aber auch dieses Gericht erfolgt nicht in der Höhe, sondern, insofern darüber überhaupt eine Aussage gemacht wird, auf der Erde im Jerusalemer Hinnomtal[71]. Mithin kann in diesen Texten von einem Jenseitsgericht im strengen Sinne nicht die Rede sein.

Unsere Bedenken richten sich aber nicht nur gegen das von Michel vorausgesetzte Vergeltungsgericht in der Höhe. Auch die Annahme, daß die frühe Apokalyptik überhaupt mit einem generellen Aufstieg der Menschengeister *post mortem* gerechnet hat, ist unbewiesen. Zwar belegen 1 Hen 104,2 und Dan 12,3 die Vorstellung, daß die Gerechten und

---

67. Cf. Dan 12,3; Jub 23,30f; 1 Hen 104,2; syrBar 51,3.9f; ferner Weish 3,7f; 5,15.
68. Cf. Dan 12,2; 1 Hen 51,1f; 92,3f; 4 Esr 7,32f; ferner PsSal 3,12.
69. Zur späteren Ausmalung des Zwischenzustands in der Unterwelt cf. 4 Esr 7,75-101.
70. Cf. 1 Hen 22,10f; 103,5-8. Zur gesamten Vorstellung cf. Marie-Theres WACKER, *Weltordnung und Gericht. Studien zu 1 Hen 22* (FzB, 45), Würzburg, 1982, pp. 178-200.
71. Cf. 1 Hen 27,2f; und dann 4 Esr 7,36.

ihre Lehrer[72] in himmlische Regionen erhoben werden. Aber erstens erfolgt dieser Aufstieg nicht unmittelbar, sondern erst mit der endzeitlichen Auferweckung von den Toten, zweitens bleibt er einem Kreis von Auserwählten vorbehalten[73]. Und selbst in den späten Bilderreden Hen 37-71, die wir zur Rekonstruktion der gesuchten Lehre nicht heranziehen dürfen[74], wird nur die Wohnung der Gerechten(!) bis zum Endgericht in den Himmel verlegt[75].

Schließlich erhebt sich die Frage, ob die von den Gegnern behauptete Sonderstellung der Menschen vor den Tieren noch einen Vorzug darstellte, wenn ihre Totengeister samt und sonders zum Gericht gen Himmel aufstiegen. Denn mit 4 Esr 7,65-69 und slHen 58,4-6 besitzen wir jedenfalls zwei späte apokalyptische Belege[76], die umgekehrt das Geschick der Tiere glücklich preisen, weil sie im Gegensatz zu den Menschen nicht ins Gericht müssen. Oder sollte man den Gesprächspartnern Kohelets unterstellen, daß sie meinten, die Tiere würden ebenso wie die Gottlosen von der zukünftigen Heilszeit ausgeschlossen?

Fassen wir zusammen, können wir in 3,21 weder einen bestimmten apokalyptischen Hintergrund entdecken noch die daraus deduzierte Lehre mit einer konkreten Gruppe von Gegnern zur Zeit Kohelets in Verbindung bringen. Statt dessen finden wir uns in dem Eindruck bestärkt: *3,16-21 wurde im Lichte seiner vergeltungsorientierten Nachbearbeitung in v. 17.18aγba gelesen.* Künftig dürfte also die Annahme, daß sich Kohelet in 3,21 mit einer in apokalyptisch gesinnten Kreisen vertretenen Jenseitshoffnung auseinandergesetzt habe, als widerlegt zu betrachten sein.

Sophienstr. 22   Alexander Achilles FISCHER
D-07743 Jena

---

72. Cf. 1 QS III,13; IX,12.21; 1 QSb I,1; III,22; CD XII,21; dazu Carol A. NEWSOM, *The Sage in the Literature of Qumran: The Functions of Maśkîl*, in J. G. GAMMIE & L. G. PERDUE (eds.), *The Sage in Israel and the Ancient Near East*, Winona Lake, 1990, pp. 373- 382.

73. Cf. weiter 4 Esr 7,97; syrBar 51,10; AssMos 10,9.

74. Zur Diskussion um ihr Alter cf. F. G. MARTÍNEZ, *Qumran and Apocalyptic. Studies on the Aramaic Texts from Qumran* (STDJ, 9), Leiden, 1992, p. 13 n. 19.

75. Cf. 1 Hen 40,5; 41,1f; 48,1; 61,12.

76. Zur zeitlichen Einordnung beider cf. z. B. J. SCHREINER, *Das 4. Buch Esra* (JSHRZ V/4), Gütersloh, 1981, p. 301s (1. Jh. n. Chr., nach 70); C. BÖTTRICH, *Das slavische Henochbuch*, (JSHRZ V/7), Gütersloh, 1996, p. 812s (1. Jh. n. Chr., vor 70).

ARTFUL AMBIGUITY IN ECCLESIASTES 1,1-11
A WISDOM TECHNIQUE?

I. INTRODUCTION

Interpreting a text involves a reader looking for, and hopefully picking up, clues to meaning. More reader-oriented approaches may highlight how different readers will pick up different clues, but this paper is an attempt to show how the clues embedded in the text of Ecclesiastes 1,1-11 can assist an alert reader in understanding the book of Ecclesiastes.

In relation to 1,2-11, Edwin Good has noted that there are "some perceptible stylistic techniques in this passage" that possess "a high correlation with meaning"[1]. In other words, the style of these verses, not just the content can affect the meaning of the whole. In this paper, I want to build on Good's work, yet move in a somewhat different direction.

Ecclesiastes 1,1-11 has been variously read as a description of the endless repetitiveness of life (so most scholars, reflected in the majority of English Bible translations) or, more positively, as a narration of the regular and dependable cycles of life (so, most prominently, Whybray). While commentators tend to opt for either a positive or negative reading of this section, this paper takes the lead from the apparently deliberate ambiguity of verse 6.

Verse 6 needs to be read in the light of the description of the sun in the previous verse:

וְזָרַח הַשֶּׁמֶשׁ וּבָא הַשָּׁמֶשׁ וְאֶל־מְקוֹמוֹ שׁוֹאֵף זוֹרֵחַ הוּא שָׁם: 5

הוֹלֵךְ אֶל־דָּרוֹם וְסוֹבֵב אֶל־צָפוֹן סוֹבֵב סֹבֵב הוֹלֵךְ הָרוּחַ 6
וְעַל־סְבִיבֹתָיו שָׁב הָרוּחַ:

In v. 5, the sun is said to rise, go down and hurry to the place where it rises. In v. 6, the subject of the verse (the wind) is delayed, so that the first-time reader would think that the sun is still being spoken about — going down to the south, round to the north[2], round and round it goes.

1. E.M. GOOD, *The Unfilled Sea: Style and Meaning in Ecclesiastes 1:2-11*, in J.G. GAMMIE et al. (eds.), *Israelite Wisdom: Theological and Literary Essays in Honor of Samuel Terrien*, New York, 1978, pp. 59-73, p. 72.
2. GOOD, *The Unfilled Sea* (n. 1), p. 66 argues that the reader would be aware that the sun is not the subject once they come to the phrase אֶל־צָפוֹן since the sun would not ever appear in the north in that part of the northern hemisphere.

But suddenly, unexpectedly from a reader's point of view, the wind is supplied as the subject of verse 6. This is an example of deliberate, purposeful, artful ambiguity. The text gives us, as it were, misleading clues[3] — clues that have the effect of causing the reader to still think about the sun, when the text has actually moved on to the wind. What is being asserted about the wind, could easily have been applied to the sun, and this gives the reader cause to reflect. If a re-reading of verse 6 gives a different meaning to that of a first-time reading, is it not worth re-reading the rest of the passage to see if there are other less blatant clues that may have been overlooked? When Good starts to read through these verses his initial response is "that every expression appears to have more than one possible meaning"[4]. In other words, this passage is full of words and expression with a broad semantic range, which makes it an ideal seedbed for ambiguity. Let us, therefore, look back at some of the details.

II. AMBIGUITY IN ECCLESIASTES 1,1-11

Verses 1-3

In v. 1, there is uncertainty about the figure described as Qohelet. The appositional phrase, בֶּן־דָּוִד מֶלֶךְ בִּירוּשָׁלָם, is an apparent allusion to David's son, Solomon. Yet, Solomonic authorship is not explicitly asserted, and many scholars would date the book much later than Solomon on linguistic or ideological grounds. Furthermore, the reference in 1,16 to 'all who were before me over Jerusalem' (similarly 2,9) presupposes a long line of rulers, which would preclude Solomon. For such reasons, most perceive in the opening chapters of the book, a Solomonic fiction that initially teases the reader with the possibility of a Solomonic provenance but, in the end, only alludes to his situation.

In v. 2, there is the well-known dispute about the meaning of הֶבֶל, but this is a matter to which we will return later. Just as important is the uncertainty about the reference that הַכֹּל is הֶבֶל. Is הַכֹּל meant to include all things, even God or piety, or does it just refer to everything short of this? There appears to be a more restricted use of הַכֹּל in 3,19, and there is a tension with 3,11, where God made הַכֹּל 'beautiful' or perhaps 'suitable' in its time. The precise ambit of הַכֹּל is not explicitly spelt out.

---

3. I.J.J. SPANGENBERG, *Irony in the Book of Qohelet*, in *JSOT* 72 (1996) 57-69 has most recently studied the related topic of irony in Ecclesiastes. At p. 61, he notes that two marks of irony are an intention to mislead and a double meaning. This could be said of ambiguity in general, with irony being one use to which ambiguity is put.

4. GOOD, *The Unfilled Sea* (n. 1), pp. 64-65.

Verse 3 is particularly difficult. Is this a rhetorical question implying the answer 'no', or is it a genuine question? Is it answered by v. 2 or by v. 4, or is the verdict left open? In terms of its detail, does לָאָדָם refer to humanity in general, or an individual human being? Is עָמָל a reference to hard labour, or simply to any kind of work, or perhaps even the wealth that comes from one's work (e.g. Ps 105,44)? The word יִתְרוֹן appears to be a commercial word for the surplus left over, but is the focus on the here and now, or, as Ogden has proposed, on "wisdom's reward both here and after death"[5]? What, too, is the significance of the phrase תַּחַת הַשֶּׁמֶשׁ? Does it mean 'leaving God out of consideration' (so Kidner, Eaton, Farmer), or is it equivalent to 'on earth' as opposed to 'in heaven'[6]? The clustering of so many words with wide ranges of meaning is surely not merely an accidental feature of the text.

Verses 4-8

In vv. 4-8, the alternative meanings are found in the unit as a whole. If, as Whybray argues, v. 4 does not answer v. 3 but rather introduces vv. 5-8, then v. 4 presents the central theme which is developed in the verses that follow. Yet, even if this is agreed, the thrust of both v. 4 and the verses which follow is open to dispute. Whybray, for example, claims that the text does not assert that there is anything futile about human life cycles, but rather the focus is that, even though periods of time pass, new ones come, and the earth stands as it is — that is, that there are regular cyclical processes that are then outlined in vv. 5-7[7]. Murphy, on the other hand, represents the majority of scholars when he suggests that vv. 4-7 are not a simple nature poem but rather they "epitomize the fruitless nature of human activity that is expressed in v. 8 and is reflected

5. G.S. OGDEN, *Qoheleth* (Readings — A New Biblical Commentary), Sheffield, 1987, p. 29. His argument supporting this view is found on pp. 22-26. On a slightly different tack, K.A. FARMER, *Who Knows What is Good? A Commentary on the Books of Proverbs and Ecclesiastes* (International Theological Commentary), Grand Rapids, 1991, p. 153 sees the issue in v. 3 as permanence ("any *permanence*, anything which can be grasped and kept ("gained")"), not value.

6. D. KIDNER, *A Time to Mourn, and a Time to Dance: Ecclesiastes and the Way of the World* (Bible Speaks Today), Leicester, 1976, p. 23 argues that the observation point of the book is at ground level. M.A. EATON, *Ecclesiastes: An Introduction and Commentary* (Tyndale Old Testament Commentaries), Leicester, 1983, p. 57 comments, "When a perspective of faith is introduced 'All is vanity' is still true, but it is not the whole picture; 'under the sun' it is the whole truth". FARMER, *Who Knows* (n. 5), p. 154 suggests that "Qohelet does not include God's activities in the category of what is done 'under the sun'".

7. R. N. WHYBRAY, *Ecclesiastes 1.5-7 and the Wonders of Nature*, in *JSOT* 41 (1988) 105-112, pp. 105-107. See also G.S. OGDEN, *The Interpretation of* דור *in Ecclesiastes 1.4*, in *JSOT* 34 (1986) pp. 91-92.

upon in vv. 9-11"[8]. The passage in vv. 4-7 is, on this view, not written in praise of nature, but merely a foil for his conclusions about the useless activity of human beings.

A brief survey of vv. 4-7 reveals that both these readings can arise out of the text. When we turn to v. 4, are we talking about periods of time or human generations? Is the observation in v. 4a optimistic or pessimistic — all new generations will die, or that after each generation that passes, a new one comes? In terms of v. 4b, does 'earth' refer to the physical earth, or, as Fox has suggested, the world of people ('le monde' instead of 'la terre')[9]? Is the implication of v. 4b that despite much movement nothing really is achieved or changed, or is it that the earth or world can still be relied upon as regular or stable?

In v. 5, is there a depiction of the rising and setting of the sun describing the regular and dependable cycle of nature, or is it a picture of pointless repetition? The Hebrew root שָׁאַף has the sense of 'gasp, pant, sniff' and can be used negatively of a runner breathing heavily out of exhaustion in a race, or positively of one who is panting with eagerness to get underway[10].

We have already looked at some of the ambiguity of v. 6 (that of the delayed subject), but there is also the question of whether the blowing of the wind is part of the regular pattern of nature, or a further example of useless or unproductive activity.

This uncertainty is also present in v. 7, but there is an additional ambiguity as well. The Hebrew text can be read as referring to a water cycle (the water returning to the place *from* which it flows, likely to be understood beneficially), or to the constant flow of water into the sea (the water continually flowing to the place *to* which it flows), without making any difference[11].

Verse 8 clearly contains reflection on the preceding verses, but the nature of the reflection is moot. Is it a reflection on 'all things' or 'all words'? The balance of v. 8 (where the root דבר is used to refer to speech) suggests 'words', but דָּבָר is used in v. 10 to mean 'thing' not 'word'. Is the NRSV right to suggest 'wearisome' as a translation of יְגֵעִים? It is translated as 'weary' in its only other two uses in the Old Testament (Deut 25,18; 2 Sam 17,2), but Whybray points out that the more common cognate noun and verb generally mean either labour or the product of labour — that is, wealth, produce, property. Thus,

8. R.E. MURPHY, *Ecclesiastes* (WBC), Dallas, 1992, p. 9.
9. M.V. FOX, *Qohelet 1.4*, in *JSOT* 40 (1988) p. 109.
10. WHYBRAY, *Ecclesiastes 1.5-7* (n. 7), p. 108.
11. WHYBRAY, *art. cit.*, pp. 108-110.

Whybray, following Lohfink, suggests that it could mean purposeful or effective activity here, giving the meaning 'all things are constantly in activity'[12]. He notes that one's reading of this section is strongly influenced by one's translation of this word. If we were to read it as he suggests, then the balance of the verse tells of how humanity is speechless in response to the cycles of nature, and their eye and ear are incapable of taking it all in. Yet, if one were persuaded by a translation like 'wearisome', then this would paint a negative gloss over vv. 4-7.

In this crucial central section, therefore, there are two ways of reading these verses. Scholars have tended to opt for one or the other, but the deliberate use of ambiguity in v. 6 might alert the reader to look for its wider use throughout this section.

Verses 9-11

We will deal with these verses in less detail, as the central point has already been made. Examples of ambiguity here include the translation value of the tenses in v. 9; the implications of תַּחַת הַשֶּׁמֶשׁ (noted above in relation to v. 3); the meaning of דָּבָר in v. 10; and whether רִאשֹׁנִים in v. 11 has in view former people, former events, or, even former times, which may cover both people and circumstances.

III. THE MEANING OF הֶבֶל IN ECCLESIASTES

Many of these details have been discussed in a plethora of scholarly writings, and there is not space to explore them here. Indeed, the fact that most readers or commentators have decided many of these matters, and preferred some translations to others, ought not to blind us to the existence of so much uncertainty on a first reading of the text. On a re-reading of the passage, it appears that what seemed to be a straightforward pericope is in many ways purposefully, deliberately, even artfully, enigmatic. It does not surrender its meaning in a transparent way.

In the light of this observation, it is worth re-examining the meaning of הֶבֶל in v. 2. This has a literal sense of 'breath' or 'breeze' (e.g. Isa 57,13), but is almost always used metaphorically in the Old Testament[13]. Over half the uses of this word occur in Ecclesiastes, but outside this book it commonly means what is useless or worthless. The NRSV opts for 'vanity'; the NIV chooses 'meaningless'; while some other versions choose a

---

12. WHYBRAY, *art. cit.*, p. 107.
13. R.N. WHYBRAY, *Ecclesiastes* (NCBC), Grand Rapids, 1989, p. 36.

number of different words to translate הֶבֶל throughout the book. Fox has suggested the existentialist category of 'absurd'; Crenshaw sees a cross between 'ephemeral' and 'futile/absurd'; Fredericks has argued for 'transience'; Whybray suggests mostly 'futility', but 'brevity' in 6,12; 9,9 and 11,10[14].

One stimulating suggestion has been that of Graham Ogden who builds on earlier suggestions by Staples ('unknowable, incomprehensible, a mystery'), and by Good ('incongruous or ironic'). Ogden examines the contexts in which it is used in Ecclesiastes (3,16-19; 6,1-2; 4,7-8; 8,14); the parallel and complementary phrases (striving after wind, a sore affliction, an unhappy business) and the calls to enjoyment which punctuate the book. He suggests that הֶבֶל "has a very specific meaning: it identifies the enigmatic, the ironic dimension of human experience; it suggests that life is not fully comprehensible"[15]. Life is unable to be fully fathomed, and must be lived with many questions left unanswered.

In the light of this debate, we return to our passage. Might not this very passage be indicating the ambiguity found in this sage's observations on life? Life is puzzling or enigmatic because, on the one hand, there are many regular, dependable cycles in nature, but, on the other hand, there is much pointless repetition. This reality is not so much futile, or absurd, or meaningless, but rather it is complex, ambiguous, enigmatic.

Is it not possible — indeed likely — that Ecclesiastes, like Job, was written to correct a misunderstanding of the nature of proverbial wisdom? Job's friends held on to such a rigid doctrine of retribution that they could read his sinfulness off from his suffering. Instead of seeing retribution as only part of God's truth, they rewrote Job's life. They fossilised or calcified a single truth, failing to see that the doctrine of retribution is only a partial perspective, and needs to be held in tension with other truths about how God runs his world.

The book of Ecclesiastes also seems to be written as a corrective to certain misunderstandings of retribution. While Qohelet does not deny that God has created order, he wants to assert in addition that our perception of this order is often confused and confusing. Life is ambiguous, enigmatic. It is, in any event, much more complex than an entirely posi-

14. M.V. Fox, *Qohelet and His Contradictions* (JSOT SS, 71) Sheffield, 1989, pp. 29-48; J.L. Crenshaw, *Ecclesiastes* (OTL), Philadelphia, Westminster – London, 1987, pp. 57-58; D.C. Fredericks, *Coping with Transience: Ecclesiastes on Brevity in Life* (Biblical Seminar, 18), Sheffield, 1993, pp. 11-32; Whybray, *Ecclesiastes* (n.13), p. 36.
    15. Ogden, *Qoheleth* (n. 5), p. 14.

tive phenomenon, or an entirely negative one. Life is both purposeful and puzzling. It is a matter of 'both/and', not 'either/or'.

It is not surprising, therefore, to find in wisdom literature this ambiguous or complex understanding of life reflected in the literary style of the text. Ecclesiastes 1,1-11 seems to introduce the theme of ambiguity by the concentration of many ambiguous words, phrases and ideas. This is literary artistry at its best. It is not that a positive or negative reading alone is intended, but that the reader needs to see both the regularity and seemingly pointless repetition are true to life.

IV. ARTFUL AMBIGUITY IN THE WISDOM CORPUS

An interesting confirmation of this might be to consider other areas of the wisdom corpus where there may be further artful ambiguity. A number of examples suggest themselves from the book of Ecclesiastes — the time poem in 3,1-8; the metaphor in chapter 12 (variously interpreted as referring to death, aging, a house, even meteorological phenomena); the epilogue with its endorsement of Qohelet's words, as well as the call to fear God and obey his commands.

Yet, the use of ambiguity is not confined to Ecclesiastes. In the book of Job, there is the uninterpreted ambiguity of the Yahweh speeches, and the nature of Job's 'repentance' in 42,6. There is also the ambiguity of the epilogue, and how that squares with the doctrine of retribution in the rest of the book; the meaning of ברך in the prologue; and the nature of Job's call for a legal figure in chapters 9, 16, 19 and 31. If the Song of Songs is a wisdom book, then there is the ambiguity of working out if it if an anthology of poems, or whether the characters remain the same.

Indeed, even in the foundational wisdom book — the book of Proverbs — there is evidence of this deliberate ambiguity. In 26,4.5, for example, should one answer a fool according to their folly or not? The response of the sage appears to be that sometimes it is helpful to do so, and sometimes it is not. Proverbs yield truth, but it is the nature of proverbs to be partially true — true from a certain perspective, but not always true[16]. This is even the case with English proverbs, where 'look before you leap' is to be read together with 'he who hesitates is lost', and 'too many cooks spoil the broth' is nuanced by 'many hands make light work'.

16. See, for example, F. HOLMGREN, 'Barking Dogs Never Bite, Except Now and Then: Proverbs and Job', in Anglican Theological Review 61 (1979) 341-353.

V. Conclusions and Implications

What, then, can we say about the reason for this use of ambiguity in the wisdom writers. Childs has pointed out that Ecclesiastes was not written in a vacuum, but as a critical corrective to conventional wisdom, much as James may have been a corrective to a misunderstanding of Paul[17]. Without denying there is order in the world, Qohelet's use of ambiguity can affirm that there is also confusion and pointlessness in this order, or at the very least in our perception of it. Both aspects help the reader to understand God's world as it is. In the broader wisdom corpus, there is both the assertion of an orderly world (so Proverbs) as well as the legitimate questioning and protest about how God is ruling his world (so Job).

In Ecclesiastes 1, this paper proposes that the purposeful use of ambiguity is a way of reminding the reader that wisdom observations usually reflect part, not all, of the truth. In other words, what is being asserted from one viewpoint might need to be qualified by other perspectives. The effect of this ambiguous opening section is that the reader is warned to tread carefully. The same words can indicate both the regularity of nature and the apparent pointlessness of human activity. Both interpretations pass the wisdom test of ringing true to the sage's experiences and observations of the world. Reality is much richer than either insight stretched so far as to exclude the other. The use of ambiguity thus does not mean that the text fails to communicate its message, but rather implies that the message is more complex that it appears at first[18].

Let me finish with one important concern. If there is ambiguity or uncertain meaning in parts of scripture, what does it mean to call Ecclesiastes or the other wisdom books, the word of God? How does artful ambiguity affect one's doctrine of scripture? This requires further detailed reflection, but two observations are worth making here.

Firstly, it should be pointed out that deliberate ambiguity does not mean uncertainty of meaning. Rather, it is simply to identify a feature of the text that invites the reader to re-read the text in order to arrive at the final meaning. The meaning is, in fact, richer when it affirms two aspects which may be in tension with each other, but which are both equally true to life.

17. B.S. CHILDS, *Introduction to the Old Testament as Scripture*, London, 1979, p. 588.
18. See, for example, M.V. FOX, *The Uses of Indeterminacy*, in *Semeia* 71 (1995) 173-192, pp. 173-175. He notes significant indeterminacies in Ecclesiastes, but regards them, however, as unresolvable and leading to the view that life is absurd.

Secondly, it is a high view of scripture to base one's interpretation on what is in the text, and all that is in the text. Certain techniques, such as ambiguity, should not be ruled out by *prima facie* assumptions, but rather the biblical books should be re-examined to discern whether or not they are present. As Fox has pointed out in relation to Ecclesiastes, "a reading faithful to this book, at least, should try to describe the territory with all its bumps and clefts, for they are not mere flaws, but the essence of the landscape"[19].

Ridley College   Lindsay WILSON
The University of Melbourne
160 The Avenue
Parkville, Victoria 3052
Australia

19. M.V. FOX, *Contradictions* (n. 14), p. 28.

THE SIGNIFICANCE OF AMBIGUITY IN
ECCLESIASTES 2,24-26

The חֲכָמִים of ancient Israel built the theological foundation of their movement in a theological area prone to shifting and upheaval. On the one hand, the wise upheld the sovereignty of God and its byproduct, the stability of creation[1]. On the other hand, the wise affirmed the freedom of humanity to achieve its potential, to order its private world. Though wisdom provides the ability to steer one's own life[2] (Prov 1,5: תַּחְבֻּלוֹת), it also affirmed that ultimately God and not wisdom is sovereign (Prov 21,30). One might argue that the theological premises of wisdom are by nature ambiguous[3].

Out of this awareness, this paper will examine an expression of wisdom's theological ambiguity as exhibited in Eccles 2,24-26. This writer proposes that Qoheleth modifies the wisdom perspective associated with certain *Tôb-Sprüche* in Proverbs[4] through the combination of a new form of *Tôb-Spruch*[5] (אֵין טוֹב) and certain types of ambiguity in Eccles 2,24-26.

AMBIGUITY: A DEFINITION

Before discussing the significance and types of ambiguity in Eccles 2,24-26, it is important to define the term "ambiguity". Generally, the

---

1. W. ZIMMERLI, *The Place and Limit of the Wisdom in the Framework of the Old Testament Theology*, in *SJT* 17 (1964) 146-158, p. 148.

2. *Ibid.*, p. 149.

3. J.G. WILLIAMS, *Those Who Ponder Proverbs: Aphoristic Thinking and Biblical Literature*, Sheffield, The Almond Press, 1981, pp. 17-34.

4. Originally, this article included a contextual study of *Tôb-Sprüche* in relation to Yahweh-sayings in Proverbs. In summary, the comparative form, טוֹב מִן, is used 21 times in the book of Proverbs. The majority of the occurrences are found in Prov 10,1-22,16. By using the categories of relative value (which describes a situation that is sometimes good) and an absolute value (a situation or meaning that is always good), one discovers that fifteen of the *Tôb-Sprüche* reflect a situation that is relative in nature. Furthermore, 8 of 15 *Tôb-Sprüche* are juxtaposed with a Yahweh-saying (cf. Prov 15,16-17; 16,8.19; 17,1; 19,22; 22,1; 28,6) in a relative context. Theologically, this is suggestive of a carefully constructed answer to life's ambiguities. Even if a situation is less-than-ideal, the sage can have confidence in the sovereignty of God to help assuage the pain of an ambiguous circumstance.

5. Based on a similarity of form and function, it seems likely that there is a connection between טוֹב מִן and אֵין טוֹב. See G. OGDEN, *The 'Better'-Proverb (Tôb-Spruch), Rhetorical Criticism, and Qoheleth*, in *JBL* 96 (1977) 493-494; G. BRYCE, *'Better'-Proverbs: An Historical and Structural Study*, in *Seminar Papers, SBL*, 1972, p. 351; G. OGDEN, *Qoheleth's Use of the 'Nothing is Better'-Form*, in *JBL* 98 (1979) 339-350, p. 342.

term implies multiple meanings[6]. However, "ambiguity" should not be understood as deceitfulness. Instead, at the basic level of reading the text, different options regarding the meaning of a word or phrase surface. Especially, if the context supports more than one meaning[7].

AMBIGUITIES IN ECCLESIASTES 2,24-26

Qoheleth adopted and modified the traditional *Tôb-Spruch* by "appending to it a clause which provides grounds for validating the values proposed... In each case a postfixed כִּי clause is the means of expressing the validation"[8]. This modification allows Qoheleth to use the *Tôb-Sprüche* as a literary device to express conclusions drawn from his observations about life[9]. However, Qoheleth also modifies the *Tôb-Sprüche* by preemptive statements (3,22; 6,11) that relativize the "good" expressed in the series of *Tôb-Sprüche* in Eccles 4,1-16 and 7,1-12[10]. Furthermore, it is important to note that the preemptive statements emphasize God's freedom in regard to the future (3,15.22; 6,10-12; 7,13-14) and humanity's inability to anticipate it regardless of one's wisdom[11].

This theological tension between God's freedom as a comfort, as exhibited in the context of certain *Tôb-Sprüche* in Proverbs, and God's freedom as a limitation of wisdom, as reflected in the context of certain *Tôb-Sprüche* in Ecclesiastes, seems to be especially evident in Qoheleth's contextual use of the אֵין טוֹב sayings[12]. The אֵין טוֹב sayings seem to re-

6. W. O'CONNOR, *Princeton Encyclopedia of Poetry and Poetics*, Princeton, Princeton University Press, 1974, s.v. ambiguity, pp. 18-19; W.G.E. WATSON, *Classical Hebrew Poetry: A Guide to its Techniques*, Sheffield, JSOT Press, 1984, p. 237; *Webster's New International Dictionary of the English Language*, 2nd unabridged ed., s.v. "ambiguity, ambiguous."

7. P.R. RAABE, *Deliberate Ambiguity in the Psalter*, in *JBL* 110 (1991) 213-227, pp. 213-214. Raabe, at the conclusion of his article, addresses the concern that some readers might invent ambiguity that is not in the text. His answer to the issue is threefold: 1) be careful not to base ambiguity solely on the basis of cognate languages (while this would seem to strike at the heart of my first category, concerning the word חוש, this word's most basic meaning, "to be hasty", does not fit the context, which in my estimation opens the door to consider the second meaning of the term in Biblical Hebrew, as well as the most agreed upon cognate among scholars as a means of testing the significance of lexical ambiguity); 2) context is the most important control. Context should anticipate and echo the ambiguity; 3) theological significance should be involved in the ambiguity. *Ibid.*, p. 227.

8. OGDEN, *'Better'-Proverb* (n. 5), p. 495. This literary development is found in Eccles 4,9.17 (5,1); 6,3-4; 7,2.3.5-6; 9,4.

9. *Ibid.*, p. 497.

10. C.L. SEOW, *Ecclesiastes: A New Translation with Introduction and Commentary* (AB, 18C), New York, Doubleday, 1997, pp. 67 and 186.

11. *Ibid.*, pp. 250-251.

12. OGDEN, *Qoheleth's Use of the 'Nothing is Better' Form* (n. 5), pp. 340-342.

flect the tension between God's sovereignty and humanity's limitations by setting forth advice "on how to cope with a life which is God-given but fraught with enigmas such that man's limited knowledge and ability to comprehend it leave him without the final and absolute answers for which he craves"[13]. Therefore, this section of the paper will explore certain types of ambiguity in Eccles 2,24-26 that influence one's reading of the אֵין טוֹב form. The result of the contextual ambiguity is tension between God's gift of pleasure and the limitation of humanity's wisdom to control God's gifts.

LEXICAL AMBIGUITY[14]

The first example of ambiguity is the use of the term יָחוּשׁ in Eccles 2,25. Almost without exception scholars begin a discussion about חוּשׁ by stating that the common meaning of the term "hasten" does not fit the context of Eccles 2,24-26[15]. Scholars then turn their attention to cognates and develop a list of alternative understandings of חוּשׁ[16]. While there is still no consensus among scholars, when one considers the ancient versions, as well as the two major options among scholars, there appears to be two basic opinions in regard to חוּשׁ: "to enjoy" or "to worry"[17]. The polyvalent nature of the word may imply a deliberate ambiguity in the choice of חוּשׁ.

13. *Ibid.*, p. 342.
14. For a description of lexical ambiguity, see S. ULMANN, *Semantics: An Introduction to the Science of Meaning*, New York, Barnes & Noble, Inc., 1962, pp. 158-167; WATSON, *op. cit.* (n. 6), pp. 237-238.
15. A. LAUHA, *Kohelet* (BKAT, 19), Neukirchen, Neukirchener Verlag, 1978, p. 58; R. MURPHY, *Ecclesiastes* (WBC, 23a), Dallas, TX, Word Books, 1992, p. 25; SEOW, *op. cit.* (n. 10), p. 139.
16. A list of cognates include 1) Akkadian, *hâšu*, "to hasten" or "to worry" (See F. ELLERMEIER, *Das Verbum* חוּשׁ *in Koh. 2, 25: Eine exegetische, auslegungsgeschichtliche und semasiologische Untersuchung*, in *ZAW* 75 (1963) 197-217); 2) Akkadian, *hašāšu*, "to rejoice" (See L. LEVY, *Das Buch Qoheleth*, Leipzig, Hinrich's, 1912, pp. 77-78) or Ugaritic, *ḫšt*, "to enjoy" (See M. DAHOOD, *Qoheleth and Recent Discoveries*, in *Bib* 39 (1958) 302-318, pp. 307-308), 3) Arabic, "to abstain from, refrain" (See R. GORDIS, *Koheleth – The Man and His World: A Study of Ecclesiastes*, 3rd ed., New York, Schocken Books, 1968, p. 227), 4) Arabic root "to gather" (See SEOW, *op. cit.* (n. 10), p. 140).
17. Whitley summarizes the ancient versions by stating "The Septuagint, Theodotion and the Peshitta read ישתה (will drink) for יחוש, as in verse 24. So the Vulgate paraphrases *et deliciis affluet ut ego* (and abound in delights as I). On the other hand, Aquila, Symmachus and Syro-Hexaplar presuppose יָחוּשׁ "to experience pain". So likewise the Targum reads חששׁא, "feeling" or "anxiety". C.F. WHITLEY, *Koheleth: His Language and Thought* (BZAW, 148), Berlin/New York, Walter de Gruyter, 1979, p. 28. De Waard argues that the Septuagint's reading of חוּשׁ as πίεται may simply be a generic rendering meaning "to enjoy". J. DE WAARD, *The Translator and Textual Criticism (with Particular Reference to Eccl 2,25)*, in *Bib* 60 (1979) 509-529, p. 522.

If חוּשׁ is polyvalent, then Qoheleth may be focusing the reader's attention upon v. 25 in particular as a hinge around which vv. 24 and 26 turn[18]. If the reader understands חוּשׁ as "enjoyment", then the two halves of v. 25 are synonymous and serve as an explanation of v. 24[19]. A person can eat, drink, and discover good in one's toil because God makes it possible (חוּץ מִמֶּנִּי). Reading from this perspective, Qoheleth seems to be affirming the positive gifts of God. This would certainly be in line with the traditional usage of the *Tôb-Sprüche* in Proverbs, which affirms God's freedom as a comfort in the midst of ambiguous circumstances (see n. 4).

On the other hand, if one were to read חוּשׁ as "worry" or "agitation", a meaning found not only among certain cognates, but in Job 20,2 and Isa 28,16, then the second half of v. 25 is antithetical to the first part. The translation would be "For who can eat and who can worry apart from him". This interpretation of v. 25 forces the reader to v. 26 in order to discover the nature of the agitation suggested by חוּשׁ[20]. It is in the destinies of the אָדָם שֶׁטּוֹב and the חוֹטֵא that the contrast of v. 25 between "eating" and "worrying" is exemplified[21]. The implication is that God is responsible for pleasure and worry, thus making the freedom of God, not a comfort, but a painful enigma. This certainly seems to be an unique contextual modification of the אֵין טוֹב saying coined by Qoheleth.

If Qoheleth is using חוּשׁ in an ambiguous manner, then perhaps his purpose is to lead the reader to think of God's sovereignty both in a positive and puzzling light. Indeed, this ambiguous reading of the text may be Qoheleth's unique way of challenging the wisdom movement to focus more upon God's freedom in supplying טוֹב and less upon wisdom's ability to discover and develop טוֹב[22].

GRAMMATICAL AMBIGUITY

The final example of ambiguity in Eccles 2,24-26, which calls attention to God's sovereignty and wisdom's limitation, is the concluding phrase of v. 26: גַּם־זֶה הֶבֶל וּרְעוּת רוּחַ. Oftentimes, a phrase or clause is positioned at the end of a text so that one is unsure exactly how to relate

18. This tends to be supported by a word count of vv. 24-26: v. 24 contains 18 words, v. 25, 7 words, and v. 26, excluding the *hevel* judgment as a concluding formula, contains 18 words.

19. G. OGDEN, *Qoheleth*, Sheffield, JSOT Press, 1987, p. 49.

20. R.N. WHYBRAY, *Ecclesiastes* (NCBC), Grand Rapids, William B. Eerdmans Publishing Co., 1989, p. 64.

21. For a similar understanding of v. 25 see SEOW, *op. cit.* (n. 10), p. 140.

22. WHYBRAY, *Ecclesiastes* (n. 20), pp. 62-63.

it to what went before[23]. This ambiguous function of the phrase can certainly be demonstrated by the wide differences of opinion among scholars in their interpretation of the *hevel* judgment in relationship to vv. 24-26. Beginning with its most immediate context, Ogden and Whybray argue that the *hevel* judgment is related only to v. 26a, arguing on the basis of the immediate referent of גַּם־זֶה in v. 24b. Their interpretation is that Qoheleth finds an exact scheme of retribution confusing or enigmatic[24.] Gordis expands the referent of the *hevel* judgment to include all of vv. 24-26, including the advice to find pleasure in one's toil[25]. Finally, Crenshaw argues that the *hevel* judgment is the conclusion of the entire pericope which stretches from 1,12-2,26[26].

Beginning with the entire pericope, one must admit that it seems likely that the original reader could understand the final *hevel* judgment as the conclusion of 1,12-2,26. This is based on the recurring refrain of הֶבֶל וּרְעוּת רוּחַ in 1,14; 2,11.17.26. In particular, it is significant that the complete *hevel* judgment occurs at generally accepted seams in the overall pericope[27]. This would lead the reader to the conclusion that the final *hevel* judgment is related to the preceding sections and is the summation of them all. If this is a possible understanding, it is important to recognize that each of the *hevel* judgments relates to some failure of the wisdom enterprise (understanding, 1,12-18; accomplishments, 2,1-11; advantages in light of death, 2,12-17; and retribution, 2,18-26). Thus, as one views 1,12-2,26 as a textual unit, one is met with the dismal failure and ineffectuality of wisdom and the mysterious sovereignty of God.

Another reading suggests that the *hevel* judgment relates to only 2,18-26. This is based on the recurring phrase גַּם־זֶה הֶבֶל which occurs in 2,20.21.26. As one examines the referent of each conclusion, issues regarding toil stand out[28.] In particular, a chiastic pattern based on theme is noted: one's lack of control over the use of wealth in v. 20, one's lack of comfort from toil in v. 21, and one's lack of control over retribution in regard to wealth in v. 26. Another indication of a connection with 2,18-26 is the repetition of חָכְמָה וְדַעַת in vv. 21 and 26. Therefore, should one read the final *hevel* judgment of v. 26 as a final commentary on 2,18-

---

23. RAABE, *art. cit.* (n. 7), pp. 223-224.

24. OGDEN, *Qoheleth* (n. 19), p. 49; WHYBRAY, *Ecclesiastes* (n. 20), p. 64.

25. GORDIS, *op. cit.* (n. 16), p. 228.

26. J.L. CRENSHAW, *Ecclesiastes: A Commentary* (OTL), Philadelphia, The Westminster Press, 1987, p. 91.

27. Most commentators divide 1,12-2,26 into four or five sections: either 1,12-18; 2,1-11; 2,12-17; 2,18-23; 2,24-26 or 1,12-18; 2,1-11; 2,12-17; 2,18-26. For a chiastic interpretation of 1,12-2,26, see SEOW, *op. cit.* (n. 10), p. 144.

28. M.V. FOX, *Qohelet and His Contradictions*, Sheffield, The Almond Press, 1989, pp. 185-186.

26? If so, then the issue of no control and no comfort from wealth becomes dominant. This certainly seems to undercut Qoheleth's advice in the form of the אֵין טוֹב saying[29]. Indeed, the final *hevel* judgment reminds the reader that God's freedom coupled with wisdom's limitation is a bitter pill to swallow.

The final possible reading of the *hevel* judgment is in its immediate relationship to v. 26. This interpretation suggests that the emphasis on retribution found in v. 26a is not reliable. Texts which are reminiscent of v. 26, such as Prov. 13,22 that affirm the triumph of the wise over the foolish, are not necessarily true in every circumstance. Instead, God determines who enjoys wealth and who gathers wealth only to lose it[30].

The end result of the grammatical ambiguity of the *hevel* judgment in v. 26b is that the reader is invited to conclude from a broad context (1,12-2,26) or a restrictive context (2,26) that God is in control of life, and wisdom cannot guarantee success in life. Therefore, Qoheleth's unique *Tôb-Spruch* in Eccles 2,24-26, unlike certain uses of the *Tôb-Sprüche* in Proverbs (see n. 4), does not communicate comfort in the presence of God's sovereignty and life's ambiguities, but resignation.

CONCLUSION

It is obvious that a deliberate shift has taken place between the use of the *Tôb-Sprüche* in Proverbs and Qoheleth's use of אֵין טוֹב in Eccles 2,24-26. Not only has there been a syntactical modification, but also a theological modification. No longer is the sovereignty of God a comfort as in the context of certain *Tôb-Sprüche* in Proverbs. Instead, God's freedom is a reminder, through the ambiguities in Eccles 2:24-26, that ultimately pleasure and wisdom are limited by the Divine will and not capitalized on by humanity's wisdom.

New Orleans Baptist Theological Seminary   Rick W. BYARGEON
3939 Gentilly Blvd
New Orleans, LA 70126
U.S.A.

---

29. Ogden disagrees with this assessment by arguing that v. 21 is partly true, but so is v. 26. OGDEN, *Qoheleth* (n. 19), p. 49. However, Loader argues that when one reads v. 21 in light of v. 26 the arbitrary nature of God's gifts is emphasized. See J.A. LOADER, *Ecclesiastes: A Practical Commentary*, Grand Rapids, William B. Eerdmans Publishing Co., 1986, p. 32.

30. SEOW, *op. cit.* (n. 10), pp. 157-158; OGDEN, *Qoheleth* (n. 19), p. 49; WHYBRAY, *Ecclesiastes* (n. 20), p. 64.

THE SIGNIFICANCE OF אֲשֶׁר IN QOH 7,26:
"MORE BITTER THAN DEATH IS THE WOMAN,
IF SHE IS A SNARE"

In regard to Qoh 7,26: "And I find woman more bitter than Death, she is a snare, her heart is a net, and her arms are chains" (NJB), Whybray notes that "the unexpected introduction of this reference to woman into the discussion has perplexed commentators from very early times"[1]. It is no surprise that Krüger has recently proposed again an alternative interpretation, seeing in v. 26 a reference to Lady-Wisdom[2]. But for most critics, this verse is about "woman" as such. The exegetical concern has, instead, been focused on whether or not this verse describes a "pessimistic image of woman"[3]. On the one hand, the attitude toward woman presented here by Qohelet (and in v. 28) has been regarded as misogynous[4] or anti-feminist[5]. Further, Qohelet is to be considered "almost surely a bachelor"[6], because "he did not succeed in finding a wife"[7]. On the other hand, this verse can be thought of as a quotation, in which case the author should not be regarded as a "woman-hater"[8]. We agree with this latter opinion, but with some reservations. The reason is: even if v. 26 should be regarded as a quotation, it is still difficult to tell what the author's personal view about woman is,

---

1. R.N. WHYBRAY, *Ecclesiastes. Based on the Revised Standard Version* (NCBC), London, 1989, p. 125.

2. Th. KRÜGER, «*Frau Weisheit» in Koh 7,26?*, in *Bib* 73 (1992) 394-403; cf. E.W. HENGSTENBERG, *Commentary on Ecclesiastes: with Treatises on Song of Solomon, Job, Sacrifices, etc.*, New York, 1860, pp. 184-187. See further G.S. OGDEN, *Qoheleth* (Readings — A New Biblical Commentary), Sheffield, 1987, pp. 119-125, who understands "woman" in 7,26 in a metaphorical sense, interpreting the verse: "an untimely death is more bitter than death itself" (p. 123).

3. H.P. MÜLLER, *Neige der althebräischen «Weisheit». Zum Denken Qohäläts*, in ZAW 90 (1978) 238-264, p. 252.

4. F. DELITZSCH, *The Book of Ecclesiastes* (Commentary on the Old Testament in Ten Volumes, 6), Edinburgh, 1877, reprinted 1984, pp. 332-334.

5. J.A. SOGGIN, *Introduzione all'Antico Testamento* (BCR, 14), Brescia, ⁴1987, p. 487.

6. R. GORDIS, *Koheleth — The Man and His World* (TSJTSA, 19), New York, ³1973, p. 306.

7. M.V. FOX, *Qohelet and His Contradictions* (JSOT SS, 71), Sheffield, 1989, p. 243. See a critical observation of N. LOHFINK, *Nachträge*, in M. GILBERT (ed.), *La Sagesse de l'Ancien Testament* (BETL, 51), Leuven, ²1990, p. 419.

8. This aspect has been advanced most convincingly by N. LOHFINK, *War Kohelet ein Frauenfeind? Ein Versuch, die Logik und den Gegenstand von Koh., 7,23-8,1a herauszufinden*, in M. GILBERT (ed.), *La Sagesse de l'Ancien Testament* (BETL, 51), Leuven, ²1990, pp. 259-287.

because of the ambiguity of the particle אֲשֶׁר. The significance of this particle, however, has not received due attention from the scholars[9].

Because v. 26 is presented in a wider context, our first task is to appreciate the overall structure of the text, in order to discover a possible connection between v. 26 and the verses which precede and follow it. We will then proceed to examine v. 26, in which Qohelet makes use of אֲשֶׁר in conjunction with "woman". In the course of our analysis we will attempt to describe what is the author's own opinion and the view that he is criticizing. For the purpose of this paper, we will not discuss here all the related verses in detail.

I

The first person usage of 7,23 is an unmistakable indication of a new beginning, which implies that the foregoing unity ends with the second person discourse in v. 22[10]. The unit does not include 8,1b, which introduces a topic concerning the advice on how one should comport oneself in the presence of a King in 8,1b-4[11]. The root חכם in 7,23; 8,1a, and the rhetorical questions beginning with "who" in 7,24 and in 8,1a, constitute an *inclusio*, by which Qohelet's investigation begins and ends.

Qohelet begins to introduce his own past intellectual experiment[12] accompanied "by wisdom", where the feminine demonstrative זֹה[13] refers to what follows (7,23a). This introductory phrase is followed by a twofold exposition.

First exposition (vv. 23b-24): This reveals that, contrary to the intention expressed in the first person[14], the threefold assertion in vv. 23bβ-24 emphasizes that wisdom of any kind is utterly beyond human reach: 1) Wisdom is remote from me; 2) That which exists is far remote; 3) Who can comprehend (מצא) it?

Second exposition (vv. 25-29): Qohelet uses again the expression "I turned" in v. 25, which marks a new observation from the point of view of theme and vocabulary[15]. This has two distinct purposes[16]: he intends (1) "to

9. For the recent significant study on אֲשֶׁר in 7,26, see I. RIESENER, *Frauenfeindschaft im Alten Testament? Zum Verständnis von Qoh 7,25-29*, in A.A. DIESEL et al. (eds.), *"Jedes Ding hat seine Zeit..."* . FS D. Michel (BZAW, 241), Berlin-New York, 1996, pp. 195-197.

10. Cf. F.J. BACKHAUS, *»Denn Zeit und Zufall trifft sie alle«. Studien zur Komposition und zum Gottesbild im Buch Qohelet* (BBB, 83), Frankfurt am Main, 1993, p. 234.

11. For a detailed argument in favor of a literary unit 7,23-8,1a, see LOHFINK, *War Kohelet ein Frauenfeind?* (n. 8), pp. 272-277.

12. כל זה + verb with perfect tense in the first person refers to what the author has experienced; cf. 8,9; 9,1 (with masculine demonstrative).

13. The feminine demonstrative זו is used with an anaphoric function in 2,2.24; 5,18 and with a cataphoric function in 5,15; 9,13. See, however, R.E. MURPHY, *Ecclesiastes* (WBC, 23A), Dallas, 1992, pp. 69, 71, who understands זו in 7,23 as referring back to the wisdom sayings in 7,1-22.

14. Cf. the cohortative אחכמה followed by *waw* adversative in v. 23b.

15. Although "I turned" in v. 25 marks a new observation (cf. LOHFINK, *War Kohelet ein Frauenfeind?* (n. 8), p. 276), the passage that begins here is linked to the preceding

understand and to explore and to seek out wisdom and 'conclusion'"; (2) "to understand wickedness, foolishness, folly and madness"[17]. This introductory statement is followed by a progressively structured triple assertion centering round מצא and אשר, but with a stylistic variation (vv. 26-29)[18]:

v. 26	אשר...	מוצא אני	ו
v. 27-28	אשר...	מצאתי	ראה זה
v. 29	אשר...	מצאתי	ראה זה לבד

Waw in v. 26 presents a *continuum* nuance, whilst the predicate-participle מוצא indicates an iterative[19]. V. 26, vv. 27-28 and v. 29 are constructed in the same manner with verb + object clause; while in v. 26, the whole phrase "more bitter than death (is) the woman" has the function of an object clause of מוצא אני, the object clause in vv. 27-28 and v. 29 begins with אשר. In these latter verses, Qohelet adds ראה זה so as to underscore what he himself has discovered in his life, while, by inserting an adverb לבד in the latter, he draws careful attention to his consideration on the *status* of humankind.

With regard to the style of the two *Discoveries* (vv. 23bβ-24 and vv. 26-29), both are expressed by parallelism, but only the second *Discovery* contains an introductory phrase.

There seems to be a logical development of the theme in the I° Exposition, where the key word חכם is thoroughly considered. But, it is not easy to see any rigorous connection between Intention and Discovery of the II° Exposition; if Qohelet has intended to understand "what is wisdom" (or בקש חכמה), and "what is wickedness/folly" (or לדעת רשע/ הסכלות)[20], one would have expected that both or either of these terms

---

one by the theme-words מצא and חכם, and to the following by בקש, מצא, ידע, חשבון (חשבנות in 7,29b) and חכם.

16. Cf. the construction ל + inf. cst. indicating a purpose or the intention of the author.

17. Even if the conjunction *waw* before כסל and הוללות is lacking, we consider the four substantives as direct object of the infinitive לדעת; cf. J.Y.S. PAHK, *Il canto della gioia in Dio. L'itinerario sapienziale espresso dall'unità letteraria in Qohelet 8,16-9,10 e il parallelo di Gilgameš Me. iii*, Napoli, 1996, p. 86. For the structural similarity between 1,17; 7,25; 8,16, see *Ibid.*, pp. 85-88.

18. The threefold structure represents Qohelet's favorite style; among the many instances in the Book, see esp. 8,17 marked by the phrase "cannot find" and 9,5-6, where Qohelet uses the structure: אין; אין עוד; אין עוד לעולם. OGDEN, *Qoheleth* (n. 2), p. 121, according to whom, the "final summary" of Qohelet's search comes in two parts, vv. 27-28 and v. 29, fails to see this carefully studied structure of the author.

19. Cf. LOHFINK, *War Kohelet ein Frauenfeind?* (n. 8), pp. 277-278; B. ISAKSSON, *Studies in the Language of Qoheleth* (SSU, 10), Stockholm, 1987, p. 66.

20. Read 1,17, where wisdom and folly are connected together; wisdom is known by its opposite, folly. For the semantic ambience of "folly" opposed to "wisdom", see T. DONALD, *The Semantic Field of "Folly" in Proverbs, Job, Psalms and Ecclesiastes*, in VT 13 (1963) 283-292, p. 289.

(or at least their semantic equivalents) be included in the Discovery. Instead, the author introduces into the discussion a clear reference to *woman*. Could the term "woman" itself be considered as indicating (personified) "wisdom" or "wickedness"/ "folly"? Or could it be possible to think that what Qohelet has found out about woman from his dialogue with traditional wisdom beliefs, is concerned with folly? More probably the latter. The woman described in v. 26bβc responds to "wickedness"/"folly" and "being captured by her" (v. 26dβ) is caused by not following the way of wisdom, but by pursuing the way of folly.

The remoteness of wisdom is summarized in 8,1a, which recapitulates 7,23bα-24 and is reminiscent of vv. 25.28 as well: the MT מי כהחכם in 8,1aα, read as מי כה חכם (so LXX)[21] corresponds to אחכמה in v. 23bβ and to מי ימצאנו in v. 24. The clause מי יודע פשר דבר in 8,1aβ corresponds to מי ימצאנו in v. 24 (and to ידע חכמה in v. 25a) and to לא מצאתי in v. 28a.

The structural process of the unit may be set out in the following schematic manner:

	Thematic key words	
Introduction to the past investigation made by wisdom		7,23a
I° Exposition:		
Intention to be wise and	חכם	23bα
Discovery	חכמה	23bβ-24
1) she (wisdom) is remote from me (23bβ)		
2) that which exists is far remote (24a)		
3) who can comprehend it? (24b)		
II° Exposition		
Intention to understand (ידע)		25
wisdom/conclusion/wickedness... and	רשע/הסכלות – חכמה	
Discovery		26-29
1) And I find (that) (26)	אשה	
2) see, I have found that (27-28)	אדם – אשה	
3) see, I have only found that (29)	אלהים – אדם	
Conclusion - recapitulation of I° and II° *Exposition*	חכם	8,1a
1) no one is so wise		
2) no one knows (ידע) the meaning of the matter		

21. The context indicates Qohelet has recognized the remoteness of wisdom to all (7,23b-24) and comprehended (מצא: v. 27) that there is something which he has not understood (לא מצא: v. 28a). If there should be a logical sequence in these verses, 8,1aβ can only mean that no one is so wise as to know the meaning of the (above mentioned) matter: there is a limit even to the wise man's intellectual capacity. Consequently, we prefer to read, with LOHFINK, *War Kohelet ein Frauenfeind?* (n. 8), p. 260, n. 10, מי כה חכם (who is so wise? = no one is so wise!).

The above diagram sets out clearly Introduction, I° Exposition (= Intention + Discovery), II° Exposition (= Intention + Discovery) and Conclusion[22].

II

In this structure of the unit, 7,26 is the first of the three parallel observations of the II° Exposition. The verse reads:

> And I find that more bitter than death is the woman,
>
> אֲשֶׁר (הִיא) is a snare, her heart is a net, her hands are bonds.

The אֲשֶׁר by itself has a varied significance. Most commentators parse it either as a relative adjective with the independent personal pronoun הִיא serving as a copula[23], or as a causal conjunction. If one adopts the former, it becomes obvious that Qohelet speaks about "a particular kind of woman"[24]. In the latter case, instead, one supposes that "he [Qohelet] is directing his remarks against womankind as a whole"[25].

According to these interpretations of אֲשֶׁר, Qohelet seems to remain a misogynist. Yet, it is observed that the author should not be considered as a woman-hater, for the participle form מוֹצֵא, having a double accusative (אֶת־הָאִשָּׁה and מַר)[26], introduces a traditional wisdom, which the author does not accept. Qohelet would have only said, adding a motivational phrase beginning with אֲשֶׁר:

22. Slightly different is the observation of F. ELLERMEIER, *Qohelet. Teil I, Abschnitt 1. Untersuchungen zum Buche Qohelet*, Herzberg, 1967, p. 75, who classifies vv. 23abα and 25 as *Vorsätze*. See further J.A. LOADER, *Polar Structures in the Book of Qohelet* (BZAW, 152), Berlin-New York, 1979, pp. 50-54, who divides the passage (7,23-8,1) into three subsections, vv. 23-25, 26-28 and 7,29-8,1. Loader fails to see the intention-discovery structure in the passage.

23. MURPHY, *Ecclesiastes* (n. 13), p. 74. According to P. JOÜON – T. MURAOKA, *A Grammar of Biblical Hebrew* (Subsidia biblica, 14/I-II), Roma, 1991 (= *JM*), § 158g, the retrospective subject pronoun in a nominal clause is commonly used with an adjective or participle. See further R. GORDIS, *Was Koheleth a Phoenician? Some Observations on Methods of Research*, in *JBL* 74 (1955) 103-114, p. 110; C.F. WHITLEY, *Koheleth — His Language and Thought* (BZAW, 148), Berlin-New York, 1979, p. 41 (he argues that the separate pronoun has a function of repeating and emphasizing the subject of a relative clause). The proposal of M.J. DAHOOD, *The Independent Personal Pronoun in the Oblique Case in Hebrew*, in *CBQ* 32 (1970) 86-90, pp. 89-90, who reads אֲשֶׁר־הִיא as אַשְׁרֵי הִיא ('the feet of her') appears to be unconvincing: cf. A. SCHOORS, *The Preacher Sought to Find Pleasing Words. A Study of the Language of Qoheleth* (OLA, 41), Leuven, 1992, pp. 30-31, 48-49.

24. M.A. EATON, *Ecclesiastes: An Introduction and Commentary* (TOTC, 16), Leicester-London, 1983, p. 116. H.W. HERTZBERG, *Der Prediger* (KAT, XVII/4), Gütersloh, 1963, p. 157, has already said of "eine Art von Frauen"; likewise, V. D'ALARIO, *Qo 7,26-28: un testo antifemminista?*, in D. ABIGNENTE et al. (eds.), *La donna nella Chiesa e nel mondo*, Napoli, 1988, p. 230.

25. FOX, *Contradictions* (n.7), p. 241.

26. D. MICHEL, *Untersuchungen zur Eigenart des Buches Qohelet* (BZAW, 183), Berlin-New York, 1989, p. 227. Likewise, ISAKSSON, *Language of Qoheleth* (n. 19), p. 66, maintains that אֶת־הָאִשָּׁה is the direct object of the verb מוֹצֵא.

"Ich finde da dauernd (als ein Untersuchungsergebnis), bitterer als der Tod sei die Frau, insofern sie (...)"[27].

Another possibility, which we prefer, is the understanding of the syntax of 7,26 proposed by Schoors: the word "woman" is subject of the nominal clause, introduced by the particle את[28]. We have an analogous expression in 4,3, where we find את אשר[29]. The clause "more bitter than death (is) the woman" is an asyndetic nominal clause of the transitive verb "to find" with the possible ellipsis of אשר[30]. It results:

"And I understand[31] that more bitter than death is the woman,
אשר (...)".

The verse thus understood leads us again to think that Qohelet has a very negative view about woman, for v. 26abα can only introduce Qohelet's own conclusion. This aspect is confirmed by the presence of the principle verb "to find". Further, if one translates the אשר either with "because" or "that", Fox is right in his assertion that "this passage remains irreparably misogynistic"[32].

But it must be admitted that such a perspective does not reconcile with the author's general view about woman, as observed by more commentators. In fact, Qohelet's recommendation to his male students to live all the fleeting days in the company of their own wives (9,9; cf. Prov 5,18b-19), suggests a very different attitude toward woman. If the author has not had any positive view about woman, how could he recommend his students to marry one? Could this represent another element of contradiction and be interpreted as a painful irony[33]? This con-

27. MICHEL, *Untersuchungen* (n. 26), p. 238.

28. SCHOORS, *The Preacher Sought* (n. 23), pp. 188, 191. He observes in this regard that את with the subject is limited to later texts (see the bibliography in *Ibid.*, p. 191, n. 355); cf. B.K. WALTKE – M. O'CONNOR, *An Introduction to Biblical Hebrew Syntax*, Winona Lake (IN), 1990, § 10.3.2.b.c.

29. We confront the Hebrew texts, 4,3 (text indicated by SCHOORS, *The Preacher Sought* (n. 23), p. 191) and 7,26:

4,3 = A + מן + B + את אשר + nominal clause ‏וטוב משניהם את אשר עדן לא היה

7,26 = A + מן + B + את + noun ‏מוצא אני מר ממות את־האשה אשר היא

If we have to parse, in 4,3, the nominal clause את אשר־עדן לא היה as a logical subject of the comparative clause (thus the translations of *RSV*, *NJB*, *EÜ* and *TOB*), it is most probable that the substantive האשה introduced by the particle את functions likewise as a logical subject of nominal clause; see P.P. SAYDON, *Meanings and Uses of the Particle*, in *VT* 14 (1964) 192-210, p. 209, who notes that the particle את introduces, in 4,3, a subject of the verb היה; cf. J. ELWOLDE, *The Use of 'ēt in Non-biblical Hebrew Texts*, in *VT* 44 (1994) 170-182, p. 178.

30. Cf. *JM*, § 157b.

31. On מצא "to understand", see A.R. CERESKO, *The Function of Antanaclasis (mṣ' "to find" // mṣ' "to reach, overtake, grasp") in Hebrew Poetry, Especially in the Book of Qoheleth*, in *CBQ* 44 (1982) 551-569, pp. 566-567.

32. FOX, *Contradictions* (n. 7), p. 238.

33. A. LAUHA, *Kohelet* (BKAT, 19), Neukirchen-Vluyn, 1978, p. 141.

textual consideration does not permit us to adopt either the causal meaning, or the relative for the particle אֲשֶׁר. One asks consequently if it is possible to detect another significance of this particle. It is necessary to read more closely the following two verses, where Qohelet gives another view of woman.

The syntax of vv. 27-28 is difficult and much discussed[34]. On the one hand, there is no doubt that the first person of מָצָאתִי in vv. 27-28a is Qohelet himself; what is expressed here represents the author's personal thought formed from his own experience: "See, I have found - says Qohelet[35], adding one thing to another to find out[36] a conclusion[37] - that "my soul has sought continuously, but I have not found out". On the other hand, the first person of מָצָאתִי in v. 28b considered as a quotation, is, instead, the one who originally pronounced it in the wisdom tradition: "One man among a thousand I found, but a woman[38] among all these I have not found". That the author does not share such an opinion of others is self-evident by the negative particle לֹא preceded by the main verb מָצָאתִי, with the first person being Qohelet. It becomes obvious, therefore, that Qohelet *knows* the very fact that he - ironically enough - *has not yet accepted* (found out the truthfulness of) the saying of v. 28b[39]. Qohelet's wisdom did not suffice to apprehend the traditional sayings[40] despite his scientific (or inductive) method. Even though some

---

34. As SCHOORS, *The Preacher Sought* (n. 23), pp. 57, 138, rightly remarks, the parallelism between vv. 27-28 and v. 29 suggests that the principal verb מָצָאתִי in v. 27 has a dependent object clause עוֹד־בִקְשָׁה נַפְשִׁי וְלֹא מָצָאתִי, introduced by אֲשֶׁר and preceded by זֶה (cf. DELITZSCH, *Ecclesiastes* (n. 4), p. 333; Qoh 9,1; Gen 5,1). From the syntactical point of view, v. 28a has, then, its asyndetic object clause (v. 28b); for the most obvious example of the ellipses of אֲשֶׁר in Qohelet, cf. 5,12 with 6,1.

35. We read אָמַר הַקֹּהֶלֶת instead of the MT אָמְרָה קֹהֶלֶת (cf. 12,8).

36. The construction לְ + inf. cst. describes a finality, whose aim has not yet been attained; cf. E. PODECHARD, *L'Ecclésiaste* (EB), Paris, 1912, p. 387.

37. The phrase אַחַת לְאַחַת לִמְצֹא חֶשְׁבּוֹן explains the method ("induktive Methode": L. LEVY, *Das Buch Qoheleth. Ein Beitrag zur Geschichte des Sadduzäismus kritisch untersucht*, Leipzig, 1912, p. 111). In this sense, אַחַת לְאַחַת, being an adverbial accusative of manner (cf. W. GESENIUS, *Hebräische Grammatik*, völlig umbearbeitet von E. KAUTZSCH, Hildesheim-Zürich-New York, 1985, § 118q), corresponds to בְּחָכְמָה in 7,23.

38. The Hebrew word אִשָּׁה is to be understood as elliptical usage for "eine wahre Frau" (MICHEL, *Untersuchungen* (n. 26), p. 229) or "a woman such as ought to be" (DELITZSCH, *Ecclesiastes* (n. 4), p. 334).

39. Cf. LOHFINK, *War Kohelet ein Frauenfeind?* (n. 8), p. 280.

40. MICHEL, *Untersuchungen* (n. 26), p. 231, refers to Sir 6,6, while L. SCHWIENHORST-SCHÖNBERGER, *Nicht im Menschen gründet das Glück (Koh 2,24). Kohelet im Spannungsfeld jüdischer Weisheit und hellenistischer Philosophie* (HBS, 2), Freiburg, ²1996, pp. 177-178, to Song of Songs. This latter considers v. 28b as a quotation introduced by אֲשֶׁר, seeing a strict parallel in Cant 3,1f and 5,6, where recur three identical terms, such as נֶפֶשׁ/מָצָא/בִּקֵּשׁ in a loving context. He argues further that a woman, represented by נַפְשִׁי, does not find out any man (אָדָם אֶחָד), though the traditional wisdom

sages in the wisdom tradition would do so, Qohelet does not accept this
unflattering opinion of woman. He never agrees with the saying which
affirms the inferiority of woman to man. Neither does he give any misogynous pronouncement about a woman in the Book as a whole.
Qohelet doubts if any sage could comprehend this popular saying, for he
questions "Who is so wise?", "Who knows the meaning of the [above
mentioned] matter?" (8,1a). This observation is closely linked to the
first chapter of the Book and to 8,16ff. In this former case, there appears
a reflection on wisdom, while in this latter, the quest for wisdom is further developed, as in 7,23ff, by the reference to woman.

At an earlier stage, Qohelet announced his determination to explore "by
wisdom" all that happens under the sky (1,13; cf. 2,3) and affirmed that
his quest for wisdom ended in failure: one cannot "understand wisdom"
and pursuing her is similar to grasping after the wind (1,17). He has never
pretended to know everything: "The crooked cannot be made straight"
(1,15; cf. 7,13). As in 1,13ff, Qohelet expresses in 7,23 also, that he has
already "proved" all this by wisdom (נסה בחכמה)[42] and revealed the inac-
cessibility of wisdom of any kind to humans (vv. 23bβ-24)[43].

And later, in the context of 8,16-9,10 Qohelet underscores again that
no sage is able to comprehend all that happens under the sun[44]. Nevertheless, he does not hesitate to command the enjoyment of life *with*
(עם!) one's 'wife' (cf. 4,9-12). His recommendation is in accordance
with the OT appreciation of the benefits a good wife brings: "He who

would claim that "one man among a thousand I found": it is the woman who is in search
of אדם. But nowhere in Qohelet is presented any beloved one as an object to "search and
find". Further it is difficult to see any change of the speaker between the person of בקשה
נפשי and that of לא מצאתי: the subject is invariably Qohelet. See also the critical observation made by RIESENER, *Frauenfeindschaft* (n. 9), p. 201, n. 23.

Nor does the proposal of FOX, *Contradictions* (n. 7), p. 242, seem to be convincing;
Fox prefers to follow Ehrlich's conjectural emendation of אשר to אשה; according to this
understanding, it is Qohelet (the first person of מצאתי in v. 28a) who is in search of a
woman. Such emendation was already proposed by F. PERLES, *A Miscellany of Lexical
and Textual Notes on the Bible*, in *JQR NS* 2 (1911/12) p. 131, but there is no manuscript
evidence for that reading: J.B. DE ROSSI, *Variae Lectiones Veteris Testamenti*, 4 voll.
(Parmae 1784-1788) gives no variation in this regard. See the critical observation made
by J.L. CRENSHAW, *Ecclesiastes* (OTL), London, 1987, p. 147.

41. The term פשר is *hapax legomenon*, but found often in the Aramaic of Daniel and
in the Qumran literature (also with the form פשר הדבר: cf. *TWAT* VI, 810-816 (Fabry—
Dahmen), c. 814). J.L. CRENSHAW, *The Expression mî yôdēaʿ in the Hebrew Bible*, in *VT*
36 (1986) 274-288, p. 286, argues that "Qoheleth's use of mî yôdēaʿ functioned to call
into question the entire wisdom enterprise".

42. For the expression נסה בחכמה, cf. Deut 33,8; Judg 2,22; 3,1.4; 2 Kings 10,1; Qoh
2,1 with שמחה.

43. Cf. LOHFINK, *War Kohelet ein Frauenfeind?* (n. 8), p. 274.

44. The author uses the triple expression לא מצא, "do not find/comprehend" in 8,17;
cf. 11,5.

finds a wife finds a good thing"[45]. The joy of life in Qohelet is described as one's portion (חלק, 9,8). As I have argued elsewhere[46], there is nothing which leads us to think of a hedonistic style of life. Rather, the author describes the woman as one who is to be loved by man and as one who is given by God (9,9). In that context, Qohelet never gives any definition of the moral quality of a woman, apart from the assertion that all humans, represented by "the just and the wise", are full of wickedness (רע) in their lifetime and all destined to death (9,1-3).

Though Qohelet has dedicated himself to understanding and searching for "conclusion" (v. 25) until he find it (v. 27)[47], he has failed to verify the credibility of the traditional wisdom saying about woman (v. 28b). What he has found is that humans "pursued many *questionable things*"[48]. Humans have spoken many proverbial sayings, but these can only be doubtful efforts, because there are certain things that cannot be understood. Qohelet's own experiment only attests that he knew a woman could act as a snare[49]. This view corresponds to the traditional

45. Prov 18,22; cf. Sir 26,1-18; 36,22-25.
46. PAHK, *Il canto della gioia* (n. 17), pp. 250-260.
47. The singular noun חשבון appears in Qoh 7,25.27; 9,10, while the plural חשבנות in 7,29 and in II Chr 26,15. In Sir 42,3 the noun חשבון refers to reckoning or keeping accurate accounts. PODECHARD, *L'Ecclésiaste* (n. 36), p. 382, remarks that חשבון in Qohelet could be equivalent to wisdom as in 7,25 and 9,10. But the author's intention is to find out חשבון by the inductive method (אחת לאחת) in v. 27. That which is attained by such a method can be a kind of (calculated) conclusion. For the various meanings of חשבון, see further O. LORETZ, *"Frau" und griechisch-jüdische Philosophie im Buch Qohelet (Qoh 7,23-8,1 und 9,6-10)*, in *UF* 23 (1991) 245-264, pp. 258-260.
48. For this definition of חשבנות, cf. WHITLEY, *Koheleth* (n. 23), p. 70. See further LORETZ, *"Frau"* (n. 47), p. 259. The parallelism of the two stichoi in v. 29b leads us to note that חשבנות רבים, translated by "many questionable things", is in contrast to ישר ("straightforward", "upright"). As noted above, Qohelet observes that humans are full of wickedness (9,3). If ישר can be thought of, in some extent, the opposite conception to רע in the wisdom tradition (cf. Job 1,1; Prov 16,17; 28,10), one supposes a possible relation between חשבנות and רע. If this is the case, human's quest for many questionable things can be nothing but wickedness.
49. KRÜGER, *«Frau Weisheit»* (n. 2), p. 402, sees, here in v. 26, a reference to Lady-Wisdom. Confronting Sir 6,23ff, he argues that "Nach V. 26 hat Kohelet "gefunden", *daß* "die Frau (Weisheit) bitterer ist als der Tod", *wenn* sie so ist, wie sie in der Tradition dargestellt wird, mit der er sich hier auseinandersetzt". Yet, there is no indication that Lady (Wisdom) is more bitter than death, either in the tradition or in the Qohelet text. Wisdom gives life, not death! (cf. Qoh 7,12; Prov 3,18; 8,35-36). The above cited text of Sirach describes, after all, the benefits — not the pejorative aspect such as death! — the personified wisdom gives to those who put their feet into her fetters, "For in the end you will find rest in her and she will take the form of joy for you: her fetters you will find a mighty defence, her collars, a precious necklace. Her yoke will be a golden ornament, and her bonds be purple ribbons" (Sir 6,28-31, *NJB*). In addition, it is difficult to maintain that "Wenn "die Frau" (Weisheit) so ist, (...), dann ist es gerade der "Sünder", der von ihr gefangen wird!". Can Wisdom capture the sinner so as to bestow her benefits? "The senseless does not stay with her for long!" (Sir 6,20, *NJB*). Is it not rather "He who is

wisdom: a woman, or, better, an evil woman (Prov 6,24), being a "deep pit"[50], could bring about the fall of man; the wickedness of certain women, against whom the wisdom tradition warns (cf. Sir 25,19), could reduce a man even to death or lead him down to Sheol (cf. Prov 5,1-5.20-23). If such a woman can in certain circumstances ensnare him, this simply demonstrates the quality expressed in v. 26bβc, when there would surely be a crucial danger to man. How must one save oneself from the wicked/alien woman[51]? Who will be ensnared by her? Qohelet gives answer to these problems: "He who pleases God escapes her, but the sinner is captured by her" (v. 26d; cf. 2,26). This assertion not only represents Qohelet's own comment to v. 26a-c which can be a quotation, cited from an old *topos* celebrated in the wisdom literature (cf. Prov 7,27; 5,4 with 9,13)[52], but also serves significantly in choosing the right way on the part of his male students who seek the love of a woman (9,9). The teachings of Qohelet are not to demonstrate, if a woman might be dangerous to man or not. Rather, the author studies the traditional wisdom regarding a woman and sees - objectively - in v. 26abα a possible danger which a woman may cause to his students. Therefore, the readers are challenged to see the tragedy which a woman may cause and to remain as one "who is pleasing to God" (v. 26, *NJB*); yet, not every woman should be thought of as a snare *in se*[53]. The conclusive conviction of Qohelet in 7,29 that "God made all (male and female) straightforward" favors this interpretation. If any wise person attempts to define Qohelet with any of the anthropological terms, such as a woman-hater, then he/she would be far remote from the intention of the author.

Our analysis of the text suggests some practical conclusions:

– v. 26abα in itself describes a negative view about woman;
– but the general view of Qohelet about woman does not offer any misogynistic idea. The credibility of the traditional wisdom remains unverified despite his inductive reflection;

---

pleasing to God" (cf. Qoh 2,26; 7,26d) or the disciplined, that will enjoy her fruits? In our opinion, the possibility of regarding אשה as a reference to Lady-Wisdom must be rejected. See further LORETZ, *"Frau"* (n. 47), pp. 261-262.

50. Prov 22,14; 23,27; cf. 18,7.

51. Cf. אשה זרה in Prov 2,16-19; 5,1-4; 6,24-26; 7,22-23; J. COOK, אִשָּׁה זָרָה *(Proverbs 1-9 Septuagint): A Metaphor for Foreign Wisdom?*, in ZAW 106 (1994) 458-476.

52. MURPHY, *Ecclesiastes* (n. 13), p. 76, refers to Prov 2,16-19; 5,1-4; 7,22-23; 9,13-18. Cf. LORETZ, *"Frau"* (n. 47), p. 246; J. VÍLCHEZ LÍNDEZ, *Eclesiastes o Qohelet*, Estella (Navarra), 1994, p. 326.

53. Cf. Sir 9,3-5.13 Heb; P.J. BOTHA, *Through the Figure of a Woman Many Have Perished: Ben Sira's View of Women*, in OTE 9/1 (1996) 20-34, p. 24.

- in the OT, an evil woman, being a deep pit, could reduce a man even to death: there are certain cases where she is like a hunting-net. Between "being a deep pit" and "to be reduced to death", there is a conditional situation, i.e., only if such a woman ensnares man, then she can cause the fall of man;
- Qohelet's past investigation is aimed at understanding wisdom and folly, arriving at some conclusions. He arrives at the understanding from the tradition that a woman could act as a net, but does not agree with the saying that there is any difference - from the point of view of moral quality - between man and woman. If one pursues the way of folly, he will be captured by such an evil woman.

This cumulative series of conclusions suggests that the particle אשר in 7,26 is to be parsed as a conditional nuance, which is rare, but attested to in the OT[54]. That the conditional clause envisages circumstance in which an evil woman could create a more-bitter-situation than death seems to be self-evident[55]. Thus, Qoh 7,26 can be translated:

> "And I understand that more bitter than death is the woman, if [56] she is a snare, her heart a net, her hands bonds".

From this standpoint, Qohelet should not be regarded as a "woman-hater", as observed by Lohfink, for he simply recognizes the conditional situation regarding the woman. Qohelet was so wise that he could weigh the traditional wisdom sayings about women and teach his students what he himself examined. The author of the epilogue could only describe the intellectual-empirical quality of the author in this way: "Qoheleth taught the people what he himself knew, having weighed, studied and emended many proverbs" (12,9, *NJB*).

The Catholic University of Korea   Johan Y.S. PAHK
Songsim Campus
43-1 Yokkok 2-Dong, Wonmi-gu
Puchon City, Kyonggi-do 422-743
South-Korea

54. Cf. Lev 4,22; Deut 11,27 (LXX translates אשר with ἐάν): the conditional value is determined here by the parallel clauses. See *JM*, § 167j; B.K. WALTKE – M. O'CONNOR, *op. cit.* (n. 28), § 38.2d; L. KOEHLER – W. BAUMGARTNER, *Hebräisches und aramäisches Lexikon zum Alten Testament: Lieferung I*, neu bearbeitet von W. BAUMGARTNER, unter Mitarbeit von B. HARTMANN – E.Y. KUTSCHER, Leiden, ³1967, p. 95b; F. ZORELL, *Lexicon Hebraicum Veteris Testamenti*, Romae, 1984, p. 88b.

55. One may say in this case that the clause followed by אשר "is the author's commentary" to the preceding clause, as noted by K. BALTZER, *Women and War in Qohelet 7:23-8:1a*, in *HTR* 80 (1987) 127-132, p. 128.

56. J. ELLUL, *La raison d'être. Méditation sur l'Ecclésiaste*, Paris, 1987, p. 305, translating אשר with causal nuance, proposes another possibility: "quand elle devient"; cf. *TOB*.

A RE-INTERPRETATION OF ECCLESIASTES 2,12b

In Eccles 2,12b we read:

מֶה הָאָדָם שֶׁיָּבוֹא אַחֲרֵי הַמֶּלֶךְ אֵת אֲשֶׁר־כְּבָר עָשׂוּהוּ׃

Both the translation and the interpretation of this passage are disputed. In the Revised Standard Version, we find the following translation of verse 12: "So I turned to consider wisdom and madness and folly; for what can the man do who comes after the king? Only what he has already done." But this translation is based on an emended text and other interpretations are possible. Moreover, the textual transmission of the last word of the sentence is ambiguous. In 68 Hebrew manuscripts[1] we find the variant reading: עָשָׂהוּ instead of עָשׂוּהוּ (singular instead of plural). Various interpretations have been given. In this short contribution, the probability of these interpretations will be considered and the possibility of a new understanding of the text will be discussed.

Survey of various solutions[2]

a) The passage stands at the wrong place.

According to a number of scholars, the passage has been misplaced. See, for example, the suggestion by LAUHA in his commentary: "Es ist also anzunehmen, daß der Satz aus irgendeinem anderen Textzusammenhang versehentlich hierher versetzt worden ist"[3]. There is, however, no compelling reason to concur with this suggestion. There is no other place in the book where the passage fits any better than here. Moreover, no convincing explanation has been given as to why the passage would have been misplaced by some scribe.

---

1. Cf. R. GORDIS, *Koheleth – The Man and His World. A Study of Ecclesiastes*, New York, Schocken Books, ³1955, p. 221; A. SCHOORS, *The Preacher Sought to Find Pleasing Words. A Study of the Language of Qoheleth* (OLA, 41), Leuven, Departement Oriëntalistiek – Peeters, 1992, p. 156.

2. A more elaborate survey can be found in D. LYS, *L'Ecclésiaste ou que vaut la vie? Traduction, introduction générale, commentaire de 1/1 à 4/3*, Paris, Letouzey et Ané, 1977, pp. 232-235. His own solution is to insert מֶלֶךְ after הַמֶּלֶךְ (haplography). In this way, he arrives at the following translation: "Car que sera l'homme qui succédera au roi, régnant sur ce qu'il a déjà réalisé?".

3. A. LAUHA, *Kohelet* (BKAT, XIX), Neukirchen-Vluyn, Neukirchener Verlag, 1978, p. 53. See also W. ZIMMERLI, *Prediger* (ATD, 16,1), Göttingen, Vandenhoeck & Ruprecht, ²1967, p. 159.

b) Emendation of אַחֲרֵי הַמֶּלֶךְ

Some commentators[4] take the reference to the king to be a later addition to the text, the word now pointed אַחֲרֵי, 'after', having originally been intended to be read אַחֲרַי, 'after me'. However, this emendation is unnecessary[5]. Qoheleth stresses the fact that the other person is a mere successor to the wise and rich king *par excellence*, to wit: himself.

c) A relative clause

Other commentators read אֵת אֲשֶׁר־כְּבָר עָשׂוּהוּ as a relative clause referring to the successor or to the king himself, "whom they have made already"[6]. This interpretation, however, does not account for the addition of אֵת before אֲשֶׁר[7]. Moreover, the function of such a relative clause within the present context remains unclear.

d) Insertion of יַעֲשֶׂה after מֶה

The addition of the verbal form יַעֲשֶׂה after מֶה[8] enables us to translate the first part of verse 12b as follows: "What can the man do who comes after the king?"[9] If we assume that the question ends after הַמֶּלֶךְ, there are two possibilities. If the singular עָשָׂהוּ is the original reading, then the subject is the king: "Only what he (the king) has already done" (*RSV*). If we stick to the plural עָשׂוּהוּ, then the verb has a general subject: "Only what has been done already"[10]. Schoors remarks: "In the general context of the Solomonic role assumed by Qoheleth, the former solution seems preferable"[11].

---

4. See e.g. K. GALLING, *Der Prediger* (HAT, 1,18), Tübingen, Mohr, ²1969, p. 90, and LAUHA, *op. cit.*, pp. 40 and 42.

5. Cf. R.N. WHYBRAY, *Ecclesiastes* (NCBC), Grand Rapids & London, Eerdmans & Marshall, Morgan & Scott, 1989, p. 57.

6. Cf. N. LOHFINK, *Kohelet* (NEB), Würzburg, Echter Verlag, 1980, p. 28: "den König [...] den sie einst eingesetzt haben". See also SCHOORS, *op. cit.*, p. 157, n. 56.

7. Cf. LYS, *op. cit.*, p. 231.

8. See e.g. GALLING, *op. cit.*, p. 90; LAUHA, *op. cit.*, pp. 40 and 42; SCHOORS, *op. cit.*, p. 156; C.F. WHITLEY, *Koheleth. His Language and Thought* (BZAW, 145), Berlin, De Gruyter, 1979, p. 24. Note, however, that ZIMMERLI, *op. cit.*, p. 160, and D. MICHEL, *Qohelet* (EdF, 258), Darmstadt, Wissenschaftliche Buchgesellschaft, 1988, p. 132, insert יַעֲשֶׂה after הַמֶּלֶךְ. L. SCHWIENHORST-SCHÖNBERGER, *"Nicht im Menschen gründet das Glück" (Koh 2,24). Kohelet im Spannungsfeld jüdischer Weisheit und hellenistischer Philosophie* (HBS, 2), Freiburg, Herder, 1994, p. 70, concurs with MICHEL.

9. Translation in SCHOORS, *op. cit.*, pp. 156-57.

10. Cf. GALLING, *op. cit.*, p. 90; ZIMMERLI, *op. cit.*, p. 160. See also H.W. HERTZBERG, *Der Prediger* (KAT XVII, 4), Gütersloh, Mohn, 1963, p. 76: "Das, was sie schon lange taten". The third person plural refers to Solomon's predecessors (*ibid.* p. 90).

11. SCHOORS, *op. cit.*, p. 157.

However, there are several problems with the addition of יַעֲשֶׂה to the first half of the clause:

1. It did not occur in the *Vorlage* of the LXX nor do we find it in any Hebrew manuscript.

2. There is no reason as to why the author or a scribe would drop this essential word. Some say that the omission can be explained through *homoioteleuton*[12], others through *aposiopesis*[13]. But these explanations are not very convincing[14]. If "What can a man do" was meant by the author, he would not have omitted the verb, because מֶה הָאָדָם as such is a common expression as we will see (cf. below under e).

3. The assumption of a question and answer creates "an exceedingly harsh construction"[15]. Moreover, we are dealing here with a rhetorical question. This means that no answer is needed. Therefore, it is unlikely that אֵת אֲשֶׁר־כְּבָר עָשָׂהוּ constitutes a separate sentence[16]. It must be a part of the rhetorical question itself.

4. The remark that no king can accomplish something new, nicely fits within the context of Eccles 1,9-11 but not here. It does not give a reason for Qoheleth's intention to consider wisdom and folly.

e) Parallels to מֶה הָאָדָם

But there is also no need for the addition of יַעֲשֶׂה to the first half of the clause. The expression מֶה הָאָדָם gives good sense. It means "What is the man?" in the sense of "What is the nature or value of man?" For the expression, there is a close parallel in Ps 8,5:

מָה־אֱנוֹשׁ כִּי־תִזְכְּרֶנּוּ וּבֶן־אָדָם כִּי תִפְקְדֶנּוּ׃

"What is man that thou art mindful of him, and the son of man that thou dost care for him?" (*RSV*).

Another, even closer parallel we find in Ps 144,3:

יְהוָה מָה־אָדָם וַתֵּדָעֵהוּ בֶּן־אֱנוֹשׁ וַתְּחַשְּׁבֵהוּ׃

"O LORD, what is man that thou dost regard him, or the son of man that thou dost think of him?" (*RSV*).

However, if we do not alter the beginning of the passage, we have the problem that the connection with the latter half of it seems unclear.

---

12. Cf. e.g. WHITLEY, *op. cit.*, p. 148.
13. Cf. e.g. B. LANG, Review in *Bib* 62 (1981) 428-35, p. 433.
14. *Pace* J.L. CRENSHAW, *Ecclesiastes. A Commentary* (OTL), Philadelphia, Westminster Press, 1987, p. 83.
15. Cf. GORDIS, *op. cit.*, pp. 220-221.
16. *Pace* LYS, *op. cit.*, p. 231.

Gordis[17], however, thinks that he found the solution. He explains: "The verb יבוא governs את and means 'come with, hence bring'". As proof-text he refers to Deut 31,7:

$$\text{כִּי אַתָּה תָּבוֹא אֶת־הָעָם הַזֶּה אֶל־הָאָרֶץ}$$

"for you shall go with this people into the land" (*RSV*).

Gordis comes then to the following translation of Eccles 2,12b: "Of what value is the man coming after the king with what he (sc. the king) has already done?" Gordis elucidates: "Koheleth, in his assumed role of Solomon, wishes to assure the reader that he has experienced the ultimate in both wisdom and pleasure and that there is no need for any one else to repeat the experiment"[18]. Nevertheless, for the meaning 'bring' a *hiphil* of בוא and not a *qal* would have been more likely. Also the word order would be rather unusual. In Deut 31,7 we see that תָּבוֹא is immediately followed by אֶת־הָעָם הַזֶּה.

A NEW SOLUTION

Although I reject the interpretation given by Gordis, I concur with him that we are dealing here with a rhetorical question stressing the unique character of Qoheleth's experience.

Possibly, the core of the problem lies in the meaning of אֶת אֲשֶׁר. The combination אֶת אֲשֶׁר is used four times in Qoheleth. Except for our passage, we find אֶת אֲשֶׁר in 4,3; 5,3; 7,13 – twice as object of a clause (5,3; 7,13); once as subject (4,3).

In general, there are several possibilities to translate אֶת אֲשֶׁר. In most cases, the addition of אֶת indicates that the following relative pronoun אֲשֶׁר has been substantivised and used in the accusative. But there are more meanings for this combination[19]. Therefore, it is appropriate to look for another meaning for אֶת אֲשֶׁר than 'that which' or 'whom'[20].

If we agree that אֶת אֲשֶׁר־כְּבָר עָשָׂהוּ is part of the question which begins with מֶה הָאָדָם, the combination אֶת אֲשֶׁר must serve as a conjunction. But what kind of conjunction? In this respect, the following passage in

17. GORDIS, *op. cit.*, p. 221.

18. GORDIS, *op. cit.*, p. 221; see also CRENSHAW, *op. cit.*, p. 84, who adduces a parallel from an Egyptian wisdom text 'The Instruction for King Merikare'.

19. In D. CLINES (ed.), *Dictionary of Classical Hebrew*, vol. I, Sheffield, Sheffield Academic Press, 1993, pp. 432-434, we find a survey of these possibilities. Note, however, that in this dictionary (p. 430) אֶת אֲשֶׁר־כְּבָר עָשׂוּהוּ is translated as "what they have already done".

20. See also the translation by A.J. ROSENBERG, who renders אֶת אֲשֶׁר with 'concerning that': "[...] for what is the man who will come after the king, concerning that which they have already done". A.J. ROSENBERG, *The Five Megilloth, vol. II, Lamentations, Ecclesiastes. A New English Translation*, New York, Judaica Press, 1992, p. 21.

1 Kings 8,31 can be of importance: אֵת אֲשֶׁר יֶחֱטָא אִישׁ לְרֵעֵהוּ, "If a man sins against his neighbour". Note the deviant wording of this conditional clause in the parallel passage 2 Chron 6,22: אִם־יֶחֱטָא אִישׁ לְרֵעֵהוּ.

The parallel in Chronicles makes it clear that אֵת אֲשֶׁר can have the same meaning as אִם and can serve as a conjunction introducing a conditional clause. Therefore, I suggest that we interpret אֵת אֲשֶׁר here in the same way. If we follow this suggestion and adopt the reading עָשָׂהוּ instead of עָשׂוּהוּ, we come to the following translation of Eccles 2,12b: "For what is the man who will come after the king, if he [= the king] has already done it?"

But does this translation make sense? I think, it does. Verse 12 constitutes the connection between the preceding passage on Qoheleth's experiment in acquiring wealth (vv. 4-11) and the following passage on the value of wisdom in verses 13-16. In the first half of verse 12, Qoheleth announces: "So I turned to consider wisdom and madness and folly" (*RSV*). Then he gives the reason why he decided to investigate wisdom and folly. He uses the conjunction כִּי to elucidate his decision. And then follows a rhetorical question in which the abilities of a person who wants to repeat his experiment are questioned.

In the preceding, Qoheleth had stressed the fact that he surpassed any other person who ever lived in Jerusalem before him (Eccles 1,16; 2,7.9). Now he explains that his superiority extends also to the future. Because he has done everything in order to find meaning in human life, a person who comes after him will never have more opportunity than the king himself to investigate human destiny. For he will not have the same qualities and possibilities as his predecessor, the king. So he can never do more than the king has already done[21]. Now it becomes also clear why the author speaks of הָאָדָם שֶׁיָּבוֹא אַחֲרֵי הַמֶּלֶךְ, "the man who will come after the king", avoiding to designate this person as 'the king's son'. He does not talk about a successor to the throne but he means any future searcher for the meaning of life, any other teacher of wisdom who seeks "to find pleasing words" (Eccles 12,10).

In conclusion, the meaning of Eccles 2,12b can be summarized as follows: Qoheleth's search for wisdom and folly is unique and cannot be surpassed. Whoever undertakes a similar quest after him, will never outdo Qoheleth. His conclusions regarding the value of human life are final, unto this very day.

Celebesstraat 13-15   K.A.D. SMELIK
NL-3312 XB Dordrecht

---

21. The *Leitwort* עשׂה links 2,12b with the preceding passage 2,4-11.

GOTTES SOUVERÄNITÄT ANERKENNEN

Zum Verständnis der »Kanonformel« in Koh 3,14

Koh 3,14 – Übersetzung und Gliederung

    a   Ich erkannte,
    b   daß alles,
    c   was der Gott macht,
    d   es ist für eine längere Dauer.
    e   Dazu ist nichts hinzuzufügen
    f   und davon ist nichts wegzunehmen,
    g   aber der Gott hat bewirkt,
    h   daß man ihn fürchten kann.

Voraussetzungen

Die Diskussion über Herkunft, Entwicklung und Bedeutung der sogenannten »Kanonformel« (»Zu diesem ist nichts hinzuzufügen und von
diesem ist nichts wegzunehmen«) ist vor allem durch Wolfram Herrmann[1] und in der Folge durch Hans-Peter Müller[2] in die Kohelet-
forschung getragen worden. Daß sowohl die anfänglich gern gebrauchte
Bezeichnung »Ptahotepformel« als auch die vereinzelt nach wie vor benutzte Bezeichnung »Kanonformel« zur Benennung dieser Wendung
höchst problematisch sind, wurde bereits des öfteren aufgezeigt. Erstere
deshalb, weil die Ägyptologen gezeigt haben, daß die maßgebliche Stelle in der Lehre des Ptahotep anders übersetzt werden muß[3], zweitere,
weil der Begriff des »Kanons« in der Theologie an ein verbindliches
Korpus von autoritativen Schriften denken läßt, was aber bezüglich dieser Wendung in Koh 3,14 in keiner Weise zutreffend ist.

Vor allem Eleonore Reuter[4] hat auf das Scheitern jeglicher Versuche
hingewiesen, sämtliche altorientalischen, biblischen und frühjüdischen
Vorkommen dieser Formel auf eine konkrete Quelle zurückführen zu
wollen, oder einen völlig linearen Entwicklungsstrang der Wendung auf-

---

1. Siehe W. HERRMANN, *Zu Kohelet 3,14*, in *WZ(L).GS* 3 (1953/54) 293-295.
2. Siehe H.P. MÜLLER, *Theonome Skepsis und Lebensfreude. Zu Koh 1,12-3,15*, in *BZ* 30 (1986) 1-19, p. 16.
3. Siehe z.B. S. MORENZ, *Gott und Mensch im alten Ägypten*, München, ²1984, p. 25.
4. E. REUTER, *Nimm nichts davon weg und füge nichts hinzu. Dtn 13,1, seine alttesta-mentlichen Parallelen und seine altorientalischen Vorbilder*, in *BN* 47 (1989) 107-114.

zuzeigen. Doch scheint mir auch ihre Einteilung der Vorkommen in drei Anwendungsbereiche[5] verkürzt und damit unzutreffend.

Vielmehr muß man jedes einzelne Vorkommen der Formel zunächst im Rahmen des jeweiligen eigenen Binnenkontexts betrachten. Ich habe dies in einem kürzlich erschienenen Aufsatz ausführlich dargelegt[6].

Dieses eben aufgezeigte Scheitern verführte zahlreiche Koheletkommentatoren dazu, nur kurz auf die allgemeine Bekanntheit dieser Formel bereits im Alten Orient und deren Anwendung auf das Tun Gottes durch Kohelet hinzuweisen, um dann gleich zum nächsten Vers überzugehen. Damit wird man aber der fundamentalen Bedeutung dieser Wendung in Koh 3,14 für das Verständnis des Gottesbildes im gesamten Koheletbuch nicht gerecht.

Sie steht nämlich in direktem Zusammenhang mit den Begriffen »עולם« und »Gottesfurcht«, die wiederum für die Charakterisierung des Tuns Gottes und der angemessenen menschlichen Reaktion darauf Schlüsselbegriffe darstellen. In diesem Kontext kommt ihr die Funktion einer Erkenntnis über Gott zu, die die Koheletforschung – will sie zu Aussagen über das Gottesbild bei Kohelet kommen – nicht übergehen darf. Diese These soll nun im einzelnen erläutert werden.

1. *Der Bereich des עולם*

V. 3,14 ist im Kontext des Teilabschnittes 3,10-15 zu sehen, der wiederum die Interpretation des vorangehenden Gedichtes 3,1-8 darstellt; v. 9 bildet die Überleitung vom Gedicht zur Interpretation. Neben אלהים, das in diesem kurzen Abschnitt sechs mal vorkommt, treten – in Weiterführung der Gedanken des Gedichts – diverse Lexeme aus dem Wortfeld »Zeit« als Leitworte auf. Darunter ist v.a. עולם wichtig, das von den Begriffen עת und מראש ועד־סוף abgesetzt wird. עולם wird m.E. sowohl in 3,11 als auch in 3,14 in der Bedeutung »längere Dauer«[7] gebraucht, was übrigens auf alle עולם-Vorkommen bei Kohelet außer 12,5 zutreffen dürfte[8]. Zudem fungiert es hier als Zeitbegriff[9]. V. 11 führt den עולם im

---

5. *Ibid.*, p. 114.

6. A. VONACH, *Die sogenannte »Kanon- oder Ptahotepformel«. Anmerkungen zu Tradition und Kontext einer markanten Wendung*, in *Protokolle zur Bibel* 6 (1997) 73-80.

7. Zu einer adäquaten Wiedergabe von עולם bei Kohelet – insbesondere in 3,11 und 3,14 – sind zahlreiche Vorschläge gemacht worden. So hat bereits Ellermeier Koh 3,11 als »Tummelplatz der Phantasie« (F. ELLERMEIER, *Qohelet I,1. Untersuchungen zum Buche Qohelet*, Herzberg, 1967, p. 310.) bezeichnet. Einen guten Überblick über die verschiedenen Varianten bietet J. VILCHEZ, *Eclesiastés o Qohélet* (Nueva Biblia Española, Sapienciales, III), Estella, 1994, pp. 237-240.

8. Zu עולם im Sinne von »längere Dauer« siehe H.D. PREUSS, *Art.* עולם, in *TWAT* V, Stuttgart/Berlin/Köln/ Mainz, 1986, pp. 1144-1159, esp. p. 1156; F.J. BACKHAUS, *Denn Zeit und Zufall trifft sie alle. Zu Komposition und Gottesbild im Buch Qohelet* (BBB, 83),

Sinne einer Zeit ein, die zwischen עת und מראש ועד־סוף liegt. Daß dem Menschen der עולם in den Verstand gegeben wurde, heißt, daß der Mensch fähig ist, über den jeweiligen Augenblick und auch über seine eigene Lebenszeit hinaus zu denken[10]. Das Ganze der Welt und insbesondere der göttliche Bereich als gesamter sind ihm jedoch nicht zugänglich. עת – so lehrt das Gedicht in 3,1-8 – bezeichnet die einzelnen Augenblicke des konkreten menschlichen Lebens, die der Mensch erlebt und selbst mitgestalten kann. מראש ועד־סוף beschreibt einen nur für Gott überblickbaren Bereich; es ist im Grunde jene Zeitkategorie, die wir heute mit Ewigkeit – und zwar sowohl die Vergangenheit als auch die Zukunft betreffend – bezeichnen würden.

V. 14a-d wirft nun noch etwas mehr Licht auf diese Setzung von v. 11. Das gesamte Tun Gottes ist nicht der für das menschliche Tun charakteristischen Begrenzung und Kurzlebigkeit unterworfen, sondern Gott tut alles für die längere Dauer. Das heißt, Gottes Tun ereignet sich in einer zeitlichen Kategorie, in die der Mensch einen Einblick, nicht aber den vollen Überblick, und in der er auch keine aktive Handlungsmöglichkeit hat. Dies bedeutet für den Menschen konkret, daß ihm das Tun Gottes zwar nicht direkt und unmittelbar zugänglich ist, daß er aber befähigt ist, hinter dem Weltgeschehen und auch hinter dem, was ihm sein eigenes Leben bietet, das Wirken Gottes erkennen zu können. Damit können auch zunächst sinnlos scheinende Zeitabschnitte im eigenen Leben neu als sinnvoll erkannt werden; dadurch nämlich, daß man sie als einzelne Teile in ein größeres Ganzes eingefügt und von Gott gegeben sehen kann.

Diese Fähigkeit, über die eigene Lebensdauer hinauszudenken, bietet dem Menschen die Möglichkeit, einen agierenden Gott zu erkennen, auch ohne daß dieser aktiv und spürbar in die konkrete Lebenswelt eingreift. עולם ist also insofern ein Schlüsselbegriff im Buch Kohelet, als er einerseits den zeitlichen Bereich oder besser die zeitliche Kategorie darstellt, in der sich alles Tun Gottes ereignet. Andererseits hat der Mensch in diesen Bereich auch so weit Einblick, daß er Gott als einen Handelnden und dem Menschen Verschiedenes Gebenden erkennen kann. Trotz-

---

Frankfurt, 1993, p. 123; I. WILLI-PLEIN, *Am Anfang einer Geschichte der Zeit*, in *TZ* 53 (1997) 152-164, p. 163, n. 33.

9. Diese Ansicht vertritt auch Jenni, der über Koh 3,11 schreibt: »Von den zahlreichen Deutungen, die bisher gegeben worden sind [...], werden diejenigen, die in עולם [...] einen Zeitbegriff sehen am meisten Wahrscheinlichkeit beanspruchen dürfen.« (E. JENNI, *Art. עולם*, in *THAT* II, Gütersloh, ⁴1993, pp. 228-243, p. 242.).

10. So auch L. SCHWIENHORST-SCHÖNBERGER, *Nicht im Menschen gründet das Glück. Kohelet im Spannungsfeld jüdischer Weisheit und hellenistischer Philosophie* (HBS, 2), Freiburg i. Br., 1994, p. 107; sowie G. OGDEN, *Qoheleth* (Readings – A New Biblical Commentary), Sheffield, 1987, p. 55.

dem bleibt am Gesamtwerk und am Wesen Gottes vieles für den Menschen geheimnisvoll.

2. Die Opposition »nichts hinzufügen – nichts wegnehmen«

Auf diese Voraussetzung folgt nun in v. 14e.f die Wendung, daß
diesem Tun Gottes nichts hinzuzufügen und davon nichts wegzunehmen sei. Daß hier mit אין und nicht mit לא verneint wird, und daß es
sich auch um keine apodiktische Aussage handelt, zeigt, daß der
Koheletautor nicht einfach Dtn 4,2 und 13,1 zitiert. Er bedient sich
vielmehr der bekannten Opposition, um seine Sicht des Tuns Gottes zu
verdeutlichen. Daß er hierzu ein oppositionelles Begriffspaar verwendet, stellt eine augenfällige Parallele zum Gedicht in 3,1-8 dar, in dem
Oppositionen unter anderem dazu dienten, die Umfassendheit und
Vielschichtigkeit des menschlichen Lebensbereiches[11] und speziell des
menschlichen Tuns zu schildern. Dementsprechend wird auch hier in
3,14e.f das Tun Gottes ganz allgemein, im umfassenden Sinn also, angesprochen.

Sicher bedeutet die Wendung an dieser Stelle auch, daß Gottes Tun in
sich vollkommen ist, und es daher keinerlei Korrekturen bedarf[12]. Vor
allem aber will sie die Freiheit und Souveränität Gottes unterstreichen.
Dadurch nämlich, daß Gottes Tun im und für den עולם geschieht, der
Bereich des aktiven und freien menschlichen Handelns aber nur innerhalb der jeweiligen עת liegt, ist es dem Menschen nicht möglich, Gottes
Tun direkt zu beeinflussen. Der Mensch kann Gott weder ganz »in die
Karten schauen«, noch sein Werk prinzipiell verändern. Dies macht
Gott aber nicht zu einem unnahbaren und völlig unerkennbaren Despoten[13], sondern es beläßt ihm vielmehr sein Gottsein, bzw. es macht sein
Gottsein eigentlich gerade aus. Denn was wäre das für ein Gott, wenn
man als Mensch sein Tun lenken oder gar für sich vereinnahmen könnte? Gegen die Möglichkeit der Vereinnahmung Gottes auch im kultischen Bereich wendet sich dann Koh 4,17-5,6.

---

11. Zu diesem Verständnis des Gedichtes siehe auch N. LOHFINK, *Gegenwart und
Ewigkeit. Die Zeit im Buch Kohelet*, in *GL* 60 (1987) 2-12, p. 4; sowie T. KRÜGER, *Theo-
logische Gegenwartsdeutung im Kohelet-Buch* (Unveröffentlichte Habilitationsschrift),
München, 1990, p. 252.

12. So L. SCHWIENHORST-SCHÖNBERGER, *op. cit.*, p. 109; T. KRÜGER, *Die Rezeption
der Tora im Buch Kohelet*, in DERS., *Kritische Weisheit. Studien zur weisheitlichen
Traditionskritik im Alten Testament*, Zürich, 1997, pp. 173-193, p. 181.

13. Diese öfters vorgeschlagene Deutungsrichtung vertreten z.B. W. ZIMMERLI, *Predi-
ger* (ATD, 16), Göttingen, ³1981, pp. 168ff; A. LAUHA, *Kohelet* (BK, 19), Neukirchen-
Vluyn, 1978, p. 70; D. MICHEL, *Untersuchungen zur Eigenart des Buches Qohelet*
(BZAW, 183), Berlin/New York, 1989, pp. 69-72; H.P. MÜLLER, *op. cit.*, pp. 16f.

Die Opposition »nichts hinzufügen – nichts wegnehmen« hat somit bei Kohelet eine doppelte Funktion für die menschliche Gotteserkenntnis. Zum einen erkennt der Mensch darin die Vollkommenheit des göttlichen Tuns an, zum anderen unterstreicht sie die Souveränität Gottes. Der Mensch ist fähig zu begreifen, daß Gottes Tun seinem direkten Einflußbereich entzogen ist. Damit erkennt er aber auch den ihm von Gott zur Verfügung gestellten Lebensraum und seine Lebenszeit als Bereich, in dem er frei handeln kann. Dies verdeutlicht die formale Parallele der Verwendung von Oppositionsbegriffen zur Beschreibung der jeweiligen Bereiche.

3. *Gottesfurcht*

Nun hätte man aber die Wendung an dieser Stelle mißverstanden, würde man v. 14g.h von ihr loslösen. Ja es scheint geradezu charakteristisch für Kohelets Gebrauch dieser Opposition zu sein, daß er sie mit v. 14g.h weiterführt. Aufgrund des Subjektwechsels läßt sich mit adversativem Anschluß übersetzen: »Aber der Gott hat bewirkt, daß man ihn fürchte«. Der Begriff der Gottesfurcht erscheint hier erstmals im Buch Kohelet, daher ist seine genaue inhaltliche Konnotation an dieser Stelle von besonderer Bedeutung. Das Imperfekt יראו wird dem hier gegebenen Kontext entsprechend wohl am besten modal wiedergegeben[14]. Außerdem verstehe ich mit Michael Fox und anderen עשה im Sinne von »bewirken«[15]. Somit besagt v. 14g.h, daß Gott selbst es ist, der die Gottesfurcht ermöglicht. Der Mensch wird nicht zur Gottesfurcht gezwungen, sondern sie wird ihm von Gott her als Antwort auf dessen Tun angeboten; ob der Mensch sich dieser Möglichkeit bedient, liegt in seiner eigenen Entscheidungsfreiheit.

Daß also das Tun Gottes im Kontext des עולם geschieht, heißt – um die Gesamtaussage der Formel nochmals zusammenzufassen – daß der Mensch Gott als einen frei Handelnden und dem Menschen seinerseits Handlungsfreiheit und Freude Gewährenden erkennen kann, ohne ihn aber völlig zu durchschauen und ohne in sein Tun aktiv eingreifen zu können. Wohl aber kann er dem so erfahrenen Gott durch ein gottesfürchtiges Leben Antwort geben. Angesichts dieser Erkenntnisse ist wohl nicht anzunehmen, daß Gottesfurcht hier als »auflehnungs- und erwartungsloses Sich-Abfinden mit der Übermacht«[16] zu verstehen ist.

---

14. Vgl. L. SCHWIENHORST-SCHÖNBERGER, *op. cit.*, pp. 109f.
15. Siehe M.V. FOX, *Qohelet and his Contradictions* (JSOT SS, 71), Sheffield, 1989, pp. 194f.
16. H.P. MÜLLER, *op. cit.*, p. 16.

Vielmehr scheint mir die logische Reaktion auf einen so erfahrenen Gott eine Haltung von Ehrfurcht und Demut zu sein, die das realistische Bewußtsein der eigenen menschlichen Grenzen mit einschließt.

In diesem Sinne kann man Gottesfurcht hier durchaus im klassisch weisheitlichen Verständnis sehen; als gläubige Ehrfurcht nämlich, die sich in einer ethisch-sittlichen Lebensgestaltung zu erkennen gibt[17]. Freilich bedeutet »ethisch-sittliche Lebensgestaltung« hier nicht das Festhalten an einem ganz bestimmten Verhaltenskatalog. Wenn jemand aber im Glauben an einen Gott, der dem Menschen Freiheit, Freude, aber auch Verantwortung für sein Tun gegeben hat, lebt, dann hat dies vielmehr automatisch Auswirkungen auf die Lebensgestaltung dieses Menschen. Unter dieser Rücksicht müßten dann meines Erachtens auch die weiteren Gottesfurchtstellen des Koheletbuches gesehen werden. Auch die Erweiterung der Gottesfurcht um das Halten der Gebote in Koh 12,13 bereitet bei einem solchen Verständnis keine Schwierigkeiten mehr[18]; denn die Gebote eines Gottes, dem man mit gläubiger Ehrfurcht antwortet, wird man auch prinzipiell zu halten geneigt sein. Im Gegenteil; gerade diese in 3,14 geschilderte Erkenntnis eines Gottes, dessen Tun über dem Tun des Menschen steht, der aber dem Menschen innerhalb seines eigenen Lebensbereichs – der עת – Eigenverantwortung und Handlungsfreiheit gewährt, läßt die sich bietenden freudigen Lebensmomente einerseits und eine prinzipielle Lebensgestaltung im Wissen um einen solchen Gott andererseits sinnvoll und förderlich erscheinen.

Gottesfurcht wird also hier eingeführt als Ermöglichung einer Antwort des Menschen auf das Tun Gottes, das er in einem gewissen eingeschränkten Ausmaß wahrnehmen kann. Die Antwort äußert sich in einer ehrfürchtigen Haltung diesem Gott gegenüber und wirkt sich entsprechend auf bestimmte Lebenshaltungen aus.

Ausblick

Vers 3,14 im allgemeinen und die darin verwendete und erweiterte Opposition, daß dem Tun Gottes nichts hinzuzufügen und davon nichts wegzunehmen sei, im besonderen, erweisen sich als Schlüssel für das Verständnis der Begriffe עולם und Gottesfurcht im gesamten Koheletbuch. Da beide Begriffe vor allem das Verhältnis zwischen Gott und

---

17. Siehe dazu auch R.N. WHYBRAY, *Ecclesiastes* (NCBC), London, 1989, p. 75; T. KRÜGER, *op. cit.* (n. 11), p. 268.

18. Mit M.V. FOX, *Frame-Narrative and Composition in the Book of Qohelet*, in *HUCA* 48 (1977) 83-106 und T. KRÜGER, *op. cit.* (n. 12), p. 173, n. 4 gehe ich davon aus, daß das Koheletbuch von *einem* Verfasser stammt, der sich mehrerer literarischer Ebenen und »Stimmen« bedient.

Mensch beschreiben, stellen sie Eckpfeiler für die Theologie dieses Buches dar. In 3,14 wird Gottesfurcht innerhalb des Koheletbuches eingeführt und das einzige Mal mit עולם gemeinsam im selben Vers genannt. Damit kommt diesem Vers eine besondere Bedeutung für die Beurteilung des Gottesbildes bei Kohelet zu, und die vermeintliche Kanonformel wird zu einer Art Glaubensbekenntnis.

Alttestamentliches Institut   Andreas VONACH
Karl-Rahner-Platz 3
A-6020 Innsbruck

OLD AGE FRAILTY VERSUS COSMIC DETERIORATION?

A Few Remarks on the Interpretation of Qohelet 11,7-12,8

Many Biblical exegetes are in agreement that Qoh 12,3-4 should be understood in terms of an allegory on the frailty of the aging human body based on the image of a house[1]. According to some scholars the allegorical interpretation appears to be losing ground[2]. Nevertheless, other scholars still uphold this approach respecting the present passage[3]. This paper does not necessarily reject or intend to replace the reading of the passage in terms of an allegory. However, it is proposed that the passage be read in terms of a different allegory, namely not of the old age of the human body, but an allegory which deals, albeit perhaps indirectly,

---

1. See J. LOADER, *Prediker. Een praktische Bijbelverklaring* (Tekst & Toelichting), Kampen, Kok, 1984, p. 149; W. C. KAISER & M. SILVA, *An Introduction to Biblical Hermeneutics*, Grand Rapids, Michigan, Zondervan, 1994, p. 102. The allegorical approach is reflected in translation, inter alia, in *Today's English Version*, and the *Contemporary English Version*.

2. See I.J.J. SPANGENBERG, *Die Boek Prediker*, Kaapstad, N G Kerk-Uitgewers, 1993, p. 173.

3. Arguments which favour this approach include among others, the literary context, namely that a youth is addressed (11,9; 12,1) and advised to enjoy life while he is young, before (אד אשר לא 12,1b. 2.6, a circumstantial conjunction, according to H. C. LEUPOLD, *Exposition of Ecclesiastes*, Grand Rapids, Michigan, Baker, 1974, p. 276), the dismal days (ימי הרעה), that is, the days of old age, overtake him. Further, certain "domestic" expressions in the passage seem to be slanted towards such an understanding. Thus the "trembling of the guards" would indicate the weakening of the legs, "grinders" would refer to teeth, "windows" to the eyes, and "doors" to ears (vv. 3-4). The aged show fear, move slow, and eventually die (v. 5). One example usually quoted in this connection is Barzillai, the Gileadite, who hid behind the ailments of his old age as an excuse to decline king David's invitation to accompany him (2 Sam 19,31-38), see J.H. KROEZE, *Die Woorde van die Prediker*, Johannesburg, De Jongh, 1975, p. 130. Part of Qoh 12,5 reads: ותפר האביונה, translated as "desire fails" (NRSV). According to E. R. WENDLAND, *The Cultural Factor in Bible Translation*, Stuttgart, UBS, 1987, pp. 102-103, this translation veils a euphemism, an expression which he translates as, "the caper-berry is exhausted". He finds a double metonymy here in which the berry substitutes for the potion that is made from it, and the potion replaces its intended effect, namely as an aphrodisiac to increase one's sexual desire. This argument supports the opinion that the passage deals with the ills of old age. Further support to read the passage as an allegory can perhaps be gleaned from a comparison of the legs of the beloved to pillars of marble (Cant 5,15). The problems of old age appear in other ancient Near Eastern literature as well, e.g. the *Enuma Elish*. See R. HARRIS, *Gendered Old Age in Enuma Elish*, in M. E. COHEN et. al. (eds.), *The Tablet and the Scroll. Near Eastern Studies in Honour of W. W. Hallo*, Bethesda, Maryland, CDL Press, 1993, pp. 111-115; G. W. COATS, *Saga, Legend, Tale, Novella, Fable, Narrative Forms in Old Testament Literature* (JSOT SS, 35), Sheffield, 1985, p. 135, n. 70.

with the "old age" of the *globe* and the *cosmos*. Certain scholars have pointed out that in the distant past certain scientific astronomical occurrences accompanied by cosmological disruptions were embodied or expressed in mythical language. This paper does not purport to prove (or disprove, for that matter) the theses surrounding the possible relation(s) between natural phenomena of cosmological occurrences and mythical imagery as asserted by proponents of these ideas. Part of these ideas are scientifically verifiable, the rest of the conclusions are open to criticism[4].

To examine these possibilities, a brief discussion of a somewhat different approach of ancient myths is in order. De Santillana and Von Dechend[5] were at pains to show that, contrary to what was believed in the past, some (Norse and other North and West European) myths appear to have been vehicles of scientific facts in antiquity. This means representing the frame of a world age or a system for veiling technical terminology of an advanced astronomical science behind the everyday language of myth. In their search for the origins of scientific thought these authors stumbled upon what they imagine was in ancient time a link between myth and astronomy, particularly where "number" gave the key. In early times measures and counting provided the armature, the

---

4. Exegetes are currently confronted with archaeological and geological studies combining astronomical material with astrological views, and which lay claim to Biblical texts. In some cases these ideas are based on a sub-apocalyptic text and are presented as popular science. See R. BAUVAL – A. GILBERT, *The Orion Mystery*, London, Mandarin, 1996; R. BAUVAL – G. HANCOCK, *Keeper of Genesis. A Quest for the Hidden Legacy of Mankind*, London, Heinemann, 1996; A. G. GILBERT & M. COTTERELL, *The Mayan Prophecies. Unlocking the Secrets of a Lost Civilization*, Shaftesbury, Dorset, Element, 1995; A. G. GILBERT, *Magi. The Quest for a Secret Tradition*, London, Bloomsbury, 1996, and many others. Perhaps the recent renewed interest in the cosmos generally inspired these views (*Astronomy Now*, 11, 3 (1997) 41-52). This practice constantly crops up in bestsellers against the backdrop of renewed attention given worldwide to alleged theological and sociological impact of the concept of the "Millennium". These views were severely criticized by D. THOMPSON, *The Time of the End – Faith and Fear in the Shadow of the Millennium*, London, Sinclair-Stevenson, 1996, pp. 223-225. This author claims that the views set forth in these books carry the fingerprints of the controversial New Age Movement all over them (*ibid.*, pp. 3ff.). See the recent study of F. FERNÁNDEZ-ARMESTO, *Millennium, A History of Our Last Thousand Years*, London, Bantam, 1995. In connection with the turn of the millennium bold statements are made on, *inter alia*, possible pending global disasters. Information in support of these ideas is gleaned and calculated from ancient myths, especially mythical calendars. Some authors have seized upon this occurrence of the precession of the equinoxes and possible related phenomena and popularized the information with the aid of ancient calendars, certain maritime discoveries and other facts by using them as a basis for certain predictions, see G. HANCOCK, *Fingerprints of the Gods. A Quest for the Beginning and the End*, London, Mandarin, 1996, pp. 169-176.

5. G. DE SANTILLANA – H. VON DECHEND, *Hamlet's Mill: An Essay on Myth and the Frame of Time*, Ipswich, Mass, Gambit, Macmillan, 1969, p. ix, 45, 49, 58 (also: New York, St. Martin's Press, 1969; and Boston, D. R. Godine, 1992).

frame on which the rich texture of real myth was to grow. These sets of ideas included, inter alia, references to the turning of a *millwheel*, with the accompanying phenomenon of such a millwheel bursting asunder from its props, breaking, and causing disaster. One case will suffice to explain the occurrence. In these myths the turning of a mill or quern grounded out gold, peace and plenty. In many of the traditions two maidens, known as Fenja and Menja, were indentured to turn such a millwheel. Something went awry which forced the two giantesses to work day and night without rest. They became angry and while everyone was asleep, turned the mill at such a speed that its props, though cast in iron, burst asunder. Later the mill was stolen, the turning had to continue under new management, grounding out salt, and still later it sank to the bottom of the sea, now grounding out rocks and sand, creating a whirl-pool, the *Maelstrom*[6]. According to De Santillana and Von Dechend there are indications that this mythical picture of a rotating millwheel, the breaking free from its props, and the resultant disaster, represent re-spectively the luminous dome of the rotating celestial sphere, including the earth, and interruption of this rotation by cosmological disaster. They allege that these archaic myths, especially those in connection with the millwheel, the whirlpool, and the tree, contain, or conceal, in terms of an *allegory* (a thought tool) information about the scientific established phenomenon[7] known as the *precession of the equinoxes*[8]. Observed from the earth, the sun apparently moves through all twelve houses of the zo-diac, an occurrence which is the result of this natural phenomenon of the precession of the equinoxes, that is, the slow oscillation of the earth's

6. *Ibid.*, p. 89-90.
7. *Ibid.*, p. 57-58.
8. A complete description of this natural phenomenon is beyond the scope of this pa-per since it belongs to the field of "astrophysics" which include the study of mathemat-ics, numbers, measuring, and geometry. The phenomenon was perhaps known long be-fore Hipparchus described it in 127 B. C., and it is well-known that the origins of myth cannot be dated with any precision, *Ibid.*, pp. 26 and 57-58. For a scientific explanation of this phenomenon, see C. A. RONAN, *The Natural History of the Universe*, London, Doubleday, 1991, p. 200. Precession must be distinguished from the earth's rotation around its own axis. The problem of precessional cycles amounting to 26 000 years will not be discussed here, except to mention that in spite of the fact that most scientists are convinced of the high age of the earth (see L. ALBERTS, *Christianity and the Enquiring Mind*, Vereeniging, CUM, 1996, pp. 34-67), a few maintain that it is only a few thousand years old, see the letter by J. Kies in *Die Kerkbode*, 7 March 1997, p. 13. However, these opposing views do not effect the present reasoning in any way. Any attempt to determine (a) date(s) when the mythical imagery concerned entered the Biblical texts is hampered by its appearance in earlier (Judg) and later Biblical books (Mt). On the other hand, a late dating for Qohelet follows from the language (post-Biblical Hebrew of the Mishnah). The influence of Hellenistic philosophy on the author has often been assumed, as well as Egyptian and Babylonian influence (R. RENDTORFF, *The Old Testament, An Introduction*, Philadelphia, Fortress, 1986, p. 266). However, this remains disputed.

axis through a few degrees, completing a cycle at the end of more or
less 26 000 years. This movement can be compared to the circle described by the point of a slow spinning top. Traditionally transitions
from one completed cycle of this phenomenon to a following one, have
been regarded as ill-omened. Thus, at the completion of such a cycle,
the occurrence is allegedly followed by cosmological and global disaster. In this connection it was noted that key images and symbols in ancient myths, notably the derangement of the heavens, are also to be
found imbedded in the ancient traditions of worldwide cataclysm[9]. An
assumed link between the phenomenon of the precession of the equinoxes and certain ancient mythical tales dealing with the theme of global and cosmic catastrophe, finds expression, *inter alia*, in the figure
4320 (or its fractions, halving and multiples)[10]. Thus the meaning of
the mythical presentation runs that the turning of the millwheel represents the revolving of the heavens (the celestial bodies), including the
rotation of the earth. The mill's bursting asunder from its props, and
the subsequent breaking of the mill, represent the stars being thrown
out of kilter, as well as disasters which take place on the globe. An accompanying phenomenon of the latter relates to the mythical *tree*
which probably stands for the axis of the earth respectively the heavens, since the latter extends through the whole of the starry sky. When
the disruption of the mill takes place, this tree as axle, as pillar is
shaken accordingly. The millwheel falling into the ocean also creates a
whirlpool (the Maelstrom), which gushes up through its axle[11].

9. HANCOCK, *op. cit.* (n. 4), pp. 201-221.
10. The figure 4 320 represents the number of years required for the equinoctial sun to
complete a precessional shift of 60 degrees, that is, 2 zodiacal constellations. The number
2 160 (4 320 ÷ 2) represents the number of years required for the sun to pass completely
through one of the 12 zodiacal constellations; 2 160 x 12 = 25 920, the number of years
in one complete precessional cycle. Veiled in various ways, this number constantly crops
up in for example, the (Egyptian) Osiris myth (cf. the number of the conspirators, 72 x 60
= 4 320), Norse myth (cf. the 432 000 fighters who sallied forth from Valhalla to do battle
with the wolf, Fenrir, the latter who chases the sun, overtakes it and extinguishes its rays,
whereupon disaster strikes the earth, the earth loses its shape, and the stars coming adrift
in the sky, thus the theme of catastrophe is mixed with the quite separate theme of precession. In ancient Chinese traditions references to a universal cataclysm were said to have
been written down in a text containing 4 320 volumes; the Babylonian historian Berossus
(3rd century B. C.) ascribed a total reign of 432 000 years to the mythical kings who ruled
the land of Sumer before the great flood. The latter author ascribed 2 160 000 years (= 4
320 000 ÷ 2) to the period between creation and universal catastrophe. See HANCOCK, *op.
cit.* (n. 4), pp. 262, 273-276. Without doubt, numbers played an important role in ancient
literature. Apart from the prominent place given to numbers in Daniel and Revelation, see
C.J. LABUSCHAGNE's intricate "logotechnische" analyses of Deuteronomium
(*Deuteronomium* [POT], Nijkerk, Callenbach, vol. IA, IB, 1987; II, 1990).
11. DE SANTILLANA – VON DECHEND, *op. cit.* (n. 5), pp. 437-451.

Those who espouse these views, claim that traces of these myths can be found in certain Biblical texts[12]. The prime example quoted in this respect comes from the Old Testament, namely *Samson's grinding at the mill* in prison (Judg 16,21). This portrayal is followed afterwards by the *disaster* of the temple of Dagon, when Samson removed the main *pillars* of that temple from their foundations (Judg 16,29.30). In the chapters leading up to these incidents, a falling millstone (Judg 9,53) appears in the context of dramatic occurrences, the breaking down of a tower (8,9.17, cf. 9,47-53), the destruction of a city and the killing of its people (9,45; cf. 7,13-14; Dan 2,34-35.45). According to the New Testament, two women will be *grinding* meal together (compare Fenja and Menja), one will be taken and one will be left (Mt 24,41; Lk 17,35). These New Testament references are important, because the scene in which they are portrayed, forms part of an apocalyptic-eschatological context, which deals with approaching global disaster. Mt 18,5-6 adds to this climate when it states that if someone is a cause of stumbling to one who has faith in Jesus, it would be better for him to have a *millstone* hung around his neck and be drowned in the depths of the sea[13]. A similar story crops up when Alexander of Macedon had the cook Andreas thrown into the *sea* with a *millstone* around his neck[14]. These examples also remind of the millstone falling into the sea as told in the episodes of the mythological tales of Fenja and Menja.

This paper deals with some aspects of the mythical imagery concerned, but only in so far as these impact on selected passages in Qohelet. The aim is to place a "grid" containing several mythical concepts over the indicated passages. Obviously this grid cannot account for everything in the book, and will appear fragmentary. However, this way of reasoning is not an attempt to revive the old "myth and ritual" school[15], but takes into account the impact of non-biblical literature on

12. The Book of Enoch (1 Enoch) often refers to celestial bodies, mostly in relation to the movement of time and seasons. Here, one aspect to the point stands out. As a result of the sins of its inhabitants the earth at some stage "will be brought low", and "will be afflicted and shaken" (1 Enoch 65,1.3). Ethiopic *'aṣnana*, inter alia, renders κλίνειν, see John 19, 30: καὶ κλίνας (τὴν κεφαλὴν), the "bowing" or "tilting" (of the head). This description, applied to the earth, may portray the earth's axis moving from its fixed position. See M. BLACK, *The Book of Enoch or 1 Enoch*, Leiden, E. J. Brill, 1985, pp. 62, 239, 386-419.

13. See Isa 28,16; Ps 118,22; Mt 21,42.44; Lk 20,18; Mk 12,10. The potter's wheel (Egyptian Khnum and Jer 18-19) probably belong here, since this wheel was also part of the cosmological instrumentation related to the millwheel, see DE SANTILLANA – VON DECHEND, *op. cit.* (n. 5), p. 388.

14. DE SANTILLANA – VON DECHEND, *op. cit.* (n. 5), p. 313.

15. Comp. S. H. HOOKE and others, *Myth and Ritual: Essays on the Myth and Ritual of the Hebrews in Relation to the Cultic Pattern of the Ancient Near East*, London, Ox-

the text. The warning against "ruthless identifying"[16] must be kept in mind when comparing the Old Testament, and in the present case, Qohelet, with ancient myths. The study is limited to the possibility of understanding Qoh 11,7-12,8 in terms of an allegory based on mythological and cosmological imagery set in an apocalyptic key, perhaps complementary to the allegory of human old age. Thus certain indications may direct the exegete to understand the passage concerned in the context of the cosmos, that is, in connection with the behaviour of the sun, moon and stars, perhaps portrayed as deteriorating.

Qoh 12,8 is a precise and verbatim resumption of the opening line of the book in 1,2, and could serve as a frame for the whole book, 12,9-12 serving as an addendum[17]. Following 1,2, that is from verse 3ff. the author reflects on the permanence of man's labour *under the sun* (v. 3), the coming and going of generations (vv. 4 and 11), the exhaustion caused by these ever returning constants (v. 9a) of which there is nothing new *under the sun* (v. 9b.10a), man's habit of never-ending talk, his desire to see (v. 8b), to hear (v. 8b), but especially the permanent rising and setting of *the sun* (v. 5), the incessant blowing of the wind (v. 6), and the cyclical movement of water (v. 7). However, in contradistinction to this presentation, at the end of the book (in 11,7-12,8) there are hints that the ongoing mundane activities and the constant movement of celestial bodies, including the earth, will undergo a change, that their regular functions will deteriorate, or at least diminish, so that the rays of the sun will not shine on earth any more, the moon will become invisible, rain will not cease. There appears to be a cluster of thoughts at the end of the book in connection with serious disturbing changes of an apocalyptic character that will perhaps take place in the cosmos and on the globe. In this connection it must be kept in mind that apocalyptic perspectives seem to become more pronounced towards the end of (albeit prophetic) books that contain such material[18]. This could apply to Qohelet in the light of what has been discussed so far[19]. Further evidence that an apoca-

---

ford, 1933; *The Labyrinth: Further Studies in the Relation between Myth and Ritual in the Ancient World*, London, Oxford, 1935; *Myth, Ritual, and Kingship*, London, Oxford, 1958.

16. DE SANTILLANA – VON DECHEND, *op. cit.* (n. 5), p. 427.

17. Qoh 1,2: הֲבֵל הֲבָלִים אָמַר קֹהֶלֶת הֲבֵל הֲבָלִים הַכֹּל הָבֶל, and 12,8: הֲבֵל הֲבָלִים אָמַר הַקּוֹהֶלֶת הַכֹּל הָבֶל, and see M. FISHBANE, *Biblical Interpretation in Ancient Israel*, Oxford, Clarendon, 1991, pp. 30-32.

18. See Isa 56-66; Ezek 38-39; Dan 7-12; Zech 12-14. Cf. P.D. HANSON, *Apocalyptic Literature*, in D.A. KNIGHT – G.M. TUCKER (eds.), *The Hebrew Bible and its Modern Interpreters*, Chico, California, Scholars Press, 1985, pp. 480-481.

19. At the beginning of Qohelet (ch. 1) the incessant cyclical movement of the celestial body, the sun, the constant return of the elements (wind, water), and the function of

lyptic-eschatological perspective dominates these passages comes from the twice repeated reference to God's threat to *judge* (במשפט, Qoh 11,9; 12,14). The latter feature is part and parcel of the apocalyptic view[20]. Another indication that apocalyptic-eschatological views play a role here can be inferred from the reference to the *grasshopper* (which "drags itself along", or: "is a burden" – Qoh 12,5d). It is conceded that this phrase may be related to a metaphor for "hip", "penis", or "knuckles", or even "early summer"[21]. The latter possibilities would support the interpretation of the present passage as an allegory of the aging human body (see note 3). However, these insects (or any of their variety) were very much part of the apocalyptic scenario of the Old Testament (Joel 1,4;2,5.21) and the New Testament (Rev 11,3.7-11).

רעה – Disaster

It is conceded that Qoh 11,1-6 may be interpreted in terms of advice given to a farmer (practising husbandry). However, 11,2 warns that "disaster (רעה) may happen on earth". The possibility that רעה (in 11,2) can refer to (natural) disaster finds support in 12,1b where the reader is warned that days of רעה are on their way. The warning in 11,2 is preceded by a suggestion that a person's bread should be send out on the waters. This could refer to a river, but perhaps it means a flood, because verse 3 states that clouds full of water will empty themselves on the earth, as if heavy rains were on their way. This way of reasoning may be supported from Qoh 12,2 which reads: "before the sun and the light of day give place to darkness, before the moon and stars grow dim and the clouds return after the rain". Again, the instruction given to the farmer to keep his "investments" in different places and sow when the appropriate time arrives, could be explained in the light of the irregularity of rainfall, but it could also hint at timely preparation before the רעה strikes (11,3).

---

human faculties to the point of boredom, add to an atmosphere created to highlight a theme of the book, namely the meaninglessness (הבל) of life. In the intermediate chapters, 2,1 through 11,6 (encapsulated by chapters 1 and 11,7ff. which, *inter alia*, deal with the universe), the focus falls on and zooms in on the life of men and women. The lives of human beings are fenced off by the two references of the repetitive aspect (ch. 1) and possible disturbances (in the cosmos and) on earth (11,7ff.). In connection with the inclusive aspect, there seems to be a similar structure or tendency in Genesis where chapter 1 (vv. 14-18) deals with (the creation of) the sun, moon, and stars, and later returns to these celestial bodies in Joseph's dream (37,9).

20. D.S. RUSSELL, *The Method and Message of Jewish Apocalyptic, 200 BC -100 AD*, Philadelphia, Westminster Press, 1976, p. 380.

21. W.L. HOLLADAY, *A Concise Hebrew and Aramaic Lexicon of the Old Testament*, Leiden, E. J. Brill, 1971, p. 95.

Consider the words in 11,7: "the pleasant sight of the sun", followed by the inversion, "days of darkness" (11,8b), and subsequently by the statement on the darkening of the sun (12,2: תֶחְשַׁךְ הַשֶׁמֶשׁ). This could indicate the natural day-night sequence (comp. Gen 1), but also the apocalyptic darkness described by some prophets, (e.g. Joel 2,1b-2a; Amos 5,18). The book of Daniel contains both wisdom thought (Daniel is reckoned as a wise courtier)[22] and apocalyptic material[23]. This observation seems to confirm the possibility that Qohelet, as wisdom literature, contains apocalyptic material[24]. In apocalyptic literature disaster is often expressed in terms of darkness. Thus the expression, *days of darkness* (Qoh 11,8), represents a situation which will prevail for some time. This is followed by a summons to youth to enjoy the time before the unhappy days set in, that is, before darkness eclipses the sun, the light, the moon and the stars, and it keeps on raining (12,2). Heights will be a source of fear for people, and it will be dangerous to go out on the streets (v. 5ab, see v. 4a).

THE MILLWHEEL

Against this background the impression is created that the *turning of the mill* slows down, or is about to come to a standstill (twice referred to in vv. 3-4. See the *NRSV*, v. 3: "the women who grind cease working because they are few"; and v. 4: "the sound of the grinding is low", probably as a result of the mill slowing down). The *pulley* at the well falls and breaks (v. 6), the latter occurrence perhaps emphasized by the breaking of the pitcher. The idea that the Hebrew הטחנה (12,4) or הטחנות (12,3) means (a) (molar) *tooth/teeth*, stems from an allegorical interpretation (on human old age) of the passage. However, as far as can be determined, nowhere in the Old Testament are these words used for a tooth or teeth, only for a *mill* (Exod 11,5; Num 11,8; Deut 9,21; 24,6; Judg 9,53; 16,21; 2 Sam 11,21; Isa 3,15; Lam 5,13; Job 31,10; 41,15; Prov 31,15). The latter observation is perhaps supported by the fact that הטחנה (12,4) and הטחנות (12,3) take the feminine form, which in turn evokes

---

22. W.L. HUMPHREYS, *The Motif of the Wise Courtier in the Book of Proverbs*, in J. GAMMIE et al. (eds.), *Israelite Wisdom*, Montana, Scholars Press, 1978, pp. 177-189.

23. J.J. COLLINS, *The Apocalyptic Vision of the Book of Daniel*, Missoula, Montana, Scholars Press, 1977.

24. S.J. DE VRIES, *Observations on Quantitative and Qualitative Time in Wisdom and Apocalyptic*, in GAMMIE, *op. cit.* (n. 22), pp. 263-276. But see D. MICHEL, *Weisheit und Apokalyptik*, in A.S. VAN DER WOUDE (ed.), *The Book of Daniel in the Light of New Findings* (BETL, 106), Leuven, Peeters, 1993, pp. 413-434.

the custom of the ancients to reserve the work of grinding grain for women[25].

Combined with the idea that Qohelet 11,2-3 possibly mentions global (cosmic?) deterioration, the reference in 12,3-4 to a mill slowing down, may, in the light of what was considered so far, represent a picture of threatening global disaster, or rather a timely admonition, a feature which is also a characteristic of wisdom literature[26], to be prepared for such occurrences. In 12,6 reference is made to הגלגל, probably the "wheel" or rather "pulley", used to draw water from the cistern. This object falls at (or in) the cistern and it breaks. Thus another indication of something which is used in a rotating function, but then loses that function when it breaks. This idea reminds of the falling and breaking of the (mythical) millwheel. This leads to a situation of having no water, highlighted by the breaking of the water pitcher.

PILLARS AND TREES

In ancient myth the phenomenon of a millwheel that breaks, is accompanied by pillars that give way. The Old Testament refers to the pillars of the heavens and the earth, "trembling" (Job 9,6; 26,11), but kept steady by Yahweh (Ps 75,3; see Prov 9,1). At the entrance to the Temple of Solomon, there were two pillars (Jachin and Boaz), a typical ancient Near Eastern phenomenon in temple construction[27]. It is tempting to extend the "trembling of the guards of the house" (in Qoh 12,3) to the pillars at the entrance of, or supporting, a building, in the light of Isaiah 6,4 and Amos 9,1. However, except in one case, the verbs and nouns differ in the respective texts (Qoh 12,3, שמרי בית יזעו, ינעו; Isa 6,4, ינעו, אמות הספים, and Amos 9,1, הכפתור, ירעשו, and הספים). Nevertheless, the resemblance between "trembling guards" (which could refer to pillars) and the mythical pillars giving way, must be noted.

The idea of global and cosmic disaster perhaps hinted at in the passages under discussion, may be developed further. Qoh 11,3 mentions a *fallen tree*. The possibility that this text can be understood in terms of a violent natural occurrence, is supported by the indication of (torrential?)

25. See the *NRSV*, 12,3: "The women who grind". It was probably a disgrace for men to do this work (Judg 16,21; Lam 5,13), cf. A. VAN DEURSEN, *Bijbels Beeldwoordenboek*, Kampen, Kok, 1970, p. 30.

26. R.N. WHYBRAY, *Qohelet the Immoralist? (Qoh 7:16-17)*, in J. GAMMIE et al. (eds.), *op. cit.* (n. 22), pp. 192, 196, 198, 200.

27. C.L. MEYERS, *Jachin and Boaz in Religious and Political Perspective*, in *CBQ* 45 (1983) 167-178.

rains in verse 3a, followed by the reference to the fallen tree in verse 3b, the latter probably the result of the former. In ancient myths a tree stood for many things[28], and the motif of a "world tree" was widespread in antiquity[29]. In the light of the fact that the ancients were oriented towards the skies, they viewed a tree, *inter alia*, as the mythological axis of the millwheel, and applied to the axis of the earth. Although mythical allusions in the book of Daniel are still debated[30] it may be concluded that Dan 4,10 probably presents such a mythical world tree as being in the "midst", or "inside" the earth, בְּגוֹא אַרְעָא (Aramaic). However, the Septuagint version of this text does not read "in the centre". Nevertheless, in the Septuagint version of Dan 4,11 this tree reaches cosmic proportions, for even the *sun* and the *moon* dwell in its branches[31]. However, in Daniel the mighty king is portrayed under the figure of this gigantic tree, which is subsequently cut down[32]. In ancient myth, the tree is often portrayed in the same cosmological terms as being shaken, or cut down, an occurrence which in turn refers to the shaking of the axis of the earth, and thus the earth itself. This cosmic presentation of the tree in Daniel supports the possibility as stated above, namely that the fallen tree (Qoh 11,3) may have connotations of cosmic disaster. In ancient myth the breaking of the mill, the cutting down of the tree, and disaster often appear in close proximity[33]. Perhaps the falling of the tree points to a disruption of the rotation of the earth's axis, with catastrophic results. In the New Testament, Rev 6,13 reads: "The *stars of the sky fell* on the *earth* as the fig *tree* drops its winter fruit when *shaken* by a gale" (author's italics). This text is preceded by a reference to the sun becoming black as sackcloth, and the moon like blood. For the present purpose the interrelatedness of the references to the stars thrown out of kilter, a tree, and the tree shaken by a gale, must be noted.

Also in the case of the tree the impression is created that the way things are presented at the beginning of Qohelet appears as very calm, and in a sense stationary. In 2,5-6 the author of the book tells how he used to plant *fruit trees* and watered *young trees*. However, towards the end of the book, in 11,3, reference is made to a *fallen tree*. An idea

---

28. J.G. FRAZER, *The Golden Bough*, Kent, Papermac, p. 752.

29. L.F. HARTMAN – A.A. DI LELLA, *The Book of Daniel* (AB, 23), New York, Doubleday Company, Inc., 1980, p.176.

30. HANSON, *op. cit.* (n. 28), p. 481.

31. Dan 4,11: καὶ ἡ ὅρασις αὐτοῦ μεγάλη ἡ κορυφὴ αὐτοῦ ἤγγιζεν ἕως τοῦ οὐρανοῦ καὶ τὸ κύτος αὐτοῦ ἕως τῶν νεφελῶν πληροῦν τὰ ὑποκάτω τοῦ οὐρανοῦ ὁ ἥλιος καὶ ἡ σελήνη ἐν αὐτῷ ᾤκουν καὶ ἐφώτιζον πᾶσαν τὴν γῆν.

32. HARTMAN – DI LELLA, *op. cit.* (n. 29), p.176.

33. DE SANTILLANA – VON DECHEND, *op. cit.* (n. 5), p. 238.

which seems to support the idea of global or perhaps cosmic deterioration, in the light of the mythical role of a shaking tree as an expression of cosmic disaster. Again: it was pointed out earlier that the guards of the house (Qoh 12,3) may refer to pillars, "trembling" as it were. This reminds of Amos 9,1, and Isa 6,4, but the fallen tree in Qohelet may be a veiled way of referring to the world tree being shaken, or cut down, which in turn could signify apocalyptic upheaval.

THE WHIRLPOOL

Except for the motif of "the betrothed at the well" episodes (Gen 24,11; Exod 2,15-21), the well, or cistern, or pit as pictured in the Old Testament is usually the scene of fairly dramatic occurrences (cf. Gen 21,19; 26, 18-26; 37, 20; Jer 38,6). This must be kept in mind when considering the meaning of אֶת־בּוֹרְאֶיךָ in Qoh 12,1 and אֶל־הַבּוֹר in verse 6. First, the expression in 12,1: אֶת־בּוֹרְאֶיךָ, may be translated as 'your creator', or, if taken as בּוֹרְךָ, translated as 'grave', or 'cistern'[34]. In Qoh 12,6 on the other hand, this word may be translated as, '"at", or "in" the cistern' (אֶל־הַבּוֹר). It is possible that the latter two references (12,1 and 12,6) function as the beginning and end of a "ring-composition" (an inclusion) encapsulating at least part of the passage concerned (12,1-12,6). If this is correct, the undisputed form, בּוֹר, in 12,6 may lead the exegete to read the same form in 12,1. The possibility exists that בּוֹר may be a reference to the whirlpool dramatically created by the millwheel falling into the ocean, according to ancient myth. According to Qohelet the wheel, or pulley falls into the cistern. Another reminder of the mythical millwheel breaking, falling into the ocean, and creating the whirlpool.

THE "SILVER CORD"

Another factor to be considered comes from the words of 12,6: "Before the silver cord is snapped", or "removed", / יֵרָתֵק / יְרֻחַק / לֹא־יִרְחַק אֲשֶׁר עַד יִנָּתֵק חֶבֶל הַכֶּסֶף, a text which causes interpreters some problems. Note the play on words: חֶבֶל (12,6a) / הֶבֶל (12,8). But whether one reads רחק

---

34. In Jewish catacombs of ancient Italy a third of the inscriptions quote Biblical verses in Latin: the grave is called *domus aeterna*, "the eternal home" (Qoh 12,5). This occurrence, although of a different date than the writing of Qohelet, perhaps supports the reading of בּוֹרְךָ, as "your grave" (12,1). See B. KEDAR, *The Latin Translations*, in M.J. MULDER – H. SYSLING (eds.), *Mikra*, Assen - Maastricht, Van Gorcum, and Minneapolis, Fortress, 1990, p. 308.

רתק,, or even נתק, the specific verb is perhaps not decisive for determining the meaning of the expression. The reason for this is that the silver cord may perhaps be understood in terms of the ancient myths as the "Milky Way". One way in which the ancients understood the Milky Way was that it represented some sort of a cord or band around the star framework, to keep all the stars in position[35]. When it is stated that the cord will snap (12,6), it may refer to the stars being thrown out of kilter. This possibility supports the view that Qohelet may reveal some form of pending apocalyptic disaster.

THE WATER PITCHER

Lastly, the *water pitcher* (Qoh 12,6) evokes the apparent movement of the sun from the present age of Pisces to the next age of *Aquarius* (presented as a water bearer with water pitcher)[36]. The *breaking* of the pitcher is perhaps a reminder of the completion and transition of the ages (in this case perhaps the end of the age of Aquarius), and the alleged accompanying upheavals.

CONCLUSION

The conclusion of this paper is provisional upon its findings. There seems to be evidence in this passage in Qohelet of a wise warning against, or typical wisdom speculation on a threatening global natural disaster of an apocalyptic nature in the light of wisdom's concern with creation/the cosmos (Job 38,1-39, see v. 30; 40,6-41, see v. 34)[37].

Apart from what was discussed in connection with Qohelet, other parts of the Old Testament seem to confirm this association of images. In Job (9,6-10; 26,11, cf. 1,19; Ps 75,3-4) the reference to the *shaking* of the *earth* appears in close proximity to that of the *stars* (see Jer 4,24; Isa 13,13; Joel 2,10; 3,16; Hag 2,6.21b; Ezek 38,19-20). In the apocalyptic Isa 24 there appears to be a vivid scenery of all these items in the same context. Scenes of the *heavens* and the *earth* staggering (24,1.3.4.18b. 19.20.23), combine with the olive *tree* being beaten and losing its fruit (24,13), a threefold reference to the *pit* (but presented as a snare, vv. 17-18; a prison, v. 22 and a dung-pit, 25,10b), while *doors* are shut because

35. DE SANTILLANA – VON DECHEND, *op. cit.* (n. 5), pp. 230-233; 242-249; 264-265.
36. *Ibid.*, p. 301.
37. See H.-J. HERMISSON, *Observations on the Creation Theology in Wisdom*, in GAMMIE, *op. cit.* (n. 22), pp. 43-57.

Yahweh's wrath is expressed by *disaster* in the *streets* (24,10.11; 27,20.21). It is difficult to deny the resemblances with what has been discussed above. Other related ideas come from the Jewish tradition of David's removing and replacing the shard over the pit at the time of the building of the Temple in Jerusalem[38]. The ark's coming to rest on Mount Ararat and the waters subsiding fall in the same category as that of the shard which stops the waters gushing up from the deep (pit). According to later traditions the Child cast stones in the well at Bethlehem, while the star of the Magi fell into the same well (see Rev 8,4ff; 9,1; 19,20; 20,10.14)[39].

The Biblical author(s) of Qohelet thus probably used the mythical imagery concerned for their own purposes, perhaps without fully associating themselves with myths containing information of the Universe any longer. However, this suggestion calls for further study.

5 Pinegrove Place   H.A.J. KRUGER
3610 Pinetown
South Africa

38. L. GINZBERG, *The Legends of the Jews* (trans. H. Szold), Philadelphia, Jewish Publication Society, 1947, Vol. IV, p. 96.
39. DE SANTILLANA – VON DECHEND, *op. cit.* (n. 5), pp. 219ff, 422-424.

QOHELET 12,1a: A RELATIVELY UNIQUE STATEMENT
IN ISRAEL'S WISDOM TRADITION[1]

In the rapidly changing society of the third century B.C.E.[2] Qohelet deals with an understanding of human life. The main theme of the Book of Qohelet is man, as W. Zimmerli rightly stated[3], more explicitly man in relationship to God, to man and to life and death. In his book, in which observation and instruction complexes occur in alternation[4], he tries to offer a modus vivendi.

In my opinion, Qohelet holds no optimistic view of man. In Qohelet's view he is a suppressor of man (e.g. Qoh 3,16; 4,1), without helping each other (Qoh 4,1). He is mortal, transient (Qoh 5,17.19); youth and strength are temporary (Qoh 9,9; 11,10), although God had laid עולם in him (Qoh 3,11), eternity[5], that is: his רוח (Qoh 12,7). Man pursues הבל. In my opinion, the term הבל in Qohelet points to different things; I see the following meanings of the word הבל in the Book of Qohelet: it points to the absurdity[6] or vanity[7] of human acting (Qoh 2,11), secondly to the incomprehensibility[8], the enigma[9] of life (Qoh 3,11), and thirdly it points to the fact that man and things are fading away[10]. Qohelet argues that man has to live accepting the limitedness of life (Qoh 5,17-19; 9,7-

1. I should like to express my gratitude to drs. M. van Krimpen, who gave me valuable suggestions for improving the English translation.

2. See e.g. D. MICHEL, *Koheletbuch*, in *TRE* 19, Berlin-New York, 1990, 345-356, p. 352; O. KAISER, *Qoheleth*, in J. DAY – R.P. GORDON – H.G.M. WILLIAMSON (eds.), *Wisdom in Ancient Israel*. FS J.A. Emerton, Cambridge, 1995, pp. 83-93; ID., *Beiträge zur Kohelet-Forschung*, in *TR* 60 (1995) 1-31, p. 17; A. SCHOORS, *Qoheleth: A Book in a Changing Society*, in *OTE* 9 (1996) 68-87, pp. 68-72; C.R. HARRISON Jr., *Qoheleth Among the Sociologists*, in *BibInt* 5 (1997) 160-180.
3. W. ZIMMERLI, *"Unveränderbare Welt" oder "Gott ist Gott"? Ein Plädoyer für die Unaufgebbarkeit des Predigerbuches in der Bibel*, in H.G. GEYER e.a. (eds.), *Wenn nicht jetzt, wann dann?* FS H.-J. Kraus, Neukirchen, 1983, pp. 103-114, esp. 110-111.
4. S. DE JONG, *A Book on Labour: The Structuring Principles and the Main Theme of the Book of Qohelet*, in *JSOT* 54 (1992) 107-116.
5. Cf. N. LOHFINK, *The Present and Eternity: Time in Qoheleth*, in *TD* 34 (1987) 236-240, p. 239: "eternal referent". R.E. MURPHY, *On Translating Ecclesiastes*, in *CBQ* 53 (1991) 571-579, p. 573, translates 'temporal duration'; in his view eternity is too strong.
6. M.V. FOX, *The Meaning of HEBEL for Qohelet*, in *JBL* 105 (1986) 409-427.
7. D. BERGANT, *Vanity (Hebel)*, in *The Bible Today* 22 (1984) 91-92.
8. MURPHY, *On Translating* (n. 5), p. 573.
9. G.S. OGDEN, *'Vanity' it certainly is not*, in *BTrans* 38 (1987) 301-307.
10. N. LOHFINK, *Von Windhauch, Gottesfurcht und Gottes Antwort in der Freude*, in *BiKi* 45 (1990) 26-32, p. 26.

12)[11]. In this life under the shadow of death, man is summoned to enjoy life as long as it is possible. Man has to enjoy life because life is a gift of God (Qoh 3,11-14; 5,17) and man is God's creation (Qoh 3,11; 7,29; 11,5). Life is to be lived in fellowship with others (Qoh 4,12), with industry (Qoh 4,5; 10,18), and with care (Qoh 11:1-6).

Qohelet's central ethical instruction is *carpe diem*[12]. It is typical of Qohelet that this instruction is founded in creation theology.

An example of Qohelet's use of creation theology can be found in Qoh 12,1a, וזכר את בוראיך בימי בחורתיך. Three remarkable elements can be found in this statement:

1. In biblical wisdom literature the verb ברא occurs only here[13];
2. In biblical wisdom literature only here and in Job 32,22; 35,10 a personal relationship between God and man is supposed;
3. The word combination בימי בחורתיך occurs in the Old Testament only here and in Qoh 11,9 (בימי בחורותך).

In my opinion Qoh 12,1a is part of the pericope Qoh 11,7 -12,7. The demarcation of the pericope of which Qoh 12,1a forms a part, is object of much discussion. I list some views: Qoh 11:1-12:8[14]; Qoh 11,1-12,7[15]; Qoh 11,7-12,8[16]; Qoh 11,7-12,7[17]; Qoh 11,9-12,8[18]; Qoh 11,9-12,7[19]; Qoh 11,9-12,6[20]; Qoh 12,1-8[21]; Qoh 12,1-7[22].

---

11. E. SCHEFFLER, *Qohelet's Positive Advice*, in *OTE* 6 (1993) 248-271.

12. L.G. PERDUE, *Wisdom and Creation. The Theology of Wisdom Literature*, Nashville, 1994, pp. 237ff.; L. SCHWIENHORST-SCHÖNBERGER, *»Nicht im Menschen gründet das Glück« (Koh. 2,24). Kohelet im Spannungsfeld jüdischer Weisheit und hellenistischer Philosophie* (HBS, 2), Freiburg u.a., ²1996.

13. S. LEE, *Power Not Novelty: The Connotations of* ברא *in the Hebrew Bible*, in A.G. AULD (ed.), *Understanding Poets and Prophets*, FS G.W. Anderson (JSOT SS, 152), Sheffield, 1993, pp. 199-212, esp. 210.

14. G.A. BARTON, *A Critical and Exegetical Commentary on the Book of Ecclesiastes* (ICC), Edinburgh, 1993, pp. 179ff; D.C. FREDERICKS, *Life's Storms and Structural Unity in Qoheleth 11.1-12.8*, in *JSOT* 52 (1991) 95-114.

15. A. FISCHER, *Skepsis oder Furcht Gottes? Studien zur Komposition und Theologie des Buches Kohelet* (BZAW, 247), Berlin-New York, 1997, p. 252.

16. R.B.Y. SCOTT, *Proverbs. Ecclesiastes* (AB, 18), Garden City (NY), ²1974, pp. 253ff; M.V. FOX, *Qohelet and his Contradictions* (JSOT SS 71), Sheffield, 1989, p. 156; G.S. OGDEN, *Qoheleth xi 7 – xii 8: Qoheleth's Summons to Enjoyment and Reflection*, in *VT* 34 (1984) 27-38; R.E. MURPHY, *Ecclesiastes* (WBC, 23A), Dallas 1992, pp. 111ff; M.J.H. VAN NIEKERK, *Qohelet's Advice to the Young of His Time – and to Ours Today? Chapter 11:7-12:8 as a Text of the Pre-Christian Era*, in *OTE* 7 (1994) 370-380; J.A. LOADER, *Prediker* (T&T), Kampen, ²1995, pp. 147ff; C.-L. SEOW, *Ecclesiastes* (AB, 18C), New York e.a., 1997, pp. 47 and 346ff.

17. A. LAUHA, *Kohelet* (BK, XIX), Neukirchen-Vluyn, 1978, pp. 204ff; H. WITZENRATH, *Süß ist das Licht...: Eine literaturwissenschaftliche Untersuchung zu Koh 11,7-12,7* (ATSAT, 11), St. Ottilien, 1979; J.L. CRENSHAW, *Ecclesiastes* (OTL), Philadelphia, 1987, pp. 181ff; J. NEGENMAN, *Prediker* (Belichting van het Bijbelboek), Boxtel –

I choose the above-mentioned demarcation on account of the following arguments:

- The pericope Qoh 11,1-6 is a self-contained unit, with its own theme. In Qoh 11,7 the theme is changing,
- Qoh 12,8 is redactional, due to the clause אמר הקוהלת[23]. This verse repeats the idea of Qoh 1,2. Together these verses form an inclusion[24].

Within this pericope Qoh 11,7-12,7 one can find two inclusions:

- ימי בחור(ו)ת(י)ך   Qoh 11,9; 12,1
- נתן רוח – ברא   Qoh 12,1.7. God is subject of both verbs. In Ps 104,30, תשלח רוחך יבראון, ברא and שלח רוח are paralleled[25].

The following terms relate Qoh 11,7-8 with the continuation:

- הבל   Qoh 11,8.10
- זכר   Qoh 11,8; 12,1
- עינים   Qoh 11,7.9
- שמח   Qoh 11,8.9

Leuven – Brugge, 1988, pp. 84 and 92; Chr. KLEIN, *Kohelet und die Weisheit Israels. Eine formgeschichtliche Studie* (BWANT, 132), Stuttgart – Berlin – Köln, 1994, p. 150; J.S. REITMAN, *The Structure and Unity of Ecclesiastes*, in *BS* 154 (1997) 297-319, p. 319.

18. N. LOHFINK, *'Freu dich, junger Mann...' Das Schlußgedicht des Koheletbuches (Koh 11,9-12,8)*, in *BiKi* 45 (1990) 12-19; ID., *Grenzen und Einbindung des Kohelet-Schlußgedichts*, in P. MOMMER e.a. (eds.), *Altes Testament – Forschung und Wirkung*, FS H. Graf Reventlow, Frankfurt etc., 1994, pp. 33-46; ID., *Freu dich, Jüngling – doch nicht, weil du jung bist. Zum Formproblem im Schlussgedicht Kohelets (Koh 11,9-12,8)*, in *BibInt* 3 (1995) 158-189.

19. D. MICHEL, *Qohelet* (EdF, 258), Darmstadt, 1988, p. 166; L.G. PERDUE, *Wisdom* (n. 12), p. 232.

20. H.-P. MÜLLER, *Der unheimliche Gast. Zum Denken Kohelets*, in *ZTK* 84 (1987) 440-464, p. 442.

21. M.A. BEEK, *Prediker, Hooglied* (POT), Nijkerk, 1984, p. 127; M.V. FOX, *Aging and Death in Qohelet 12*, in *JSOT* 42 (1988) 55-77; B.C. DAVIS, *Ecclesiastes 12:1-8 – Death, an Impetus for Life*, in *BS* 148 (1991) 299-318.

22. F. ROUSSEAU, *Structure de Qohelet I 4-11 et plan du livre*, in *VT* 31 (1981) 200-217, p. 213.

23. KLEIN, *Kohelet* (n. 17), p. 150.

24. W. ZIMMERLI, *Das Buch Kohelet – Traktat oder Sentenzensammlung?*, in *VT* 24 (1974) 221-230, p. 228; J.L. CRENSHAW, *Ecclesiastes* (n. 17), p. 189.

25. In Qoh 3,14 occurs the combination of creation [עשה] and ירא. God creates, God acts, 'so that man will fear before him.' The consequence of Gods acting as a Creator is that man fears God. The theme of the fear of God occurs further in Qoh 5,6; 7,18; 8,12-13 and 12,13. In my opinion the advice זכר את בוראיך is a synonym of the advice 'fear God!'. In the Old Testament the terms זכר and ירא occur sometimes in one context, e.g. Isa 54,4; 57,11; Ps 111,5. So this may be a wider inclusion in Qoh 12.

I conclude from these data that the statement of Qoh 12,1a has a two-fold function: it is the conclusion of Qoh 11,7ff (a passage existing of 10 lessons[26]) and the introduction of Qoh 12,1ff (the description of the last part of life and the death). The pericope Qoh. 11,7-12,7 can thus be divided into three parts: Qoh 11,7-8 / 9-12,1a / 12,1a-7. For that reason I disagree with G.S. Ogden; in his opinion the הבל-phrases in Qoh 11,8.10 and 12,8 have a concluding function[27]. The theme of the passage Qoh 12,1a-7 is clear. Here the dismantling of life in the old age is described. Man is mortal. At the very end death comes. The second part, Qoh 11,9-12,1a, is addressed to man in the prime[28] of life. In the contrast within the pericope בחור denotes not only the youth, but the man who is active, who has the power to go wherever he wants (Qoh 9,7-10). In Qoh 11,7-8 the themes of life and death (the "days of darkness") are introduced.

Nearly at the end of his book Qohelet summarizes his teachings. Themes which he developed in foregoing parts of the book, are repeated. The themes of life and death that dominate the pericope Qoh 11,7-12,7, are present in the whole book. The theme of death is elaborated in Qoh 12,1ff more explicitly than elsewhere in the book. Qoh 11,7ff has the same combination of the words שמח and זכר as Qoh 5,17-19[29]. The verb נתן (Qoh 5,17.18) returns in Qoh 12,7. The notion that God is the Creator of all, developed in Qoh 3,11-14; 7,14.29; 11,5, returns in Qoh 12,1a. Here Qohelet makes use of Israels particular creation terminology -ברא- to denote God as the Creator[30].

However, the term בוראיך is much disputed. Commentators draw attention to the fact that God is always called אלהים (37x) in Qoheleth, secondly to the fact that a religious exhortation -to remember God- is not fitting at this point[31]. Some commentators expect an exhortation to think about death or an exhortation "to reflect on the joys of female compan-

---

26. 1. Qoh 11,8: בכלם ישמח
   2. Qoh 11,8: ויזכר את ימי החשך
   3. Qoh 11,9: שמח בחור בילדותיך
   4. Qoh 11,9: ויטיבך לבך בימי בחורותך
   5. Qoh 11,9: והלך בדרכי לבך
   6. Qoh 11,9: (והלך)במראי עיניך
   7. Qoh 11,9: ודע כי על כל אלה יביאך האלהים במשפט
   8. Qoh 11,10: והסר כעס מלבך
   9. Qoh 11,10: והעבר רעה מבשרך
   10. Qoh 12,1: זכר את בוראיך בימי בחורתיך

27. OGDEN, *Qoheleth xi 7 – xii 8* (n. 16), pp. 29-30.
28. SEOW, *Ecclesiastes* (n. 16), p. 346.
29. OGDEN, *Qoheleth xi 7 – xii 8* (n. 16), pp. 35ff.
30. MÜLLER, *Der unheimliche Gast* (n. 20), p. 453.
31. R.B. SALTERS, *Exegetical Problems in Qoheleth*, in *Irish Biblical Studies* 10 (1988) 44-59, pp. 56-57.

ionship before old age and death render one incapable of sensual pleasure"[32].

Some alternatives have been proposed. Some exegetes delete Qoh 12,1a[33]. A. Lauha writes in the introduction to his commentary on Qohelet[34]: "... sein Gott ist nicht der Gott des israelitischen Glaubens: das Verhältnis des Menschen zu Gott ist bei ihm anders als allgemein im Alten Testament. Kohelet kennt jenen Gott nicht, der für den Menschen ein »Du« ist und mit dem man ein Gespräch haben kann.... Gott ist fern.... Für den alttestamentlichen Glauben ist zuversichtliches Vertrauen charakteristisch. Das kennt Kohelet nicht. Er hat nur Achtung vor dem unbegreiflichen Despoten." M.V. Fox offers an important counter-argument: when Qoh 12,1a is deleted, Qoh 12,1b-7 lacks its main clause, he rightly states[35]. Sometimes the text is emended: בורך, "your pit", that is: 'your grave'[36], בארך, "your well", as metaphor for 'your wife' (Prov 5,15)[37], בראיך or בריך, "your health"[38]. When Qoh 11,7-12,7 is read not as an isolated pericope in the Book of Qohelet, but as a part of the whole Book of Qohelet, than the theme 'creation' does not surprise. In the pericope Qoh 3,11-19 we can find the same cluster of themes: life – creation – שמח – death. Moreover, the image of God as a Creator often occurs in Israels wisdom literature[39].

By means of the possessive pronoun Qoh 12,1a has been phrased as a personal advice, like Qoh 11,9-10. Mostly Qohelet's vocabulary is descriptive; yet more passages in the book have been formulated as a personal advice like Qoh 12,1a: 2,1; 4,17-5,7; 7,9-14; 7,16-22; 8,3; 9,7-10; 10,4; 10,20-11,6. The personal pronoun in בוראיך has its influence on the meaning of the term ברא. S. Lee concludes at the end of her article on ברא that the verb carries the connotation of divine sovereignty and power. This power is here part of a relationship. Neither in the Book of Proverbs nor elsewhere in the Book of Qohelet such a personal relationship between God and man is supposed, only in Job 32,22, עשני, and Job 35,10, עשי. That is the relative uniqueness of the statement in Qoh 12,1a.

32. CRENSHAW, Ecclesiastes (n. 17), p. 185.
33. BARTON, Ecclesiastes (n. 14), p. 185; LAUHA, Kohelet (n. 17), pp. 204 and 209; MICHEL, Qohelet (n. 19), pp. 166-167.
34. LAUHA, Kohelet (n. 17), p. 17.
35. FOX, Aging and Death (n. 21), p. 72.
36. E.g. SCOTT, Proverbs. Ecclesiastes (n. 16), p. 253.
37. E.g. CRENSHAW, Ecclesiastes (n. 17), pp. 181 and 185.
38. J.R. BUSTO SAIZ, בוראיך(Qoh. 12,1), Reconsiderado, in Sef 46 (1986) 85-87; R.B. SALTERS, Exegetical Problems (n. 31), p. 57.
39. PERDUE, Wisdom (n. 12); S. DE JONG, God in the Book of Qohelet: A Reappraisal of Qohelet's Place in Old Testament Theology, in VT 47 (1997) 154-167, pp. 165-166.

In the Old Testament the participle בֹּרֵא is used 13x in respect to God: Isa 40,28; 42,5; 43,1.15; 45,7 (2x).18; 57,19; 65,17.18 (2x); Amos 4,13; Qoh 12,1. Only in Isa 43,1 and Qoh 12,1 a possessive pronoun is connected to this participle. In Isa 43,1 the participle occurs in the singular, in Qoh. 12:1 in the plural. This plural, mostly not translated, however, is essential. It agrees with the plural אלהים. The plural expresses that God is the God *par excellence* and the Creator *par excellence*, the real God and the real Creator. In its contents Qoh 12,1 is in harmony with Isa 45,12; 54,5. In Isa 45,12 mankind is depicted as a creation of God, in Qoh 12,1 the individual man. One finds here an important connection between prophecy and wisdom. In my opinion the Book of Qohelet has to be read not only separately, but also as a part of the canon. It has many elements in common with other books. In my opinion it is possible that Qohelet quotes Deutero-Isaiah in Qoh 12,1a; at least Qoh 12,1a is a reaction on Deutero-Isaiah. However, Deutero-Isaiah's theology of redemption is completely lacking in Qohelet.

Qohelet's God is a remote God. Man is not capable of finding out the work of that God (Qoh 8,17; 11,5). In Qohelet's opinion there is an immense gap between God and man (Qoh 5,1). S. de Jong rightly observes the strong concentration on the limitation of man in comparison with God's greatness[40]. Yet at the end of the book Qohelet tries to bridge this gap. Just as in Israel's prophecy, in the Book of Qohelet a personal relation between God and man is indicated, although on only one single place. Man is not on his own. The God who has to be feared, is the Creator of man. So Qohelet indicates a basic security for man. Hence this anonymous speaker with his own accents has to be placed not too far from the mainstream of Old Testament theology[41].

Oranjestraat 17   A.J.O. VAN DER WAL
NL-2131 XN Hoofddorp

40. DE JONG, *God in the Book of Qohelet* (n. 39), p. 166.
41. Cf. H. JAGERSMA, *Het boek Prediker*, in E. EYNIKEL (ed.), *Wie wijsheid zoekt, vindt het Leven. De wijsheidsliteratuur van het Oude Testament*, Leuven-Boxtel 1991, pp. 105-117, esp. 115-116.

CHARACTER AND COSMOLOGY
RHETORIC OF QOH 1,3-3,9

Recently, C. L. Seow has demonstrated that by imitating the style of the royal inscription, Qoheleth highlights his achievements as king in Qoh 1,12-2,11 and subsequently shows their ephemerality[1]. This insightful proposal raises other questions: How then does Qoheleth specifically point out the ephemerality of his own achievements? and Why does he do so at the beginning of his discourse?

Before directly responding to the questions above, I will at first defend the unity of Qoh 1,3-3,9 by identifying certain key rhetorical techniques by which Qoheleth's argument proceeds.

As Figure 1 indicates, 1,3-3,9 exhibits a chiasm[2]: The whole unit is framed by both the thematic question, "What is the net gain?" (1,3 [A]; 3,9 [A']) and two poems about cosmology (1,4-11 [B]; 3,2-8 [B'])[3]. The middle section, 1,12-3,1 [C], also displays a chiasm which is signaled by the repetition of certain words: 1,12-15 [C1] begins with תַּחַת הַשָּׁמַיִם and עִנְיָן רָע נָתַן (1,13), which Qoheleth repeats in 2,24-3,1 [C1']; while 1,16-18 [C2] concludes with 1) הוּא plus the *hebel* judgment (1,17b) and 2) the words כַּעַס and מַכְאוֹב (1,18), 2,12-23 [C2'] ends with the same words in reversed order (2,23); and 2,1-11 [C3] begins and ends with the particle הִגֵּה and the *hebel* judgment (2,1, 11).

In addition to the chiastic structure, 1,12-3,1 [C] exhibits three rhetorical techniques that compel Qoheleth's audience to acknowledge the continuity of his argument[4].

---

1. C. L. SEOW, *Qohelet's Autobiography*, in A.B. BECK et al. (eds.), *Fortunate the Eyes That See: Essays in Honor of David Noel Freedman in Celebration of His Seventieth Birthday*, Grand Rapids, 1995, pp. 275-287.

2. On other opinions of the chiastic structure of cc. 1-3, see C. L. SEOW, *Ecclesiastes* (AB, 18C), New York, 1997, pp. 142-144; A. FISCHER, *Beobachtungen zur Komposition von Kohelet 1,3-3,15*, in ZAW 103 (1991) 72-86. FISCHER has already pointed out the inclusio of the thematic questions in 1,3 and 3,9 (*ibid.*).

3. Here, cosmology means "how the world is understood to work." H. GESE has already noticed the existence of two forms of order expressed by the two poems. See *Crisis of Wisdom in Koheleth*, in J. CRENSHAW (ed.), *Theodicy in the Old Testament* (Issues in Religion and Theology, 4), Philadelphia, 1983, pp. 141-153, esp. 147-148.

4. I omit the evidence of the continuity of 1,12-2,11. For that matter, see SEOW, *Qohelet's Autobiography* (n. 1), p. 275; E. BONS, *Zur Gliederung und Kohärenz von Koh 1,12-2,11*, in BN 24 (1984) 73-93.

Figure 1: Structure of Qoh 1.3-3.9

A. Thematic Question (1.3)

   B. Cosmology I (1.4-11)

      C. Main argument (1.12-3.1)
         1. Introduction: Qoheleth as king (1.12-15)
         2. Qoheleth as the wisest (1.16-18)
            3. Qoheleth as the wealthiest (2.1-11)
         2'. Qoheleth's character deconstructed by wisdom (2.12-23)
      1'. Conclusion: God as decision-maker (2.24-3.1)

   B'. Cosmology II (3.2-8)

A'. Thematic Question Revisited (3.9)

First, 2,24-3,1 [C1'] is symmetrical to 1,12-15 [C1]: Each unit begins with a remark (1,12-14a; 2,24-26bα), moves to the *hebel* judgment (1,14b; 2,26bβ), and closes with a short saying (1,15; 3,1). This symmetry between 1,12-15 [C1] and 2,24-3,1 [C1'], on the one hand, supports my proposal for the chiastic structure of 1,12-3,1. On the other hand, it highlights differences of emphasis between 1,12-15 [C1] and 2,24-3,1 [C1']: an autobiographical remark focusing on Qoheleth (1,12-14a) versus a concluding statement focusing primarily on God (2,24-26bα); "All is *hebel*" (1,14b) versus "This is also *hebel*" (2,26bβ); simple parallelism (1,15) versus chiastic parallelism (3,1).

Second, Qoheleth uses anaphora, the "repetition of the same word at the beginning of successive clauses"[5], in 2,11-12 and 2,17-18. In the former Qoheleth employs וּפָנִיתִי אֲנִי ("I turned") in 2,11a and repeats it in 2,12a; in the latter וְשָׂנֵאתִי ("I hated") is found in 2,17a and 2,18a. Moreover, each anaphora brackets the *hebel* judgment (2,11b.17b), and each *hebel* judgment is characterized by the following elements: 1) both contain the expression, הֶבֶל וּרְעוּת רוּחַ, which recurs four times in 1,12-3,1 (1,14b; 2,11b.17b.26bβ; cf. 4,4; 6,9); 2) the subject of each sentence is הַכֹּל ("everything"), which is employed as the subject of the *hebel* judgment only three times in 1,12-3,1 (1,14b; 2,11b. 17b; cf. 3,19); and 3) each *hebel* judgment begins with a particle (וְהִנֵּה in 2,11b and כִּי in 2,17b), which is also true in 1,14b (וְהִנֵּה).

Against many commentators who have suggested that the *hebel* judgments in 2,11b and 2,17b evaluate only what is discussed immediately prior (2,3-10 and 2,12-16 respectively)[6], I would propose another way to

---

5. P. TRIBLE, *Rhetorical Criticism: Context, Method, and the Book of Jonah*, Minneapolis, 1994, p. 248.

6. For example, it has been suggested that the subject of the first *hebel* judgment is

explain the function of the *hebel* judgment in conjunction with anaphora. There is a technique called prolepsis, a rhetorical device that features "an attribute or epithet that will have relevancy later"[7]. This technique is applicable here; the *hebel* judgments in 2,11b and 2,17b are prolepses, evoking in advance a general conclusion that will become apparent later (2,18-23). Qoheleth presents a conclusion of his argument to his audience in the middle of the discourse without providing sufficient reasons for such a conclusion. Furthermore, the anaphora in 2,11-12 and 2,17-18 functions as a repetitive resumption to indicate the continuation of the discourse. Thus, while a general conclusion is given in advance, Qoheleth can continue his argument from 2,1-11 to 2,12-17 to 2,18-23.

Third, there is paronomasia, "a wordplay on similarly sounding words"[8], between 2,3b and 2,24a. Whereas the question in 2,3b starts with אֵי־זֶה טוֹב, the sentence in 2,24a begins with אֵין־טוֹב. The difference between the two is the demonstrative, which comprises only one syllable. Moreover, אֵי־זֶה is usually translated as "which?", in the sense of "choosing one out of two or many"[9], instead of "what?" as in 2,3b, which is the only attestation of this usage in Biblical Hebrew[10]. The evidence above, thus, suggests that 2,24a is a conclusion in response to Qoheleth's search for goodness in human life declared in 2,3b.

My analysis so far suggests that 2,12-3,1 is not an independent unit but the continuation of 1,12-2,11. How, then, does Qoheleth deconstruct his own achievement in 2,12-3,1? In other words, how does Qoheleth show the ephemerality of his unchallenged, authoritative position of power and wisdom as king (1,12; 1,16; 2,9a)?

First, he introduces himself as king in 1,12 and deconstructs the superiority of his kingship in 2,12b[11]. Qoheleth does not find any uniqueness

"portion" in 2,10 (G. Ogden, *Qoheleth*, Sheffield, 1987, p. 42); "pleasure" in 2,10 (R. N. Whybray, *Ecclesiastes* (NCBC), Grand Rapids, 1989, p. 55); or "labor and toil" (M.V. Fox, *Qohelet and His Contradictions* (JSOT SS, 71), Sheffield, 1989, p. 39).

7. R.A. Lanham, *A Handlist of Rhetorical Terms: A Guide for Students of English Literature*, Berkeley, 1968, p. 81.

8. Trible, *Rhetorical Criticism* (n. 5), p. 250.

9. 11,6 is a good example of this usage.

10. L. Koehler – W. Baumgartner (eds.), *The Hebrew Lexicon of the Old Testament*, vol. 1, trans. M. E. J. Richardson, Leiden, 1994, p. 38.

11. A short comment is needed on 2,12b. In 1,12-3,1, the word מֶלֶךְ is seen only here and in 1,12, where Qoheleth introduces himself as "king over Israel in Jerusalem." In 1,12-3,1, the word "Jerusalem" is only found twice other than in 1,12 (1,16; 2,9b); in both verses Qoheleth claims his superiority (wisdom and wealth) over anyone who was in Jerusalem. Hence, it is possible to regard 1,12 (kingship) as another self-characterization of Qoheleth to claim his superiority over others.

What, then, is distinctive about kingship if not wisdom and wealth? 2,12b says that, since any king, including Qoheleth himself, does whatever his predecessors have already done, kingship itself will not grant Qoheleth any superiority to others in terms of *what*

in being king, because a king only repeats what has been done by other kings before; kingship alone cannot provide any superiority because of the repetitive nature of projects that a king undertakes. Interestingly, this repetitive nature of reality has already been expressed in 1,10, where Qoheleth declares that there is nothing new under the sun and uses the word "כְּבָר" ("already"), which is also present in 2,12b. Kingship, defined as the king's ability to do many different projects, shares the same characteristic of repetition with the first cosmology in 1,4-11.

Second, Qoheleth characterizes himself as the wisest king in Jerusalem in 1,16, declares his intention to utilize this wisdom to know more about wisdom and folly in 1,17a, and begins reflecting on wisdom and folly in 2,12a. This reflection leads Qoheleth to conclude that there is no profit for the wise over the fool because both will be forgotten and die (2,16). Since death visits all, and both the wise and the fool are soon forgotten, is the distinction between the wise and the fool ultimately meaningful? Notably, the lack of remembrance (זִכָּרוֹן) in human affairs has already been pointed out in 1,11, which is the last line of the poem on the first cosmology (1,4-11).

Finally, Qoheleth examines his self-characterization as the wealthiest. This is closely linked to Qoheleth's search for profit and goodness in 1,12-2,11, where Qoheleth begins to test everything under the sun with wisdom (2,3). After producing much wealth as a result of his search (2,4-8), Qoheleth sees himself as "the greatest in possession of cattle" (2,7b) and "the greatest of all" (2,9a), that is, the wealthiest king of all who have been in Jerusalem before. However, this self-characterization is deconstructed in 2,18-19, where Qoheleth considers the one who will inherit his wealth: he has to give it away as inheritance to someone whom he himself cannot determine. Apparently, the impact of death is implicit in Qoheleth's argument here because the absence of the owner is necessary for someone to inherit the wealth of that person. Death is closely related to the non-remembering reality expressed in 1,11, as noted before, and the reality of death deconstructs the superiority of Qoheleth's self-characterization as the wealthiest.

---

kind of project he can undertake. Qoheleth distinguishes the ability to undertake a variety of projects from the accumulated result of these projects, that is, wealth. In other words, kingship, as is defined by Qoheleth, is about the ability to carry out *different projects*, but wealth is about the sum of what a human can produce out of many projects. Thus, in 2,12b Qoheleth says the following: although a king claims his superiority over others based on his ability to undertake projects different from them, this claim of superiority is invalid because of the repetitive nature of the king's projects; some projects appearing new are not new. Moreover, since Qoheleth's kingship is at stake in 2,12b, כִּי at the beginning of 2,12b functions as a causal particle: *because* kingship, the ability to carry out different projects, provides no superiority to others (2,12b), Qoheleth omits kingship from his reflection and moves to discuss wisdom (2,12a).

To conclude, in 2,12-3,1 Qoheleth reflects on his self-characterization as the wisest, wealthiest king in conjunction with the poem on the first cosmology in 1,4-11, and it is this cosmology that deconstructs his own unchallenged position as king, which he assumed in 1,12-2,11.

Why, then, does Qoheleth do as he does in 1,12-3,1? On the surface level, Qoheleth demonstrates the ephemerality of his self-characterization as the wisest, wealthiest king, but what is the impact of 1,12-3,1 upon Qoheleth's whole argument? I will suggest three implications.

First, Qoheleth points out that the prerogatives which kingship entails, such as ability to do a variety of projects, wisdom to obtain profit, and accumulated wealth, are not ultimately profitable for humanity, because what is unavoidable for Qoheleth, who as king possesses such prerogatives, is surely unavoidable for those not enjoying his position. Qoheleth deals with a similar theme on wealth later (e.g., 5,10-17; 6,1-6) and argues its ephemerality as well as its unprofitability.

Second, Qoheleth clarifies how God rules human affairs. At the very beginning, Qoheleth claims to be able to decide what projects to undertake in 2,1-11 (2,10a), in spite of the fact that God is the inscrutable taskmaster (1,13b.15). However, after reflecting on wisdom and wealth, Qoheleth acknowledges that enjoyment is available only through God, not through his own wisdom or wealth (2,24). Thus, the focus of 1,12-3,1 moves from Qoheleth (1,12-15 [C1]) to God (2,24-3,1 [C1'])[12]. How, then, can Qoheleth correlate God to his reflection without mentioning God in 1,16-2,23?

As mentioned above, the first cosmology in 1,4-11 supports Qoheleth's argument to deconstruct his own achievement and leads him to acknowledge that God rules human affairs. Thus, the connection between God and cosmology is clear: Qoheleth seems to imply that cosmology represents how God the ruler deals with human life. This relationship between God and cosmology becomes explicit later when Qoheleth reflects on the second cosmology (3,2-8 [B']): God does everything suitably according to its timing (3,11a). The second cosmology represents how God determines the timing of a variety of activities in human affairs.

Finally, Qoheleth begins to characterize himself as a sage who is able to correlate cosmology to human affairs. It has been acknowledged that

12. The asymmetry between 1,12-15 [C1] and 2,24-3,1 [C1'] is illuminating in this regard: instead of Qohelet (1,12-15 [C1]), God is in the spotlight in 2,24-3,1 [C1']; while the autobiographical style is attributed to Qoheleth in 1,12-15 [C1], the first common singular personal pronoun in 2,24-3,1 [C1'] refers to God (2,25)! See J. DE WAARD, *The Translator and Textual Criticism (with Particular Reference to Eccl 2, 25)*, in *Bib* 60 (1979) 509-529 for a text-critical analysis of 2,25.

Qoheleth's self-characterization as king is not sustained beyond chapter 2[13]. Rather, as my analysis above has shown, Qoheleth presents himself as king, only in order to deconstruct the unchallenged, authoritative position that kingship represents. Thus, his self-characterization as king is merely a means to achieve certain goals, namely, to point out the ephemerality of human achievements and to portray God as the inscrutable ruler. At the same time, the very deconstruction of Qoheleth's self-characterization suggests that Qoheleth the speaker can correlate cosmology to human affairs in a remarkably profound way: the correlation is the very means by which he deconstructs his own authoritative position.

Who, then, can correlate cosmology to human affairs? The chiastic pairing of 1,16-18 (C2: Qoheleth as the wisest) and 2,12-23 (C2': Qoheleth's character deconstructed by wisdom) sheds some light on this. Though Qoheleth denies the superiority of wisdom to folly (2,12-17), he reflects on human achievements through the very wisdom of which he has the most (1,16-18; cf. 1,13a; 2,3). There is a slight differentiation with regard to the role of wisdom here. It is wisdom-as-the-means-to-gain-superiority-to-folly that Qoheleth deconstructs; however, he still treasures wisdom-as-the-means-to-reflect-on-human-affairs[14]. In some areas wisdom still triumphs. Thus, Qoheleth begins to characterize himself as a sage who has wisdom to reflect on human affairs in terms of cosmology. Qoheleth's self-characterization as a sage fits well with the statement of the epilogist (12,9) as well as with Qoheleth's own statement in 8,1-2.

Qoheleth is portrayed as a skilled rhetorician: he is able to imitate an Ancient Near Eastern genre, to characterize himself as someone who is superior to anyone imaginable, to deconstruct his self-characterization as king in order to re-characterize himself as sage, to correlate human affairs to cosmology, and to prepare his audience for points that Qoheleth is about to make later. It is this very ability to speak well that may have prompted his name "the preacher"[15].

Union Theological Seminary in Virginia   Naoto KAMANO
3401 Brook Road
Richmond, VA 23227, U.S.A.

13. See, for example, J.L. CRENSHAW, *Ecclesiastes* (OTL), Philadelphia, 1987, p. 29.

14. Cf. See M.V. FOX, *Wisdom in Qoheleth*, in L.G. PERDUE et al. (eds.), *In Search of Wisdom: Essays in Memory of John G. Gammie*, Louisville, 1983, pp. 115-131. He divides wisdom in Ecclesiastes into three basic aspects: ingenuity, good sense, and intellect. The aspect of wisdom as intellect, which is unparalleled in other wisdom literature according to Fox, roughly corresponds to wisdom-as-the-means-to-reflect-on-human-affairs here.

15. I would like to thank William P. BROWN, Craig A. VONDERGEEST, and Brian D. RUSSEL for reading the earlier draft of this manuscript, refining my English, and offering insightful comments.

QOHELETH AND THE/HIS SELF
AMONG THE DECONSTRUCTED*

Heraclitus said some 25 centuries ago, 'You could not discover the limits of the self, even by travelling along every path: so deep a *logos* does it have' (frag. 45). So, the self is not a modern invention, but it has relatively recently undergone something of an ideological transmutation. It has transformed from something of which we could be certain, or of which we at least spoke confidently, to something so diverse and impossible to define that it is, as James Olney describes, 'infinitely difficult to get at...it bears no definition; it squirts like mercury away from our observation'[1]. The problem is culturally evident. In the early 1970s American popular culture suffered a 'minor crisis' when the notion was put about that the real Paul McCartney of the Beatles had died a few years previously and been replaced by the winner of a Paul McCartney look-alike contest. The furore ceased when people came to accept that as long as the face and the voice were essentially the same, it mattered little who the flesh and blood person actually was[2]. The veracity of Paul McCartney's self was reduced to the quality of an audio-visual image. Errol Flynn, that swashbuckling cinematic heartthrob of the 30s and 40s: impotent. Walt Disney, the supposed genius behind the early animated 'Disney' characters: could not draw Mickey Mouse to save his life. These are the judgments of a recent UK television series, BBC's *Reputations*, which examines inexplicable (or perhaps disturbingly explicable?) paradoxes between the private and public personas of such complex characters ranging from Bertrand Russell to John Wayne. The series is just one example of how traditional ways of talking about and defining the self — ways in which we understand a public or private persona, a visual[3] or textual persona — are being questioned and overturned.

* This paper is taken mostly from chapter 7, 'Qoheleth and the Self', of my *A Time to Tell: Narrative Strategies in Ecclesiastes* (JSOT SS), Sheffield, Sheffield Academic Press, forthcoming.
1. James OLNEY, *Metaphors of Self: The Meaning of Autobiography*, Princeton, New Jersey, Princeton University Press, 1972, p. 23.
2. So Michael SPRINKER, *Fictions of the Self: The End of Autobiography*, in J. OLNEY (ed.), *Autobiography: Essays Theoretical and Critical*, Princeton, Princeton University Press, 1980, p. 322.
3. Jonathan Alter, in an incisive piece on the O.J. Simpson case in *Newsweek International* ('Television's False Intimacy', 27 June 1994, p. 25), argued that the public at large fell victim to the false intimacy created by television. The Janus face of the television

Cultural concerns about the self are in turn reflected in our academic concerns. Questions of self are being raised in many quarters: cultural studies, history, literature, biblical studies. Critics inspired by Barthes, Foucault and Derrida have argued (to a wide and receptive audience) that the self is a construct determined by its socio-linguistic context, whose only reference is itself and nothing more. Authors can no longer hide behind texts for the simple reason that they are dead. As Barthes wrote in 1968, in his classic essay, *The Death of the Author*, the linguistic subject 'I' is 'empty outside of the very enunciation which defines it'[4], and at least one critic has observed that the death of the author has heralded the death of the self[5]. Stephen Best and Douglas Kellner state the case harshly: postmodern criticism has gone as far as to 'valorize' the 'pulverization of the modern subject'[6], and we have thereby been 'thrown into apocalyptic doubt about all previous beliefs about humanness and all courses of actions that such beliefs sustained'[7]. Anthony Paul Kerby neatly sums up the deconstructed position in his recent book, *Narrative and the Self*: 'self arises out of signifying practices rather than existing prior to them as an autonomous or Cartesian agent'[8]. This statement forces Kerby into the unfortunate position of regarding the computer named HAL in Stanley Kubrick's film *2001* as more of a person than a preverbal child[9]. The problem of referentiality is the most serious for the deconstructive theory of the subject[10], but most especially for Mr

personality given to the world is at one time friendly, yet born of violence. The visual image elicits judgments. We are invited to decide for ourselves who is speaking the truth. The frame of reference that people in the US made use of in their time of disillusionment was that of Simpson's media character, which, while familiar, was unknowable.

4. R. BARTHES, *The Death of the Author*, in ID., *Image, Music, Text* (ed. and trans. S. HEATH), London, Fontana Press, 1977, 142-48, p. 145.

5. So SPRINKER, *Fictions of the Self* (n. 2), pp. 324-25.

6. Steven Best and Douglas Kellner, cited in J. Richard MIDDLETON – Brian J. WALSH, *Truth Is Stranger Than it Used to Be* (Gospel and Culture), London, SPCK, 1995, p. 51.

7. MIDDLETON – WALSH, *loc. cit.*

8. A.P. KERBY, *Narrative and the Self* (Studies in Continental Thought), Bloomington, Indiana University Press, 1991, p. 1.

9. KERBY, *op. cit.*, pp. 70-71 and 123 n. 11.

10. Cf. KERBY, *op. cit.*, p. 14. See also Michel FOUCAULT, *What is an Author?*, in *Partisan Review* 42 (1975) 603-14, where he argues that the self (particularly as author) can no longer exist outside of its enunciation. Foucault's arguments suffer overall from the conflicting notions that writing refers only to itself, yet, in order for it to create the space through which the *subject* (does he mean author?) can continually disappear (which 'transference' is, for Foucault, the 'true' function of authorship) it must pass outside itself, by which is assumed a notion of self (see esp. pp. 604 and 608). This is, in my view, the most potent critique *against* the deconstruction of the subject: that in order for meaning to occur, some kind of *referential* movement (not necessarily metaphysical!) must take place. Further on the problem that referentiality poses to postmodernism, see B. POLKA, *Freud, Science, and the Psychoanalytic Critique of Religion: The Paradox of Self-Referentiality*, in *JAAR* 62/1 (1994) 59-81, esp. pp. 67-68, 74 and 78-81.

Kerby since he cannot exist. To summarize, then: the present impasse in speaking about the self is coming to terms with its death.

And what do we find when we turn to the most 'individual' book of the Old Testament? The story of a man who, as John Paterson said, suffers from 'I trouble', and whose 'ego seems to have few friends'[11]. Readers of autobiography naturally *expect* the source of its cohesion to be the author's self, and Qoheleth's text is, by any critical standard, an autobiography. His narration is fused together by an iterative first-person narrator. Whatever historicity the reader may or may not assume, one comes from Qoheleth's narrative with an impression (which some have thought overbearing) of individuality. This quality has inspired such titles of articles and books as *Old Man Koheleth*[12], *The Intimate Journal of an Old-Time Humanist* and *The Inner World of Qohelet*[13]. Qoheleth's use of the first-person form among the wisdom-oriented books of the Hebrew Bible is largely unique[14] and the relentless individualism of his narrative has prompted such labels as 'confessions', 'memoirs' and 'autobiography'. Like confessions or memoirs, autobiography is concerned with the events of the life of the primary narrator. The label 'autobiography', then, while seemingly anachronistic, is nonetheless appropriate.

Qoheleth's choice of the autobiographical form strikes me as strategic for his content matter; for, as Georges Gusdorf remarks, '[the autobiographer] believes it a useful and valuable thing to fix his own image so that he can be certain it will not disappear like all things in this world'[15]. This applies particularly well to Qoheleth who observed a traditionally stable 'realm of meaning' to be a 'pursuit of wind'. Qoheleth thus reflects and juxtaposes the life he narrates to us against the transience and absurdity that he has observed and knows to be real. A generation comes and another goes, the earth will remain and Qoheleth has ensured his place under the sun. (Ironically, *he* has been remembered and will doubtless continue to be.) His idea of self is in a sense easy to 'extract'

11. J. PATERSON, *The Intimate Journal of an Old-Time Humanist*, in *Religion in Life* 19.2 (1950) 245-54, p. 251.

12. E. STONE, *Old Man Koheleth*, in *Journal of Bible and Religion* 10 (1942) 98-102.

13. F. ZIMMERMANN, *The Inner World of Qohelet*, New York, Ktav, 1973.

14. For example, Proverbs strikes up the personal narrative posture only twice: 7,6-27 where the story of a senseless youth is told and 24,30-34 where the narrator offers an aetiology for the saying, 'A little sleep, a little slumber...' But cf. also, Prov 4,1-3, the Dame Wisdom speeches (1,22-33; 8,4-36) and the dialogue of 'the man' (נאם) to Ithiel and Ucal (30,1-9).

15. G. GUSDORF, *Conditions and Limits of Autobiography*, in OLNEY (ed.), *Autobiography* (n. 2), p. 30. William P. BROWN has, separately from myself, formulated part of this conclusion in arguing that Qoheleth immortalizes himself through the (royal) autobiographical form (*Character in Crisis*, Grand Rapids, Eerdmans, 1996, p. 122).

— it is not a discourse on the subject, obviously, but the concerns of what actually makes a person truly wise (and for Qoheleth this means truly human) are at the forefront more than in perhaps any other biblical text.

Qoheleth was a king (of sorts!), a builder of vineyards, of parks, of gardens; a wealthy man. He made these things *for himself* (לי, 'for me', is an operative word in his ch. 2 boastings). In other words, he virtually 'made' himself and leads us to believe that, as a result, he considered himself a man of great importance. That importance was both social and intellectual, for *he defined himself* in terms of status and material wealth. His intellectual ability had even become part of that status ('I said... "Behold, I have become great and increased in wisdom more than all who were before me over Jerusalem"', 1,16). It was this 'definition' of himself that he set out famously to test in ch. 2, wherein is found a full-blown interest in the constitution of his own self, one that results in a concern for action: What is the best humanity can do given their situation? (In this regard, it is no coincidence that most of Qoheleth's advice to his reader occurs towards the end of his narration, after the majority of his experiences have been related. As William Brown states, 'The bulk of the book...consists of a person who, like Job, shares his personal discoveries and bares his soul, but without dialogic partners'[16].)

To clarify the matter, in Qoheleth's concern for the formation of his own self is implied a wider view of the self. That is, his self-reflective language acts metaphorically as a way to understand the concept of self as a whole. His narrated experience is a way of observing the development of the self over the expanse of time. As autobiography it becomes a way for readers to examine the arenas in which the formation of the self might take place. We look hard at Qoheleth's self (he gives us no choice) and our gaze is returned.

Qoheleth's narrative further involves the process of 'redoubling' the self. As autobiographer, he is capable of distinguishing himself from his (narratorial) past point of view. That is, because he is aware that he is narrating his own subjective past (since the 'event of self-consciousness is inseparable from the history of saying "I"'[17]), he transcends it and creates two characters in the process: the one whom we envision writing or speaking — in real time — and the one about whom is written or of whom is spoken — in narrated time. Qoheleth sees himself seeing with the same eyes. He sees a youthful king who saw that his life was abhor-

---

16. BROWN, *Character in Crisis* (n. 15), p. 121.
17. Calvin Schrag, cited by GUSDORF, *Conditions and Limits of Autobiography* (n. 15), p. 38.

rent. He sees a sensitive sage who saw that the oppressed had no comforter to comfort them. Qoheleth understands the process of (failed and,
by implication, successful) understanding. In such a way he transcends
himself. Both *the* self as *subject* and Qoheleth's self, through this reflective redoubling, are brought into the sharpest relief[18].

To summarize the positions so far, then: the deconstructed notion of
self heralds the death of the author and of the subject. The self is dead
because we cannot find it. There is no referential link available that enables interaction with Another — with a person. The most important implication from this is that since the self can only be a product of language (and not vice-versa), self-existence is made difficult to affirm,
establish and/or communicate. Qoheleth's narrative demonstrates a concern for character formation and reflection on experience through autobiography, cohesion, the redoubling of the self and so on; through all of
which Qoheleth leaves an indelible impression on readers.

These two positions are made incongruous by the fact that Qoheleth's
involves a reading experience, while the deconstructive is a broad theory
that, while encompassing reading, attempts to account for human communication in general. They are, however, able to be linked by three
points. (1) The deconstructive is discussed and formulated through writing *and* reading. (2) Both positions are credal. The first is founded on a
reading hunch and yet can be discussed critically, while the second asks
us to believe that, contrary to our expectations, we do not exist outside
of the enunciations that define us. (3) The positions are made 'convers-
able' in that Qoheleth's claims about his own self, as we have seen,
amount to claims about the subject and the self in general. His *treatment*
of the subject forces us to look hard at it — and 'What you look hard at',
said Gerard Hopkins, 'seems to look hard at you'[19].

18. Both H. Fisch and William P. Brown have observed this phenomenon in
Ecclesiastes. For Brown it is because Qoheleth cites his 'accomplishments' as failures
that he makes his narrated self a 'stranger' and therefore separates his 'reputation' (public
image) from his individuality or essence. Qoheleth thereby 'steps out of himself' and creates a ghost (BROWN, *Character in Crisis* [n. 15], pp. 130-33). Fisch sees in Qoheleth's
'self-duplication' an 'ironic mode' which, by its smiling awareness of what happens to
itself, constitutes something 'near the very ground and origin of all irony'. Fisch comments further that 'even as the philosopher contemplates himself as the passive *object* of
a universal *process*, his active contemplation of this process in the language of philosophy detaches him from the process, affirms his freedom and independence as a *subject*...
Irony brings together man as object, immersed in the world, and man as a subject, capable
of rising superior to pains and pleasures' (H. FISCH, *Qohelet: A Hebrew Ironist*, in ID.,
Poetry with a Purpose: Biblical Poetics and Interpretation [Indiana Studies in Biblical
Literature], Indianapolis, Indiana University Press, 1988, pp. 158-78, esp. 169; italics
Fisch's).

19. Cited in OLNEY, *Metaphors of Self* (n. 1), p. 33.

Qoheleth's view shares an interesting trait with the deconstructive. He acknowledges that he cannot discover the reasons why things happen the way they do, and in this he is sceptical of ideologies that he has received[20]. In fact, just as the deconstructive competes with the Cartesian, Qoheleth's way of accounting for experience, as has been widely noted, competes within its own canon by overturning received ideas. But the similarity ends here.

Qoheleth tests a way of accounting for his 'youthful' experience — one that is not unlike the deconstructive position — and is wholly dissatisfied by it. As the reader follows Qoheleth on his self-journeying (and this decidedly more intensely than in any other biblical book) the question of fate is a constant sub-text. What will be the end result of testing wisdom *with* his heart? How will his self (part Qoheleth, part Solomon, part disillusioned, part full of life) fare in the face of the absurd world? For Qoheleth attempted first to define himself in terms of wealth and reputation, and this failed miserably. In this respect it was the media-based image of self (one connected to the death of self) that Qoheleth tried and tested. He did attempt to define his own identity in reference to a public persona — based on material wealth and so on — and this failed him. That failure was itself absurd. For Qoheleth, the self was in need of a more substantial base for definition than the experience of extreme folly and mirth could offer. In the end result, the self must be further defined by an honest confrontation with the absurd. And beyond this 'self-test' we find some germane observations: relationships do fail (many are based on envy, 4,4); the attempt to understand God fails (3,11, *passim*); and Qoheleth asks repeatedly of human striving and of toiling for good things, For what purpose — what advantage — are these? Qoheleth's is the failure of living, for not only is it better never to have been born (cf. esp. 4,1-3 and ch. 6) but the day of death is better than the day of birth (7,1). To put it another way, the failure of living is the failure of the self to achieve definition satisfactorily — otherwise life is not absurd but merely meaningless.

Qoheleth also raises distinctly 'modern' questions of sincerity such as those we put to our John Waynes and Walt Disneys. The combination of the autobiographical form and the frame narrator's historical presentation form an invitation to question the sincerity of Qoheleth's 'I'. When we read 'I' we want to know if the author of that 'I' is telling the truth[21].

---

20. Further, see my discussion of Qoheleth's ideological clashes with the frame narrator in *A Time to Tell* (n. 1), esp. chapter 4.

21. That is, the 'I's narrator *or* historical author. The distinction can become blurred.

When there is *only* 'I', the witness to what the 'I' asserts becomes nothing less than the very integrity of that speaker. Does the speaker offer a true reflection of (narrated) experience? The frame narrator reflects this concern when he finds it necessary to assert that Qoheleth did in fact write words of truth with integrity (12,10). And yet how can he know that Qoheleth was, like Job, truly יָשָׁר, upright? This is a question of character, and character is a question of identity. Just what kind of person are we dealing with? (The Hellenistic Broadcasting Corporation would have had a field-day.)

Ultimately Qoheleth's narrating stance sets apart his idea of the self from the nihilism of the deconstructed self in its assertion of what it means to be human. In Qoheleth's acknowledgment of the failure of living he affirms the reality of the experience of those who live. By saying that the stillborn is better off than the living he affirms that it is because there is a defining faculty in the individual that that person, while living, is prevented from being consigned to the designation, 'cipher of words'. By thinking, by reflecting on events, by centring the place of experience and by feeling the weight of absurdity so deeply, he acknowledges that the self is not simply a mental peg on which to hang his ideas and observations. The self is at the centre. The movement of expression is from Qoheleth's mind/heart, soul and spirit *to* speech. Furthermore, each of these terms relates to *Another* and/or affirms the authenticity of the self. The לב is the place of שמחה where God answers and where the act of feeling life is not feared but is affirmed. Although not linked directly to God, the נפש establishes the primacy of existence by rejecting death as an alternative to vexatious existence. The רוח returns to God who made it — the self's origin — and the (intellectual) comprehension of its experience is thereby asserted. Qoheleth's is an existence not of words and the constructs of speech but of his self *outside of* the words that enunciate its presence, for those words are regardless הבל in the end and ultimately fail to express life's brightest and darkest experiences. God answers humanity not with words in the wind, but with joy in the heart, in the innermost and secret places.

The crisis in which the self has lost its privileged place, and in which we can find no more 'causal efficacy for the self', is alien to Qoheleth's world, in which the causes, if absurd, for the failure of the self are brutally clear. The world and the self's relationship to it are not as they

This is true in the case of Ecclesiastes due to the fictional premises of the frame narrative. I use the word 'author' to denote the character who says 'I' since Ecclesiastes, despite its fictional premise, is autobiography and assumes the telling of someone's life. The 'I' therefore makes the kind of claim to truth I am here discussing.

should be. This places every individual in Qoheleth's world (everything and everyone under the sun) under the vexatious curse of futile toil and circular existence. To state it another way, the concreteness of Qoheleth's experience is what defines his personhood. As Dietrich Bonhoeffer put it, 'the person, as a conscious person, is created in the moment when he is moved, when he is faced with responsibility, when he is passionately involved in a moral struggle, and confronted by a claim which overwhelms him. *Concrete personal being arises from the concrete situation*'[22]. Qoheleth's rejection of a world in which nothing is fixed and everything is in flux, is that against which he rallies and rejects; the opposite of which he therefore values.

Qoheleth's 'younger' self, split from his older, telling self, is remarkably like the postmodern self, one 'consumptive of images and experiences [a self which] will likely prove to be even more insatiable than its modern [colonial and imperial] ancestor'[23]. Like Qoheleth's media-based self, it is found wanting. Here is a qualitative popular appeal of Ecclesiastes and something that might even go towards explaining its inclusion in the canon: its truthfulness in describing the human condition; then as now. As Roger Lundin says of the cultural, postmodern self, 'There is no goal for [its] actions...save the fulfilment of its desires'[24]. And this is a driving force of Qoheleth's story: the fulfilment of desire and the inability to contain or achieve it; for Qoheleth and those he observes find לא־תשבע, no satisfaction, no fulfilment of desire (1,8; 4,8; 6,3; cf. 6,7 and the waning of desire in the closing poem).

At least one scholar has made a case for Qoheleth espousing elements of deconstruction, such as, for example, the undermining of traditional ways of knowing[25]. And I have heard people in the 'guild' of biblical studies refer to Qoheleth as a sort of bedfellow of postmodernity. While it is true that Qoheleth displays a subversive tendency to undermine what is generally 'accepted', he does not take the further step of carnivalizing the practice. That is a wholly new enterprise. Qoheleth did not 'play with the text' of his ancestors. He brought into question their

22. From Dietrich BONHOEFFER's doctoral thesis, *Sanctorum Communio (Communion of Saints)*, cited in J. de GRUCHY (ed.), *Dietrich Bonhoeffer: Witness to Jesus Christ* (The Making of Modern Theology), London, Collins, 1988, p. 46 (italics mine).

23. MIDDLETON – WALSH, *Truth Is Stranger Than it Used to Be* (n. 6), p. 55.

24. Cited in MIDDLETON – WALSH, *Truth Is Stranger Than it Used to Be* (n. 6), p. 59.

25. See S. SCHLOESSER, *"A King is Held Captive in her Tresses": The Liberating Deconstruction of the Search for Wisdom from Proverbs through Ecclesiastes*, in J. MORGAN (ed.), *Church Divinity*, Bristol, Cloverdale Corporation, 1989–90, 205-28, esp. 210-11.

ways of knowing by bitterly detracting the results and thereby heralded a wholly new set of values embodied in an honest confrontation that evil and injustice which found no easy answers.

University College Chester   Eric S. CHRISTIANSON
Parkgate Road
Chester CH1 4BJ
England

KOHELET – PHILOSOPH UND POET

Vorbemerkungen zur Reimkunst in Israel

Merkwürdig schwer hat sich die alttestamentliche Forschung damit getan, die Besonderheiten der Poesie Israels wiederzuerkennen[1]. Schon angesichts der chiastischen Anaphorik mit einem unverkennbaren Endreim bereits im 1. Kapitel der Gen (1,27) ist es mir unverständlich, daß Heinrich Ewald schreiben konnte:

>»Die Hebräische dichtung kennt... den reim noch garnicht, obwohl das Hebräische als bloße sprache zu ihm hätte einladen können«[2].

Herder hat seinen Eutyphron sagen lassen:

>»Lied (als »eigentliche Poesie) ist nur ein Einziges darinn (sc.: im AT); Lamechs Lied...«[3]

Dabei sind die Ausführungen über die poetischen Wesenszüge alttestamentlicher Schriften bei beiden Autoren faszinierend und haben nicht viel an Aktualität eingebüßt. Zudem sind wichtige Charakteristika für die Reimkunst bereits gesehen, aber nicht genügend beachtet worden[4]. Eduard König lehnt Reim und Stabreim für Israels Poesie ab[5], obwohl er

---

1. Z.T. lag es daran, daß es offenbar eine (MSS=)Gegenbewegung gegen die alten Reime gegeben hat (s. dazu meinen Beitrag *Kohelets Urteil über die Frauen*, in *ZAW* 108 (1996) 584-593, speziell: pp. 584-586).

2. H. EWALD, *Die poetischen Bücher des Alten Testaments*, I, Göttingen, 1839, p. 104 (vgl. auch p. 105, Anm. 3). Kohelet zeigt nach Meinung Ewalds das »völlige ermatten und sichauflösen des rhythmus«, und »dies übrigens ganz dichterische buch« mache auch »in der form... so einen ganz merkwürdigen übergang zu einer ganz anderen entwicklung der literatur« (*op. cit.*, p. 129f). Im Bd. II (2. Aufl., Göttingen, 1867), pp. 267-329 hat er Koh kommentiert.

3. J.G. HERDER, *Vom Geist der ebräischen Poesie*, I (1782), *Werke*, XXXIII, 1826, pp. 319f.

4. Herder hat das Vorkommen von »Wortspiel« und »Schall-Aehnlichkeit« im Alten Testament sehr wohl bemerkt, aber er sucht sogleich eine Abgrenzung vorzunehmen »von der schlechten Kunst, die der Engelländer 'the art of punning' nennt« (*Werke*, XXXIV, p. 280). Ewald schreibt (*op. cit*, p. 5), daß »man sich... hütet die begriffe über griechische und lateinische poesie zu unvorsichtig in die fragen über die althebräische zu mischen«. »Abwechslungen« seien in ihr »sehr frei geblieben... aber eben deswegen in desto grösserer menge und mannigfaltigkeit« vorliegend und erfordern »desto grössere aufmerksamkeit um sie richtig zu verstehen« (p. 111). Trotz solcher Einsichten vermochte sich die alttestamentliche Wissenschaft offenbar nie ganz von den Maßstäben griechischer und abendländischer Poesie zu lösen.

5. E. KÖNIG, *Stilistik, Rhetorik, Poetik in Bezug auf die biblische Literatur*, Leipzig, 1900, p. 329; pp. 355-357.

ausführlich auf die »Quellen des Wohllauts« eingeht[6] und verschiedene Formen von Assonanz aufzeigt[7]. Das Buch Kohelet rechnet er »als Ganzes zur Prosa«[8]. In neuerer Zeit hat Karl Georg Kuhn zwar die Meinung widerlegt, der Reim sei vor der Pijut-Dichtung in Israel nicht nachweisbar[9]; aber auch er schreibt: »die paar Reimverse des Alten Testaments zählen nicht«[10]. Mit weiteren Urteilen dieser Art (z.B. James K. Kugel) habe ich mich bereits auseinandergesetzt[11]. Als Beispiele einer neuen Hinwendung zur Erforschung der Poesie Israels im allgemeinen sei besonders Alonso-Schökel gewürdigt[12]; für Koh speziell sei auf Aarre Lauha und Hagia Witzenrath hingewiesen[13].

Außer dem für den Alten Orient (und Ägypten) typischen PM (*Parallelismus membrorum*)[14] ergeben sich aus der Beschäftigung mit der alttestamentlichen Poetik als weitere Charakteristika: 1. daß das ὁμοιοτέλευτον[15] nur ein Stilmittel neben anderen ist, die eingesetzt werden, um Euphonie zu bewirken; 2. daß somit prosodische Formeln innerhalb eines Poems wechseln können[16] und 3. reimlose Verse (»Waisen«) nicht als störend empfunden wurden. (In abgeschwächter Weise gibt es für alles dieses auch Beispiele in der Geschichte der abendländischen Poetik, aber dies im einzelnen zu belegen, würde den Rahmen dieses *Short Paper* sprengen.)

6. *Op. cit.*, pp. 285-360, vor allem p. 285.

7. *Op. cit.*, p. 300 (»Ploke«).

8. Eine gelegentliche Verwendung poetischer Stilmittel stellt König bei Koh nicht in Abrede: *Poesie und Prosa in der althebräischen Literatur abgegrenzt*, in ZAW 37 (1917-18) 145-187, speziell p. 154.

9. Gegen Ismar ELBOGEN, *Der jüdische Gottesdienst in seiner Entwicklung*, Berlin, 1913, 3. Aufl. 1931, p. 293, mit einem Hinweis auf einen älteren Text des Achtzehn-Bitten-Gebets in der Geniza von Kairo, wobei er zudem eine Rückübersetzung des Vaterunsers ins Aramäische von Enno Littmann (1912) anführt: K.G. KUHN, *Achtzehngebet und Vaterunser und der Reim* (WUNT 1), Tübingen 1950.

10. *Op. cit.*, p. 26. Mit dieser Meinung ist Kuhn auch in die 17. Aufl. des »Großen Brockhaus«, Bd. 15, Wiesbaden, 1972, p. 600, gelangt.

11. H.-F. RICHTER, *Das Liedgut in der »jahwistischen« Urgeschichte*, in WO 25 (1994), pp. 78-108, speziell p. 79f.

12. L. ALONSO-SCHÖKEL, *Estudios de poética hebrea*, Barcelona, 1963, dtsch.: *Das Alte Testament als literarisches Kunstwerk*, Köln, 1971, vor allem pp. 30-76.

13. A. LAUHA, *Kohelet* (BKAT XIX), Neukirchen-Vluyn, 1978, p. 10: Koh »Meister der Stileffekte« und Hinweis auf Reime bei ihm; H. WITZENRATH, *Süß ist das Licht... Eine literaturwissenschaftliche Untersuchung zu Koh 11,7-12,7* (Arbeiten zu Text und Sprache im Alten Testament, 11), St. Ottilien, 1979, wobei Frau Witzenrath allerdings stärker als ich zur Vorsicht bei der »Analyse von Vers, Rhythmus und Strophe« mahnt (p. 51).

14. Vgl. dazu das sumerische Gebet des Bilgamesch in *TUAT* II, p. 714f; J. ASSMANN, *Parallelismus membrorum*, in LÄ IV, Sp. 900-910; W. VAN DER MEER – J.C. DE MOOR (eds.), *The Structural Analysis of Biblical and Canaanite Poetry* (JSOT SS, 74), Sheffield, 1988.

15. Zu Problemen beim Einsatz dieses Stilmittels, vgl. RICHTER, ZAW 108 (1996) p. 584f.

16. In diesem Zusammenhang sei auf das sehr hilfreiche kleine Nachschlagewerk von W. BÜHLMANN – K. SCHERER, *Stilfiguren der Bibel* (BibB 10), Fribourg, 1973, hingewiesen.

Wie so oft in der Wissenschaft zeigt sich auch hier, daß Differenzen zumindest teilweise auf Definitionsfragen beruhen können. Wenn man den Begriff »Reimpoesie« nur auf solche Formen anwenden will, die unseren abendländischen Kriterien entsprechen, läßt sich dagegen nicht viel sagen. Aber die bunte Mannigfaltigkeit der (Reime einschließenden) Euphonik des Alten Israels einfach ignorieren zu wollen, würde dem Geist des Alten Testaments nicht gerecht werden und eine Verarmung des Blickfeldes bedeuten[17].

1. *Kohelets zyklisches Weltbild*

Israel hatte ein linear-historisches Zeitverständnis durch seine Besinnung auf die Heilstaten Gottes gewonnen[18], und so galt auch für seine Zukunftserwartung:

> »Das einzige, woran Israel sich halten kann, ist ein neues Geschichtshandeln Jahwes«[19].

Teilte Koh diese von prophetischer Verkündigung getragene Konzeption? Zweifellos nicht. Er lehnte sie explizit ab[20], und vor diesem Hintergrund gewinnen die Aussagen Kohelets über eine Wiederkehr von Gleichartigem[21] ihre Bedeutung. Leider wurde dieser Bruch mit Israels Geschichtsverständnis bisher hauptsächlich nur unter dem Gesichtspunkt einer eventuellen Abhängigkeit von anderen – vor allem griechischen[22] —Betrachtungsweisen diskutiert. Nun ist für die historische Wissenschaft die Einmaligkeit und Irreversibilität aller Ereignisse maßgeblich geworden. Aber hier geht es vor allem darum, Koh als Denker den Platz einzuräumen, der ihm gebührt. Er ist der Mann, der in Israel als erster[23]

17. Da auf die Fülle der Literatur zu Israels Poetik hier nicht eingegangen werden kann, sei vor allem auf ALONSO-SCHÖKEL, *op. cit.* (n. 12), verwiesen, der jeweils am Schluß eines Kapitels ausführliche Verzeichnisse bringt, sowie auf O. LORETZ – I. KOTTSIEPER, *Colometry in Ugaritic and Biblical Poetry* (UBL, 5), Altenberge, 1987, pp. 118-150.

18. G. VON RAD, *Theologie des Alten Testaments,* II, 5. Aufl., München, 1968, pp. 108-133, bes. p. 115.

19. *Ibid.,* p. 127.

20. 1,9-11; 3,19-21; 7,10; Koh 9,1-3 und 5-6 könnten sich sogar auf prophetische Deutungen beziehen. Auch die (späteren) Sadduzäer haben diesen wohl skeptisch gegenüber gestanden (R. LEVY, *Sadduzäer,* in *Jüdisches Lexikon,* IV,2, Sp. 36f).

21. Nicht eine Wiederkehr desselben; darauf weist mit Recht O. LORETZ, *Qohelet und der Alte Orient,* Freiburg – Basel – Wien, 1964, p. 255, hin.

22. Zum Einfluß griechischer Philosophie auf Koh neuere Untersuchungen von R. BRAUN, *Kohelet und die frühhellenistische Popularphilosophie* (BZAW, 130), Berlin, 1973, und dazu die Literatur-Angaben sowie das Register bei A.A. FISCHER, *Skepsis oder Furcht Gottes?* (BZAW, 247), Berlin 1997, p. 288. Abgewogene Urteile darüber bei D. MICHEL, *Qohelet* (EdF, 258), Darmstadt, 1988, p. 65 und L. SCHWIENHORST-SCHÖNBERGER, *»Nicht im Menschen gründet das Glück« (Koh 2,24)* (HBS, 2), Freiburg, 1994, p. 274 und Kontext.

23. Allerdings müßte man die ins Hiob-Buch eingefügten Diskussionen sicherlich mitnennen.

den Schritt von der altorientalischen Weisheit, an der Israel eigenständig
partizipiert hatte, zur Philosophie im eigentlichen Sinn vollzogen hat.
Und zu diesem seinen Weltbild gehört nun einmal die zyklische Sicht[24],
die der Anfang seines Büchleins zum Ausdruck bringt, und zwar mit einer eindrucksvollen onomatopoetischen Untermalung seiner Gedanken[25].

Zunächst fält sie als Euphonie auf. Worauf diese beruht, wird deutlich, wenn man die einzelnen Klangelemente näher betrachtet.

<u>Die Klangfigur[26] von Koh 1,2-3</u>

2 a[27]	hab(i)l	habalīm		
b			'amar qōhilt[28]	
c	hab(i)l	habalīm		
d	ha=kul[l]			
	habl			
3 a			mah yitrōn	l=h[a]='adam[29]
b	b=kul[l]		'amal=ō[30]	
c	ša=yi'mul			
			taht ha=šamš[28]	

24. Diese wird zwar von LORETZ, *op. cit.* (Anm. 21), p. 255, bestritten. Aber über-
zeugend M. HENGEL, *Judentum und Hellenismus* (WUNT, 10), Tübingen, 1969, p. 221:
»Natur und Geschichte erscheinen ihm (Koh) als ein scheinbar sinnloser Kreislauf«,
und das dort angefügte Zitat von H. RICHTER, *Die Naturweisheit des Alten Testaments
im Buche Hiob*, in ZAW 70 (1958) 1-20, spez. p. 19: In Koh 1,5-7 »wird die Natur
weder um ihrer selbst willen betrachtet, noch soll sie zum Lobe Jahwes hinführen. Diese Naturbeobachtungen werden vielmehr in den Dienst einer bestimmten Weltanschauung gestellt, sie sollen eine philosophische These erhärten und beweisen.« Vgl. auch O.
KAISER, *Die Sinnkrise bei Kohelet*, in *FS A. Köberle*, Darmstadt, 1978, pp. 3-21, spez.
p. 12f.

25. Ein erheblicher Teil der Forscher bezweifelt, daß 1,2 und 12,8 von Koh stammen. Aber die Rede in der 3. Person kann durchaus ein bewußtes Stilmittel sein; die
onomatopoetische Form spricht m.E. für die Authentizität dieser Verse. Platon läßt So-
krates seine Worte sagen, Kierkegaard benutzte ebenfalls Pseudonyme, und der Anony-
mus, der sich als den Kohelet bezeichnet, kann auch über diesen einmal in der 3. Person
sprechen. Und als solcher läßt er dann ja auch Salomo reden (wie Spr 8,4-10 die Weisheit).

26. Zum Begriff »Klangfigur« vgl. auch RICHTER, ZAW 108 (1996), p. 585, Anm. 13
(zu Euripides). – Es sei daran erinnert, daß auch die neuzeitliche Dichtung Wohlklang
nicht nur durch den Endreim erzeugt (s. die auch innerhalb der Strophen erfolgte Wiederkehr von a=, ei= und ö=Vokalismen z.B., die Goethes »Heidenröslein« so anmutig wirken läßt; denn die Endreime sind nicht einmal durchweg perfekt (schön:sehn/
Freuden:Heiden).

27. Die Numerierung ist nur ad-hoc gedacht und entspricht zudem nicht der
Skandierung der MSS oder der Wolfgang Richters, an dessen *altebr. Wiedergabe ich
mich anlehne (W. RICHTER, *Biblia Hebraica Transcripta* [ATSAT, 33.13], St. Ottilien,
1993).

28. Im MSS-Text ist die Onomatopoesie noch deutlicher, und vielleicht gab es schon
bei Koh Segolate (vgl. meine Erwägung aufgrund der LXX: *WO* 25 (1994], p. 102).
Durch diese entstehen weitere Assonanzen. Das Kolon 3c beginnt und endet mit š (konso-
nantischer Klangzirkel).

Daß die Anaphorik den Gedanken der Sinnlosigkeit unterstreichen soll, versteht sich von selbst. Aber über die Wiederkehr der Wörter hinaus werden die Silbenklänge dem angepaßt, was der Text zur Sprache bringen möchte[31].

Der onomatopoetische Stil wechselt im nächsten Vers. Wieder ist eine (Anfangs=)Anaphorik eingesetzt, aber jedes der drei Kola ist durch ein langes ō geprägt, das jetzt die sinnlose Wiederkehr des Gleichartigen unterstreicht:

4 a	dōr			hōlik	
b	w'=dōr	bā(')			
c			w'=ha='arṣ		
	l'='ō	= lam		'ōmidt[32]	
5 a		w'=zaraḥ	ha=šamš		
b		w'=bā(')	ha=šamš		
c					w'='il maqōm=ō[33]
d				šō'ip	
				zōriḥ	
	hū(')	šam[m]			
6 a				hōlik	'il darōm
b				w'=sōbib	'il ṣapōn
c				sōbib	
d				sōbib	

Eine oft schon festgestellte[34] Seelenverwandtschaft zwischen Koh und Arthur Schopenhauer zeigt sich auch, wenn letzterer für die Sinnlosigkeit des Daseins ähnliche Bilder verwendet:

> »Die Erde wälzt sich vom Tage in die Nacht; das Individuum stirbt; aber die Sonne selbst brennt ohne Unterlaß ewigen Mittag«[35].

29. Vokalischer Klangzirkel: mah... 'adam.

30. Chiastische Assonanz: mah yitrōn / 'amal=ō.

31. Ähnlich bei Friedrich von Schiller:
»Sieh da,
sieh da,   Timotheus:
Die Kra =niche   des Ibykus!«
Inwieweit solch eine Euphonie jeweils durch Reflexion zustande kommt oder ein bloßes Empfinden – »zufällig« wäre wohl ein unpassendes Wort –, scheint mir ein zweitrangiges Problem zu sein.

32. Falls Koh schon Segolate kannte, müßten selbstverständlich ha='aræṣ und 'ōmædæt untereinandergesetzt werden.

33. w'='il maqōm=ō zeigt einen chiastischen Vokalismus zum Schluß von 4c: l'='ōlam 'ōmidt.

34. Z.B. E. RENAN, L'Ecclésiaste traduit de l'hébreu avec une étude sur l'âge et le caractère du livre, Paris, 1882, p. 90.

35. A. SCHOPENHAUER, Die Welt als Wille und Vorstellung, I (Werke, II, her. J. FRAUENSTÄDT), 2. Aufl., Leipzig, 1922, p. 331; vgl. auch zum zyklischen Weltbild, Bd. II (Werke, III), p. 545.

Eine andere Klangfigur bei Koh weist noch deutlicher lautmalende Züge auf. Wie in einem Chorlied der Antigone des Sophokles der Rhythmus den dort geschilderten Aufbruch eines Mannes unterstreicht[36], so hier bei Koh der Einsatz von ל und מ[37] das langsame Fließen von Wasser:

7 a	kul[l]	ha=naḥalīm hōlikīm	
	ʾil		ha=yam[m]
b		w'=ha=yam[m]	ʾēn-an=[h]u(w)[38] malē(')[38]
c	ʾil	maqōm	
		ša=ha=naḥalīm hōlikīm	
d		šam[m]	
	him šabīm[39]		
e			la=likt[38]

Obwohl das Gedicht mit V. 8 endet, behandle ich diesen erst im nächsten Paragraphen und gehe zunächst zu V. 9 über, der das zyklische Weltbild wieder unterstreicht und zudem vollendete Anfangs- und Endreime aufweist:

9 a	mah ša=hayā	
b		hū(') ša=yihyæ
c		u=[40]
	mah ša=niʿśā	
d		hū(') ša=yi[ʿ]ʿaśæ[41]

(e schließt dann disassonant das kleine Poem ab:)
w'=ʾēn kul[l] ḥadaš taḥt ha=šamš[42].

36. 106-109:   τὸν λευκάσπιν Ἀργόθεν ἐκ
φῶτα βάντα πανσαγία
φυγάδα πρόδρομον ὀξυτέρῳ
κινήσασα χαλινῷ (u.s.w.)

Daß im Gegensatz zu dem flotten, marschmäßigen Rhythmus des griechischen Chorliedes in Koh 1,2-8 der langsam sich vollziehende Kreislauf durchklingt, dürfte evident sein.

37. Die Zahl der Konsonanten in V. 7 (MSS) beträgt 60; davon sind 9 bloße Grapheme, dazu 3 Anfangs-Alef, so daß ein Rest von 48 konsonantischen Phonemen bleibt. Die Mehrzahl dieser bilden die nicht grundlos so bezeichneten Liquida (mem: 12; lamed 10; nun: 4), insgesamt 26, so daß nur 22 (mit Anfangs-Alef 25) konsonantische Phoneme auf den Rest fallen.

38. Disassonant

39. Schlagreime.

40. W vor m wird von selbst zu u (MSS!).

41. Sollen die Zischlaute zudem noch die Form eines (rhetorischen) Gesprächs onomatopoetisch untermalen? Vgl.: dtsch.: »Getuschel«!

42. SCHOPENHAUER, op. cit., Bd. I (Werke III), p. 329 (kein Direktzitat aus der Vulgata!): »Quod fuit? Quod est. Quod erit? Quod fuit.« – FISCHER, Skepsis oder Furcht Gottes?, p. 21; sieht in dem Buch Koh das Dokument eines »Schulbetriebs«. So dienten

2. Die Negierung der Sinnfrage

Das Dasein in seiner endlosen Wiederholung von Gleichartigem, ohne Fortschritt, Sinn und Ziel, ist somit *hæbœl*. Zumindest aus der Warte des Menschen bleiben die Fragen nach dem Wozu ohne Antwort.

(An 1,7 schließt sich V. 8 zunächst reimpoetisch an:)

8 a   kul[l] ha=dabarīm yagiᵉᵉīm⁴³   Alle Worte sind unzulänglich⁴⁴.

Der Stil wechselt nun und geht in bloße Anfangs-Anaphorik über:

b   lō(') yūkal⁴⁵ 'īš l'=dabbir   Nicht ist ein Mensch Meister der Rede⁴⁵;
c   lō(') tiśbaᶜ ᶜayn l'=r'ōt   Nicht wird ein Auge gesättigt beim Sehen;
d   w'=lō(') timmalē(') 'uzn   Nicht wird ein Ohr befriedigt beim
    miš=šmuᶜ   Hören⁴⁶.

Entweder will Koh hier nur an menschlicher Geschwätzigkeit und Neugier Kritik üben, oder er will den philosophischen Gedanken zum Ausdruck bringen, daß alle Erkenntnis nur eine Approximation ist. Wahrscheinlich aber ist eine solch alternative Fragestellung für ihn unangebracht: Er will beides sagen.

Anthropozentrisch wird die Sinnfrage auch in der auf V. 9 folgenden Sentenz⁴⁷ negiert:

	althebr. Text	Imitation⁴⁸
10 a	yiš dabar ša=yē'amir⁴⁹	Es gibt ein Wort, das man oft sagt:
b	r'ē(h) zæ ḥadaš hū(')	»Sieh, das ist neu, das gibt's erst heut!«
c	k'bār hayā l'=ᶜōlamīm	Doch schon seit undenklichen Jahren

die poetischen Reflexionen zur »Lehrrede«, bei der sogar die zeitgenössischen griechischen Naturwissenschaften gleichsam Pate gestanden haben können. Aber ist Koh 1,4-8 wirklich Didaktik einer »Kohelet-Schule«? Oder will hier nicht vielmehr ein philosophischer Dichter seinen Reflexionen und Stimmungen Ausdruck verleihen?

43. Schlagreim (bei Übersetzung nicht berücksichtigt).

44. Andere Deutung: »Alle Worte ermüden«.

45. Nach der von der *BHS* vorgeschlagenen Konjektur *yklh*: »Nicht hört ein Mensch auf zu reden« (wenig einleuchtend).

46. 8a+b und 8c+d bilden jeweils einen PM.

47. Dem Buch Koh liegt keine einheitliche Konzeption zugrunde, sondern es ist eine Sammlung von Sentenzen: Kurt GALLING, *Der Prediger* (HAT, 1,18), 2. Aufl., Tübingen, 1969, p. 76, wobei allerdings auch die Abschwächung dieser These durch Walther ZIMMERLI, *Das Buch Kohelet – Traktat oder Sentenzensammlung?*, in *VT* 24 (1974) 221-230, Beachtung verdient.

48. Die Imitation möchte lediglich den Sinn für die so oft verkannte Reimpoesie Israels stärken; sie kann keine Übersetzung im eigentlichen Sinn sein (z.B. wird das Suffix -nū (10d) erst in 11b (wo es gar nicht steht) berücksichtigt, u.a.m.). – Vgl. zum Problem »Imitation« auch F. ELLERMEIER, *Qohelet*, I, Herzberg, 1967, bes. p. 156 und Kontext.

49. Das Niphal gibt einen besseren Sinn und paßt rhythmisch gut. Da eine Änderung des Konsonantenbestandes mit ihm nicht erfolgt, habe ich keine Hemmung, es einzusetzen.

d ʼašr hayā mil=lʼ=panē=nū   Gab's das, seit einer Ewigkeit.
11 a ʼēn zik[ka]rōn   Vergessen die Erinnerung
 b lʼ=[h]a=rī(ʼ)šōnīm⁵⁰   An jene, die hier vor uns waren!
 c wʼ=gam lʼ=[h]a=ʼaḥrōnīm   Dies droht auch unseren Nachfahren
 d ša=yihyū   In spätrer Zeit.
 e lō(ʼ) yihyæ la=him zikkarōn   Denn jedwede Erinnerung
 f ʿim[m] ša=yihyū   An unsre Zeit
 g lʼ=[h]a=ʿaḥrōnā   Fehlt in der spätren Welt.

Das Leben ist ein Wahrnehmen des Augenblicks. Der Gedanke an den
Tod wird nicht verdrängt. Im Gegenteil! Koh 12 mahnt:

1 a wʼ=zkur ʼat bōrʼ(ē)=ka⁵¹   Denk dran: ein Grab dein Schicksal ist,
 b bʼ=yamē baḥūrōt-ē=ka   Jetzt, wo du noch bei Kräften bist!
 c ʿad ʼašr lō(ʼ) yabōʼū   Noch trifft nicht zu,
 d yamē ha=raʿ[ʿ]ā   Daß die Tage kommen,
 e wʼ=higgīʿū šanīm   Da Leid dich wird plagen
 f ʼašr tō(ʼ)mir   Und du sprechen wirst:
 g ʼēn l=ī ba=him   Es fehlt diesen Tagen
 h ḥipṣ   Mir Freude⁵².
2 a ʿad ʼašr lō(ʼ) tiḥšak ha=šamš Noch wird nicht dunkel die Sonne,
 b wʼ=ha=ʼōr wʼ=ha=yariḥ   Das Licht und der Mond,
 c wʼ=ha=kōkabīm   Und die Sterne sind da.
 d wʼšābū ha=ʿābīm   Doch Wolken stets wieder sind nah
 e ʼaḥar ha=gašm   Nach dem Regen.
3 a bʼ=[h]a=yōm ša=yazūʿū   Eines Tages beben
 b šomirē ha=bayt   Die (stets) das Haus bewacht;
 c wʼhitʿawwitū   Gekrümmt dann einhergehen
 d ʼanašē ha=ḥayl   Die Männer, (einst) voll Kraft.
 e wʼbaṭʼlū   Es ruhen (von der Pflicht)
 f ha=ṭōḥinōt   Die mahlenden Frauen;
 g kī miʿ[ʿ]iṭū   Ihrer viel blieben nicht.
 h wʼ=ḥašakū   Und das Licht
 i ha=rōʼōt   Weicht dem Grauen
 j bʼ=[h]a=ʼurubbōt   Will durchs Fenster man schauen⁵³.
4 a wʼ=suggarū   Öffnen etwa sich nicht
 b dalataym bʼ=[h]a=šūq   Die Türen zur Straße,

50. Chiastische Vokalfolge in 11ab (e-i-(a?)-o/a-i-o-i) Zufall?
51. SCHWIENHORST-SCHÖNBERGER, *op. cit.* (Anm. 22), p. 227 und p. 332, wendt sich
gegen eine Konjektur oder den Verdacht eines späteren Einschubs. Viele lesen wie er mit
MSS *bwrʼyk* (denk an deinem Schöpfer). Ich halte die Konjektur (*bōr* = Brunnen, Grab)
für den Gedanken Kohelets besser entsprechend. *EÜ* auch: Grab.
52. Trotz der Mischung von Assonanzen und »Waisen« ist der reimpoetische Charakter dieses Gedichts wohl kaum zu überhören. Daher soll die Imitation fortan genügen, um
dies zu verdeutlichen.
53. Die bisher von Koh gebrauchten Bilder werden in Kommentaren und Übersetzungen gedeutet, so daß ich hier aus Raumgründen nicht auf sie eingehe, wenn ich die Deutung teile. Das ist im folgenden jedoch nicht mehr der Fall.

c b'špal qōl ha=ṭaḥnā   Weil der Schlag der Mühle[54] versagt?
d w'=yaqūm   Doch er kann aufstehn[55],
e l'=qōl ha=ṣippu(w)r   Wenn der Hahn[56] kräht
f w'yaśiḥū[57]   Und es zwitschern
g kul[l] banōt ha=šīr   Alle »Töchter des Liedes«[58].

Vers 5 läßt sich am besten in Klangfiguren darstellen, und der Imitationsversuch trifft die Euphonie Kohelets nicht annähernd.

5 a gam mig=gabuh   Eine Anhöhe gar wirkt (jetzt)
     yīra'ū   furchtbar.
  b w'ḥatḥattīm b'=[h]a=dark Das Dunkel unheimlich bedroht[59].
  c w'=yani(')ṣ[ṣ]   Und der Baum erscheint im
     ha=šaqid   Blütenkleid
  d w'=yistabbil ha=ḥāg[60]   Und das Fest[61] nahet herbei[62].
  e (disassonanter Strophenaus- An ihm erntest du –
     klang:) b=ō tipræ 'abīyōnā   Eine Kaper[63].

---

54. Die Deutung auf Ohren und Stimme überzeugt mich nicht. Zwar sind die »Müllerinnen« in 3f offensichtlich die Zähne; aber deswegen mit LAUHA, op. cit. (Anm. 13), p. 212, zu schließen, daß auch »die Mühle konsequenterweise den Mund und das Geräusch der Mühle das Reden der Menschen« meinen müsse, leuchtet mir nicht ein. Mit qōl kann sogar das Rascheln eines Blattes bezeichnet werden (Lev 26,36). קול הטחנה könnte sich somit auch auf den Herzschlag beziehen. In diesem Fall wären die geschlossenen Türen zur Außenwelt nicht mehr Metapher und 4a-c gäbe eine rhetorische Frage wieder.

55. Koh hätte – wenn die Deutung hier von 4a-c richtig sein sollte – durch ein literarisches Verzögerungsmotiv die Spannung erhöht: Es scheint noch einmal gutgegangen zu sein.

56. Nur von einem Vogel ist die Rede; aber dieser könnte auch ein Hahn sein, ohne daß ich behaupten will, diese Deutung sei zwingend.

57. Es erscheint mir einleuchtender, yśḥw (statt yśḥw) zu lesen; śyḥ kann auch »singen« bedeuten. »Zwitschern« setze ich in der Imitation für »singen« nur ein, um deutlich werden zu lassen, daß mit dem schönen Bild »Töchter des Liedes« wohl Vögel gemeint sind.

58. Manche Kommentare (z.B. MICHEL, Qohelet, p. 166) deuten bnwt hśyr auf Stimmen.

59. Parallelismus membrorum.

60. Auch bei der Lesart ha=ḥagab bliebe eine Assonanz gewährt.

61. Das Erntefest: sarkastisch für den Tod und die Totenfeier.

62. Das Hitpael von sbl – ein Hapaxlegomenon in der BH – wird als »mühsam sich fortschleppen« gedeutet (GESENIUS, Hebräisches und aramäisches Handwörterbuch, 17. Auflage, Berlin, 1962, p. 535). Sollte das Subjekt hier aber nicht eine Heuschrecke, sondern ein Fest sein, wird es fraglich, ob eine Aussage über das Tempo impliziert ist (vgl. griech. φέρεσθαι).

63. Wörtl.: »wirst du als Frucht eine Kaper (als Bild für hæbæl) vorweisen«. – Die seit der LXX nachgewiesene und MSS folgende Leseweise – etwa EÜ: »... Die Heuschrecke schleppt, die Kaperknospe platzt« – muß, ungeachtet ihres Alters, nicht die ursprüngliche Sinngebung Kohelets gewesen sein.
Einleuchtender erscheint mir,   statt   wystbl hḥgb wtpr h'bywnh
                                zu lesen: wystbl hḥg bw tprh 'bywnh.
Aber selbstverständlich bin ich mir des hypothetischen Charakters dieser Skandierungsänderung bewußt.

f kī hōlik[64] ha'=adam[65]   Denn der Mensch schwindet hin
g 'il bēt 'ōlam=ō[66]   In sein Ewigkeitshaus,
h w'sababū   Und es laufen
   b'=[h]a=šūq[67]   da draußen
i ha=sōpidīm   Die, die trauern (um ihn)[68].
   (Koh wechselt jetzt wieder den Stil und geht zum PM über:)
6 (I A)   a 'ad 'ašr lō(') yir[r]ahiq[69]   Bis (schließlich) der silberne Faden
                                             reißt
  (I B)   b w'=tarōṣ[70] gullat ha=zahab   Und die goldene Schale entzweit,
  (II A)   c w'=tiššabir kad[d] 'al   Am Wasserbrunnen der Krug
             ha=mabbū'   zerschellt,
  (II B)   d w'=narōṣ[71] ha=galgal[l] 'il Und das Schöpfrad zerbricht an dem
             ha=bō(')r   Quell.
7 (III A) a w'=yašūb ha='apar 'al   Und der Staub kehrt zurück zur Erde,
             ha='arṣ
           b k'=ša=hayā   An seine Statt.
  (III B)[72] c w'=ha=rūh tašūb 'il   Doch kehrt auch die Ruach zu Gott
             ha='ilōhīm[73]   zurück,
           d 'ašr natan-a=h[74]   Der sie gegeben hat?
8 a hab(i)l habalīm   »Nichtig, welche Nichtigkeit!«
  b 'amar ha=qohilt   Sagt der Kohelet,
  c ha=kul[l] habl   »(Nichtig), alles Nichtigkeit!«[75]

3. Kohelets Einstellung zur Religion

Kohelets Lebensstil ist geprägt durch Skepsis, Furcht vor Gott[76] und ein Bekenntnis zur Lebensfreude[77], deren Bejahung er mit dem griechischen Philosophen Epikur teilt. Doch gibt es zwischen Koh und ihm gerade im Verhältnis zur Religion erhebliche Unterschiede[78]. Israels Gott

64. Kleiner Klangzirkel mit i.
65. Kleiner Klangzirkel mit a.
66. Kleiner Klangzirkel mit o.
67. Assonanz zum vorhergehenden Wort.
68. Im Hebr. wird der Vokalismus des Anfangs von 5f (kī hōlik) am Schluß von 5i (sōpīdim) wieder aufgenommen; in der dtsch. Imitation habe ich statt dessen einen Endreim gesetzt.
69. MSS: K; zu Varianten s. BHS.
70. W. Richter: tarūṣ.
71. Anfangskreuzreim 6b/d: w'=tarōṣ / w'narōṣ.
72. Antithetischer PM mit der Besonderheit, daß das 2. Glied eine rhetorische Frage ist.
73. Chiasmus in 7ac: yašūb / tašūb.
74. 7b und 7d bilden einen Kreuzreim.
75. Wie bereits gesagt – m.E. Stilmittel von Koh, nicht Zusatz von anderer Hand; anders dagegen 12,9-14.
76. Nicht alternativ, wie in dem Titel des Buchs von FISCHER (Anm. 22).
77. Daß Koh wirklich lebensfroh gewesen ist, ist mehr als zweifelhaft. Sein Denken erweckt eher den Eindruck eines Ankämpfens gegen immer wieder nahende Depressionen. Dafür sprechen Stellen wie 2,1-2; 4,1-3 u.dgl.
78. T. TYLER, Ecclesiastes, London, 1874, zu Koh 5,(17-)19, sah in מענה die ἀταραξία (zitiert nach P. HEINISCH, Griechische Philosophie und Altes Testament, in BZ

spielt im Denken Kohelets eine ungleich größere Rolle als die griechische Götterwelt bei Epikur[79]. Dieses Resümee, das auch Schwienhorst-Schönberger am Ende seines Buches zieht, ist sicher – trotz Differenzierungen in Einzelfragen[80] – nicht anfechtbar.

Daß Gott ein *Deus absconditus* ist, der für den Menschen kein »Du« ist und zudem das »für den alttestamentlichen Glauben... zuversichtliche Vertrauen« nicht besteht, ist oft bemerkt worden[81]. Ein Gott gegebenes Gelübde flößt Koh solche Furcht ein, daß er dringend von einem solchen abrät (5,1-6). Und dies tut er, obwohl in seinem Denken eine Erfahrung eine ausschlaggebende Rolle spielt: Es ist nicht zu erkennen, daß Frömmigkeit immer belohnt und Gottlosigkeit immer bestraft wird. Auch zweifelt er daran, daß es eine ausgleichende Gerechtigkeit nach dem Tod geben wird (2,13-17; 6,16-21; 7,15; 8,10-14).

Ein Schlüsselwort zum Verständnis der religiösen Einstellung Kohelets ist wohl 7,16f:

16 a	'al tihy ṣaddīq harbē(h)	Sei nicht allzu fromm[82],
b	w'='al tithakkam yōtir	Um Weisheit nicht allzu bemüht!
c	la=mah tiššōmim	Warum willst du dich aufreiben?
17 a	'al tirša' harbē(h)	Sei nicht zu hemmungslos[82],
b	w'='al tihy sakal	Und werde kein Narr!
c	la=mah tamūt	Warum willst du sterben
d	b'lō(') 'itt-i=ka	Vor deiner Zeit?

Es bleibt also eine Furcht vor Gottes Strafe, auch wenn Koh ihr Eintreffen bei einem Frevler nicht immer (!) erkennen konnte.

So sehr sich eine gewisse Geistesverwandtschaft zu Koh in der Wertung des Lebens als sinnlos erscheinendes Leiden bei Arthur Schopenhauer zeigt, so unterschiedlich ist bei beiden die aus dieser Einsicht ge-

---

(1913), 3-80, spez. p. 68). Zur Frage eines möglichen Einflusses der Epikuräer auf Koh, vgl. SCHWIENHORST-SCHÖNBERGER, *op. cit.* (Anm. 22), pp. 260-269 und 274-332, bes. p. 274 Anm. 5.

79. H. DIELS, *Ein epikureisches Fragment über Götterverehrung (Oxyrrh. Pap. II n215)*, in *SPAW* (1916) 886-909, spez. p. 903: θεὸς δὲ μὴ προσάγε ἐνταῦθα (Diels übersetzt den Passus sehr frei: »... die Angst vor den Göttern mußt du zu Hause lassen«). Doch darf trotz der ἀταραξία, die Epikur den Göttern zuschreibt (M.P. NILSSON, *Geschichte der griechischen Religion*, II (Handbuch der Altertumswissenschaft 5,2 II), München, 1950, p. 239f), diesem völlige religiöse Indifferenz nicht nachgesagt werden (vgl. dazu A.-J. FESTUGIÈRE, *Epicure et ses dieux*, Paris, 1946, bes. p. 99).

80. SCHWIENHORST-SCHÖNBERGER, *op. cit.*, p. 332. Auf die Differenzen bei den Stellen Koh 12,1 und 7 wurde bei deren Erörterung bereits hingewiesen.

81. LAUHA, *op. cit.* (Anm. 13), p. 17. – Weitere Literatur dazu s. bei MICHEL, *Qohelet*, pp. 95-103. – Koh 5,1: »Gott ist im Himmel, und du bist auf der Erde.«

82. Die hebr. Wörter צדיק und (das der Verbform תרשע entsprechende Adjektiv) רשע scheinen mir so am besten wiedergegeben zu sein. Ähnlich auch die *EÜ*: «Halte dich nicht zu streng an das Gesetz... Entferne dich nicht zu weit vom Gesetz...».

zogene Konsequenz. Die Erhebung asketischer Lebensweise als »Heiligkeit«, die Schopenhauer als Ideal aufstellt[83], dürfte geradezu das Gegenteil von Kohelets Lebensstil sein, und ersterer hat es auch so empfunden[84]. Eine Formulierung wie die, wenn es Gott gäbe, müßte diesem die Erschaffung der Welt »dann freilich mißrathen seyn«, die Schopenhauer äußert[85], widerspräche bei Koh dem Respekt vor dem Schöpfer.

Selbst wenn Gott dem Menschen aus unerklärlichen Gründen so viel עמל auferlegt hat, entspricht doch andererseits die Freude am Essen und Trinken und den Annehmlichkeiten dem, was er uns zubilligt; – doch ein Rest kindlicher Glaubenshaltung bleibt bei Koh (2,24; 3,12-13.22; 5,18-19; 6,9; 9,7ff; 11,7ff). Im krassen Gegensatz zu Paulus wäre der Satz »Φάγωμεν καὶ πίωμεν, αὔριον γὰρ ἀποθνήσκομεν«[86], von ihm entschieden bejaht worden.

4. Die ethischen Konsequenzen

Die Ablehnung eines Anhäufens von Reichtümern ist bei Koh, der vermutlich selbst durchaus vermögend gewesen ist[87], nicht ethisch oder religiös begründet[88]. Sie ist rein pragmatisch motiviert: Reichtum bringt עמל mit sich, und dieses Wort scheint speziell in diesem Zusammenhang soviel wie »Streß« zu bedeuten (2,10-11; 4,8 u.ö.).

Mit den ausgebeuteten Menschen zeigt Koh tiefes Mitgefühl (4,1-3) – auch wieder eine Gemeinsamkeit mit Schopenhauer[89]. Allerdings bietet der eine so wenig wie der andere Vorschläge oder gar Initiativen zur Linderung des Elends. Ob Koh 11,1 als eine Mahnung zu Großzügigkeit im sozialen Bereich zu werten ist, wie oft angenommen, bleibt fragwürdig[90]. Jedoch übt Koh auch scharfe Kritik an den ungerechten Machtverhältnissen, wobei die dem Königtum gegenüber freundliche Einstellung, die ihm von den meisten Übersetzungen zugeschrieben wird[91], meiner

---

83. SCHOPENHAUER, op. cit. (Anm. 35), pp. 452ff u.ö.

84. Das Zitat von Koh 7,4 bei SCHOPENHAUER, op. cit., p. 731, ist wohl ein Mißverständnis; aber schon bald danach distanziert er sich heftig vom Alten Testament und seinem Optimismus, den er »zum Theil empörend« nennt, und führt dabei Koh 9,7-10 an (p. 741).

85. SCHOPENHAUER, op. cit., II (Werke, III), p. 718.

86. 1 Kor 15,32, das bekanntlich dabei Jes 22,14 LXX zitiert.

87. S. dazu KAISER, art. cit. (Anm. 24), p. 5.

88. Vgl. dazu D. MICHEL & L.E. KECK & J. MAIER, art. »Armut«, in TRE 4, pp. 72-85.

89. SCHOPENHAUER, op. cit., II (Werke, III), p. 663 und Kontext.

90. ELLERMEIER, op.cit. (Anm. 48), pp. 253-268, bringt gewichtige Gegenargumente; allerdings für direkt widerlegt (so GALLING, op. cit. [Anm. 47], p. 119) halte ich eine Interpretation von Koh 11,1 in sozialethischer Hinsicht damit noch nicht.

91. Z.B. die EÜ: »Trotzdem ist es ein Gewinn für das Land, wenn das bebaute Feld einem König untersteht«.

Überzeugung nach die Intention verkennt:

5,7   Wenn du Unterdrückung eines Armen und Mißachtung von Recht und Ge-
        rechtigkeit im Lande siehst, wundere dich nicht darüber! Denn ein Mächti-
        ger deckt[92] einen anderen und über ihnen stehen (wieder) Mächtige.

5,8   a w'=yitrōn 'arṣ b'=[h]a=kul[l]   Und der Ertrag für das Land bei
                                          alledem?

      b hū(')[93] malk   (sarkastisch:) Es ist ein König

      c l=ō[94] śadæ niʿbod   Für ihn müssen wir »ackern[95]«.

Was für die Reichtümer gilt, trifft auch für die Weisheit bei Koh zu:
Beides hat seinen relativen Wert, aber bleibt *letztlich* ohne יתרון (2,12-
23)[96]. Dieser Gedanke kommt auch in einer Klangfigur zum Ausdruck:

6,7   kul[l]   ʿamal   ha='adam l'=pī=hu(w)
                                       w'=gam
8   lō(') timmalē(')
                        ha=napš
                                              kī
              mah   yōtir[97]
                        l'=[h]a=ḥakam min ha=ksīl
              mah   l'=[h]a=ʿanī
                                          yōdiʿ
      l'=hluk   nagd   ha=ḥayyīm
9   ṭōb   mar'ē(h)
                        ʿēnaym
      mi[n]=hluk   napš   gam   zǣ
                        habl
      (disassonant:) w'=rʿūt rūḥ.

6,7   Alle Mühsal des Menschen ist das, was für ihn bestimmt ist; und zudem
        wird seine Nephesch nicht befriedigt.

8   Denn was für einen Vorteil hat (schon) ein Weiser vor einem leichtfertig
        (Dahinlebend)en? Was für einen ein Armer, (auch wenn) d(ies)er ver-
        steht, im Urteil seiner Zeitgenossen (recht) zu wandeln.

9   Besser, sein Augenmerk auf Schönes zu richten, als ein Dahingehen der
        Nephesch[98]. (Doch) auch das ist nichtig und Windhascherei.

92. שמר könnte auch bedeuten: »paßt auf, belauert« (Michel: »wacht über«), aber
die Wiedergabe bei Loretz und der *EÜ* gibt hier einen guten Sinn.
93. K: hī('); Q: hū(').
94. Eine geringfügige Konjektur לו statt לְ (oder לְשָׂדֵהוּ statt לְשָׂדֶה) ist m.E. die beste
Lösung.
95. »... Land bearbeiten« ist zwar im Gegensatz zu dem umgangssprachlichen Wort »ak-
kern« eleganteres Deutsch und zudem wörtliche Übersetzung; aber die Intention Kohelets
wird durch das Wort »ackern« ganz genau getroffen. – Der Text könnte auch Lauten: »Ihm
gehört das bebaute Land« (niʿbad). – LORETZ, *op. cit.* (Anm. 21), p. 263, nimmt an, im Text
habe ursprünglich מכל statt מלך gestanden; auch GALLING, *op. cit.*, p. 101f, nimmt eine kleine
Konjektur vor und kommt bei dem immer noch kommentierbedürftigen Vers zu einer inhaltlich ähnlichen Aussage wie ich: Ein König ist kein Ausweg aus dieser Notlage.
96. Das Lieblingswort יתרון steht hier nicht, wohl aber das zugehörige Verb יתר (6,8).
Einen relativen Vorteil spricht Koh der Chokma nicht ab: 2,13f.
97. mah yōtir annähernd chiastisch vokalisiert zu timmalē(').
98. = Siechtum, Tod. Im Gefolge der LXX (πορευόμενον ψυχῇ) wird das

Es ist hier kein Raum, näher auf den Vorzug der Lebensfreude vor
dem Trauern und Grübeln bei Koh einzugehen (7,1-10 vor allem)[99];
so verweise ich auf die Textanalyse Michels, die ich für zutreffend
halte[100].

5. Ästhetische Gesichtspunkte in der Philosophie Kohelets

Wenn von der Chokma nur noch die Mahnung übrigbleibt, zu essen,
zu trinken[101], sich am Eros zu erfreuen (3,5b; 9,9; 11,9), es seinem
Haupt nicht an Salböl fehlen zu lassen und stets weiße Kleider zu tragen
(9,8)[102], ist dann die Lebensauffassung Kohelets eine rein ästhetische?
Sören Kierkegaard hat in seinem Roman *Entweder – Oder?* erst eine
solche uns vor Augen geführt und dann ihr die ethische gegenübergestellt[103]. Es ist interessant, daß eines der wichtigsten Kriterien für diese
Differenzierung – die positive Einstellung zur Ehe – eher Koh der letzte-
ren zuweisen würde[104]. Seinem Denken kann man Ehrlichkeit und Ver-
antwortungsbewußtsein nicht absprechen. Allerdings bringt Koh mit seinem Sarkasmus und seiner Ironie Salz und Pfeffer in die alttestamentliche
Chokma, und wer in ihm nur einen Tradenten althergebrachter und be-
währter Moral an bra-lernwillige Schüler sieht, verkennt ihn.

Zu seiner Freude an den schönen Dingen gehört gewiß auch jene am
sprachlichen Wohlklang, an der Poesie. Die Sänger und Sängerinnen
seiner »Königstravestie« zählen allerdings zu der Üppigkeit, die vielleicht einmal in seiner Jugend von ihm bewundert oder erstrebt wurde,
die er aber als *hæbæl* zu verwerfen gelernt hat (2,8.11). Aber die in 12,2
und 12,4 verwendeten Bilder (einschließlich der – wenn die hier vorge-

---

Hapaxlegomenon נפש הלך als »Zügellosigkeit der Begierde« (GESENIUS, *Wörterbuch*, 17.
Aufl. p. 181: »sich ergehen, umherschweifen«) gedeutet. Selbst wenn נפש das erste Mal
in diesem Vers mit »Begierde« treffend wiedergegeben wird, das Wort ist bekanntlich in
seiner Bedeutungsfülle schillernd. Ungleich häufiger bedeutet הלך »sterben«: vgl. Gen
15,2; Jes 38,10; Ps 39,14; Hiob 14,20; 19,10.

99. Mit Recht hat Erasmus herausgehört, daß Koh hier eine gewisse Sympathie für
den כסיל äußert und so wird von ihm in seinem humorigen Büchlein *Encomium moriae*
(*Das Lob der Thorheit*, aus dem Lat. übers. von Heinrich HIRSCH, Leipzig, o.J., p. 134)
7,4 zitiert. Allerdings hat er als Endziel des Lobes der μωρία die des Evangeliums 1 Kor
1,18 im Blick. – כסיל bedeutet mehr »leichtfertig, unbekümmert«, erst daraus erwächst
die Bedeutung »töricht«; s. RICHTER, *ZAW* 108 (1996) p. 587.

100. MICHEL, *Qohelet*, pp. 148f, und *BZAW* 183 (1989), pp. 126-137.

101. Stellenbelege s. oben §4.

102. Die Parallelen im Gilgamesch-Epos X,3,6-13 (*ANET*, p. 90) und Ägypten
(*ANET*, p. 467) u.a. sind zu beachten, doch besagen sie nicht – wie GALLING, *op. cit.*
(Anm. 47), p. 113, mit Recht sagt –, daß Koh sie gekannt hat.

103. S. KIERKEGAARD, *Gesammelte Werke*, I, Jena 1922, spez. p. 396.

104. Der Harem in der Königstravestie wird als *hæbæl* abgelehnt (2,8); s. RICHTER,
ZAW 108 (1996), pp. 589-592.

schlagene Deutung richtig sein sollte − der Vögel als banōt ha=šīr[105]) sprechen für liebevolle, auch sonst erkennbare Naturbeobachtung. Ins Grau des Alltags wird Farbe gebracht.

Kohelet ein Philosoph und Poet.

Fregestraße 12   Hans-Friedemann RICHTER
D-12159 Berlin

---

105. Die Stuttgarter Jubiläumsbibel (1941) kommentiert »Töchter des Gesangs« als »Vogel- und Menschenstimmen«; New English Bible: »song-birds«.

KOHELET'S MINIMALIST THEOLOGY

הוא ענין רע נתן אלהים לבני האדם לענות בו

It is a grievous business that God has given human beings to keep them busy.

In order to express both my hopes for this meeting and also my gratitude for the Book of Kohelet, I would like to offer a mildly midrashic reading of Qoh 1,13: Don't read only רָע (grievous), read also רֵעַ (friend); and may the Book of Kohelet, grievously difficult to understand, become for us an ענין רֵעַ, a "subject of friendship that God has given us to discuss and argue over."

I. *Hebel* and Kohelet's Quietism

My paper is part of a larger work in progress, tentatively entitled *Joyous Kohelet*, on Kohelet's minimalist theology. Because of time restrictions, I can focus on only one of its aspects, Kohelet's quietism.

What is perhaps most theologically troublesome with Kohelet is the absence of those forms of spirituality that seem to us mandatory: cult, revelation, covenant, a personal relationship with God. In Kohelet all individual appetites and preoccupations (חפץ) become explained by pre-determined cosmic patterns and balances. The main question is posed at the start: in such a universe what is to be derived from human effort? In other words, isn't quietism the logical approach to life? For if everything has its preordained moment, of what possible use are my efforts, anticipations, anxieties, even prayers? Is it not true that even our wisdom is tainted – indeed, driven – by our being so up-tight (here termed כעס, anger; 1,18; 7,9)? Shouldn't perfect acceptance and conformity with God's will, as expressed in the order of things, be the true focus of our spiritual approach?

To grasp the peculiar flavor of vanity (הבל) and chasing after the wind (רעות רוח) in Kohelet, we may have to divert our religious gaze from the very fullness of God's creation and, along with the Dalai Lama and others, develope a deeper awareness of the emptiness that surrounds creation and that seems to be its very support. We may also have to turn from our tense notions of frustration and woe, to withdraw from our forever expansive hatreds and dogmatisms and especially attachments (Qoh 7,8-10). In short, and like *La Princesse de Clèves* or Edith Wharton's lovers in *Age of Innocence,* we may have to relearn to appreciate the tranquility of the void more than the turbulence of the passions.

Despite our western cult of passion – the most vehement form of which may not be romantic love or even scientific curiosity but moral rectitude and religious justification – there has always been a minority opinion. What prevents us from making positive use of הבל may be a רעות רוח which has turned sour on its own extravagances. Kohelet's particular brand of indifference has struck some critics as upper-crust, as a numb and snooty aloofness from all wordly things. One wonders, though, whether we are not dealing here with a particular form of mental asceticism, with philosophical detachment, apathy, passivity, abandon, a mistrust of that passionate intensity that we occidentals have come to view as the very hallmark of the spiritual life or, indeed, of any life worth living whatever.

The Vanity or void that is of particular interest to the Preacher is thus neither cosmological nor even anthropological – in the sense of referring to "the worldly realities with which humans must deal"[1]: it is a human invention. As Montaigne put it, "Ce n'est pas merveille que le hazard puisse tant sur nous, puisque nous vivons par hazard" ("It is small wonder that chance has such power over us since we live by chance")[2]. Kohelet's moral point here is to stop increasing הבל and, through recognition and self-limitation, to come to accept and enjoy our lives. For when we remove the objects from the light, the light itself remains, giving greater delight than any of the objects or, indeed, all of them together.

II. רעות רוח

Kohelet experimented, gave his heart rein to excessive curiosity, only to discover later that "the soul can never be filled, satisfied" (6,7) and concluded that all is הבל and רעות רוח. Whatever הבל means, it is closely associated with רעות רוח. Indeed, just as humans bring הבל into the world through blind and senseless pursuits, so too our "chasing after wind" both characterizes and creates an "afflicted spirit" (the two senses of רעות רוח). Conversely and even more to Kohelet's point, it is the spirit's or heart's excessive desires that chase the wind. Indeed, the phrase הבל ורעיון רוח (4,16) equates vanity with a *desire* for wind.

I shall now examine several passages from a quietistic perspective.

A) The Cosmology (1,3-11)

What profit for humans from so much labor [I will return to this translation later] that they labor under the sun? (Qoh 1,3)

Just as, according to the Stoics, human nature is part of universal Na-

---

1. R. MURPHY, *Ecclesiastes* (World Biblical Commentary, 23A), Dallas, 1992, p. 4.
2. M. DE MONTAIGNE, *Essais*, ed. P. Villey, Paris, 1963, II,1, p. 337.

ture, for Kohelet humans exist "under the sun". From the juxtaposition with the cosmology that follows, we learn that what is affirmed about the cosmos is asserted about human existence as well. This point is also made by the use, in the cosmology, of psychological terms and metaphors to describe the elements: רוח (wind and also spirit), the sun's "panting desire". Here are the details:

> 1,4: People are born and die (or, if you prefer, generations come and go), forever striving to advance and effect change, but the earth (or, if you prefer, the people of the earth) remains the same, unchanged.
>
> 1,5: The sun rises and sets, "desiring" to reach its place. Each day the process is repeated.
>
> 1,6: The winds blow in a circular fashion.
>
> 1,7: Despite their efforts to fill the sea, which is never filled (=satisfied 1,8), the rivers themselves return to their point of departure.

Of the many things that can be said of this cosmology, let me stress the following three points:

> 1) the fact of universal movement;
> 2) each movement has a definite and limited goal, called its place;
> 3) each self-contained process is repeated indefinitely.

Item three, the cyclical regularity of all things, has captured the attention of critics, but the other two elements are equally important: in the natural world "under the sun" the universal movement (of desire, perhaps) is characterized by limited ends. Seneca puts it this way:

> Natural desires are limited, but those which spring from false opinion have no stopping point, for there are no limits to the false. When you are traveling on a road, there must be an end; but when astray, your wanderings are limitless [cf. Qoh 10,15]. Therefore, withdraw from vain things (*vanis*); and when you would know whether what you seek is based on a natural or a blind desire, consider whether it can stop at any definite point. If you find, after having travelled far, that there is a more distant goal always in view, you may be sure that this condition is contrary to nature. (Letter to Lucilius, #16)[3]

Thus, beyond their regularity or cyclicality, natural desires (both in the elements and in humans) have definite limits and visible ends. What thus may seem to us as a dreadful annoyance – that there is nothing new etc. – is in fact viewed by Kohelet as a guarantee against a more serious inconvenience. For it is UNnatural, linear desires that seek the new, imagining places where there is no memory of past things; and it is the limitation of desires to their natural boundaries that saves us from the

---

3. SENECA, *Ad Lucilium Epistulae Morales*, ed. and trans. R.M. GUMMERE, 3 vols, London, 1967; cf. also MONTAIGNE, *op. cit.*, p. 1011.

vanity of the false infinite. From this point of view the opening motto "all is vanity" is neither ontological nor epistemological. It is a moral preacher's caution against the vanity that we multiply (6,11) through our blind and extravagant desires and pursuits.

B) More is less (1,3)

One important lesson of the Seneca passage is that, if our labors are to avoid wearisome vanity, they must be limited. Let us now return to our translation "SO MUCH labor" (1,3). It is customary to interpret this verse in terms of the preceding one, forcing the conclusion that human vanity is part of universal vanity. Thus, כל is understood as "any", with Kohelet insisting that NO effort has any value. When we later must admit that "something does accrue from the various activities that occupy human beings during their waking hours"[4], we must then rely on the notion of death's finality – a false strategy, in my view, since it displaces the debate to the other world. Rather, I propose a return to Michael V. Fox's notion that extra effort does not *adequately* compensate our efforts[5], but I would shift the focus of the complaint from the nature of things to the human subject. Now, if the following section (1,12-2,26) might well be entitled "the futility of toil and effort"[6], then the opening cosmology can be viewed not at all as an introductory general complaint on such a state of affairs but rather precisely the opposite: it offers observations on how the universe functions in its natural state and, by implication, how humans SHOULD behave as well.

The sorry state of *human* affairs is appropriately given immediately after the cosmology: as opposed to the limited desires of the natural elements, the world of איש, of humans, is one of excess:

> SO MANY things in ceaseless activity:
> No one can express them all
> The eye is never satisfied with seeing
> Nor the ear filled with hearing. (Qoh 1,8)

In other words, while it is true that human speech and eye and ear are "incapable of taking it all in"[7], Kohelet makes the crucial *moral* argument that humans SHOULD NOT TRY TO DO SO! These words are thus neither a complaint on the universe's monotonous futility nor even prima-

---

4. J.L. CRENSHAW, *Ecclesiastes* (The Old Testament Library), Philadelphia, 1987, p. 60; see R.N. WHYBRAY, *Ecclesiastes* (The New Century Bible Commentary), London, 1989, pp. 83-84, on 4,4.

5. M.V. FOX, *Qohelet and His Contradictions* (JSOT SS, 71), Sheffield, 1989, p. 68.

6. WHYBRAY, *op. cit.*, p. 47.

7. R.N. WHYBRAY, *Ecclesiastes 1.5-7 and the Wonders of Nature*, in *JSOT* 41 (1988) 105-112, p. 107.

rily a lingering admiration of nature's wonders. Rather, they take note of the vanity of our boundless striving for what we imagine to be fulfillment. Indeed, our endless pursuit of newness, our ceaseless curiosity, our pretense to have invented the world anew is based on a blissful ignorance not only of nature but of history as well:

> Someone claims: "Look, this is new!"
> It has already happend for aeons. [He is simply unaware, since]
> There is no memory of former things
> [people make no effort to remember. In the same way, tit-for-tat],
> They too will be forgotten. (Qoh 1,10-11)

C) Qoh 8,8 (I translate according to Radak [Rabbi David Kimhi, 1160?-1235?], in his commentary to Ps 1[8]):

> Humans do not rule over their spirit, to inhibit the spirit – just as there is no rule over the day of death or escape in a war – and passion (רֶשַׁע) will not save its possessor.

Radak goes on to explain:

> The wicked (רשעים) are those who are passionate (חרדים) in acquiring money and their heart's desires in this world and make no distinction between good and evil, and embezzle and steal and kill because of their heart's passion.

We might think that this is a standard diatribe against materialism, focussing on the *goal* of desire (money and other forms of wealth). But Radak thinks that the real evil is desire itself:

> For the meaning of wickedness (רֶשַׁע) is passion (חרדה).

He then cites, in addition to 8,8, Qoh 7,17: אל תרשע הרבה, "Don't be too wicked". Might one then conclude that Kohelet gives license to be somewhat wicked? But, rather: don't be too passionate. For "too much" leads not only to emotional disturbance[9] but also to depravity.

In our endless studies of such key concepts as רעות רוח and עמל, we have become stalled on the act and its result, while neglecting the cause. Thus, עמל means both labor and its result, wealth, to be sure. But in the בכל עמלו we have not noticed the רעיון לבו (2,22), the heart's unnatural desires that produce the "overdoing"[10], perhaps a workaholism[11], in the first place.

8. Rabbi David KIMHI, *Commentary on Psalms* [in Hebrew], Jerusalem, 1967.
9. FOX, *op. cit.*, p. 235, citing 1,18.
10. FOX, *op. cit.*, p. 54.
11. R K. JOHNSTON, *"Confessions of a Workaholic" : A Reappraisal of Qohelet*, in *CBQ* 38 (1976) 14-28.

CONCLUDING POSTSCRIPT

In conclusion, although I have used a rather refined and restricted religious concept to characterize a neglected area of Kohelet's spirituality, it seems to me that his quietism is of the practical sort, and this in several senses. First of all, Kohelet does not present a treatise, a systematic proof of the necessity of quietism, since that would undermine his general point of knowledge's insufficiency and, more dangerously, further its enormous pretense. Secondly, a usual quietism based on a radical trust in only God in the abstract would be but another occasion for pretense, for a secret feeling of supremacy over the spiritual approaches of others. No, his general sense is that things must be worked out practically, must be consistent in every detail with the quotidian character of our personal existence and reflexion. Thus, thirdly and to protect against a radical quietism, the Catalogue of the Times (3,1ff), teaches that many projects and desires are appropriate *in their natural time*.

In order to introduce our students to Kohelet as a manual for living well, let us not forget such sensible texts as Montaigne's essay on vanity (*Essais* 3,9), or Seneca's praise, over all worldly honors and passions, of tranquil retirement (Letter #36).

My friends, "Die Sonne tönt nach *alte* Weise" (*Faust* I, "Prologue in Heaven"). When the sun rises every morning, we may still, with Kohelet's help, recover the sense, a hint of eternity perhaps, that there is nothing new: Thank God!

Ben Gurion University of the Negev   T. Anthony PERRY
Beer-Sheva, Israel

LIBERTÉ DE DIEU OU DESTIN?
UN AUTRE DILEMME DANS L'INTERPRÉTATION DU QOHÉLET

L'emploi du mot מִקְרֶה dans le livre du Qohélet est une confirmation ultérieure de la singularité de notre texte par rapport aux autres livres de l'Ancien Testament; מִקְרֶה en effet pourrait évoquer une force mystérieuse qui détermine les événements, tandis que dans toute la Bible le principe de la souveraineté absolue de Dieu est affirmé d'une façon incontestable[1]. On peut se demander alors si en abordant le thème du destin de l'homme Qohélet n'a pas été influencé par la littérature grecque, puisque l'ouvrage est situé très probablement à l'époque hellénistique[2].

Notre analyse part des textes où l'on retrouve le mot מִקְרֶה, sans oublier d'autres passages qui traitent des thématiques semblables (3,22; 8,5-8; 9,6.9.11-12). Il faut délimiter aussi l'aire sémantique où le thème en question se pose. Outre מִקְרֶה, les substantifs עֵת, פֶּגַע, חֵלֶק sont également importants pour notre recherche. En ce qui concerne les termes זְמָן et עוֹלָם, nous en tiendrons compte indirectement pour une mise au point de la problématique concernant le destin.

Le mot מִקְרֶה revient, on le sait, sept fois: 2,14.15; 3,19 (ter); 9,2.3, le plus souvent dans un contexte différent.

En 2,14-15 la question de Qohélet a pour objet l'avantage effectif de la sagesse: en théorie sa valeur est indiscutable et on pourrait épouser aussi la thèse traditionnelle selon laquelle le sage est illuminé et bien orienté dans la vie, tandis que celui qui est insensé marche dans les ténèbres (2,14). Mais si ensuite le sage et l'insensé ont le même destin, à quoi bon toute cette sagesse? Qohélet en appelle alors à une réalité irréfutable, qui est l'objet de l'expérience de tous les hommes, pour mettre en question un principe fondamental de la tradition: la supériorité de la sagesse sur la folie au niveau existentiel.

---

1. Cf. P. MACHINIST, *Fate, miqreh, and Reason. Some Reflections on Qohelet and Biblical Thought*, in Z. ZEVIT et al. (eds.), *Solving Riddles and Untying Knots. Biblical, Epigraphic and Semitic Studies in Honor of Jonas C. Greenfield*, Winona Lake, 1995, pp. 159-175; O. KAISER, *Schiksal, Leid und Gott. Ein Gespräch mit dem Kohelet, Prediger Salomo*, in M. OEMING – A. GRAUPNER (eds.), *Altes Testament und christliche Verkündigung. FS A.H.J. Gunneweg*, Stuttgart, 1987, pp. 30-51; ID., *Determination und Freiheit beim Kohelet/Prediger Salomo und in der Frühen Stoa*, in *NZSTh* 31 (1989) 251-270.

2. Cf. L. SCHWIENHORST-SCHÖNBERGER, *"Nicht im Menschen gründet das Glück (Koh 2,24). Kohelet im Spannungsfeld jüdischer Weisheit und hellenistischer Philosophie*, Freiburg, 1994, spéc. pp. 233-332.

En 3,19 le problème est encore le destin final de l'homme, qui cette fois rejoint celui de la bête; face à la mort il n'y a aucune différence et toutes les prétentions de supériorité de l'homme par rapport aux animaux s'écroulent misérablement puisqu'ils aboutissent tous à la même demeure. La mort est le destin naturel de tous les êtres vivants. Le verbe הלך, employé en 3,20 avec היה et שׁוב, nous ramène à Qo 1, 4-11, à la conception de circularité, selon une vision des cycles qui est propre à la pensée de l'ancien Orient comme à celle de la philosophie grecque. En ce qui concerne le contexte, le thème du destin est encadré par Qohélet dans une vision très large, qui embrasse le jugement de Dieu sur l'histoire et au-delà de l'histoire (3,17).

Dans ses argumentations Qohélet utilise des instruments logiques qui sont propres au style philosophique, puisqu'il donne le primat à l'expérience mais en même temps il nie toute validité à ce qui dépasse la réalité sensible. De plus, la structure logique de l'argumentation s'exprime d'une façon satisfaisante dans les figures de rhétorique qui caractérisent le style de cet auteur si singulier[3]: la répétition, qui attire l'attention sur le thème fondamental (ter מִקְרֶה); l'interrogation qui rend problématique la position de l'interlocuteur, mettant en discussion l'hypothèse d'un sort différent de l'homme par rapport à celui de la bête (3,21)[4]. La conclusion, concernant le rôle de l'homme dans la vie, reconduit au présent, la seule réalité qui justifie l'existence (3,22). L'autre interrogation du v. 22 a comme but de mettre en question la possibilité de connaître l'avenir. Ce problème, qui occupe une position particulièrement importante dans la problématique du livre (6,10-12)[5], exerce une fonction décisive pour cerner et définir le rôle que l'homme a dans le monde; celui-ci doit s'orienter exclusivement vers le présent.

En 9,2-3 la perspective change de nouveau parce que Qohélet aborde cette fois le problème de la rétribution, cependant la thèse fondamentale reste la même: tout le monde partagera le même sort. Dans ce passage Qohélet se rapporte à cinq catégories: juste et impie; bon et méchant; pur et impur; celui qui offre des sacrifices et celui qui ne les offre pas;

---

3. Sur les figures de rhétorique dans le Qohélet cf. V. D'ALARIO, *Il libro del Qohelet. Struttura letteraria e retorica* (SupRivBib, 27), Bologna, 1993, pp. 183-237.
4. Cf. A. SCHOORS, *Koheleth: A Perspective of Live after Death?*, in *ETL* 61 (1985) 295-303; V. D'ALARIO, *"Chi sa se lo spirito dell'uomo sale in alto...? (Qo 3, 21). Un testo problematico sul tema dell'immortalità*, in G. LORIZIO (ed.), *Morte e sopravvivenza. In dialogo con X. Tilliette* (Saggi, 32), Roma, 1995, pp. 211-222.
5. Cf. D'ALARIO, *Il libro del Qohelet* (n. 3), pp. 115-116; 216-218. Sur le rapport que Qohélet entretient avec l'apocalyptique cf. L. ROSSO UBIGLI, *Qohelet di fronte all'apocalittica*, in *Henoch* 5 (1983) 209-232; D. MICHEL, *Weisheit und Apokalyptik*, in A. S. VAN DER WOUDE (ed.), *The Book of Daniel in the Light of New Findings* (BETL, 106), Leuven, 1993, pp. 413-434.

le jureur et celui qui a peur de jurer. Mais puisqu'il n'y a pas de sort différent parmi ceux qui se comportent d'une façon différente, on explique ainsi pourquoi le cœur de l'homme est rempli de méchanceté et de démence. Qohélet en appelle à cette donnée empirique, qui revête une forte valence anthropologique, pour prouver l'insuffisance de la doctrine traditionnelle sur la rétribution.

Les versets de conclusion du chapitre (9,11-12) insistent sur cette réflexion, se référant à cinq autres catégories: agiles, forts, sages, prudents, intelligents. Le pouvoir de nivellement de la mort agit aussi au niveau des capacités; si elles ne sont pas garanties durant la vie, elles le sont encore moins au moment de la mort: le temps (עֵת) et le hasard (פֶּגַע) n'épargnent personne. À ce propos le Qohélet développe en 9,12 une similitude déroutante, qu'il tire de la symbologie animale: l'homme n'est pas différent des poissons et des oiseaux, puisque son sort est également imprévisible. Tandis que מִקְרֶה désigne d'une façon générale le destin qui arrive à tous les êtres vivants, les deux autres mots, עֵת et פֶּגַע, soulignent qu'un tel destin échappe au contrôle de l'homme. Il ne s'agit pas d'un hendiadys mais de deux termes distincts, qui dénotent des aspects différents de la même réalité[6]; le mot עֵת désigne dans ce passage l'heure; פֶּגַע signifie l'événement qui tombe tout à coup sur l'homme et il a souvent une connotation négative[7]. Ce concept de hasard est très semblable au concept grec de τύχη; ce terme en effet désigne l'événement qui arrive au débotté sans que l'homme l'ait cherché[8]. Même dans cette unité le thème de la mort entraîne l'invitation à la joie qui dans ce contexte est plus approfondie (9,7-9)[9]. Mais la clé de lecture de tout le chapitre est donnée, à notre avis, par le v. 1; les œuvres des justes et des sages sont dans la main de Dieu mais l'homme ne connaît pas les senti-

---

6. Sur ce problème cf. A. SCHOORS, *The Preacher Sought to Find Pleasing Words. A Study of the Language of Qoheleth* (OLA, 41), Leuven, 1992, p. 217; J. VILCHEZ, *Eclesiastes o Qohelet*, Estella, 1994, pp. 365-366.

7. "Stoß" ou "Schlag" selon P. MAIBERGER, פֶּגַע, in *TWAT* VI, 501-508, spéc. 506. Sur l'importance du concept de hasard dans le livre du Qohélet cf. F. J. BACKAUS, *"Denn Zeit und Zufall trifft sie alle". Zu Komposition und Gottesbild im Buch Qohelet* (BBB, 83), Frankfurt am Main, 1993, spéc. pp. 274-275.

8. Voir la définition de τύχη dans M. C. NUSSBAUM, *The Fragility of Goodness. Luck and Ethics in Greek Tragedy and Philosophy*, Cambridge, 1986, p. 3: "What happens to a person by luck will be just what does not happen through his or her own agency, what just *happens* to him, as opposed to what he does or makes". Qohélet exprime le concept de hasard inattendu même par la combinaison de קָרָה מִקְרֶה et מִקְרֶה (cf 2,14.15), que nous rencontrons aussi en Rut 2,3. À ce sujet cf. קָרָה, in *TWAT* VII, 172-175 (Ringgren), spéc. 173; MACHINIST, *Fate, miqreh, and Reason* (n. 1), p. 169.

9. Sur le thème de la joie cf. J. Y.- S. PAHK, *Il canto della gioia in Dio. L'itinerario sapienziale espresso dall'unità letteraria in Qohelet 8,16 – 9,10 e il parallelo di Gilgameš Me.iii*, Napoli, 1996.

ments de Dieu à son égard parce que le jugement divin est insaisissable[10].

La lecture rapide des textes démontre que le problème du sort de l'homme est abordé par Qohélet sous plusieurs perspectives, mais on peut relever aussi des constantes: 1) la mort est le dernier destin de tous les êtres vivants et elle est inéluctable; 2) son effet est d'annuler toutes les différences aussi bien au niveau biologique qu'au niveau éthique et religieux; toute l'emphase est sur l'expression מִקְרֶה אֶחָד; 3) le thème du destin, qui est relié au problème de la cognoscibilité de l'avenir, n'est pas l'objet principal de la réflexion de Qohélet; c'est plutôt un moment important de l'argumentation qui a comme but de fonder l'éthique de la joie et du quotidien; 4) le discours anthropologique est strictement lié au discours théologique et surtout au thème du mystère de Dieu.

Pour sa conception de la mort comme destin de l'homme Qohélet semble s'alligner en quelque sorte à la pensée judaïque, mais dans ses argumentations il introduit des éléments qui provoquent une rupture décisive à l'égard de la tradition sapientiale.

L'opinion que l'homme se rapproche de la bête dans son destin réalise un renversement de la perspective par rapport au discours de la Genèse; en effet chez Qohélet on a l'impression que l'homme est plus proche de la bête que de Dieu[11]. L'emphase sur le pouvoir de la mort, qui réalise un nivellement sous tous les aspects, détruit la doctrine traditionnelle de la rétribution; franchement on ne comprend pas quel est l'avantage réel de la sagesse sur la stupidité, de la justice sur l'impiété. Enfin l'association du sort de l'homme au hasard nous oblige à formuler plusieurs questions: dans quelle mesure la pensée de Qohélet s'accorde-t-elle avec la conception que l'Ancien Testament présente sur la souveraineté de Dieu dans l'histoire? L'intervention de Dieu peut-elle s'exprimer en termes de hasard? À travers l'emploi des mots מִקְרֶה, עֵת et פֶּגַע, est-il possible que Qohélet ait introduit des éléments étrangers aux catégories bibliques? Les similitudes avec la pensée grecque sont éclatantes, mais elles ne concernent pas seulement la conception de l'inéluctabilité de la mort, qui est un *topos* de la littérature pessimiste de tous les temps. Elles concernent surtout la relation serrée que l'auteur établit entre la mort, le destin et le temps[12] et en outre sa lecture du rôle de l'homme à partir

10. On trouvera une interprétation différente dans J.-J. LAVOIE, *Vie, mort et finitude humaine en Qo 9,1-6*, in *ScEs* 47 (1995) 69-80, spéc. p. 75. Il s'agirait des sentiments humains, surtout pour la reprise du thème au v. 6.

11. À ce sujet cf. J.-J. LAVOIE, *La pensée du Qohélet. Étude exégétique et intertextuelle* (Héritage et projet, 49), Montréal, 1992, pp. 53-89.

12. Cf. J. G. GAMMIE, *Stoicism and Antistoicism in Qoheleth*, in *HAR* 9 (1985) 169-187, spéc. pp. 180-185; J. BLENKINSOPP, *Ecclesiastes 3,1-15: Another Interpretation*, in *JSOT* 66 (1995) 55-64.

d'une réflexion générale sur le destin. À notre avis, en effet, le rapprochement entre le Qohélet et l'hellénisme doit se faire au niveau du procédé rationnel plus que des contenus, pour lesquels beaucoup de comparaisons seraient possibles[13]. Son style et ses argumentations attestent que Qohélet est un sage sensible aux instances culturelles de son temps et qu'il est aussi capable d'utiliser les instruments de la logique et du style de l'époque hellénistique. Mais c'est bien la nature dialectique de ses thèses qui suscite nos questions: elles découlent de la formulation même des questions dans le livre du Qohélet. Le destin de l'homme, qui aboutit à la mort, est-il prédéterminé de sorte qu'on pourrait parler de Dieu en termes de *Fatum*? Ou, au contraire, l'entremise du hasard échappe-t-elle à tout contrôle, de l'homme aussi bien que de Dieu[14]? Cette deuxième éventualité peut se retrouver dans la philosophie grecque, où les dieux mêmes n'échappent pas à la τύχη, tandis qu'elle est vraiment impossible chez un auteur biblique. Quel est donc le rôle que la catégorie du hasard joue dans l'argumentation de Qohélet? Il faut se déplacer du domaine anthropologique à celui de la théologie, où l'on rencontre le thème de la liberté de Dieu. Son dessein est mystérieux et incompréhensible (3, 10-15; 7, 23-24; 8, 17; 11, 5.6) et même son rapport avec l'homme est indéchiffrable (9,1); Dieu en effet n'a pas donné à l'homme la clé de l'interprétation de son œuvre (3,11) et il ne lui accorde pas le pouvoir de changer son dessein dans l'histoire (1,15; 3,14; 7,13)[15]. Dans cette conception de Dieu Qohélet s'accorde soit avec les apocalypticiens[16] soit avec les historiens et les philosophes grecs[17]: tout est prédéterminé par Dieu ou par la εἱμαρμένη et rien ne peut changer. Ce trait rapproche les théologies de l'époque hellénistique, surtout le stoïcisme, et l'historiographie de la période finale du judaïsme. De là on peut aussi comprendre l'importance que ces théologies donnent à la détermination du moment historique où les hommes et les peuples se trouvent. Mais le Dieu du Qohélet ne se fait pas bloquer dans des schémas interprétatifs trop rigides. Le message de l'auteur vise à sauvegarder, par le mystère, la liberté de Dieu. Il agit en dehors des règles, sans que l'homme puisse compren-

---

13. Cf. G. RAVASI, *Qohelet*, Cinisello Balsamo (Mi), 1988, pp. 377-469.

14. Pour la littérature sur le thème de la liberté de Dieu cf. LAVOIE, *La pensée du Qohélet* (n. 11), p. 235 à la note 54.

15. Cf. V. D'ALARIO, *Chi può conoscere il disegno di Dio? Problematica e prospettiva della sapienza critica*, in M. LORENZANI (ed.), *La volontà di Dio nella Bibbia*, L'Aquila, 1994, pp. 87-111.

16. Cf. M. DELCOR, *Le Dieu des apocalypticiens*, in J. COPPENS (ed.), *La notion biblique de Dieu* (BETL, 41), Gembloux – Leuven, 1976, pp. 211-228, spéc. p. 214: "D'après les conceptions apocalyptiques, les hommes ne doivent donc pas changer ce qui a été prédéterminé par Dieu".

17. M. DELCOR, *L'histoire selon le livre de Daniel, notamment au chapitre 11*, in VAN DER WOUDE, *The Book of Daniel* (n. 5), pp. 365-385.

dre le sens des événements, puisque toute la réalité est impénétrable. À notre avis le concept de hasard (פֶּגַע), qui est familier aux Grecs mais inconnu aux apocalypticiens, est employé par Qohélet pour souligner avec emphase que les événements sont incontrôlables et qu'ils sont encore plus imprévisibles. En 8,5-8 l'entrelacement des thèmes est analogue aux textes où l'on retrouve le mot מִקְרֶה. D'abord Qohélet expose la pensée traditionnelle, selon laquelle le sage connaît le temps et le jugement. Ensuite il fait sa critique qui aboutit toujours à la même conclusion: l'homme ne peut pas connaître sa dernière heure. À ce domaine conceptuel il faut ramener les catégories de מִקְרֶה, עֵת et פֶּגַע. Il s'agit alors de comprendre l'articulation des différents niveaux.

Liberté de Dieu et destin: comment ces deux éléments s'épousent-ils? Quel est leur poids dans la vie de l'homme? On peut par ailleurs se demander si la liberté de Dieu et le destin sont vraiment deux réalités distinctes ou s'il s'agit de deux aspects différents de la même réalité. La réponse à ces questions peut naître de la compréhension de la logique profonde du texte; elle n'est pas linéaire mais dialectique. À côté du concept de Dieu qui gouverne tout, nous trouvons l'idée de sa liberté. Les concepts de temps (עֵת) et de hasard (פֶּגַע) pourraient être corrélatifs à ces deux idées théologiques. Le mot עֵת nous fait comprendre que les événements arrivent au moment opportun, tandis que l'irruption du hasard dans la vie de l'homme témoigne qu'ils échappent à son contrôle puisque l'histoire est sous la souveraineté de Dieu. Le Seigneur est le maître du temps; pour cela la connaissance même de l'histoire Lui appartient, une connaissance qui n'est pas donnée à l'homme. Deux autres termes, זְמָן et עוֹלָם, auraient exprimé d'une façon plus prégnante la conception de la souveraineté de Dieu sur le temps: זְמָן en effet renferme le sens de la détermination, עוֹלָם souligne le caractère d'invariabilité et de mystère du plan divin[18]. Qohélet se sert par contre des mots עֵת et פֶּגַע; peut-être parce qu'il n'est pas si intéressé à l'idée de la prédétermination de la mort [19] comme il l'est à exprimer le sens du moment opportun et en même temps imprévisible dans lequel l'événement arrive. מִקְרֶה est le destin naturel de tous les hommes, puisqu'ils participent à un cycle auquel toutes les générations sont soumises. Par contre les mots עֵת et פֶּגַע, qui sont liés à l'idée d'imprévisibilité, donnent la mesure de la limite gnoséologique et existentielle que l'homme rencontre[20]; en même

18. Cf. BLENKINSOPP, *Ecclesiastes 3,1-15* (n. 12), pp. 61-62.
19. Pour cette interpretation cf. MACHINIST, *Fate, miqreh, and Reason* (n. 1), pp. 169-173. Sur la méthodologie notre analyse concorde avec l'étude de MACHINIST, *ibid.*, pp. 174-175; mais nos conclusions sont différentes en ce qui concerne l'aire conceptuelle du thème du destin.
20. Cf. aussi les conclusions de F. BIANCHI, *«Ma Dio ricerca ciò che è scomparso»? (Qo 3,15b). La storia, la memoria e il tempo nel libro di Qohelet*, in RivBib 42 (1994) 59-73.

temps ils font comprendre que le destin n'est pas un mécanisme automatique, prédéterminé. Dieu se réserve la liberté de décider et d'agir dans la détermination du moment de la mort[21]; celle-ci est imprévisible selon l'homme, tandis que dans le dessein de Dieu elle arrive au moment opportun. En conclusion, l'événement défavorable, qui est interprété par l'homme en termes de hasard, exprime la liberté de Dieu. Toutes les catégories humaines en sont bouleversées et toute tentative de s'approprier la conduite divine et ses temps n'aboutit nulle part (11, 5.6). Faisant recours à l'art subtil de l'ironie et de la dialectique, Qohélet s'est mesuré courageusement avec les courants culturels de son temps sur un thème qui était controversé dans la philosophie hellénistique et dans l'apocalyptique judaïque. Ses argumentations sur le destin et sur le temps cependant ne sont que fonctionnelles à une thèse générale: la démonstration des limites de l'homme et l'affirmation de la toute-puissance de Dieu.

Pontificia Facoltà Teologica   Vittoria D'ALARIO
    dell'Italia Meridionale (Sez. San Luigi)
via Epomeo, 257
I-80126 Napoli

---

21. Sur ce trait de la théologie de Qohélet cf. V. D'ALARIO, *Dall'uomo a Dio. L'itinerario della sapienza nella ricerca di Qohelet*, in E. BIANCHI (ed.), *Cercare Dio* (PSV, 35), Bologna, 1997, pp. 39-50.

THE ANATOMY OF THE WISE MAN
WISDOM, SORROW AND JOY IN
THE BOOK OF ECCLESIASTES

I. THE PROBLEM

Much has been written about the search for joy in the book of Ecclesiastes[1]. However, no work of which I am aware has considered Qohelet's investigations in the light of his positive attitude towards sorrow. Not only does the author of Ecclesiastes associate grief (מכאוב) and sorrow (כעס) with wisdom (1,18; 2,23), he actually advocates meditation on the gloomier aspects of existence: the sage seeks out mourning (אבל — 7,2.4) and values sorrow (כעס — 7,3) as a route to wisdom. A paradox results: how can Qohelet, whose exhortations to pleasure (2,24a; 3,12.22a; 5,17; 8,15a; 9,7-9a; 11,7-12,1a) have impelled one commentator to call him a "Preacher of Joy"[2], also be a "Preacher of Grief"? While a full treatment of the relationship between wisdom, sorrow and joy is outwith the scope of this paper, a study of three relevant texts (7,3; 9,3; 11,9-10) in which the terms "good" (טוב) and "evil" (רע) are associated with the mind (לב) points to the main thrust of Qohelet's thought on this question.

II. TEXT AND CONTEXT

1. *Ecclesiastes 7,3*

The translation of Eccles 7,3 has long been considered problematic, and no fewer than three different interpretations have been offered for this verse. The text under consideration reads: טוב כעס משׂחק כי ברע פנים ייטב לב. The meaning of the first part of the verse is clear: "Sorrow is better than mirth". This *tob-spruch* is apparently followed by a causal כי (GKC §158b) introducing a subordinate clause containing the reason for this judgment. The beginning of this clause may be translated "by the sadness of the face". However, interpretations of the final phrase ייטב לב

---

1. Cf. e.g. C.S. KNOPH, *The Optimism of Koheleth*, in *JBL* 49 (1930) 195-99; D. BUZY, *La notion du bonheur dans l'Ecclésiaste*, in *RB* 43 (1934) 494-511; R.N. WHYBRAY, *Qoheleth, Preacher of Joy*, in *JSOT* 23 (1982) 87-98.
2. The texts are noted by WHYBRAY, *Qoheleth* (n. 1), p. 87.

diverge significantly and it is therefore to the meaning of this expression that attention should first be directed.

a. *The Moral Interpretation*

One interpretation of 7,3b finds expression in the Vulgate's translation *per tristitiam vultus, corrigitur animus delinquentis* "by the sadness of the face, the soul is corrected of wrongdoing". The phrase ברע פנים ייטב לב is thus construed as referring to the idea that suffering can improve moral character. This moral interpretation is particularly characteristic of 19th century scholarship, but has not recommended itself to more recent commentators[3].

Such an understanding of 7,3b provides a possible reason for Qohelet's judgment that sorrow is better than mirth. However, the notion that suffering can improve personal morality appears to be quite alien to the author of Ecclesiastes. Certainly he considers the topic of wrongdoing, but only as symptomatic of the general injustice of existence (4,1-3; 5,7 [Eng. 8]; 7,15; 8,10-11). Indeed, Qohelet seems to accept the presence of a certain amount of wickedness in humanity as a whole (7,17.20). More importantly, there is no real suggestion of moral self-improvement in the immediate context of the verses surrounding 7,3; these appear to be more concerned with the acquisition of wisdom.

b. *The "Joy" Interpretation*

Currently, most commentators argue that the expression ברע פנים ייטב לב *reinterprets* 7,3a[4]. That is to say, Qohelet seeks to qualify or partially undermine the judgment that "Sorrow is better than mirth". Part of the rationale for so doing is to harmonize Qohelet's statement about the superiority of sorrow to pleasure with those which he makes elsewhere urging the enjoyment of life as a positive good. A somewhat similar approach can be seen in the work of those who argue that Qohelet's advocacy of sorrow in 7,1-4 is "tongue in cheek"[5], the work of glossators[6], or reflective of an ongoing dialogue within the book[7].

3. e.g., F. DELITZSCH, *Ecclesiastes*, Grand Rapids, 1982; German original: *Hoheslied und Kohelet*, Leipzig, 1875, p. 315; T. TYLER, *Ecclesiastes*, London, 1874, pp. 97-98; E.H. PLUMPTRE, *Ecclesiastes*, Cambridge, 1881, p. 161.

4. So, e.g., R.N. WHYBRAY, *Ecclesiastes*, London, 1989, p. 114.

5. WHYBRAY, *Ecclesiastes* (n. 4), pp. 113, 118; M.V. FOX, *Qohelet and his Contradictions* (JSOT SS, 71), Sheffield, 1989, pp. 226-27.

6. A.H. MCNEILE, *An Introduction to Ecclesiastes*, Cambridge, 1904, pp. 22-23; G.A. BARTON, *Ecclesiastes*, Edinburgh, 1908, pp. 138-39; E. PODECHARD, *L'Ecclésiaste*, Paris, 1912, p. 371.

7. N. LOHFINK, *Kohelet* (Die Neue Echter Bibel), Würzburg, 1980, pp. 50-54; R.E. MURPHY, *Ecclesiastes*, Dallas, 1992, pp. 61-63.

The argument that 7,3b is intended to undermine the first part of the verse finds support from the use of the phrase ייטב לב elsewhere in the OT in contexts suggestive of joy or contentment (Ruth 3,7; Judg 19,6.9; 1 Kings 21,7). The translation offered by the *NEB*, "a sad face may go with a cheerful heart" for this part of the verse is characteristic of most recent commentators. This interpretation is not without its problems however.

Firstly, the particle כי in 7,3 can only be translated causally. If 7,3b were indeed a reinterpretation of the opening proposition of the verse, one would expect כי to be used in an adversative sense. This, however, would require a negative formulation in the opening clause. The grammatical evidence thus makes it unlikely that 7,3b qualifies the first part of the verse. The resultant translation, "Sorrow is better than mirth, for a sad face may go with a cheerful heart" makes no sense. An adequate justification for the superiority of sorrow to mirth must be provided by 7,3b.

Elsewhere in the OT, כעס is said to reside in the לב of the individual (1 Sam 1,8; Eccles 11,9)[8]. Since the context of 7,3 concerns the experience of sorrow, it would be strange if the expression ייטב לב meant "the heart may be cheerful" when the exterior of the sage clearly shows signs of sadness (cf. Neh 2,2). The evidence of Prov 14,13 ("The heart may be sad even in laughter and the end of joy may be grief") adduced by commentators to the contrary only serves to underline the fact that sadness is a deep inner disturbance which contrasts with the sometimes superficial nature of mirth.

c. *The "Wisdom" Interpretation*

Another possible interpretation of 7,3 disregards the meaning of the phrase ייטב לב elsewhere in the OT and accordingly translates "Sorrow is better than mirth, for when the face is sad, the mind improves"[9]. Although at first sight problematic, this reading deserves more consideration than it has hitherto received.

Firstly, this translation provides an adequate reason in 7,3b for Qohelet's statement in the first part of the verse. Sorrow is shown to be superior to mirth because it is conducive to the acquisition of wisdom. This does not contradict Qohelet's exhortations to enjoy life, though it does present a paradox: wisdom obtained through sadness may allow one to take appropriate advantage of what life has to offer. Qohelet

8. כעס in *TDOT* 7,284 (Lohfink).
9. PODECHARD, *L'Ecclésiaste* (n. 6), p. 366; R. GORDIS, *Koheleth: The Man and his World*, New York, 1968, p. 268; R.B.Y. SCOTT, *Proverbs Ecclesiastes*, New York, 1965, p. 234. Fox construes similarly (*Contradictions* (n. 5), p. 228).

twice issues a warning against allowing sorrow to take over one's life (5,16; 7,9): it is not to be a permanent part of the sage's experience.

Secondly, the interpretation offered by Podechard, Gordis and Scott takes account of the connection between wisdom and sorrow in 1,18; 2,23; 7,1-4, and is in keeping with the wider context of the OT where sorrow is located in the mind of the individual. Both of these pieces of evidence are passed over by other interpretations. Nevertheless, although this reading is probably the correct one, the use of the expression ייטב לב elsewhere in the OT should not be ignored: it is essential to understanding Qohelet's wordplay in 7,3. Ordinarily one would say that "the mind becomes good" (ייטב לב) when pleasure is experienced. Qohelet is aware of both this expression and the related טוב לב (Prov 15,15; Esther 5,9) which he uses in 9,7. In 7,3, however, he makes the point that "the mind becomes good" through sorrow too — in a way superior to pleasure — for it is the lasting "good" of wisdom which the sage gains. Thus, it is the phrase ייטב לב which is reinterpreted in the light of 7,3a and not *vice versa*. Ambiguity is (theoretically) avoided by the use of the causal כי which precludes the more usual meaning of ייטב לב as well as the location of the proverb in the immediate context of 7,1-4.

A picture of the sage emerges in 7,3 which one might call "the anatomy of the wise man": his mind is associated with sorrow (כעס), and this is reflected on his exterior, which is said to be "evil" (רע). Nevertheless, the sorrow in the sage's mind improves it (יטב) in the sense that it engenders wisdom.

2. *Ecclesiastes 9,3*

In contrast to the situation of the sage, Qohelet says of human beings in 9,3: "...a single fate is for all, and also the mind of humanity is full of evil: madness is in their mind during their lives — and afterward off to the dead". All commentators have understood Qohelet's statement that "the mind of humanity is full of evil" (לב בני האדם מלא רע) in a moral sense. Thus, when the term טוב is associated with the mind, it is construed as joy, but when its opposite רע occurs in the same context, it is interpreted as referring to wickedness.

Qohelet does imagine humanity as predisposed to wickedness: this is expressed in his statement that "the minds of human beings are fully set to do evil" (8,11). Yet there is an essential difference between this statement and that of 9,3. Moral evil is defined by action, not by thought; hence the use of the phrase עשׂה רע "to do evil" in these contexts (4,17; 8,11.12). Outside its occurrence in this phrase, the term רע may mean "harm, harmful" (8,3.5.9; 9,12), "grievous" (1,13; 2,17; 4,8; 5,13; 6,2) or "bad thing" (4,3; 9,3) but it has no moral nuance.

Another problem with this moral interpretation of 9,3 is that in 8,11 moral evil as expressed by the phrase "to do evil" is attributed to the deity's tardiness in punishing human misdeeds. In 9,3, "evil" in the mind is somehow linked to the inevitability of death. While there is a logical connection between a lack of divine justice and human wrongdoing, it is difficult to see one between the presence of death and the same. Concerning Qohelet's apparent use of the phrase ייטב לב to indicate the presence of wisdom in the human mind, it is worth noting that the presence of רע in the mind in 9,3 is placed parallel to הוללות ("madness"). The latter term is most often used by Qohelet in conjunction with סכל√ ("folly") and typically denotes irrational thought or behaviour (1,17; 2,12; 7,25)[10]. In the context of 9,3 therefore, רע probably has a meaning equivalent to הוללות and would best be interpreted as referring to irrationality rather than to moral evil *per se*.

Further evidence for this suggestion comes from 10,13 in which Qohelet describes the behaviour of the fool: "The beginning of his speech is folly (סכלות), and its end, complete madness (הוללות רע)". The translation given here is that of Gordis, but others have also cited the possible use of the term רע in conjunction with הוללות as intensifying the force of Qohelet's judgment about the fool's irrational behaviour, rather than making a moral qualification about the nature of the fool's madness[11].

While no logical connection exists between the reality of death and human evil, there is a clear link between death and human ignorance. The state of death is described as one in which "there is no work, nor device, nor knowledge nor wisdom..." (9,10). Living and dead are comparable in terms of knowledge: "the living know that they will die, but the dead know nothing" (9,5 cf. 9,1). 9,3 contributes to this theme by demonstrating that the thought of the living is characterised by folly: it is filled with "madness" (הוללות) and "irrationality" (רע), "and afterwards — off to the dead", where just as in life "there is no knowledge nor wisdom".

The sage differs from the rest of humanity: the natural state of the human mind is characterised by the term רע, but his mind is טוב. This

10. DELITZSCH in fact interprets רע in the light of the term הוללות as referring to the moral evils of hedonism (*Ecclesiastes* (n. 3), pp. 357-58).

11. GORDIS, *Koheleth* (n. 9), pp. 192, 194; J.L. CRENSHAW, *Ecclesiastes*, Philadelphia, 1987, p. 174. K. GALLING (*Der Prediger* (HAT, 18), Tübingen, 1969, p. 116) and W. ZIMMERLI (*Das Buch des Predigers Salomo* (ATD, 16/1), Göttingen, 1980, p. 231) are similarly cautious about understanding the term רע in a moral sense here.

idea finds further expression in the final passage to be considered in this paper.

3. *Ecclesiastes 11,9-10*

In 11,9-10, Qohelet's main exhortation to joy occurs: "Rejoice, young man, in your youth: let your mind cheer you (יטיבך לבך) in the days of your youth. Walk in the ways of your heart and in the sight of your eyes,...Remove sorrow (כעס) from your mind and put away evil (רע) from your flesh..."

This passage presupposes the same state of affairs as we find earlier. The expression ויטיבך לבך implies the presence of טוב within the mind. Therein is also located כעס, with רע on the sage's exterior, all as in 7,3. Interestingly, despite the fact that the MT is supported by all the Versions, some commentators emend ויטיבך לבך to ויטב לבך "let your heart be cheerful"[12], supporting the dubious translation of ייטב לב in 7,3 as "the heart may be cheerful".

No emendation is in fact required. In 11,9-10 Qohelet enjoins the sage to consider the positive aspects of existence. In doing so the mind "cheers" the sage (ויטיבך לבך). Following this spread of טוב outwards, "evil" is banished from the sage's exterior (העבר רעה מבשרך), and sorrow from his mind (הסר כעס מלבך). The wise mind is not burdened by sorrow forever: at the appropriate moment, wisdom can drive out sadness and transform the anatomy of the wise man. Hitherto, it has been argued that Qohelet's message of joy in 11,9-10 is aimed at everyone[13]. The language employed by Qohelet demonstrates that this is not the case, however. It is directed towards the follower who has taken his advice in 7,1-4 to seek out sorrow by contemplating the finite nature of existence.

III. CONCLUSION

Qohelet envisions a sequence in the sage's development. While sorrow is experienced in the course of his meditations upon the world, this act leads ultimately to wisdom. This in turn enables the sage to appreciate life's benefits. It is not without purpose that Qohelet confronts the

---

12. CRENSHAW, *Ecclesiastes* (n. 11), p. 181; MURPHY, *Ecclesiastes* (n. 7), p. 111. The emendation is also suggested in *BHS*. However, E. GLASSER (*Le procès du bonheur par Qohelet*, Paris, 1970, p. 164) and FOX (*Contradictions* (n. 5), pp. 278-79) are correct in following the MT.

13. G. OGDEN, *Qoheleth XI 7-XII 8: Qoheleth's Summons to Enjoyment and Reflection*, in *VT* 34 (1984) 27-38, p. 32.

reader with the examples of injustice which he has seen (3,16; 4,1-3; 5,7 [Eng. 8]; 9,11; 10,6-7). The author leads his disciple along the same painful path as himself to accrue wisdom, but then encourages him to take the essential next step and find enjoyment in life. Only after the mind has been improved by wisdom (ייטב לב — 7,3) can it make the sage rejoice (ויטיבך לבך — 11,9).

Qohelet's parting message in 11,8-12,7 contains not one but two exhortations: one should "rejoice" (11,8.9) but also "remember" death (11,8; 12,1)[14]. Qohelet's follower will indeed have pondered death, for it is the consideration of this phenomenon which leads to wisdom. By combining the two actions, Qohelet's hope is to find for himself and for others a joy compatible with wisdom, untainted by the "folly and madness" (1,17; 2,2.3.13) which defines it at the beginning of his quest.

Department of Theology & Religious Studies Dominic RUDMAN
King's College London
Strand
London WC2R 2LS
United Kingdom

---

14. This idea is evident in the work of H. WITZENRATH (*Süss ist das Licht...: Eine literaturwissenschaftliche Untersuchung zu Kohelet 11:7-12:7* (ATSAT, 11), St. Ottilien, 1979), whose findings are schematized by G. OGDEN (*Qoheleth* (Readings: A New Biblical Commentary), Sheffield, 1987, pp. 193-94). Most commentators see the problematic בוראיך "your creator" as an oblique reference to death or emend to בורך "your grave." A recent exception is CRENSHAW (*Ecclesiastes* (n.11), pp. 181, 185) who reads בארך "your wife".

HUMAN DESTINY IN EMAR AND QOHELET

The following essay is an attempt to show the bearing of two wisdom texts from Emar[1] about human destiny on the interpretation of Qohelet. No claim is made about the influence of the Emar tradition in Qohelet, let alone a possible genetic relationship between them.

The first text, Emar VI.4:767[2], begins with the following affirmation:

> (1) Destinies have been designed by Ea. (2) Portions have been distributed according to the decree of the god. (3) It has been that way since the days of old. (4) It has been declared from the beginning[3].

Qoh 1,9 contains a similar observation on the immutability of destinies: "What has been is what will be, and what has been done is what will be done; and there is nothing new under the sun". The idea that destinies are sanctioned by divine power appears in Qoh 3,14-15: "I know that whatever God does – it will be forever; there will be no adding to it and substracting from it, and God has acted so that they will be afraid in his presence. That which is, already has been; that which is to be, already has been; and God brings back what has already been pursued".

Destiny is mentioned again in the last line of the Emar text. There is thus a kind of inclusio with the first line:

> (24) This is human destiny.

1. These are cuneiform texts from the late 14th – early 12th centuries B.C. that were found in Tell Meskene, ancient Emar, about 95 km southeast of Aleppo at the elbow of the Euphrates, excavated between 1972-76. Since 1976 the tell has been submerged in the artificial Lake Assad. Official excavations before the building of the lake have yielded over 800 tablets. A considerable number of other tablets from Emar are in private collections or still circulating among antiquity dealers. For a useful summary of the texts found at the site, see M. DIETRICH, *Die akkadischen Texte der Archive und Bibliotheken von Emar*, in *UF* 22 (1990) 25-48.
2. This is a Sumerian-Akkadian bilingual text. The siglum refers to the editio princeps by D. ARNAUD, *Recherches au pays d'Aštata – Emar VI/4*, Paris, 1987, pp. 359-365. For a synoptic edition of the Emar text and the extant versions from Ugarit, see M. DIETRICH, *"Ein Leben ohne Freude..."*, *Studie über eine Weisheitskomposition aus den Gelehrtenbibliotheken von Emar und Ugarit*, in *UF* 24 (1992) 9-29. Some parallels with Qohelet have been pointed out by W. LAMBERT, *Some New Babylonian Wisdom Literature*, in J. DAY – R. GORDON – H. WILLIAMSON (eds.), *Wisdom in Ancient Israel. FS J. Emerton*, Cambridge, 1995, pp. 38-42 and recently also by C. UEHLINGER, *Qohelet im Horizont mesopotamischer, levantinischer und ägyptischer Weisheitsliteratur der persischen und hellenistischen Zeit*, in L. SCHWIENHORST-SCHÖNBERGER (ed.), *Das Buch Kohelet. Studien zur Struktur, Geschichte, Rezeption und Theologie* (BZAW, 254), Berlin/New York, 1997, pp. 192-196. The unrecoverable lacunae are shown as [xxx].
3. *ina pī ālik pāni*, literally, 'in the mouth of the predecessor'.

This literary phenomenon makes the twenty-four line composition a unit in itself[4]. More importantly, this literary device leads the reader, ancient or modern, to retrace the text and re-create it mentally. Each reading will therefore result in a new understanding. The Book of Qohelet uses a similar technique. The words of Qohelet start at 1,2 in a quotation-like expression of an ancient editor: "Utter futility! says Qohelet, Utter futility! Everything is futile". Then toward the end, at 12,8, the text has, "Utter futility! says Qohelet. Everything is futile". At this point the reader finds the way back to 1,2 and hence a fresh encounter with the text can take place.

While demonstrating the futility of all efforts to understand the meaning of human existence, Qohelet develops new insights into life using the concept of enjoyment, שמחה. However, the precise sense of enjoyment is not easy to isolate. Instead of spelling out his idea of enjoyment, Qohelet posits it as a polar opposition to the theme of futility. This is especially clear before 8,14[5]. Furthermore, he argues that human destiny, חלק (literally, 'portion'), while rooted in futility, nevertheless also allows for "joy in the heart". It is interesting to note that, whereas the Hebrew word חלק reflects human acceptance, the Akkadian word *uṣurtum* connotes divine agency.

Let us go back to Emar. After a triple statement about the immutability of destinies given above (lines 1-4), there follows a statement about the total separation between the divine and human spheres (lines 5-8) and the inevitability of death (lines 9-10):

> (5) Beings are different from one another. (6) Some dwell above, [some dwell below]. (7) Some are as unattainable as the faraway heavens, (8) Some are as unknown as the deep underworld.
> (9) The whole of life appears just like the twinkling of an eye. (10) Human life is not everlasting.

At this point the sage starts to question the ways of liberation from death according to traditional Mesopotamian wisdom, namely, longevity (line 11), renewed life (line 12), exploits (line 13), might (line 14), exploits (line 15), renewed life (line 16), and longevity (line 17). Note the concentric arrangement of the seven ideals.

---

4. The end of the composition is also clear from the four-line colophon immediately after line 24. Before the discovery of Emar, a version of the same composition had been unearthed at Ugarit and published by J. NOUGAYROL in *Ugaritica* 5 (1968) 291-304, text # 164-166. But the interpretation was seriously hampered by the badly preserved state of the fragments. For the difference between the Emar and Ugarit versions, see DIETRICH, *Leben* (n. 3), esp. p. 13.

5. See my short note, *The Theme of Enjoyment*, in *Biblica* 73 (1992) 528-532, esp. p. 530.

(11) Where is King Alulu who lived for 36,000 years? (12) Where is king Entena who went up to the heavens? (13) Where is Gilgamesh who [managed to trace life back] like Ziusudra? (14) Where is Huwawa[6] who [xxx]? (15) Where is Enkidu who [performed] mighty deeds on earth? (16) Where is Bazi? Where is Zizi? (17) Where are the Great Kings who lived from days of old until now?

But in the next line, all these seven ideals are said to be non-existent:

(18) In fact, they have never been conceived; they have never been born.

This statement is very audacious, even iconoclastic. It does not only challenge, but completely dismantles the validity of the tradition simply by bringing up the realities of life. Such a denial is unheard of in the Mesopotamian tradition. It was in Syria, that is, the western periphery of the cuneiform culture, that intellectuals had a license to question the canonical teaching of Mesopotamian wisdom. Such freedom is also enjoyed by Qohelet, especially in the royal experiments (Qoh 1,12-14. 17-18; 2,1-23), where he challenges some basic tenets of traditional wisdom.

It is true that at the beginning of this century scholars had already noted that the Gilgamesh tradition deals with the questions of the futility of the search for life. The recognition of such a vain search constitutes wisdom[7]. But one may note that the question raised in Qohelet and in the Emar text is slightly different. No longer does the focus of the problem lie in the search for life as in Gilgamesh's journey to find the tree of life, which nonetheless ends in failure. The question now is about the meaning of this present life. The Syrian sage and Qohelet are bothered – or to use Qohelet's own word – vexed by the traditional conviction that destinies are immutable. The Emar sage asks about the meaning of life (line 19) and suffering (line 21).

(19) A gloomy life[8], what advantage does it have over death? (20) O, young man, whose god [xxx] firmly.

The question elicits a new insight: joy in the heart is the reasonable alternative to choose (lines 21-22).

---

6. Huwawa was a mighty giant protected by seven layers of dazzling radiance. In the Gilgamesh legend, he was killed by the joined forces of Gilgamesh and Enkidu. It is not accidental that this line is found between the lines which mention these two heroes. There is a touch of irony in this arrangement.

7. See the ample documentation in J. PAHK, *Il canto di gioia in Dio. L'itinerario sapienziale espresso dall'unità letteraria in Qohelet 8,16-9,10 e il parallelo di Gilgameš Me. iii*, Napoli, 1996, pp. 33-71.

8. Akkadian *balāṭu ša lā namāri* 'a life without light'. Dietrich renders it as 'ein Leben ohne Freude', which captures the sense, but loses the allusion to the underworld where darkness reigns. The imagery of darkness for the afterlife appears in Qoh 11,8.

(21) Cast off all griefs, ignore troubles! (22) *dinānu [ḫ]ud lib[bi] ištēn ūmu[akkal] ešeret šāru [lillika]* 'instead of joy in the heart of a single day, a period of 36,000 [years of silence will come]'[9].

The statement in line 22 is to be interpreted as a warning: failure to consider the invitation to cast off grief and ignore trouble (line 21) will bring eternal silence, that is, death. Thus one will know what death is like by just missing a single day of joy. Seen from a more positive angle, joy of the heart can neutralize the threat of death. And this leads to a new understanding of what true human destiny is (lines 23-24).

(23) May Zirash[10] rejoice in a son like you! (24) This is human destiny.

The word *this*, Akkadian *annûm*, in line 24, points back to the long statement in lines 19-23 that expresses the core of the message of the text. This development of thought compares well with Qohelet's search for a better understanding of human destiny. Like the Emar text, throughout the book, Qohelet also challenges the ideals of traditional teaching: wisdom and toil (1,12-2,24); knowledge of God (3,1-13); righteousness (3,16-22); wealth (5,9-19); divine retribution (8,10-15); individual destiny (9,1-10); longevity (11,7-12,7). All these amount to nothing. Qohelet proposes an alternative to these futile ideals: to rejoice in life[11]. This alternative is very much like what is found in lines 19-24 of the Emar text.

The common ground is all the more evident in Qoh 5,17-19: (17) "This is what I see to be good: that it is appropriate to eat and drink and look on good things in the toil that one does under the sun the few days of life that God has given, for that is one's portion חלקו. (18) Likewise everyone to whom God gives wealth and possessions and whom God enables to eat from them and to accept his portion חלקו and rejoice in his toil – this is the gift of God. (19) Indeed, he should not worry over the days of his life, for God *inspires*[12] him with joy in his heart". Though Qohelet takes it for granted that human lots are already cast and therefore, like lines 1-4 of the Emar text, immutable, in v. 19 he proposes the appropriate way to face it.

Some comment on a subtle literary phenomenon in the Emar text and Qohelet is appropriate here. As mentioned before, the last line (line 24)

9. The restoration of the last word of the line (*lillika* 'will come') is based on a version preserved at Ugarit *ana dinān ḫud libbi ūmakkal ūm qūli* 10 ŠÁR.MU.MEŠ *lillika* 'instead of joy of the heart of a single day there will come a period of silence of 36,000 years'.

10. Zirash is the goddess of beer.

11. Cf. R. N. WHYBRAY, *Qoheleth, Preacher of Joy*, in *JSOT* 23 (1982) 87-98.

12. Understanding מענה as the hiphil of ענה 'to answer', i.e., 'to make someone find an answer', 'to inspire'; see also my *Theme of Enjoyment* (n. 6), p. 530.

of the Emar text echoes the beginning of the text. Similarly, Qoh 12,8 forms an inclusio with 1,2. Yet in both cases the inclusio is not perfect and, presumably, is not meant to be perfect. Line 24 of the Emar text contains the singular noun 'destiny', Akkadian *uṣurtum*, in contrast to the plural 'destinies', Akkadian *uṣurātum*, in line 1. It seems that, whereas in line 1 the sage gives back what traditional Mesopotamian wisdom has to say about various destinies of humankind, here in line 24 he expresses his own understanding of human destiny. Qohelet uses a similar technique. In 12,8 the Hebrew text mentions הבל הבלים 'utter futility' only once, not twice, as in 2,1[13]. It is likely that here Qohelet wants to suggest that though absurdity is still part of human life, it is not as overwhelming as before. The Emar text provides a useful parallel to this suggestion. At the end of the composition, true destiny (singular *uṣurtum*) is affirmed: to let good living transform one's life for the better (lines 21-23). Qohelet himself repeatedly and steadily affirms that one's portion is to enjoy good life despite the absurdities one may experience, as in 2,24; 3,13.22; 5,17; 8,15; 9,7-10; 11,9-10. Each of these passages is a response to some form of absurdity in life. This is Qohelet's new attitude toward הבל.

The other text, Emar VI.4:778, in Akkadian, was written as a debate (*dabābu*) between a father and a son, as mentioned explicitly in the last line (line 114)[14]. This form allows a critical discussion about traditional values without being disrespectful. After a prologue containing an invitation to listen to wisdom (lines 1-8), the father communicates his instructions (lines 8-84; only the better preserved lines 8-10 and 71-73 are translated here). These maxims will suffice to illustrate the world-view of traditional wisdom.

(1) Listen to the counsel, o Šūpē[-amēli], (2) whose mind Enlil-banda[15] has opened; (3) the wise counsel, o Šūpē-amēli, [on whom Enlil-banda has bestowed] understanding.
(4) From his mouth there will come out decisions for (5) the future. For men and women [he will pronounce blessings]. (6) Like a firstborn child [his counsel] will come out. [He will utter] prudent prayers.
(8) O, my son, [beware,] your month may be ruined. Therefore, if a journeying landowner [is going to abandon] (9) his cornfield, beware, you shall

13. In 12,8 a few Hebrew manuscripts and the Pesitta add הבל הבלים after the word הקוהלת; undoubtedly an effort to make 12,8 conform with 1,2.
14. Editio princeps by ARNAUD, *Recherches* (n. 2), pp. 377-382; for a synoptic edition of the Emar text and the versions from Ugarit and Boghazköy, see M. DIETRICH, *Der Dialog zwischen Šūpē-amēli und seinem 'Vater'. Die Tradition babylonischer Weisheitssprüche im Westen*, in *UF* 23 (1991) 33-74; the appendix by G. KEYDANA, pp. 69-74, gives the Hittite version from Boghazköy.
15. The name means the Lord of Wisdom.

conclude [a contract and proceed] (10) to acquire his cornfield.

......

(71) [Do not acquire] a well-groomed [man]. (72) His price is half a silver mina[16], (but) his earning is four shekels[17] of silver. (73) Give no one advice about the price. (74) Discard your feeling, [take away] your mind from him! (75) Give him one or [two] months of punishment.

At this point the son questions the teaching of traditional wisdom (lines 85-87). He brings his father back to reality: the miserable human condition despite all appearances (lines 88-90); accumulated wealth turned into a useless thing by death (lines 99-106); complete separation between the world of the living and the realm of the dead (107-113). Ignorance of the afterlife is also frequently mentioned in Qoh 3,11.22b; 6,12; 7,14.24; 8,7.17; 10,14.

(85) The son opened his mouth to speak, (86) addressing his father, the counsellor: (87) "I have silently listened to the word of my father. Let me speak now!"
(88) Are we doves, birds that languish? (89) Or the most restless of the strong bulls, the mighty heavenly bull? (90) We are just beasts of burden!
......
(99)...Father, you have built a house. (100) You made [its entrance] high, with a storeroom ten cubits large. (101) [Wh]at did you carry with you? The granary of your house is full, (102) and the store[room] full of grain. On the day (103) of your destiny (*ina ūmi šīmātīka*), nine sacrifices are counted (104) on your [he]ad from among your property: (105) flocks of goats, changes of clothing [...] (106) [the enti]re wealth is bread and tribute[18].
(107) [Many] are those who eat food during the day. Many are those who become pale because of thirst. (108) [Ma]ny of us can see the sun. Many (109) [of us will so]journ in vast darkness. (110) [In the under]world people will lie down. (111) [Eresh]kigal is our mother, we are her sons! (112) Shutters [have been put] at the entrance to the underworld (113) *[aš-šum b]alṭu* (TI.LA-*tum*) *lā* (NU) *idaggalū mītūti* (BA.ÚŠ-*ti*) '[so that the l]iving cannot see the dead.'
(114) These [xxx] the father and the son put together in a debate.

In lines 106 and 113 the sage, in the words of the son, suggests that what really matters is what one can enjoy in the world of the living, because, as is clear from lines 107-113, what happens in the afterlife is beyond human understanding. This is also Qohelet's view.

---

16. The word for mina is supplied from the Akkadian text from Boghazköy.
17. The word for shekels is supplied from the Akkadian text from Boghazköy.
18. Reading *[gabb]a mašru* (NÍG.TUKU) *šū akalu* (NINDA) *u biltu* (GÚ.UN). I read the sign *šū* as a copula, rather than the 3sg. m. suffix - *šū* 'his'. The meaning is that real wealth consists of things that one can actually consume or spend, rather than accumulated foodstuff and possessions.

To conclude, here are the four basic themes commonly shared by the two Emar texts and Qohelet:

1. The Syrian sage understands that destinies are fixed by divine force with their own logic. Qohelet also finds that human understanding cannot grasp divine activity.
2. Destinies and lots are therefore unalterable. According to Qohelet, human beings have no control over the flux of events in life.
3. It is a mere illusion to try to change destinies. Qohelet even establishes that human efforts to improve their conditions are doomed to nonsense.
4. Despite all this, one thing is worth doing: to try to find meaning in the realities of life. And indeed Qohelet states in 5,18-19 that to enjoy life – to take reality as it is – is to find God's own answer. Once found, it constitutes a solution to the enigma of destinies.

Pontificio Istituto Biblico   Agustinus GIANTO
via della Pilotta 25
I-00187 Roma

ASPECTS OF THE RELATIONSHIP BETWEEN
THE SEPTUAGINT VERSIONS OF KOHELET AND PROVERBS

The Septuagint versions of Proverbs and Ecclesiastes differ dramatically in respect of various textual issues. When one studies the latter after researching Proverbs the differences simply seem so large that one inevitably wonders whether these two translation units could actually belong to the same corpus[1]. However, when one takes a closer look at LXX Ecclesiastes one actually discovers a number, albeit a small number, of correspondences between these versions, one being the fact that no one of these texts has been prepared in the Göttingen edition.

As textual basis for this comparison I make use of the available publications, primarily the pocket edition by Rahlfs. Where necessary I also utilize the edition by Holmes & Parsons. I have chosen to discuss a small number of aspects of the relationship between these two texts. It is not posssible to address the full extent of the relationship between Ecclesiastes and Proverbs within the space of the current contribution. For the sake of argument I distinguish between the translator's approach on a macrolevel and a microlevel.

I. THE MACROLEVEL

1. *Textual Issues*

The first observation to be made when these two LXX versions are compared is that Proverbs has many more textual differences than is the case with Ecclesiastes. There is a large number of plusses in Proverbs. Each chapter has its own peculiar added strophes and interpretations. Chapter 9 for one has a total amount of 17 stichs added as well as an additional number of smaller textual differences including some minusses in comparison to MT. In chapter 6 a whole passage of three stichs on the bee has been added in conjunction with the ant. In by far most of these cases I have argued that the translator of Proverbs actually brought about these changes in comparison with MT and the other textual witnesses (see n. 1). This applies also to another characteristic of Proverbs, the question of changed order of chapters towards the end of the book.

---

1. Cf. J. COOK, *The Septuagint of Proverbs – Jewish and/or Hellenistic Proverbs?* (SVT, 69), Leiden, 1997. This article is largely based upon the results of this book.

There are no major differences of this order in the book of Ecclesiastes. I could only locate a limited number of smaller differences in
Ecclesiastes, the first being Eccles 2,15:

> MT: Then I said in my heart, "what befalls the fool will also befall me,
>   why then have I been so exceedingly wise?"
>   And I said in my heart that this is also absurd.

> LXX: And I said in my heart,
>   "As the experience of the fool is
>   so also it will happen to me,
>   and to what purpose have I gained wisdom?"
>   I also said in my heart,
>   *"Because the fool speaks of his abundance,*
>   this is also absurd".

It is difficult to decide whether the phrase printed in italics is indeed an
addition by the translator, or whether it is the result of the transmission of
the text. Because the translator generally sticks to his parent text it would
be possible to argue that this actually represents a deviating Hebrew text.
The problem is that there is no additional evidence for such a parent text.
BHS (Horst) does mention NT parallels (Matt 12,34 and Luke 6,45) in this
regard. It is therefore possible that this phrase could have become part of
the Ecclesiastes text in the course of the transmission of the text itself.

There is a large number of additions in LXX Proverbs. One example
occurs right in the beginning of the book (Prov 1,3). For the sake of
contextuality I treat verse 2 and 3 together. In this regard the rules of
thumb formulated by De Lagarde[2] are useful in determining the Old
Greek also in this context.

Proverbs 1,2-3

לָדַעַת חָכְמָה וּמוּסָר לְהָבִין אִמְרֵי בִינָה:
לָקַחַת מוּסַר הַשְׂכֵּל צֶדֶק וּמִשְׁפָּט וּמֵישָׁרִים:

2 That men may know wisdom and instruction,
  understand words of insight,
3 receive instruction in wise dealing,
  righteousness, and justice, and uprightness.

2 γνῶναι σοφίαν καὶ παιδείαν
  νοῆσαί τε λόγους φρονήσεως
3 δέξασθαί τε στροφὰς λόγων
  νοῆσαί τε δικαιοσύνην ἀληθῆ
  καὶ κρίμα κατευθύνειν

---

2. P.A. DE LAGARDE, *Anmerkungen zur griechischen Übersetzung der Proverbien*,
Leipzig, 1863, p. 3.

2 To learn wisdom and instruction,
   as well as to understand words of insight,
3 *and* to receive the inventive dealing of (in) *words*,
   as well as to understand true justice and *to make correct decisions.*

Verse 2 is translated relatively literally, although the translator shows signs of competence in the Greek language. He uses the conjunction τε solely in the first 6 verses. Where in the MT an *ellipsis* occurs in verse 3 the translator applies νοῆσαί. That this is actually an exegetical rendering is borne out by the limited way in which the verb νοέω is used in Proverbs. It appears in Prov 1,2 (בין), 3 (שׂכל?) and 6 (בין); 8,5 (בין); 16,23 (שׂכל); 19,25 (בין); 20,24 (בין); 23,1 (בין); 28,5 (בין); 29,7 (בין) and 19 (בין) and 30,18 (פלא). Hatch-Redpath chose שׂכל as the equivalent for νοέω in Prov 1,3. However, I think the translator probably took verse 2 into account in this regard, harmonizing without a reference to an underlying Hebrew reading.

Verse 3 contains other possible exegetical renderings, one being the phrase στροφὰς λόγων for מוּסָר. The Greek word στροφή occurs only four times in the LXX, but frequently in other Greek sources. It appears once in Wis 8,8, once in Sir 39,2, in Ps Sol 12,2 and here in Proverbs. Sir 39,1-11 is devoted to the wise, describing the true, enigmatic nature of his studies. In this context the combination στροφαῖς παραβολῶν is used to describe the "problematic" nature of the sayings studied by the wise. The same nuance is found in Wis where this lexeme is used in conjunction with αἴνιγμα. In the context of Wis 8,8 wisdom is described as the source of knowledge concerning "the past, the future, the intricate nuances of arguments and riddles, and even signs and wonders".

The combination of στροφὰς λόγων occurs also in this passage. Apparently it is a technical term even though it does not appear abundantly. It is therefore evident that the translator of Proverbs had the same intention of stressing the nuance of "problematic, complicated" with these words. If he therefore actually had the same Hebrew reading as MT[3], which seems more than probable to me, then it would seem as if he interpreted מוּסָר as coming from the verb סור (the Hofʿal masc part) "to turn aside, to withdraw, to evade". A hint as to the possible interpretation of this lexeme is in fact found in Sir 6,22, where the Hebrew indeed reads מוסר, "For discipline is like her name, she is not obvious to many". According to this interpretation מוּסָר indeed has to do with the "enigmatic, problematic".

---

3. A. BARUCQ, *Le livre des Proverbes* (Sources bibliques), Paris, 1964, p. 48, takes it as a free interpretation.

If the translator indeed had the same reading as MT, then the verbal form νοῆσαι could be an infinitive as a rendering of the Hif inf of שׂכל. It is nevertheless also possible to argue that the infinitive has been added in conjunction with the previous verse. However, this would then leave λόγων unaccounted for. In this regard the combination of στροφὰς λόγων is instructive, for λόγων seems to have been added in conjunction with the previous verse in order to explicate מוּסָר. The translator consequently created an antipole of the combination λόγους φρονήσεως in verse 2. This is a specific technique that this translator used extensively in the book of Proverbs[4].

The final two stichs in verse 3 also do not represent a literal rendering of the MT. Δικαιοσύνη is probably taken from צֶדֶק, but ἀληθῆ seems to be an addition either as an adjective or as a noun referring to "truth" (τὰ ἀληθῆ). I also think κρίμα is the equivalent for מִשְׁפָּט, whereas κατευθύνειν has been introduced in connection with ישר (וּמֵישָׁרִים) by the translator. This Greek verbal form occurs in Prov 1,3 (מֵישָׁרִים); 4,26 (כון); 9,15 (ישר); 13,13 (-); 15,8 (ישר) and 21 (ישר); 21,2 (תכן); 23,19 (אשר) and 29,27 (ישר). As can be seen, all these lexemes are semantically related.

It seems strange that מוּסָר is apparently rendered differently in these two verses. This Hebrew lexeme occurs 28 times in Proverbs. In practically all these passages one Greek lexeme, παιδεία, was used as the equivalent. This is not the normal practice of this translator; even though he does it in some instances, he tends to vary expressions. In verse 2 מוּסָר is thus translated relatively literally as a noun παιδεία; however, in verse 3 it is brought into connection with the root סור, as I argued above. Again, this could be the result of the translator's free approach, or he could have misunderstood the Hebrew. Not to be forgotton is another possible Hebrew reading, which was suggested by De Lagarde[5]. He accepts a deviating parent text and in the process he seems to underestimate the translator's input.

Whereas there are an additional two examples of larger additions in LXX Ecclesiastes (2,15 and 7,22), Proverbs contain a multitude of appropriate examples.

---

4. Cf. my contribution to the Festschrift for J.A. Sanders: *Contrasting as a Translation Technique in the LXX Proverbs*, in C.A. EVANS & S. TALMON (eds.), *From Tradition to Interpretation: Studies in Intertextuality in Honor of James A. Sanders*, Leiden, 1997, pp. 281-292.

5. DE LAGARDE, *Anmerkungen*, p. 5.

2. Differences in the Order of Verses and Chapters

At the last *Colloquium Biblicum Lovaniense* I demonstrated that the translator of Proverbs actually adapted his parent text for "theological" reasons[6]. This applies to the conspicuous correspondence between Prov 29,27 and 31,10, where the translator followed the contrast in his parent text between these two passages in order to adapt his version. In the meantime I have located also other purposeful adaptations by the translator where he actually followed thematical perspectives in order to adapt his subject matter. A key to this interpretation is found in the fact that this translator emphatically observed all the proverbs in this book exclusively as Proverbs of king Solomon. He consequently removed references to other kings, Agur and Lemuel. In addition Prov 31,1-9 which has the king as subject is placed immediately before Prov 25,1-8 where the principal figure is also the king[7].

I could find not a single example of a deliberately changed text of this order in Ecclesiastes. The most comparable textual phenomenon is where parts of verses are read in conjunction with a previous or a following verse. This is the case in Eccles 1,6 where the phrase ἀνατέλλων αὐτὸς ἐκεῖ is part of the previous verse in MT. This does, however, not represent a true textual difference, as it is just a matter of versing. Similar examples abound in LXX Proverbs.

3. On the Syntactical Level

A definite difference between the books under scrutiny is the literary approach followed by the persons responsible for each version. In LXX Proverbs the translator consistently takes into account the larger picture of his parent text. Therefore he also had a different understanding of the coherence of passages, with the result that he structures certain passages in a syntactically different way. It becomes clear that he was not in the first place interested in the details of his subject matter, but in its intention. He goes to great lengths to realise this intention. In Prov 1, for example, he brings about nuanced changes in order to stress certain issues, especially religious issues. The translator's different view of verse 32, for instance, has implications for the macrostructure of practically the whole passage. He made a nuanced and significant connection between

6. J. COOK, *Exodus 38 and Proverbs 31 – A Case of the Different Order of Verses and Chapters in the Septuagint*, in M. VERVENNE (ed.), *Studies in the Book of Exodus, Redaction – Reception – Interpretation* (BETL, 126), Leuven, 1996, p. 543.
7. Cf. J. COOK, *The Septuagint of Proverbs – Jewish and/or Hellenistic Proverbs?*

this verse and the previous verses. The term κακοί of verses 28 ff., which in the final analysis has as antithesis, the "fools" (οἱ δὲ ἄφρο-νες) of verse 22, is made to refer also to those who wronged the innocent. These fools are then killed, and not the innocent, as seen by MT. The Greek translator thus followed the syntax of the Hebrew to some extent, but, expressed the individual clauses in a typically Greek linguistic manner. In some instances he brings about nuanced changes in order to deliberately express specific meanings. This is the case in verses 22, 23 and 32 where he clearly structured his translation so as to emphasise a religious theme, the contrast between the good and the bad.

This stress on religious issues is at stake in Prov 2 as well. Chapter 2 is divided neatly into two parts by the use of the exclamation particle ὦ in verse 13 to bring about this significant dichotomy. He then applies dualisms in order to contrast the good and the evil. Prominent contrasts in this chapter are ὁδοί δικαιωμάτων (verse 8) and ἄξονοι ἀγαθοί (verse 9); ὁδοί εὐθείας and ὁδοί σκότοι (verse 13); τρίβοι σκολιαὶ and καμπύλαι αἱ τροχιαὶ (verse 15); ὁδός εὐθείας in verse 16 and τρίβοι εὐθείας in verse 19 and τρίβοι ἀγαθαί and τρίβοι δικαιο-σύνης in verse 20. The negative poles are ὁδός κακός (verse 12); ὁδοὶ ἀσεβῶν and οἱ παράνομοι in verse 22. Other highly significant contrastive terms are βουλὴ καλὴ in verse 11 and κακὴ βουλὴ in verse 17.

There are many more appropriate examples in the book of Proverbs, to some of which I shall return below, for they are closely related to the issue of what I have chosen to call his "theological" approach. This translator has a specific interest in religious issues which in the final analysis also influences his rendering of his parent text. The same can not be concluded of Ecclesiastes. The fact that there are practically no additions already is an indication of the minimalist approach of this translator. There is no deliberate attempt by this translator to account for the larger picture as in the case of Proverbs. One thing is for sure, this can not be the result of the subject matter of the corpus, for both belong to the genre of wisdom. On a microlevel there are, nevertheless, indications of the translator interpreting in a small number of cases. However, not at all to the same extent as in LXX Proverbs.

II. THE MICROLEVEL

The same basic minimalist approach as demonstrated above in connection with Ecclesiastes is located in other grammatical spheres as well. This is totally contrary to the book of Proverbs which together with LXX Job represents a unique translated unit in the whole corpus of

Septuagintal writings[8]. I have already demonstrated that contrary to the Greek version of Ecclesiastes the translator of Proverbs creatively approached his parent text. This is not only observed on the macrolevel, but also on the semantical levels. As far as lexical items are concerned, the translator of Proverbs exhibits a unique approach of unity and diversity. In a preselected corpus of some 8 chapters (1, 2, 6, 8, 9, 24, 29 and 31) I determined that this translator applies a total of 30 *hapax legomena*. An interesting feature in this regard is that the final chapter (31) actually contains the largest number of hapaxes! Moreover, a large number of lexemes are used only or primarily in Proverbs. The same does not hold true for Ecclesiastes where consistency is the order of the day.

1. *The semantical level*

The translator of Eccles seems to stick basically to his *Vorlage*. The literal translation is observed in all facets of the translation. Lexical items are used rather consistently, totally different to the way the translator of Proverbs treated his subject matter. It is also not possible to be exhaustive in this regard, therefore I make a selection of categories for the purposes of the analysis.

Nouns

– Hapax legomena

I encountered the following hapaxes, which represents a representative but not an exhaustive number:

ἀνθέμιον Eccles 12,6 (גלה); ἀντίρρησις Eccles 8,11 (פתגם); βούκεντρον Eccles 12,11 (דרבון); δόκωσις Eccles 10,18 (מקרה); ἐντρυφήμα Eccles 2,8 (תענוג); ἔντριτος Eccles 4,12 (שלש); ἐπικοσμέω Eccles 1,15 (תקן); ἐπικραταιωθῇ Eccles 4,12 (תקף); κόπωσις Eccles 12,12 (יגיעה); κόσμιον Eccles 12,9 (תקן).

A number of nouns in Ecclesiastes occur in a limited number of instances, for example the two occurrences in the whole of the LXX of διαπονέω (Eccles 10,9 and 2 Macc 2,28), rendering עצב. Κοπέω Eccles 10,15 (יגע); Jdt 13,1 is another example. A number of lexemes are used three times in the LXX such as ἔκτρωμα Eccles 6,3 (נפל); Num 12,12 (מות); Job 3,16 (נפל) and λύσις Eccles 7,30 (פשר); Wis 8,8; LXX Dan 12,8 (*).

– The following lexemes appear solely in wisdom literature:

'Αμφιβλήστρον Eccles 9,12 (מצודה); Ps 141,10 (מכמר); Job 1,15 (חרם). 16 (מכמרת) and 17 (חרם); εὐτονία Eccles 7,7 (מתנה); Wis 8,3; 2

---

8. Cf. my contribution to the IOSCS-congress held in Cambridge, 1995, "Aspects of the Relationship between the Septuagint Versions of Proverbs and Job".

Macc 14,42; 4 Macc 6,5.9.13. 23. 27; 10,3 and 15; ματαιότης Psalms
(13x); Prov 22,8 and Eccles (32x). In Eccles it is consistently used as
equivalent for הבל with minor differences in 6,11 and 7,1.

– Consistent renderings
The consistent way the translator approaches his subject matter is clear
from the way specific Hebrew lexemes are rendered.

περισσεία is found in Eccles 1,3 (יתרון); 2,11 (יתרון); 2,13 (יתרון 2x);
3,9 (יתרון); 3,19 (מותר); 5,8 (יתרון); 5,15 (יתרון); 6,8 (יותר); 7,12 (יתרון);
10,10 (יתרון); 10,11 (יתרון); ἐπιστρέφω appears umpteen times in the
Bible, and in Eccles 9x, always for שוב; κύκλοω is used many times in
the LXX, and in Eccles 1,6; 7,26; 9,14; 12,5 it translates סבב; πνεῦμα
occurs many times in the LXX; 20x in Eccles always for רוח; ποίημα
occurs 20x in Eccles, always for מעשה: Eccles 1,14; 2,4.11.17;
3,11.17.22; 4,3.4; 5,5; 7,13; 8,9.14 (2x).17 (2x); 9,7.10; 11,5; 12, 14;
μόχθος consistently acts as equivalent for עמל in the 20 occurrences in
Eccles.

Particles

The rendering of particles makes for interesting reading.

καί γε: וגם in 1,11; 3,13; 5,15; 6,3.7; 7,6.18; 8,17; 9,3.11 (3x); 10,3;
11,2; BUT גם in 1,17; 2,1.7.8.14.15 (2x).19.21.23 (2x).24.26; 3,11;
4,4.8 (3x).11.14.16 (2x); 5,9.16.18; 6,5.9; 7,14.21.22; 8,10.12.14.16;
9,1 (2x).6 (2x).12.13; 10,20; 12,5. There are two exceptions; 2,9 (אף)
and 3,18 (המה).

σὺν is consistently used as equivalent for the nota accusativus את.

Verbs

Verbs exhibit similar trends in that consistency is the rule in most instances.

הלך. Qal: In Eccles 1,4.6 (2x).7 (3x); 2,14; 3,20; 4,17; 5,14; 6,4.6.8
(2x).9; 7,2 (2x); 8,3; 9,7.10; 10,3.7.15 and 12,5 πορεύω is used,
whereas in 2,1 and 9,7 δεῦρω and in 5,15 ἀπέρχομαι are applied.

Other verbal themes unfortunately are not used abundantly as can be
observed in the following examples: Pi 4,15 and 11,9 (περιπατέω);
8,10 (πορεύω); Hi 5,14 (πορεύω); 10,20 (ἀποθέρω).

אמר. In Eccles 1,2.10; 2,1.2.15; 3,7.18; 5,5; 6,3; 7,10.23.27; 8,4.17;
9,16; 12,1 and 8 εἶπω is used. In 1,16 λέγω and in 10,3 λογίζομαι are
applied. This is the sole example of the latter in Eccles.

אכל. In practically all instances in Eccles (2,24.25; 3,13; 4,5; 5,10.11.18; 6,2; 8,15; 9,7 and 10,17) φάγω is used. The sole exceptions are 5,10 and 10,16 where the verb ἔσθιω is applied. In 5,16 no equivalent has been offered.

Conclusion

As a preliminary conclusion to the translation technique the translator of Ecclesiastes followed, it is clear to me at least that he should be described as a literal translator, but not a mechanical one. On this level there are practically no correspondences between the two corpora compared here. I have formulated the lexical approach of the LXX Proverbs as one of *diversity* and *unity*[9]. I would argue that the approach of LXX Ecclesiastes should be defined as one of *unity*, for the characteristic of this translator is *consistency*. However, as I indicated above there is a small number of examples where the translator, who clearly had an excellent knowledge of both the Greek and Hebrew languages, did in fact nuance his translation. In Eccles 1,9 the lexeme חדש is rendered by means of πρόσφατον and in the next verse the translator used καινόν. These are the sole examples of this Hebrew lexeme in Kohelet. In chapter 10 the translator uses two verbs as equivalent for a single Hebrew verb in two adjacent verses. In verse 16 ἐσθίω is used to render אכל and in verse 17 the verb is φάγομαι. This is, however, not the rule and is also not at all of the same nature as, on the one hand, Proverbs, or, for that matter, on the other hand, the Pentateuch which generally seem to be on the more literal side. As far as LXX Proverbs is concerned these differences in the final analysis have their origin in the historical context in which the translator operated and the ensuing "theological" approach he had. But before I address this issue let me first of all discuss briefly a number of examples where the translator indeed interpreted his *Vorlage*, or had to cope with a problem in this text.

III. THE TRANSLATOR'S INPUT

In Eccles 1,5 the verb δύνω is used as equivalent for בוא. This verb does not appear abundantly in the OT and it is a stereotype in terms of the whole LXX, for it is consistently used as equivalent for the rising of the sun (Gen 28,11; Lev 22,7; Deut 23,12; Judg 14,18 and 19,14; 2 Kingdoms 2,24; 3,35; 3 Kingdoms 22,36; 2 Paralip 18,34; Tob 2,4 and

---

9. J. Cook, *op. cit.* (n. 1).

7; Job 2,9; Eccles 1,5; Amos 8,9; Micah 3,6; Isa 60,20; 1 Macc 10,50 and 12,27).

Eccles 1,10 in MT reads יֵשׁ דָּבָר שֶׁיֹּאמַר. LXX has the reading ὃς λαλήσει καὶ ἐρεῖ. This is an interpretation, also because MT offers an antecedent for the pronoun הוּא[10]. In Eccles 1,18 the Hebrew word כַּעַס is interpreted as γνώσεως in the LXX. This could be the result of a deviating parent text reading דעת. In Eccles 3,18 the equivalent for the adverb שָׁם is missing. In Eccles 4,1 the verbal form τὰς γινομένας is used as an interpretation of נעשׂים. In Eccles 5,5 LXX has the reading τοῦ θεοῦ for הַמַּלְאָךְ in MT. This could of course be based on the Hebrew reading הָאֱלֹהִים. The Peshitta has a similar reading, but it is possible that it goes back to the LXX. It is difficult to decide this issue for this is the sole example of the Hebrew lexeme in Eccles. It is possible that the translator actually experienced some problem with the logics of the clause; the reference to the messenger and God seems discrepant and it could therefore be a deliberate adaptation by the translator.

The translator in some cases interpreted his parent text differently from the MT. The reading τοῦ δούλου in Eccles 5,11 is based on a different vocalization of העבד. In a number of instances the translator interchanged consonants. The preposition ב for כ could have occurred in Eccles 7,12 and 9,10. In the first instance the LXX testifies to a reading of בצל and כצל. In Eccles 9,10 MT reads בכחך whereas LXX has ὡς ἡ δύναμίς.

More difficult is the difference in Eccles 7,10 where LXX reads ἐν σοφίᾳ and MT מחכמה. It must be possible that the translator actually deliberately interpreted, although he could of course have had a *Vorlage* with the preposition ב. The fact that the translator generally renders literally makes the reading בחכמה more probable.

The consonants ח and ה have clearly been interchanged in Eccles 7,14 where LXX reads ζάω for היה. In the same chapter, verse 22 the ד and ר have been interchanged. LXX reads the equivalent of ירע (κακώσει) for ידע and דעת for רעת in Eccles 8,6 (γνῶσις). The translator also read שׂנא for שׂנא in Eccles 8,1 which is indicated by the reading μισηθήσεται.

The continuous text was also divided differently from MT. In Eccles 8,1 the MT has מי כהחכם (who is like the wise?) but the LXX translator understood it as מי כה חכם (who is so wise?). In other cases the text was understood differently. In Eccles 7,24 the phrase ὑπὲρ ὃ ἦν should be retroverted to משׁהיה, which represents a difference from MT מה־שׁהיה.

10. M.V. Fox, *Kohelet and his contradictions* (JSOT SS, 71), Sheffield, 1989, p. 172.

IV. On the "Theological/Ideological" Level

In various publications I have argued that the Proverbs version of the Septuagint represents a unique translated unit in the whole of the LXX corpus of translations. It is therefore possible to formulate a definite "theological" approach for this translator. I have demonstrated that this translator indeed had a more conservative outlook towards his parent text than actually occurs in this Semitic text itself. In the process he actually reacted in what I called an "anti-Hellenistical" way, for he nuanced his parent text in such a way that any possible misunderstanding of its intention would be avoided. Consequently he made use of typical Jewish exegetical traditions such as in Prov 2,11.17 and in Prov 10,13. The law plays a much more prominent role in this translation than formerly suspected by scholars[11]. These are all signs of the "Jewishness" of this translator. He evidently had an excellent schooling in Greek literature and philosophy, but he consistently applied these perspectives in order to make clear the intention of his parent text. An appropriate example is the application of Greek literary traditions in Prov 10,18 in order to make an "anti-Hellenistic" statement as to the dangers of Greek philosophy to the Jewish reader[12]. He also applied perspectives which he most probably obtained from Aristotle's *Historia Animalium* in Prov 6,8, where the parable of the bee and the ant is neatly inserted into the LXX.

The same approach certainly is not to be found in the version of Ecclesiastes. This translator basically stuck to his parent text in a literal manner, using what I would like to call a minimalist approach. The translator of Proverbs, on the contrary, exhibits a maximalist approach. It is on the face of it, strangely enough, exactly on this level that there is a conspicuous correspondence between LXX Proverbs and Ecclesiastes. To me it would seem that they both had the same contention, namely to make clear the intention of the parent text. However, they followed diametrically opposed approaches. The one, Proverbs, seems to be preoccupied with explaining the intention of his parent text, in order to avoid possible misunderstanding. In the process he explicates, mostly adding strophes and offering pertinent interpretations. The other, Ecclesiastes, is intent on rendering as truly as possible his parent text. That he was also steeped in the Greek literature is evident from the way he nuanced his

---

11. Cf. J. Cook, *The Law in Septuagint Proverbs*, in *JNSL* 23 (1997) 211-223.
12. Cf. J. Cook, אִשָּׁה זָרָה (*Proverbs 1-9 Septuagint): A Metaphor for Foreign Wisdom?*, in *ZAW* 106 (1994), p. 473.

Greek text. However, he clearly had a different view on what it meant to translate from that of the translator of Proverbs.

This different approach towards texts can in my view only be understood against the background of divergent historical contexts. Scholars (inter alia Barthélemy[13]) have identified the translator of Ecclesiastes as Aquila. In his view the LXX version is the first edition of Aquila mentioned by Jerome, and the fragments that were identified by Origen as Aquilan actually represent Aquila's second edition. Hyvärinen[14] is of the opinion that one should perhaps rather talk about a school in this regard. He points to significant deviations in LXX Eccles from Aquilan techniques in lexical and syntactical matters and argues against an Aquilan origin for LXX Eccles. Michael Fox[15] refers to it being an Aquilan type translation. Be this as it may, it would seem as if this translation came into being in the post-Aquilan era. This at least testifies to a post-Christian translation which most probably took place in Palestine. I have argued that the Septuagint version of Proverbs should be placed also in Palestine, but in a period much earlier, probably the 2nd century BCE[16].

Final Conclusion

I have endeavoured to treat specific aspects of the relationship between two wisdom texts from the Septuagint. To me it is clear that these translation units differ dramatically as far as most facets of their rendering are concerned. However, in one aspect they correspond, both translators being intent to render the intention of their parent texts as clearly as possible. In this sense the Greek version of Proverbs could strangely enough be seen as a forerunner of the literal pre-Origenic translational activities. Because of the time gap between the various translations different modes of translation were followed by different translators.

Department of Ancient Near Eastern Studies   Johann COOK
University of Stellenbosch
7600 Stellenbosch
South Africa

13. D. BARTHÉLEMY, *Les devanciers d'Aquila* (SVT, 10), Leiden, 1963, pp. 21-33.
14. K. HYVÄRINEN, *Die Übersetzung von Aquila*, Lund, 1977, p. 98.
15. FOX, *Kohelet and his Contradictions*, p. 172; cf. also J. JARICK, *Aquila's Koheleth*, in *Textus* XVIII (1995) 131-139.
16. COOK, *The Dating of Septuagint Proverbs*, in *ETL* 69 (1993), 383-399, p. 398.

INDEXES

ABBREVIATIONS

AB	The Anchor Bible
ABRL	Anchor Bible Reference Library
ACEBT	Amsterdamse cahiers voor exegese en bijbelse theologie
AF	Archivio di Filosofia
AJSL	American Journal of Semitic Languages and Literatures
AnBib	Analecta Biblica
ANET	Ancient Near Eastern Texts Relating to the Old Testament, ed. J.B. PRITCHARD
ANETS	Ancient Near Eastern Texts and Studies
ANRW	Aufstieg und Niedergang der römischen Welt
ATD	Das Alte Testament Deutsch
ATSAT	Arbeiten zu Text und Sprache im Alten Testament
AUSS	Andrews University Seminary Studies
BASOR	Bulletin of the American Schools of Oriental Research
BAT	Die Botschaft des Alten Testaments
BBB	Bonner biblische Beiträge
BC	Biblischer Commentar über das AT
BCR	Biblioteca di Cultura Religiosa
BDB	F. BROWN – S.R. DRIVER – C.A. BRIGGS, A Hebrew and English Lexicon of the Old Testament
BEATAJ	Beiträge zur Erforschung des Alten Testaments und des Antiken Judentums
BETL	Bibliotheca Ephemeridum Theologicarum Lovaniensium
Bib	Biblica
BibB	Biblische Beiträge
BibInt	Biblical Interpretation
BiKi	Bibel und Kirche
BJ	Bible de Jérusalem
BK(AT)	Biblischer Kommentar. Altes Testament
BN	Biblische Notizen
BOT	De Boeken van het Oude Testament
BS	Bibliotheca Sacra
BTB	Biblical Theology Bulletin
BThSt	Biblisch-theologische Studien
BTrans	The Bible Translator
BWANT	Beiträge zur Wissenschaft vom Alten und Neuen Testament
BZ	Biblische Zeitschrift
BZAW	Beihefte zur Zeitschrift für die alttestamentliche Wissenschaft
CBC	Cambridge Bible Commentary
CBQ	Catholic Biblical Quarterly
CBQ MS	Catholic Biblical Quarterly. Monograph Series

CE	Cahiers Evangile
COT	Commentaar op het Oude Testament
DBS	Dictionnaire de la Bible. Supplément
DJD	Discoveries in the Judaean Desert
DSD	Dead Sea Discoveries
EB	Études bibliques
EdF	Erträge der Forschung
EstBíb	Estudios Bíblicos
ETL	Ephemerides Theologicae Lovanienses
EÜ	Einheitsübersetzung
EurHS	Europäische Hochschulschriften
ExpT	Expository Times
FAT	Forschungen zum Alten Testament
FOTL	The Forms of the Old Testament Literature
FzB	Forschung zur Bibel
GK	W. GESENIUS – E. KAUTZSCH, Hebräische Grammatik/Hebrew Grammar
GL	Geist und Leben
HAL	Hebräisches und Aramäisches Lexikon zum Alten Testament, von L. KOEHLER und W. BAUMGARTNER, neu bearbeitet von W. BAUMGARTNER *et al.*
HAR	Hebrew Annual Review
HAT	Handbuch zum Alten Testament
HBS	Herders biblische Studien
HKAT	Handkommentar zum Alten Testament
HNT	Handbuch zum Neuen Testament
HSAT(K)	Die Heilige Schrift des Alten Testament (KAUTZSCH)
HSS	Harvard Semitic Studies
HTR	Harvard Theological Review
HUCA	Hebrew Union College Annual
ICC	The International Critical Commentary
Interpr	Interpretation
ITC	International Theological Commentary
JAAR	Journal of the American Academy of Religion
JBL	Journal of Biblical Literature
JJS	Journal of Jewish Studies
JLS	Journal of Literary Studies
JNES	Journal of Near Eastern Studies
JNSL	Journal of Northwest Semitic Languages
JQR	Jewish Quarterly Review
JSHRZ	Jüdische Schriften aus hellenistisch-römischer Zeit
JSOT	Journal for the Study of the Old Testament

JSOT SS	Journal for the Study of the Old Testament. Supplement Series
JTS	Journal of Theological Studies
KAI	Kanaanäische und aramäische Inschriften
KAT	Kommentar zum Alten Testament
KHAT	Kurzer Handcommentar zum Alten Testament
LÄ	Lexikon der Ägyptologie
LD	Lectio Divina
MLM	*Mûsar lammēbîn*
NCBC	New Century Bible Commentary
NEB	Neue Echter Bibel
NEB	The New English Bible
NIB	New Interpreter's Bible
NIV	The Holy Bible. New International Version
NRSV	New Revised Standard Version
NRT	Nouvelle revue théologique
NZSTh	Neue Zeitschrift für systematische Theologie
OBO	Orbis Biblicus et Orientalis
OLA	Orientalia Lovaniensia Analecta
OLP	Orientalia Lovaniensia Periodica
OLZ	Orientalistische Literaturzeitung
OTE	Old Testament Essays
OTL	Old Testament Library
OTS	Oudtestamentische Studiën
Pléiade	Bible de la Pléiade, Paris 1961-62
POT	De Prediking van het Oude Testament
RB	Revue biblique
REB	The Revised English Bible
RivBib	Rivista Biblica
RQ	Revue de Qumran
RSR	Revue des sciences religieuses
RSV	Revised Standard Version
RTL	Revue théologique de Louvain
RTP	Revue de théologie et de philosophie
SBB	Stuttgarter biblische Beiträge
SBG	Skrifuitleg vir Bybelstudent en Gemeente
SBL DS	Society of Biblical Literature. Dissertation Series
SBL MS	Society of Biblical Literature. Masoretic Studies
SBL RBS	Society of Biblical Literature. Resources for Biblical Study
SBL SCS	Society of Biblical Literature. Septuagint and Cognate Studies
SBL SP	Society of Biblical Literature. Seminar Papers
SC	Sources chrétiennes

ScEs	Science et Esprit
Sef	Sefarad
SJT	Scottish Journal of Theology
SSU	Studia Semitica Upsaliensia
StANT	Studien zum Alten und Neuen Testament
STDJ	Studies on the Texts of the Desert of Judah
SupRivBib	Supplementi alla Rivista Biblica
SVT	Supplements to Vetus Testamentum
TD	Theology Digest
TDOT	Theological Dictionary of the Old Testament
THAT	Theologisches Handwörterbuch zum Alten Testament
ThEv	Theologia Evangelica
ThViat	Theologia Viatorum
TOB	Traduction Œcuménique de la Bible
TOTC	Tyndale Old Testament Commentaries
TR	Theologische Rundschau
TRE	Theologische Realenzyklopädie
TSAJ	Texte und Studien zum Antiken Judentum
TSJTSA	Texts and Studies of the Jewish Theological Seminary of America
TUAT	Texte aus der Umwelt des Alten Testaments
TWAT	Theologisches Wörterbuch zum Alten Testament
TZ	Theologische Zeitschrift
UBL	Ugaritisch-Biblische Literatur
UF	Ugarit-Forschungen
VT	Vetus Testamentum
VuF	Verkündigung und Forschung
WBC	World Biblical Commentary
WBG	Wissenschaftliche Buchgesellschaft
WeltBib KK	Die Welt der Bibel. Kleinkommentare zur Heiligen Schrift
WO	Die Welt des Orients
WUNT	Wissenschaftliche Untersuchungen zum Neuen Testament
WZ(L)	Wissenschaftliche Zeitschrift Leipzig
ZAW	Zeitschrift für die alttestamentliche Wissenschaft
ZDMG(.S)	Zeitschrift der Deutschen Morgenländischen Gesellschaft (Supplementa)
ZTK	Zeitschrift für Theologie und Kirche

INDEX OF AUTHORS

INDEX OF BIBLICAL REFERENCES

13,26	218	39,14	448
14,3	119	49,12	312
14,20	289, 448	57,6	293
15,5	216	57,8	289
15,24	289	62,10	227
19,2	293	66–67	153
19,10	448	73	196
19,23	218	75,3-4	410
20,2	370	75,3	407
21,23-26	349	88,11	354
21,34	227	88,49	26
22,4	119	90	253
23,6	47	90,3	349
26,5	354	90,4	290
26,11	407, 410	90,10	347
28	223, 229	93,20	294
28,23.27	222	94,12	216
30,23	34	103,17-18	162
31,10	406	104,24	129
32,22	414, 417	104,29-30	350
33,33	217	104,30	415
34,14-15	350	105,44	359
34,24	222	110,4	347
34,27	313	111,5	415
35,10	414, 417	112	164, 191
35,11	216	112,1	162
36,26	222	115,3	152
38-41	249	116,11	19
38,1-39	410	118,22	403
38,5	207	119	146
38,16	222	119,63	162, 164
40,6-41	410	119,79	162
41,15	406	119,108	216
42,6	363	119,161	162
42,8	147	126,2	228
		128,1	162
PSALMS		134,4	294
1	143, 146, 189, 196	139,1-3	220
1,5	122	139,23-24	221
7,15	291	141,10	487
7,16	292	143,2	119
8,5	387	144,3	387
8,6	294	145,3	222
8,14; 10	196	146,4	350
19	146		
34,13	26	PROVERBS	
34,22	196	1-9	163
36,6-10	42	1	163, 485
39,7	263	1,2-3	215, 482-484

SUBJECT INDEX

HEBREW WORDS

GREEK WORDS

BIBLIOTHECA EPHEMERIDUM THEOLOGICARUM LOVANIENSIUM

29. M. DIDIER (ed.), *L'évangile selon Matthieu. Rédaction et théologie*, 1972. 432 p. FB 1000.

*30. J. KEMPENEERS, *Le Cardinal van Roey en son temps*, 1971.

SERIES II

31. F. NEIRYNCK, *Duality in Mark. Contributions to the Study of the Markan Redaction*, 1972. Revised edition with Supplementary Notes, 1988. 252 p. FB 1200.

32. F. NEIRYNCK (ed.), *L'évangile de Luc. Problèmes littéraires et théologiques*, 1973. *L'évangile de Luc – The Gospel of Luke*. Revised and enlarged edition, 1989. x-590 p. FB 2200.

33. C. BREKELMANS (ed.), *Questions disputées d'Ancien Testament. Méthode et théologie*, 1974. *Continuing Questions in Old Testament Method and Theology*. Revised and enlarged edition by M. VERVENNE, 1989. 245 p. FB 1200.

34. M. SABBE (ed.), *L'évangile selon Marc. Tradition et rédaction*, 1974. Nouvelle édition augmentée, 1988. 601 p. FB 2400.

35. B. WILLAERT (ed.), *Philosophie de la religion – Godsdienstfilosofie. Miscellanea Albert Dondeyne*, 1974. Nouvelle édition, 1987. 458 p. FB 1600.

36. G. PHILIPS, *L'union personnelle avec le Dieu vivant. Essai sur l'origine et le sens de la grâce créée*, 1974. Édition révisée, 1989. 299 p. FB 1000.

37. F. NEIRYNCK, in collaboration with T. HANSEN and F. VAN SEGBROECK, *The Minor Agreements of Matthew and Luke against Mark with a Cumulative List*, 1974. 330 p. FB 900.

38. J. COPPENS, *Le messianisme et sa relève prophétique. Les anticipations vétérotestamentaires. Leur accomplissement en Jésus*, 1974. Édition révisée, 1989. XIII-265 p. FB 1000.

39. D. SENIOR, *The Passion Narrative according to Matthew. A Redactional Study*, 1975. New impression, 1982. 440 p. FB 1000.

40. J. DUPONT (ed.), *Jésus aux origines de la christologie*, 1975. Nouvelle édition augmentée, 1989. 458 p. FB 1500.

41. J. COPPENS (ed.), *La notion biblique de Dieu*, 1976. Réimpression, 1985. 519 p. FB 1600.

42. J. LINDEMANS & H. DEMEESTER (ed.), *Liber Amicorum Monseigneur W. Onclin*, 1976. XXII-396 p. FB 1000.

43. R.E. HOECKMAN (ed.), *Pluralisme et œcuménisme en recherches théologiques. Mélanges offerts au R.P. Dockx, O.P.*, 1976. 316 p. FB 1000.

44. M. DE JONGE (ed.), *L'évangile de Jean. Sources, rédaction, théologie*, 1977. Réimpression, 1987. 416 p. FB 1500.

45. E.J.M. VAN EIJL (ed.), *Facultas S. Theologiae Lovaniensis 1432-1797. Bijdragen tot haar geschiedenis. Contributions to its History. Contributions à son histoire*, 1977. 570 p. FB 1700.

46. M. DELCOR (ed.), *Qumrân. Sa piété, sa théologie et son milieu*, 1978. 432 p. FB 1700.

47. M. CAUDRON (ed.), *Faith and Society. Foi et société. Geloof en maatschappij. Acta Congressus Internationalis Theologici Lovaniensis 1976*, 1978. 304 p. FB 1150.

48. J. KREMER (ed.), *Les Actes des Apôtres. Traditions, rédaction, théologie,* 1979. 590 p. FB 1700.

49. F. NEIRYNCK, avec la collaboration de J. DELOBEL, T. SNOY, G. VAN BELLE, F. VAN SEGBROECK, *Jean et les Synoptiques. Examen critique de l'exégèse de M.-É. Boismard,* 1979. XII-428 p. FB 1000.

50. J. COPPENS, *La relève apocalyptique du messianisme royal. I. La royauté – Le règne – Le royaume de Dieu. Cadre de la relève apocalyptique,* 1979. 325 p. FB 1000.

51. M. GILBERT (ed.), *La Sagesse de l'Ancien Testament,* 1979. Nouvelle édition mise à jour, 1990. 455 p. FB 1500.

52. B. DEHANDSCHUTTER, *Martyrium Polycarpi. Een literair-kritische studie,* 1979. 296 p. FB 1000.

53. J. LAMBRECHT (ed.), *L'Apocalypse johannique et l'Apocalyptique dans le Nouveau Testament,* 1980. 458 p. FB 1400.

54. P.-M. BOGAERT (ed.), *Le livre de Jérémie. Le prophète et son milieu. Les oracles et leur transmission,* 1981. *Nouvelle édition mise à jour,* 1997. 448 p. FB 1800.

55. J. COPPENS, *La relève apocalyptique du messianisme royal. III. Le Fils de l'homme néotestamentaire.* Édition posthume par F. NEIRYNCK, 1981. XIV-192 p. FB 800.

56. J. VAN BAVEL & M. SCHRAMA (ed.), *Jansénius et le Jansénisme dans les Pays-Bas. Mélanges Lucien Ceyssens,* 1982. 247 p. FB 1000.

57. J.H. WALGRAVE, *Selected Writings – Thematische geschriften. Thomas Aquinas, J.H. Newman, Theologia Fundamentalis.* Edited by G. DE SCHRIJVER & J.J. KELLY, 1982. XLIII-425 p. FB 1000.

58. F. NEIRYNCK & F. VAN SEGBROECK, avec la collaboration de E. MANNING, *Ephemerides Theologicae Lovanienses 1924-1981. Tables générales. (Bibliotheca Ephemeridum Theologicarum Lovaniensium 1947-1981),* 1982. 400 p. FB 1600.

59. J. DELOBEL (ed.), *Logia. Les paroles de Jésus – The Sayings of Jesus. Mémorial Joseph Coppens,* 1982. 647 p. FB 2000.

60. F. NEIRYNCK, *Evangelica. Gospel Studies – Études d'évangile. Collected Essays.* Edited by F. VAN SEGBROECK, 1982. XIX-1036 p. FB 2000.

61. J. COPPENS, *La relève apocalyptique du messianisme royal. II. Le Fils d'homme vétéro- et intertestamentaire.* Édition posthume par J. LUST, 1983. XVII-272 p. FB 1000.

62. J.J. KELLY, *Baron Friedrich von Hügel's Philosophy of Religion,* 1983. 232 p. FB 1500.

63. G. DE SCHRIJVER, *Le merveilleux accord de l'homme et de Dieu. Étude de l'analogie de l'être chez Hans Urs von Balthasar,* 1983. 344 p. FB 1500.

64. J. GROOTAERS & J.A. SELLING, *The 1980 Synod of Bishops: «On the Role of the Family». An Exposition of the Event and an Analysis of its Texts.* Preface by Prof. emeritus L. JANSSENS, 1983. 375 p. FB 1500.

65. F. NEIRYNCK & F. VAN SEGBROECK, *New Testament Vocabulary. A Companion Volume to the Concordance,* 1984. XVI-494 p. FB 2000.

66. R.F. COLLINS, *Studies on the First Letter to the Thessalonians,* 1984. XI-415 p. FB 1500.

67. A. PLUMMER, *Conversations with Dr. Döllinger 1870-1890.* Edited with Introduction and Notes by R. BOUDENS, with the collaboration of L. KENIS, 1985. LIV-360 p. FB 1800.

68. N. Lohfink (ed.), *Das Deuteronomium. Entstehung, Gestalt und Botschaft / Deuteronomy: Origin, Form and Message*, 1985. XI-382 p. FB 2000.

69. P.F. Fransen, *Hermeneutics of the Councils and Other Studies*. Collected by H.E. Mertens & F. De Graeve, 1985. 543 p. FB 1800.

70. J. Dupont, *Études sur les Évangiles synoptiques*. Présentées par F. Neirynck, 1985. 2 tomes, XXI-IX-1210 p. FB 2800.

71. *Recueil Lucien Cerfaux*, t. III, 1962. Nouvelle édition revue et complétée, 1985. LXXX-458 p. FB 1600.

72. J. Grootaers, *Primauté et collégialité. Le dossier de Gérard Philips sur la Nota Explicativa Praevia (Lumen gentium, Chap. III)*. Présenté avec introduction historique, annotations et annexes. Préface de G. Thils, 1986. 222 p. FB 1000.

73. A. Vanhoye (ed.), *L'apôtre Paul. Personnalité, style et conception du ministère*, 1986. XIII-470 p. FB 2600.

74. J. Lust (ed.), *Ezekiel and His Book. Textual and Literary Criticism and their Interrelation*, 1986. X-387 p. FB 2700.

75. É. Massaux, *Influence de l'Évangile de saint Matthieu sur la littérature chrétienne avant saint Irénée*. Réimpression anastatique présentée par F. Neirynck. *Supplément: Bibliographie 1950-1985*, par B. Dehand-schutter, 1986. XXVII-850 p. FB 2500.

76. L. Ceyssens & J.A.G. Tans, *Autour de l'Unigenitus. Recherches sur la genèse de la Constitution*, 1987. XXVI-845 p. FB 2500.

77. A. Descamps, *Jésus et l'Église. Études d'exégèse et de théologie*. Préface de Mgr A. Houssiau, 1987. XLV-641 p. FB 2500.

78. J. Duplacy, *Études de critique textuelle du Nouveau Testament*. Présentées par J. Delobel, 1987. XXVII-431 p. FB 1800.

79. E.J.M. van Eijl (ed.), *L'image de C. Jansénius jusqu'à la fin du XVIIIᵉ siècle*, 1987. 258 p. FB 1250.

80. E. Brito, *La Création selon Schelling. Universum*, 1987. XXXV-646 p. FB 2980.

81. J. Vermeylen (ed.), *The Book of Isaiah – Le livre d'Isaïe. Les oracles et leurs relectures. Unité et complexité de l'ouvrage*, 1989. X-472 p. FB 2700.

82. G. Van Belle, *Johannine Bibliography 1966-1985. A Cumulative Bibliography on the Fourth Gospel*, 1988. XVII-563 p. FB 2700.

83. J.A. Selling (ed.), *Personalist Morals. Essays in Honor of Professor Louis Janssens*, 1988. VIII-344 p. FB 1200.

84. M.-É. Boismard, *Moïse ou Jésus. Essai de christologie johannique*, 1988. XVI-241 p. FB 1000.

84A. M.-É. Boismard, *Moses or Jesus: An Essay in Johannine Christology*. Translated by B.T. Viviano, 1993, XVI-144 p. FB 1000.

85. J.A. Dick, *The Malines Conversations Revisited*, 1989. 278 p. FB 1500.

86. J.-M. Sevrin (ed.), *The New Testament in Early Christianity – La réception des écrits néotestamentaires dans le christianisme primitif*, 1989. XVI-406 p. FB 2500.

87. R.F. Collins (ed.), *The Thessalonian Correspondence*, 1990. XV-546 p. FB 3000.

88. F. Van Segbroeck, *The Gospel of Luke. A Cumulative Bibliography 1973-1988*, 1989. 241 p. FB 1200.

89. G. THILS, *Primauté et infaillibilité du Pontife Romain à Vatican I et autres études d'ecclésiologie*, 1989. XI-422 p. FB 1850.
90. A. VERGOTE, *Explorations de l'espace théologique. Études de théologie et de philosophie de la religion*, 1990. XVI-709 p. FB 2000.
91. J.C. DE MOOR, *The Rise of Yahwism: The Roots of Israelite Monotheism*, 1990. *Revised and Enlarged Edition*, 1997. XV-445 p. FB 1400.
92. B. BRUNING, M. LAMBERIGTS & J. VAN HOUTEM (eds.), *Collectanea Augustiniana. Mélanges T.J. van Bavel*, 1990. 2 tomes, XXXVIII-VIII-1074 p. FB 3000.
93. A. DE HALLEUX, *Patrologie et œcuménisme. Recueil d'études*, 1990. XVI-887 p. FB 3000.
94. C. BREKELMANS & J. LUST (eds.), *Pentateuchal and Deuteronomistic Studies: Papers Read at the XIIIth IOSOT Congress Leuven 1989*, 1990. 307 p. FB 1500.
95. D.L. DUNGAN (ed.), *The Interrelations of the Gospels. A Symposium Led by M.-É. Boismard – W.R. Farmer – F. Neirynck, Jerusalem 1984*, 1990. XXXI-672 p. FB 3000.
96. G.D. KILPATRICK, *The Principles and Practice of New Testament Textual Criticism. Collected Essays*. Edited by J.K. ELLIOTT, 1990. XXXVIII-489 p. FB 3000.
97. G. ALBERIGO (ed.), *Christian Unity. The Council of Ferrara-Florence: 1438/39 – 1989*, 1991. X-681 p. FB 3000.
98. M. SABBE, *Studia Neotestamentica. Collected Essays*, 1991. XVI-573 p. FB 2000.
99. F. NEIRYNCK, *Evangelica II: 1982-1991. Collected Essays*. Edited by F. VAN SEGBROECK, 1991. XIX-874 p. FB 2800.
100. F. VAN SEGBROECK, C.M. TUCKETT, G. VAN BELLE & J. VERHEYDEN (eds.), *The Four Gospels 1992. Festschrift Frans Neirynck*, 1992. 3 volumes, XVII-X-X-2668 p. FB 5000.

SERIES III

101. A. DENAUX (ed.), *John and the Synoptics*, 1992. XXII-696 p. FB 3000.
102. F. NEIRYNCK, J. VERHEYDEN, F. VAN SEGBROECK, G. VAN OYEN & R. CORSTJENS, *The Gospel of Mark. A Cumulative Bibliography: 1950-1990*, 1992. XII-717 p. FB 2700.
103. M. SIMON, *Un catéchisme universel pour l'Église catholique. Du Concile de Trente à nos jours*, 1992. XIV-461 p. FB 2200.
104. L. CEYSSENS, *Le sort de la bulle Unigenitus. Recueil d'études offert à Lucien Ceyssens à l'occasion de son 90ᵉ anniversaire*. Présenté par M. LAMBERIGTS, 1992. XXVI-641 p. FB 2000.
105. R.J. DALY (ed.), *Origeniana Quinta. Papers of the 5th International Origen Congress, Boston College, 14-18 August 1989*, 1992. XVII-635 p. FB 2700.
106. A.S. VAN DER WOUDE (ed.), *The Book of Daniel in the Light of New Findings*, 1993. XVIII-574 p. FB 3000.
107. J. FAMERÉE, *L'ecclésiologie d'Yves Congar avant Vatican II: Histoire et Église. Analyse et reprise critique*, 1992. 497 p. FB 2600.

108. C. BEGG, *Josephus' Account of the Early Divided Monarchy (AJ 8, 212-420). Rewriting the Bible*, 1993. IX-377 p. FB 2400.

109. J. BULCKENS & H. LOMBAERTS (eds.), *L'enseignement de la religion catholique à l'école secondaire. Enjeux pour la nouvelle Europe*, 1993. XII-264 p. FB 1250.

110. C. FOCANT (ed.), *The Synoptic Gospels. Source Criticism and the New Literary Criticism*, 1993. XXXIX-670 p. FB 3000.

111. M. LAMBERIGTS (ed.), avec la collaboration de L. KENIS, *L'augustinisme à l'ancienne Faculté de théologie de Louvain*, 1994. VII-455 p. FB 2400.

112. R. BIERINGER & J. LAMBRECHT, *Studies on 2 Corinthians*, 1994. XX-632 p. FB 3000.

113. E. BRITO, *La pneumatologie de Schleiermacher*, 1994. XII-649 p. FB 3000.

114. W.A.M. BEUKEN (ed.), *The Book of Job*, 1994. X-462 p. FB 2400.

115. J. LAMBRECHT, *Pauline Studies: Collected Essays*, 1994. XIV-465 p. FB 2500.

116. G. VAN BELLE, *The Signs Source in the Fourth Gospel: Historical Survey and Critical Evaluation of the Semeia Hypothesis*, 1994. XIV-503 p. FB 2500.

117. M. LAMBERIGTS & P. VAN DEUN (eds.), *Martyrium in Multidisciplinary Perspective. Memorial L. Reekmans*, 1995. X-435 p. FB 3000.

118. G. DORIVAL & A. LE BOULLUEC (eds.), *Origeniana Sexta. Origène et la Bible/Origen and the Bible. Actes du Colloquium Origenianum Sextum, Chantilly, 30 août – 3 septembre 1993*, 1995. XII-865 p. FB 3900.

119. É. GAZIAUX, *Morale de la foi et morale autonome. Confrontation entre P. Delhaye et J. Fuchs*, 1995. XXII-545 p. FB 2700.

120. T.A. SALZMAN, *Deontology and Teleology: An Investigation of the Normative Debate in Roman Catholic Moral Theology*, 1995. XVII-555 p. FB 2700.

121. G.R. EVANS & M. GOURGUES (eds.), *Communion et Réunion. Mélanges Jean-Marie Roger Tillard*, 1995. XI-431 p. FB 2400.

122. H.T. FLEDDERMANN, *Mark and Q: A Study of the Overlap Texts*. With an *Assessment* by F. NEIRYNCK, 1995. XI-307 p. FB 1800.

123. R. BOUDENS, *Two Cardinals: John Henry Newman, Désiré-Joseph Mercier*. Edited by L. GEVERS with the collaboration of B. DOYLE, 1995. 362 p. FB 1800.

124. A. THOMASSET, *Paul Ricœur. Une poétique de la morale. Aux fondements d'une éthique herméneutique et narrative dans une perspective chrétienne*, 1996. XVI-706 p. FB 3000.

125. R. BIERINGER (ed.), *The Corinthian Correspondence*, 1996. XXVII-793 p. FB 2400.

126. M. VERVENNE (ed.), *Studies in the Book of Exodus: Redaction – Reception – Interpretation*, 1996. XI-660 p. FB 2400.

127. A. VANNESTE, *Nature et grâce dans la théologie occidentale. Dialogue avec H. de Lubac*, 1996. 312 p. FB 1800.

128. A. CURTIS & T. RÖMER (eds.), *The Book of Jeremiah and its Reception – Le livre de Jérémie et sa réception*, 1997. 332 p. FB 2400.

129. E. LANNE, *Tradition et Communion des Églises. Recueil d'études*, 1997. XXV-703 p. FB 3000.

130. A. Denaux & J.A. Dick (eds.), *From Malines to ARCIC. The Malines Conversations Commemorated*, 1997. ix-317 p. FB 1800.
131. C.M. Tuckett (ed.), *The Scriptures in the Gospels*, 1997. xxiv-721 p. FB 2400.
132. J. van Ruiten & M. Vervenne (eds.), *Studies in the Book of Isaiah. Festschrift Willem A.M. Beuken*, 1997. xx-540 p. FB 3000.
133. M. Vervenne & J. Lust (eds.), *Deuteronomy and Deuteronomic Literature. Festschrift C.H.W. Brekelmans*, 1997. xi-637 p. FB 3000.